Foundations

of

International

Politics

VAN NOSTRAND POLITICAL SCIENCE SERIES

Editor

FRANKLIN L. BURDETTE
University of Maryland

PLISCHKE, E.—*Conduct of American Diplomacy*, 2nd Ed.

DIXON, R. G., JR., and PLISCKHE, ELMER—*American Government: Basic Documents and Materials*

SPROUT, HAROLD and MARGARET—*Foundations of National Power*, 2nd Ed.

LANCASTER, LANE W.—*Government in Rural America*, 2nd Ed.

JORRIN, M.—*Governments of Latin America*

TORPEY, WILLIAM G.—*Public Personnel Management*

PLISCHKE, ELMER—*International Relations: Basic Documents*, 2nd Ed.

GOODMAN, WILLIAM—*The Two-Party System in the United States*, 2nd Ed.

DILLON, CONLEY H., LEIDEN, CARL, and STEWART, PAUL D.—*Introduction to Political Science*

SWARTZ, WILLIS G.—*American Governmental Problems*, 2nd Ed.

BAKER, BENJAMIN—*Urban Government*

ZINK, HAROLD, PENNIMAN, HOWARD R., and HATHORN, GUY B.—*American Government and Politics: National, State, and Local*

ZINK, HAROLD—*Modern Governments*, 2nd Ed.

HENDEL, SAMUEL—*The Soviet Crucible: Soviet Government in Theory and Practice*

LINEBARGER, P. M. A., DJANG, C., and BURKS, A. W.—*Far Eastern Governments and Politics: China and Japan*, 2nd Ed.

HATHORN, GUY B., PENNIMAN, HOWARD R., and ZINK, HAROLD—*Government and Politics in the United States*

MADDOX, RUSSELL W., and FUQUAY, ROBERT F.—*State and Local Government*

SHARABI, H. B.—*Governments and Politics of the Middle East in the Twentieth Century*

ANDREWS, WILLIAM G.—*European Political Institutions*

SPROUT, HAROLD and MARGARET—*Foundations of International Politics*

Foundations
of
International
Politics

by
HAROLD
and
MARGARET
SPROUT

D. VAN NOSTRAND COMPANY, INC.

Princeton, New Jersey • Toronto • London • New York

D. VAN NOSTRAND COMPANY, INC.
120 Alexander St., Princeton, New Jersey (*Principal office*)
24 West 40 Street, New York 18, New York

D. Van Nostrand Company, Ltd.
358, Kensington High Street, London, W.14, England

D. Van Nostrand Company (Canada), Ltd.
25 Hollinger Road, Toronto 16, Canada

Library of Congress Catalog Card No. 62-20143

First Published August 1962
Reprinted June 1963

★ ★ ★

Contents

v

PART IV: INTERNATIONAL POLITICS IN TRANSITION

PART I: THE STUDY OF INTERNATIONAL POLITICS

INTRODUCTION

★ ★ ★

The Study of International Politics in a Period of Revolutionary Change

THIS BOOK IS addressed primarily to young people everywhere. Upon their shoulders will fall responsibility for coming to terms more effectively than their elders have with the rapidly changing facts of life in our revolutionary age.

Non-American readers will undoubtedly discern an American perspective. Since we have lived most of our lives in the American milieu, it would scarcely be possible for us to divorce ourselves completely from American viewpoints and ways of looking at the international scene. However, the book is in no sense a treatise on American foreign policy; nor is it intended to be an apology for American perspectives and actions. Except for the final chapter, we have tried to keep the book as descriptive, analytical, and free from policy-bias as possible.

The book is not focused specifically on current problems and events. As we write these introductory pages, the cold war has reached a new climax in the Communist squeeze-play on Berlin and in the resumption of nuclear-weapons testing. Each day brings in a fresh grist of news about internal disorder in the Congo, Angola, Algeria, and elsewhere. Brazil has just escaped a bloody civil war that might have split the Americas even more deeply than the Castro revolution in Cuba. The Belgrade Conference of the Uncommitted Nations has just closed, with the "experts" disputing about the motivations and influence of the emerging nations of Asia and Africa. Congress is waging its annual battle with the Administration over aid to the underdeveloped countries.

By the time this book reaches its readers, most of these and other current events will appear in different perspective. Some problems will have been resolved; others will appear even more refractory and dangerous. It is fruitless to compete with the newspapers and the daily newscasters in chronicling events upon the international stage. It should be much more fruitful to establish a frame of ideas, some basic background information, and a mode of thinking creatively about the rapidly changing international scene. This, rather than discussion of current problems, is what is attempted in *Foundations of International Politics*. The key word in the title is "foundations."

International politics—by which is meant those aspects of the interactions and relations of independent political communities in which some element of opposition, resistance, or conflict of purpose or interest is present—affects deeply the life of everyone. This is so whether one thinks much about it or not. It is likely to become even more so during the next half century, unless some tragic accident or miscalculation should unleash the multimegaton bombs and transform a good part of the earth into a radioactive desert.

Wars have disrupted the lives of two living generations. Millions of men now approaching retirement bear the scars of World War I—the war of 1914-1918 that was fought to make future wars impossible and to make the world safe for democracy. Other millions, now in the prime of life, were torn from families, schools, and jobs to fight World War II— the war of 1939-1945, fought to save mankind from Nazism and other forms of tyranny. A few years later, Americans and others were fighting again, this time in Korea, to stem the march of Communism. Violence and killing have repeatedly accompanied the recent and continuing struggles of colonial peoples to win political and economic independence. There is constant danger that these "brush fires," as they are sometimes called, may spread and get out of control; there is widespread fear that they might even trigger off a third world war, far more destructive than anything hitherto experienced.

Today, young men in America and in many other countries are still compelled to interrupt education and career for military service. Hundreds of thousands of young Americans are deployed overseas. American military posts encircle the Eurasian strongholds of Communist rule. Military installations have perceptibly altered the American domestic landscape. Jet planes and ballistic rockets roar aloft and streak across the sky. Air-raid sirens and fallout shelters remind us of the precarious balance of destructive forces that encompass us.

In view of these manifest perils, it would be easy to succumb to a fatalistic pessimism and to view international politics in our time as a macabre advance from crisis to crisis to the ultimate irreversible catastrophe. We reject such pessimism *in toto*. No one can *predict* that multimegaton H-bombs will not bring the human story to a sudden violent end. But this book rests upon the opposite assumption: the assumption that no such catastrophe will occur. For reasons that are self-evident, any other assumption would reduce the study of international politics, or indeed any subject, to futility. Besides, as we shall attempt to demonstrate, the shape and trend of world events offer rational grounds for faith that the Cold War is not a preview of a total war of extermination but rather a difficult stage in a continuing adjustment of human expectations, institutions, and behavior to the realities of the nuclear age.

Under these conditions the cost of the role of Superpower is heavy and seems likely to grow heavier. This cost is not generally appreciated, owing largely to the methods of collecting taxes. Every family of four in the United States is paying approximately $1,000 per year on the average towards support of our huge military establishment, which, we are constantly told, still falls far short of adequacy. Congress votes additional billions annually to strengthen the alliances by means of which we strive to counterbalance the military power arrayed against us. Additional tax dollars are allocated, generally grudgingly, towards support of the Department of State and Foreign Service, towards alleviating famine and other catastrophes in impoverished foreign lands, towards creating higher living standards in faraway countries which most Americans could not even locate upon a map. Congress allocates relative small amounts, still more grudgingly, for the Voice of America, for cultural and educational exchanges of persons, for exhibits of American products at international fairs, and for other activities designed to win friends, influence people, and confound our adversaries.

All this outpouring of wealth and effort is accompanied by a continuing barrage of arguments and counterarguments, carried on in public for the purpose of swaying American opinions. One set of voices demands a "crash program," a convulsive attempt to regain our former commanding lead in military engineering. Others plead for "fallout shelters" and other preparations against the day of the "inevitable" holocaust to come. Still others deplore the concentration on "military hardware," while we neglect the battles against hunger and disease going on in Asia, Africa, Latin America and elsewhere. For still others the road to survival leads via Madison Avenue to the "battle for men's minds."

Press, radio and television bombard us with news (mostly alarming) from Moscow, Peking, the Congo, and the scores of other distant places.

We have to reckon with the possibility that obscure events in Katanga or Tashkent or Kuala Lumpur or some other faraway place could trigger a political chain reaction that would bring devastating rockets hurtling down from the stratosphere. Even if that ultimate catastrophe is avoided, there is little ground for complacence, for other perils confront us on every side.

There is abundant evidence that millions of Americans, perhaps an overwhelming majority, pay little attention to these matters. One hears the prevailing mood of America characterized as apathetic, defensive, and lacking in imagination and initiative. Walter Lippmann, one of America's most insistent critics, spoke as follows towards the end of 1959:

> The critical weakness of our society is that for the time being our people do not have great purposes which they are united in wanting to achieve. The public mood . . . is defensive, to hold on and to conserve, not to push forward and to create. . . . The strength of the Soviet regime . . . is that it is above all else a purposeful society in which the main energies of the people are directed and dedicated to its purposes. This sense of purpose accounts for the astounding success of the regime in science and in technology both civilian and military. . . . In our encounter with the Soviet rulers, in the confrontation of the two social orders, the question is whether this country can recover what for the time being it does not have—a sense of great purpose and of high destiny.*

This was one of the main themes of President Kennedy's Inaugural Address in January 1961. He appealed to Americans to "ask not what your country can do for you—ask what you can do for your country" in the struggle "against the common enemies of man: tyranny, poverty, disease and war itself."

What part the ordinary private citizen can and should attempt to play with respect to foreign affairs is a baffling question. Plainly we all pay the piper when our politicians muck things up. Plainly also, most of us can do little or nothing to affect the day-by-day unfolding of world events, whatever their impacts on our lives. But no one denies that public opinion plays some role in international as well as in domestic affairs. Politicians, even the most cynical of them, want public support for their projects and go to great lengths to obtain it.

The citizen's dilemma is evident. Most of us can give no more than intermittent and superficial attention to the "problems" and "crises" that afflict our world. For only a few are politics and public affairs a full-time

---

* From "Today and Tomorrow," Sept. 17, 1959; reproduced by permission of the author.

occupation. Nevertheless, we repeat, public support is sought for international projects and policies. Periodically we go to the polls to pass judgment on the results achieved by our chosen leaders. Yet such judgments, it is clear, cannot rise above the level of public knowledge and understanding.

America needs, and will continue to need, more men and women capable of thinking imaginatively and prudently about the baffling and refractory problems of our revolutionary age. America shares the ever shrinking surface of our planet with some hundred-odd independent political communities. These nations stand for widely differing notions of what constitutes the good life. They differ in their standards of what is right and justifiable. The claims and demands of each collide with others. Their leaders command a varied array of instruments with which to assert their demands and to annoy other nations. Two of them (with others almost certain to follow) possess weapons systems capable of turning a considerable part of the earth into a radioactive desert. Our ability to call the tune (never as great as many Americans have fatuously imagined) has shrunk markedly in recent years. Too many of our fellow citizens, it would appear, have yet to learn the lesson of the *sputniks*.

Given this state of affairs, the issue confronting us here might be stated as follows: What frame of concepts and theories, and what kinds of factual knowledge, will be most helpful in preparing Americans to discharge responsibly and wisely their responsibilities as citizens of one of the leading nations in the world of tomorrow?

Some educators contend that the study of history—our own and that of other countries and regions—provides the best preparation. Scarcely any educated person will deny that history enriches almost any area of human experience. It is also undeniable that historical momentum—the pulls of tradition, habit, and familiar values and ideals—is one of the very important foundations of all political behavior. One could not hope to understand the behavior of the actors upon the international stage without some knowledge of the cultural heritage which differentiates each from all the others. At the same time, a nation's heritage can sometimes guide its leaders into a dead-end street and to the edge (and even over the edge) of a precipice. This danger seems especially acute in our time. This is so because we are living in an age of revolutionary change.

In lengthening historical perspective, the two world wars of this century appear increasingly as but especially violent and destructive phases of a many-faceted and continuing revolutionary upheaval. Scarcely any aspect of our environment is stable. Nearly everything is in flux.

Perhaps the most important (if slightly banal) statement that one can make about international politics in the twentieth century is that change is its most important feature.

This has been said many times and in many ways. Nowhere has it been said more forcefully than in the preamble of the Republican Party's Platform in 1960:

> The United States is living in an age of profoundest revolution. The lives of men and of nations are undergoing such transformations as history has rarely recorded. The birth of new nations, the impact of new machines, the threat of new weapons, the stirring of new ideas, the ascent into a new dimension of the universe—everywhere the accent falls on the new.

This passage sounds a theme which runs through every chapter of this book on the *Foundations of International Politics*. We shall be concerned with, among other things:

(1) Changes in the international objectives and strategies of nations;

(2) Changes in their relative capacities to affect in desired ways the behavior of other nations;

(3) Changes in the modes of conducting diplomacy and other techniques of international statecraft;

(4) Changes in the relative utilities of military weapons and non-military instruments and techniques;

(5) Changes in the political roles and operational modes of the United Nations and other international organizations; and, above all else—

(6) Changes in the physical and social environment to which the actions and accomplishments of nations are related.

A few examples will suffice in this preview to indicate the scope, magnitude, and significance of changes that are transforming the national policies, transnational interactions, and international institutions which constitute, in the aggregate, what may be called the international political system.

Let us take, first, the phenomena of scientific and technological advance. These, in our view, are the master variables, to which almost all other changes and transformations are directly or indirectly related. We have already alluded to the revolutionary advances in military technology. So stark and frightening is the apparatus of destruction unlimited, as to overshadow almost equally revolutionary effects of technological advances in other fields. Preoccupation with H-bombs, ICBM's, biological weapons, and other destructive agents tends to crowd from attention the international consequences of advances in transportation, communications, economic productivity, and other nonmilitary "miracles" of our age.

Consider, for example, the effects of the more or less ostentatious display of affluence to which Americans (and to a lesser degree Europeans too) have been treating Asians, Africans, and Latin Americans in recent years. Soldiers, civil servants, businessmen, and tourists have carried to the farthest corners of the earth the amenities that are taken for granted in America. They have been (unintentionally in the main) carriers of the message that common people in the West (especially in the United States) enjoy goods and services available to only a tiny minority in pre-industrial societies, which these days are euphemistically called "underdeveloped countries."

One extremely important aspect of the technological revolution is the progressive conquest of disease. Everywhere death rates are falling, not because the causative micro-organisms are less virulent, but because techniques for combatting them are so much more effective than they were even as recently as twenty-five years ago. A by-product of falling death rates is rapid increase of population. This is taking place nearly everywhere in the world today. In some countries the increase is so rapid as to be called explosive. This population explosion and the varying reactions to it pose some of the most baffling and refractory issues that cut across the frontiers of nations.

Consider another by-product of the technological revolution: the rising consumption of raw materials. Increasing mechanization of economic production, transportation, and household economy makes ever heavier demands on the earth's shrinking reserves of fossil fuels and other nonrenewable materials. This pressure comes, moreover, not only from the more highly industrialized countries but from the populous underdeveloped countries as well. By Western standards consumption of fuels and other raw materials is very low in most of Asia, Africa, and Latin America. But every step towards economic modernization—and many of these countries are taking giant steps—increases their need and intensifies their demands for more foodstuffs, fuels, fibers, and minerals.

In the aggregate these latecomers greatly outnumber the populations of Western Europe, the United States, and the Soviet Union combined. Their capacity for growth is likewise potentially greater. Western observers are prone to underestimate the future demands of these rising peoples. The underdeveloped countries may not meet their production targets this year, or next. But their rate of economic growth seems likely to be much more rapid than most Western observers have anticipated. These peoples who are belatedly experiencing the industrial revolution, will need, will claim, and will take a much larger share of available foodstuffs and raw materials; and they will do so at the very time when the demands of the older industrial economies are likewise on the rise.

Human relations, both within nations and between them, are assuming radically altered patterns, sometimes smoothly and quietly, frequently with explosive violence. One thinks immediately of the Communist revolutions which have transformed with so much violence and brutality so many nations within the memory of living people. But Communism and social change are not synonyms. There are many kinds of social transformation going on today in Asia, in Africa, and elsewhere. Political leaders who are guiding these movements seem destined to play increasingly important roles upon the international stage.

By no means least are the changes that are transforming the international political system. Millions of men and women alive today can remember when the Society of Nations consisted almost exclusively of states ruled by Europeans or the descendants of Europeans. As late as 1900, the international political system was predominantly a white man's system, run mainly by and for the benefit of the white race.

Even as late as 1945, the political map of Africa included only four independent states. In one of these, the Union of South Africa, a small white minority of European descent ruled with an iron hand over a predominantly colored population. Another African state, Egypt, was still a British protectorate (we would call it a satellite today), occupied by British troops and ruled indirectly from London. Only in Liberia and in Ethiopia could populations of indigenous African race and culture claim an even tenuous autonomy. Since 1945 the number of independent African states—states ruled by Africans for the benefit of Africans—has multiplied many times. The political emancipation of Asia has been no less spectacular. In the words of *The New York Times* (June 20, 1960), "Western imperialism and colonialism are in precipitate retreat in Africa and Asia."

These and other variables are reflected in the transformation that has taken place in the United Nations. This was recently described as follows by *The New Statesman* (London, August 13, 1960):

> The United Nations was created to be the symbol and instrument of Great-Power unanimity, expressed through the Security Council. As such it could not function in the Cold War. Instead, by a series of fortunate precedents, it has become the instrument of the desires of the small powers—who by sheer numbers now control the Assembly

—not only to avoid commitment to the major blocs, but to prevent them from coming into contact in sensitive areas [such as the Near East and Sub-Saharan Africa].*

The significance of change in the environment, policies, and interactions of states derives not merely from its pace and momentum but also from the differential character of the transformations taking place. That is to say, changes are occurring at different rates in different countries and regions, and at different rates among different factors within particular countries and regions. These differentials add still another dimension to the political relations of nations. Differential changes erode alliances and modify historic antagonisms. Differential changes alter the respective capacities of governments to impose their demands on other governments and peoples. In these and other respects, differential change sets the stage for new policies, new strategies, new alignments, and other innovations in the international political system.

New voices, new ideas, new demands, altered capabilities, all emphasize the ubiquity of change in our revolutionary age. Statesmen and their constituents may or may not perceive and come to grips with the changes taking place all around them. They may even set their faces stubbornly against change, and strive (as reactionaries have striven from time immemorial) to freeze the existing order or even to turn back the clock.

Governments have repeatedly resorted to shooting war in their desperate desire to resist revolutionary movements and upheavals. War to preserve or restore a status quo has proved repeatedly to be a tricky business, often yielding results precisely the opposite of what was intended. To put it bluntly, shooting war, especially on a large scale and fought to the bitter end, is a deadly effective revolution-breeder. The Allies in the French Revolutionary and Napoleonic Wars won a Pyrrhic victory when they shipped Napoleon off to St. Helena and restored the Bourbon monarchy in France. Nothing they could do could halt the spread of radical democratic ideas all over the Western world. The Russo-Japanese War of 1904-5 nearly toppled the Czarist monarchy, and prepared the ground for successful revolution a decade later. World War I, fought to make the world safe for democracy (in the words of Woodrow Wilson), had instead the effect of communizing the vast Russian Empire, Balkanizing Eastern Europe, and setting the stage for Hitler and lesser Fascists whose perverted nationalism and reckless behavior led straight into World War II. The Fascist dictators were ultimately defeated, but at the price of further spreading revolutionary communism. One of the persistent illusions of conservative politicians (an illusion even more pervasive among their professional military staffs) has been the optimistic assumption that lawless violence on the vast scale of modern war can serve the purposes of law and order. Modern total war is a good deal like mob violence raised to the nth power. He who transforms whole populations into lawless mobs becomes a prisoner (and often a victim) of the violent upheavals that ensue. One wonders uneasily how long many national leaders will continue to disregard this fundamental principal of politics.

Skillful and prudent leaders in a period of revolutionary change may be able to guide events to some extent. But change cannot be halted, not in our time. Change dominates too many sectors of human activity, and the pace and momentum are too great. Ability to lead the way and adjust with a minimum of violence and ruin is one of the supreme tests of statesmanship in a revolutionary age.

The shifting attitudes and strategies of even the more conservative nations reflect the profound instability of international politics in the twentieth century. We should not forget, for example, that the United States government and millions of Americans have changed their minds about Russia at least five times since 1914. We should not forget that American politicians and their experts, in 1945, were perfecting plans to complete the destruction of modern industry in Germany and Japan, thereby de-industrializing as well as totally disarming the nations held chiefly responsible for World War II. We should never forget that these projects were enthusiastically supported by a large and vocal segment of our press and public. We should not forget how the late Professor Nicholas J. Spykman (of Yale) was denounced for folly and almost for treason when he predicted in 1942 (after the Japanese attack on Pearl Harbor) that the United States might one day need a strong Japan as an ally against an awakened, united, and dangerously aggressive Chinese nation.

In the light of these and many other uncertainties and changes in the political patterns of our world in recent years, who would venture to predict what NATO will be like ten or even five years hence? Or what the course will be of Soviet-American relations? Or the consequences of Soviet-Chinese struggles for primacy in the Communist Realm? Or the trend of American, as well as of Soviet and Chinese, relations with the politically awakened and increasingly articulate and active peoples of southern Asia, the Near East, Sub-Saharan Africa, and Latin America?

Given these and other possibilities latent in the present unstable posture of international relations, does it seem likely that the bipolarization of power and influence around Moscow and Washington is the ultimate pattern of international politics? Or that the Soviet-American struggle will continue indefinitely to dominate the international scene? Or that our allies will acquiesce in the idea that cold war is the only alternative to total war with the Soviet Union? Or that the Communist Camp will hold together forever?

One discerns an inclination in some quarters within the United States these days to reduce all international issues to the bipolar struggle between Washington and Moscow, and to seek solutions largely in terms of nuclear hardware. Military and quasi-military conceptions of power have heavily influenced American thinking about international politics ever since World War II. Too many of us have ignored the patent limitations of military power in general, and in particular under the conditions prevailing since the middle 1950's. Preoccupied with projects for regaining primacy in superweapons (projects which are unquestionably important and possibly vital to our survival), American politicians and their expert staffs may have seriously miscalculated the utilities of less lethal instruments of policy.

We have witnessed the emergence of a conception (sparked by certain mathematicians) of international politics as a "game," carried on by "nations," envisaged as so many players around a grandiose gaming table. The value of their "hands" is calculated mainly in terms of H-bombs, ICBM's, and other military hardware. Preoccupation with the "rules" and "strategy" of the game often distracts attention completely from what this game is all about—namely, the fears, yearnings, aspirations, and expectations of the flesh-and-blood human beings who compose the hundred-odd political communities in the Society of Nations.

Such ways of thinking about international politics have failed palpably, in our judgment, to prepare us for much of what is happening upon the international stage these days. It is one of the central themes of this book, that the influence of a Nehru or a Nkruma or, for that matter, a Macmillan or even a Khrushchev is by no means simply a function of the distribution of military forces or even of military potentialities. Every statesman speaks out of an environment, out of a geographic and social context. The impact of his words or other actions depends in large part on how his personality and the context out of which he speaks are perceived and construed by other governments and by his own and other constituencies. But the effects of his actions may also depend in some degree on the properties of the environment itself, on the opportunities and limitations latent in that environment, which may or may not be accurately perceived and assessed in advance of action. The personal magnetism of an inspiring leader may be more influential than the most ominous threats. Under certain conditions, scientific, economic, or even artistic accomplishment may outweigh the most impressive military demonstrations in the scale of international prestige.

Foundations of International Politics represents an attempt to provide a framework within which to think fruitfully about the issues raised in the foregoing paragraphs. The book is a direct descendant of our *Foundations of National Power,* first published in 1946 and revised in 1951. The new book, like its antecedent, is concerned with the sources of national strength and weakness, with the patterns of power and influence in the Society of Nations, and with changes in these patterns through time. But the present book has a broader focus. This is indicated in the slight but important change of title.

The new book is organized into four groups of chapters. Part One deals with some of the intellectual tools and operations involved in any systematic study of international politics. Part Two presents a frame of concepts and principles designed to give shape and structure to the subject as a whole. Part Three presents a scheme for identifying, classifying, and judging the relevance and significance of various sets (or clusters) of factors which may affect the policies and strategies of nations and their respective power and influence in the international political system. Part Four presents a view of this system both in historical perspective, and with reference to the changes—global, regional, and other—taking place in the system today.

Finally, a few words on the educational philosophy represented in this volume. In recent years, teachers of political subjects have extended their intellectual horizon in all directions. Aspects formerly touched lightly or not at all have come to be regarded as significant. Cognate specialties, to which teachers of politics are turning increasingly, include geography, demography, economics, the physical sciences and technologies, and the cluster of disciplines—psychology, sociology, anthropology, and others— known collectively as the behavioral sciences.

These cognate fields of learning were always relevant and significant for the study of politics. The difference today is simply that political analysts are coming more generally to appreciate their relevance. This recognition appears to derive mainly from two interrelated trends: from the increasing complexity and interdependence of our world, and from the consequent enlarging scope of political action. When, for example, the growth of population threatens nearly everywhere to outrun the means of subsistence, and governments are playing an ever increasing role in attempts to cope with this problem, the data and theories of demography, geography, economics, technology, and the behavioral sciences acquire a political relevance and urgency that can no longer be ignored.

The extended horizons of political investigation and analysis confront the teacher of international politics with a dilemma. He cannot ignore the collateral fields because those provide so much of the data and so many of the concepts and theories out of which political problems are defined and political strategies are fashioned. At the same time, the teacher of international politics cannot possibly become really expert in more than one or two of these cognate fields. He has no effective alternative but to depend heavily on other specialists for specialized knowledge. Yet most of these specialists are not themselves primarily concerned with the political bearings and implications of their researches.

For this reason, if for no other, the problem of preparing teaching materials in international politics has become progressively more difficult and unmanageable. More and more teachers are asking whether international politics can any longer be effectively taught with conventional textbooks. Not only do international problems lead one over an intellectual landscape too large for any single textbook to encompass, but in addition, the subject is shot through with controversy. Education here involves not only the building of a fund of knowledge drawn from many specialties, but also the development of a mature critical faculty.

These conditions have inspired numerous experiments, nearly all of which involve anthologies, or collections of readings, drawn from many sources. These have evolved a long way from the so-called "source book" of the 1920's and 1930's. Today one can choose from well-selected collections which include some of the finest interpretative writing bearing on international problems. In most of the newer collections, moreover, the editor provides helpful notes or short essays designed to show how and why the selected readings contribute to a better grasp of the subject. Finally, anthologies of this kind provide a welcome change of literary pace, different styles, different perspectives, different interpretations.

Anthologies, however, even the best of them, exhibit well-known limitations. Variety of perspective is achieved at some cost, often heavy cost, in lack of coherence. As supplementary assignments, anthologies may or may not "track" well with the principal text in the course. Moreover, there is the refractory human tendency to neglect collateral readings which supplement the "cold dope" of a conventional textbook.

One possible way to meet these difficulties is to integrate text and readings into a single coherent entity. This is precisely what is attempted in *Foundations of International Politics*. The book represents an attempt to combine the virtues of a text with the richness of a carefully selected anthology or a library reserve shelf. The book offers a rather more systematic presentation than any anthology or collection of readings, and greater diversity of viewpoint and interpretation than a straight text. With a view to integrating text and readings more effectively, the latter are not segregated from the former. Quoted selections are incorporated into the chapters at the point of relevance. We hope this will help to overcome one of the shortcomings of anthologies.

Foundations of International Politics does not present a connected narrative of international events. It is not, and is not intended to be, a compendium of recent international history. International crises and other events occur—and quickly pass into history. The future may resemble the past in certain important respects; but in our revolutionary period the future seems likely to be less like the past than in more stable times. This speculation evokes the question: What kinds of knowledge will contribute most to the anticipation and understanding of international problems ten to twenty years hence? No one can be sure. But we have kept this question constantly before us; and what is said and what is left unsaid in the following chapters represent an effort to provide a frame of concepts, theories, and basic knowledge of enduring value in our swiftly changing world.

With this objective in view, we have tried also to make the book as non-polemical and non-policy-oriented as possible. We recognize the difficulty of achieving even approximate objectivity in a subject so controversial and so nationalistically colored as international politics. We have attempted to meet this challenge in two ways: by making our own viewpoint and bias as explicit as possible, and by presenting opposing viewpoints and theses in the words of some of their more capable and eloquent advocates.

In sum, the function of the book, as we conceive it, is not to argue for or against particular policies, but rather to promote understanding of a complicated subject. To this end, the book outlines an approach, provides a frame of reference, describes a few useful tools of analysis, presents a modest fund of basic knowledge and a representative sampling of interpretative writing. The function of the book, in short, is to provide the basic and essential ingredients for clearer thinking about the international problems that seem likely to affect our individual lives and our national destiny in the years ahead.

Speaking still more specifically, and from a purely American standpoint and perspective, *Foundations of International Politics* is intended (hopefully) to contribute something towards a clearer understanding of how our United States has arrived where we seem to be, where we seem to be heading, what we seem to be up against, and what appear to be our national assets and liabilities. The book stands or falls on the help it can provide in casting up the accounts and taking stock of the solvency of America's strategy in the revolutionary age into which we have been propelled willy-nilly, and from which there is no exit or line of retreat.

CHAPTER ONE

★ ★ ★

Intellectual Tools and Perspectives in the Study of International Politics

A SUBJECT CALLED international relations began to appear in the curricula of American colleges and universities before World War I. These courses were taught chiefly by scholars trained in history and in international law, and reflected strongly the approaches and perspectives of those ancient and respected disciplines.

After World War I, international studies put out new branches. Formation of the League of Nations inspired the introduction of courses on international organization. The term *international relations* acquired new dimensions, some of them nonpolitical. Largely for this reason, some teachers and writers began to use the term *international politics* to denote the interactions and relations of organized national communities, especially those transactions which involved some element of opposition or resistance or struggle or conflict.

During the 1930's, scholars who specialized in international politics moved progressively away from the approaches and perspectives of diplomatic history and international law. Writing on international political subjects became more analytical, topical, and schematic. In this, international political analysts were following a trail blazed by some of the great pioneers in the development of social science. Broadly speaking, the trend was towards more formal modes of analysis, more explicit concepts, a growing collection of models and theories, and technical vocabularies.

Most of the recent writings on international politics reflect the influence of these newer tools and approaches. This book is no exception.

The reader will find in the following chapters some technical vocabulary, numerous conceptual schemes, analytical models and theories—all introduced for just one purpose: to stimulate insights and to promote understanding of the activities called international politics.

Those who attempt to use the newer tools of political analysis occasionally run into resistance. This comes, in part, from those who believe that intuition is inherently superior to more formal approaches and theories, which are sometimes contemptuously dismissed as mere "methodology." Resistance comes also from disillusioned souls who expected much from the newer tools and approaches, and have become disappointed and even cynical because of the comparatively meager results thus far achieved.

These two kinds of criticism can perhaps be illustrated by a homely analogy. The first set of critics can be likened to the carpenter who goes on using familiar tools after new (and possibly more efficient) tools are invented. The second are like the carpenter who builds a house with the new tools, dislikes the finished structure—and throws away the tools.

Every complex human activity develops special concepts and theories, and technical vocabularies to express them. In order to comprehend any specialized activity one has to learn its technical terms and theories. Take baseball, for instance. This game has a formidable vocabulary, words used with highly specialized meanings: diamond, outfield, the grass, mound, strike, ball, double play, sacrifice, fielder's choice, triple, and many others. Baseball also has inspired elaborate theorizing regarding the conditions or odds favoring one strategy in preference to some other: for example, when to walk a hitter deliberately; when to sacrifice to advance a base runner; when to attempt a play at the plate; and a great many other strategies. The spectator rarely learns as much about the game as the professional who devotes most of his time to it. Nevertheless, most knowledgeable people would probably agree that it is impossible to understand baseball without learning most of its jargon (technical vocabulary), some of its theory, and something about the reasoning that may underlie choice of strategy.

Much the same can be said of international politics. In order to understand the moves and countermoves upon the international stage, and the operational results that flow therefrom, one needs to know the vocabulary of statecraft, something of the kinds of intellectual operations that are involved, and the concepts and theories, both old and new, that may be utilized in political analysis and interpretation.

This opening chapter is designed to bring these matters into focus at the outset. We hope that it will be read by everyone who reads the book at all. If this is done, we believe that it will help one to read the ensuing chapters more effectively, and thereby get ahead with the business of identifying and forming judgments about the conditions and events which are shaping the destinies of nations, our own included, in these days of revolutionary change.

Language, the basic tool

The most basic tool of political analysis and communication is language. Discussions of international politics, as of political affairs in general, are carried on almost exclusively in the verbal language of everyday speech. This is sometimes called the literary language, to distinguish it from the mathematical language of numbers. We say that the literary language is *almost* exclusively the language of politics because there have been attempts, increasingly numerous in recent years, to describe and explain political events and relationships in the language of numbers. One could cite many books and articles on political subjects in which liberal use is made of statistics, formulas, and equations.

Political scientists are divided regarding the fruitfulness of such efforts, and seem likely to continue so. In any case, the language of mathematics or any other nonverbal notation will not soon displace the everyday verbal language as the chief medium of political discourse and communication. However, before considering some of the characteristics of the verbal language, one should note well that simple mathematical ideas can be expressed in words as well as in numbers and other nonverbal symbols.

One such idea is relative size or relative frequency of occurrence. When one says that A is greater than B, or that there are more of A than of B, or that A occurs more frequently than B, one is thinking mathematically, albeit at a very elementary level.

This mode of thinking contrasts with "either . . . or," "yes . . . no" modes of thinking. Instead of contrasting blacks and whites, one compares shades of gray, so to speak. This comparative mode rejects absolutism. In the words of Harold Lasswell (Professor of Law in Yale University), the "either . . . or" mode tends to "rigidify thinking" and to reduce complex relationships to a simplicity rarely confirmed in the world of affairs.

Comparing relative size, or frequency of occurrence, or other aspects of a problem has many uses in international political analysis. For example, instead of asserting that China's international behavior is aggressive and India's nonaggressive, it may be more enlightening to say that China's behavior is *more* aggressive than India's in such-and-such respects. Instead of asserting that China is or is not a "Great Power," it may be more informative to say that, with respect to certain specified aspects of power, China has more or less, or is stronger or weaker, than India.

Relative size, relative frequency, etc., are very elementary mathematical ideas. But they are none the less useful. Indeed, this mode of thinking is generally more fruitful in political analysis than the "either . . . or," "yes . . . no" mode, for it evokes comparisons that reveal significant differences between states in policies, power and influence, and in the changes occurring in these phenomena through time.

The verbal language is more closely linked than the mathematical language to particular national cultures or groups of cultures. Broadly speaking, $E = mc^2$ (one of the basic descriptive statements of modern physics) conveys the same meaning to a Russian as to an American scientist. But this clearly is not the case with the verbal language, as anyone learns when he translates from one language to another. For example, the notion of causation—*A determines* (or *influences* or *affects,* etc.) *B*—is much more sharply delineated in English and other Western languages than in many Asian and African languages. Even where the language is ostensibly the same, as in Britain and America, for example, words and phrases may carry quite different connotations, in some instances fundamentally different ideas. Linguistic frontiers present one of the most refractory obstacles to effective diplomacy or other transnational communication.

Even within a single cultural milieu, the language of everyday speech is a most imprecise medium. Imprecision springs from numerous sources. One of these is poetic license, of which more will be said in a moment. Another source of imprecision is multiple meaning. Hundreds of words in common use stand for two, or often as many as five to ten, different referents. With regard to a single referent, moreover, a word may be overlain with multiple connotations or different shades of meaning. Connotations of many key terms in political discourse trigger off prejudices that obstruct rational thinking and frustrate communication. The vocabulary of political discourse includes a large assortment of terms which normally denote only the vaguest abstractions. These and other properties of words render it difficult to carry out precise analyses or to formulate precise hypotheses and theories in the language of everyday speech. Nevertheless, we repeat, the verbal language is the basic tool with which the political analyst and interpreter of events has to make do.

A pernicious source of imprecision is *poetic license*. The poet Shelley began a famous poem about a skylark with the familiar lines

> Hail to thee, blithe Spirit!
> Bird thou never wert.

Judged by the standard canons of meaning, this statement is patently nonsense. In everyday speech a skylark is a bird, whether Shelley says so or not. But in the context of the poem, the contradiction is not offensive, though contradiction there indisputably is. The man of letters justifies playing fast and loose with words, since for him words are like colors in a painting or sounds of different pitch and timbre in music. Using words to evoke moods, regardless of accepted meanings, is inherent in the art of poesy, and is appropriately called poetic license.

However, poetic license does not end with poetry. It has invaded other fields in which verbal precision is of the essence of fruitful discourse. Writers who purport to speak scientifically, or at least precisely, about social behavior and relationships also play fast and loose with the verbal language. Consider, for example, the following sentence from a highly regarded work of serious scholarship: "The mountains . . . have pushed the Japanese out upon the seas. . . . Sea routes have beckoned the Japanese abroad."*

We shall return to this passage when we come to examine the nature of man's relations to his environment. Here we are concerned simply with its figurative use of language, usage which amounts to a sort of poetic license. Such rhetoric, prevalent in books and articles on social subjects, is a fanciful and inexact mode of expression. Poetic license may infuse otherwise dreary prose with some sense of struggle and drama, but its rhetoric is likely to be an obstacle to precise description and explanation. It is as inappropriate in social science as it is appropriate in poesy.

Multiple meanings of words may or may not produce confusion. It depends in considerable degree on the audience. Take the word *power*, for example. This is a technical term of political discourse. Yet the word carries several distinct meanings outside the boundaries of political discourse altogether. There is a mathematical concept of power: "the product arising from the continued multiplication of a number into itself." In the vocabularies of physics and engineering, power denotes "the rate of transfer of energy, as in work done by an engine." Then there is an optical concept of power: "the degree to which an optical instrument magnifies." Probably most of the readers of this book will suffer no confusion from these nonpolitical meanings of the word *power*. But what

---

* From p. 5 of *Japan, Past and Present*, by E. O. Reischauer. Copyright 1946 by Alfred A. Knopf, Inc.; reproduced by permission.

of the two distinct meanings of power which one encounters *within* the frame of political discourse? One speaks of the power of Congress, and of the power of the United States. The first means *legal authority* to act; the second, *actual capacity* to affect human behavior—two distinct and different referents.

To confuse matters still more, *power* in the political as distinct from the legal sense, carries various shades of meaning. To some readers of this book, we imagine, power will connote effective military force conceived in terms of prospective ability to win wars. To others, power may convey the idea of ability to override opposition by means of threats as well as actual warfare. In some contexts, power seems to connote only physical coercion; in others, noncoercive influence as well. Since power is a key term in the vocabulary of international politics, and since it carries different connotations or shades of meaning, its use presents constant risk of imperfect communication. It will be desirable, of course, to define such words very carefully. But so sloppy are prevailing linguistic habits in America, even among well-educated people, that there can be no assurance whatever that the most careful and precise definitions will be heeded when the term recurs in discourse.

The probability of imprecision increases whenever the term triggers prejudices or other emotional responses. Take the word *communism*, for example. A teacher of government wrote on the blackboard the following formula: "From each according to capacity; to each according to need." He asked his students to comment on this formula as a basis of public policy. Initial responses were generally favorable. Students pointed out that this seemed to be the basis of free education, free highways, various welfare services, graduated income taxation, and other accepted policies. Then someone said: "It sounds like communism to me!" Whereupon everyone who had supported the formula hastily retracted. The emotional connotation of communism was sufficient to block further rational thinking on the subject.

Communism is also a good example of the vagueness which plagues so many terms in the vocabulary of international politics. Communism, democracy, freedom, security, aggression, justice and many other political terms not only mean different things to different people, but also to most people what is connoted is vague and imprecise. If the reader has any doubt about this, let him invite his friends to define the terms listed above. Vague reference is clearly another obstacle to precise thinking about political events.

It would be difficult to overstress the importance of explicit definitions, especially for technical terms. Since the meaning of a word has to be described by recourse to other words, there are manifestly limits to the precision that can be achieved. This is especially the case with words in everyday use (power is a good example) which acquire technical meanings in the context of special subjects. But words are the basic tools of political analysis and communication. For better or for worse we are stuck with the verbal language. The most anyone can do is to be as explicit and precise as possible in the choice and definition of these verbal tools.

Every sector of human activity, as already emphasized, has technical words and idioms. To the uninitiated, technical language is apt to be confusing, often meaningless. Technical terms which a person does not understand are simply jargon so far as he is concerned. The average American sports fan has no difficulty understanding a broadcast of a baseball game. But let him switch to a British broadcast of a cricket match, and listen to him complain of the incomprehensible jargon (incomprehensible to him) in which the broadcast is phrased. The average American male is apt to react similarly to instructions for knitting a sweater or for making a cake.

Used in appropriate context, technical terms constitute a sort of shorthand, designed to speed up communication. One technical term may express a concept that would otherwise require a sentence or even a paragraph or more. Take *cathexis*, for example. This is a term borrowed by sociologists and some political scientists from the vocabulary of psychoanalysis. Cathexis can be defined as "concentration of desire upon some object or idea"—eight words to do the work of eight letters. Or consider *empathy*, another term in common use in sociopolitical discourse. Empathy can be defined as "imaginative projection of one's consciousness into another being"; or more simply, as "imagining sympathetically how things appear to the other fellow"—one short word in place of eight or nine.

There has been a mushroom growth of technical vocabularies in all the social sciences. In general this seems to reflect attempts to attain greater precision and economy in expression of concepts and theories. One of the requisites for effective reading and communication in any special field is to learn its technical vocabulary. This is no less true of international politics than of economics or biology or knitting.

We shall endeavor throughout this book to use few unfamiliar terms. We shall make do as far as possible with terms in common use. But it will be necessary to define these terms with care, especially since many of them are used loosely and imprecisely in ordinary discourse.

Kinds of intellectual operations

Words are employed to communicate various kinds of intellectual operations. One of the requisites of clear thinking is to be able to distinguish between the intellectual operations represented by (1) descriptive statements, (2) explanatory statements, (3) predictive statements, (4) engineering statements, and (5) normative statements. Any newspaper provides exhibits of all five types: after reading this section, let the reader go through one or two news stories and editorials, identifying the different kinds of statements exemplified therein.

Clear-cut understanding of these different patterns of thought is useful in any subject. It is especially important in international politics. This is a realm in which prejudices are rampant and passions run high. It is a realm in which dispassionate contemplative thought is too rarely encountered and immensely difficult to achieve. Hence the importance of differentiating at the outset between description, explanation, prediction, prescription, and polemical argument and disputation.

Descriptive statements are designed to communicate an image of an object, a state of mind, a sequence of events, a layout in space, or some other state of affairs. A descriptive statement answers such questions as What is it? What is it like? Where is it? What happened? When did it happen?

Any newspaper provides scores of descriptive statements. For example, on September 14, 1959, *The New York Times* told its readers: "The Soviet Union hit the moon with a space rocket early this morning." On the same front page was a news story which began: "Washington was engaged this weekend in the most painstaking preparations ever made for the reception of an official visitor to the United States. The preparations are for Premier Nikita S. Khrushchev. . . ."

Description always involves selection. A great deal more could be said about any subject than is ever said. Whether the story is about a space rocket hitting the moon or the Soviet Premier's visit to the United States or the state of the Atlantic Alliance or the economic development of China, a particular description includes only a limited selection of the infinite number of things that could be said about the subject. What is said in a particular description depends, of course, on the context in which the description is given. Frequently, by his selection of "facts" the speaker gets into a descriptive statement a certain explanatory slant. That is to say, he conveys a certain meaning that is not inherent in the "facts" per se.

Explanatory statements are statements designed to interpret or give meaning to an object, a state of mind, a sequence of events, a layout in space, or other state of affairs. An explanatory statement typically answers the question: Why? In the context of human affairs, explanatory statements more specifically answer the questions: How was it possible for a given event or state of affairs to occur? Or, with reference to a choice or decision: How did it come about that the given choice or decision was taken? In answering these questions, one usually asserts correlations or other meaningful connections between the condition or event to be accounted for and collateral or antecedent conditions and events.

Explanatory statements are not quite as easy to identify in newspaper or other discourse. Such statements generally do not take the simple form of "*x* happened because . . ." or "*A* chose *x* because . . .". Here are a couple of samples from the same issue of the newspaper quoted above:

> Professor A. C. B. Lovell, director of the Jodrell Bank radiotelescope [in Britain] called the [Soviet moon] shot "a brilliant demonstration of the advanced stage of Russian science and technology."

In a feature article on Soviet art and literature, it was stated:

> Only occasional echoes of the battles on the artistic front are heard in the West because the Soviet censorship often refuses to pass dispatches that touch on vital aspects of the controversies.

Explanation is a complex idea, with many ramifications. Whole books have been written about it. The subject as a whole is far beyond the compass of this discussion. But two or three points should be noted here. Explanatory statements invariably refer to past events, or to past or currently existing states of affairs. In the idiom of logic, the process of explanation consists typically of locating the necessary or the necessary-and-sufficient antecedent conditions of the event or state of affairs to be explained.

Without going into technical detail, one may define a necessary condition as something in the absence of which the given event or state of affairs could not have occurred. Thus, an engine with a thrust capable of pushing a rocket beyond the effective counterpull of the earth's gravitation is a necessary condition of travel into outer space. Or, to take another example, access to iron ores and various other raw materials is a necessary condition of the existence of a steel industry.

In general, one can define a sufficient condition as anything, the presence of which renders it highly probable that the event or state of affairs will occur. Thus, assuming the requisite necessary conditions to be present (available goods and services), a favorable Congressional vote was the sufficient condition for the inauguration of the famous European aid program popularly known as the Marshall Plan.

The necessary and sufficient conditions of an event or state of affairs are established by the application of suitable explanatory propositions (also called explanatory hypotheses or "laws"). More will be said about these explanatory propositions when we come to consider the relationships between environmental factors and policy decisions and the operational results of decisions, later in this chapter. For the moment, we leave the subject of explanation by saying that "meaning" is given to an event or state of affairs by the application of some hypothesis or theory which may be (but usually in practice is not) set forth explicitly.

Predictive statements assert that a given event or state of affairs will occur at some future time. A predictive statement may, of course, be simply a blind guess or the result of drawing numbers from a hat or throwing dice. We are concerned here not with that kind of prediction, but rather with predictions which are derived by extrapolating past and present trends, or by applying explanatory propositions to assumed sets of future conditions. Predictive statements of this type are derived from the formula: If conditions are so-and-so, then such-and-such will occur.

Excellent illustrations of this predictive process are the population projections constructed by demographers. Such a projection, for example, might deal with American population growth during the next twenty-five years. The first step would be to construct a sort of matrix of assumed environmental conditions. Thus, for example, the demographer might assume that there will be no general war during the given period; that there will be no radical change in the economic standard of living; that the average American family size will remain about as at present; that the birth and death rates will show such-and-such trends; etc. Within some such matrix of assumed conditions, the demographer applies the formula: If conditions are so-and-so, then such-and-such will occur.

All rational policy making, and all rational study of trends in the policies and capabilities of nations, involve this kind of reasoning. Its essential ingredients are explanatory propositions that serve as logical premises which, when applied to assumed future conditions, yield predictive statements. Thus prediction resembles explanation in its logical structure. It differs from explanation in that the predicted event or state of affairs, and at least some of the necessary and/or sufficient conditions, have not yet occurred.

There is much argument these days as to the limits of fruitful prediction in the realm of human behavior. Prediction also presents some special difficulties for the political analyst. We shall return to these later.

Description, explanation, and prediction may all enter into the intellectual operations which we call *scientific*. A government report defines science as "systematic knowledge and methods of discovering new knowledge, especially knowledge arranged in a logical structure or theory which is constantly under test and revision." The American physicist, Henry DeWolf Smyth, divides scientific knowledge into three categories: that which we *know* to be so or will occur: that which we *believe* to be so or will occur; and that which we *guess* to be so or will occur.

It is evident that a great deal more is *known* about certain phenomena (for example, radiation) than about others (for example, how the Cold War appears to Russian peasants). But a common feature of all *scientific* investigation and analysis, the feature which distinguishes scientific statements from engineering and normative statements, is the quest for knowledge without regard necessarily to the practical uses to which such knowledge may be put.

Engineering statements represent intellectual operations that are performed for the purpose of affecting a course of events. Engineering may be regarded as an aspect of technology, about which a great deal will be said in this book. To quote again from the report cited just above: "By technology we mean a systematic body of methods for the achievement of human purposes in any field." As Smyth puts it: "Science seeks knowledge; technology seeks utility."

One ordinarily thinks of engineering and technology as applied *physical* science. But the intellectual operations involved in building a bridge are not very different from the kind of intellectual operations involved in planning and executing a foreign policy. Both are designed to manipulate conditions and events so as to accomplish a desired purpose.

Engineering or manipulative or policy-oriented operations contrast with descriptive, explanatory, and simple predictive operations, which are essentially contemplative rather than manipulative. Explanatory statements deal with events that have already occurred, and hence (by definition) cannot be manipulative or policy-oriented. Predictive statements which relate simply to the future implications of assumed conditions are likewise free from overtones of engineering or policy making.

A particular form of predictive statement, however, is manipulative or policy-oriented—indeed, is the very essence of engineering and policy-making. We refer to the form of prediction which answers the question: If *x* is to occur, what must be done? Or, alternatively, what must be done in order to get *x*? In more general terms: What course of action will accomplish a given purpose? Applied to our immediate subject, we have such questions as What can the United States do to combat Chinese influence in Southeast Asia? How can NATO be strengthened? How can we change the prevailing image of the United States in India?

In each question, the purpose to be achieved is given. The problem is simply one of selecting an effective means to the given end. In solving this kind of problem, one makes in effect a prediction that if so-and-so is done, the desired end will be accomplished. The problem and its solution are logically analogous to any engineering probem. For example, given the end—to build a bridge across the Hudson River—the problem is to determine what type (or alternative types) of structure will do the job effectively with the resources available. The political scientist and the civil engineer alike solve their engineering problems by applying suitable propositions with regard to the properties of their respective materials and the consequences of utilizing these in certain ways.

Engineering-type analysis can also yield negative predictions. The civil engineer's knowledge of materials and processes may enable him to tell the sponsors that their projected bridge cannot be built with any materials and structures known, or with the funds available, or for other reasons. Or like the builders of the medieval cathedrals, he may not know whether his materials and methods will suffice, and can only proceed with a large element of faith and guesswork.

Similarly, an expert public-relations consultant to the Department of State might have to report that no instrumentalities and techniques which the United States government commands would accomplish very much towards counteracting Chinese influence in Southeast Asia. Or, alternatively, that nothing much can be accomplished with the appropriations available. Or, that he believes certain methods are likely to be effective, though he really doesn't know.

There is a great deal more uncertainty in political than in physical engineering these days. It is comparatively rare for a policy maker and his staff to justifiably say with confidence: we know what will happen if we adopt such-and-such a strategy. The intellectual approach and operations involved are essentially similar; the degree of faith and guesswork is generally much greater.

The engineer—be his problem political or mechanical—may or may not approve of the purposes for which his expert knowledge is demanded. There is no intrinsic reason why a physicist-turned-engineer should not do first-rate work on nuclear-weapons development, even though he totally disapproves of his government's policy of building such weapons. Comparably, an economist and a political scientist who are against all foreign aid should nevertheless be able to give sound *technical* advice to the government on how to formulate and administer a foreign-aid program.

Discrepancies between the expert's personal values and preferences (his notions of what is good and right and proper) and the exercise of his expertise are everyday occurrences in the relations of lawyer and client. Such discrepancies are also prevalent in any bureaucratic (hierarchical) organization in which subordinates are expected to work loyally for the boss whether they like his policies or not.

What is involved here is the problem of multiple roles. On the one hand, the expert is the embodiment of specialized knowledge, the use of which on assigned tasks may or may not fit in with his scheme of values. On the other hand, he is a citizen, a member of the community with more or less positive convictions as to what is good, right, and proper. If the two roles conflict, *and if he cannot keep them separate*, he becomes at best an inefficient worker and at worst a menace to the organization which he serves.

This brings us finally to *normative statements*. These are statements which express a preference in terms of right or wrong, good or bad, desirable or undesirable, proper or improper. Here is a first-rate example, culled from *The Observer*, the distinguished London newspaper. What purports to be a straight news story, in 1957, on the psychological impact of the first Soviet space satellites, opens with the headline: "SPUTNIKITIS WILL DO AMERICANS GOOD." Why? Because from these events "must spring a multitude of changes, a surprising number of which will be all to the good." Clear-cut normative statements expressing moral preferences of a British journalist and his paper! Then follows some prophecy, non-normative in itself: "Americans will never again enjoy quite the same sort of luxurious defense politics, nor for a very long time disrespect their international opponents quite so wholeheartedly."*

Every policy-oriented prediction—that is, every engineering statement as defined a few paragraphs back—proceeds from some value or preference or image of a future state of affairs desired by someone. But an engineering statement is not thereby a normative statement. If the formula runs "In order to get x, do y," it is an engineering statement—a prediction that if one does y, x will occur. If however, the formula runs "x is good; therefore y should be done if y will produce x," then the statement becomes normative.

Every society, every social group, every individual exhibits conceptions of what is good, right, and proper. Many people profess to believe that their values are universally valid. This is an unproved and unprovable position. Disputation about whose values are best rarely leads to any

* By Patrick O'Donovan, October 13, 1957. Copyright by The Observer, Ltd.; reproduced by permission.

fruitful result. Consider, for example, a proposition to which most Americans unquestionably subscribe: that democracy is better than communism. This proposition means no more and no less than that the person saying so prefers democracy to communism.

In the context of political action, normative statements frequently take the form of policy prescriptions: The United States should (or should not) recognize Red China; nuclear weapons should (or should not) be outlawed; the United States should (or should not) encourage the practice of birth control in India; etc. In such statements the value or norm may be implicit rather than explicit; but policy prescriptions are normative none the less.

Such statements, we repeat, express moral preferences; that is to say, the ethical norms which the speaker desires to see prevail. It is fruitless to brand such statements as right or wrong, good or bad, in accordance with any universal standard. They are right or wrong, good or bad, only in the sense that they conform to or deviate from the standard set by a given individual or social group or community as a whole.

One can estimate the engineering (that is, operational or practical) consequences of any policy prescription. One can find out something, for example, as to what may be the operational consequences of opening up diplomatic relations with Red China. Also, one who commands the necessary votes or the "big battalions" or sufficiently persuasive public relations experts or other effective instruments, may be able to make his values (that is, his preferences) prevail. But might does not make right in any ultimate moral sense; and that holds also for persuasion, bribery, intimidation, pressure, and all the other ways of influencing human behavior.

Popular discussion of international affairs—in newspapers and over the air—tends to be strongly ethnocentric in all countries. Even books and articles that purport to be scholarly frequently embody more or less disguised pleas for national viewpoints or policies. Dispassionate contemplative analysis of the behavior of nations has become a scarce commodity these days.

Not only public discussion but virtually all government-sponsored reporting and research are heavily loaded with national viewpoints and values. A typical example was furnished in 1959 by the Draper Committee. President Eisenhower appointed this committee of distinguished citizens to investigate the extent to which military and economic aid to foreign countries could buttress the security of the United States. Judging from the published reports, the Draper Committee and its research staff never deviated in the slightest from the assumption that the purpose of Soviet economic aid is to enslave recipient nations, whereas the purpose of American aid is to liberate them. This position stands in marked contrast to that of the Soviet government. Just as frequently and just as emphatically, Soviet spokesmen have asserted precisely the opposite: that it is the Soviet Union that liberates and the United States that seeks to enslave.

A considerable number of educators and others appear to believe that such partisanship is unavoidable. According to this view, a person can never divest his discourse of values. Discussion of international affairs, runs the argument, may be critical, but it can never be dispassionate. It will always be partisan. Hence the sensible course is to accept the inevitable: make all teaching and discussion of international subjects frankly and openly partisan, value-loaded, and policy-oriented.

Some in our midst would go still further. They would argue that we are caught up in a life-and-death struggle with evil and implacable enemies. Under these conditions they see no place whatever for dispassionate or contemplative "ivory tower" analysis of international conditions and events. The function of education and public discussion, they appear to contend, should be to close the ranks and consolidate support behind whatever policies and strategies our government happens to be following at the moment.

This attitude carries a dangerous implication. It is common knowledge that people feel intensely for or against a particular administration or a particular ideology or a particular policy or a particular nation or foreign lands and peoples in general. But it is less generally recognized that people may pay a heavy price for their partisanship. Too much preoccupation with parochial values and norms distorts one's perception of conditions and events as well as one's judgments regarding their meaning and implications. This is the point of Falstaff's remark, "The wish was father to the thought." To the extent that the wish prevails over the thought, one limits his capacity to describe and to explain, to predict and to evaluate, what is happening in the real world.

To recognize this is not to imply that anyone can divest himself of ethical norms, in particular those which prevail strongly in the local and national communities of which he is a member. Nor are we suggesting that one should even try to do so. Shared ideals, values, and preferences are an essential ingredient of the social cement which binds people together in communities, and without which a sense of community could scarcely exist at all. Our point is rather that one should be alert to the tendency of values and norms to dominate judgment. It is a primary function of formal education to teach to distinguish between the different kinds of intellectual operations outlined above. Only when they are distinguished does it become possible to come to grips with the problems which stir so deeply the emotions of nearly everyone in these troubled and swiftly changing times.

Actor and observer

We come next to two concepts nearly always implicit in descriptive, explanatory, predictive, and polemical discourse. These are the concepts of actor and observer.

The concept of actor is derived from the vocabulary of the theater. In that context an actor is a person who represents a character, or acts a part in a play. In the broader theater of public affairs, an actor may be defined as the persons or group whose behavior is being described, explained, or predicted. In political discourse, as in the vocabulary of the theater, the concept of actor is always associated with the concept of role: the position or status which the actor occupies in the political system under discussion. Thus, in order to discuss political actions meaningfully, it is necessary to identify the *political system* (international, national, local, or other), the *unit of action* (nation-state, head of government, legislative body, citizen pressure group, or other), and that unit's *role* in the system (foreign policy making, or other).

It is customary to treat nation-states as the acting units in the system which we call international politics. It is also customary to attribute personality and other human traits to these corporate entities. In Chapter 2, we examine some of the implications and consequences of this usage and suggest cautions. Here it is sufficient to emphasize that the ultimate acting units of all social systems are human persons. Diplomacy, transnational propaganda, subversive activities, foreign-aid programs, technical assistance to underdeveloped countries, and military operations are initiated and carried out not by intangible abstractions but always by human persons acting in describable roles defined by law and practice. When one speaks of action by the state, he is necessarily (though perhaps not consciously) speaking of action by human persons authorized to perform in certain ways as agents of the national political community.

Political events and situations can be viewed from either of two points of observation. One is the viewpoint of the political actor in the situation. The other is the viewpoint of someone who (from the side lines, as it were) observes, analyzes, describes, explains, or predicts the actor's behavior and evaluates his performance.

The man on the side lines is in a position a little like that of the drama critic who watches the play from a seat on the aisle. In the universe of public affairs, nonactor reporting and evaluating is performed by numerous categories of persons: journalists, teachers, research specialists, as well as just interested citizens. Persons who perform this function are variously called reporters, commentators, analysts, observer-analysts, or simply observers. The term *observer* has the merit of emphasizing the distinction between actor and nonactor.

The academic study of international politics falls exclusively within the category of *side-line* observation. Scholars write *about* international politics. Teachers lecture and conduct classroom discussions *about* international politics. Students read *about* international politics. Hence the importance of appreciating the characteristics and limitations of the role of observer.

An observer can examine political decisions and situations from two perspectives. He can attempt to see things as these are seen by the political actor under observation. This is variously called "probing the mind" of the actor, reconstructing the actor's "image of the situation," "putting oneself into the actor's position," etc. Or the observer can proceed from his own independent viewpoint. These two approaches can be illustrated diagrammatically like this:

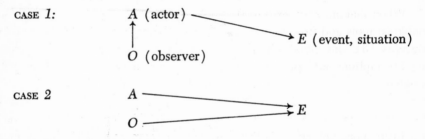

CASE *1:*   A (actor) — ↗ E (event, situation)
              ↑
              O (observer)

CASE 2   A —↘
                  → E
              O —↗

In Case 1, all O can do is to infer A's view or image of E on the basis of agreed rules of evidence. This is all O can do because O is not A. It is no more than a figure of speech to say, as is often said, that O can "penetrate" or "probe the mind" of A; or that he can observe the situation "through A's eyes" or put himself "into A's shoes" or, in short, make himself into A. O can take cognizance of what A says. He may supplement such evidence by making assumptions as to how things are likely to appear to persons in A's position and status. But all O gets in the end is *his own image* of A's image of the situation, motivations, and purposes and mode of thinking, choosing, and deciding.

How to infer another person's motivation, knowledge, and mode of thinking and acting has occupied jurists and philosophers of history from time immemorial. The conclusions of jurists are represented in the complicated rules governing what is and what is not admissible as evidence in court. Historiographers have laid down somewhat different rules of evidence to govern verbal reconstructions of the behavior of historical personages. Investigation of these issues leads one ultimately into a morass of controversy regarding "reality" and "knowledge."

It is unnecessary for us to delve deeply into these philosophical controversies. It will suffice if (when reading any description, explanation, or prediction of a government's purposes and strategies, or of the interactions of two or more governments through time, or of other operational results of political decisions) one keeps clearly in mind that he is reading *someone's version* of reality; that this someone may be either one of the actors in the situation, or (more probably) a sideline observer; that the discourse always reflects in some degree the perspective of the particular narrator; and that his perspective and image of reality depend not only on his access to events and reports of events but also on his own cultural background through which all perception and thinking are filtered.

Some analytical tools and procedures

When making a systematic study of any subject, one employs various analytical tools and procedures, including: (1) the process of analysis, (2) concepts, (3) conceptual schemes, (4) models, (5) hypotheses and theories, (6) assumptions and premises, (7) facts and factors, (8) constants and variables.

ANALYSIS

In its more limited sense, the process of analysis consists of separating or resolving something into its constituent parts or elements. So defined, analysis precedes systematic description, explanation, and prediction. Analysis normally precedes synthesis in building bridges, drafting government policies, or performing any other engineering operation. Analysis may or may not precede expressions of moral preference.

The term *analysis* is also used to denote all the intellectual operations performed in connection with a given problem. In this broader sense, we shall repeatedly use such expressions as foreign policy analysis, capabilities analysis, international system analysis, etc.

CONCEPTS

A concept is simply the name given to a class of objects, activities, qualities or other phenomena. Since the subject of international politics is concerned only with *empirical* phenomena—that is, phenomena locatable in space—every concept in this book has some empirical referent.

Empirical concepts divide into two general classes: those which refer to so-called "concrete structures," and those which refer to so-called "analytic" qualities, properties, or aspects of concrete structures. Concrete structures are physically separable; analytic aspects are not. A table is a concrete structure; its shape, height, and weight are analytic aspects of it. The United States is a concrete structure; democratic form of government is an analytic aspect. The British Isles is a concrete structure; insularity is an analytic aspect.

The clearer and more precise the reference, the more useful will a concept be for most purposes. This is emphatically so with respect to engineering statements which prescribe what must be done if a desired result is to be achieved. Sometimes, however, the purpose of discourse is not to enlighten but to confuse and muddy an issue, to inflame passions, to sway people by appeals to the "heart." For such purposes, it may be more effective to avoid sharply defined referents. Blurred reference is characteristic of much *popular* use of such terms as democracy, communism, peace-loving, war-mongering, aggression, security, intervention, national honor, national interest, limited war, and the like.

CONCEPTUAL SCHEMES

Concepts may be systematically arranged in sets of various kinds for various purposes. Such a set is called a conceptual scheme. A conceptual scheme can be likened to a collection of filing boxes, into which one sorts elements or aspects of a process or a state of affairs. Conceptual schemes, built in accordance with an ordered set of principles and relationships, are called taxonomies.

As a general rule, conceptual schemes are more useful if concrete structures and analytic aspects are not intermingled in parallel categories. In the following two examples, the first is based on concrete structures, the second on analytic aspects:

CONCEPTUAL SCHEME BASED ON CONCRETE STRUCTURES
TARGETS OF INTERNATIONAL POLITICAL ACTION
Human targets
    Officials of target state
    Other persons and groups of target state's population
    Target state's population as a whole
Nonhuman targets
    Target state's territory
    Particular structures upon target state's territory

CONCEPTUAL SCHEME BASED ON ANALYTIC ASPECTS
METEOROLOGICAL ASPECTS OF CLIMATE
Atmospheric temperature
Relative humidity
Barometric pressure
Precipitation
Air circulation
Other aspects

Another canon of classification is that parallel categories should exhaust all cases covered by the classifying principle employed. Since the five aspects of climate, in the example just above, do not quite exhaust the observable properties, one includes a residual category labeled "other aspects."

Still another, and very important, canon of classification is that parallel categories should be mutually exclusive. That is to say, data should fit into no more than one category. This is very difficult, indeed almost impossible, to achieve with conceptual schemes built around terms in common use in discussions of international politics. Suppose, for example, one desires to classify the different kinds of functions performed in the conduct of foreign affairs. Here are some of the terms in common use: diplomacy, negotiation, declaration, material aid, technical assistance, economic warfare, public relations, psychological warfare, subversion, sabotage, intervention, cold war, hot war, limited war, total war, etc. These terms have evolved over the years without much rhyme or reason. The more or less firmly established meanings and connotations of almost every one of them overlap those of one or more of the others. In short, the terminology of international action is a hodgepodge of imprecise and overlapping concepts. It is no exaggeration to characterize this as a state of semantic chaos which poses a formidable problem at the very threshold of any serious political analysis.

Any conceptual scheme has built into it a set of reasons for the particular categories selected. Such reasons may or may not be made explicit. But some rationale underlies every conceptual scheme. For example, any taxonomy of the "elements" or "foundations" of national power is virtually certain to include a category labeled "geographical position," or "geographical location," or some equivalent term. Why? Certainly not because location has any intrinsic or inherent political quality or value! Inclusion of this category will be found in every case to depend upon some such proposition as: A state's geographical position affects significantly its ability to influence in desired ways the behavior of other nations, because . . . From this point the proposition may take various forms. But the point to emphasize here is that every conceptual scheme, every classification, rests upon some set of justifying propositions. Thus the very process of constructing a conceptual scheme carries the builder some way along the road towards a "theory" of his subject.

Conceptual schemes are invaluable analytical tools. They reveal relationships and evoke insights and explanatory hypotheses. Numerous conceptual schemes are utilized in the opening chapters of this book. These deal with such phenomena as (1) targets of political action, (2) kinds of instrumentalities employed in the practice of statecraft, (3) ways in which such instrumentalities are utilized, (4) kinds of effects produced by different techniques, (5) factors that enter into deliberations and calculations of policy makers, (6) sources of national strength and weakness, (7) composition and characteristics of the Society of Nations . . . etc.

MODELS

The term *model,* like *power,* has many shades of meaning. Everyone is familiar with the scale models which are reduced replicas of ships or other objects. It is common knowledge that such scale models are not exact replicas, but simplified designs intended to display and emphasize only selected features of the original.

A familiar example of scale model, widely used and indispensable in the study of international affairs, is the geographical globe, which presents a simplified design of the intricate configuration of lands and seas which cover the earth. Political boundaries, likewise simplified, may be sketched in on a globe; so may mountain ranges, railroads, and other physical features of the landscape.

Flat maps represent another kind of model in common use, also invaluable in the study of international politics. As is well known, it is mathematically impossible to transfer any design from a sphere to a plane without distortion. Shapes may be distorted, as may areas or directions or some combination of these properties.

The simplifications and distortions which characterize all models of the earth's surface affect our conceptions of reality. At the same time, no one seriously proposes that globes and maps should be banned from classrooms or maps from newspapers. It is recognized that these models are valuable tools for acquiring knowledge about the earth and about human activities related to the earth.

Nor do most people feel uncomfortable in the presence of charts and graphs of various kinds—to depict business trends, flow of commerce, growth of population, and a great many other phenomena. These charts and graphs are models, symbolic devices for focusing attention on particular aspects of reality. When we read popular accounts of scientific achievements, we accept without hesitation various pictorial devices for illustrating the structure of atoms and molecules, and other facts about the physical universe. Though most of us do not understand them well, we likewise accept the mathematical equations by which scientists describe this universe more precisely. All these devices, we repeat, are models.

Military strategy is another field in which men have proliferated models. The so-called *war game,* worked out with diagrams and other symbols, is a model designed to simulate operations as these might occur in the event of real war. Simulated behavior of one kind or another forms the basis of research into many other kinds of human activity.

In addition to maps, charts, graphs, equations and other devices already noted, the term *model* has also come to denote any orderly set of interrelated concepts and propositions designed to show how some institution or process functions. This kind of model may be quite useful in the study of international politics. We have (1) decision-making models, designed to illuminate the processes by which statesmen decide what is to be undertaken, (2) capability models, designed to help identify the factors which set limits to what a government can accomplish, and (3) international-system models, designed to cast light on the patterns of interaction in the Society of Nations.

More will be said about these specific kinds of models later on. Here it will suffice to observe that all explanations, and all predictions that involve something more than a throw of the dice are based on images regarding the ways things are arranged and how they function in the real world. Such images, even though never set down in ink or print, are models. They are models in the sense that a map is a model, or a diagram of a molecule is a model. That is to say, certain aspects of reality are abstracted from the totality and form the basis of a simplified picture or description of how things work, how people behave, what will happen, etc.

People often deny that they think in terms of models. Such denials are no more than quibbles over the meaning of words. Laboratory experiments as well as everyday experience show that people do make assumptions about their universe, and that they do form pictures in the mind, so to speak. However described and labeled, such images constitute a person's set of working models, to which he relates his choices and decisions and without which he could scarcely survive a single day in our complicated modern world.

HYPOTHESES, THEORIES, ASSUMPTIONS, PREMISES

Let us suppose that we are waiting at a traffic light to cross a busy street. The light turns green, and we step confidently from the curb. In stepping into the street, one is proceeding on the basis of a prediction (rarely verbalized) that adverse traffic will obey the signal. In effect, such a prediction is simply an inference (generally instantaneous and subconscious or nearly so) from a "picture in the mind" (generalized model) of how a "typical" motor car driver behaves when he comes to a red traffic light. The pedestrian rarely has any specific knowledge about the drivers of oncoming cars. He usually knows nothing about their individual driving habits. But he does have a "picture in the mind" of how drivers normally behave in the given locality; and he predicts driving behavior on the expectation of probable conformity to that hypothetical norm.

Such a model, we repeat, is not a description or image of any specific person's behavior. It carries no built-in guarantee that the image of typical behavior fits any particular person. No behavioral model or any other model can possibly anticipate individual deviations from the hypothetical norm.

Models are generally derived from observation of events. However derived, a model is useful to the extent that it helps one to understand or to predict events in the real world. If it does so, the model is said to be confirmed. The process of confirmation or disconfirmation involves the formulation of hypotheses, theories, assumptions, and premises.

Let us return to our street-crossing example. Suppose that we are newly arrived visitors from a country with different traffic rules and driving patterns. We watch the flow of traffic and the alternation of green and red signals. On the basis of what we see, we formulate a *working hypothesis:* green means go; red means stop; and vehicles almost invariably obey the rules. This working hypothesis is a generalized description of patterned activities—in this case, response of vehicle drivers to traffic signals. As further observation demonstrates that cars do *in fact* obey the rules, and that it is safe to cross the street when the red signal stops adverse traffic, the hypothesis is said to be confirmed. Then, and then only, strictly speaking, does a hypothesis become a theory.

In practice, this distinction is not rigorously observed. Propositions advanced without confirmation or proof are often called theories. Conversely, propositions, such as the one that made Darwin famous, are often called hypotheses—thus, the Darwinian hypothesis—long after experts have accepted the hypothesis as confirmed.

In due course, a theory hardens into a firm expectation that future cases will provide further confirmation. When this stage is reached, a theory comes to be regarded sometimes as manifest *common sense*. It is then frequently referred to as an *assumption*. This usage is not free from risk of ambiguity because the word *assumption* is also used to denote elementary rules or *axioms* which are used in building hypotheses, and accepted as self-evident without confirmation—as, for example, the Euclidean axiom that a straight line is the shortest distance between two points.

At any stage in the evolution from trial hypothesis to firm expectation, the proposition—in our example, that drivers obey traffic signals—may constitute the *major premise* (also called explanatory hypothesis, or "law") from which future events are predicted by logical deduction.

Some historians, geographers, political scientists and other students of human affairs have contended that every human being is unique. From this premise they argue that human behavior is unpredictable. But such persons, we have noticed, do not hesitate to cross a busy street when the light turns green. In stepping from the curb, they are acting upon a premise that is just the opposite of their contention of the uniqueness of human behavior.

Generally, such inconsistency is more apparent than real. No one will argue that any two human beings, or social groups, inanimate objects, or other "concrete structures" are exactly alike in all respects. Nor will anyone deny that units of the same class or type—whether human beings or ships or anything else—have qualities, properties, traits, characteristics, or aspects in common. Indeed, it is by the discovery of common properties that one derives concepts, gives names to them, and arranges them in various kinds of conceptual schemes.

Smith and Jones are unlike in many respects; but they are both human beings, they cannot survive without oxygen to breathe, they are United States citizens, they are presidents of corporations, they dislike socialism, and they have countless other traits in common. Britain and Japan are unlike in many respects; but their homelands are islands, they are relatively poor in indigenous mineral bodies, they are heavily dependent on foreign trade, and have many other aspects in common. Hypotheses, theories, assumptions and logical premises are derived, in the main, by abstracting and generalizing selected common aspects, properties, traits, etc., not by searching fruitlessly for identical total entities.

No model and no hypothesis or theory, we repeat, embodies all the phenomena which, in the real world, constitute the concrete units under consideration. The essence of a model, as of explanatory propositions, is the selection of one factor or some limited set of factors which are deemed to be strategic (that is, highly significant) for the state of affairs or events to be explained. In a sense it is redundant to call these tools *limited-variable* models, hypotheses, and theories. We do so here simply to emphasize that this is a character of all models, hypotheses, and theories.

The fact that no model or explanatory proposition takes into account all possibly relevant factors does not make these intellectual tools less useful. On the contrary, the abstraction of similar limited aspects from different concrete units that are unique in their respective totalities and the derivation of general descriptions from such abstractions form one of the most powerful techniques by which modern man reduces his complicated universe to some kind of intelligible and increasingly manageable order.

If repeated observations show that where factor *a* is present, there event *x* occurs, we then have empirical justification for concluding that *a* is the cause—or more precisely, the *sufficient condition*—of *x* (as described on page 26). That is to say, we conclude that the presence of *a* justifies a prediction that *x* will probably occur. In many instances it may prove to be impossible to locate *the* sufficient condition of *x*. But it may still be possible, in such instances, to identify several strategic (that is, immediate and important) *necessary conditions*. And it may be feasible, looking towards the future, to predict the conditions that must prevail in order to make possible the occurrence of *x*.

Consider, for example, a geopolitical hypothesis, to be examined critically in Chapter 12: that the relative power and influence of states varies in proportion to their relative utilization and control of inanimate energy. This hypothesis rests upon a limited set of variables—coal, oil, hydroelectric power, etc.—and holds, in its extreme form, that these factors are *the sufficient condition* of differences in the power and influence of nations. This is equivalent to saying: Where *a*, there *x*. As will appear later in this chapter, such a hypothesis represents a form of environmental determinism.

But, the critic may ask, what about other sources of political power and influence, such as manpower, skills, economic equipment, social organization, etc.? Consideration of such factors may lead one to the conclusion that control of inanimate energy does not *by itself* explain satisfactorily the differences that are observed in the international influence of nations, even though this set of factors certainly *helps to explain* such differences. This conclusion shifts "inanimate energy" to the category of necessary but not sufficient conditions. In doing so, one modifies the original hypothesis. Instead of saying that where energy is abundant, power is great, the hypothesis now says that ability to control and utilize energy is one of the necessary conditions of international influence. This amounts to saying that where energy is not abundant, influence is unlikely to be great.

By now it should be apparent that we are using the term *theory* in a narrower sense than is usual in political discourse. Examination of the so-called classics of political science—Aristotle's *Politics*, Machiavelli's *Prince*, Montesquieu's *Spirit of the Laws*, Hobbes' *Leviathan*—reveals two kinds of discourse subsumed under the label *political theory*. One consists of ethical arguments regarding various kinds of rule. The other consists of generalized descriptions and explanations of institutions and processes of political rule. Typical of the first are the criteria by which men have weighed their preferences for various forms of government, and the arguments by which they have defended particular forms, or, alternatively, incited other men to revolt. It might clarify the study of government and politics a good deal, if such discussions of political norms and values were called political *philosophy*. This would leave the term political *theory* to denote generalized descriptions and explanations of how political institutions and processes work. It is in this latter sense that we are using the terms *hypothesis* and *theory* throughout this book.

FACTS AND FACTORS

Hypotheses and theories are derived from facts, and facts are utilized to test hypotheses. The dictionary tells us that a fact is "something declared to have happened, or to have existed." To this definition one should add that, in practice, facts are phenomena *as observed and reported by someone*. Facts may be imprecise impressions of untrained observers, or very precise observations of trained specialists. Facts may come unsorted; or they may come in tidy packages, such as statistical tables, maps, etc.

Such prepackaging is useful, indeed essential, especially when one has to cope with enormous masses of data. But as we shall see repeatedly in later chapters, the packages prepared by economists, sociologists, and other specialists may sometimes fail to fit the needs of the political analyst. Public opinion polls may not ask the questions we want answered. National economic statistics may not tell us what we want to know about military outlays and foreign aid.

A fact becomes a *factor*, to quote the dictionary again, when it is identified as "one of several circumstances, influences, elements or causes which produce a result." The definition is silent as to how one is to identify such factors. The question is easy to answer in general terms, though often very difficult in specific cases. In general, identification of factors is achieved by applying explanatory propositions as discussed earlier in the chapter.

The link between facts and theories may be denied. How often one hears: "I have no theory; I simply let the facts speak for themselves." Facts never speak for themselves! Even the purest description or chronicle of events involves an element of interpretation. No one can report everything. What one observes and records, what he retains and discards, how he arranges the data which he calls facts, all reflect an exercise of judgment as to what is relevant and significant. By the very act of selecting and ordering data and by the verbal or other symbols employed in presenting these, even the purest empiricist indulges in explanation and interpretation, protests to the contrary notwithstanding. As a famous economist is said to have observed: "The most vicious theorists are those who claim to let the facts speak for themselves."

CONSTANTS AND VARIABLES

Phenomena may vary in space or through time or both. Variation in space means uneven or irregular distribution. Spatial variation is nearly always a significant dimension of international politics. Such variation is the basis of all geopolitical hypotheses, in which the relations of nations are explained or predicted on the basis of the irregular layout of lands and seas, the irregular conformation of the land's surface, the uneven distribution of mineral bodies and other natural resources, regional variations of climate, uneven distribution of population, and still other spatial variations.

Whether phenomena observed to be unevenly distributed in space are also *significantly* variable through time depends on the rate or amount of change during the period involved in the problem in hand. Suppose, for example, the problem is to compare the relative abilities of the United States and the Soviet Union to supply tractors to Nigeria during the next two months. In this problem, uneven distribution in space would certainly be relevant, whereas variations of the spatial variables through time would probably be rather inconsequential. In plain English, what would matter would be stocks of tractors on hand or in production in the two countries. If, however, the time span in the problem is lengthened to two years, the time factor might become much more important. That is to say, one would have to calculate trends in the productive capacities of Soviet and American industries as well as relative capacities at a given time.

Variations through time, and especially different rates of variation in different places, are especially important when one attempts to project longer-term trends and patterns of international politics. Population, technology, economic development, weapons systems, military forces in being, transnational ideologies, the morale and discipline of national populations under stress, and many other clusters of phenomena change significantly through time at different rates in different countries and regions. This fact of differential change was emphasized in the Introduction. It is probably the most significant aspect of international politics in our time.

Heredity and environment

All human activities take place within limits of variation set by human heredity and environment. This is a truism of behavioral and ecological science. But the implications and mechanisms involved are not self evident. Since both hereditary and environmental concepts and theories have important bearings on political actions and outcomes, it will be well to give a little attention to these matters at the outset.

First, some definitions. By heredity we mean all the structures of the human organism which can be transmitted genetically from one generation to the next; by environment, all phenomena locatable in space which set limits to the activities of the human organism, excepting the limits set by heredity. This concept of environment includes both phenomena *physically external* to and *separable* from the person under consideration and his *image* of reality as internalized by the sensory processes of perception. Additional terms are needed to denote these two aspects of environment, to which we shall return after a further note on heredity.

Human activities involve both sets of limits, genetic and environmental. For example, neither heredity nor environment alone can provide a complete explanation of man's inability to fly through the air without mechanical assistance. A person jumps from a high window and flaps his arms—but he falls to the ground. One bystander says that gravity (an environmental factor) pulled him down. Another contradicts him, saying that human beings, unlike most birds, lack wings capable of sustaining flight (a hereditary factor). Both are right, but neither explanation is complete; it takes both to account for the event.

The theory of evolution rests upon the assumption that hereditary characters change (that is, undergo mutation) through time. With regard to human heredity, the rate of change has been so gradual as to justify students of politics treating heredity as a constant within the time-spans involved in such studies. However, the release of huge quantities of radioactive materials into the atmosphere opens up the possibility of more frequent and radical human mutations in the future. All this is still very speculative and controversial. No politically significant mutations resulting from radioactive fallout are known to have occurred to date; and, so far as we are aware, no precise predictions of such mutations have received widespread support from experts in the biological sciences. Hence one is probably on sound ground in still treating heredity as a constant through time in the context of international politics.

Heredity, however, presents other facets of interest to the student of international politics. One is the widespread belief that there are significant inheritable differences in intellectual ability, in capacity to function in different climates, and in other characteristics, among the various "races" of mankind. The policies of Nazi Germany were overtly predicated upon an assumption that ethnic groups classified as "Nordics" possess superior genetic endowment. Many people in many countries have shared this or comparable belief in the hereditary superiority of one race over another.

That such racist beliefs have affected the motivations and decisions of statesmen and their constituents is well known. That such beliefs—quite apart from any evidence confirming them—have had a bearing on legal rules, social taboos, or other restrictions affecting the utilization of human resources, and hence on the relative capabilities of nations, is also well known. Whether the various races of mankind do *in fact* embody genetic differences which, if taken into account, would help significantly to explain or to predict distributions of political power and influence in the Society of Nations, is a question on which all evidence known to us is negative or at least inconclusive. Hence, in the present state of knowledge, one has to conclude that there is no scientific basis for treating genetic variations among races as having any calculable international significance whatever.

There still remain to be considered the undeniable differences (not among races but) among individuals, either of the same or of different races. We refer in particular to the personal qualities of great and not so great individuals who play roles upon the international stage: Churchill, Roosevelt, Hitler, De Gaulle, Stalin, Khrushchev, Mao Tse-tung, Nehru, Castro, and scores and hundred of others. It is generally agreed that heredity is related to the qualities of leadership. But there is no agreement whatever as to the *relative* importance of heredity and environment in the making of leaders. As things stand today, the bearing of heredity on leadership constitutes one of the unpredictable intangibles in political analysis and interpretation.

Environmental concepts and theories

Turning to the other set of limitations—those derived from environment—certain distinctions must be observed if one is to avoid confused thinking about human behavior and accomplishment. The general concept of environment was defined above as all empirical factors (excepting hereditary factors) that set limits to human activities. So defined, environment includes not only tangible objects, human as well as nonhuman, at rest and in motion. Environment also includes institutions, laws, customs, and other social patterns as well. Defined in this way, environment is equivalent to the French word *milieu*.

In analyzing a particular outcome, performance, or state of affairs, it is generally possible to identify certain elements of the total environment that appear to be strategic (that is, very immediate and important). These specific elements constitute the *operational* environment of the actor in that situation. The operational environment (the factors which an outside observer judges to be relevant and significant in explaining an event or state of affairs) should be distinguished from the environment as it appears to the actor in the situation. His image of reality we shall call his *psychological* environment.

A person's psychological environment consists *not* of phenomena external to his physical being. On the contrary, his psychological environment consists of *ideas* derived from his perception of conditions and events *interpreted* in the light of his conscious memories and subconsciously stored knowledge.

An individual's psychological environment may or may not correspond closely to his operational environment. The linguistic expert B. L. Whorf once characterized the psychological environment of a person ignorant of those aspects of the physical universe which one cannot perceive directly and can conceive only within a frame of scientific theories and inferences. For such a person

> the earth is flat, the sun and moon are shining objects of small size that pop up daily above an eastern rim, move through the upper air, and sink below the western edge; obviously they spend the night somewhere underground. The sky is an inverted bowl made of some blue material. . . . Bodies . . . fall because . . . there is nothing to hold them up. . . . Cooling is not a removal of heat but an addition of "cold"; leaves are green . . . from the "greenness" in them. . . .*

On the same issue, the British geographer K. G. T. Clark says:

> An African with no experience of the world outside his native forest, transported by magic carpet to one of our own [brick] houses, would perceive what we also perceive, a prevailingly red object of a certain shape. But because his previous experience vastly differs from ours it is impossible he should perceive it as a house. Yet in physico-chemical terms the house is the same whoever looks at it. In our two perceptions there is something in common, the objective element, and something different, the subjective element. Human geographers, and others who study phenomena embracing human action and its results, are up against complications due to the fact that the reaction of man to a given physical background is apt to be strongly colored by this subjective element in his apprehension of that background. The way we have . . . been shaped in the past influences the reactions of the present.†

* From "Language, Mind, and Reality," by B. L. Whorf, in *ETC*, Spring 1952, pp. 167, 172. Copyright 1952 by The International Society for General Semantics; reproduced by permission.
† From "Certain Underpinnings of Our Arguments in Human Geography," by K. G. T. Clark, in *Transactions and Papers, 1950,* Institute of British Geographers, No. 16, pp. 15, 20. Copyright 1952 by George Philip and Son, Ltd., London; reproduced by permission.

The study of human behavior tends to concentrate on human images and perspectives, sometimes to the virtual exclusion of the operational environment. For example, the British historian David Thomson says:

> It is not a river itself that matters as a geographic feature; it is whether the inhabitants of both its banks think of it as a main artery of their common life, or as a "natural frontier" between them.*

To similar effect, another British historian, R. C. Collingwood, says:

> The fact that certain people live . . . on an island has in itself no effect on their history; what has an effect is the way they conceive that insular position.†

To this the geographer O. H. K. Spate replies that "people cannot conceive of their insular position in any way unless they live on an island." ‡

Spate's rejoinder is patently contrary to experience. From time immemorial, men have formed opinions and shaped their actions on the basis of inaccurate images of their environment. One thoroughly investigated demonstration of such a discrepancy and its consequences was the now all-but-forgotten panic produced in 1938 by Orson Welles's vivid radio broadcast of an imaginary landing near Princeton, New Jersey, of invaders from Mars. A more recent example was the epidemic of reports of flying saucers and other unidentified objects in the sky during the later 1940's, when millions of people were very jittery about atomic bombs, rockets, and other new gadgets of the nuclear age. To contend that "people cannot conceive their insular position in any way unless they live on an island" is equivalent to saying that they cannot conceive of nonexistent invaders from outer space or that they cannot perceive nonexistent flying objects.

One can distinguish two kinds of psychological events in the above examples. On the one hand, individuals may perceive what does not exist or may fail to perceive what does exist. On the other hand, since what is perceived is interpreted in the light of past experience, individuals with different backgrounds may interpret quite differently the same perceived objects or events.

It is possible, of course, to carry these points too far. The fact that the human species has survived (so far) indicates that there must be considerable congruence between conditions and events as people conceive them to

---

* From "The Springs of Nationalism," by David Thomson, in *The Listener*, London, May 5, 1960. Copyright 1960 by the British Broadcasting Corporation; reproduced by permission of publisher and author.

† From p. 200 of *The Idea of History*, by R. C. Collingwood. Copyright 1946 by Oxford University Press; reproduced by permission.

‡ From p. 423 of "Toynbee and Huntington: A Study in Determinism," in *Geographical Journal*, London, Dec. 1952, p. 423.

be and as these actually are in the real world. Man's increasing mastery over the physical universe seems to confirm this hypothesis and to suggest that congruence between image and reality is one of the conditions of technological advancement. One may also go a step further and speculate that individuals with similar cultural background tend to perceive and interpret conditions and events rather similarly. Otherwise it is difficult to imagine how social institutions could survive and continue to function even as well as they do on the whole.

The term *real world*, in the preceding paragraph, poses a philosophical issue about which men have argued since the days of Plato, and probably long before. That issue is whether there *is* any reality apart from someone's perception of it. We do not propose to re-argue this issue. We simply assume that there is a real world, distinct from someone's image thereof, though knowable only through the processes of perception from which are derived concepts and theories about reality. The distinction between image and reality is a fruitful one, and we shall continue to use it.

Perhaps the reader is asking: What has all this to do with international politics? The answer is: A great deal.

In the study of international politics, one is concerned with *both* the attitudes and decisions of statesmen and their constituents, *and also* the outcomes or operational results of decisions. In general, only the concept of psychological environment is relevant in the analysis of attitudes and decisions; and only the concept of operational environment in the analysis of outcomes and operational results. Environmental factors are related very differently to these two aspects of action.

In the explanation and prediction of attitudes and decisions, one is dealing not with a set of conditions external to and separable from the environed individual. One is concerned rather with some kind of psychological interaction between the individual's felt needs and his stored knowledge, on the one hand, and the signals or messages conveyed to him via his sensory organs, on the other. That is to say, what matters in shaping human attitudes and decisions (and in explaining these) is not how the real world actually is, but rather how it is perceived or imagined to be by the individuals under consideration. This elementary proposition, self-evident though it clearly is, is constantly neglected in discussions of foreign policy and the interactions of nations.

When the task is to explain a decision made in the past, it may be possible to reconstruct more or less plausibly the intellectual operations that actually took place. This procedure breaks down if the necessary historical evidence has been destroyed or is for other reasons unavailable. The procedure will not work at all, of course, when the task is to predict decisions not yet taken. Under these conditions, the alternative to pure guessing is to draw inferences on the basis of the actor's probable conformity to a set of hypothetical norms. This amounts to reasoning from a "model" of typical behavior, as described in the street-crossing example described earlier in this chapter.

Such behavioral models are almost never so labeled. They usually appear as assumptions (oftener implicit than explicit) which a writer makes with regard to the person or group whose attitudes and decisions are under examination. In general, such assumptions relate mainly to the actor's purposes and motivation, to the accuracy and completeness of his information, and to his mode of utilizing such information in formulating alternatives and taking decisions.

Careful reading will usually yield clues as to a writer's behavioral assumptions. One may discover, for example, that he assumes one set of statesmen to be predominantly acquisitive and power-hungry, but another set to be altruistic and self-abnegating. With regard to the extent of an actor's information (that is, his knowledge of the environment in which he is operating), one may discover writers assuming anything from perfect knowledge to total ignorance. Assumptions relating to a decision maker's mode of utilizing information turn mainly on the issue of rationality, as rationality is conceived by the person making the analysis.

One further assumption is almost always present. The observer (the person doing the explaining) tacitly assumes that his own image of the situation corresponds closely to that of the actor (the person or group whose activities are being explained or predicted). Given this final assumption, the observer proceeds to explain the actor's past choices and to predict his probable future choices, simply by imagining how a "rational" person (such as the observer himself) would behave in the circumstances.

What we have just been describing are the rock-bottom elements of what is commonly called *behavioral analysis*, or the *behavioral approach*. It is essentially a *probabilistic form of reasoning*. Its essence is reasoning from assumptions regarding what would be normally expectable behavior in the context under consideration. Thus, starting with a given past decision and the set of environmental facts which the observer deems to have been relevant, he reasons backward to an explanation of the decision. Starting with a set of environmental facts and assumptions regarding the actor's purposes, knowledge, and intellectual habits, he reasons forward to a prediction of the probable future decision.

These intellectual operations may or may not be self-evident. In a sense, what we have described is a little like the scaffolding which the workman takes down when the house is finished. But it is generally possible to infer from the context of a conversation or piece of writing how the conclusions were reached. We believe that the probabilistic model outlined above will be found to fit rather closely a good deal of political discourse in general, and discussions of international politics in particular.

When, as often happens, the speaker or writer tacitly assumes that his own national perspective and values are shared by actors of other nationality, and when, as is still oftener the case, this assumption fails to fit observable facts, the reasoning outlined above can lead to dangerously untenable conclusions. When this occurs, the root of the trouble generally will be found to lie in failure to recognize that differences in national perspectives and values may be highly consequential and hence significant in the explanation or prediction of national reactions to conditions and events.

There seems to be growing awareness of the significance of these basic behavioral differences among nations. This awareness is reflected in increasing use, on the part of those who study international politics, of ideas and theories developed by those anthropologists, sociologists, psychologists and other specialists who have probed more deeply into social patterns which differentiate each national culture from all others. We shall take up these matters further in Chapters 3 and 16.

Thus far we have been examining the relations of environmental factors to attitudes and decisions. We turn now to the quite different kind of relationship between environment and outcomes or operational results of decisions. The basic proposition here is that environmental factors can affect outcomes, results, and accomplishments, regardless of whether the actors in the situation perceived and took these factors into account. In the analysis of outcomes and results, the issue of choice and decision is bypassed completely. The task is rather to identify the factors which significantly affected the outcome of whatever was attempted. In this type of analysis, the operational environment is conceived as a sort of channel or matrix, within which the undertaking runs its course, a matrix which affects the course of the action and the outcome of a given decision or strategy of action.

These environmental limits may vary from time to time and from place to place. The limits implicit in one set of factors (for example, Atlantic winds and currents) may vary with changes in other factors (for example, changes in ship design and mode of propulsion). Thus the westerly winds which handicapped westward crossings in the days of sail, became relatively insignificant limitations in the later era of steamships. Though the limits vary, some set of limits is present at any given place and time and affects the outcome of any attempted course of action.

A particular set of limits may circumscribe broadly or narrowly; that is to say, the environment may leave room for much, little, or no range of *fruitful* choice. Under conditions of primitive technology, the limits are generally very restrictive. As men attain more efficient tools and skills, accumulate capital, and perfect their social organization, the limits are pushed back, and the range of fruitful choice widens.

Before men learned how to build mechanical flying machines, gravitation imposed an *absolute* limit on human flight. Today the size of a particular person's bank account or the state of his credit may just as effectively prevent *him* from riding in airplanes. Or he may have enough money to do so, but prefer to spend it on "the horses." In the second and third cases, the limitation is one of preference when available resources are insufficient to cover all desires.

An exciting aspect of history is mankind's progressive mastery over his physical environment. Broadly speaking, each new scientific hypothesis formulated, each new tool invented, each new skill acquired, each new application of nonhuman energy to get something done, has enlarged somebody's range of effective choice. Yet, as the late Isaiah Bowman once put it: "For all his independence and ingenuity," man "can never wholly escape from his environment. He cannot move mountains without floating a bond issue." He "conforms to many defective layouts because it would cost him too much to alter them," * even where he clearly has the technical knowledge and necessary equipment to do so. That is to say, with advances in technology and accumulation of capital, the question: Can it be done? tends increasingly to give way to the question: Is it worth the cost?

How does one go about identifying opportunities and limitations latent in the environment, with reference to a particular activity? Mainly by applying general explanatory propositions—the major premises of formal logic. We can try this out on the example, cited above, of the problem of transnavigating the Atlantic. In that example, the environmental factors given were winds and currents which, north of about forty degrees north latitude, move generally towards the east.

> PROPOSITION 1. Until well into the nineteenth century, the design of square-rigged sailing ships was such that they could not sail close to the wind—that is, with the wind blowing at an angle much forward of a right angle to the keel of the ship.
> PROPOSITION 2. Redesign of sailing ships to enable them to sail closer to the wind reduced somewhat the limiting effects of headwinds and adverse currents.

* From *Geography in Relation to the Social Sciences*. Copyright 1934 by Charles Scribner's Sons; reproduced by permission.

PROPOSITION 3. The development of internally powered ships reduced these limitations to a level where they no longer affected significantly the westbound courses of ships crossing the Atlantic.

In environmental theory, limitations on performance may be operative irrespective of human knowledge and decisions. In the example just cited, Atlantic winds and currents limited certain movements of pre-nineteenth-century ships irrespective of the desires and decisions of shipmasters. But *explanatory propositions* to account for outcomes and performances do not exist apart from human observation and thought. Such propositions are formulated by someone; they are strictly man-made in every respect—creative acts of imagination. Generally, though not necessarily, such propositions are derived from observed events. There is no certainty that any two observers will formulate identical hypotheses or regard the same hypothesis as relevant and sufficient in a given case. However, in any given society and historical period, there is likely to be considerable agreement as to how things work and why.

It is never inevitable that a given person or group will discover the limits of fruitful choice before reaching a decision. Nor is there any ground for assuming, as a general rule, that prior discovery of the limits would necessarily affect the decision taken. For reasons better known to psychiatrists, people often persist in courses which they recognize to be futile, even self-destructive.

In the explanation of outcomes and performances, some decision, some project or undertaking is *always taken as given*, not as an event to be explained. Similarly, in estimating future possibilities. The function of this kind of analysis is to identify and evaluate the environmental factors as well as the qualities of the acting units themselves which set limits to what can happen *subsequent* to a given decision, or undertaking. This frame of reference is technically called environmental *possibilism*. It is, broadly speaking, an important part of the intellectual framework within which the international capabilities of states are calculated. This will receive fuller consideration in Chapter 4.

Environmental "influences" reconsidered

In the light of the foregoing brief discussion of the relationships of environmental factors to attitudes and decisions, on the one hand, and to outcomes and results of decisions, on the other, it remains to examine critically the deterministic or near-deterministic rhetoric in which these relationships are frequently phrased. A few examples, picked almost at random, will illustrate this tendency.

Consider, first, a sentence from a textbook on the history of seapower:

England, *driven* to the sea by her sparse resources to seek a livelihood and to find homes for her burgeoning population, and sitting athwart the main sea routes of Western Europe, seemed *destined by geography* to command the seas.* [Italics added.]

We offer, next, a few sentences from a highly regarded book on modern Japan:

The mountains of Japan have *pushed* the Japanese out upon the seas, *making* them the greatest seafaring people of Asia. . . . Sea routes have *beckoned* the Japanese abroad. . . . The factor of geographic isolation during . . . two thousand years has *helped fashion* national traits which eventually and *almost inevitably*, *led* Japan to political isolation and to crushing defeat in war.† [Italics added.]

Third, from a work on economic resources, an assertion that invention of the basic steel furnace in the 1870's (an invention which made it possible to produce high-grade steel from acidic ores abundant in the provinces of Alsace and Lorraine, annexed by Germany after the French defeat of 1870)

led inevitably to Germany's industrial hegemony on the continent" of Europe in the final quarter of the nineteenth century.‡ [Italics added.]

Fourth, the opening sentence of an article on the economic development of Iran:

The political affairs of men and nations have always been *profoundly affected* by water.§ [Italics added.]

These are typical examples of environmentalistic rhetoric. In each instance some attitude, decision, or state of affairs is asserted to be determined or influenced or in some other way causally affected by conditions, forces, or factors present in the environment. Sometimes the alleged cause is a social situation; sometimes it is a man-made mechanism; very frequently the alleged causative factor is a feature of the nonhuman physical environment.

How is one to construe such rhetoric? Manifestly mountains do not

---

* From p. 44 of *The United States and World Sea Power*, by E. B. Potter et. al. Copyright 1955 by Prentice-Hall, New York; reproduced by permission.

† From pp. 5, 8, of *Japan: Past and Present*, by E. O. Reischauer. Copyright 1946 by Alfred A. Knopf, Inc., New York; reproduced by permission.

‡ From p. 648 of *World Resources and Industries*, rev. ed., by E. W. Zimmermann. Copyright 1951 by Harper & Brothers, New York; reproduced by permission.

§ From "Enterprise in Iran," by D. H. Lilenthal, in *Foreign Affairs*, October 1959, p. 132. Copyright 1959 by Council on Foreign Relations, New York, reproduced by permission.

push; sparse resources do not drive; sea routes do not beckon; steel furnaces do not lead inevitably to anything or anywhere.

One possible hypothesis is that speakers who employ such rhetoric are expressing a naive teleology. Indeed, one can find plenty of instances in which a literal interpretation of a passage allows no other alternative. Take, for example, the following sentences in a standard treatise on resources and industrial development:

> Nature . . . does infinitely more than merely set the outer limits within which human arts and wants can operate. *She makes suggestions* and man is wise enough to listen. At times this suggestive power of nature is very evident, as in cases when *she lures* man by rich rewards or *blocks* his road with *discouraging threats.* More often *nature speaks* with a less audible *voice.* In ways hardly noticed by man *she affects* the development of human arts and wants. It is human willingness to respond to even these *suggestions* of *nature* that marks man as homo sapiens. . . .* [Italics added.]

Another possible hypothesis is that deterministic and near-deterministic statements, especially those imputing purposeful activities on the part of a personified Nature, are simply examples of the sort of poetic license described earlier in this chapter: a figurative and fanciful mode of expression employed to infuse prose with a synthetic atmosphere of high drama.

Quite often, it would appear, such rhetoric is neither teleology nor poetic license, but a sort of verbal shorthand. Take the verb *influence.* This is easily the most overworked verb in the environmentalist's vocabulary. The essence of dictionary definitions of influence is "some activity on the part of a person or thing that produces without apparent force an effect on another person or thing." Thus, for example, a police officer blows his whistle and traffic stops. There is no physical contact between the affecting agent and the affected unit. The effect is produced without apparent force.

By a sort of analogical extension, a writer slips into the habit of speaking of geographical location or climate or mountains or a new machine or some other nonhuman human factor of environment as influencing people to do so-and-so. Construed in context, such statements as those quoted above may be merely equivalent to saying that the influenced person or group took cognizance of the environmental facts in question; that he (or they) evaluated it with reference to their felt needs and desires; and that he (or they) then acted in the light of the conclusions thus reached. Depending on the verb employed—determine, lead inevitably, drive, beckon,

---

* From p. 11 of *World Resources and Industries*, rev. ed., by E. W. Zimmermann. Copyright 1951 by Harper & Brothers, New York; reproduced by permission.

influence, or some other—such rhetoric can be construed as expressing the speaker's estimate of the odds that the environed person or group would recognize and heed the limitations and opportunities latent in the environment. Thus when one reads that the "sea routes beckoned the Japanese abroad," perhaps all that the passage means or was intended to mean is that substantial numbers of Japanese persons, at a certain stage of Japanese history, envisaged more attractive opportunities in seafaring than in farming or other pursuits ashore.

This conclusion suggests that environmentalistic rhetoric, when employed to explain attitudes and decisions, may reflect the kind of probabilistic reasoning described on page 50. What was there called the "model of typical behavior" included, it will be recalled, assumptions as to purpose, knowledge, and mode of relating knowledge to purpose in making decisions. Such a behavioral model carries a built-in assumption that people are capable of choosing among alternatives. But that is *not* equivalent to saying that *all* choices, which by definition are *possible* choices, are equally *probable* choices. The essence of probabilistic thinking about behavior is that some choices are regarded as more probable than others. The function of the model is to enable one to arrange a set of possible choices in order of estimated degrees of probable occurrence. By reference to the assumptions of normally expectable behavior, the analyst eliminates as very improbable or less improbable those choices which would represent greater or lesser deviations from the hypothetical norm.

Though this kind of reasoning appears to be implicit, if not explicit, in most predictions of behavior, one should always keep in mind its limitations. First, it is manifestly better suited to predicting the odds of occurrence in a large aggregate of units, than to pinpointing the choice of a specific unit. Second, no behavioral model can be any more valid than the historical experience from which it is derived.

With respect to the first point, a market analyst, for example, may be able to predict within a more or less calculable range of error how many persons per thousand in a given country will buy new automobiles next year. But if he should attempt to identify specific purchasers of next year's automobiles, the incidence of error would increase enormously. That is to say, the statistical methods employed in handling large aggregates of data might prove quite unfruitful when one comes to predicting the behavior of particular members of the aggregate. Yet it is the decisions of specific units—heads of state, cabinets, foreign offices, etc.—with which the student of international politics is usually concerned. This is not to contend that probabilistic reasoning based upon assumptions of normally expectable behavior, is fruitless. It is the best, often indeed the only, analytical tool one has for this purpose. But it is a tool of limited utility at the present level of knowledge regarding the springs of human behavior.

The second limitation relates to the validity of generalizing from historical experience. Assumptions as to what is normally expectable behavior in any context are derived ultimately from historical evidence. The process, it would appear, is more or less as previously described in the street-crossing example, on page 39. The relevance of past experience, however, may vary. It all depends on the rate and scale of change through time. If the kind of behavior at issue exhibits relatively stable patterns through a given time span, precedents are manifestly more trustworthy guides than in periods of rapid and radical change.

This principle is exemplified in numerous unconfirmed predictions in the late 1940's and 1950's, that one or another international crisis—Berlin blockade (1948), Korean attack (1950), etc.—was the opening move of World War III. In each case the predicted general war failed to occur. Study of these episodes suggests a possible recurring source of error. The prophets of World War III were manifestly reasoning from patterns of the pre-1914 and pre-1939 periods. Yet the enormous increase in the destructiveness of weapons, together with the concentration of superweapons in American and Russian hands during that period, created a situation without any precedent. Under those conditions, statesmen repeatedly exhibited a caution unknown in earlier periods. They might bluster and threaten; they might hurl insulting epithets that would have started the armies marching in the past; but they showed extreme reluctance to pass the point of no return. In consequence the outcomes of pre-1945 crises offered much less reliable guidance to the probable course of post-1945 crises than might otherwise have been the case.

Though nearly all historical experience has lost some predictive value in our era of revolutionary change, such experience is clearly more relevant in some fields than in others. The point is simply that the rapid and differential changes which characterize almost every sector of our environment today add a baffling uncertainty to the task of predicting future decisions and interactions upon the international stage.

Finally, one should be alert to possible significant differences in the way people behave as individuals and as members of complex decision-making groups or organizations. Such differences have become more clearly understood and more widely appreciated in recent years, with the development of knowledge and theories regarding communications and the operations of complex organizations. Broadly speaking, significant differences between individual and organizational behavior may extend to motivations and purposes, to the amount and accuracy of information available to the decision maker, and to the mode of framing alternative strategies and choosing among them. We shall return to these issues in Chapter 3.

Concepts and theories of strategy

Recent development of concepts and theories of strategy has added a new set of analytical tools for the study of international politics. Strategy used to be an essentially military concept. In one of the older dictionaries it is defined as "the science or art of employing the armed strength of a belligerent to secure the objects of a war." Since World War II a much broader concept of strategy has taken form. Today the term is applied to operational plans in all sorts of situations involving the interaction of adverse parties: labor disputes, legislative processes, law enforcement, and a great many others. In the context of international politics, strategy has come to denote the operational plans in accord with which governments manipulate *all kinds* of instrumentalities—nonmilitary as well as military— in their efforts to accomplish desired objectives vis-à-vis other nations, including allies and neutrals as well as potential or declared enemies.

This broadening of the concept of international political strategy has coincided with the development of so-called game theory. This development dates from the publication in 1944 of a book, by John von Neumann (professor of mathematics at the Institute for Advanced Study) and Oskar Morgenstern (professor of economics at Princeton University), entitled *The Theory of Games and Economic Behavior*. This pioneering work and others dealing with game theory have inspired numerous attempts to apply this kind of analysis to the Cold War and other phenomena of international politics.

It may be doubted whether formal game theory has much to contribute at this stage to the analysis or solution of international problems. But the notion of international politics as a game with describable rules, moves, stakes, and payoffs has certainly stimulated interest in strategy. In America, heightened interest in international strategy has tended to focus on the problem of deterrence: how to prevent potential enemies, the Soviet Union in particular, from attacking the United States or our allies.

This consuming preoccupation with deterrence arises, of course, from the mutually destructive potentialities of nuclear weapons systems, a condition which will receive further attention in Chapter 8. There is a very widespread belief that *military* war, fought with nuclear weapons, would likely ruin the victor as well as the vanquished. This belief has stimulated a great deal of new thinking about international strategy. One result is a revival of the idea—widely current within political communities, and formerly applied in the sphere of diplomacy and war—that most situations exhibiting conflict of purpose or interest are *ipso facto* situations with potentialities for bargaining. Another product of recent thinking about international strategy is the idea that satisfactory solutions are generally those in which each side gains enough to make acceptance of a compromise solution seem preferable to the mutually suicidal risks inherent in full-scale war.

When one begins to think about international conflict, strategy, and deterrence in such terms, the question arises whether students of international politics may not derive fruitful insights from analogous bargaining and deterrence situations in other spheres of human behavior. This question, among others, is dealt with by Thomas C. Schelling (professor of economics at Harvard), in a book entitled *The Strategy of Conflict*. This book should be read *in toto,* but the following short selection from it will suffice perhaps to indicate the perspective which concepts and theories of strategy can give to the study of international politics.*

We can be interested in [the strategy of conflict] . . . for at least three reasons. We may be involved in a conflict ourselves; we are all, in fact, participants in international conflict, and we want to "win" in some proper sense. We may wish to understand how participants actually do conduct themselves in conflict situations; an understanding of "correct" play may give us a bench mark for the study of actual behavior. We may wish to control or influence the behavior of others in conflict, and we want, therefore, to know how the variables that are subject to our control can affect behavior. . . .

But, in taking conflict for granted, and working with an image of participants who try to "win," a theory of strategy does not deny that there are common as well as conflicting interests among the participants. In fact, the richness of the subject arises from the fact that, in international affairs, there is mutual dependence as well as opposition. Pure conflict, in which the interests of two antagonists are completely opposed, is a special case; it would arise in a war of complete extermination, otherwise not even in war. For this reason, "winning" in a conflict does not have a strictly competitive meaning; it is not winning relative to one's adversary. It means gaining relative to one's own value system; and this may be done by bargaining, by mutual accommodation, and by the avoidance of mutually damaging behavior. If war to the finish becomes inevitable, there is nothing left but pure conflict; but if there is any possibility of avoiding a mutually damaging war, of conducting warfare in a way that minimizes damage, or

* The following selection is from pp. 3-20 of *The Strategy of Conflict,* by T. C. Schelling. Copyright 1960 by the President and Trustees of Harvard College; reproduced by permission of the author and the Harvard University Press.

of coercing an adversary by threatening war rather than waging it, the possibility of mutual accommodation is as important and dramatic as the element of conflict. Concepts like deterrence, limited war, and disarmament, as well as negotiation, are concerned with the common interest and mutual dependence that can exist between participants in a conflict. . . .

To study the strategy of conflict is to take the view that most conflict situations are essentially bargaining situations. They are situations in which the ability of one participant to gain his ends is dependent to an important degree on the choices or decisions that the other participant will make. The bargaining may be explicit, as when one offers a concession; or it may be by tacit maneuver, as when one occupies or evacuates strategic territory. It may, as in the ordinary haggling of the market-place, take the status quo as its zero point and seek arrangements that yield positive gains to both sides; or it may involve threats of damage, including mutual damage, as in a strike, boycott, or price war, or in extortion.

Viewing conflict behavior as a bargaining process is useful in keeping us from becoming exclusively preoccupied either with the conflict or with the common interest. To characterize the maneuvers and actions of limited war as a bargaining process is to emphasize that, in addition to the divergence of interest over the variables in dispute, there is a powerful common interest in reaching an outcome that is not enormously destructive of values to both sides. A "successful" strike is not one that destroys the employer financially, it may even be one that never takes place. Something similar can be true of war. . . .

Deterrence has been an important concept in criminal law for a long time. . . . It has figured prominently enough for one to suppose the existence of a theory that would take into account the kinds and sizes of penalties available to be imposed on a convicted criminal, the potential criminal's value system, the profitability of crime, the law-enforcement system's ability to apprehend criminals and to get them convicted, the criminal's awareness of the law and of the probability of apprehension and conviction, the extent to which different types of crime are motivated by rational calculation, the resoluteness of society to be neither niggardly nor soft-hearted in the expensive and disagreeable application of the penalty and how well this resoluteness (or lack of it) is known to the criminal, the likelihood of mistakes in the system, the possibilities for third parties to exploit the system for personal gain, the role of communication between organized society and the criminal, the organization of criminals to defeat the system, and so on.

It is not only criminals, however, but our own children that have to be deterred. Some aspects of deterrence stand out vividly in child discipline: the importance of rationality and self-discipline on the part of the person to be deterred, of his ability to comprehend the threat if he hears it and to hear it through the din and noise, of the threatener's determination to fulfill the threat if need be—and, more important, of the threatened party's conviction that the threat will be carried out. Clearer perhaps in child discipline than in criminal deterrence is the important possibility that the threatened punishment will hurt the threatener as much as it will the one threatened, perhaps more. There is an analogy between a parent's threat to a child and the threat that a wealthy paternalistic nation makes to the weak and disorganized government of a poor nation in, say, extending foreign aid and demanding "sound" economic policies or cooperative military policies in return.

And the analogy reminds us that, even in international affairs, deterrence is as relevant to relations between friends as between potential enemies. (The threat to withdraw to a "peripheral strategy" if France failed to ratify the European Defense Community Treaty [in 1954] was subject to many of the same disabilities as a threat of retaliation [in case of Soviet attack on the West]. The deterrence concept requires that there be both conflict and common interest between the parties involved; it is as inapplicable to a situation of pure and complete antagonism of interest as it is to the case of pure and complete common interest. Between these extremes, deterring an ally and deterring an enemy differ only by degrees. . . .

The deterrence idea also crops up casually in everyday affairs. Automobile drivers have an evident common interest in avoiding collision and a conflict of interest over who shall go first and who shall slam on his brakes and let the other through. Collision being about as mutual as anything can be, and often the only thing that one can threaten, the maneuvers by which one conveys a threat of mutual damage to another driver aggressing on one's right of way are an instructive example of the kind of threat that is conveyed not by words but by actions, and of the threat in which the pledge to fulfill is made not by verbal announcement but by losing the power to do otherwise.

Finally, there is the important area of the underworld. Gang war and international war have a lot in common. Nations and outlaws both lack enforceable legal systems to help them govern their affairs. Both engage in the ultimate in violence. Both have an interest in avoiding violence, but the threat of violence is continually on call. It is interesting that racketeers, as well as gangs of delinquents, engage in limited war, disarmament and disengagement, surprise attack, retaliation and threat of retaliation; they worry about "appeasement" and loss of face; and they make alliances and agreements with the same disability that nations are subject to—the inability to appeal to higher authority in the interest of contract enforcement.

There are consequently a number of other areas available for study that may yield insight into the one that concerns us, the international area. Often a principle that in our own field of interest is hidden in a mass of detail, or has too complicated a structure, or that we cannot see because of a predisposition, is easier to perceive in another field where it enjoys simplicity and vividness or where we are not blinded by our predispositions. It may be easier to articulate the peculiar difficulty of constraining a Mossadeq [Persian prime minister who sanctioned seizure of the British oil industry in Iran in 1951] by the use of threats when one is fresh from a vain attempt at using threats to keep a small child from hurting a dog or a small dog from hurting a child.

None of these other areas of conflict seems to have been mastered by a well-developed theory that can, with modification, be used in the analysis of international affairs. . . .

What would "theory" in this field of strategy consist of? What questions would it try to answer? What ideas would it try to unify, clarify, or communicate more effectively? To begin with, it should define the essentials of the situation and of the behavior in question. Deterrence— to continue with deterrence as a typical strategic concept—is concerned with influencing the choices that another party will make, and doing it by influencing his expectations of how we will behave. It involves confronting him with evidence for believing that our behavior will be determined by his behavior.

But what configuration of value systems for the two participants— of the "payoffs," in the language of game theory—makes a deterrent threat credible? How do we measure the mixture of conflict and common interest required to generate a "deterrence" situation? What communication is required, and what means of authenticating the evidence communicated? What kind of "rationality" is required of the party to be deterred—a knowledge of his own value system, an ability to perceive alternatives and to calculate with probabilities, an ability to demonstrate (or an inability to conceal) his own rationality?

What is the need for trust, or enforcement of promises? Specifically, in addition to threatening damage, need one also guarantee to withhold the damage if compliance is forthcoming; or does this depend on the configuration of "payoffs" involved? What "legal system," communication system, or information structure is needed to make the necessary promises enforceable?

Can one threaten that he will "probably" fulfill a threat; or must he threaten that he certainly will? What is the meaning of a threat that one will "probably" fulfill when it is clear that, if he retained any choice, he'd have no incentive to fulfill it after the act? More generally, what are the devices by which one gets committed to fulfillment that he would otherwise be known to shrink from, considering that if a commitment makes the threat credible enough to be effective it need not be carried out. What is the difference, if any, between a threat that deters action and one that compels action, or a threat designed to safeguard a second party from his own mistakes? Are there any logical differences among deterrent, disciplinary, and extortionate threats? . . .

This brief sample of questions may suggest that there is scope for the creation of "theory." There is something here that looks like a mixture of game theory, organization theory, communication theory, theory of evidence, theory of choice, and theory of collective decision. It is faithful to our definition of "strategy": it takes conflict for granted, but also assumes common interest between the adversaries; it assumes a "rational" value-maximizing mode of behavior; and it focuses on the fact that each participant's "best" choice of action depends on what he expects the other to do, and that "strategic behavior" is concerned with influencing another's choice by working on his expectation of how one's own behavior is related to his.

There are two points worth stressing. One is that, though "strategy of conflict" sounds cold-blooded, the theory is not concerned with the efficient *application* of violence or anything of the sort; it is not essentially a theory of aggression or of resistance or of war. *Threats* of war, yes, or threats of anything else; but it is the employment of threats, or of threats and promises, or more generally of the conditioning of one's own behavior on the behavior of others, that the theory is about.

Second, such a theory is nondiscriminatory as between the conflict and the common interest, as between its applicability to potential enemies and its applicability to potential friends. The theory degenerates at one extreme if there is no scope for mutual accommodation, no common interest at all even in avoiding mutual disaster; it degenerates at the other extreme if there is no conflict at all and no problem in identifying and reaching common goals. But in the area between those two extremes the theory is noncommittal about the mixture of conflict and common interest; we can equally well call it the theory of precarious partnership or the theory of incomplete antagonism. . . .

Both of these points—the neutrality of the theory with respect to the degree of conflict involved, and the definition of "strategy" as concerned with constraining an adversary through his expectation of the consequences of his actions—suggest that we might call our subject the *theory of interdependent decision.*

Threats and responses to threats, reprisals and counter-reprisals, limited war, arms races, brinkmanship, surprise attack, trusting and cheating can be viewed as either hot-headed or cool-headed activities. In suggesting that they can usefully be viewed, in the development of theory, as cool-headed activities, it is not asserted that they are in fact entirely cool-headed. Rather it is asserted that the assumption of rational behavior is a productive one in the generation of systematic theory. If behavior were actually cool-headed, valid and relevant theory would probably be easier to create than it actually is. If we view our results as a bench mark for further approximation to reality, not as a fully adequate theory, we should manage to protect ourselves from the worst results of a biased theory.

Furthermore, theory that is based on the assumption that the participants coolly and "rationally" calculate their advantages according to a consistent value system forces us to think more thoroughly about the meaning of "irrationality." Decision-makers are not simply distributed along a one-dimensional scale that stretches from complete rationality at one end to complete irrationality at the other. Rationality is a collection of attributes, and departures from complete rationality may be in many different directions. Irrationality can imply a disorderly and inconsistent value system, faulty calculation, an inability to receive messages or to communicate efficiently; it can imply random or haphazard influences in the reaching of decisions or the transmission of them, or in the receipt or conveyance of information; and it sometimes merely reflects the collective nature of a decision among individuals who do not have identical value systems and whose organizational arrangements and communication systems do not cause them to act like a single entity.

As a matter of fact, many of the critical elements that go into a model of rational behavior can be identified with particular types of rationality or irrationality. The value system, the communication system, the information system, the collective decision process, or a parameter representing the probability of error or loss of control, can be viewed as an effort to formalize the study of "irrationality." Hitler, the French Parliament, the commander of a bomber, the radar operators at Pearl Harbor, Khrushchev, and the American electorate may all suffer from some kinds of "irrationality," but by no means the same kinds. Some of them can be accounted for within a theory of rational behavior. . . .

The apparent restrictiveness of an assumption of "rational" behavior—of a calculating, value-maximizing strategy of decision—is mitigated by two additional observations. One, which I can only allege at second hand, is that even among the emotionally unbalanced, among the certified "irrationals," there is often observed an intuitive appreciation of the principles of strategy, or at least of particular applications of them.

The second observation is related to the first. It is that an explicit theory of "rational" decision, and of the strategic consequences of such decisions, makes perfectly clear that it is not a universal advantage in situations of conflict to be inalienably and manifestly rational. . . . It may be perfectly rational to wish oneself not altogether rational, or—if that language is philosophically objectionable—to wish for the power to suspend certain rational capabilities in particular situations. And one *can* suspend or destroy his own "rationality," at least to a limited extent; one can do this because the attributes that go to make up rationality are not inalienable, deeply personal, integral attributes of the human soul, but include such things as one's hearing aid, the reliability of the mails, the legal system, and the rationality of one's agents and partners. In principle, one might evade extortion equally well by drugging his brain, conspicuously isolating himself geographically, getting his assets legally impounded, or breaking the hand that he uses in signing checks. In a theory of strategy, several of these defenses can be represented as impairments of rationality if we wish to represent them so. A theory that makes rationality an explicit postulate is able not only to modify the postulate and examine its meaning but to take some of the mystery out of it. As a matter of fact, the paradoxical role of "rationality" in these conflict situations is evidence of the likely help that a systematic theory could provide.

And the results reached by a theoretical analysis of strategic behavior *are* often somewhat paradoxical; they often do contradict common sense or accepted rules. . . . It is not invariably an advantage, in the face of a threat, to have a communication system in good order, to have complete information, or to be in full command of one's own actions or of one's own assets. Mossadeq and my small children have already been referred to; but the same tactic is illustrated by the burning of bridges behind oneself to persuade an adversary that one cannot be induced to retreat. . . .

The well-known principle that one should pick good negotiators to represent him and then give them complete flexibility and authority— a principle commonly voiced by negotiators themselves—is by no means as self-evident as its proponents suggest; the power of a negotiator often rests on a manifest inability to make concessions and to meet demands. Similarly, while prudence suggests leaving open a way of escape when one threatens an adversary with mutually painful reprisal, any visible means of escape may make the threat less credible. The very notion that it may be a strategic advantage to relinquish certain options deliberately, or even to give up all control over one's future actions and make his responses automatic, seems to be a hard one to swallow.

Many of these examples involve some denial of the value of skill, resourcefulness, rationality, knowledge, control, or freedom of choice. They are all, in principle, valid in certain circumstances; but seeing through their strangeness and comprehending the logic behind them is often a good deal easier if one has formalized the problem, studied it in the abstract, and identified analogies in other contexts where the strangeness is less of an obstacle to comprehension.

Here perhaps we perceive a disadvantage peculiar to civilized modern students of international affairs, by contrast with, say, Machiavelli or the ancient Chinese. We tend to identify peace, stability, and the quiescence of conflict with notions like trust, good faith, and mutual respect. To the extent that this point of view actually encourages trust and respect it is good. But where trust and good faith do not exist and cannot be made to by our acting as though they did, we may wish to solicit advice from the underworld, or from ancient despotisms, on how to make agreements work when trust and good faith are lacking and there is no legal recourse for breach of contract. The ancients exchanged hostages, drank wine from the same glass to demonstrate the absence of poison, met in public places to inhibit the massacre of one by the other, and even deliberately exchanged spies to facilitate transmittal of authentic information. It seems likely that a well-developed theory of strategy could throw light on the efficacy of some of those old devices, suggest the circumstances to which they apply, and discover modern equivalents that, though offensive to our taste, may be desperately needed in the regulation of conflict.

Concepts and theories of social systems

System is a familiar term in political discourse. People speak of the American political system, the Soviet system, democratic and communist systems, the historic European States System, the balance-of-power system, the bipolar system, the inter-American system, the United Nations system, and many, many others.

Some concept of system underlies every branch of organized knowledge. One speaks of chemistry, physics, biology, psychology, economics, and other university disciplines as systems of concepts and theories. One speaks of the solar system, climatic systems, atoms and molecules as systems, plants and animals as biological systems. All sorts of man-made machines are conceived as mechanical systems. Sociologists analyze various kinds of social systems: state, family, church, business corporation, and others.

All concepts of system have a common core of meaning. This can be defined as a set of elements or components or units which are observed to exist or to function in accordance with a discernible pattern. Kenneth E. Boulding (professor of economics at the University of Michigan) characterizes every such system as

> a structure or complex of individuals of the order immediately below it—atoms as an arrangement of protons and electrons, molecules of atoms, cells of molecules, plants, animals and man of cells, social organizations of men. The "behavior" of each individual is "explained" by the structure and arrangement of the lower individuals of which it is composed or by certain principles of equilibrium or homeostasis according to which certain "states" of the individual are "preferred." Behavior is described in terms of the restoration of these preferred states when they are disturbed by change in the environment.*

The term *homeostasis*, in the passage above, is the familiar concept of the self-regulating mechanism. A thermostat built into a refrigerator or into a domestic heating system or other heat-exchanging mechanism, for example, keeps the temperature of a given air-space within a prescribed range of variation. The governor on a motor, to take another example, keeps the shaft from turning faster or slower than a prescribed range of variation. An autonomic mechanism built into the human organization keeps the body's temperature normally within a narrow range close to 98°F. Failure of the self-regulating mechanism may destroy the machine or the organism, or at least impair its efficiency.

* From "General Systems Theory—The Skeleton of a Science," by K. E. Boulding, in *General Systems*, Vol. 1 (1956), pp. 11, 13. Copyright 1956 by the Society for the Advancement of General Systems Theory; reproduced by permission.

Boulding and others contend that social systems exhibit properties analogous to homeostasis. A family, a fraternal order, a political community, or other organized social group penalizes those of its members who deviate too widely from approved norms, standards, and values. Failure to check such deviation may destroy the group or transmute it into something quite different. This is roughly what happens when a political revolution occurs.

Somewhat similar is the concept of equilibrium or balanced power which has been associated with the Society of Nations for several hundred years. When one nation-state or group of states becomes too strong or too aggressive, other governments enter into alliances and increase their military budgets to restore the balance of power. This historic principle and practice has been recently described as a sort of international homeostasis.

Useful as this concept may be, we would put in a word of caution with regard to it. Concepts and theories which purport to explain political systems by means of analogies drawn from machines and biological organisms may yield fruitful insights. But such analogies present certain dangers. They impart to political discourse a certain deterministic flavor, a certain automatic self-regulating behavior beyond the control of the human persons who comprise the system under consideration.

Neither a nation-state nor any international system is a self-regulating mechanism. Nor do political systems bear any striking resemblance to biological organisms. For reasons that should become more and more apparent as we proceed, analogies comparing political systems either to machines or to organisms are more apt to confuse and mislead than to clarify and enlighten. This is not to contend that system is an unfruitful concept. On the contrary! The point is rather that in describing social systems in general, and political systems in particular, one should be aware of the pitfalls latent in analogies drawn from biology and mechanics.

This cautionary word is not intended to belittle the important place which the idea of system has in many kinds of political analysis and interpretation. This idea appears in many contexts and at different levels of study and analysis: specifically, in the study of international politics, at the level of the individual acting units (states, nations, governments), and at the level of interaction among these units.

At the level of the individual unit, some concept of system underlies nearly all analysis of foreign policy (about which more will be said in Chapters 3 and 6). In recent years, the emphasis at this level has become increasingly on "organizational behavior," or decision-making in complex organizations such as those which formulate the diplomatic, military, and economic policies of any national political community.

In the study of foreign policy, the viewing point is characteristically that of the "national actor." However, by shifting the viewing point successively from one actor to another in an ongoing course of interaction, the decision-making approach takes on certain of the qualities of a more general systemic approach.

Focus on an individual acting unit (state, nation, government) poses questions regarding the characteristics of decision-making within *that* national political system. Taking an overview of the international system stimulates search for regularities as well as differences in the behavior of the various national systems which comprise the international system. Focus on the international system also stimulates hypotheses regarding types of actions and interactions which tend to preserve the system, those which tend to restore the system to a "steady-state," and those which tend to disrupt the system or to transmute it into a different kind of system.

Most analyses of political systems, both international and national, are carried on within a framework of concepts and theories which has recently become known as structural-functional requisite analysis. We shall not attempt to describe this type of analysis in detail. In essence it involves formulating hypotheses regarding the conditions and events which made it possible for a given system to come into existence, and upon which the system's continued operation and survival depend. Broadly speaking, structural and functional requisites are equivalent to the "necessary conditions" involved in explanations, described briefly on page 26 above. Examples of requisite analysis will be found at numerous places in this book: for example, in Chapter 2, where we attempt to formulate the requisites of the modern nation-state, and to use these as a basis for identifying significant differences between national and international political systems in existence today.

The essential principles of requisite analysis are not new, but they have special utility in a revolutionary age such as ours. They help one not only to form judgments as to the conditions and events which made a given system possible in the first place, and upon which its future depends. By comparing postulated requisites with observed changes in conditions—changes either in the units of the system or in their environment—one may be alerted to impending changes in the system itself. In a word, structural-functional requisite analysis may lead one to a better understanding of a system both in a state of equilibrium and in process of breakup or transformation.

There have been numerous international systems, recognized as such, in the past. One of the most thoroughly studied, though mainly from the standpoint of narrative history, was the European States System, generally dated from about 1650. That system evolved from a regional to a world-wide system in the eighteenth and nineteenth centuries, and then went to pieces in the twentieth. While it lasted, its members developed modes of action and interaction which will be considered in Chapter 2.

Today, various less-than-global groupings have been characterized as international systems: the United Nations, East-West bipolarism, the Communist Camp, the Anti-Communist Coalition, the Organization of American States, and others. We shall have to consider in what sense these are international political systems, later on in the final chapters of the book.

Students of international politics have begun quite recently to explore the possible extension and application of concepts and theories regarding political systems at the national and subnational levels. One line of inquiry has sought to discover fruitful analogies from the historic processes involved in the formation and breakup of nation-states and empires. The hypothesis underlying such investigations seems to be that similar processes may be at work both globally and regionally in the Society of Nations today.

The intellectual apparatus of any science or body of knowledge has to meet one test: Does it help people to think more clearly and more fruit-fully about the real world: what that world is like and how it functions. Every technical term, every analytical procedure, every model and construct, every hypothesis and theory, stands or falls ultimately on the degree to which it meets this test.

In utilizing some of the newer analytical tools, one need not belittle the older ones. Narrative history, for example, has yielded rich insights into the purposes, strategies, and accomplishments of the actors upon the international stage. But more formal and systematic modes of analysis and interpretation may prove especially helpful in projecting trends and in estimating future possibilities and probabilities in the rapidly changing international scene of today.

PART II: THE INTERNATIONAL POLITICAL SYSTEM AND ITS ELEMENTS

CHAPTER TWO

★ ★ ★

The International Political System

SEARCH FOR THE origins and antecedents of modern international politics would take one far back into a dim and remote age in the lands bordering the Mediterranean Sea. There, after centuries of recurrent disorder and fighting, one political community, Rome, emerged triumphant over all rivals. Then for a brief period, dating from about the beginning of the Christian era, Roman administrators and soldiers imposed on the Mediterranean and West European peoples a regime of public order which came to be known as the *Pax Romana*, the Roman Peace.

Gradually but inexorably this system of public order went to pieces. Historians have attributed the collapse of Roman power to various causes which need not concern us at this point. As the temporal power of the Caesars deteriorated, the spiritual authority of the Christian Church of Rome expanded and grew stronger. But the Papacy lacked the physical resources that would have been required to preserve the *Pax Romana*. The Empire disintegrated into fragments. The ideal of a politically unified world was lost—but not quite completely.

Many of the European fragments of the Roman Empire gradually coalesced into political communities of a somewhat different kind. These eventually came to be called nation-states, national states, nations, states. The rulers, or "sovereigns," of these European national communities were linked together loosely by two sorts of bonds: kinship through inter-marriage, and formal adherence to the Christian faith. These bonds did not prevent recurrent wars, which became more destructive with the development of cannon, small arms, and other advances in military technology. But kinship and the religious heritage did provide a basis for a rudimentary international order identified by such labels as the Family of Nations and Christendom.

In due course, this so-called Family of Nations became known also as the Society of Nations, and in more recent times as the International Community. At no time has the collection of legally sovereign national political communities ever constituted a family or a society or a community, as these terms are now generally understood. Nevertheless, they are deeply rooted in usage, and we shall continue to use one of them, Society of Nations, to designate the aggregate of national communities which constitute the units of the international political system, and with which the study of international politics is primarily concerned.

International relations and international politics

A great deal of movement and communication goes on among these national political communities. Some of this communication and movement involves only private individuals and groups. Into this category goes much transnational commerce and finance, international sports events, tourism and other private travel, private letters and telegrams, news reporting through various media, circulation of books, magazines and other reading matter, etc. But a large and increasing proportion of transnational activity involves governments directly: ceremonial visits by heads of state and other official representatives, diplomatic negotiations and conferences, various public relations activities, government grants of capital, other goods, and technical services, espionage and subversion, and military operations of many kinds. Moreover, even transactions which appear to be unofficial, involve governments indirectly, in the sense that no one can travel or send a letter or telegram or transmit news or carry on commerce or invest money or engage in any other transnational activity without at least implicit assent of one and generally of two or more national governments.

This complex of *trans*national activities—transnational in the sense that they cut across the boundaries and jurisdictions of national states— is loosely called international relations. The term *international relations* suffers from ambiguity and lack of clear focus. In addition to the above sense of *all* transnational events, it is also used to denote only transactions involving the *organized* political communities variously called nation-states, nations, and states. The term *international relations* suffers from further ambiguity in that it is sometimes used to denote *all* interstate transactions; and again only those which exhibit some conflict of purpose or interest. For transactions of the latter type we favor the term *international politics* which appears in the title of this book.

In delimiting the subject in this manner, we are not saying that the study of international politics is unconcerned with the activities of private persons and groups: for example, private business corporations producing oil in Arabia or the Associated Press gathering news in the Soviet Union or athletic teams competing in Olympic Games or even ordinary "garden variety" tourists on the loose. Such persons and groups, and their multifarious activities, are components of the environment in which international politics is conducted; and as such they may be significantly related to the interactions and relations of *organized* political communities. To a limited extent, private persons and groups may some-times act in a semi-official capacity as temporary agents of the national community to which they belong. They may also affect significantly the prestige of that community, and hence the ability of the community as a whole to accomplish certain purposes vis-à-vis other national communities. The test in every case is whether *organized national communities* are inter-acting. If so, the transaction and the environmental setting in which it occurs may (if the transaction involves some conflict of purpose or interest) fall within the sphere of international politics, as defined above.

Much the same can be said of various kinds of *trans*national organiza-tions. Some of these are associations of private persons or of domestic corporate groups: for example the International Political Science Associa-tion or the International Chamber of Commerce. In others the members are nation-states, acting through official delegates or representatives: the United Nations Security Council and General Assembly, the Organization of American States, the North Atlantic Treaty Organization, and many others. A few intergovernmental organizations—the European Coal and Steel Community, for example—show signs of developing into *supra*national systems of action—supranational in the sense that, for certain purposes, their corporate decisions attain precedence over those of the nation-states which they comprise. To the extent that *trans*national organizations, whether private or intergovernmental in structure, become *supra*national, *inter*national politics will become *supra*national politics and will acquire one of the essential characters which differentiate a *national* from an *international* political system—namely, a structure of authoritative decision-making. This is the goal of the United World Federalists and others who favor the development of a genuine world government. But we are still a long way from that goal. For the foreseeable future, it will be more realistic to regard *trans*national organizations, like the transnational activi-ties of private persons and groups, as components of the environment in which organized national political communities interact.

The further delimitation of international politics to include only transactions and relationships involving in significant degree some conflict of purpose or interest is in accord with general usage, domestic as well as international. A great many of the transactions of national governments involve an element of opposition, or resistance, or struggle, or conflict. When the conflict of purpose or interest is significant—that is, when it is the essence of the situation—the transaction is called political. Conflict need not involve hostility in either a legal or a psychological sense. Conflict of interest and purpose may characterize transactions among allies or with uncommitted nations, as well as between avowed enemies.

The element of conflicting purpose or interest differentiates a political from an administrative issue. Once the conflict of purpose or interest has been resolved, to quote from E. H. Carr (British historian and former diplomat):

> the issue ceases to be "political" and becomes a matter of administrative routine: . . . When states cooperate with one another to maintain postal or transport services, or to prevent the spread of epidemics or suppress the traffic in drugs, these activities are described as "nonpolitical" or "technical." But as soon as an issue arises which involves, or is thought to involve, the power of one state in relation to another, the matter at once becomes "political." While politics cannot be satisfactorily defined exclusively in terms of power, it is safe to say that power is always an essential element of politics.*

Some authorities go to the extreme of defining international politics exclusively as a "struggle for power" among nation-states, and even to conceiving of power mainly as military coercion actual or threatened. These are controversial issues. We shall have to deal with them in due course. But for the moment it will suffice to regard as within the scope of a study of international politics all transactions and relationships between or among organized independent national communities which exhibit some significant conflict of purpose or interest, regardless of whether military or nonmilitary forms of action are involved.

Some consequences of state personification

To say that the acting units of international politics are the organized national communities known as states, and to leave it at that, would be to sidestep several controversial but important issues.

States have no physical existence apart from the human beings who constitute their membership. Nevertheless it has long been customary to speak as if states were themselves physical persons. Most of the literature of diplomacy and war has been written in a vocabulary which attributes

---

* From p. 102 of *The Twenty Years Crisis, 1919-1939*, 2d ed., by E. H. Carr. Copyright 1946 by Macmillan & Co., London; reproduced by permission of St. Martin's Press, Inc., New York.

personality to the state. It is standard usage to speak *as if* the state possessed a humanlike will, and *as if* it were capable of perceiving, thinking, feeling, desiring, hating and otherwise behaving like a flesh-and-blood human being.

Such usage is well-nigh universal. One hears that Germany does this; France wants that; Britain is angry; China is inscrutable; and so on. In the eyes of most writers and readers such expressions are not merely standard usage; they are preferred usage. Personification of the state is most frequently defended as a semantic shorthand to save time and print. It may take a sentence or even a paragraph or more, to say exactly who is doing the thinking or the acting that is succinctly attributed to the state-as-a-person.

Such usage is undeniably a timesaver; but it has other, less desirable consequences as well. Verbal personification of the state evokes dramatic rhetoric, exemplified by the following passage from a serious political article:

> The liberated Europe . . . [of the late 1940's] consisted of ruined states *crouching* more or less *submissively* at the *feet* of a major and a minor *archangel, talking* English to each other. France was the first to receive promotion to nominal archangel rank, but without *wings* and with a different language on *her lips.* . . . [Italics added.]

No doubt many writers and editors, and probably most of the readers of this book, like such rhetoric. One can imagine them defending it enthusiastically as colorful and dramatic. But what kind of image does the above passage (and countless others comparably picturesque) evoke? Does this image conform to anything observable in the real world? Does such rhetoric foster fruitful thinking about the complex *human* relationships which we call international politics?

It is elementary common sense that the state is not a biological organism. Very few people these days would contend seriously that any corporate abstraction *as such* possesses human characters. Yet there is plenty of evidence that by ascribing personality to the state, people slip into behaving *as if* the state were a biological organism, *as if* it did have a humanlike personality, and *as if* the state *as state* exhibited humanlike capacities of thinking, feeling, desiring, deciding, acting and reacting. Numerous consequences flow from such ways of thinking.

It is easy for individuals to identify with *la patrie, das Vaterland,* my country. Americans who would not readily identify with President Eisenhower or President Kennedy find no difficulty in identifying with an abstraction called America, symbolized by the flag, the statue of liberty, and many other symbols. Such identification affects behavior in many ways.

People become emotional about their country and make great sacrifices in its name. They even submerge their interpersonal standards of right and wrong in the slogan: My country, may she always be right; but right or wrong, my country.

Another consequence of behaving as if states were superpersons is the universal habit of ascribing humanlike virtues and vices to states *as states*. As so much of the literature of international politics shows, this kind of thinking pushes into the background the human beings who alone are capable of moral or immoral behavior and who perform all the operations attributed to the state.

State actions are explained and defended, not in terms of the human individuals who did the acting, but in terms of *national* honor, *national* prestige, *national* security, *national* interest, *national* necessity, *raison d'état*, and similar verbalisms. Built into such expressions is an implicit concept of the state as a tangible, physical reality, a sort of superhuman person, an entity with an identity and behavioral apparatus similar to but independent of the human persons who compose it and alone give it tangible reality. From this mode of thinking, we repeat, flow judgments regarding the moral character of states *as states*, regarding the motivations of states *as states*, and other aspects of the behavior of *states*.

This mode of speaking and thinking sets the stage for a conception of international politics as a sort of game played by superpersons around a supergameboard. In recent years it has become fashionable to talk about international politics in this idiom. Numerous theories of international politics have been formulated in these terms. We have already noted some aspects of this theorizing, in Chapter 1. We shall have more to say about it later on. For the moment, it will suffice to indicate one or two by-products of the application of so-called game theories to international politics.

One of these is a set of psychological presuppositions about political motivation. The players in the game of international politics are generally assumed to play according to a set of rules for generally similar stakes. These are usually expressed in terms of desire for power, aggrandizement, and survival. Such psychological presuppositions may be quite fruitful at a very high level of abstraction. But they tell one little or nothing about the *differences* between national communities, differences in attitudes and in motivations and purposes, which find expression in the human persons who transact business with the human representatives of other national communities.

Another by-product of viewing states as persons and international politics as a game has been the paradoxical one of dehumanizing the whole business. Experts spin theories about the game and its strategies, much as if they were manipulating a deck of cards or a set of chessmen. They disregard (if indeed they do not largely forget, in their preoccupation with the game) what politics is ultimately all about—namely, the accommodation of conflicting human claims and interests, ideals, and aspirations.

Still another by-product of regarding states as humanlike persons and politics as a game is (in the words of a British writer) a "pervasive implication that the game is somehow given, that it is for the players to adapt themselves to it rather than change the rules to suit their own convenience."*

This deterministic taint is clearly discernible in a good deal of recent American writing about international politics. What is, is! The Cold War, the armaments race, espionage and counterespionage, these and other features of the contemporary international scene are treated more or less as immutable givens. In this view, one may deplore the state of the world. He may, figuratively speaking, wring his hands in despair over the predestined folly of his fellow men. But little or nothing can be done to alter the course of predetermined events. Human beings become, in this pessimistic view, mere chips in a swiftly flowing current. They are caught in the current, in a channel from which they cannot escape.

It should be plain by now that important consequences flow from the manner in which one conceives of the acting units of international politics. One way to avoid some of the consequences of state personification is to focus as sharply as possible on the human persons who act in the name of the state. It is not always possible, nor is it always worth the effort, to identify the precise persons who are acting as agents of the state in a given situation. But it is both possible and fruitful to keep clearly in mind that action by a state is action by human persons who are authorized to act as agents, in the name of the national political community which they represent.

The anatomy of statehood

The political communities comprised in the Society of Nations all have certain attributes in common. These include population, territory, government, economy, and a national culture. These features are requisites in the sense that the nation-state (as we know it) would not and could not exist in their absence.

* From David Marquand in *The New Statesman*, London, June 18, 1960, p. 904. Copyright 1960 by The Statesman and Nation Publishing Co.; reproduced by permission.

POPULATION

The state, a form of social organization, manifestly could not exist without a population. The persons who constitute a state's membership are called *nationals* (in international law), *subjects* (in the vanishing vocabulary of monarchism), and *citizens* (in the idiom of everyday speech).

The body of citizens changes continuously. Citizens die; others are born into citizenship. Immigrants become citizens by a process called naturalization. Emigrants may renounce their citizenship and accept membership in another state. At any given time a state's membership may be defined as all persons who owe allegiance to that state and enjoy the legal status of citizen. This aggregate of citizens is sometimes designated the *body politic*; more commonly *the* people—for example, the American people, or the British people.

The term *people*, however, has certain other connotations as well. Colonial populations legally owe allegiance to the imperial sovereign, but are not usually included as part of *the* people of the imperial state. Conversely, the term *people* may refer to the population of a colony or other political community which is not a full-fledged member of the Society of Nations. It is normally evident, from the context of a discussion, in what sense the term *people* is being used.

States vary enormously in size of population. Four have a population exceeding 100 millions. These four are:

China ("People's Republic")	about 650 millions
India	about 400 millions
Soviet Union	about 210 millions
United States	about 180 millions

The next eight in order of population size are:

Japan	about 95 millions
Indonesia	about 90 millions
Pakistan	about 90 millions
Brazil	about 65 millions
West Germany	about 55 millions
United Kingdom	about 52 millions
Italy	about 50 millions
France	about 45 millions

Of the seven most populous states, six are wholly or partly in Asia (including Japan and Indonesia, which occupy islands in the far Western Pacific). The United States and Brazil (ranking fourth and eighth respectively) are in the American hemisphere. Not until we reach number nine (West Germany) do we come to a strictly European country.

At the opposite end of the scale, one discovers several new states in Africa with a population of less than one million, and several in Central America and the Near East with less than two millions—not to mention the politically insignificant statelets or quasi-states of Monaco (famous for gambling), Liechtenstein, and one or two others.

Size, of course, is not the only facet of population that interests the student of international politics. The policies and capabilities of states may be significantly related to the internal make-up of a state's population, and to its physical and intellectual qualities. We shall return to these and other aspects of population later, especially in Chapter 13.

TERRITORY

Territory is the second attribute of statehood. A state's territorial boundaries may be in dispute. More than one government may lay claim to the same piece of territory. A government-in-exile may claim jurisdiction over territory from which it has been ejected. In every case, however, a state has a geographical base. Without territory the state (as we know it) would not and could not exist.

When one speaks of a state primarily in its territorial aspect, the term in common use is *country*. Again usage is not consistent. The term *country* may also refer to the territory of a political community, such as a colony, which lacks other essential requisites of statehood. There is a tendency to use the terms *country* and *state* interchangeably. Journalists are addicted to this careless usage. It will further clarify if the term *country* is used only in the sense indicated at the beginning of this paragraph: to denote the state in its territorial or geographical aspect.

States differ in geographical size as widely as in population. On a scale of largest to smallest (excluding colonial dependencies), the Soviet Union stands far out in front. This huge country is considerably more than twice as large as the next in size. The following table shows, in round numbers, the comparative size of the six largest states:

Soviet Union	approximately 7.9 million sq. mi.
China ("People's Republic)	approximately 3.8 million sq. mi.
Canada	approximately 3.8 million sq. mi.
United States (50 States)	approximately 3.6 million sq. mi.
Brazil	approximately 3.3 million sq. mi.
Australia	approximately 2.9 million sq. mi.

At the other end of the scale, one discovers a number of states with ten thousand square miles of territory or less. These include the Near Eastern states of Lebanon and Israel and the Central American state of El Salvador. The five largest European countries (excluding the Soviet Union, which is Eurasian rather than strictly European) lie closer to the small than to the large end of the scale.

France	approximately 212,600 sq. mi.
Spain	approximately 194,900 sq. mi.
Sweden	approximately 177,500 sq. mi.
Finland	approximately 130,100 sq. mi.
Norway	approximately 125,000 sq. mi.
Poland	approximately 120,000 sq. mi.

The United Kingdom (England, Scotland, Wales, and Northern Ireland) totals only 92,000 square miles, comparable to Illinois and Indiana combined. West Germany is only slightly larger, with an area of 95,000 square miles.

If one adds the oversea territories governed directly or indirectly from London, the total for the British Empire was more than two million square miles in 1960. (That total included, of course, none of the members of the British Commonwealth, all of which are full-fledged sovereign states.) Comparably, the area of numerous other European states, and a few non-European states, would be considerably increased if the basis of comparison is area-of-rule rather than area of the ruling state.

One could compare many other facets of the territorial aspect of states: for example, their location, geographical shape, structure of boundaries, landscapes, climates, and soils, forests, mineral bodies, and other useful materials. These facets may have important bearings on the policies and international capabilities of states. Later we shall go into some of these features of the physical environment in which national policies are formulated and executed—chiefly in Chapters 9, 10, 11, and 12.

GOVERNMENT

A third attribute of statehood is government. The essence of government is effective command of and legal authority to exercise a monopoly of organized violence within a state's geographical space. Under conditions prescribed by international law, this authority may extend onto the high sea, and also to certain limited situations inside the territory of other states.

If a government is unable to maintain a monpoly of organized violence —that is, an effective police power—within its territory, it has a revolt on its hands or is suffering military defeat inflicted by outside forces. In the first case, the legitimate government (called, in international law, the *de jure* government) either puts down the revolt or it eventually ceases to be a government. If the rebels take over, their organization of power becomes the *de facto* (that is, effective) government. In the normal course of events, the *de facto* government is recognized by a sufficient number of the more influential members of the Society of Nations, as the legitimate successor of the dispossessed regime and is thereby transformed into the *de jure* government.

In the case of military defeat, inflicted by the forces of other states, several outcomes are possible. The state may cease to exist as an independent political community, as happened when the Soviet Union annexed the states of Lithuania, Latvia, and Estonia in 1940. Or the military victors may displace the defeated state's government and install another one, which is substantially what happened in Germany after World War II. Or the victors may permit the defeated government to survive and continue to function, with or without alterations, as happened after the defeat of Japan in 1945.

Governments differ widely in the principles upon which they are founded, in institutional structure, and in mode of functioning. Since governments are the primary acting units of international politics, it will be necessary to investigate (in Chapter 6) how such differences may affect the purposes, strategies, and operations of particular states, and also the distribtuions and patterns of power and influence in the Society of Nations.

ECONOMY

The fourth attribute of statehood—an economy or system of producing and distributing goods and services—also presents many variations. National economies vary both in what is produced and distributed and in the manner in which these functions are performed. An economy may exist in communities which lack some of the other requisites of statehood. But it is impossible to conceive of a modern state without an economy. Thus some set of arrangements for producing and allocating goods and services is not merely an attribute; it is a genuine requisite for the existence of a political community. Indeed, everywhere in the modern world, the function of ruling and the function of producing and allocating goods and services have become closely interrelated aspects of the state as an on-going social system.

Our interest in national economies, as in governmental systems, is centered mainly on their relation to the external policies and capabilities of states. Stage of economic development, productivity of the economy, extent of dependence on imported foodstuffs and raw materials, patterns of allocation and consumption—all these and other aspects of a nation's economy may affect significantly the role which its government plays upon the international stage. We shall be especially interested (in Chapter 14) to compare the features and operational characteristics of certain communist and private-enterprise economies, and of the economic systems of Red China, India, and other nations in process of rapid modernization.

UNIFYING CULTURE

By unifying culture we mean the aggregate of shared values, norms, habits, and customs which give to members of a population a sense of belonging to a common community, and which in varying degrees give unity, direction, and purpose to the behavior of the population. Without substantial consensus on what is desirable and right, and undesirable and wrong, no sense of community is likely to exist. Without some sense of community no state could survive.

A people with a strong sense of community, manifested by shared values and ways, which may or may not include political norms specifically, is said to have a common *nationality*. In more aggressive manifestations, the phenomena of nationality are called *nationalism*. Observed similarities in the behavior of people of common nationality are frequently called *national character*. In everyday speech nation has become a synonym for state. Thus we speak of a nation acting so-and-so; and we call our subject inter*national* politics even though the reference is to the political interactions and relations of states.

This usage is imprecise, but it has certain virtue. Nation is a less abstract concept than state. It carries a rather stronger political connotation than *people*. Hence nation can be used appropriately instead of state or people whenever the reference is to a government plus the body of citizens, especially when the intent is to emhasize the political community rather than the corporate entity.

Many facets of national culture are among the more important foundations of international politics. Nations differ widely with respect to internal unity and solidarity, discipline and morale, ability to carry on in affluence and in adversity. Nations differ in their ideals and values, in their tolerance for austerity, in their demands for luxury and easy living. They differ in their degree of tolerance for foreign people and for alien ways and ideas. They probably differ, above all, with respect to the point at which catastrophe would overwhelm them. These and other aspects of national culture will be dealt with in later chapters, especially in Chapter 16.

Status and stature in international politics

A political community acquires membership and status in the Society of Nations when and only when a sufficient number of the more influential members have taken some appropriate step to "recognize" its claim to become a member of the Society of Nations. Recognition is remotely analogous to being voted into a club—if one can imagine a club without precise by-laws governing admission of new members.

By some appropriate policy declaration, or by entering into diplomatic relations, a government indicates its intention to regard the new state as a member of the Society of Nations, or its intention to treat a new regime as the effective (*de facto*) or rightful (*de jure*) successor to the displaced regime in a pre-existing state. But international law sets no precise norm as to which states or how many must recognize the new state or new regime in order to legitimize its status.

A great deal of misunderstanding beclouds the subject of recognition. Denial of recognition or withdrawal of recognition (by severing official relations with a foreign government) has nothing to do with that government's actual existence. Statements in the 1950's and early 1960's to the effect that it was "unrealistic" for the United States government to pretend that the Chinese Communist government did not exist miss the point altogether. Such denial or (in the opposite case) withdrawal of recognition represents an attempt either to exclude the political community in question from the international political system or to brand its government as an outlaw legally unqualified to speak for its community in dealings with other members of the Society of Nations.

This principle of legitimacy by recognition was firmly established in the international law of the European States System in the seventeenth and eighteenth centuries. It was in accordance with this principle that the European monarchs denied recognition to the revolutionary regime in France following the Revolution of 1789. During the nineteenth century the concept of governmental legitimacy lay dormant most of the time, as the European system expanded into a global system by the generally routine recognition of non-European members. On various occasions, the act of recognition (or the denial of recognition) was employed for other policy purposes (of which more in Chapter 4). But the really important aspect of recognition in our century has been a return to the eighteenth century principle of legitimacy. This principle has been asserted in numerous contexts, but especially in connection with the international legitimacy of Communist regimes. The United States and numerous other states denied recognition to the Communist regime in Moscow following the Revolution of 1917-18. (The United States persisted in this policy until 1933.) The United States has followed the same course since 1949 with respect to Communist China. In these and lesser instances, one avowed basis of denial has been the asserted lack of convincing evidence that the non-recognized regime intends to observe in good faith the obligations imposed by international law and by the charters of the United Nations and other international organizations.

Recognition as a test of status (however ambiguously and imprecisely the principle works in practice) operates today as the route of entry into the present nonideological international system. If the system of Communist states (now, from our Western perspective, a refractory subsystem within *the* global system) should acquire more and more important members, a time might come when the non-Communist national communities would become marginal members or even outlaws of a globally dominant Communist international system, as the Soviet Union was in the 1920's. This is manifestly not an imminent contingency. But it is clearly implicit and sometimes explicit in the utterances of Khrushchev, Mao Tse-tung, and other major prophets of Communism. (This aspect of international Communism is dealt with further in Chapters 17 and 20.)

Leaving for now the subject of recognition, we turn to another aspect of status and stature in the Society of Nations. This is the principle of international law that all nation-states are legally sovereign and equal members of the Society of Nations. National political communities differ widely in size of population, geographical area, form of government, stage of economic development, and national character. But once admitted by the process of recognition, they are all legally equal, and legally entitled to exercise virtually exclusive jurisdiction throughout their geographical space.

In actuality, nations differ enormously in their respective abilities to order their internal or domestic affairs and to affect conditions and events beyond their territorial borders. *It is one of the main theses of this book that differences in international power and influence are a function of the differences in the anatomy of statehood outlined in the preceding section.* Just how this is so will be continuously in the forefront of our discussion throughout the book. For the present we merely emphasize that enormous differences in power and influence do exist.

The fact as well as the importance of such disparities is evident if one compares the activities of such great states as the United States, the Soviet Union, Red China, or Great Britain, on the one hand, with states such as Jordan, Ethiopia, or Afghanistan. It is such differences which set the political, as distinguished from the legal, patterns of the Society of Nations.

Gradations of power and influence are recognized in the everyday vocabulary of international politics. States are commonly called "Powers." They are graded according to their impacts on other nations. The term *Great Power* is historically associated with the European States System (about which more will be said later in the chapter). The Great Powers were originally those states which had effectively insisted on being a party to any general settlement of international affairs in Europe. After 1870, this group included Britain, Germany, France, Russia, Austria-Hungary, and (somewhat marginally) Italy. By 1914 two non-European states—the United States and Japan—had also come to be regarded as Great Powers, mainly because each had effectively asserted its military primacy within its own geographical region: the United States in the Western Hemisphere, Japan in Eastern Asia. The revolution of 1917 temporarily eliminated Russia from the list. Military defeat did the same for Germany. The Austro-Hungarian Empire broke up under the impact of defeat and permanently disappeared from the list of Great Powers.

World War II had shattering effects on the so-called power relations of states. The primacy of the United States and the Soviet Union became generally accepted. But virtually everything else has been uncertain. Relatively, if not absolutely, the power position of Britain, France, Germany, Italy, and Japan has declined. Meanwhile, since the Communist triumph of 1949, Red China's international prestige has soared. To a lesser degree the same can be said of India. Under Nehru's leadership, India has come to exert an international influence nearly comparable to some of the greater European states. Below this level, almost everything is in flux, reflecting fundamental changes that are transforming the hierarchy of power and influence in the Society of Nations.

The term *Superpower* appeared during World War II. To date this term has been applied to only two states—the United States and the Soviet Union. The term reflects the almost universal recognition that the capabilities of these two nations to influence events anywhere in the world far outstrip those of any others. The term *Superpower* has largely superseded the term World Power. Down to World War I, the only state accorded the status of World Power was Great Britain, upon whose empire (it was often reiterated) "the sun never set." After 1920 Americans rather generally fancied that the United States too had become a World Power. But neither foreign attitudes nor objective events confirmed this self-image of the United States until after World War II.

International political systems

International political transactions exhibit patterns of various kinds. One speaks, for example, of an international equilibrium or balance of power, of bipolarism, polycentrism, and other patterns. Such patterns undergo change through time, as, for example, the transformation of the polycentric "balance of power" which more or less prevailed prior to World War II, into the bipolar pattern which transiently prevailed for a few years thereafter. International political patterns have long been regarded as constituting the elements of an international political system, for example, the historic European States System.

Numerous sets of patterns can be identified in the international politics of our time. There is a global pattern, and there are regional and other less-than-global patterns. The global international system includes all hundred-odd members of the Society of Nations. This system can be conceived as the direct descendant of the European States System which took form in the seventeenth and eighteenth centuries. That earlier system has evolved into a global system within the past seventy-five years or so. We shall call it the international political system.

This global system attained a degree of institutionalization in the League of Nations and associated international organizations formed after World War I. The United Nations represents a further development of systemic institutions. But the United Nations organizations are not synonymous with *the* international political system, as we are using the term. Nor is the international political system coterminous with the United Nations. Not all states are members of the United Nations, and by no means all of the important political transactions of general international significance take place within the United Nation's institutional framework.

Numerous sets of less-than-global interaction patterns are more or less evident. We think it fruitful to treat these as subsystems of the international political system. The oldest are the Inter-American System, now institutionalized in the Organization of American States, and the British Commonwealth which has evolved from the British Empire of the last century. The so-called Communist Camp in Eastern Europe and Asia is a regional subsystem which (since Castro's revolution in Cuba) begins to exhibit interregional ramifications. Another subsystem is the Anti-Communist Coalition within which, in turn, one can identify subsystems: in particular the Atlantic Community, which operates through the North Atlantic Treaty Organization and other institutions. Inside the Atlantic Community one finds the European Economic Community (popularly known as the Common Market) and numerous other manifestations of slowly maturing integrative movements in Western Europe. Other regional international systems may be in the making in the Near East, in Southern Asia, in Sub-Saharan Africa, and elsewhere.

All of these less-than-global international systems are linked in various ways to the global system. Take the Inter-American System, for example. This system evolved out of the Monroe Doctrine. At first it was simply a policy of the United States to resist certain kinds of European activities in the Americas deemed likely to endanger the security of the United States. In the course of time this United States policy evolved into a hemispheric system in which the defense of the Americas became a joint responsibility of all the American republics. At the same time, each of these republics has a set of relationships with non-American states; and first one and then another non-American Great Power has attempted by various means to extend its influence over the American region. Similar linkages could be described between the global system and all other international subsystems.

What we are suggesting, in effect, is that one can discern a certain confederative principle in the Society of Nations. This is remotely analogous to the functional federative structure of many national political systems. The United States, for example, is composed not only of fifty States which form the American Federal Union, but also of thousands of local political systems: counties, townships, villages, cities, school districts, sanitary districts, port authorities, and many others. Some hierarchy of political subsystems exists in every large and populous country, whatever its form of government or brand of political ideology.

Having said this, one should immediately emphasize a significant difference in the membership of national and subnational systems, on the one hand, and international systems, on the other. The constituent units of nearly all national and local political systems are human persons. The same person may be simultaneously a United States citizen and a member (say) of a county, a village, a school district, and other local political systems. The laws of a state may give to business and other corporations a sort of quasi-citizenship for certain limited purposes. But human persons are the primary building blocks of every national political system and subsystem known to us. The constituent units of international political systems, in contrast, are other political systems: specifically, the systems called nation-states. Thus the "population" of the global system and its various subsystems differs in a very strategic sense from the population of the United States or any other constituent unit of the international community.

After population, it will be recalled, territory was stated to be one of the attributes of statehood. International political systems frequently have a permanent headquarters. This is roughly analogous to a state's capital or seat of government. But territory—even a permanent headquarters—is not a requisite of the global international political system.

Passing over for a moment the third attribute of statehood—government—we may compare international and national political systems with respect to the additional requisites of nation-states, economy and unifying culture. No international system has an economy even remotely resembling the economy of a nation-state. One of the weaknesses of the United Nations and most other international organizations is their lack of authority and facilities to determine who shall produce what, how much, and for what purposes. However, rudimentary beginnings of an internationally controlled economy may be observed in the working of the European Coal and Steel Community and certain other organizations. If the United Nations should one day acquire authority and effective control over the production, distribution, and use of nuclear energy, it might represent a decisive step towards establishment of a truly international economy. (It should be noted that international economy is being used here in a sense different from prevailing usage in economics. By international economy we mean a system of supranational control, not merely distribution across national borders.)

The fifth requisite—unifying culture—is more difficult to compare. Clearly there is no international culture analogous to the myths, rituals, and other norms that provide the unifying social cement of national communities. Efforts to promote a sense of identification with international organizations—by means of a United Nations flag or other symbols—have thus far produced relatively little discernible effect. But studies of the historical processes from which nation-states have emerged in the past suggest that analogous processes may possibly be laying the foundations for a unifying supranational culture which could have profoundly significant effects on the future development of international political systems.

Returning now to the third attribute of statehood—government—one notes perhaps the most significant contrast of all. A feature of nearly all international political systems today is *interaction in the absence of authoritative decision-making*. The units of international political systems are states. These states are legally independent, sovereign, and equal. In this respect, international systems differ from national systems. To repeat what was said earlier, every nation-state has an internal organization of power, called a government. Such a government is invested with legal authority to make decisions binding on everyone subject to the system's jurisdiction as defined by law. No such authority is invested in the United Nations. Nor has any regional or other less-than-global organization to date achieved a decision-making authority as binding on its members as is the authority of even the most loosely structured national state.

In practice, this dichotomy is not as clear-cut as the above statement might imply. In many legally sovereign states, the government's authority may be more or less limited with respect to certain parts of the country or certain groups within the country. On the other hand, certain international organizations—for example, the European Coal and Steel Community—are invested with *functions* which constitute *in effect,* if not in legal theory, some actual curtailment of the decision-making authority of the constituent states.

The same *functional tendency* of international systems to encroach on the decision-making autonomy of national systems is discernible at the very highest level—in the General Assembly of the United Nations. It is all too easy to focus on recurrent assertions of national autonomy reflected in the right of a single Great Power to block, by exercise of veto in the Security Council, a public censure or other *international* action adverse to its claims of interest. What may be less generally appreciated are the formidable and growing pressures that may be brought to bear on even the most powerful states—the U.S.A. and the U.S.S.R.—by the concerted nonviolent public speeches and resolutions of the lesser states in the General Assembly.

These developments may possibly indicate a trend of great portent. From the perspective of the twenty-first century, the 1960's might even appear to have been the critical decade in which the global system was undergoing radical transformation. Be that as it may, the system still must be regarded (from our limited contemporary perspective) as mainly, though not quite completely, a system of interaction in the absence of central authoritative decision-making institutions.

The interactions, which characterize international political systems, originate as demands and responses-to-demands on the part of the authorized spokesmen or agents of the constituent states. Statesmen support or implement or back up their demands by manipulation of various kinds of instrumentalities, such as diplomatic missions, public relations experts, subversive agents, goods and services, saboteurs, military forces, and still others. These instrumentalities are likewise brought into play to parry and resist adverse demands, pressures, and attacks from abroad. Statesmen and their fellow citizens carry on within a set of environing conditions which set limits to what is or can be accomplished. Thus, in a broad and rather imprecise fashion, one can conceive of an international political system as a set of constituent units (states, organized political communities), interacting (demands and responses) in patterns (instrumentalities, techniques, strategies) within an environment (physical and social) which sets limits to the probable variations in the behavior both of the units and of the system of which they are components.

Changes in the relations of particular units of the system tend to evoke corrective counteractions. This phenomenon is remotely analogous to the function of a thermostat in a heating system or a governor in an engine, though (as strongly emphasized in Chapter 1) this analogy can be most misleading if carried too far or applied literally. We shall see how this return-to-normal principle has operated in response to the attempts of national statesmen to maintain an equilibrium or balance of power within the historic European States System and its more recent successors.

If conditions change too profoundly or too rapidly, any corrective actions may prove ineffective. In that case, one of two events will occur. The system may simply collapse and disappear, as might easily happen in case of a general war fought to a finish with thermonuclear explosives. Or the system may be transformed into another kind of system, as actually has happened several times in the past. Such transformations have usually been gradual; contemporary observers often did not appreciate the significance of what was happening: for example, the consequences of the rise of Japanese and American power which transformed the nineteenth-century Europe-centered system into the early-twentieth-century global system; or the subsequent transformation of the polycentric Great Power system into the bipolar system temporarily dominated by the Soviet Union and the United States.

All social systems develop routines and momentum. This is the concept of the "going concern" familiar to everyone. Every family, every business, every government, indeed every social organization, develops routines. These permeate every level of organized human activity. They are reflected in the precedents of courts and foreign offices, in religious and patriotic rituals, in the ordinary processes of day-to-day living. People behave from hour to hour, often from minute to minute, on the confident assumption that trains and planes will run more or less on schedule, that the milkman and the postman will arrive as usual, that groceries will line the shelves of the supermarkets, that physicians and hospitals will be available if needed, that the water in the tap and the milk in the bottle are safe to drink, and so on ad infinitum. One of the unanswered riddles of the nuclear age is: What would devastating nuclear war do not merely to human life and nonhuman physical structures but to the human habits and routines which keep a modern organized society in business? We shall return to this issue again and again.

This same property is manifest in international political systems. These too are going concerns with momentum. These traits are embodied in the forms and styles of action and interaction and in the norms and institutions of what may be euphemistically called the international community. Most of the time statesmen follow the strategies to which they are habituated. Barring catastrophic changes such as full-scale nuclear war, powerful stimuli are required to uproot old patterns and establish new ones in the political relations of states. Those most prone to do so, it would appear, are the spokesmen of national communities which have recently passed through or are in process of radical internal transformations. Such governments are likely to produce serious and disruptive effects on established international patterns. This happened following the French Revolution of 1789. The international systemic effects of the Russian Revolution of 1917 were even more disruptive. Comparably disturbing consequences are accompanying the upheavals in Asia, Africa and Latin America. For this as well as other reasons, the study of international political systems in the 1960's is the study of human relations in flux, with old patterns breaking up and new ones not yet clearly discernible or firmly established.

These matters will form the main themes of the concluding chapters. But a brief preview of the historic international political system, and its successive transformations, is inserted at this point, with a view to providing a sort of chart and compass to guide us through the intervening explorations of the foundations of international politics.

The historic European states system

The international political system of today is the direct descendant of the historic European States System. That system took form a little over three hundred years ago, at the close of the religious wars following the Protestant Reformation. The founding event is usually given as the Peace of Westphalia of 1648. Actually, the system was the outcome of a long-drawn-out sequence of earlier events.

In a still broader sense, the historic European States System, and the concepts and principles upon which it rested, should be regarded as but an aspect of the evolving civilization which emerged several thousand years ago around the eastern end of the Mediterranean Sea. We have a rich historical record of the spread of this civilization into the western borderlands of the Mediterranean, thence northward into the rest of the

European peninsula of Eurasia, and eventually overseas into the Americas, Australia, New Zealand, with beachheads in Africa and Asia. The history taught in American schools and universities has been mainly the history of this so-called Western civilization. The ideas about international affairs generally prevailing in America today are likewise products of this civilization.

Other histories—at least as ancient—are derived from the civilizations indigenous to the so-called monsoon lands of Asia, especially India and China. (These lands take their name from the monsoon winds that blow landward from the seas during the summer, bringing heat and dampness, and seaward in winter, bringing to the coastal lands cooler and drier air from the continental interior.)

Only within the last generation or so has the march of events compelled Americans to give much serious attention to these non-Western civilizations. Past generations of Americans, and Europeans too, generally regarded Indians, Chinese, and other "Asiatics" as inferior races, "inscrutable" orientals, "heathen" to be converted to Christianity, and potential customers for the products of Western factories. A few Americans and Europeans periodically voiced fear of the "yellow peril," but remarkably few envisaged the East as a region of great political potential. It is easy these days to forget how recently most of the populous lands of southern and eastern Asia were colonies or satellites of Western empires, and how generally it was expected that they would remain so indefinitely.

Long before Marco Polo, Vasco da Gama, and other European adventurers and traders penetrated to the lands of eastern and southern Asia, the "Eastern" civilizations had developed their own rules for dealing with foreigners. These rules differed in significant respects from those which evolved in Europe. But for the superior technology, especially in firearms, developed by Europeans from about the fifteenth century onwards, it is quite possible that Asian concepts of international relations, rather than European, would eventually have blanketed the earth.

By the seventeenth and eighteenth centuries, the European System appears from this distance to have become a loose association of hereditary rulers—kings, princes, dukes, etc.—linked by ties of kinship and a formal adherence to either Catholic or Protestant Christianity. Hence as already noted, the historic European System came to be known as the *Family of Nations*, and to be piously identified with *Christendom*.

The basic principle of the European States System, to paraphrase the words of the British historian R. S. Mowat, was "equipoise" or balanced power, periodically readjusted with a view to enabling each sovereign to keep what he already possessed, and to prevent any member of the system from coercing or despoiling the rest. Since there was no superauthority, equilibrium had to be maintained or restored—if at all—by the states which themselves composed the system.

Besides the general principle of equilibrium through balanced power, the historic European System also embodied the implementing principles of *legitimacy* and *rightful intervention*. The regimes who had participated in establishing the system, plus those whom charter members of the club should recognize as rightful, legal, *de jure* rulers, alone were legitimate. Any of these regimes, threatened by revolt from within or by attack from outside its territorial borders, was entitled to call on the other legitimate governments for aid. And the rules of the system—called international law—not only recognized the legality of such intervention, but imposed on all members a positive obligation to take whatever actions might be necessary to preserve or restore an endangered *status quo* and thereby to reestablish equilibrium in the system as a whole.

These principles worked imperfectly at best. Much of the time they did not work at all. The territorial, commercial, or other ambitions of rulers and their influential subjects conflicted more often than not with whatever sense of responsibility they might have felt for maintaining international order. That the principle of equilibrium could be manipulated at all without any central organization of power was attributable to a number of conditions. Throughout its existence, the European States System never included fewer than five major members. These Great Powers, as they were called, differed in territorial size, population, and other characteristics. But until the system began to break up, no member was sufficiently powerful to dominate the rest and thereby transform the system into something radically different.

Numerous efforts to do so were made. The most nearly successful was that of France under Napoleon I. Each attempt brought forth opposing coalitions and led to a general war. In the end each bid for hegemony in Europe was defeated and a multilateral equilibrium was reestablished.

The historic European System functioned most effectively during the century, 1815-1914. In the words of a recent Government Report, that was a century in which

no single power could realistically aspire to dominate the world. England, with firm control of the seas, acted as a check on the ambitions of any of the land Powers. England was not strong enough, and did not aspire to dominate the European Continent. She acted as a balance wheel to preserve the balance of power between the

European continental land empires. No nation outside of Europe had the command of modern technology or an industrial base sufficient to make plausible a general challenge to European leadership. Economic institutions based on the gold standard and centered on the London capital market provided an economic framework within which large portions of the world, including the United States, were able to make tremendous forward strides in developing their economies. The principles of the common law and of political institutions based on the notion of public responsibility began to spread out to the far corners of the world. Above all, wars up to 1914 were kept limited in their geographic extent and in the objectives of the participants.*

Following the Congress of Vienna (which restored the system after the French Revolutionary and Napoleonic Wars, and ushered in the century of relative international stability), there emerged a further operating principle. This was the principle of concerted action by the Great Powers to maintain the international equilibrium in Europe. This Concert of Europe, as it was called, found expression in numerous diplomatic conferences which dealt more or less successfully with various threats to the peace. But the Concert of Europe foundered eventually on the rocks of rival alliance-building.

The European States System had shown from the outset a tendency to evolve towards fewer effective units by the circular process of building alliances in order to counter alliances. When the rulers of one state felt threatened by the actions of others, they looked for allies. The resulting alliance would stimulate a sense of anxiety in other countries and evoke counteralliances. The effect (in the terminology of a generation ago) was the tendency for a complex multilateral equilibrium to evolve towards a simple bilateral balance.

This tendency came to dominate the system between 1870 and 1914. In the resulting political climate of growing anxiety, stress, and fear, the level of peacetime armaments rose to unprecedented heights. This armaments race contributed progressively to instability of the System as a whole. During the final critical decade of recurrent alarms and diplomatic crises, culminating in the outbreak of a general war in 1914, Europe was repeatedly described as a Continent divided into two armed camps, and the political relations of the Great Powers as a condition of international anarchy.

* From "The Purposes of U.S. Military and Economic Assistance," prepared by the Washington Center of Foreign Policy Research, Annex A to the Report of The President's Committee to Study the U.S. Military Assistance Program, 1959, p. 2. U. S. Government Printing Office, Washington, D.C.

From European to global system

The men who operated the European States System, from its origin until late in the nineteenth century, were responsible for the extension of European rule to Asia, Africa, and the Americas. When the thirteen North American colonies made good their bid for independence, European sovereigns recognized the new republic, albeit reluctantly, and thereby accepted the principle that communities of Europeans transplanted overseas might become at least marginal members of the European System. But European statesmen did not accept so readily the idea that political communities of non-European origin could become members of their system. In particular, Asians and Africans were regarded as heathen barbarians. Such peoples were beyond the pale of civilized Christian nations. It was legal to trade with them and it was proper to send missionaries to convert them to Christianity. But the heathen had no rights which Europeans felt compelled to respect. International law was made by Europeans, administered by Europeans, for the benefit of Europeans. Only civilized Christian nations had "rights" under international law; and such nations were, by European definition, either European nations or nations of European origin and culture. (The continuing impact of these propositions will be examined in Chapter 18.)

International law and morality justified, in European eyes, the extension of European rule overseas. This expansion of Europe continued at an accelerating rate until about the end of the nineteenth century. By 1900 nearly all of Africa, the Near and Middle East, Southern and Eastern Asia, and the islands of the Pacific had come under the direct or indirect rule of one or another of the European imperial powers.

This empire-building was an extremely important function of the European States System. Ever since the fifteenth century, voyages of exploration and discovery, followed by commercial and colonial adventures, had occupied the energies of some of Europe's most aggressive and restless ruling classes. Disputes between European nations were repeatedly eased by giving one or both sides "compensation" overseas. That is to say, Asian, African, and Pacific lands and peoples were parceled out to Europeans as a means of keeping the peace in Europe. It is no mere figure of speech to say, as has often been said, that non-Europeans were regarded simply as pawns of European international politics.

By 1900, however, this game was largely finished. There were no more non-European lands and peoples to barter for the sake of order in Europe. This condition inspired one of the most important political essays of modern times. We refer to the lecture entitled "The Geographical Pivot of History" which Sir Halford J. Mackinder delivered to the Royal Geographical Society in London in January 1904. The opening sentences of that lecture read as follows:

> When historians in the remote future come to look back on the group of centuries through which we are now passing, and see them foreshortened, as we today see the Egyptian dynasties, it may well be that they will describe the last 400 years as the Columbian epoch, and will say that it ended soon after the year 1900. . . . In 400 years the outline of the map of the world has been completed with approximate accuracy. . . . But the opening of the twentieth century is appropriate as the end of a great historic epoch, not merely on account of this achievement, great though it be. The missionary, the conqueror, the farmer, the miner, and, of late, the engineer, have followed so closely in the traveller's footsteps that the world, in its remoter borders, has hardly been revealed before we must chronicle its virtually complete political appropriation. In Europe, North America, South America, Africa, and Australasia, there is scarcely a region left for the pegging out of a claim of ownership, unless as a result of a war between civilized or half-civilized powers. Even in Asia we are probably witnessing the last moves of the game first played by the horsemen of Yermak the Cossack and the shipmen of Vasco da Gama.
>
> Broadly speaking, we may contrast the Columbian epoch with the age which preceded it, by describing its essential characteristic as the expansion of Europe against almost negligible resistances, whereas medieval Christendom was pent up into a narrow region and threatened by external barbarism. From the present time forth, in the post-Columbian age, we shall again have to deal with a closed political system, and none the less that it will be one of worldwide scope. Every explosion of social forces, instead of being dissipated in a surrounding circuit of unknown space and barbaric chaos, will be sharply re-echoed from the far side of the globe, and weak elements in the political and economic organism of the world will be shattered in consequence. . . .*

Mackinder did not exaggerate. When he spoke, the march of events had already eroded the foundations of the European System at many points. The Moslem Ottoman Empire in the Near East and North Africa had acquired an ambiguous status, half in, half out of the System. The industrialization of Japan had begun in the 1870's. By winning a quick military victory over China (1894-95), Japan became a "Power" to be reckoned with in Eastern Asia. By her alliance with Britain (1901), Japan was grafted into the European System. The Spanish-American War (1898), accompanied by United States annexations in the middle and

---

* From *The Geographical Journal*, 1904, Vol. 23, pp. 421 ff.

western Pacific, together with active American opposition to European partition of the moribund Chinese Empire, brought the United States into the inner circle of the European System via the same Far Eastern route. During the Administration of Theodore Roosevelt (1901-1909), the United States Government repeatedly took a hand in European and Asian affairs. Roosevelt mediated peace between Japan and Russia (1905), participated in the settlement of the Moroccan Crisis (1907), and sent the American fleet around the world (1908-9) as a public demonstration of American military power and interest in transoceanic conditions and events. Thus by 1914 the European System was clearly on the way to becoming a polycentered global system, even though the European Great Powers still wielded far greater power and influence than the non-European members of the system.

World War I and the Paris Peace Conference (1919) completed the transformation of the European System from a continental to a global system. The League of Nations (the charter of which constituted the first section of the peace treaties of 1919) was conceived not as a continental or regional, but as a universal organization. It never approached universality, but it was none the less global in conception as well as in membership.

Article 10 of the Covenant of the League obligated all members "to respect and preserve as against external aggression the territorial integrity and existing political independence of all members of the League. . . ." Article 16 provided that "should any member of the League resort to war in disregard of its covenants . . . it shall ipso facto be deemed to have committed an act of war against all other members of the League. . . ." These and other sections of the League Covenant envisaged a universal application of the principle of collective intervention long implicit in the historic European System.

Perhaps equally important in the transformation of that system was its progressive dissociation from Christendom. That identification gradually evaporated during the nineteenth century. But there remained just a vestige of it, in the notion that the Great Powers—including those geographically located in other parts of the world—represented a *European* tradition. Differ as they might in ambition, conflict as they might in their national policies, compete as they might for colonies and for military primacy— there remained, nevertheless, a myth of common cultural heritage and the unity of Western civilization. Even Japan was often spoken of as a sort of stepchild of Europe, since the Japanese had borrowed freely from Germany and other European countries in the process of modernizing their civil government, military forces, and national economy.

There was truth as well as myth in the nineteenth-century concept of the unity of Western civilization. Despite great and widening differences between the more democratic and the more despotic nations, the practice of most conformed rather closely to a well understood vocabulary and etiquette of diplomatic intercourse, and to a substantial body of private and public law. The terms *Family of Nations* and *Society of Nations* meant considerably more to most diplomats, international lawyers, and businessmen than simply labels for a mere congeries of potentially warring political communities.

The Russian Revolution (1917) smashed beyond repair the myth of any cultural or political solidarity implicit in the Society of Nations. In a manner reminiscent of the efforts of European monarchs to break the French Revolution in the 1790's, the Great Powers (in 1917) sent military expeditions to Russia to help throw out the Communist pretenders. When these military interventions all failed, an attempt was made to outlaw the Communist regime by refusing it diplomatic recognition. In the end, however, Russia, transmuted into the Soviet Union, was re-admitted into the Society of Nations, as one by one the other Powers recognized the Communist Government and entered into diplomatic relations with it.

The impact of these events on the international political system appear more clearly in retrospect than they did at the time. It would take many years and much unpalatable and frustrating experience to learn how Communists would react in diplomatic negotiations, international conferences, and other operating situations. The Bolsheviks introduced the technique of diplomacy by vilification and developed subversion into an art never previously imagined.

The Fascist revolutions—especially the Nazi revolution in Germany—introduced still other disruptive influences and practices. Hitler too, to the bewilderment of respectable professional diplomats everywhere, rejected the traditional norms, if not the traditional forms and rituals. He specialized in ostentatious perfidy and repudiated the principle of common responsibility for international order and the status quo. His satellites in spirit—Mussolini in Italy, Franco in Spain, Peron in Argentina, and still lesser Fascist fry—played according to these unorthodox rules as much as they dared or felt expedient.

In the meantime, an accelerating rate of invention in military technology was tipping the scale towards offensive warfare. Motorization increased tactical mobility on land. The airplane was transformed from an instrument of reconnaissance and close support for ground forces into an independent weapon of great and rapidly growing potentialities. In consequence of all these developments, the patterns and norms of the international political system were, by 1939, in a state of chaos, and the system itself was manifestly on the threshold of a major transformation.

Bipolarism

World War II transformed the international political system from a polycentered into a bipolar system. As already stated, the alliance-building that went on in the traditional system trended in this direction. Prior to 1900, however, Britain's strategy of playing the role of "balancer," in which firm and continuing commitment to either side was avoided, prevented the bipolarizing tendency from dominating Europe completely. Until 1939 the United States played sporadically and erratically a somewhat analogous role on a global scale. But the military and political events of 1933-1945 shattered any semblance of the old polycentered equilibrium, and created conditions which, at least temporarily, prevented reestablishing the global system on any such basis.

It took time for most people to grasp the full implications of the altered profile of power and influence in the Society of Nations. Americans rather generally expected the wartime coalition to continue indefinitely into the postwar years. It was mainly Russian behavior which destroyed the grand alliance. Whether from fear, or from ambition (and that will be debated for a long time to come), the Soviet government drew tightly into its sphere of influence or "orbit" a protective zone of Communized political commmunities in Eastern and Southeastern Europe—Poland, Czechoslovakia, Hungary, Rumania, Bulgaria, Yugoslavia (until 1948) and Albania. Unsuccessful efforts were made to build a similar protective zone along the southern border of the Soviet Union. In the Berlin blockade (1948-49) a major attempt was made to end the four-power occupation of that city, and to deal a smashing blow to the prestige of the Western Powers. With Soviet approval, if not active clandestine direction, the Communist regime in northern Korea attempted in 1950 to take over by force the whole Korean peninsula opposite Japan.

Under the leadership of the United States, the West responded with the Truman Doctrine (1947), the Kennan-inspired strategy of containment (1947), the Berlin airlift (1948-49), the Marshall Plan of economic aid to hasten European recovery (1949-   ), the Atlantic Alliance (1949), military resistance in Korea (1950-53), and other moves in a global strategy of preventing the geographical extension of Soviet-sponsored Communist rule.

These actions and counteractions, accompanied by Soviet success in breaking the American monopoly of nuclear weapons, have led to what is frequently called a military stalemate. This constitutes, in effect, a new form of international equilibrium, upon a radically different basis from any previously achieved. In the traditional system, military power was distributed among several (usually five or more) Great Powers which did not differ widely in their respective capacities to wage a major war. The operators of that system systematically cultivated the myth that the mission of national armaments was, first, to deter aggression, and, second, to repel it. But resort to large-scale violence remained everywhere a recognized technique of statecraft. Indeed the obligations of collective security, implicit in the international law of the eighteenth century, and explicitly embodied in the Covenant of the League of Nations, envisaged the transformation of limited war to global war if necessary to bring down a declared aggressor against the system or any of its constituent units.

The equilibrium which took form in the 1950's rested upon quite different postulates. Since the advent of the hydrogen bomb—first in the United States, soon thereafter in Russia, then in Britain, with other possessors in prospect—it has been strongly urged, and rather widely believed, that general war has ceased to be an effective and fruitful technique of statecraft. A general war not involving the United States and the Soviet Union would be a contradiction in terms. Such a war not involving unrestricted use of *all* available weapons is difficult to imagine.

It is predicted, with few dissents, that all-out attack with thermonuclear weapons could utterly wreck the economy of any country so attacked. But it is just as firmly believed that such an attack could not, at present or in the near future, paralyze the *military capacity* of the nation attacked to retaliate with comparable devastating counterstrikes against the aggressor's own cities and industrial regions. As long as this state of affairs continues—a state of affairs that could be terminated in a number of ways to be considered later on—it seems unlikely that any sane head of government would deliberately take so great a risk.

This state of affairs was characterized at the time of Premier Khrushchev's visit to the United States in 1959, as a "true balance of terror." The author, Cyrus L. Sulzberger, of *The New York Times*, continued:

> Five years ago it was still conceivable, in the event of open conflict, that Russia could have been totally destroyed without being able to totally destroy the United States. This is no longer imaginable. By its remarkable breakthrough in manufacture of missiles and hydrogen explosives the U.S.S.R. ended the kind of preventive war theory once entertained by certain unofficial but nevertheless important Americans. That sort of reasoning is no longer just immoral; it is also deprived of logic. For, quite as surely as our own land and sea based planes and missiles could entirely ravage Khrushchev's homeland, just as surely his land and sea based missiles could ravage Eisenhower's

homeland. War as a contemplated policy became replaced by suicide as a contemplated policy. This is acceptable to no one.*

We shall have to defer until later a more detailed and critical consideration of the implications latent in the present military situation. For the moment, we merely note what may be a few of the more obvious political consequences of the thermonuclear stalemate. One of these, it would appear, is to transfer the weapons of mass destruction from the category of active instruments of statecraft to the category of inactive deterrents. For the first time since the formation of the European States System, it may be realistic to say that the primary function of armaments (or at least certain weapons) is to prevent resort to unlimited violence. For the time being at least, the all-important function of these superweapons has become to hold the ring, as it were, while less destructive instruments and techniques—diplomacy, public relations, propaganda and psychological warfare, economic aid and technical assistance, economic pressures, and possibly strictly limited use of conventional military force—are brought to the center of the stage and into action.

After bipolarism—what?

There has been some tendency to regard bipolarism as the ultimate stage in the evolution of the international political system. Many discussions of Soviet-American relations, in particular, appear to assume: that the present reciprocal identification of *the* enemy will stand for years and decades to come; that Moscow and Washington will continue to press the costly search for the ultimate weapon to break the present nuclear stalemate; that in the meantime, each side will continue to wage cold war with all nonviolent, or at least less violent, weapons available; and that the rest of mankind will be drawn inexorably into the political orbit of one side or the other.

Such assumptions are beginning to appear dubious to many students of international politics. As will be repeatedly emphasized in this book, ours is an age of rapid and differential changes. The next twenty years may well see changes in the international political system as drastic as those which have disconfirmed so many of the dogmatic expectations of the past twenty years. Various portents are clearly visible on the horizon.

One of these is the manifest determination of additional nations to produce and control nuclear weapons. It seems possible that the members of the so-called nuclear club may increase to six or seven or more during the next few years. It seems scarcely credible that this can happen without

* From *The New York Times*, September 30, 1959. Copyright 1959 by the New York Times Company; reproduced by permission.

profoundly altering the attitudes and strategies that now prevail in Moscow and in Washingon, and producing equally profound changes in the distribution of power and influence in the Society of Nations.

Another straw in the wind is the manifest increase in the effective influence of the less powerful nations. One apparent by-product of the present Soviet-American nuclear deadlock has been to give relatively greater effective choice and more maneuverability and leverages to some of the governments not possessing nuclear weapons or even very strong conventional military forces. This is especially discernible with respect to those non-European states whose peoples were until recently the colonial subjects of European empires. Those who rule in the Near and Middle East, in Southern and Southeastern Asia, and to an increasing extent in Sub-Saharan Africa and Latin America, are demonstrating their ability to defy with impunity the fiat of the greatest Powers. These nations are shaping their own destiny and affecting events beyond their own frontiers to a degree that would have seemed incredible as recently as twenty years ago. The obverse of this trend is the equally unanticipated effects of the Moscow-Washington deadlock on the ability of either side to manipulate and exploit for its purposes these emerging nations, whose leaders have quickly learned the value of concerted action and of strategies which from the perspectives of Washington and of Moscow appear frequently as an unpleasant and inconvenient form of diplomatic blackmail.

A third apparent effect of the revolutionary rise and destructiveness of the superweapons, still controlled mainly in Washington and in Moscow, is to foster a desire in many quarters either to contract out of the game altogether or to play an uncommitted role between the Superpower blocs. This tendency towards neutralism, either passive or active, is notorious in the Near East and in Southern Asia. It has taken firm root in Africa. It appears to be gaining ground in Latin America and even in Western Europe; and there are hints that the same tendency lurks also beneath the heavily censored news from behind the Iron Curtain.

Thus, as we embark upon an examination of the foundations of international politics, we are confronted at the outset by unmistakable signs that the international political system is still in process of transition. The early postwar bipolarism, which evolved from the pre-1939 polycentered balance-of-power system, seems likely to be only a passing phase in a continuing transformation, again towards a polycentered system. Numerous possibilities are latent in this most recent trend, provided events continue to point in the directions suggested above. We shall return in the final group of chapters to these new trends and to the changes which they may portend for the future structure and working of the international political system.

CHAPTER THREE

★ ★ ★

International Actions and Interactions

THE TRANSACTIONS AND relationships which exhibit conflicts of purpose or interest between nation-states can be analyzed in terms of projects and undertakings, on the one hand, and outcomes or results, on the other. Often the distinction between undertakings and outcomes is not clear-cut. Indeed, what appears to be an undertaking in one perspective may in a different perspective appear to be the result of an earlier undertaking. Nevertheless, the analytic distinction between undertakings and outcomes should help us to gain a clearer picture of the ways of international politics.

It has been said that the essence of undertakings is decision-making. The steps in formulating a project and in putting it into operation may be simple or complex, few or many. Implicit in every decision is some notion of purpose or end towards which the decision is oriented; some image of the situation or state of affairs with reference to which the decision-maker feels impelled to act; and some mode of reasoning by which he links up purpose and image in a choice of what to do or not to do.

In the study of statecraft, one is confronted typically with quite complicated and prolonged deliberations prior to the taking of decisions. Directly or indirectly, substantial numbers of persons are likely to participate in most official decision-making processes. Reduced to barest essentials, one may conceive of a decision-making organization (such as a government or a business corporation) as normally including: (1) offices, agencies, departments, etc. whose incumbents are invested with legal authority to act with reference to particular kinds of issues or subject matter; (2) information flowing into the system (sometimes called *inputs*); (3) more or less standardized routines for sifting evidence and framing alternatives; and (4) the choice of a course of action or inaction (sometimes called the *output*).

In a typical case, the decision-making unit (which may be a single person or a group) approaches an issue or problem with certain purposes and presuppositions in mind and some image of the situation. He (or they) may seek further information, or it may be provided more or less as a matter of routine in accordance with the working rules of the system. He (or they) may take the new information into account or disregard it as irrelevant or inconsequential for his (or their) purposes. The deliberations may take any of numerous forms: individual study and cogitation, interpersonal conversations or exchange of written opinions, formal conferences, with or without side-symptoms of emotional strain manifested by walking the floor, beating the chest, biting the fingernails, or other irrational behavior.

In the end, the decision will take the form of action vs. inaction, or action $_1$ vs. action $_2$. Whatever the end product, the essential variables can be regarded as including the decision-makers' conception of what is to be undertaken (end, goal, purpose, objective, idea of national interest); what are believed to be the relevant facts, situation, or state of affairs; and the deliberative processes, irrational as well as rational, by which that image is related to the purpose in view.

It is helpful in dealing with policy-making to draw another analytic distinction: between *action* and *reaction*. Such a distinction is arbitrary and artificial in the sense that every action is in some degree a reaction to some earlier action by someone. However, it is necessary to cut into the seamless web of events somewhere. The question, Where? is determined by the way in which one formulates the problem to be investigated.

This distinction can be illustrated from the Suez crisis of 1956. In July of that year, President Nasser of Egypt issued a decree "nationalizing" the Canal: that is to say, he took it away from the private company that owned and operated it, and put it under the administration of the Egyptian Government. If one decides to start his analysis of the subsequent crisis with this nationalization decree, rather than go into earlier antecedent events, the decree becomes the initial or initiatory *action*. This action evoked protests from the British, French, and other governments. These protests were *reactions*: that is, responses to the action. (It should be remembered, as noted above, that the initiatory action itself was a reaction to earlier events, including the abrupt termination of negotiations for a loan to build a huge dam on the upper Nile, which in turn could be explained in terms of still earlier events.) After the initial reactions, there followed weeks of declarations and counterdeclarations, negotiations and recriminations, threats and finally military intervention.

All these, together with the subsequent withdrawal of the intervening forces, the stationing of a United Nations force in the Canal Zone, and other events, can be viewed as a complex of interlocking chains of *interaction*.

Patterns of actions and interaction

When one analyzes the part played by a government involved in a complex of interactions, it is generally possible to come to some conclusion as to the purposes (ends, intentions, motivations) which the acting statesmen had in view. Thus, in the Suez example, the explicit, publicly asserted objective of the British Government was to prevent Nasser from gaining exclusive control over the Canal, which (it was felt) might endanger its use by other nations. Some observers also inferred from British words and deeds an implicit ancillary objective to oust, or at least to curtail the prestige of, the Egyptian president, who was widely regarded in those days as a dangerous troublemaker and potential Soviet satellite. Still others read into British actions a determination to show the world that Britain was still a Great Power who could not be pushed around by any petty Near Eastern despot.

Associated with the ends or purposes to be accomplished, the student of international politics also looks for patterns in the actions and interactions themselves. Some of these patterns—those that relate to the means employed to accomplish desired ends—are called strategies. Everyone is familiar with the military concept of strategy—the plan by which a commander deploys combat forces. As stated in Chapter 1, strategy has an analogous meaning in the context of international statecraft as a whole. In this context we may define strategy as the particular combination in which a government deploys various instrumentalities, nonmilitary as well as military, in pursuit of desired objectives vis-à-vis other states.

Thus, returning again to the Suez case, the British Government, in attempting to oust Nasser's agents from the Canal administration, impounded Egypt's financial assets in British banks, brought trade with Egypt to a standstill, negotiated with other governments for concerted economic and moral pressures on Egypt, ostentatiously assembled military forces, threatened military intervention, entered into joint military arrangements with France, and finally launched a military attack accompanied by a barrage of verbal propaganda.

From such raw materials the student of international politics assembles the patterns which in the aggregate constitute the *foreign policy* of a state.

One can do this with reference to a single episode, such as Suez. One can do it more fruitfully with reference to the whole range of a state's foreign relations viewed through some more or less extended span of time. Both in the context of a single episode and in the broader context of a state's regional and global relations, foreign policy can be defined as the scheme or pattern of ends and means explicit or implicit in that state's actions and reactions vis-à-vis other states or the members thereof.

Almost everyone interprets such events from his own particular nationalistic perspective. The Russians think of their country as surrounded and threatened by the plane and missile bases of "aggressive capitalist Powers." With very few exceptions, Americans take just the opposite view. From our perspective, it seems to be the Russians who are threatening a coalition of "peace-loving" democracies who have no aggressive designs on anyone. H-bombs, long-range bombing planes, and ICBM's in Russian hands, we regard as weapons for potential aggression, but in our hands as necessary instruments of defense. Any American who should argue that the behavior of the United States is neither significantly more nor less aggressive on the whole than the Soviet Union's would run the risk of having most of his fellow citizens brand him as either a knave or a fool.

Even if it is nearly impossible in the present state of the world to divest oneself of nationalistic bias, it is certainly possible to establish a few guidelines for classifying foreign policies. This involves, first of all, establishing some general hypotheses regarding national policy objectives and strategies.

Experts disagree as to the degree to which governments plan ahead in this field. At one pole, there are those who contend that statesmen normally proceed with more or less definite preconceptions of what to do and how to go about it. At the other pole, one finds other experts who contend that events, many of which are beyond control, tend to shape national objectives and strategies. More frequently, disagreement is over not whether there is planning and premeditation, but rather how much and what kind.

A veteran British diplomat, Sir Harold Nicolson, is one of the foremost sceptics on this issue. He says:

> Nobody who has not watched "policy" expressing itself in day-to-day action can realize how seldom is the course of events determined by deliberately planned purpose, or how often what in retrospect appears to have been a fully conscious intention was at the time governed and directed by that most potent of all factors—"the chain of circumstance." Few indeed are the occasions on which any statesman sees his objective clearly before him and marches towards it with undeviating strides; numerous indeed are the occasions when a decision or event, which at the time seemed wholly unimportant, leads almost fortuitously

to another decision which is no less incidental, until, little link by link, the chain of circumstances is forged.*

Nicolson's chain-of-circumstance hypothesis is certainly more accurately descriptive of the day-to-day conduct of foreign relations than of the longer-term definition of foreign-policy objectives and strategy. However derived —whether by deliberate conscious planning or by day-to-day improvisation —the foreign policy of any state reveals in historical perspective certain patterns and characteristics. These constitute what is sometimes called a state's foreign-policy style.

Long-term objectives tend in most states to be defined in such broad concepts as national security, national prosperity, the white man's burden (a late-nineteenth-century European idea, meaning a self-assumed obligation to rule and "civilize" the nonwhite races), manifest destiny (the slogan of American expansionism in the mid-nineteenth century), and other general slogans and formulas. In shorter-term perspective, a state's purposes and strategies may be described in more operational terms, such as securing compliance to its specific demands, creating a favorable mood in the government and populace of other countries, building certain alliances, strengthening allies, weakening potential enemies, etc.

In day-to-day conduct of foreign affairs, the chain-of-circumstance approach seems to be more or less prevalent in all states. This is an aspect of what the British have traditionally called "muddling through." The same point of view was expressed in the State Department's historic assertion that American foreign policy was being made on a "twenty-four-hour basis" during the early stage of the Japanese invasion of central China, in August 1937.

Veteran diplomats have often been heard to contend that this is generally the safest and most practical approach to most international problems. From this position follows the view, sometimes expressed by experienced professionals, that "policy-planning staffs" in foreign offices have limited value because no one can know what the future will be like or how one will want to react to unfolding events. In its most extreme form, this point of view is summed up in the old gag: "How do I know what I think until I hear what I say?"

Such a negative approach, it must be obvious, would surrender all initiative to adversaries. It is an approach more attractive to statesmen whose highest desire is to hold the line, to defend the status quo, to react rather than to seize the initiative. No government, however reactionary or

---

* From pp. 19-20 of *The Congress of Vienna,* by Harold Nicolson. Copyright 1946 by Harold Nicolson; published by Harcourt, Brace & World, Inc., New York; reproduced with their permission.

static its viewpoint, adheres consistently to so negative an approach. There are many degrees of planning, both short-term and longer-term. It is helpful to know, and generally possible to find out a good deal, about a particular government's approach to foreign policy: whether it tends to be positive or negative, active or passive, initiatory or reactive, planned or opportunistic.

At the opposite pole from the chain-of-circumstance interpreters stand those who see foreign policy as the manifestation of a conscious and deliberate pursuit of power. This thesis appeared in one or two texts in the 1930's. It was forcefully presented in controversial books by the British historian E. H. Carr and the American political scientist F. S. Schuman. But it remained for Nicholas J. Spykman, a Dutch-born Yale professor, to elevate the thesis that pursuit of power is the basic objective of foreign policy into a dogma which became widely accepted as a self-evident axiom of international politics.

Spykman's thesis is succinctly stated in the introduction to his influential book, *America's Strategy in World Politics*, published in 1942, a few months after the Japanese blitz on Pearl Harbor. Spykman said:

> International as well as national affairs are influenced by love, hate, charity, by moral obligation and the hope of material gain, by the moods and psychological abnormalities of rulers, and by the emotional affiliations of peoples. International society is, however, a society without a central authority to preserve law and order, and without an official agency to protect its members in the enjoyment of their rights. The result is that individual states must make the preservation and improvement of their power position a primary objective of their foreign policy.*

Spykman spoke at a critical moment in history. Though few people sensed at the time the magnitude of what was in process, World War II was transforming the historic international system. The United States was shifting from a relatively passive role to a position of predominance in the Western world. The Soviet Union was on the threshold of an explosive economic, political, and military expansion. Total war on an unprecedented scale had at least temporarily subordinated all aspects of international relations to a ruthless struggle for total military victory.

Under those conditions Spykman's message left a heavy imprint on American thinking about foreign affairs. A decade earlier, his book might have found its way to library shelves, to gather dust and be forgotten. Because of its timing and the mood of the moment, the book began to appear upon the desks of top-level Washington executives. Spykman was

---

* This quotation and the longer one which follows are from pp. 7, 12-25 of *America's Strategy in World Politics*, by N. J. Spykman. Copyright 1942 by Harcourt, Brace & World, Inc., New York; reproduced with their permission.

widely quoted in the press and in academic lecture halls and classrooms. *America's Strategy in World Politics* was probably read by more people in America during World War II than was any other book on international politics. Because this book represents a crucial turning point in American thinking about foreign affairs, and because its imprint on American thinking is still discernible, we reproduce some further excerpts showing Spykman's conception of politics in general, and of international politics in particular:

Spykman on international politics

Human beings have invented a great variety of techniques designed to win friends and influence people. These different methods can be classified under four broad headings: persuasion, purchase, barter, and coercion, although this does not mean that every endeavor to make others do our bidding can be neatly pigeonholed into one of these categories. On the contrary it will be found that most successful policies are a judicious mixture of all four. The relative amount of each of the ingredients differs from case to case, from individual to individual, from community to community, and it is the community which defines what is acceptable and what is condemned. Where freedom and individual dignity are cherished, persuasion is more acceptable than coercion and the use of the latter is usually restricted as between individuals. The state alone, not the citizen, can legally coerce by means of the night stick, tear gas bomb, and sub-machine gun.

From an ethical point of view power can be considered only as a means to an end. It is, therefore, important that the use which is made of it should be constantly subjected to moral judgments, but to hope for a world that will operate without coercion and to decry man's desire to obtain power is an attempt to escape from reality into a world of dreams. Man creates society through cooperation, accommodation, and conflict, and all three are essential and integral parts of social life. He works together with others for common ends and creates the instruments of government for that very purpose. He accommodates himself to his fellows by shaping his conduct in conformity to common values and by accepting the normative pressure of custom and the rules of law. But he also accepts conflict for personal gain or impersonal ideal. Strife is one of the basic aspects of life and, as such, an element of all relations between individuals, groups, and states. A world without struggle would be a world in which life had ceased to exist. An orderly world is not a world in which there is no conflict, but one in which strife and struggle are led into political and legal channels away from the clash of arms; are transferred from the battlefield to the council chamber and the courtroom.

For groups as for individuals there are two forms of approach to desired objectives in case of opposition and conflict, direct action and "political action." The first means that the group acts directly upon the individuals whose cooperation is necessary to achieve the desired result. The second means that the group tries to achieve success through the use of the coercive power of the state. A great deal of modern economic life involves group struggle in the form of direct action: sharecroppers against landowners, farmers against milk distributors, industrial unions against trade unions, labor unions against employers, and industrial corporations among themselves. Many a western railroad and pipeline owes its present right-of-way not to a court decision but to the successful outcome of a bloody battle at strategic points between the forces of opposing companies.

An industrial dispute may start with a negotiation between an employer and a labor union. If negotiation fails, the parties may attempt mediation or accept arbitration. They may, on the other hand, refuse the peaceful solution and declare war in the form of a strike or a lockout. In that case the opponents will have tried all the possible methods of influencing each other's behavior, including persuasion, purchase, barter, and coercion. The strength of the group will obviously influence its choice of method, but it would be a mistake to assume that power is important only in the case of coercion. On the contrary, the fact that the labor union is powerful may make a test of strength unnecessary and successful negotiation that much easier.

The union and every other group is, therefore, forced to devote itself not merely to the pursuit of its objectives but also to the constant improvement of its strength. Any association, however simple its purpose, which depends for the realization of its objectives on the actions of other men or groups becomes involved in the struggle for power and must make not only self-preservation but also improvement of its power position a primary objective of both internal and external policy.

Labor unions, like all groups operating within the state, have an alternative method to their objective. If the direct aproach is too difficult, they can try an indirect route through the legislature and attempt to obtain the use of the law-making power of the state. It is sometimes possible to achieve rewards for labor through legislative definitions of minimum standards which cannot possibly be obtained by direct action on employers. The Woman's Christian Temperance Union may act directly through persuasion and the picketing of saloons, or it can act indirectly through the Eighteenth Amendment. It is to this technique in the national sphere that the term "political activity" is applied, the struggle for control of the government for the purpose of serving individual or group interest.

To the extent that private groups intend to work through government agencies they must add to their broad power objective the specific task of increasing political strength. For one particular kind of group, the political party, political power is the main object and *raison d'être*. It exists for the purpose of influencing public policy, and it can achieve its aim only by winning elections in competition with other political parties. The struggle for power is here so near the surface that it is easily visible, and everybody is, therefore, willing to agree that for the political party the improvement of its relative power position must be a constant endeavor. When the war chest is depleted more quickly than filled, when loyalty weakens, when organization and discipline deteriorate, the party will be on its way out, to be replaced by one of its competitors.

There are a great many instances when political action in the form of indirect pressure through the legislature is not possible. The group may be without political power because sex or property qualifications have disfranchised its members. The issue may be one in which the government cannot act because of constitutional restrictions, budget limitation, or lack of administrative agencies. In that case the group will have to choose between direct action and political activity of a special kind aimed at constitutional amendments, the extension of government power, changes in the distribution of authority, and the creation of new agencies. Political activity is then directed not at the use of the existing instruments of government but at their modification and the creation of new ones.

Groups which must operate within the power organization called the state must conduct their external policy within the limits of the permissible methods. In theory the state reserves to itself the legal monopoly of physical force, and only those forms of coercion which are free from physical violence are permitted. There are obviously wide differences in the ability or willingness of different states to enforce this principle and great variations in the same state at different times, running all the way from "perfect order" to "complete anarchy." . . .

In international society, as in other social groupings, there are observable the three basic processes of cooperation, accommodation, and opposition. Not only individuals and groups but also states maintain the three types of social relations. They have cooperated for common ends and created the instruments of international administration in the fields of communication and transportation without which modern international intercourse would be impossible. They have, through acceptance of common values, developed modes of accommodation by building out of custom and precedent a body of rules called international law. States have often obeyed these rules voluntarily and have been willing to adopt peaceful procedures for the settlement of disputes. But they have also accepted conflict and used coercion including war for the achievement of their national objectives.

The situation which characterizes the relations of groups within a state only in periods of crisis and breakdown of central authority is normal for the relations of states within the international society. It is the so-called sovereign independence of states, the absence of higher authority, and the freedom from external restraints that give to interstate relations their peculiar character of anarchy.

This historical state system consisting of sovereign independent units has been subject to two processes, conquest and confederation, which, if successful, might have changed its basic character. But neither process could ever achieve more than partial success. There have been strong and vigorous states which conquered their neighbors and enslaved the weak, but not even the gigantic empires of antiquity managed to absorb the states beyond their regional control and integrate them into simple hegemonic systems. Equally unsuccessful has been the process of the delegation of power from below. There have been confederations in all historical periods, but they were always partial and limited, partial in the sense that they included only a small number of states and limited in the sense that the interstate organizations were formed for specific and usually administrative purposes. Illustrations of international cooperation and limited confederation are many, but there has never been a case of the actual transfer of military power and political authority from individual states to the organs of an international community.

The essential difference between the international community and the national community as conditioning environments for group behavior is, therefore, the absence in the former of a governmental organization capable of preserving order and enforcing law. The international community has never, in fact, guaranteed the member states either life, liberty, property, or the pursuit of happiness, whatever the paper provisions of international conventions may have stipulated. Each individual state has continued to depend for its very existence, as much as for the enjoyment of its rights and the protection of its interests, primarily on its own strength or that of its protectors.

Self-preservation used in connection with states has a special meaning. Because territory is an inherent part of a state, self-preservation means defending its control over territory; and, because independence is of the essence of the state, self-preservation also means fighting for independent status. This explains why the basic objective for the foreign policy of all states is the preservation of territorial integrity and political independence.

In addition to the primary task of survival, the foreign policy of states is directed at a great many specific objectives which can be classified in different ways. They are geographic, demographic, racial, ethnic, economic, social, and ideological in nature and include such items as: the acquisition of naval bases, the limitation of immigration, the assimilation of minorities, the search for access to raw materials, markets, and investment opportunities, the protection of the social order against disruptive alien forces, the encouragement of cultural relations, and the restriction of the trade in dangerous drugs.

The same two methods which are used in the national sphere for promoting group interests are used in the international sphere for promoting state interests. States may use the direct method, acting immediately upon other states; they may use such international organizations as exist; or they may devote their foreign policy to the creation of new instruments. The relative importance of each of these methods is, however, very different from that which prevails in the national sphere. The character of international society . . . makes direct power over other states far more useful than ability to influence international organizations. [The reader should remember that Spykman was writing in 1942. Whether he would hold to this statement today, were he still alive, no one can say.] . . .

Direct action from state to state has remained the normal and most prevalent form of approach. It represents the most characteristic expression of foreign policy. Absence of international government is responsible not only for the significance of direct action but for the fact that there is no community restraint on the methods used. In international society . . . the struggle for power is identical with the struggle for survival, and the improvement of the relative power position becomes the primary objective of the internal and the external policy of states. . . .

Because power is in the last instance the power to wage war, states have always devoted considerable effort to the building of military establishments. But the relative power of states depends not only on military forces but on many other factors—size of territory, nature of frontiers, size of population, absence or presence of raw materials, economic and technological development, financial strength, ethnic homogeneity, effective social integration, political stability, and national spirit. In the struggle for power these items become important secondary objectives. They have value in themselves, and they are means to power.

The power position of a state, however, depends not only on its own military strength but also on that of its potential enemies. This means that there is a second approach to power apart from the enlargement of one's own war equipment. Its purpose is to influence directly the power position of other states, to weaken some, to strengthen others. To achieve this aim, states are willing to use their military power not only for the protection of their own territory but also for the protection of the territory of others, not for any altruistic reasons but because the continued existence of the third state contributes to their own security. . . .

But willingness to support other states has not been motivated solely by a desire for the security of a frontier or a zone of special strategic significance, but also by a desire to stop the expansion of some great state which after further growth might become a menace. The policy is then directed at the prevention of hegemony, a power position which would permit the domination of all within its reach. . . .

Experience has shown that there is more safety in balanced power than in a declaration of good intention. To preserve the balance requires action not only against the neighbor that becomes too powerful but also against distant states. As a matter of fact, the best period for the application of this policy is before continued expansion makes the growing state a neighbor. . . .

It is obvious that a balance-of-power policy is in the first place a policy for the Great Powers. The small states, unless they can successfully combine together, can only be weights in a balance used by others. But although they are stakes rather than players, their interest in the outcome of the game is none the less great. A small state is a vacuum in a political high pressure area. It does not live because of its own strength but because nobody wants its territory or because its preservation as a buffer state or as a weight in the balance of power is of interest to a stronger nation. When the balance disappears, the small states usually disappear with it.

Since the Renaissance and the Reformation, the balance of power has been a favorite topic of speculation among the political philosophers of Europe. After Emperor and Pope had lost their function as keystones in the European political order, a search began for a new integrating principle. It was found in the "balance of power," which became the subject of learned discourses. . . . If all states were held in check, no state could win a war; and, if no state could win a war, then no state would start a war or threaten war. Equilibrium is balanced power, and balanced power is neutralized power. A society in political equilibrium is a society in which force is useless and in which men will, therefore, live happily by the reign of law and devote themselves to the arts and graces.

To the men of learning it seemed obvious that states ought to pursue a balance-of-power policy; that the law of nature and Christian ethics both demand such a policy. States ought to direct their diplomacy not merely at counterbalancing specific threats to themselves but at establishing a balanced system for the whole of the international society. They ought to pursue a balance-of-power policy not merely to preserve their own relative power position but to preserve peace.

Statesmen have always been eager to accept from the theologian and the philosopher the correct formulation of the ethical precepts that should guide foreign policy, and since the seventeenth century all power politics has, therefore, been presented not as a crude attempt to survive in a tough world but as a noble endeavor aimed at the establishment of political equilibrium and the preservation of order.

Formulated in those terms the success has not been overwhelming. We might search for an explanation in the fact that the process is not guaranteed and that not all statesmen are good technicians, but it is perhaps safer to explain the result on the theory that they were not really interested in achieving a balance. There are not many instances in history which show great and powerful states creating alliances and organizations to limit their own strength. States are always engaged in curbing the force of some other state. The truth of the matter is that states are interested only in a balance which is in their favor. Not an equilibrium, but a generous margin is their objective. There is no real security in being just as strong as a potential enemy; there is security only in being a little stronger. There is no possibility of action if one's strength is fully checked; there is a chance for a positive foreign policy only if there is a margin of force which can be freely used. Whatever the theory and the rationalization, the practical objective is the constant improvement of the state's own relative power position. The balance desired is the one which neutralizes other states, leaving the home state free to be the deciding force and the deciding voice.

It would seem that this objective does not require quite the accuracy in measuring which the search for a perfect equilibrium would require, but, even so, the task is full of difficulties. It is easy to balance mechanical forces because they can be measured, but there is no measuring stick for political power. Are two states balanced, is their power equal, is the relationship between the two sets of alliances in equilibrium? On that question there is usually profound disagreement. The relative power remains a purely subjective judgment. Each state always feels that the other one needs balancing. In so far as the power concerned is in the last instance a power to wage war, it might be assumed that the military men would know the answer, but theirs is an opinion equally subjective, even if a little more expert. The most learned generals have disagreed as often as the statesmen. The only objective test of relative strength is to fight the war and see who wins, but this is hardly a helpful guide to the state that wants to decide whether to fight or not.

The second difficulty lies in the fact that the elements contributing to strength are not static but dynamic; they do not stay put. A new economic development, a new raw material, a new weapon, a new martial spirit may produce the most profound inequality between states that only a few years before had been approximately equal. Besides, in a world of states of equal strength, what is there to prevent the combination of two of them against a third?

Another problem which sometimes appears is the discovery that the state selected to be the ally in the opposition to the growing power has already made a deal with the opponent, and the chance for a balance has been missed. Similar unfortunate results may flow from the fact that statesmen occasionally believe in the innocence of other statesmen. This permits some of them to achieve enormous expansion by the accretion of small additions of territory. The state of Lusitania announces that it has only one very limited aim, the incorporation of a little territory of the state of Mauritania after which the true balance will have been established, and it will never aspire to another square foot of land. The demand is so small, the request so modest that it is obviously not worth fighting for. It will, of course, be discovered afterwards that there is still no perfect balance, that there is still need for an additional piece of territory. This even smaller piece is likewise not worth fighting for. It lies perhaps in a region outside the immediate interest of the state which must decide how to act, and so its annexation goes unopposed. It is by this process of gradual conquest that most of the successful hegemonies have been established.

An actual balance-of-power policy operates along several lines, boundary-making, compensation, the creation of alliances, and varying degrees of intervention in wars, grading all the way from slight deviations from neutrality to full participation as an ally. Boundary-making is important at the end of a war, and historically the Great Powers have always demanded to be heard at the peace settlement even if they had not participated in the conflict. Under the theory of compensation, states have permitted other states to grow provided they themselves obtained an equal accretion of strength and prestige. It was under this principle of compensation and in the name of the balance of power that the Treaty of Westphalia parceled out the small German principalities among Austria, Bavaria, Brandenburg and Sweden; that Poland was divided four times; that Africa was carved up; and that plans were laid for the partition of China.

In addition to boundary-making and compensation, nations have used systems of alliances to check the growth of a dynamic power. The least expensive and, therefore, the most preferable method would be for a state to encourage an alliance between third parties strong enough to ward off the danger. But this is seldom possible, and the state must be prepared to make its own positive contribution and become part of the alliance. The alliance may stipulate merely a limited contribution in the form of a fixed sum of money, a specific number of ships, or a defined number of soldiers. There is, however, little protection in such limitation. If the survival and continued independence of the ally is really important for the state's own security, its assistance may have to go far beyond the original promises. It will, in fact, have to be increased to whatever is necessary to assure victory and security.

The purpose of the alliance, like the purpose of all power politics, is to achieve the necessary margin of safety in the field of action. But the margin of security for one is the margin of danger for the other and alliance must, therefore, be met by counter-alliance and armament by counter-armament in an eternal competitive struggle for power. Thus it has been in all periods of history. One state successfully conquers adjacent territory and makes each new conquest the stepping-stone for further expansion, each accretion of power the means for further enlargement. Power tends to grow and diffuse through wider areas, and the states in the vicinity have the choice between collective defense and ultimate absorption.

The weak states of the Tigris-Euphrates Valley allied themselves against their stronger rivals and preserved their independence for centuries, until Hammurabi finally established the Babylonian Empire. A new and inconclusive struggle for power then emerged over a much wider area between the Egyptians, the Assyrians, the Hittites, and the Persians with the smaller states in the region being used as buffers and weights. The Greek city-states maintained a precarious balance by means of the Delian and Peloponnesian Leagues under the leadership of Athens and Sparta, but they failed to combine against the menace of Macedonia. Rome, the victorious, found no league to stem her vast expansion, and defeated her enemies one by one. Had they known how to combine, Carthage, Egypt, and Macedonia might have preserved their independence far longer and confined Rome within the boundaries of Europe.

Modern European history begins with the struggle for power among the Italian city-states which was later transferred to the national states over an ever-widening area eventually including the whole world. When the House of Hapsburg under Charles V attained such vast domains that it threatened to become a menace to other states, these states combined to check its ascendancy. Similar was the fate of the hegemonic aspirations of Spain under Philip II, France under Louis XIV and Napoleon, and Germany under Kaiser Wilhelm II. . . .

In this endless story of struggling states, there have been short periods in which an approximation to balanced power prevailed, not because anybody wanted it or tried to achieve it, but because two states or two sets of states were trying to upset it in different directions. Such a situation is inherently unstable because all parties are constantly attempting to destroy it, but while it lasts it brings mankind important benefits as the philosophers had promised. In an international society in which states are intent on preserving their independence, both against world conquest and against world government through federation, balanced power is the only approximation to order. . . . [Spykman, it should be remembered, was describing the international political system as it appeared to him in 1942. He did not live to witness the bipolarization of power and the emergence of a sort of equilibrium deriving from threats of massive retaliatory attack with thermonuclear weapons.]

The idea of international politics as an interminable struggle carried on by national statesmen to improve the power positions of their respective states has attracted many adherents. Whether or not this idea fits the real world of the 1960's depends in part on how one defines power, and in part on the level of abstraction at which one is speaking. In prevailing American usage, the term *national power* carries a strong connotation of military capability. In this idiom, a Great Power is a nation capable of winning a great war. But some nations, manifestly incapable of winning great wars, have exerted great influence in the Society of Nations, Spykman and many others to the contrary notwithstanding. Moreover, nonmilitary sources of influence seem paradoxically to increase as military weapons become more destructive.

If national power be defined so as to include *all* the means, non-military as well as military, by which a government overcomes resistance and affects in desired ways the behavior of other nations, then power becomes, *by definition*, the primary value in statecraft. But this formula provides no basis for differentiating the more specific objectives of different nations. And it is these specific objectives with which both statesmen and their constituents are deeply concerned. In Chapter 4, we shall return to this and other aspects of the concept of power in international politics, but for the present our problem is to discover more specific and fruitful categories for classifying and comparing national foreign policies.

This problem engaged the attention some years ago of Arnold Wolfers (Director of the Washington Center of Foreign Policy Research). Wolfers deals with the objectives of foreign policy under the title—

The pole of power and the pole of indifference *

States are not single-purpose organizations like hospitals, golf clubs, or banking establishments. At one and the same time people expect from them not only external security, but such widely differing things as colonial conquest, better control over foreign markets, freedom for the individual, and international lawfulness. Between goals such as these, relatively scarce means must be parceled out in order of preference and by a constant process of weighing, comparing, and computing of values. Because policy-makers, like all men, seek to maximize value in accordance with ever-fluctuating value patterns, one would anticipate great variation in their choice unless something compelled them to conform.

The number of conceivable ends is much larger than is indicated by broad categories such as "security," "aggrandizement," or "international order." Policy-makers must decide whether a specific increment of security is worth the specific additional deprivations which its attainment through power requires. However, for purposes of analysis it is permissible to limit the discussion to a few representative types of goals. It need only be kept in mind that these typical bundles of related ends are not sharply divided from one another and that no actor is likely to be found pursuing a single type of objectives all the time. He may be out for security today, for conquest tomorrow.

The goals of foreign policy can be classified under the three headings of "goals of national self-extension," "goals of national self-preservation," and "goals of national self-abnegation." For actors other than states, corresponding categories would have to be chosen.

The term "self-extension" is not used here in a derogatory sense, although some goals which belong in this category may deserve moral condemnation. It is meant to cover all policy objectives expressing a demand for values not already enjoyed, and thus a demand for a change of the status quo. The objectives may vary widely. The aim may be more "power as an end in itself" or domination over other peoples or territorial expansion; but it may also represent a quest for the return of lost territory, or the redress of legitimate grievances, such

* From "The Pole of Power and the Pole of Indifference," by Arnold Wolfers, in World Politics, October 1951, pp. 39-64. Copyright 1951 by Princeton University Press; reproduced by permission.

as termination of unjust discriminations, the emancipation from foreign control or imposition on others of an ideology or way of life.

Self-preservation is meant to stand for all demands pointing toward the maintenance, protection, or defense of the existing combination of values, usually called the status quo. The term "self-preservation" is not without ambiguity. The national "self" which states seek to preserve can undergo a wide variety of interpretations. It may be considered to include only national independence and the territorial integrity of the homeland; or it may be held to embrace a whole catalogue of "vital interests," from safety belts and influence zones to investments and nationals abroad. Another variable makes the notion of self-preservation even more elusive and therefore often convenient as a cloak for other purposes. To preserve possessions does not merely mean to defend them when they are actually under attack. Status quo powers regularly demand that the threat of such attack be reduced at least to the points of giving them a reasonable sense of security.

Thus, the quest for security—the preservation goal *par excellence*—points beyond mere maintenance and defense. It can become so ambitious as to transform itself into a goal of unlimited self-extension. A country pursuing the mirage of absolute security could not stop at less than world domination today. A change to self-extension in the name of security often occurs at the close of a war. Victims of attack who were entirely satisfied before hostilities are rarely content, if victorious, to return to the *status quo ante*.

Self-abnegation, finally, is meant to include all goals transcending—if not sacrificing—the "national interest," in any meaningful sense of the term. It is the goal of those who place a higher value on such ends as international solidarity, lawfulness, rectitude, or peace than even on national security and self-preservation. It is also the goal of individuals, groups, or regimes who at the expense of the nation as a whole use their influence within the decision-making process to promote what might be called "subnational" interests.

This may appear to be a category which only a Utopian could expect to find in international politics, at least as far as idealistic self-abnegation is concerned. How could any nation dare indulge in altruistic pursuits—or allow its interests to be sacrificed to interest of a group—and yet hope to survive? While the discussion of compulsion and penalties must be further postponed, it is worth pointing out, nevertheless, that the United States was powerful enough in 1918 to permit Woodrow Wilson to indulge in self-abnegation goals without much harm to American interests and that little Denmark, too weak to seek self-preservation through power, limited its foreign policy largely to humanitarian causes and yet in the end survived Hitler's conquest. There is also the case of governments like that of Communist Czechoslovakia which for the sake of party doctrine and power are ready to promote the transnational cause of world communism, though it mean sacrificing all but the outward appearances of national sovereignty and independence. Highest devotion to national interests and aspirations, even if spread more widely over the globe today than ever, is not the only possible attitude of actors in international affairs. Exponents of world government are not necessarily Utopians for hoping that peoples and governments some day will commit an act of radical national self-abnegation and abdicate as soverign entities in favor of a world state.

Cases in which self-abnegation goals have precedence over national self-preservation may be rare in an era in which nationalism and the ethics of patriotism continue unabated. This does not preclude the possibility, however, that where influential groups of participants in the decision-making process place high value on a universal cause such as peace, pressures exerted by these groups may affect the course of foreign policy. It may lead to a more modest interpretation of the national interest, to more concern for the interests of other nations, to more concessions for the sake of peace, or to more restraint in the use of power and violence. Whether the nation will profit or suffer in the end from the success of such "internationalist," "humanitarian," or "pacifist" pressures depends on the circumstances of the case; whichever it does, the abnegation goals will have proved themselves a reality.

Wolfers' classification of the goals of foreign policy—as expansive, protective, and self-abnegatory—represents only one of numerous ways to cut the foreign-policy pie. But Wolfers' scheme has the merit of breaking out of the sterile axiom that politics is a struggle for power, and its equally sterile corollary that maximization of power is the highest goal of foreign policy. The Wolfers scheme could be used to compare a single state's foreign policy at different periods in its history, or to compare the policies of two or more states in the same or different historical periods.

Explanations of political action

In this section we shall examine certain problems and difficulties that confront anyone who tries to understand or to predict the purposes and operations of any government. There will be numerous cross references to passages in Chapter 1. The reader should find it helpful to review passages from that chapter as these are cited in the present context.

It is possible to describe the interactions of governments—their demands and responses to demands—with a minimum of theory. It is also generally possible to discover in historical perspective certain recurring patterns in the foreign policies of particular nations: for example, the historic American avoidance of military alliances, the British strategy of preventing any one nation from dominating the European Continent, repeated Russian attempts to gain control of ice-free ports, and many other historic patterns that could be cited. Such descriptions, we repeat, can be derived with a minimum of theory. But in order to take the next step—to explain how it came about that certain decisions were taken or to predict the limits within which future decisions seem likely to vary—more explicit theories may be helpful. At a minimum, one will need a set of hypotheses as to what constitutes typical or normally expectable behavior on the part of the government under consideration.

Our first proposition is that statesmen are capable of choosing, and do in fact choose, among alternative courses of action. This premise may seem like elementary common sense. But politicians often defend their actions, both to themselves and to their constituents, by contending that conditions and events compelled them to do what they did do; that they had no choice to do otherwise. Journalists and ordinary private citizens are even more fond of this kind of deterministic rhetoric. Every day brings examples. When American marines went ashore in Lebanon in 1958 to buttress a deteriorating local situation, defenders of the action argued that there was nothing else for President Eisenhower to do.

This kind of rhetoric *never* means what it appears to mean. The statesman always has alternatives. When he says that a situation compels him to choose a given course, he simply means that he rejects other courses— with his reasons for the choice frequently left unspecified. The first essential of clear thinking about foreign policy and political action in general is to rid oneself once and for all of the notion that statesmen are mere chips in a fast flowing stream of history.

Our second proposition is that policy-making is normally a deliberative process. Rarely if ever is an important political decision as instantaneous and reflexive as, say, the motorcar driver's twist of the wheel to avoid a collision. The essential elements of the deliberative process of policy-making can be classified in various ways. We conceive them to include: (*a*) the *personal* motivations of those responsible for acting in the name of the state; (*b*) their *official* ideas of national interest, purposes, goals, etc.; (*c*) their mental image of the environment or situation in which they are operating; and (*d*) their mode of utilizing such knowledge in formulating demands on other states or responding to demands made on them by other governments.

Our third proposition is that personal motives and official purposes frequently do not coincide. A spokesman for a democratic community may feel personal repugnance towards all Communists. Yet in his representative capacity he may have to negotiate and bargain with Communist adversaries. He may personally oppose making concessions, yet be persuaded that it is politically expedient and in the national interest to do so. Countless examples could be cited to illustrate the thesis that a statesman's official role may limit his freedom to follow his personal preferences and inclinations. Conversely, it could also be just as plausibly demonstrated that the statesman's personal preferences may bias his official conceptions of the national interest.

What results from the psychological interplay between a statesman's personal inclinations and his concept of the national interest has been endlessly debated. This was one of the underlying points at issue in the selections above from Spykman and Wolfers. Spykman argued that pursuit of more power is the overriding goal of all governments. Wolfers urged a more functional approach and described three specific orientations discernible in the foreign policies of different states—expansion, defense, and self-abnegation. An implication of Wolfers' argument is that certain similarities do appear in the policy objectives of most states, but that states differ significantly in the priorities assigned to specific objectives; and that in practice these differences are likely to be more significant than the similarities.

If one takes this position, he will be sceptical of across-the-board generalizations about all international politics being simply a struggle for power. That is not to argue that one cannot find patterns more or less common to the policies of all states. The point is rather that it is generally more profitable to compare less-than-global groupings of states: as, for example, the Communist Camp, Latin America, Western Europe, the new nations of Africa, or other groupings. Frequently, one may find it still more fruitful to compare the policy patterns of single states: as, for example, France and Great Britain, or China and India, or the Soviet Union and the United States. The importance of differentiating national patterns and, to a lesser degree, regional patterns becomes still more apparent when one enlarges the focus to include strategies as well as objectives of policy. This view contradicts a basic assumption of certain applications of game theory, to which we shall come in a moment.

Turning to the policy-maker's mental image of the environment or situation in which he is operating, the starting point of analysis is our fourth proposition, that what matters in decision-making is how the actor imagines things to be, not how they actually are. The American debacle at Pearl Harbor dramatically illustrates this basic axiom. During the early days of December 1941 the American commanders at Pearl Harbor were making plans to meet an early Japanese attack—somewhere. But the possibility of an air strike against Pearl Harbor itself apparently did not enter into their calculations at all. The approaching Japanese task force, readying its planes for the Sunday dawn attack, was indubitably there. It was part of the operational environment which was to affect decisively the outcome on that fateful morning, the 7th of December. But the approaching fleet remained unperceived and hence unrelated to the defensive preparations going on at Pearl Harbor. It formed no part of the psychological environment of the American commanders there. So far as their decisions were concerned, the enemy fleet did not exist—until the attack actually began.

One could cite a great many examples of more or less serious discrepancies between conditions as statesmen or military commanders have imagined these to be and as they actually were. In the War of 1812, the Battle of New Orleans was fought in the erroneous belief that a state of war still continued. The Battle of the Bulge caught the Western Allies unprepared in December 1944 because of faulty evaluation of intelligence reports at various headquarters. The Monroe Doctrine was proclaimed in 1823 with reference to a threat of European aggression in the Americas that had already subsided before Monroe spoke. American missile and satellite research after World War II proceeded on a widely held but mistaken assumption of a comfortable margin of superiority over Russian science and engineering. Attitudes are formed and policy decisions are taken again and again on fragmentary and often quite defective estimates of the situation.

Such mistakes sometimes lead to fatal or near-fatal outcomes. Napoleon's and Hitler's invasions of Russia are classic examples. Two startling examples of near-fatal discrepancy between a statesman's image of the situation and the actual state of affairs are provided in Hugh Baillie's report of an interview with Neville Chamberlain (the British Prime Minister who tried to appease Hitler at Munich in 1938 and who continued in office until the disastrous defeats of 1940).

This interview took place in the autumn of 1939, after the German armies had conquered Poland and less than a year before the aerial blitz on London and other British cities. Baillie (then president of the United Press) asked Chamberlain about the air-raid defenses plainly visible in Britain. To this the Prime Minister replied:

> Yes, all these things are quite necessary. . . . But of course there will never be a successful air raid on London. We have an impenetrable barrage all along the east coast . . . through which no hostile aircraft can penetrate. [Later in the interview, Chamberlain predicted] Hitler will have a mutiny on his hands if he attempts to go through this coming winter [1939-40, the winter of the so-called "phony war" that preceded the sensational German conquests of Norway, Denmark, Holland, Belgium, and France] without using his ground forces. He cannot keep such a big army idle all through the winter months. The

morale of the German troops is already impaired by reading our pamphlets which we drop on them from airplanes.*

One wonders these days whether comparable errors underlie the mental images of American, Russian, Chinese, and other policy-makers. One wonders too what may happen when the scientists and engineers have provided fully automatic missiles. A manned bomber can be recalled in flight if a mistake in reconnaissance is discovered in time. Perhaps techniques can be perfected for the recall or deliberate destruction of missiles in flight. But the fact remains that each technological advance that shortens the time span between decision and operational result may increase the risk of disastrous and possibly irreparable mistakes in intelligence.

A complicating feature of most on-going situations is the near certainty that the operational environment will change significantly during the course of interaction. The Suez case of 1956 exemplifies this complication. Let us suppose, for the purpose of the illustration, that the decision of the British Cabinet to use military forces to reoccupy the Canal was predicated on some such intelligence estimate as follows: that the operation could be executed swiftly; that the Egyptians would be unable either to offer effective resistance or to block the Canal; that the Arab peoples would not disrupt the production and flow of oil to Europe contrary to their manifest economic interest; that the Soviet government would keep its hands off; that the United States and Canadian governments and peoples would accept a *fait accompli;* that the United Nations could offer no serious opposition; that the public opposition which was dividing Britain internally would collapse as soon as British forces were reestablished in the Canal Zone.

In this case as stated here, a significant aspect of the situation was the potential responses of various governments to the decision to intervene. Such responses, if and when they should occur, would then become part of the operational environment in which the decision would be carried out. But these responses did not actually exist prior to the decision to intervene. That is to say, the policy-makers' expectations as to what responses their actions would evoke were (prior to the actions) an aspect of their psychological environment. But the congruence or discrepancy between their expectations and the operational environment could not be conclusively established until after some overt actions were taken. This added a complicating element of uncertainty to the decision-makers' problem—an uncertainty inherent in most human interactions.

This complication, however, does not invalidate in the slightest the

* From pp. 144, 145 of *High Tension: The Recollections of Hugh Baillie.* Copyright 1959 by Hugh Baillie; published by Harper & Brothers, New York; reproduced by permission.

proposition that environmental factors become related to policy decisions only to the extent and in the manner that these are perceived and taken into account in the decision-making process. The Suez example simply demonstrates that the decision-makers' estimate of the situation may have to include not merely conditions that exist or events that occur prior to the moment of decision but also predictions as to how the operational environment may change as the decision is carried into successive stages of execution.

Discrepancies between the policy-maker's image of the situation (that is, his psychological environment) and the real world (his operational environment) become highly significant when the problem is to explain or to predict the outcome or results of a given course of action; but that is an entirely different kind of problem, to which we shall come in the next chapter. For the present we simply emphasize once again that conditions and events affect policies only to the extent that the policy-makers take cognizance of them.

The distinction between things as they appear and as they actually are —so important to the policy-maker—is likewise important to anyone who observes and interprets events from the sidelines. In order to comprehend what governments are up to—why the policy-makers of State A pursue certain objectives by means of certain strategies—one must try to discover how conditions and events appear to them. How do they "size up" the situation?

The popular tendency is to assume that statesmen know what they are doing. This assumption is implicit in the venerable axiom that "politics is the art of the possible." This cliché is sometimes quoted as a description of typical policy-making behavior, sometimes as a precept for the guidance of statesmen. In either context it implies that those who make political decisions can be assumed, in the main, to have knowledge of the situation sufficiently accurate and complete to enable them to know the limits of what is possible.

Alongside these assumptions, one generally encounters still another, already discussed in Chapter 1. That is the assumption that the sideline interpreter of political events normally perceives and "sizes up" a situation about as the operators do themselves. All of these assumptions are debatable.

One should never take for granted that a specific head of government or a specific foreign minister or a specific legislative assembly or other specific decision-making unit does in fact command *effectively* the wide range of knowledge required to conduct adequately the foreign affairs of a modern state. It is still more dubious to assume that a newspaper editor or other political commentator or a college teacher and his students will be able (simply by applying common sense) to view situations and events through the eyes (figuratively speaking) of generals, diplomats, civil servants, and politicians.

The sideline observer always functions under handicaps, difficult to surmount but not insurmountable. He has to reconstruct at second hand from what statesmen say and do a description of their image or estimate of the situation. He nearly always views events at some distance, often at great distance. He may have to surmount linguistic, ideological, and other barriers to communication. He has to make do with insufficient and often contradictory evidence. At best, his inferences regarding the operators' ideas and outlook rest on rather arbitrary decisions as to the relevance and weight to be attached to various kinds of evidence. And all the evidence is filtered through the observer's own culture-biased spectacles.

Consider, for a moment, what Russian leaders say about their defense problem. Anyone who accepts their words at face value is likely to come to the conclusion that they are genuinely apprehensive about the plane and missile bases with which the United States has partially encircled Soviet territory. Should one accept this Russian image at face value? If not, by what criteria does one discriminate between what to believe and what to doubt. Merely to ask such questions is sufficient to suggest some of the difficulties which confront anyone who undertakes to interpret the foreign policies of another nation.

The more one studies the governmental organization of any state, the more he is likely to be impressed by the remoteness of the men at the top from the real world in which their decisions are executed. What passes for information of the situation at the higher levels consists, more often than not, of generalizations and abstracts, several stages removed from on-the-spot observations. On most issues the individuals or groups responsible for major decisions will have little time—sometimes no time at all—to cross-check what has been prepared for them at lower working levels of the organization.

Let us assume, for purposes of illustration, that the British Cabinet's decision to send military forces to reoccupy Suez (in the autumn of 1956) was predicated on a firm expectation that the job could be finished quickly. How did Sir Anthony Eden and his colleagues come to such a conclusion? One can only speculate, of course. They probably received estimates of the situation prepared by civil servants and military staffs. Such estimates probably included statements regarding the strength and distribution of land, sea, and air forces, their state of readiness, landing craft and other transportation and handling equipment on hand, liaison arrangements with the French command, the condition of Egyptian defenses, the morale of Egyptian troops and civil population, etc. In addition, one may perhaps assume that Eden and his immediate associates had some notions of their own about British military power in general, about conditions in the Arab countries, and about the forces that would be required to do the contemplated job. But is it likely that they had much fresh personal knowledge of these matters, or the time and energy necessary to check up on their experts?

Other examples will come to mind. One occurred early in President Kennedy's Administration. During the final year of the Eisenhower Administration, Cuban exiles in the United States had been preparing a military expedition designed to bring down Castro's regime. Though evidence was somewhat contradictory, it appeared that these preparations had gone forward with the approval and support of the Central Intelligence Agency. Finally, someone gave the "go ahead" signal. The expedition went ashore, and was promptly liquidated by Cuban government forces. Kennedy immediately assumed responsibility for the decision which led to the debacle. Did he personally take the decision to go ahead? If so, did he rely exclusively on advice from the Director of the Central Intelligence Agency? However these questions are answered, they point up the dependence of the top executive on information and estimates supplied by his organization.

The above questions immediately pose others. To what extent is the head of government or other high-ranking decision-maker a virtual prisoner of the civil and military staffs who provide the data and help to shape the alternatives? Was Khrushchev, in 1961, really the dictator he appeared to be; or was he caught up in a struggle for primacy going on within the Kremlin? On the other hand, how may the known preferences of the men at the top affect the substance and angling of what their subordinates decide to tell them? To what extent may the blind spots and preferences of those who collect and process intelligence bias their own observations and calculations? In other words, to what extent is the wish father to the thought in statecraft as in other walks of life? And to what extent do such considerations affect the whole chain of communications in a complex foreign-policy-making operation?

Such questions justify doubts as to the validity of the common-sense assumption of adequate knowledge. The proposition that top-level decision-makers in a complex modern government effectively command adequate knowledge is no more than a hypothesis to be confirmed, never to be taken for granted.

When one is studying historical cases, it is sometimes possible to discover what data were actually available, recognized as relevant, and taken into account. But what is one to do with historical cases in which evidence is scanty or deemed untrustworthy? What is one to do when estimating how a given statesman or governmental agency would be likely to view a postulated future contingency? To these questions only one rational answer is possible. One has no fruitful alternative but to supplement factual knowledge with assumptions as to what information was probably available and utilized in a past instance, or would probably be so in a future contingency. That is to say, one has to fall back on a model (as described on page 56, Chapter 1) of the manner in which information is *normally* or *typically* gathered, processed, and communicated upwards through a complex governmental organization. Such a model, as already emphasized, is fallible and subject to error. It is a poor substitute for observation. But the only alternative is sheer speculation.

We come finally to the related issue of estimating how statesmen did (in past cases) or are likely to (in future contingencies) make use of information in the decision-making process. How do they react to a perceived state of affairs? How is the sideline observer to interpret decision-making behavior, especially the behavior of foreign governments? These questions have been answered in different and conflicting ways.

At one pole stand those who are sceptical of deriving any useful knowledge on this subject. Such scepticism is especially pronounced with respect to the difficulty of interpreting the behavior of persons in environments radically unlike the observer's own. This view is reflected in such statements as: It is useless to try to understand or to forecast the reactions of Chinese, or Russians, or other "inscrutable" foreigners. The classic expression of this brand of pessimism is Churchill's often quoted epigram dubbing Soviet foreign policy a "riddle wrapped in a mystery inside an enigma."

At the opposite pole, one hears it optimistically asserted that human nature is everywhere the same. Hence, according to this view, anyone can (within limits, to be sure) intuit how foreigners (even the "inscrutable" ones) are likely to react to a given state of affairs. The observer, according to this common-sense thesis, has simply to imagine how he himself would react to the conditions and events in question. This intuitive hypothesis rests upon an assumption that persons of different social class, different educational background, different social roles, different nationality, etc., will nevertheless perceive *and react* in substantially similar ways. When doubts are voiced, these are met by arguing that the observer and his subjects all function in accordance with the same universal principles of logic and human nature.

A third view, falling somewhere between these two extremes, recognizes significant variations in what is "normal" or "typical" behavior in different social environments, and holds such variation to be comprehensible across cultural frontiers. According to this thesis, it is unrealistic to expect a Chinese Communist and a London banker, for example, to react in the same way to most conditions and events. Each views the situation from his own socio-national background and perspective. Both may recognize certain so-called imperatives, such as defense against the manifest peril of nuclear attack. But national variations still remain; and it is our thesis that such variations often provide a key to understanding significant differences in national policies.

For knowledge of such variations, there is a growing tendency to seek help from specialists who have investigated most thoroughly the values, attitudes, and other behavioral patterns of different nationalities. Specifically, this has meant going to the works of psychologists, comparative sociologists, and anthropologists, to supplement impressions of casual travelers, journalists, diplomats, and other "generalists."

This has come to be called the behavioral approach to foreign policy: a descriptive even if not highly distinctive label. All approaches are behavioral, if they are designed to explain or predict the actions and interactions which constitute international politics. What is new is the more systematic comparative application of theories of motivation, perception, reasoning, etc., drawn from the more specifically behavioral sciences.

Such theories focus attention on national differences formerly neglected or ignored: differences in attitudes towards foreign lands and peoples; differences in the meaning of words and in the uses of language; differences in modes of reasoning; and many others. Applied to the study of foreign policy, the behavioral approach tends to bring to light and to emphasize significant differences between Russian, Chinese, British, American, Indian, and other conceptions of national interest and perhaps more important differences in national strategies and operations.

A contrary tendency has appeared in attempts to bring much greater precision to prediction of international events by application of so-called game theory, cited briefly on page 58 above. Most, though not all, game theorists tend to treat the state as a solid unit, an entity with a single will and voice. They envisage international politics as a game played "rationally" according to a common set of rules.

One of the leading contributors to this brand of theory is Arthur L. Burns (of the National University of Australia). Burns summarily downgrades any help to be obtained from anthropology, sociology, and social psychology. He does so because he regards what goes on inside a national political community as essentially irrelevant to that community's foreign policies, strategies, and interactions with other communities. In the Burns model, the environment that is controlling is the international environment.

From this position Burns spins out a tightly reasoned set of theorems about international politics. In his scheme, national differences are recognized to exist, but (as noted above) are treated as having little or no political significance. His whole argument appears to rest upon the hypothesis that the international political system itself imposes a set of conditions and rules which the "players" (states, not states*men*, mind you) accept and to which they react substantially alike, irrespective of whether they are Chinese or Indians or Russians or Britons or Americans. This hypothesis, if rigorously applied, leads to the conclusion that essentially the same operational rules prevail, for example, in Moscow and in Washington, or in Peking and in Delhi.*

This is a strongly mechanistic, indeed almost deterministic, model of policy-making behavior. Whether it corresponds to what happens in the real world, whether it provides reliable guidance to what may happen, is plainly debatable. In assuming irrelevance, or only slight relevance, of variables in the domestic environment of a nation's policy-makers, this brand of theory disregards a great deal of evidence in support of the contrary thesis: namely, that foreign policy is also a manifestation of a community's values, attitudes, ways of thinking, and other aspects of culture which differentiate it from every other community. As will become more and more apparent in later chapters, this is one of the central issues in any examination of the foundations of international politics.

All theories of international behavior pose a problem of special difficulty. That is the problem of predicting the actions of *specific* persons or organized groups. It will help to focus this difficulty if we compare the problem of predicting average behavior in large aggregates of units. The economic geographer predicting crop distributions, the demographer projecting population trends, the market analyst, or the election forecaster rarely if ever attempts to predict the behavior of specific individuals. Rather he predicts the odds of certain choices recurring in large aggregates of behavior. The foreign policy analyst, on the contrary, deals (by definition) with the choices of specific individuals or relatively small groups.

The foreign-policy analyst's task is rendered more difficult by the magnitude and complexity of the issues with which he has to deal. In the street-crossing example in Chapter 1 (see page 39) the observer drew a predictive inference from assumptions as to what he regarded as normally expectable behavior in a given situation and locality. But the significant variables involved in predicting when a specific individual will cross a busy

---

* The classic statement of Burns's thesis is in his paper entitled "From Balance to Deterrence," in *World Politics*, July 1957, pp. 494 ff.

street may be considerably fewer and simpler than those involved in predicting what a head of government will do about disarmament, nuclear weapons tests, technical assistance to the Congo, or almost any other international issue.

One method of resolving the difficulty of predicting specific choices is to deduce intentions (that is, objectives and strategy) from capabilities. This technique is said to be standard practice in the planning of military operations. One suspects that it also enters into diplomatic and other political planning, and likewise into the judgments of journalists and other sideline observers of the international scene.

The essence of this method is to begin by estimating what courses of action a given decision-making unit (military command, foreign office, head of government, or other) is capable of undertaking with fair prospect of success. The next step is to assume that the unit will choose rationally from the range of possible alternatives a strategy which offers relatively high promise of success. The third step is to assume that the unit being analyzed will evaluate its capabilities in the same way as the outsider making the analysis. From these assumptions, the latter calculates the range within which the decision will probably fall—by himself (the analyst) estimating the possibilities latent in the operating conditions. The fruitfulness of this line of reasoning, it is obvious, must depend in part on the tenability of the assumptions outlined above. Anyone who has read the foregoing pages will realize how dubious one or more of these assumptions is likely to be. Nevertheless, inference of intentions from estimates of the relative capabilities of the interacting parties may provide a fruitful first approximation.

Another way to cope with the formidable difficulty of predicting specific political decisions is to resort to negative prediction. By means of the same logical procedures, it may be possible to narrow the range within which a specific decision seems likely to fall. By application of suitable premises, one attempts to eliminate as *very improbable* those choices which would represent the greatest deviation from the postulated norm. He then narrows the range still further by eliminating as *quite* improbable, though somewhat less so, those choices which represent progressively smaller deviations from the postulated norm. At some point he decides that it is too speculative, with the evidence at hand, to carry this narrowing process any further. What is left is a residual estimated range of variation within which the specific choice seems likely to fall. Thus, if one cannot forecast precisely what the British Cabinet will do about nuclear weapons during the next five years, he can perhaps reach more general conclusions as to some of the choices that they are more or less likely *not* to make. The following diagram indicates schematically the procedure suggested in this paragraph:

CONTINUUM OF ALL POSSIBLE CHOICES VIS-À-VIS A GIVEN PROBLEM

VERY IMPROBABLE	LESS IMPROBABLE	ABOUT EQUALLY PROBABLE

The rationale of this procedure is self-evident. The margin of probable error is assumed to increase as one moves from the most improbable to the most probable pole of the range of all possible choices. Whether such an assumption is reasonable depends, of course, on the knowledge and insight that has gone into setting up the scale of normally expectable decision making. For negative prediction, to narrow the range of probable choice, no less than for positive prediction to "spot" a specific choice, involves the application of general propositions as to what is typical or normally expectable behavior by the decision-making unit under consideration. But negative prediction does bypass the issue of specific choice (in predicting which the probability of error may be so high as to nullify the value of the whole calculation), in favor of a less specific solution involving considerably lower probability of error.

It would be all too easy to leave a discussion of foreign-policy analysis on a note of pessimism and discouragement. In the foregoing pages we have dealt with only a few of the salient aspects of analysis and interpretation. Yet even this limited reconnaissance has uncovered difficulties that appear to resist the best available tools and methods.

It would be folly to minimize these difficulties, especially the nationalistic bias that infects nearly all thinking about the objectives and strategies of one's own and other nations. There is no escape from the conclusion that explaining and predicting the actions and interactions of national political communities is a tricky and speculative business.

However, to admit difficulties, where difficulties patently exist, is not to counsel pessimism and despair. Nor need one seek refuge in the palpably untenable conclusion that one man's guess is as good as another's.

National policies plainly exhibit discernible patterns, both in space and through time. In our era of revolutionary change, these patterns are nearly everywhere undergoing transformations. But these variations are not essentially eccentric or capricious. The patterns which differentiate the objectives and strategies of one government from another are not only describable. It is the thesis of this chapter that national projects and undertakings are also explainable, and within rather broad limits predictable as well. And it is one of the continuing themes of the book as a whole, that it is possible to identify many of the factors—both in the organization of national political communities and in the environments which encompass their policy-makers—that affect their purposes and strategies, projects and undertakings.

We turn next to the problems involved in explaining and predicting the outcomes or operational results of national projects and undertakings.

CHAPTER FOUR

★ ★ ★

Power, Political Potential, and International Capabilities

POWER IS ONE of the most common terms in the vocabulary of international politics. States are called Powers, and classified as Superpowers, World Powers, Great Powers, Second-Rate Powers, Weak Powers, etc. Statesmen concern themselves with something called the balance of power. Alliances are formed to redress the balance of power, to create a preponderance of power, or otherwise to improve the power position of the state in question. Such activities are called power politics. International politics is frequently defined as a struggle for power. Some concept of power underlies virtually every description of political interaction, domestic as well as international. The discipline of political science, of which the field of international politics is a branch, has been defined as the study of power in society.

An American historian, Carl Becker, once said:

> The simple fact is that politics is inseparable from power. States and governments exist to exert power. . . . In each country and in the world at large there is either a stable balance of power, an unstable balance of power, or no balance of power at all. But there is always power. . . . Political power exists in the world and will be used by those who have it. . . .*

The above quotation suggests the idea of a quantifiable and commensurable mass, something like a pile of bricks or a stone wall perhaps. Some such notion as this seems to be implicit in a great deal of the discussion of international politics. A mass can be measured and weighed. Hence

---

* From pp. 83-84 of *How New Will the Better World Be?* by C. L. Becker. Copyright 1944 by Alfred A. Knopf, Inc., New York; reproduced by permission.

the power of two or several states can be compared and their relative weights ascertained.

Closely linked to this way of viewing power is the thesis that the power of a national political community is a function primarily of its mobilizable and deployable military force. This has been one of the main tenets of the so-called "realist school" of international politics. Thus, for example, a leading text, published in the 1930's, asserts that

> states . . . vary in the degree to which they can clothe their national policies with force. As a consequence, only a few . . . will possess the force necessary to support their national policies effectively; and these alone constitute the Great Powers. . . . Ours is not only a world without enforceable international law but also a Great-Power world.*

The late Nicholas J. Spykman (professor of international relations at Yale University) stated, to the same effect, that the power of a state is "in the last instance the power to wage war." For *The Economist* (London magazine of business and finance), this was insufficient:

> A Great Power is a country capable of waging active and autonomous war against another Great Power. The words *active* and *autonomous* are both essential to the description [*The Economist* continued]. It is not enough to sustain a passive defense, even for a long time, if it cannot eventually go over to the attack. And for a country to be beyond question a Great Power it must be able to fight with its own resources—not necesarily with those to be found in its own territories, but with those that it can rely on being able to procure.†

As long as military war, however brutal and demoralizing, remained an effective means of supporting a government's policies (that is, its demands on other nations), such wars provided a rough-and-ready yardstick for ranking nations in a hierarchy of power, "like the chickens studied by biologists, which are found to have a definite pecking order when a feed pan is set down among them." ‡ In the intervals between wars, comparison of national military establishments provided a more or less quantifiable, if doubtfully trustworthy, substitute for war itself as a basis for ranking the Powers of the Society of Nations. By the time of World War II, such estimations commonly included latent resources which a government might turn into effective military force through an extended period of mobilization.

---

* From p. 28 of *The Great Powers in World Politics*, rev. ed., by F.H. Simonds and B. Emeny. Copyright 1937 by M. G. Simonds and B. Emeny; published by American Book Co., New York; reproduced by permission.

† From "What is a Great Power?" in *The Economist*, March 11, 1944, p. 330. Copyright by The Economist Newspaper, Ltd.; reproduced by permission.

‡ From p. 1 of *Technology and International Relations*, by W. F. Ogburn et al. University of Chicago Press, 1949.

"Force in being" plus such latent mobilizable resources was called "military potential," or more commonly, "war potential" or "power potential."

Long before the explosion of the first atomic bomb, there were grounds for doubting whether simple military comparisons could yield reliable conclusions regarding the relative power of states. The proliferation of military instruments and techniques during the nineteenth and twentieth centuries piled one complication upon another. Marine mines, automotive torpedoes, submarines, tanks, poison gas, and above all aircraft had added new dimensions to war. The ever widening industrial base and the ever lengthening list of raw materials required to support modern military forces necessitated comparisons which ramified far beyond the strictly military sphere. The totalization of war required computing the capacities of whole nations to carry on under conditions of austerity, stress, and even catastrophe on the home front. The more nearly "total" war promised to be, the less meaningful strictly military comparisons became.

Nevertheless, the advent of atomic bombs, followed within a few years by vastly more destructive hydrogen bombs, did more than merely add still newer dimensions to the traditional concept of power. Rather it put the problem in radically different perspective. Whether war-making capacity is still an adequate and fruitful index of a state's power in international politics is clearly debatable today. Despite threats and counterthreats, recurrent crises, and reckless advice from the sidelines, responsible heads of government who control these superweapons have repeatedly shown remarkable reluctance to use them, reluctance to venture too close to the brink, to the point of no return, which might accidentally bring on a war of mutual annihilation.

> There may have been a time when it was reasonable to estimate relative national power in terms of mobilizable military establishments [writes the American military critic Walter Millis], and to conclude that, short of actual war, the nation with the biggest battalions was most likely to have its way in diplomatic maneuver and negotiation. But it is patently impossible to make any such crude military calculation in terms of relative numbers of deliverable megaton bombs.
>
> As many have been recently pointing out, an increase in the size of one's hydrogen bomb arsenal may actually diminish rather than enhance one's national power on the stage of international politics. Such weapons are so appallingly destructive as to be unusable except in the direst extremity, and thus, in effect, deprive any nation which relies upon them of applicable military power in more ordinary diplomatic situations.
>
> "National power," whatever it may be, is today a resultant of many incommensurable factors, of which mobilizable military power is only

one, and even that one not easily measured in practice. In addition it is necessary to include the factors of human and raw material resources, geographic and strategic position, productivity of industrial plant, the stage of technology, domestic unity and morale, the firmness of the alliance systems, the effectiveness of statecraft and propaganda, the intangibles of "prestige." *

Millis is not arguing, nor would we argue, that military force has ceased to be an important factor in the political relations of states. The point is rather that the enormously increased destructiveness of total war, and the consequently heightened risk inherent in military actions of any kind, have had the effect of upgrading less violent and less destructive techniques of statecraft.

This trend was manifest from the day the phrase *cold war* was coined. It is becoming ever more manifest in the growing emphasis on diplomacy and conference, on subversion and nonsubversive public relations and propaganda, on economic aid and technical assistance, boycotts and embargoes, and other nonmilitary techniques of statecraft.

The threat of massive retaliation with nuclear weapons, coupled with the known destructiveness of these weapons, tends to cancel them out as active instruments of policy. Increasingly the primary function of these superweapons—perhaps the only function compatible with human survival—is deterrence. Put in different words, we may be approaching, indeed we may conceivably have reached, the point where the function of the superweapons is to hold the ring, so to speak, while less dangerous instruments are brought into play. If this is so, then capacity to provide and to make effective use of these less dangerous instruments of statecraft becomes more important than ever before. Historians of the future may conclude that ability to employ nonmilitary instruments effectively had become by the 1960's as critically important as capacity to build the most destructive thermonuclear warheads and to deliver them to distant targets.

Definitions of power

The concept of political power has undergone a subtle change during recent years. The notion of power as a quantifiable mass is giving way to the concept of power as a behavioral relationship.

Indicative of the behavioral trend in thinking about political power is a passage by Samuel H. Beer (professor of government at Harvard) in a treatise on comparative politics. In Beer's definition,

* From "U.S.—The Balance of Power—U.S.S.R.," by Walter Millis, in *New York Times Magazine*, August 2, 1959. Coyright 1959 by the New York Times Company, New York; reproduced by permission of publisher and author.

one person exercises power over another when he intentionally acts in such a manner as to affect in a predictable way the action of the other. . . . Power in society takes many forms. An obvious one is wealth—every day each of us exercises this form of power by paying money in return for goods and services. Other familiar forms are physical strength, social status, education, moral character, personal magnetism, military, legal, or managerial skill. Often we may be able to trace the power of an individual over others to one or more such factors, his "power base." . . . To speak thus of the power base does not mean that power is something that the individual or group simply "has." Power is relational. The influence that one person has over another depends not only on the power-holder, but also on the person he influences. The situation of the person influenced will certainly make a difference. The poor man will probably be more subject to the influence of money than the rich; the unarmed man more subject to the influence of force than the armed. Moreover, the interests and general psychological equipment of the person to be influenced will affect the outcome. The martyr will not be swayed by threats of violence, the dunce by appeals to reason, nor the atheist by promises of heavenly bliss. While these are examples of special individual traits, they also suggest how the culture of a society will profoundly condition the forms of power that may arise within it.*

The quoted passage was written in the context of government and politics *within* nations; but, for reasons explained in the preceding section, Beer's discussion of power is also relevant to international politics. The basic concept is interaction. The essence of interaction is demand and response. In the context of international politics those who make demands are the state's official agents, or spokesmen—persons or groups legally invested with authority to act in the name of the state. Their demands, *in order to have political quality*, must evoke some element of opposition or resistance or *conflict of interest*. But neither demands nor responses need exhibit hostile or potentially hostile quality in order to be political. Demands may be mild or imperative, highly specific or vague and general. Responses may vary all the way from amiable if reluctant compliance to angry resistance with every resource available.

The methods by which governments attempt these days to achieve compliance to their demands cover a wide spectrum—wider perhaps than ever previously. In descending order of compulsiveness, techniques of statecraft can be characterized as destructive, coercive, and influential. The meaning of destruction is self-evident. By coercion we mean bodily

---

constraint; by influence, compliance achieved without destruction or constraint. Thus, for example, an army destroys buildings and other structures, and kills people or coerces them, whereas a diplomat wins his way by verbal argument or other modes of persuasion.

Of course, verbal argument may be more "persuasive" if brute force lurks in the background. There is generally a transition zone where influence merges into coercion, a zone where it may be difficult to distinguish sharply between coercion and influence. For example, is it influence or coercion when a government gets its way by denying food to a starving nation, or by accompanying its demands with some ostentatious display of military force? Strictly speaking, both examples fall within the category of influence, since no actual bodily constraint occurs. But influence in these cases is much closer to coercion than is, for example, the diplomatic bargaining among friendly governments of roughly comparable resources and capabilities.

It might help to think more clearly about the relations of states if the word *power* could be stricken from the vocabulary of international politics altogether. However, this term is too deeply and firmly embedded to be easily uprooted at this late date. The term *power* appears repeatedly in the quoted passages in this book. The usage in these quoted selections is unfortunately by no means uniform. The remaining pages of this chapter are devoted to an attempt to work out a more satisfactory terminology with which to express the political relations of states. But before proceeding to this task, it should be emphasized that in American popular usage, the term *power* tends more often than not to denote *military* power, or at least to connote some idea of *coercion* or threatened coercion which is the essence of military power.

National power in action

One way to avoid overemphasizing the military factor in international politics is to describe the interactions of states in more functional terms. This involves, among other things, analyzing the instrumentalities and techniques employed, and the targets and effects of the various techniques. Perhaps it will help to visualize what this approach involves, if we consider for a moment a much oversimplified model of an international political system. In this model there are only two states: State 1 and State 2. Within each state there are two sources of action: the government (designated g), an organization authorized to act in the name of the state; and a constituency (designated c), comprising all persons legally subject to that government's authority. In this oversimplified two-state system one can imagine messages traveling both ways along various channels as follows:

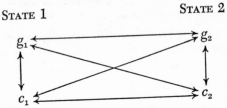

The channels g_1——c_1 and g_2——c_2 carry communications between government and constituency within a single national community. The messages in this channel may consist of laws, decrees, proclamations, public addresses, press releases, and many other kinds of messages from government to constituency. Also along this channel flow demands, appeals, critical reactions to government policies, votes, and other messages from members of the constituency to their government. Transactions that follow the government-constituency channel inside a community do not constitute international transactions by our definition of international politics. Nevertheless, they may constitute highly relevant aspects of the environment of the state's official decision-makers (that is to say, its government).

The channel c_1——c_2 carries all unofficial messages between persons or groups in different states. Along this channel flow unofficial letters, telegrams, telephone conversations, and radio broadcasts; contacts between tourists, students and other aliens with the local population; newspapers, magazines, books, and other unofficial printed matter that flows into the country from abroad; that part of international commerce and finance which is privately conducted; and unofficial transactions of many other kinds. These transactions certainly fall within the general category, international relations. They may or may not be of much significance to international *political* relations—that is relations which involve some conflict of purpose or interest between organized national communities. In all states—but especially in Communist and other totalitarian systems—it is always difficult, and sometimes impossible, to draw a sharp distinction between international communications that are official and those that are unofficial. That is to say, it is difficult to decide whether to classify particular transactions as c_1——c_2 or as g_1——c_2 or g_2——c_1.

The g_1——c_2 and g_2——c_1 channels carry messages mainly in one direction: from government to foreign constituency. A certain amount of communication does flow in the opposite direction: for example, loans by private banks to foreign governments, or, more specifically, business projects from American oil companies to the Arab states around the Persian Gulf.

In some states, the United States in particular, it is illegal for private individuals to negotiate *politically* with foreign governments. On the other hand, it is standard practice for governments to try to influence other governments by beaming propaganda at the latter's constituents. Channels g_1——c_2 and g_2——c_1 are also the channels along which flow many of the transactions designed to subvert the political system of another state. And these channels also carry many of the transactions of hot war as well as of cold.

Channel g_1——g_2 is the channel of all communications between governments. It is the channel of diplomacy and of all other intergovernmental transactions.

As we outline, in the following pages, the instrumentalities, techniques, targets, and effects of transnational actions, it will be helpful to keep constantly in mind these four sets of channels. By this means one can translate the general concept of power into more meaningful concepts of actions and interaction.

By *instruments of statecraft* is meant simply the apparatus, human as well as nonhuman, which statesmen make use of in their efforts to affect in desired ways the behavior of other nations. The nature and scope of this political apparatus is indicated in the following scheme:

(1) Nonhuman instruments which include—
   (a) Apparatus of communication
   (b) Normative ideas
   (c) Technical information
   (d) Apparatus of coercion and destruction
   (e) Other goods: foodstuffs, raw materials, capital equipment, consumer goods, etc.
(2) Human instruments which include—
   (a) Government agencies and personnel: diplomatic, military, public relations, and many others
   (b) Nongovernment agencies and personnel: banking and insurance personnel, educators, engineers, journalists, and many others

The *apparatus of communication* includes, first of all, the words and other symbols by which one government communicates with another or with nongovernmental persons inside another country. Also included, of course, are the mechanisms—printing machinery, electronic equipment, etc.—by which communication is conducted over distances greater than the carrying power of the human voice.

Normative ideas include standards of right conduct embodied in customs and laws and also systems of ideas for organizing human society and affecting human behavior. Statesmen regularly justify their demands by resort to moral or legal arguments. The use of liberal democratic ideology, communism, and other ideologies as instruments of statecraft is too well known to need further elaboration at this point.

Stocks of *technical information* have become increasingly important instruments of statecraft. By sharing scientific, engineering, administrative, military, and other kinds of knowledge, allies can be strengthened. Economic and technical knowledge enters into all so-called technical assistance programs undertaken to hasten the modernization of underdeveloped countries.

The *apparatus of coercion and destruction* has long been one of the more important kinds of political apparatus. Military apparatus includes everything from simple explosives to the most intricate and destructive modern weapons. As previously emphasized, the enormous development of firepower, most recently in the form of thermonuclear superweapons, has narrowed the limits within which military force can be effectively employed without suicidal risk to the user. Nevertheless, within these limits military equipment is still a high-priority category of political apparatus.

Nonmilitary goods and service facilities have become increasingly important instruments of statecraft in recent years. Command over goods and service facilities may give a government highly effective leverages on other nations. Depending on circumstances, this holds true for foodstuffs, raw materials, capital equipment, consumer goods, and facilities for providing transportation and for performing financial and other services.

In practice, nonhuman instruments of statecraft become operative in human hands. The apparatus of communication provides communication when someone makes use of it. The same holds for normative ideas, technical knowledge, military equipment, and nonmilitary goods and service facilities.

This brings us to the distinction between *instruments* and *techniques*. By the latter we mean the functions performed with various instruments and combinations thereof. Thus, for example, foreign offices and embassies, including their personnel, are instruments of statecraft; but diplomacy is a technique. Military forces—weapons plus the soldiers who operate them—are instruments; military operations of various kinds are techniques. A communist party in a democratic state may be an instrument of a foreign communist governemnt; subversive activities carried on by members of that party constitute a technique. Engineers, farm experts, teachers, and other specialists may be instruments; technical assistance is a technique. Economic goods of various kinds may be instruments; gifts and loans to foreign nations may be techniques.

The techniques of statecraft may be classified in various ways: with reference to the instruments employed; with reference to the targets of action; with reference to effects desired; or with reference to effects actually produced. The following break-down is based on instruments employed:

(1) Techniques linked primarily with instruments of communication:
    (a) Negotiation: diplomacy, conference, etc.
    (b) Unilateral declarations of policy
    (c) Public relations activities not specifically related to particular policies
    (d) Psychological attacks: subversion, attacks on morale, etc.
(2) Techniques linked primarily with normative ideas and/or technical knowledge:
    (a) Display of social achievements: scientific and engineering display, escorted tourism, exhibitions and fairs, etc.
    (b) Assistance in military development
    (c) Other technical assistance activities
(3) Techniques linked primarily with nonmilitary goods and service facilities:
    (a) Provision of goods and services: loans, gifts, etc.
    (b) Denial of goods and services: boycotts, embargoes, etc.
    (c) Other forms of economic action
(4) Techniques linked primarily with instruments of coercion and destruction:
    (a) Sabotage
    (b) Deterrence: display of weapons, threats of military action, etc.
    (c) Limited military operations: military intervention, limited war, etc.
    (d) Unlimited military operations: total war, etc.

Negotiation is the art of employing verbal arguments and persuasion to adjust conflicting claims and demands. Negotiation is the essence of diplomacy as traditionally conceived and generally practiced in the past. Many would contend that negotiation has been and continues to be the most important technique of international satecraft.

Perhaps the leading exponent of this view today is Hans J. Morgenthau (professor of international relations at the University of Chicago). Until the development of nuclear weapons, he says, national statesmen had a

choice among three alternatives: diplomacy, war, and renunciation. Which one of these alternatives a nation would choose in a concrete situation was a matter of rational calculation; none of them was *a priori* excluded on rational grounds. Modern technology, especially in the form of all-out atomic war, has destroyed this rational equality among diplomacy, war, and renunciation, and has greatly enhanced the importance of diplomacy. In view of that technology, there is no longer safety in renunciation or victory in war. . . . When universal destruction is the result of victory and defeat alike, war itself is no longer a matter of rational choice but becomes an instrument of suicidal despair. . . . A nation which under present conditions is either unwilling or unable to take full advantage of the traditional methods of diplomacy condemns itself either to the slow death of attrition or the sudden death of atomic destruction.*

In rebuttal to the argument, frequently heard these days, that the United Nations and other international organizations have made the older forms of diplomacy obsolete, Harlan Cleveland (Assistant Secretary of State in the Kennedy Administration) has the following to say:

The citizen, watching the United Nations at its complex work, will be less baffled if he keeps in mind the distinction between the issues which the U.N., reaching beyond the cold war, can *do* something about, and the issues on which U.N. action is necessarily limited to talk—useful, clarifying talk sometimes, but talk nevertheless. The great cold war issues will not be settled by committee work in the United Nations, because these are questions whose outcome may be more important to the Great Powers than considerations of world opinion. . . . But all [such issues, Berlin, nuclear disarmament, Communist China, etc.] are subject to negotiation, and U.N. debate performs a signal service in pushing the Great Powers toward talking with each other about them.†

Diplomatic negotiations may result in compliance by one side, rejection by both sides, or compromise. During the 1950's a state of affairs developed in which rational compromise became exceedingly difficult on the dangerous issues which divide the Communist Camp and the Anti-

---

* From "The Art of Diplomatic Negotiation," in *The State of the Social Sciences,* edited by L. D. White, pp. 404, 410. Copyright 1956 by University of Chicago Press; reproduced by permission.
† From "The Road Around Stalemate," by Harlan Cleveland, in *Foreign Affairs,* October 1961. Copyright 1961 by Council on Foreign Relations, New York; reproduced by permission.

Communist Coalition. The major Communist spokesmen, apparently believing that their bargaining position was improving and bound to improve still further, confronted the Western Powers with an increasingly arrogant and uncompromising posture. The latter, especially the Americans, had come rather generally to equate compromise with appeasement—as a fruitless attempt, by making concessions, to buy peace from an insatiable adversary.

These states of mind have rigidified diplomacy and have resulted in irrational attitudes and behavior on both sides in the Cold War. Yet it is difficult to rebut Morgenthau's thesis that diplomacy, which implies bargaining and compromise by negotiation, remains the only rational alternative to mutually suicidal violence.

The growing complexity of international problems in our time has fostered more frequent resort to multilateral conferences. These are essentially devices for carrying on negotiations involving several or many states. Cleveland's statement quoted above suggests one of the limitations of multilateral diplomacy, especially as carried on within the United Nations. The United Nations Assembly is also a prime example of another tendency of our time: the tendency of diplomacy to merge into public propaganda.

Geoffrey Goodwin (of the University of London) has characterized this practice as "forensic diplomacy." Inflammatory speeches in the General Assembly, broadcast to the ends of the earth, may have considerable value, he admits, as indicators of the "international climate." They may also serve a useful purpose of "letting off steam." But he comes to the conclusion that the "net result" of public proceedings of the U.N. Assembly is "usually to arouse slumbering suspicions and passions, to place a heavy strain on delegates' patience, and to militate against that mutual exploration of interests which is the cornerstone of true negotiation and one of the primary purposes of the Charter." But that is not the whole picture. While the Assembly resounds with impassioned speeches, heads of government and their foreign ministers have repeatedly made use of the United Nations headquarters as a common meeting place to carry on quiet exploratory conversations that may lead to highly constructive results.*

Finally, it is well to remember that diplomatic talent and expertise are not limited to the possessors of great military force. Verbal arguments, as previously emphasized, may be more persuasive if superior force lurks in the background. But the diplomatic record includes many instances in

---

* From "The Expanding United Nations: II—Diplomatic Pressures and Techniques," by Geoffrey Goodwin, in *International Affairs,* April 1961. Copyright 1961 by Royal Institute of International Affairs, London; reproduced by permission.

which gifted negotiators, representing small and weak nations, have exerted influence on events quite out of proportion to the military or economic resources at their command.

Unilateral declarations of policy are an ancient and widely used technique of statecraft. A government may proclaim publicly in its press, in its legislative chambers, over the air, or by other media of communication, what it intends to undertake or desires to see happen.

Historically, this has been a favorite American technique. Indeed the U.S. government has operated this way so frequently in the past as to inspire assertions that all we have is a declaratory foreign policy—lots of proclamations and very little follow-through. Such allegations are patent exaggerations, especially in the light of recent American practice. But it is nevertheless true that the United States has repeatedly resorted to public declarations to inform, to advise, and to warn other nations of our demands and expectations.

President Washington, for example, set this style with his public proclamation in 1793 telling the world of our intent to take no part in the European War of the French Revolution. President Monroe's historic "Doctrine," warning European monarchs to leave the Americas alone, was embodied in a public message to Congress in 1823. The Atlantic Charter of 1940 was a public declaration of postwar aims, issued jointly by President Roosevelt and Prime Minister Churchill. The Truman Doctrine of 1947 was a public declaration of American disapproval of direct or indirect aggression anywhere in the world. Many other examples, of course, could be cited.

The vocabulary and rhetoric of policy declarations—as indeed of verbal statecraft in all its forms—have undergone subtle and not so subtle changes in recent times. Formerly a rigid code of diplomatic etiquette governed the rhetoric of statecraft. Ill will and vulgarity frequently lurked behind the verbal façade, but were kept within bounds and rarely reached the level of public utterance.

The Russian Revolution of 1917 and the subsequent spread of Communism (and also of Fascism) changed all this. The Bolshevik revolutionaries introduced the technique of public defamation, vilification, vituperation, and abuse on a grand scale. This kind of verbal warfare adds a new dimension to statecraft. It has depreciated the verbal currency, as other nations have imitated in varying degrees this Communist and Fascist practice. This debasement amounts, in effect, to employing the technique of policy declaration as public propaganda beamed at the lowest and least cultured classes in a nation.

Policy declarations find a special use in connection with recognition of new states, or of revolutionary regimes in pre-existing states. As stated in Chapter 2, such a political community acquires legal status as a member of the Society of Nations by being recognized by other states. By an appropriate public declaration, or by entering into diplomatic relations, a government indicates its intention to treat the new or transmuted state as a member of the Society of Nations. By severing diplomatic relations, a government may attempt to impair the status of another state or its government. This form of action, which displays numerous variants, may represent merely a desire to bring moral, financial or other pressures to bear in support of the acting government's demands. Or, as in the case of British and French rupture of diplomatic relations with Egypt in 1956, following President Nasser's expropriation of the Suez Canal, withdrawal of recognition may constitute a frontal attack designed to bring down the government of the target state.

The value of recognition as an instrument of statecraft depends on conditions and circumstances. It has been one of the time-honored techniques employed in attempts to prevent successful revolutions. Denial of recognition was so used by the conservative monarchies of the eighteenth century. It has been so used by the United States and by other states in recent times. By granting, delaying, or denying recognition to revolutionary regimes, the United States has attempted on many occasions to exert an influence on political developments in various Latin American republics. The long delay (from 1918 to 1933) on the part of the United States in granting recognition to the revolutionary Bolshevik regime in Russia had very little if any effect on the fortunes of post-revolutionary Russia. Similarly the American attempt after 1949 to maintain the position that the refugee regime of Chiang Kai-shek upon the island of Taiwan, was the *de jure* government of all China did not prevent the successful consolidation of Communist rule over the Chinese mainland. Moreover, nonrecognition can be a two-edged weapon. By withholding recognition of Red China, the United States Government denied to itself the opportunity to observe at first hand the course of events at a dynamic turning point in the world's most populous country.

The development of modern rapid communications and the world-wide spread of literacy have greatly enlarged the opportunities for influencing people in the mass. The result has been a mushroom expansion of declaratory operations, and in particular their extension to produce a wide range of effects not immediately connected with particular official demands on other nations. Governments have borrowed and adapted the methods of commercial advertising and public relations activities in general. We have called such operations *non-policy-specific public relations*, since they are typically directed less to securing compliance with specific demands than to fostering the development of a certain mood or climate of opinion within the communities in question.

Activities of this kind have grown by leaps and bounds in recent years. They include circulation of reading matter of all kinds, radio broadcasts, exchange of teachers, students, and other persons, promotion of tourism, exhibits at international fairs, spectacular engineering stunts, and many other activities.

The intense rivalry between Russian and American scientists and engineers has provided numerous exhibits of non-policy-specific public relations activities. By being first to put man-made satellites into orbit, to send a satellite around the moon, and then to put men themselves into space satellites, the Soviet Union gave impressive demonstration of its rapid advance in basic science and engineering. These demonstrations carried obvious military implications. Rockets capable of blasting satellites into outer space could also propel ballistic missiles halfway around the world or farther. The sputniks, the moon shots, and the manned satellites, however, carried still another message, perhaps a more important one in the long run. These dazzling "firsts" were products of the forced-draft intellectual and industrial development which has taken place in Russia since the Communist revolution. Implicit in them is the theme, undeniably attractive to many leaders in the underdeveloped countries, that the Russian brand of socialism will produce quicker results for peoples struggling belatedly to climb the ladder of modern industrial civilization.

If opinion-influencing activities seek to impair, or have the effect of impairing, relations of loyalty within the target state, they fall into the category which we have called *psychological attacks*. Such attacks have come to be called subversive activities. If successful they constitute *subversion*. The subversionist labors, generally surreptitiously, to undermine the citizen's faith in his leaders and in his nation's values and policies and to transform him into a spy or saboteur for the subverting state, and may attempt to alter the basic structure of the subverted community.

A subversive organization is often called a "fifth column." The Nazis experimented with this technique with considerable success, softening up their prospective victims in advance of military invasion. The Communist governments have carried subversion to levels hitherto unknown. In this they have been assisted by local Communist parties which have provided generally compliant, if not always reliable, instruments of Moscow-directed (and in Southeast Asia, Peking-directed) subversive operations.

Closely associated with subversion is the technique of *sabotage*. Whereas the subversionist attacks the human linkages of the target nation's society, the saboteur attacks its physical links—railroads, ports, factories, etc. The methods of the saboteur are many and varied. The familiar stereotype of the saboteur surreptitiously blowing up bridges and putting ground-glass into the gears of munitions plants is a caricature that suggests merely the more obvious forms of this kind of clandestine warfare. While sabotage can be operated without subversion, successful subversion extends the opportunities for sabotage. If projects for poisoning water supplies and spreading epidemic diseases should move from the laboratory to the arena of political action, the combination of subversion and sabotage might become one of the most formidable techniques of statecraft.

Techniques utilizing economic goods and services cover a wide range of activities. *Material aid* and *technical assistance* of many kinds to improve living standards, strengthen military defenses, win allies, bind them more closely to the aid-giving state, etc., are much in the news these days. Such activities seem likely to absorb even more energy and resources in the years to come. They may well become the most important focus of struggle between the Communist and anti-Communist coalitions. The European Recovery Plan of the late 1940's (popularly known as the Marshall Plan) is the most spectacular example to date of a massive deployment of goods and services to buttress the economies and social structures of friendly nations.

Economic techniques can also be used to weaken foreign economies and to obstruct their development. Such techniques are frequently called *economic warfare*. They constitute one of the principal forms of cold war. In general, they consist of denial or restriction of goods and services or of markets and other economic opportunities. Such measures may have the effect of weakening the target state's economy, and hence its war-making capacity; or to induce its government to negotiate on more favorable terms; or to stir up unrest and possibly revolt; or to produce other adverse effects inside the target state.

The specific methods of economic warfare may include tariff restrictions, import and export controls, embargoes and boycotts, exchange controls, and other devices. A government may enter the market of a third country and outbid the target state for scarce raw materials or other commodities of strategic value. Concerted restrictive policies employed by a group of states can seriously handicap a target state, especially one that is attempting to industrialize rapidly. The partial economic blockade of Red China, in which the United States has been the dominant factor since 1950, is a contemporary example of this form of cold war.

We have previously emphasized certain recent trends in the use and utility of *military techniques*. In the absence of effective world government, national military action has been in the past the ultimate (and sometimes not so ultimate) resort of ambitious politicians and generals. The mere existence of military forces has affected in ways both obvious and subtle the behavior and relations of states. This is reflected in the traditional belief that preparation for war is the best insurance against war. This unproved and unprovable dogma finds current expression in the Soviet, American, and British strategy of nuclear *deterrence* or threat of massive retaliation with nuclear weapons in response to attack.

War is a classic technique of statecraft, and many a war in the past has paid handsome dividends to such of the victors as survived. Whether war can any longer be realistically regarded as a fruitful technique is hotly argued these days. The two world wars fought in this century wrought enormous destruction of life and property and, with very few exceptions, left the conquerors in scarcely better shape than the conquered. It is widely doubted today whether there could be any real victors at all in a future global war fought with ballistic missiles, thermonuclear explosives, disease-producing viruses and bacteria, and chemical poisons, as well as the more conventional forms of high explosives.

The "no victors in nuclear war" thesis probably requires some qualification. But these are not qualifications that should give much comfort to Americans, or to Russians either. There is, of course, the possibility that thermonuclear explosions, running into the hundreds or thousands, might make the atmosphere so radioactive as to threaten the present existence and genetic future of the entire human race. Short of such a catastrophe, there is the further possibility that global war fought with thermonuclear explosives might turn over the future of our planet to the underdeveloped countries in general, and to Communist China in particular.

This possibility arises from the well-known vulnerability of highly industrialized economies to dislocation and disruption. It is difficult, for example, to imagine Britain (where the density of population runs into hundreds per square mile and half of all food has to be imported) carrying on at all after thermonuclear devastation of the metropolitan areas of London, Birmingham, and the Midlands. The United States would be in only slightly better shape after destruction of New York, Philadelphia, Pittsburgh, Chicago, and half a dozen other great metropolitan areas. The outlook for the Soviet Union might be a little brighter. This is so because of its larger area and greater decentralization of industry, deliberately dispersed with the possibility of thermonuclear bombing in view. But it seems probable that the Soviet Union too could be crippled by all-out thermonuclear attack.

On the other hand, barring the possibility of world-wide lethal fallout,

Communist China could probably withstand a great deal more thermo-nuclear bombing than the more industrialized countries. China is still a predominantly agrarian country. It is a land of cities, towns and villages which are as yet less interdependent than is the case in Western Europe or North America or even probably in the Soviet Union. The Chinese economy is perhaps about as industrialized as Russia's was before the Revolution, or our own before the Civil War. There are comparatively few vital targets for H-bombs in China. Shanghai, Canton, Peking, and a dozen more Chinese cities could probably be obliterated without destroying China's capacity to carry on and without too seriously impairing the recuperative ability of the Chinese economy. Judging from their public utterances, Chinese Communist leaders appear to be definitely counting on these possibilities, and they seem to be looking forward without much anxiety to the World War III that might enable them to inherit the earth.

All this, of course, is in the realm of speculation. But to the extent to which such possibilities are envisaged and believed, they will have an impact on the decisions and strategies of statesmen in Washington, Moscow, London, and Western Europe. If the idea continues to spread that total war fought with thermonuclear weapons would probably bring irretrievable disaster to the present possessors of these superweapons, it seems likely that we may be on the threshold of radically new conceptions of the role and control of violence in the relations of states.

Speculation on the odds of World War III and on the possible conse-quences of such a war should not blind us to the undeniable fact that *limited military action* is still regarded almost everywhere as a permissible technique of statecraft. Early in 1959 a tabulation of limited wars was issued by the American Department of Defense. This report listed eighteen situations involving military action on a considerable scale since 1945. Six of these were civil wars and four were colonial wars. The remaining eight involved the use of military force across international frontiers. None of these operations involved confrontation of the major military forces of the United States and the Soviet Union. But in Korea and in one or two other cases, the fighting approached dangerously close to the brink of general war. The limits within which military forces can be deployed and engaged without bringing out the H-bombs and the ICBM's is one of the most furiously debated issues of our day.

Finally, military force performs still another function—that of *deterrence*. Provision of military force for the purpose of preventing attack is not a new concept. One of the most frequently asserted political maxims is that the surest way to avoid war is to prepare for it. This was a highly dubious operating principle as long as the means for immediate and decisive reprisal were strictly limited. The invention of atomic bombs, followed by the H-bomb, and the stockpiling of these weapons and their airborne carriers in massive quantities by the Soviet Union and the United States have given greater cogency to the strategy of deterrence.

This strategy, in its present-day context, poses highly controversial issue of technique. The time-honored practice of keeping new weapons secret was based upon several assumptions: (1) that secrecy could be maintained, despite espionage; (2) that sudden disclosure in combat would give significant, and perhaps decisive, tactical advantage; and (3) that precombat disclosure would enable potential enemies to contrive effective tactical defenses for the weapons in question.

Events in recent years have cast doubt on all these assumptions. Evidence seems to indicate that secrecy cannot be maintained despite the greatest precautions. If failure of deterrence means utter devastation for both sides, then the second assumption falls to the ground. If secrecy cannot be maintained, the third assumption loses its validity. In addition, the enormous premium now placed on *effective* deterrence, because of the destructiveness of thermonuclear weapons, fosters the argument that everything possible should be done to keep potential enemies accurately informed of a state's capacities for instant and utterly devastating retaliatory action.

Before leaving the techniques of statecraft, it will be useful to examine the historic distinction between peace and war. Techniques have been branded as peaceful or warlike. There was a famous treaty—the Briand-Kellogg Pact, of the late 1920's—for the "renunciation of war as an instrument of national policy." The time has come to consider what purposes are served by this distinction between peace and war.

One can note, first of all, that this distinction serves the polemical purposes of public relations and psychological attack, as when a nation is accused of "warmongering," or conversely, defends itself as "peace-loving." The distinction also entails various legal consequences. For example, insurance policies frequently include specific war risk clauses limiting liability. But does the distinction between war and peace still have much functional significance? Does it call attention to different sets of conditions and techniques? Has not the concept of *cold* war blurred, and all but obliterated, the traditional meanings of war and peace? Would it not be more realistic simply to describe the various techniques of statecraft, without reference to their allegedly peaceful or warlike character?

Operations called psychological warfare, economic warfare, cold war, etc., are going on continuously today between nations which are legally at peace. On repeated occasions military operations have been carried on—

battles have been fought and thousands of casualties incurred—without being legally treated as a state of war. The term *neutrality* formerly meant legal nonparticipation in an on-going war. Today it has come to mean a state of greater or lesser detachment from the alliances systems of the Superpowers. Whether one decides to retain or to discard the historic distinction between war and peace, he should keep clear in his mind that these terms no longer mean what they formerly did; and that there has ceased, in practice, to be any well-defined borderline between a state of war and a state of peace in the international political system.

It might be more realistic to recognize that a state's actions vis-à-vis another state or coalition can vary in posture through a broad spectrum from unrelenting hostility at one extreme to identity of purpose at the other. At the pole of hostility, the objective may be to do everything possible (or at least everything *feasible*) to destroy the target state; at the opposite pole, to do everything possible to support and protect it. Between these two extreme postures, one could locate many gradations, among which would be such concepts as cold war, armed coexistence, neutralism, etc.

Some techniques, it may be discovered, are useful only in particular relationship postures, hostile or nonhostile. Others can be bent to suit many gradations between the poles of hostility and nonhostility.

In the foregoing paragraphs we have used repeatedly the expression *target state,* and have referred to the government and public of that state as specific targets of action. By target is meant the person, group of persons, or physical objects towards which different techniques may be directed. Target in the destructive military sense is included. But the political concept of target includes a great deal besides. The term, as used in this discussion, carries a definite connotation of opposition, active or latent, to the demands of the acting state, but no necessary connotation of hostility or enmity. Thus, Great Britain, one of the states with which the United States is most closely identified, is recurrently a target of American action, without being conceived as a potential enemy under any imaginable circumstances. In short, the concept of target of action, as used throughout this discussion, does not *ipso facto* connote potential hostility or enmity, but merely some degree of opposition or resistance which action is designed to overcome.

The specific targets of action in international politics include the following:

(1) Official decision-makers of the target state
(2) Other elite groups within the target state

(3) The target state's population as a whole
(4) The target state's physical territory
(5) The man-made structures upon the target state's territory

Broadly speaking, the aim of action is to affect in desired ways the behavior of those who govern the target state and speak with authority to other governments. To this end, persuasion and pressure may be applied directly to the head of state, foreign minister, or other authorized spokesmen of the target state. But persuasion and pressure may be applied also to them indirectly, by molding the opinions and mood of influential groups or the body politic as a whole. Or the acting state may attempt to impose its demands by destroying cities or other structures or by occupying the target state's territory.

However they proceed, whatever techniques they employ, governments act to produce desired effects. Governmental officials, politicians, and their constituents normally rationalize their demands in terms of the requirements of national security against aggression. Just as consistently, their adversaries impute aggresive intentions to these same demands. We have already noted the difficulty, in the current tense posture of international relations, of evaluating dispassionately the objectives of any state's foreign policy, one's own in particular. It should be less difficult, however, and perhaps more fruitful, to concentrate for the moment on the effects produced by state actions, irrespective of what is said about underlying intentions and purposes.

Such effects may be classified broadly as policy-specific and non-policy-specific. Policy-specific effects—that is, effects directly related to specific demands—may consist of compliance to demands, compromise of conflicting demands, or rejection of demands. Non-policy-specific effects cover a range of behavior and states of affairs. The effect may be to foster a particular psychological mood, favorable or unfavorable to the demanding state. Or the effect may be to strengthen or weaken the economic or military capabilities of the target state. Or the effect may be coercion of the target state's population, military or civilian, or both; or the occupation of its territory, totally or partially; or the destruction of some part of its population and physical structures; or the destruction, partial or total, of the state as a going concern.

Table 4.1 provides a set of scales on which to locate the observed operational effects of a given set of actions. Different observers may disagree somewhat as to the effects of particular actions. But allowing for such unavoidable variations in observation and interpretation, the exercise of locating on these scales the effects of actions undertaken should serve several useful purposes. It should help one to grasp the strategy underlying a state's foreign policy. It should throw light on the relative effectiveness (or ineffectiveness) of different aspects of that strategy in the given operating situation. In particular, it should provide data for conclusions regarding the relative political potential of the two or more states involved —that is, the actual ability of each to affect the others' behavior. In this respect, Table 4.1 can be thought of as a sort of bridge connecting the concepts of political potential and political capabilities, to be described later in this chapter.

By extending the analytical scheme presented in Table 4.1, one can perform several additional operations. One can, for example, compare category by category the relative effectiveness of the strategies of two or several states. To do so would stimulate such questions as: Why is State A's strategy more (or less) effective than State B's? That is to say, why is A's impact on behavior (of various kinds) in B so much greater (or less) than B's impact on A? To ask and attempt to answer such questions is to advance along the road towards an operational conception of power and the manifestations of power in the political relations of states.

TABLE 4.1   NATIONAL POWER IN ACTION

Effect of A's specific demands on reactions of B's government
COMPLIANCE.................................COMPROMISE...................................REJECTION

Effect of A's public relations activities on the mood of B's government, other elite, or public as a whole
FRIENDLY...............................NO EFFECT...................................HOSTILE

Effect of A's actions of all kinds on the solidarity and morale of B's society as a whole
STRENGTHENED...............................NO EFFECT...................................WEAKENED

Effect of A's actions on the productivity of B's economy
INCREASED ....NO EFFECT...................................REDUCED

Effect of A's non-violent actions on the state of B's military forces
STRENGTHENED...............................NO EFFECT...................................WEAKENED

Effect of A's military actions on the state of B's military forces
STRENGTHENED...............................NO EFFECT...................................WEAKENED

Effect of A's military actions on the physical state of B's territory, non-human structures, and population
PRESERVED...............................NO EFFECT...................................DESTROYED

Concept of political potential

In view of the considerations presented in the foregoing pages, it will be useful to establish a distinctive term *other than power* to denote the overall or aggregate impact which a state exerts within the international political system. These considerations, to repeat, are: (1) the strong military connotation implicit in the term *power*; (2) the many ways besides military action whereby a state may affect the behavior of other nations; and (3) the inhibiting effect which the development of nuclear weapons appears to have had on resort to military action.

In view of these considerations, we shall henceforth reserve the term *power* to denote those demand-response relationships in which military force, active or latent, seems to be the most significant ingredient. We shall use the term *influence* to denote relationships involving conflict of purpose or interest, but no violence or significant threat of violence. Then, to cover both power (military) and influence (nonmilitary), we need a third term. For this we propose the term *political potential,* or simply *potential* used as a noun.

The reader should note that potential is a noun which, like power, has several recognized meanings. In nonscientific discourse, potential commonly denotes something that is possible though not yet existent. This idea is expressed, for example, in the familiar term *military potential,* or *war potential,* which refers to the undeveloped war-making capacities latent within a nation. The idea of latency, or capacity for future development, is more precisely expressed by the noun *potentiality* or the adjective *potential.* When we wish to express this concept of latency we shall use one or the other of these terms: for example, the military potentiality of the Soviet Union is very great; or (another example) the potential coal resources of Great Britain have significantly declined.

In the vocabularies of physical science, the noun *potential* carries a related but different meaning, a meaning that is rather difficult to express verbally with precision. About the nearest one can come is to define potential in this sense as the measure of pressure, or pull, or attraction, or simply effect that is expressed in physical systems by such terms as gravitation and voltage. These physical concepts are not directly transferrable to social systems. But they may evoke fruitful analogies. Thus by analogy we may think of the aggregate power and influence of a state in the international system as its political potential—that is to say, its *effective* pressure, pull, attraction, or simply *effect* on the behavior of other nations. Used in this sense, we repeat, political potential does not refer to undeveloped capacities, latent within a nation. Political potential is not potentiality, in short, but an effect actually observed.

The obverse of political potential is manifestly *political deference*. Political deference includes the degree of compliance or acquiescence which one state customarily accords to the specific demands of other members of the system. But we may also fruitfully put a little more into this concept as well. It is well known that members of one political community may willingly or grudgingly recognize the leadership and superior prestige of another community, even in the absence of immediate specific demands. Something like this, for example, would appear to underlie a traditional complaint of many Latin Americans that they have no recourse but to "go along with the United States."

Generally speaking, a state that ranks high overall in political deference would rank correspondingly low overall in political potential and vice versa. But an essential aspect of the phenomena of potential and deference is that most states exert potential over some and accord deference to others, and that these patterns are more or less describable. All this sounds rather imprecise and inexact, and it is so. Any attempt to rank members of the Society of Nations in the order of political potential is certain to evoke dispute. It was difficult enough to rank states in order of military power in the days when the military variables seemed fairly stable and periodic wars provided some objective test of one's judgments and predictions. It is manifestly more difficult to rank states according to their overall or aggregate impacts on other nations, when many nonmilitary variables have to be taken into consideration, and most of them are changing continuously at different rates in different countries.

Some years ago Mr. Maurice Ash, a mathematical-minded British student of international politics, devised a scheme for answering the question: "What determines, at any given moment, the exact amount of force that one state is exerting upon another? In presenting this scheme he contended that

> any analysis of power, of the forces of coercion, of politics, which cannot answer or attempt to answer this question must abandon all pretentions to being scientific and be recognized as, in fact, merely speculative.*

Walter Millis, quoted earlier in this chapter, takes a different but equally negative attitude towards estimation of political potentials. The relevant factors, he contends,

---

* From "An Analysis of Power, with Special Reference to International Politics," by M. A. Ash, in *World Politics*, January 1951, p. 231. Copyright 1951 by World Politics; reproduced by permission.

are not only incommensurable; it is difficult to compare their values as between one system and another, while all the values shift in accord with the specific situations which arise and even in accordance with one's concept of war. The power factors involved in the Western defense of Berlin, for example, are quite different from those which were involved in the attempted Western defense of Dienbienphu [the key position in Indochina which the French Army lost to Red China in 1954].*

We quote these attitudes of Ash and Millis because they are typical of a certain all-or-nothing posture towards analysis of the political relations of states. It is evident that the kind of precision and certitude to which Ash aspires, and the lack of which Millis laments, is beyond the capacity of any political analyst in the present state of knowledge. Such exactness would have been unattainable even in the good old days before Hiroshima. It is even further from attainment since the advent of superweapons has upgraded less violent techniques and more complex patterns of interaction. But that is not to say that all is mere guessing and speculation. Orders of magnitude and trends can be observed and described even when numerical quantification is impossible. Is it mere speculation, for example, to observe that the total impact of Red China in the Society of Nations is on the rise? Is it mere speculation to observe that the Suez debacle of 1956, whatever it may have revealed about the military forces of Britain and France, dealt a severe blow to their prestige and influence—that is, their political potentials—in the Near East?

There are regional as well as global patterns of potential and deference. In a rough and admittedly inexact manner these patterns can be observed and plotted in the real world of statecraft. For example, the term *satellite* used with reference to the tier of Communist-ruled states from the Baltic to the Black Sea, denotes the predominant political potential of the Soviet Union over most of Eastern Europe. The term *orbit* expresses the same idea. A term of analogous meaning was the expression *spheres of influence*, formerly used to delimit the boundaries of competing European imperial potentials in the nineteenth and early twentieth centuries in Asia and Africa. The post-1945 relationships of the United States to Western Europe and to the Western Pacific could be described in terms of American political potential. A similar pattern of relationships was implicit in the traditional concept of the Monroe Doctrine. Another expression of political potential was implicit in the nineteenth-century concept of *Pax Britannica*.

All this, it may be contended by those who seek mathematical precision

---

* From "U.S.—The Balance of Power—U.S.S.R.," in *New York Times Magazine*, August 2, 1959. Copyright by New York Times Co.; reproduced by permission of publisher and author.

in descriptions of the international political system, is loose and messy. However, this is the kind of world ours is, and the student of international politics simply has to do the best he can with a highly complex and differentially fluctuating set of variables.

Thinking about international political relationships in terms of potential and deference suggests various kinds of questions. Is it realistic, for example, to insist—as the late John Foster Dulles and many other Americans have insisted—that any nation not with us is presumed to be against us in the Cold War with the Soviet Union? Is it realistic to assume—as the above position does manifestly assume—that, between them, the political potentials of the Soviet Union and the United States blanket the earth, leaving no nation free to go its own independent way? Does not such an assumption grossly exaggerate the capacities for attracting and influencing which statesmen in Washington and Moscow can effectively wield?

Or consider another line of questions: Is it any longer realistic to think of Red China as a satellite within the Soviet political orbit? Does it not appear that China is extending its own potential and developing its own orbit? What, moreover, are the relative potentials of China and Russia in Outer Mongolia and elsewhere along the far-flung Soviet-Chinese frontier in inner Asia? Are these potentials a function merely of their respective military forces? And are Soviet and Chinese potentials in Indonesia composed of the same ingredients as in inner Asia?

If there is widespread consensus as to the general pattern of political potentials, and if the pattern remains relatively stable through a substantial period of time, then the international political system is said to be in stable *equilibrium.* If, on the other hand, there is a great deal of uncertainty or disagreement as to whose fiat runs where, if in consequence there is corresponding uncertainty as to how nations will respond to demands made on them, and if there is likewise uncertainty and disagreement as to the outcome of defiance and intransigence (in short, as to who can get away with what), then the international system is clearly unstable, and may be in process of radical transformation.

In practice, there is no fount of wisdom to which one can go for "correct" evaluation of the political potentials of states. Conclusions with respect to a particular state's potential (or conversely, the deference accorded to its demands) are judgments made by fallible human observers. Events may prove such judgments to be substantially correct or significantly in error. That is to say, a state's prestige—its accumulated reputation for making its policies prevail, for getting its way—may be significantly higher or lower than its ability to enforce its demands if the hand is called, so to speak.

Many examples of such discrepancies between predictive judgment and subsequent performance come to mind. France, during the years between the two world wars, wielded a high political potential. This rested heavily upon the widespread belief that the French army was the best in Europe and perhaps in the world. This myth was shattered by the rapid German conquest of France in 1940. During the same period, purges and other disturbances within Soviet Russia inspired widespread belief that the Communist experiment was a failure, that the Soviet Union was a house of cards and hence a negligible factor in international politics. This myth was destroyed by the German failure to conquer Russia in 1941 and by the Red Army's contribution to the ultimate smashing defeat of Germany.

Discrepancies between expectations and performance may go unchallenged for years. The gap may close with dramatic suddenness as in the examples just cited. Or it may close gradually, as expectations undergo readjustment through a considerable period of time.

The gradual liquidation of the nineteenth-century *Pax Britannica* is perhaps the best modern example of the latter process. The political potential of Britain has shrunk greatly since about 1890. There have been a few dramatic milestones in this process. Among such milestones one thinks of the Anglo-Japanese Alliance of 1902, in which Britain tacitly recognized her inability to defend single-handed her Far Eastern colonies and interests; the Washington Naval Treaties of 1922, in which Britain recognized the principle of naval parity with the United States; the Munich pact in which Neville Chamberlain attempted to buy peace by appeasing Hitler; the post-1945 financial crisis which compelled Britain to come to America for a big loan to stave off national bankruptcy; the progressive liquidation of imperial responsibilities in India, the Near East, and Africa; and the culminating humiliation of the Suez debacle of 1956.

Viewed in the perspective of half a century, the attrition of Britain's World Power position (or political potential) is clear and unmistakable. But at no point did attrition proceed catastrophically. Rather what has occurred has been a long succession of readjustments by which British statesmen have redefined their commitments and responsibilities, accompanied by fairly realistic comprehension on the part of other governments as to what was in process.

We stated in the opening paragraph of this section that political potential is an aggregative concept. It should now be clear why this is so. When one speaks of the potential of a given state, the reference is to the overall or total effect that the state's activities in the aggregate produce on the behavior of other nations. When one speaks of the international distribution of political potential, the reference is to the overall pattern of who influences whom (or conversely, who defers to whom) among the members of the Society of Nations.

In order to explain past distributions, or to predict future distributions, of political potentials in the Society of Nations, it is necessary to locate and to interpret the significance of the factors both human and nonhuman which set limits to the potentials of the interacting communities. It will be useful to have a special term to designate the ways in which such contributory factors affect the political relations of nations. For this purpose we favor the term *capabilities*.

The analysis of capabilities

The end product of an analysis of capabilities may be either an explanation or a prediction. With reference to historical cases, the analysis is designed to answer the question: How was it possible for a given state to exert an influence or to play a role which it did *in fact* exert or play? With reference to the future, capabilities analysis is designed to yield a predictive estimate as to the influence which a state could exert or the international role that it could play, either in a specific postulated contingency or in a postulated overall configuration of political relationships in the Society of Nations.

Before going any further, let us review once again the distinction between foreign-policy analysis and capabilities analysis. Whereas in foreign-policy analysis the task is to explain (or to predict) projects, undertakings, or decisions, in capabilities analysis the task is to explain (or to predict) operational results of decisions. In short, the distinction is between analyzing what is undertaken and analyzing what is accomplished.

Environmental factors enter into both types of analysis, but the relevant frames of reference and explanatory hypotheses or theories are always different. As was explained in the opening chapter and again in Chapter 3, environmental factors become related to policy decisions only to the extent that the decision-makers perceive and take these factors into account. Environmental factors may frequently affect operational results, however, even though such factors were not perceived and taken into account when the course of action was formulated and undertaken.

With respect to the making of foreign policy and to the content of policy decisions what is relevant is how the decision-maker imagines conditions to be, not how these actually are; whereas with respect to the operational results of decisions, what is relevant is how things actually are, not how the decision-maker imagines them to be. This distinction, it will be recalled from Chapter 1, is expressed by the terms *psychological* environment and *operational* environment.

On the basis of conclusions derived from actual cases (the more the better), the student of international politics builds up a more or less comprehensive picture of the role which a particular state has played, is playing, or may in the future play in the international political system. Such conclusions are commonly expressed in terms of the state's "power position," or its "international power relations." This is the concept which we have relabeled *political potential* for reasons discussed in the preceding section.

Conclusions regarding the capabilities of nations are always comparative. That is to say, the capabilities of a given state are relative to the capabilities of the other states with which it is or may be involved in demand-response relationships. There is no such thing as political capabilities in the abstract or in general—in a vacuum, so to speak—any more than there can be any concept of political potential that is not comparative.

This comparative property of the capabilities concept is frequently submerged in political and military discourse. Military planners, in particular, have been prone to deny that their projects are drawn up with particular enemies in view. It may be inexpedient for responsible politicians and officials to discuss such matters in public. But the student of international politics need not be deceived. Whenever military forces or other aspects of a state's capabilities are discussed, they are discussed, implicitly if not explicitly, in the context of relations with particular states.

This leads to yet another proposition: discussion of capabilities always takes place within some framework of policies and operational contingencies, actual or postulated. Thus, for example, one cannot speak meaningfully about the capabilities of Red China without postulating some set of propositions as to what the Chinese government is trying to accomplish, against whose resistance, by what means, in what places, over what time span, etc.

Failure to keep discussion of state capabilities within some such policy-contingency frame of reference is one of the reasons why a good deal of what has been said about the "elements" or "foundations" of national power is footless and seemingly irrelevant. The data of physical geography have no intrinsic political significance whatever. Nor have demographic, technological, economic, or any other data. Such data acquire political significance only when related to some frame of assumptions as to what is to be attempted, by whom, when and where, and vis-à-vis what adversaries, associates, and neutral bystanders.

The policy-contingency framework may be short-term and more or less specific. For example, what factors may set limits to the results of the declared American intention to regain ground lost in recent years to the Russians in military engineering and technology? What factors will affect execution of French policies in North Africa? By what criteria is one to judge the defense policy of Great Britain, which since 1957 has been based explicitly on the premise "that there is at present no means of providing adequate protection for the people of [Britain] against the consequences of an attack with nuclear weapons"?

Such relatively short-term and rather specific aspects of national capabilities shade off into longer-term and more general questions, in which policy assumptions are latent rather than explicit. By what criteria, for example, should one evaluate the thesis, propounded by a leading American geographer in the middle 1950's, that "permanent environmental restrictions of cold, drought, and continentality will never permit [the Soviet Union] to achieve strictly first-class rank"? Or the still more general thesis of the late Sir Halford Mackinder that "the grouping of lands and seas, and of fertility and natural pathways, is such as to lend itself to the growth of empires, and in the end of a single world empire"?

Hitherto most discussions of the capabilities of states have proceeded, implicitly if not explicitly, with reference to the postulated contingency of another general war. Sometimes it has been assumed that World War III will be long drawn out and more or less resemble World Wars I and II. Sometimes it has been assumed that World War III will be furious, short, and utterly devastating. Under both of these postulated contingencies, non-military capabilities have been treated as subsidiary to the capacity to wage total war.

This issue has to be faced, and it should be faced in a critical spirit. If, as we have repeatedly stressed, one of the by-products of nuclear-weapons development is to render unlimited violence—that is, total war, fought with all available weapons—a presumably ineffective technique of statecraft, it is necessary to revise somewhat the relative weight and importance given to military and nonmilitary aspects of capability. With or without an explicit strategy of avoiding total war at almost any cost, the apparatus of destruction unlimited seems to be acquiring the primary function (at least as long as the nuclear stalemate continues) of holding the ring while less destructive instrumentalities are brought into action. (We have said this before, and we shall emphasize it again, for it seems to us basic to understanding what is happening in the international arena today.) Thus, as we have also already stated, in addition to estimating the relative capabilities of states in military terms, one has to cope with the more difficult and untidy job of comparing a much wider range of functions performed by states in their respective efforts to deter possible enemies, win friends, and exert influence on the behavior of other nations.

The problem posed in the preceding paragraph is easily illustrated. Let us assume, for example, that the problem in hand is to compare the international capabilities of the United States and the Soviet Union. Now let us consider this problem in the light of three different policy-contingency assumptions. The first is the classic one, that these two nations are preparing for total war. But that is not the only assumption or even necessarily the most probable one, in the light of military, economic, and other developments over the past ten or fifteen years. Suppose, instead of the classic assumption, we choose either of two other alternatives: (1) that the Cold War, accompanied by armament competition but no large-scale military combat, will continue indefinitely; or (2) that the rise of Red China will foster both in Moscow and in Washington a felt threat so severe as to bring the Soviet Union and the United States into closer and less antagonistic relations within the next ten years or so. Is it not apparent that the qualities that would be decisive in fighting a total war may differ radically from those required for the Cold War? And that the qualities required for both of these postulated contingencies may be quite different from those required by an assumption of a trend towards Soviet-American rapprochement?

Estimates of capabilities covering all members of the Society of Nations in all imaginable contingencies would run into millions of combinations and permutations. No government—even more emphatically, no private individual—could conceivably carry out so massive a project. Nor is any such undertaking contemplated or needed. A great many contingencies— for example, the United States confronting a hostile British Commonwealth—are too improbable to justify investigation. A great many more contingencies can be dismissed for various other reasons, such as evident disparities of political potential among the nations concerned. One comes eventually, by some such process of elimination, to a hard core of contingencies which seem likely to set the major patterns of international politics in the period under consideration, and in which the relative capacities of the interacting states are not self-evident.

Putting the problem into a suitable policy-contingency framework represents only the first step in estimating a state's international capabilities. Given assumptions as to what its rulers may undertake, against whom, with what means, when and where, one can then proceed to an estimation of the relative capabilities of the interacting states. This will be found to involve far reaching conclusions as to their respective capacities: (1) to support (that is, to implement, back up, or enforce) their respective demands (policies, strategies); and (2) to resist (withstand, protect, or defend against) adverse demands (pressures, attacks) made on them.

A functional view of state capabilities

It is difficult to deal with these questions on a total or overall basis. The problem can be made more comprehensible, and the task somewhat more manageable, by breaking down the concepts of *support* and *resistance* into more specifically defined sets of functions. The following paragraphs suggest one of various possible ways of doing this. For reasons that will become clearer as we proceed, the reader will find it helpful to consider the concepts of support and resistance (which together constitute the concept of capabilities) under the following functional categories:

(1) Information-providing functions
(2) Decision-making functions
(3) Means-providing functions
(4) Means-utilizing functions
(5) Resistance-to-demands functions (to the extent that these are not covered in the preceding four categories)

INFORMATION-PROVIDING FUNCTIONS

The processes by which any government shapes its demands, attempts to support its demands, and organizes resistance to adverse demands start with appraisals of the situation. Such appraisals involve collecting, analyzing, storing, and making available information of many kinds. These functions are commonly designated by such labels as intelligence, research and analysis, etc. We shall call them simply the information-providing functions. The manner in which these functions are performed may have a decisive bearing on what a government succeeds or fails to accomplish vis-à-vis other nations.

The gathering and processing of intelligence is set up and carried on in different ways by different governments. But in some form or other, the intelligence functions constitute a vitally important step in the formulation and execution of national policies. This is not to deny that sheer intuition and luck may lead on occasion to brilliant success—in statecraft as in playing the horses. But in the long run a modern government's operations and accomplishments are not likely to rise much above the level of the information and analysis available to the decision-makers. This holds just as true for protective and defensive actions as for operations in which a government holds the initiative.

Intelligence operations may suffer from numerous kinds of deficiencies. A government may not have observers on the ground where important events are happening or about to happen. This, for example, was one of the severe handicaps which the United States government suffered throughout the 1950's, as a by-product of its refusal to recognize and enter into diplomatic relations with Red China.

Another source of weakness may be the unreliability of a government's observers. Their reports may reflect bias that seriously distorts their perception, reporting, and judgment of conditions and events. This weakness permeates all intelligence operations to some degree. It appears, for example, to have been for years a serious weakness in Russian reporting of conditions within the United States—and vice versa. Almost all observers are blinded to some extent by the values and prejudices which prevail in their own countries and in which they have been consciously or subconsciously indoctrinated.

Intelligence data may be further distorted in the sorting, sifting, and filing to which such data are subjected in the government departments where intelligence is analyzed and stored. It has been stated, for example, that the generally optimistic reports on Soviet military strength, transmitted on the eve of World War II by the American military attaché in Moscow, were heavily discounted in Washington where more pessimistic views about Soviet military power prevailed. Whether this was actually what happened or not, the point remains that the bias and prejudice of officials in the agencies where intelligence is processed can affect selection and handling of data in ways which may or may not conform to the realities of the situation.

Closely related to this deficiency is another:

In any country and at any time [writes a leading historian], political ministers have a tendency to seek to impose their preconceived notions of foreign affairs upon their agents in the field; and they are apt, moreover, to place greatest confidence in those representatives abroad whose reports confirm their own views.

German diplomats in the 19th century frequently complained that they were expected only to tell Bismarck that he was right; Hitler's ambassadors learned that it was dangerous to depart from the line established in the *Reichskanzlei*; and this sort of thing was certainly neither unknown nor unimportant in British and French diplomacy between the [two world] wars.*

Another related, though perhaps diminishing source of weakness has been the anti-intellectual bias of so-called practical men in high places.

* From "The Professional Diplomat and His Problems, 1919-1939," by G. A. Craig, in *World Politics,* January 1952. Copyright 1952 by Princeton University Press.

In our increasingly complex environment, statesmen have to consult increasingly with experts in various special fields: physicists, engineers, psychologists, anthropologists, economists, and many others. It has frequently been observed that the more conservative a politician or official is, the less likely he is to respect the judgments of learned experts. This bias is evident in the popularity in American political circles of the derogatory epithet *egghead*.

Another problem that becomes increasingly difficult to cope with is the sheer mass of intelligence required these days. Once filed, intelligence data and critical judgments thereon may not be readily available when needed. Almost anyone with government experience can recall instances when search failed to locate data which were definitely known to be filed somewhere in the department in question. Given the huge and constantly increasing volume of intelligence that flows into any capital these days, the problem of storage and recall becomes ever more difficult; and the difficulties have frequently appeared to be insurmountable.

Finally, the men at the top, the ultimate decision-makers, may or may not pay attention to information that is available. They frequently operate on their own private intuitions as to what the situation is and what they can get away with. Though one lacks definite confirmatory evidence, it seems quite likely that this is substantially how Sir Anthony Eden proceeded in connection with his ill-starred Suez project in the autumn of 1956.

Given sufficiently talented and knowledgeable executives, such freewheeling may sometimes yield effective, even brilliant results. But it is axiomatic, we repeat, that no policy-making system can rise in the long run above the level of information available to the decision-makers. Hence the quality of a government's intelligence stockpile and its capacity to keep it up to date and available have an important bearing on that government's ability to cope effectively with its problems.

DECISION-MAKING FUNCTIONS

In the context of capabilities, our interest in decisions is not to explain how it came about that certain courses of action were undertaken. Nor is the task to predict what may be undertaken in the future. In the capabilities-context, interest in decision making is rather to ascertain how the decision-making organization and practices of a government were (or may be) a source of its international successes and failures.

Most governments desire to accomplish a great deal more than is possible with the means available or at a price which they are able or willing to pay. There is a true if trite saying (already quoted), that "politics is the art of the possible." Assuming that national survival is nearly a universal value and assuming further that economy of effort is nearly always an important consideration, how effectively does a state's policy-making system combine instrumentalities and techniques in ways calculated to achieve possible ends with minimum risk and outlay of scarce resources? Ability to locate the limits of what is possible—at a level of risk and outlay deemed tolerable—is ability to estimate realistically the resources at one's command and the resistance which adverse parties can deploy in opposition. This sentence sounds very military. But the proposition holds just as certainly for nonmilitary as for military forms of action.

Limitations of various kinds may be operative in this sector. The following questions are intended to suggest kinds of information needed in making evaluative judgments with regard to the decision-making aspect of a state's international capabilities: Is the political system under consideration more (or less) flexible than other systems in adjusting to changing conditions? Do the persons who operate the system—politicians, civil servants, military officers, etc.—compare favorably (or unfavorably) in talent, education, and professional expertise with their opposite numbers in other countries? Do bias and prejudice—for example, hatred of foreigners in general, anti-communism, pro-communism, militant nationalism, etc.—affect more (or less) adversely than in other systems the ability of policy-planners and decision-makers to perceive and evaluate realistically the opportunities and limitations present in their environment? Does the system embody more (or less) effective devices than other systems, for correcting errors of observation and errors of judgment on the part of those who participate in the policy-making process? Such questions (to which one could add others similarly focused) provide a focus for investigating, from the standpoint of *quality of performance*, the decision-making structures and processes of political systems as different, for example, as those of the United States, Great Britain, France, India, China, and the Soviet Union.

The record may show skill or ineptness in choosing fruitful combinations of instruments and techniques to fit a given contingency. It may reveal failure to grasp the distinctive utilities and limitations of particular instrumentalities. Many illustrations come to mind. France in the 1920's poured valuable and scarce resources and immense effort into building the Maginot Line, a system of fortifications designed to provide impregnable defense of the country's eastern frontier across which German armies had swarmed in 1870 and again in 1914. Yet French military planners and politicians neglected the air power and mobile armored land forces which were progressively making fixed fortifications obsolete. The United States has been criticized for the failure of our politicians and civil servants to appreciate the supreme importance of the "battle for men's minds" and for their rather bungling attempts to foster in other peoples a mood more favorable and friendly to the United States and to the values for which we claim to stand.

MEANS-PROVIDING FUNCTIONS

Ability to provide the instrumentalities required by the strategy adopted is the third functional aspect of a state's international capabilities. Such instrumentalities, it should be remembered, include not merely military forces and weapons and all the items required for support of a military establishment; included also are the instruments of diplomacy, instruments of public relations, propaganda, subversion and psychological warfare, instruments of foreign aid, technical assistance, and nonviolent economic warfare.

Again, a few selected questions will help to visualize some of the lines of investigation involved in estimating a state's capacities to provide the instrumentalities of statecraft. What is the state's relative situation with respect to foodstuffs, industrial fibers, and other raw materials? What is its situation with respect to human resources: quantities and qualities of manual labor, administrative skills, scientific and other specialized skills, etc.? What are the salient characteristics of the state's economy: stage of economic development, diversity of activities, quantities and qualities of capital equipment, organization for production, etc.? How does the state's economy compare in productivity, both per capita and total GNP (gross national product)? How adaptable is the state's economy? That is, how receptive or resistant are labor and management to new machines and new processes and routines? Does the existing pattern of production provide adequately for the military and other needs of the state's international strategy? What is the system's capacity for creating new industries, providing substitutes for scarce materials, expanding production of particular industries, converting from one type of production to another, teaching new skills, etc.? What is the system's capacity for locating talent, educating and training scientists and other specialists, supporting and organizing research, etc.?

MEANS-UTILIZING FUNCTIONS

Ability to utilize effectively the instrumentalities that can be provided is the fourth functional aspect of a state's international capabilities. A government may possess a well-organized and efficiently administered foreign office and diplomatic service, and yet, for internal political or for other reasons, it may be unable to carry on very effective diplomacy. A government may possess or have access to the finest radio transmitters, newsgathering facilities, movie-making apparatus, etc.; and yet it may be unable, for a variety of reasons, to grasp the first principles of effective public relations across cultural frontiers. A state may possess the most productive and diversified economy in the world; but that is no guarantee that its government can utilize goods and services for political purposes as effectively as some other state whose economy is less productive but whose political system imposes fewer obstacles to these techniques of statecraft. A state may possess a formidable military establishment; yet its government may be unable for various reasons to employ military forces in ways that provide effective support for its demands on other nations.

The range of factors that may limit the means-utilizing ability of a state are very great. Once more a few selected questions may help to visualize what is involved. Is the state's geographical location more (or less) favorable than other given states', from the standpoint of bringing pressures effectively to bear in support of its foreign policies? Does the state's political system—especially its methods of decision making—operate more (or less) adaptably in the sphere of international relations? For example, is the system capable of making quick shifts to meet new or unexpected challenges? How adaptable is the state's population to changes in the allocation of goods and services among competing sets of consumers, especially increases in allocations to the military forces and to foreign-aid programs? Do the civic attitudes and values prevailing within the national society affect favorably (or adversely) the execution of the state's foreign policies?

RESISTANCE-TO-DEMANDS FUNCTIONS

We have included a fifth functional aspect of a state's capabilities, designed to include those aspects of resistance capacity not covered by implication in the preceding categories. A government's ability to parry demands, to resist pressures, and to defend against attacks of all kinds, nonmilitary as well as military, may be as important in the long run as its ability to seize and hold the initiative. In a sense, initiative and defense, like action and reaction, are but two sides of a single interactive process. Hence a good deal of what has already been said with reference to the four preceding categories applies to the protective or defensive activities of a government as well as to operations in which it holds the initiative.

However, ability to take as well as to give involves some additional qualities. The citizens of a state may display rather different behavior when their government holds the initiative and things seem to be going their way than they do when the nation is hard pressed on all sides. Moreover, the military maxim that an army, fleet, or air force is no stronger than its primary base holds also with respect to nonviolent sectors of statecraft.

Hence the desirability of giving some special attentions to the specifically defensive aspects of a state's capabilities.

Under this heading one requires answers to such questions as: Is the country more (or less) vulnerable than others to aerial bombardment or other forms of military attack? For example, the geographical layout of a country's cities, factories, seaports, airports, railroads, and highways may be such as to render them easy targets for airborne attacks. Is the nation more (or less) vulnerable to economic blockade or to other external economic pressures? For example, a state's economy may be heavily dependent upon imported food and raw materials by routes subject to paralyzing blockade. What is the capacity of its population to carry on under conditions of adversity, stress, or catastrophe? Are they united, or so divided internally and so deficient in common purpose as to be attractive targets for disruptive propaganda and subversive operations? In these and in many other respects a state may present a façade of strength or exhibit vulnerabilities that strongly affect the role that it can play in international politics.

Table 4.2 summarizes the five functional aspects of a state's capabilities which have been outlined in this section and suggest a schematic device for comparing the performance of two or more states at different points in time.

TABLE 4.2 CAPABILITIES ANALYSIS AND COMPARISON OF STATES' CAPABILITIES

States Analyzed and Compared: ————————➤ A B C
Aspects of Capability to Be Compared
↓

	A	B	C
(1) Intelligence Functions (ability to collect, analyze, store, recall, and utilize information in defining policy objectives and in formulating strategies for action)	A_{t_1} A_{t_2}	B_{t_1} B_{t_2}	C_{t_1} C_{t_2}
(2) Decision-Making Functions (ability to define feasible objectives, and to combine instruments and techniques of statecraft into effective strategies for attaining objectives	A_{t_1} A_{t_2}	B_{t_1} B_{t_2}	C_{t_1} C_{t_2}
(3) Means-Providing Functions (ability to provide the instrumentalities required in order to implement the strategies adopted)	A_{t_1} A_{t_2}	B_{t_1} B_{t_2}	C_{t_1} C_{t_2}
(4) Means-Utilizing Functions (ability to employ effectively the instrumentalities that can be provided and in the combinations and patterns adopted)	A_{t_1} A_{t_2}	B_{t_1} B_{t_2}	C_{t_1} C_{t_2}
(5) Resistance Functions (ability to parry demands, resist pressures, defend against attacks, and carry on under conditions of stress and catastrophe)	A_{t_1} A_{t_2}	B_{t_1} B_{t_2}	C_{t_1} C_{t_2}

In Table 4.2, the capital letters designate states to be compared. The symbols t_1 and t_2 stand for different periods in time, with reference to which the comparison is made. The introduction of the time element reflects the well-known fact that the relative capabilities of states change differentially through time. The scheme could be extended, of course, to include any number of states at any number of points in time. If, as is usually the case, in the estimation of capabilities, a predictive judgment is desired, at least one of the two or more values of the t symbol relate to some future period.

The functional approach outlined above provides a somewhat broader and more specific framework for estimating capabilities. In the past, discussions of national strength and weakness have tended to focus on Aspect 3 (ability to provide the means). Aspect 4 (ability to utilize such means effectively) and Aspect 5 (defensive strengths and vulnerabilities) have also received some attention. But Aspect 1 (information-providing) and Aspect 2 (decision-making) have hitherto been almost entirely omitted from the discussion of capabilities. The study of foreign-policy making has been directed almost exclusively to descriptions, explanations, and predictions of what actions were (or may be) undertaken. Very little attention has been paid to the ways in which a particular state's modes of making decisions may affect its level of accomplishment—its successes and failures—in transactions with other nations.

Neither the scheme outlined above nor any other will yield automatic conclusions. It is not at all like a cash register in which one pulls a lever and numbers are automatically added. The device does not and cannot eliminate the element of personal judgment. What goes into the various boxes or categories of the scheme is only what the analyst puts into them. What he puts into them will reflect his personal judgment as to what is relevant and significant. What he regards as significantly relevant will depend on the explanatory propositions which he brings to bear.

Explanatory hypotheses in capabilities analysis

One never derives conclusions about the relative capabilities of states, we repeat, merely by collecting and sorting data. Information regarding a state's geographical location and layout, its population, economic resources, economic development, military forces, weapons system, form of government, public morale—neither these nor any other set of data tell anything significant *per se* as to what a state may accomplish in its dealings with other states. The data acquire such significance only by being subjected to appropriate explanatory propositions or hypotheses. Only by means of such hypotheses is it possible to establish meaningful connections between functions and factors.

What do we mean by explanatory hypotheses? This question was discussed at some length in Chapter 1. Here are a few additional examples of the kinds of explanatory hypotheses which are utilized in capabilities analysis:

(1) The growth of air power has progressively reduced the military protective value of water barriers.

(2) Relative size of population is not *per se* a reliable index of comparative political potential.

(3) In the present state of military technology there is no effective tactical defense against aerial bombardment with nuclear weapons.

(4) The more democratic and representative a governmental system is, the less flexibility it is likely to exhibit in adapting its strategy to changes in the international situation.

(5) Taboos excluding women from certain dangerous roles in industry and military service impose a handicap on a state in comparison with other states less restrictive in this respect.

As was emphasized in Chapter 1 (page 53), such explanatory propositions do not exist ready-made in nature, to be discovered by research. Such propositions are man-made; they represent creative acts of somebody's imagination. Initially, each one is simply a working hypothesis, normally though not necessarily derived by induction from observed events. Such hypotheses serve as major premises from which conclusions as to capabilities are deduced.

Frequently, it must be admitted, there is no simple test of the tenability of such capability premises. Consider, for example, Item 3 in the list above. This proposition became in 1957 the basis of British defense policy. For obvious reasons no simple test of this premise is feasible. Such confirmation or disconfirmation as is possible has to be derived by breaking down the general proposition into more elemental propositions which have been or can be tested. Such propositions in the example cited would relate to the properties of nuclear explosives, the properties of military planes and other means of delivering nuclear bombs to their targets, the properties of defensive instrumentalities and techniques, etc.

With respect to nuclear explosives, there is a vast accumulation of experience, some of it top-secret, but much of it in the public domain and available to anyone who is competent to interpret it. There are data regarding the blast, heat, and radioactivity generated by explosions of various types and magnitudes, regarding the area and distribution of radioactive fallout, regarding the duration of residual radioactivity of various kinds, regarding the immediate and delayed effects of human exposure to radioactive materials, etc.

With respect to means of delivery, there is also a great mass of accumulated data. Such information includes the range and carrying capacity of planes of various types, the properties of ballistic missiles, the utility of submarines as launching platforms, the design and operational character-istics of the planes, missiles, submarines and other equipment of specific states.

With respect to local defense against attacks, tests under simulated conditions of war have yielded conclusions as to the odds of attacking formations and units eluding or breaking through various kinds and con-centrations of defenses—interceptor planes, gun and rocket barrages, de-fensive missiles, etc. One could derive from past experience with disasters some description of a given population's probable behavior under attack, the efficiency of various kinds of bomb shelters, fire-fighting systems, evacu-ation plans, medical care of radiation victims, anticontamination methods, emergency communication systems, and other survival schemes. Such ex-perience could be evaluated with special reference to a specific country's physical layout (Britain, in the example cited). This would involve a description of the country's size, density of settlement, size and functional relations of urban centers, their proximity to the sea, the vulnerabilities of railways, roads, airports and other facilities, etc.

It is, of course, to accumulate more information on all these and other aspects of attack and defense that tests of various kinds are run in labora-tories, on proving grounds, and (under simulated attack and disaster con-ditions) in cities and larger areas. One end product of such testing would be, in this example, a degree of confirmation or disconfirmation of the premise that "in the present state of military technology there is no effective tactical defense against aerial bombardment with nuclear weapons."

Many of the propositions employed in estimating capabilities have been so repeatedly confirmed as to be generally accepted without argument. But in our era of rapid technological and other changes, most of them have become more or less unsettled, and some are highly controversial. Take, for example, the hypothesis that scientists in a totalitarian communist state operate under ideological and other handicaps that prevent them from keeping pace with their counterparts in a "free society." Only yesterday that proposition seemed to most Americans as sound as the theory of gravita-tion. Today it is at most no more than a highly controversial hypothesis without confirmation.

The propositions (explanatory hypotheses, premises) which an analyst adjudges to be adequately confirmed and fruitful depend, as a rule, on his previous experience with the antecedents of the specific problem in hand, or on generalizations derived from other cases which seem to him to exhibit fruitful analogies. There is no guarantee whatever that any two analysts will reason from exactly the same premises or reach the same conclusions. The most that one can expect in capabilities analysis is that the premises will be made explicit, that environmental factors considered significant will be so designated, and that logical procedures will be observed. Only thus is it possible for one analyst to check the work of another, and thereby to identify the sources of conflicting conclusions.

It would be instructive to re-examine from this point of view some of the many disconfirmed capabilities predictions of our time. One might reflect, for example, on the generally unstated assumptions from which observers predicted that Nazi Germany could not stand the financial and moral strains of a long war; that the Red Army would collapse in a few weeks under the hammer blows of the German invaders in 1941; that it would take Russian scientists and engineers twenty years or more to produce an atomic bomb; and many other predictions that went wrong.

It is easier to be wise after the event. Some degree of uncertainty and some margin of error are probably inherent in all complex calculations of the capabilities of states with respect to future contingencies. But the burden of this section is that clearer understanding of the steps involved in this kind of analysis, more careful evaluation of explanatory premises, more explicitness in articulating them, and more rigor in applying them to observed "facts" should help to avoid such gross miscalculations as have so often characterized the prediction of national capabilities in the past.

PART III: SOURCES OF NATIONAL POLICIES AND INTERNATIONAL POTENTIALS

CHAPTER FIVE

★ ★ ★

The Basic Factors: Tests of Relevance and Significance

IN PART III we shall be concerned with identifying the conditions and events with which statesmen have to cope, and which make up the raw materials, so to speak, from which one constructs descriptions and interpretations of the policies, interactions, and political relations of nation-states.

Lands and seas, earth materials and climate, people and machines, ideas and institutions, and other features of the human habitat derive their international significance (if any) from certain uneven distributions of these phenomena in space or their variations through time or both. Conditions and events which affect significantly the decisions and undertakings of governments, the outcomes and consequences of those undertakings, and the resultant patterns of coercion, influence, and deference between and among nation-states—these are the variables which constitute what one means by "foundations of international politics." (Before reading further, it will be helpful to review what was said about "constants" and "variables," on page 44 of Chapter 1).

By what standards or criteria is one to decide which variables are relevant and significant in the context of international politics? The answer depends, first of all, on one's purposes and perspective. From the perspective of a head of government or a foreign office or a military headquarters or a legislative assembly or some unit of government responsible for deciding what is to be done and for doing it, the criteria of significance may appear somewhat differently than from the perspective of someone who observes and interprets events from the sideline. As already emphasized, the latter is the viewpoint of the private individual, be he a breakfast-table TV-viewer or newspaper reader or a student in college or a teacher of international politics or anyone else outside the organizations that are authorized to act on behalf of a national political community or an international organization.

From the perspective of the outside observer (and, we repeat, this is the perspective of all private citizens), one can lay down two general tests of relevance and significance:

(1) Conditions and events which *some observer perceives, infers,* or *assumes* that the official actors upon the international stage did (or are likely to) take into account in reaching decisions and initiating projects which did (or are judged likely to) evoke on the part of other nations responses in which some conflict of purpose or interest is observed, inferred, or assumed; and—

(2) Conditions and events which, in *some observer's judgment,* have substantially affected the outcome or operational results of past decisions (or are *judged* likely to produce such effects in the future).

The italicized words and phrases emphasize that criteria of relevance and significance are ultimately derived from the perspective of the observer, from the way in which he formulates issues and problems, and from the hypotheses (or theories) which he brings to bear in analyzing them. For example, if one starts from an assumption that Communists everywhere are incurably hostile to non-Communist nations, he will select and interpret "facts" rather differently than if he assumes the contrary. Or if one infers from observations of past events that governments which control H-bombs, ICBM's, and other superweapons will be extremely reluctant to risk transforming the Cold War into an unlimited shooting war, he is likely to place considerably higher value on economic aid and technical assistance programs, public relations and other psychological operations, diplomacy and international organization than if he assumes that World War III is inevitable and that the potential enemies are simply waiting for the most favorable opportunities to strike the first blow.

It would be impossible to emphasize too strongly this relationship between *perspective* (viewing point), *facts* (observed conditions and events), and *hypotheses, theories,* and *assumptions.* Unless this relationship is clearly understood and kept constantly in mind, there is no point in reading any further.

Keeping always in mind that relevance and significance are derived from the way one views and formulates issues and problems, it is possible to draw a number of general distinctions which should help in identifying and analyzing the foundations of international politics. One such distinction is that between *actor* and *environment,* described in general terms on page 46 of Chapter 1. This distinction is implicit in nearly all discussions of political events and relationships. Certain factors or variables are judged to be significant because (in the observer's judgment) they appear to account for differences between the acting units—be these individual persons or agencies of government or government as a whole or the state itself conceived as a corporate entity—whose projects and activities are being described, explained, or predicted. Other sets of variables may be deemed significant either because they appear to enter into the calculations of the acting units (that is, are comprised in their respective psychological environments), or because they appear to set limits to what those units are able to accomplish (that is, make up their operational environment).

If we break through the monolithic concept of the state as a person and focus on the *human* persons who are authorized to act in the name of the state, we may then draw a further useful distinction between those features of the human decision-makers' environment which are wholly *intranational* (that is, domestic, or internal to their state's geographical space), and those which are *extranational* or *transnational* (that is, wholly or partly external to that space).

Many of the environmental categories commonly used in discussions of international politics include subcategories of *intra*national and *extra*national factors. Take geographical configuration, for example: one can describe the layout of lands and seas without reference to national boundaries; one can also describe the geographical layout of particular countries. The same is true of natural resources, climate, population, equipment and skills, patterns of social behavior, etc. But there are also phenomena which are not readily classified into *intra*national and *extra*national categories. We refer here to phenomena which are essentially *inter*national or *trans*national in character: such as international norms (both legal and moral), international institutions (the U.N. and others), transnational communications (commerce, tourism, correspondence, and the like), transnational movements and ideologies (communism and others).

To adhere rigorously to the distinction between intranational (or domestic) and extranational (external) factors leaves certain highly important factors out of the picture. Moreover, rigorous classification on this basis overschematizes the information with which we are dealing. But the distinction has value for certain purposes. It provides one basis for comparing the environmental opportunities available to different governments and the environmental limitations operative on them. The distinction between domestic and external factors also underlies certain theories of international strategy.

According to one set of theories (described in Chapter 3), conditions and events external to a state's geographical space provide stimuli so compulsive as to obliterate or reduce to ineffectiveness conflicting stimuli coming from within the state's own body politic. Among those who argue the compulsiveness of the external environment are some of the game theorists. In one version of international game theory, the variables that matter are virtually all located in the transnational environment. These include the level of military technology, the international distribution of military forces, and a set of "rules of the game" which govern the "moves"—threats, counterthreats, military demonstrations, etc. Some exponents of international game theory come close to implying, if not actually to saying, that superweapons systems have largely superseded human beings as the ultimate determiners of national strategy.

In this near-deterministic hypothesis, the internal environment—that is, conditions and happenings inside a state's geographical space—receive scant attention. Attitudes of citizens, activities of domestic pressure groups, form of government, modes of decision-making, personal idiosyncrasies of leaders, and other factors that *differentiate* states are ignored or dismissed as relatively insignificant sources of national policies and strategies.

Critics of this hypothesis contend that it grossly oversimplifies the factors that enter into political calculations. They argue further that such theorists ignore manifest and very important differences in the behavior of governments and their constituencies; and that game theory (as thus far developed) provides little or no basis for explaining and anticipating such differences.

Some of these critics go so far as to contend that a state's external or international behavior is mainly a function of its domestic conditions. According to this second hypothesis, politicians normally give precedence to moods, attitudes, interests, and demands prevailing inside the national community. Carried to an extreme, this approach concentrates almost exclusively on the domestic environment and on the modes of policy-making within that environment. The thesis, in short, is that a state's domestic environment determines its external policies. From this perspective, it is obvious, the variables which appear significant will differ radically from those given priority from the opposite perspective.

One can take into account the undeniable relevance of domestic differentiating factors without going to the extreme of denying the significance of external factors. There is a middle position—the position taken throughout this book, and specifically in the following chapters of Part Three—that foreign policy and national strategy, especially in periods of revolutionary changes and transformations, reflect continuing, often conflicting, and seldom completely resolved tensions between domestic and external conditions and events.

Almost any case that comes to mind exemplifies this middle position. Britain's defense policy in the 1950's provides an especially clear-cut example. Throughout that decade Britain's international commitments and her military forces were continuously out of balance. There were too many contingencies to cover with the military resources which could be supported with the funds allocated thereto. In the same period a set of domestic pressures—consumer irritation with continuing postwar shortages of goods, demands for tax relief and higher pay, the rising cost of welfare services to which the Government was strongly committed, demands for abolition of military conscription, etc.—were constantly pushing the Government towards military retrenchment. But working in the opposite direction were the Government's conceptions of the Communist threat, of Britain's "vital interests" overseas, of Britain's "responsibilities as a Great Power," and her "proper role in the world." These conflicting pressures were never resolved, and the imbalance became painfully manifest in the Suez debacle of 1956. Observers might disagree as to the wisdom or folly of the Eden Government's decision to resist with military force the Egyptian seizure and nationalization of the Canal. But the unreadiness of British military forces for a task clearly implicit in British policy unquestionably contributed to what happened.

Constituency (that is, domestic public) moods, attitudes, demands and pressures may be less immediately effective in a one-party dictatorship than in a democratic political system. According to a widely held hypothesis, dictators can ignore the home front. Moreover, in moments of grave emergency, when the very future of the nation is believed to be imperiled, there is a tendency even in democratic countries to close ranks in support of the government in office. But most times in most countries—and this goes for dictatorships as well as for democracies—the art of statesmanship consists of achieving workable compromises between conflicting purposes and pressures. The relative weight given to domestic and external factors differs from country to country, and within a given country from one time to another. Such variations may be difficult to perceive in short perspective. But in the longer historical view, statesmen nearly always appear to have been the focus of conflicting demands, with expedient compromise the general rule and clean-cut choice the exception. If one accepts this proposition as a point of departure, then one must be prepared to take into account a wide range of factors, domestic as well as external or transnational.

Some of these factors are "givens"—given in the sense that they cannot be manipulated significantly to suit national purposes. The givens vary considerably from country to country. Factors within the capacity of one government to change or manipulate, may lie beyond the manipulative capabilities of another. Capacity to control or to modify the nonhuman factors within a nation's own geographical space depends on the level of its technology. Capacity to control or influence the behavior of its own citizens depends both on a government's form and operating rules and also on the instruments of control which it commands. Likewise a government's capacity to control or manipulate conditions and events outside its geographical space depends on the instruments it commands and on the overall configuration of international politics.

Certain features of the nonhuman environment are still beyond effective control of any government: for example, climate, numerous fatal and crippling diseases, etc. Frequently, in the technologically advanced societies, the issue is not so much lack of engineering techniques as ability or willingness to pay the price. For example, by the early 1960's scientists and engineers had invented several processes for desalting seawater; but the cost of doing so on a large scale was still regarded as prohibitively high. Nuclear reactors, to cite another example, provide an almost limitless source of useful energy, but at a price which in most regions is still considerably higher than the cost of coal, oil, natural gas, and other sources of energy. In general, the higher a society's level of scientific and engineering knowledge, the greater is its capacity to control or manipulate in desired ways the nonhuman factors of environment. The trend everywhere is towards ever greater technological capabilities.

Many social (that is, human) factors are nearly as resistant to manipulation as are the most refractory nonhuman factors. This is especially true of social factors beyond reach of a government's coercive power. The capacity of the United States government to alter the birth rate in China or to undermine Soviet citizens' faith in their own leaders or to retard the pace of revolutionary change in Africa is manifestly very limited. On the other hand, negotiations, public propaganda, conspiracy, economic and technical assistance, embargoes and boycotts, and military operations of various kinds and magnitudes are all utilized for the express purpose of altering the moods, attitudes, responses, and capabilities of other nations. On the whole, the ability of *any* government to manipulate conditions and events to achieve desired ends is probably more limited than Americans, Russians, and other large-scale operators upon the international stage are wont to imagine these days. The present level and trend of weaponry indicates the possibility that the custodians of these destructive machines now hold in their hands the means to terminate human history. But it may be doubted whether, in any constructive sense, today's world is anybody's exclusive oyster, ambitious rulers of great states to the contrary notwithstanding.

The above paragraphs indicate our general line of approach to the data which constitute the foundations of international politics. Our point of departure will be the governmental systems which conduct the foreign affairs of the hundred-odd national communities comprised in the Society of Nations. These governments rest upon various philosophical premises. They differ widely in organization and modes of operation. Do such differences affect significantly the style of governmental operations, the substance of national policies, and the level of national capabilities? These are the issues posed in Chapter 6.

Governments do not operate in a vacuum. Their undertakings and accomplishments upon the international stage may depend upon many features of the environment in which statesmen and their publics act and interact across national frontiers. The chapter titles of Part III indicate the categories and the order in which different sets of factors will be considered.

Chapter 7 deals with the scientific and technological revolution. Technological advance has changed our world more in the past two generations than in the preceding 10,000 years. Unless this advance is halted by nuclear war or other irreversible catastrophe, it seems likely to continue to transform our milieu in ways as yet but dimly perceived or imagined. One might also regard scientific discoveries and their engineering applications as the master set of variables. At any rate technological advance affects the meaning and significance of all other factors of our environment.

One aspect of technological change that has a special bearing on international politics is the range and destructiveness of modern weapons. This transformation of military technology began long before World War II. But the changes since 1945 dwarf everything that happened before. No one can yet be sure how the new weapons will affect the world of tomorrow, but certain implications and possibilities are becoming evident; and these will be examined in Chapter 8.

The technological revolution has profoundly altered the geographic components of the environment. The human habitat is still the earth. People still react to the earth as they imagine it to be. As in previous periods, human ideas about the earth are frequently inconsistent with the pervasive reality of our earthly habitat. In considerable degree, these discrepancies are manifestations of the time lag in human appreciation of the impacts of technological advances. More efficient machines have enabled men to change their physical environment to a greater degree than formerly. New machines and techniques have also affected the political and military meaning and significance of even the most durable earth features. These effects are investigated in Chapters 9, 10, 11, and 12.

One hears a great deal these days about the population explosion, the accelerating increase in the number of people who inhabit the earth. This increase is another consequence of technological advances which are keeping more people alive longer. The political implications of the distribution of the world's population and the prospects of its future growth constitute the subject of Chapter 13.

Technological advances foster more efficient methods of producing and distributing goods and services. Economic development, in turn, provides the basis for further technological advance. Complicated machines and skills are requisites of modern industrial society. Most of this productive capital is derived from savings, voluntary or other, provided by those who do the work. The better their tools and the greater their skills, the higher will be their output per capita, and the greater may be the savings available for more and still better equipment.

Advanced and efficient methods of production, an adequate and smoothly running transportation system—in short effective integration of human and nonhuman resources—have become requisites of power and influence in our industrial age. Variations from country to country in the magnitude of economic output and in the diversity and quality of what is produced constitute essential data for any estimation of international capabilities. The social changes which accompany transition from traditionalistic-agrarian to modern urban-industrial forms of society may also provide clues to the foreign policies and international behavior of nations at different stages of the process of modernization. These matters are looked into in Chapter 15.

Effective integration of resources depends not only on the availability of capital, labor, and raw materials; it depends also on social organization of various kinds. Organization consists essentially of working rules for securing coordinated effort. Organization may rest mainly on voluntary cooperation, as in most of the democratic systems, or more on compulsion, as in strongly authoritarian systems. No society follows one of these principles to the exclusion of the other.

The political aspect of organization will have been dealt with in Chapter 6. In Chapter 14, we shall consider the economic aspect of organization. Economic systems may rest upon different values and principles. These differences are reflected in such familiar terms as capitalism, socialism, communism, mixed economy, and others. Systems vary in adaptability and efficiency. Such variations may affect significantly the quantities and qualities of goods and services available for national purposes, including both military and nonmilitary instrumentalities of statecraft.

Economic and political organization are but two facets of the structure of national political communities. Other facets may likewise provide significant clues to their international behavior and capabilities. Nations differ with respect to the rules which govern the utilization of their human resources. They differ in their methods of locating and educating talented youth. They differ in the degree to which their citizens are united or divided on basic values and ideals. Nations differ too in their reactions to prosperity and their tolerance of adversity. They differ in their behavior under stress and in their ability to carry on in the face of catastrophe. These and many other more or less discernible patterns of behavior are frequently lumped together into a category called national character. Recently the term *political culture* has been coined to denote the patterns which differentiate the political behavior of one nation from others. We prefer the broader if less precise term *national character*. Data on behavioral patterns of which national character is composed provide very fruitful clues to the policies and capabilities of nations, as we shall attempt to show in Chapter 16.

As already noted, social patterns which are wholly or predominantly intranational or domestic (that is, internal to the geographical space of a single state) can be differentiated from patterns which are essentially international, or more precisely transnational, in the sense that they cut across the geographical space of two or more states. One set of such patterns, which we have labeled transnational images, movements and ideologies, forms the focus of Chapter 17. In that chapter we shall be exploring the manner and extent to which national policies and potentials may be affected by transnational tourism, educational and other temporary exchanges, migration, commerce, interpersonal correspondence, circulation of newspapers and other literature, radio broadcasting, the substance of ideas and ideologies in circulation, etc.

In Chapter 18, the concluding chapter of Part III, the focus is on still another set of transnational factors. These are *transnational norms and institutions*. In that chapter we shall be investigating the extent to which international legal and moral standards and the existence and functioning of international organizations of many kinds may affect the policies of states and the political potential which they exert in the international political system.

CHAPTER SIX

★ ★ ★

National Political Systems

IN THE PREVIEW of international politics and the international political system in Chapter 2 it was stated that nation-states are the primary acting units. As was also explained there, these units are themselves political systems which operate through an organization called a government. National governments vary in many ways. They differ in formal structure and in actual modes of operation. They vary widely in the degree of autonomy enjoyed by those who rule and in the degree to which these latter are responsive to moods, attitudes, and specific demands which find expression within the national community. The issue posed in this chapter is whether and in what ways particular forms of government may affect significantly the foreign policies and international capabilities of nations. Do the differences represented by such terms as democracy and dictatorship, parliamentary government and presidential government, have a bearing on national objectives, strategies, operations, and accomplishments? If so, then national political structures—in plain English, form of government—must clearly be included among the important foundations of international politics.

The attitudes of practicing politicians and officials on this issue are not in doubt. For centuries they have taken the position that the structures and operational modes of foreign governments—the governments with which they have to deal—may have a crucial bearing on their own interests and projects. They have tried on many occasions and in many ways, with varying degrees of success, both to prevent and to bring about changes in the political institutions of other nations.

One historic example is the War of the French Revolution. In the eyes of eighteenth-century European sovereigns, the French revolutionaries who pulled down the Bourbon monarchy and proclaimed France a republic were dangerous outlaws. If democratic principles should prevail in France, the virus would spread to other countries. Monarchy everywhere would be exposed to mortal peril. So reasoned the kings and princes who banded together in a war to put down the revolution and restore monarchy in France.

Repeatedly during the nineteenth century, American statesmen gave verbal encouragement to antimonarchical movements in Greece, Hungary, and elsewhere. Hostility to monarchy and to the dynastic relationships which connected the European "family" of nations appears to have been one of the considerations which evoked President Monroe's historic warning to the European Powers in 1823, not to attempt to extend their "system" to the Americas. In 1918 the United States government joined in a notoriously fruitless military venture designed to prevent Communism from taking root in Russia. After World War II, American political leaders were insistent that the defeated nations should adopt Western-style democratic constitutions. In one instance—Japan—American occupation officials played a key role in drafting such a constitution.

The men in the Kremlin are inveterate meddlers with the political institutions of other countries. Sometimes their chosen instrument has been the Red Army, as in Hungary in 1956. More commonly it has been the international conspiracy of Communist parties. By force or by subversion the Soviet government has established subservient Communist regimes in all but two of the European countries bordering the Soviet Union. Soviet statesmen apparently regard the spread of Russian-style socialist dictatorship as a high-priority objective, both for ideological reasons and for reasons associated with their own national security.

All this is but one side of the picture. In the present chapter we shall concentrate mainly on the other side of the picture—on the ways in which a nation's own political system may affect its own foreign policies, its own international operations, and its own capabilities vis-à-vis other nations.

In approaching this set of issues, it is desirable to brush away at the outset certain obstacles to clear thinking. The first is the prevalent dichotomy between democracy and dictatorship. Early writings on this subject employed the classical categories—monarchy, oligarchy, democracy—derived from the writings of the ancient Greek philosopher Aristotle. Since the Russian Revolution (1917) the tendency (in non-Communist countries and especially in the United States) has been to lump all systems of government into two loose categories: democracy and dictatorship.

This dichotomy evokes certain fruitful comparisons and insights, as the readings later in this chapter will illustrate. But the simple dichotomy misses other comparisons. For example, the international significance of operational differences between the British parliamentary and the American presidential systems may be as great as those derived from differences between either the British or the American system and the Russian Soviet system.

In American hands, the term *democracy* tends also to raise up a second obstacle to fruitful thinking. This arises from the American propensity to define democracy in terms of *American* institutions and practices. Foreign observers frequently comment on this American tendency to equate democracy with a written constitution, a bill of rights, a government of limited powers, separation of powers among coordinate executive, legislative and judicial institutions, checks and balances to prevent any part of the system from dominating the whole, periodic free elections, and a two-party system. By these criteria the United States would be the only democratic system in the world.

Such terms as democracy, dictatorship, totalitarianism, and the like are heavily value-laden everywhere. Discussions of democracy, for example, often confuse efficiency and desirability—quite dissimilar criteria. Democracy and dictatorship have become fighting words. As such they have their uses as weapons in the Cold War and on other forensic battlefields. But for purely analytical purposes, such terms contribute more to banal and value-ridden generalities than to precise and discriminating comparisons of *functional* capacities.

A third and perhaps the most serious objection to the standard terminology arises from its parochial origin. Most of the terms commonly used in classifying political systems are derived from European and American experience. This is especially true of such terms as democracy, autocracy, executive, legislative, judicial, separation of powers, responsible government, free elections, and the like. This vocabulary antedates the emerging systems of Asia and Africa. In quite a number of the political communities recently transformed from colonies to independent states there exists as yet comparatively little governmental apparatus and political practice which fits readily into the traditional Western vocabulary.

Finally, in addition to the above objections, the democracy-dictatorship dichotomy focuses too exclusively on a single aspect of government: namely, the relationship between rulers and their constituents or publics. This relationship may have a very significant bearing on a government's international behavior and capabilities. But so may other structural features of national political systems. Instead of disputing over whether democratic or dictatorial governments are, in general, more capable and efficient operators upon the international stage, it may prove more enlightening to compare specific *functional* features of differently structured national systems.

One can go about this in various ways. The following questions indicate some possible lines of inquiry. (1) How is *authority* to commit the nation and its resources to a course of action *allocated* among different parts of the governmental structure, and what effects does such allocation have on the conduct of foreign affairs? (2) How does the internal *organization* of a government affect the quality of its decisions and the conduct of its operations? (3) How and to what effect does the public *participate* in the processes of government? (4) To whom and in what ways can those who are invested with authority to act for the nation be held *accountable* for their actions? (5) How *responsive* are the government's policy-makers to moods, attitudes, and explicit demands of their constituents? (6) How much *autonomy* from public restraint does the government enjoy? (7) How do the patterns of *autonomy, responsiveness,* and *accountability* affect the decisions, operations, and accomplishments of the national system as a whole?

Key concepts in the above questions are indicated by italics: authority, accountability, responsiveness, autonomy, participation, allocation, organization. Most of these concepts enter into (though not always explicitly) the readings which follow.

Political institutions and foreign policies

Observers have asserted on many occasions that a state's form of government affects in significant ways the goals which its rulers strive to achieve and the methods which they are wont to employ. However, there is no consensus as to what these effects may be. It has been contended, and denied, that democracies are inherently more "peace-loving" and "law-abiding" than autocracies. It has been contended, and denied, that dictatorships are by their very nature more aggressive and expansionist than democracies. This clash of opinion is strikingly manifest in the following short passages on the nature of Soviet foreign policy.

The first is by Ferdinand A. Hermens (professor of political science at the University of Notre Dame). Hermens argues the thesis that rulers behave in their foreign dealings according to the same principles that govern their domestic rule; that dictators as a class are conspiratorial, distrustful, and prone to violence; and that these qualities are certain to carry over into their management of foreign affairs.

> . . . There exists [Hermens contends] a vital relationship between a country's domestic institutions and its foreign policy. The domestic political structure establishes the rules according to which power is gained and retained, and anyone who wants to make foreign policy must have won the domestic race for power first. The obstacles in this case are quite different in democracies and in dictatorships. In the former, power is acquired in a process of peaceful persuasion; in

the latter this is done in a process which necessitates the use of violence against all outsiders from the beginning, and against insiders after the conquest of power. Those who rule on peaceful persuasion, and who must, at the same time, tolerate their defeated opponents by their side, will instinctively transfer the same attitude to their partners in international relations; they will (as a rule) prefer to persuade rather than to coerce, and will (again as a rule) bring a readiness "to live and let live" to the conference table. If the representatives of top men in a totalitarian power were driven to show the same attitudes, they would be schizophrenics. Accustomed to violence and mutual destruction at home, they cannot easily conform to a pattern of trust and peaceful relationship in their dealings with foreign nations.

Furthermore, a feeling of fear is inseparable from dictatorships. . . . Evidently the psychological situation arising from this background means that a foreign power is basically as suspect as an actual or potential domestic opponent. Totalitarianism means not only the rule of a party over a nation, but also, except for periods of transition, the rule of one man over the party. . . . In the long run, the system needs the unity of action and the speed of decision guaranteed by one-man rule, which, in turn, has implications of its own. . . . [The ancient Greek writer] Herodotus has reminded us that the one-man ruler finds himself in a peculiar position: always able to act arbitrarily, he will, for several reasons, be inclined to do so. He lacks what the modern psychologist calls the "test of reality," one of the conditions for which is the possibility of a free and frank discussion among equals. A totalitarian ruler has no equals, and no one can force him to listen to unpleasant facts. . . .

A foreign policy based on unwarranted suspicion, and decided upon by a man not subjected to an efficient "test of reality," will soon lead to reactions which provide it with the appearance of objective justification. Countries which are exposed to such a policy for some time lose patience; they will take military and other measures for their defense against possible attack which can be interpreted as an attempt at "encirclement." Democracies, while usually able to handle their relations with other democracies well enough, are never free from irrationalities of their own, and these are not easily controlled when protection has to be provided against possible attack from a totalitarian opponent. . . .*

The contrasting view is by Dr. Barrington Moore, Jr. (specialist on Russian politics at Harvard University).

Concerning the . . . point, that authoritarian states tend to be expansionist, it is necessary to express reservations and doubts on

---

* From "Totalitarian Power Structure and Russian Foreign Policy," by F. A. Hermens, in *Journal of Politics*, August 1959, pp. 434 ff. Copyright 1959 by the Southern Political Science Association; reproduced by permission.

both general and specific grounds. The connection between the internal organization of a society and its foreign policy is a complex question that cannot yet be answered on the basis of simple formulas. Athens engaged in foreign conquest perhaps more than did warlike Sparta, and the Japanese, despite the militaristic emphasis of their society, lived in isolation for centuries until the time of their forced contacts with the West. To show that the authoritarian structure of any state is a source of expansionist tendencies, one would have to show the way in which these pressures make themselves felt upon those responsible for foreign policy. At this point the argument often breaks down, though there are cases where it can be shown that the rulers have embarked on an adventurous policy to allay internal discontent. But those at the apex of the political pyramid in an authoritarian regime are frequently freer from the pressures of mass discontent than are the responsible policy-makers of a Western democracy. They can therefore afford to neglect much longer the dangers of internal hostilities. Furthermore, modern events reveal the weakness of the argument that a warlike policy is the result of hostilities toward outsiders among the individuals who make up the society. In the days of total war it is necessary to use all sorts of force and persuasion, from propaganda to conscription, to make men and women fight. To regard war as primarily the expression of the hostilities of rank-and-file citizens of various states toward one another is to fly in the face of these facts.

In the case of the Soviet Union, the Nazi-Soviet Pact of 1939 shows that the rulers of modern Russia had no difficulty in disregarding the hostilities to Nazism that had been built up during preceding years, and that in this respect they enjoyed greater freedom for prompt adjustment of disputes than did other countries. Both totalitarian partners [Hitler and Stalin] were able to keep mass hostility under control as long as it suited purposes and plans based on the configuration of international power relationships. . . .

An acceptable modification of the argument that the authoritarian nature of the present Soviet regime is a source of an aggressive and expansionist foreign policy may be found along the following lines. It is probable that a certain amount of hostility toward the outside world is an essential ingredient in the power of the present rulers of Russia. Without the real or imagined threat of potential attack, it would be much more difficult to drive the Russian masses through one set of Five Year Plans after another. Yet it does not seem likely that this hostility is in turn a force that reacts back on the makers of Russian foreign policy. Their power can be more easily maximized by the threat of war than by war itself—a precarious enough situation. Nor is there evidence that mass hostility is in any way cumulative or sufficient to force the Soviet leaders into an aggressive policy. There are a number of devices for draining off internally generated hostility into channels other than those of external expansion. Military and combative sentiments, aroused for specific purposes, can be and have been directed into the socially productive channels of promoting a conquest of the physical environment. . . .*

Political institutions and international capabilities

When one turns from policies to capabilities, he finds comparable lack of agreement. We quote first a short passage from a famous book which argued the advantages of "aristocratic" forms of government in the sphere of foreign affairs. This book, entitled *Democracy in America*, was written over a century ago. It presents the reactions of a young Frenchman, Alexis de Tocqueville, who visited the United States in the 1830's.†

Statecraft in foreign affairs requires scarcely any of those qualities which are peculiar to democracy. On the contrary, conduct of foreign affairs involves the exercise of nearly all those capacities in which democracy is deficient. Democratic government facilitates the development of a nation's internal resources; it spreads material comforts, fosters a sense of community, strengthens respect for law among the different social classes—qualities which only indirectly affect the standing of a state in relation to others. But it is very difficult for a democratic government to coordinate the elements of a large undertaking, to be firm in purpose, and to carry through steadfastly in the face of obstacles. Democracy has little capacity for contriving a strategy in secret and for patiently awaiting results. These are qualities which are more characteristic of an individual person or of an aristocratic elite class. And these are precisely the qualities which in the long run make a nation, as well as an individual, dominant [over others].

If, on the other hand, one considers the defects inherent in aristocratic systems, one will find that the effects which these can produce have almost no bearing on the conduct of a state's foreign affairs. The principal failing of an aristocratic elite is its tendency to look out only for its own members and not for the masses. In foreign affairs, however, the interests of the elite are rarely different from those of the people as a whole. The propensity of democratic systems to be swayed by feeling more than by rational calculation, and to forsake long-range purpose for the gratification of momentary sentiment, was clearly observed in America on the outbreak of the French Revolution [in 1789]. It should have been as evident to Americans then as it is today [in 1835] that it was not at all in their interest to join in the bloody struggle which was about to overwhelm Europe and from which the United States could suffer no damage.

Nevertheless, public sympathy was so strong for France that only

* From pp. 396-7 of *Sovet Politics—The Dilemma of Power*, by Barrington Moore, Jr. Copyright 1950 by the President and Fellows of Harvard College; reproduced by permission.

† The following excerpt from *Democracy in America* is not a literal translation, but rather a rendering in modern idiomatic political English of the sense of the French original as it appears to us.

the steadfast will of Washington, and his immense popularity, prevented a declaration of war on England. Even so, the efforts which the rigorous rationality of that great man impelled him to make against the generous but misguided sentiments of his fellow citizens, nearly cost him the only reward which he ever claimed, the affection of his country. The majority denounced his policy, a policy which the people as a whole approve today [in 1835]. If the constitution and public esteem had not given Washington a firm hold on foreign affairs, it is certain that the [American] nation would have done precisely that which it condemns today [1835].

Nearly all nations which have exerted a large influence in international politics—those which have envisaged and carried out great projects, from the Romans to the [modern] Britons—have all been governed by an aristocratic system. The masses can be led astray by ignorance or sentiment. One can corrupt the mind of a monarch, and make him vacillate in his policies. Besides, no king is immortal. But an aristocratic elite is too numerous to be corrupted, yet not so numerous as to succumb readily to the intoxication of ill-considered sentiment. An aristocratic elite is [figuratively speaking] a steadfast man who never dies.

Eighty-odd years after De Tocqueville, a member of the British aristocracy, the politician-scholar James Bryce, took a fresh look at the venerable thesis that democratic forms of government suffer from semicrippling handicaps in the sphere of foreign relations. The following passage is from his book *Modern Democracies*, published in 1921.*

Statesmen, political philosophers, and historians have been wont to regard the conduct of foreign relations as the reproach of democratic government. The management of international relations needs— so they insist—knowledge, consistency, and secrecy, whereas democracies are ignorant and inconstant, being moreover obliged, by the law of their being, to discuss in public matters unfit to be disclosed. That this has been perceived by the people themselves appears from the fact that modern legislatures have left this department to officials, because it was felt that in this one department democracies cannot safely be democratic.

Per contra, popular leaders in some countries have, with an increasing volume of support, denounced Foreign Offices as having erred both in aims and in methods. They allege that the diplomacy of European States is condemned by the suspicion which it has constantly engendered and that the brand of failure is stamped upon it by the frequent recurrence of war, the evil which diplomacy was created to prevent.

These views, apparently opposite, are not incompatible. Oligarchies, and the small official class which in many democracies has had the

* From vol. ii, pp. 367-381 of *Modern Democracies*, by James Bryce. Copyright 1921 by the Macmillan Company, New York; reproduced by permission.

handling of foreign affairs, may have managed them ill, and yet it may be that the whole people will manage them no better. The fault may lie in the conditions of the matter itself and in those tendencies of human nature which no form of government can overcome. What we want to know is not whether oligarchic and secret methods have failed—that may be admitted—but whether democratic and open-air methods will succeed any better. . . .

A monarch is free to select his ministers and ambassadors from among the best informed and most skilful of his subjects, and in an oligarchy the mind of the ruling class busies itself with foreign relations, and knows which of its members understand and are fitted to handle them. The multitude has not the same advantage. It is ill-qualified to judge this kind of capacity, usually choosing its ministers by their powers of speech. If, instead of leaving foreign affairs to skilled men it attempt to direct them either by its own votes . . . or by instructing those who represent it in the legislature, how is it to acquire the requisite knowledge? Few of the voters know more than the most elementary facts regarding the conditions and the policy of foreign countries, and to appreciate the significance of these facts, there is needed some acquaintance with the history of the countries and the characters of the leading men. Not much of that acquaintance can be expected from the legislature. One of the strongest arguments for democratic government is that the masses of the people, whatever else they may not know, do know where the shoe pinches, and are best entitled to specify the reforms they need. In foreign affairs this argument does not apply, for they lie out of the normal citizen's range. All he can do at an election is to convey by his vote his view of general principles, and, in the case of a conflict between two foreign nations, to indicate his sympathies.

If the masses of the people have been inconstant in their views of foreign relations, this is due to their ignorance, which disables them from following intelligently the course of events abroad, so that their interest in these is quickened only at intervals, and when that happens the want of knowledge of what has preceded makes a sound judgment unlikely. They are at the mercy of their party leaders or of the press, guides not trustworthy, because the politicians will be influenced by the wish to make political capital out of any successes scored or errors committed by a Ministry, while the newspapers may play up to and exaggerate the prevailing sentiment of the moment, claiming everything for their own country, misrepresenting and disparaging the foreign antagonist. . . .

Secrecy in the conduct of diplomacy is vital in a world where each great nation is suspicious of its neighbors and obliged by its fears to try to discover their plans while concealing its own. Suppose the Ministry [Administration, in the American idiom] of a country to have ascertained privately that a foreign Power meditates an attack upon it or is forming a combination against it, or suppose it to be itself negotiating a treaty of alliance for protection against such a combination. How can it proclaim either the intentions of the suspected Power or its own counter-schemes without precipitating a rupture or frustrating its own plans? A minister too honorable to deceive the legislature may feel himself debarred from telling it the facts, some of which may have been communicated under the seal of confidence. It is all very well to say that an open and straightforward policy best befits a free and high-minded people. But if such a people should stand alone in a naughty world, it will have to suffer for its virtues. As a democracy cannot do business secretly, it must therefore leave much, and perhaps much of grave import, to its ministers. Herein the superiority for foreign affairs of a monarchy or an oligarchy is most evident.

There is force in these considerations, yet a monarchy in which the Sovereign may be either a fool, or the victim of his passions, or the plaything of his favorites, may succeed no better than a democracy. [One can, of course, substitute dictator in place of monarch, and the same argument holds.] An oligarchy is better qualified, for in it power rests with a few trained and highly educated men who keep a watchful outlook on neighboring states. . . .

[Bryce then undertakes an extended review of the international operations of three leading democratic systems, France, the United States, and Great Britain.] Summing up the results of this examination . . . we find that the case of France [1870-1920] proves that it was possible for a democracy to follow a consistent policy, the conduct of the details whereof was left in the hands of successive administrations, and safely left because the nation was substantially agreed as to the general lines to be followed. The case of the United States proves that public opinion, which is there omnipotent, is generally right in its aims, and has tended to become wiser and more moderate with the march of the years. The case of Britain shows that the opinion of the bulk of the nation was more frequently approved by results than was the attitude of the comparatively small class in whose hands the conduct of affairs had been usually left. . . .

There is another way also of reaching a conclusion as to the competence of democracies in this branch of government. Set the results in and for the three countries examined side by side with those attained in and for three other great countries in which no popular clamor disturbed the Olympian heights where sat the monarch and his group of military and civil advisers, controlling foreign policy as respects both ends and means. In Russia, in Austria-Hungary, and in Germany the Emperors and their respective advisers were able to pursue their ends with a steady pertinacity from month to month and year to year. No popular sentiment, no parliamentary opposition, made much difference to them, and in Germany they were usually able to guide popular sentiment. In choosing their means considerations of morality were in none of these countries allowed to prevent a resort to any means that seemed to promise success. Compare the situation in which Russia found herself in 1917, when the autocracy crashed to its fall, and the situations in which Austria and Germany found themselves in October 1918, with those in which that momentous year found the three free countries. The temptations and snares which surround and pervert diplomatic aims and methods in states ruled by oligarchies or despots often differ from the temptations of which popular governments have to beware. But they proved in these cases, and in many others, to have been more dangerous.

In these last few pages ends rather than means have been considered, though it is hard to draw a distinction, for most ends are means to a larger end; and the facts examined seem to show that in determining ends the voice of the people must have authority. But what is to be said as to the details of diplomacy in which, assuming the main ends to be determined by the people, a wide choice of means remains open? It has been deemed impossible for the people to know either which means are best suited to the purpose aimed at or, if the people is kept informed of them, to apply those means successfully, for in our days what is told to any people is told to the whole world. So long as each nation strives to secure some gains for itself as against other nations by anticipating its rivals in enterprises, or by forming profitable alliances, or otherwise driving bargains for its own benefit, those who manage the nation's business cannot disclose their action without damaging their chances of success. Hence even the countries that have gone furthest in recognizing popular control have left a wide discretion in the hands of their Ministers or envoys and have set bounds to the curiosity of parliamentary representatives. . . .

Following closely in the footsteps of Bryce, the American diplomat DeWitt C. Poole said in 1924:

Inefficiency in the conduct of foreign relations has always been deemed to be the grave defect of democratic government. It is plain that . . . autocratic form of government has a certain tactical advantage in pursuing its international interests. It decides more readily what it wants and has the greatest freedom of action in seeking to obtain it. Democracy must feel its way, taking account not only of the international situation but of the inner workings of its own mind, which are sometimes cumbersome and slow. This very deliberateness imparts to democratic policy, however, a greater ultimate wisdom. The wisdom of autocracies, including in that term more or less autocratic oligarchies such as Imperial Germany [1870-1918], is the wisdom of the individual or the few and may be only self-delusion. Democracy, on the other hand, suffers from the liability of the multitude to sudden heats and sentimental impulses and long intervening periods of indifference. Representative democracy is again the practical expedient. By reposing confidence for brief periods in chosen leaders, it gains in tactical mobility, retains the balanced wisdom of deliberate popular feeling, lessens the danger of unwise impulses, and bridges the periods of popular indifference.*

The optimism of the 1920's regarding the superior international capabilities of democratic forms of government was difficult to sustain in the face of the shattering events of the 1930's and World War II. Mussolini conquered Ethiopia in defiance of weak and ineffective protests from the great democratic nations, Britain, France, and the United States. Hitler repeatedly outmaneuvered his foreign adversaries until his sway reached from Norway to North Africa, and from the Atlantic to the Volga. The military-industrial oligarchy that ruled in Tokyo pushed deep into China, Southeast Asia, and the Southwest Pacific. The French surrender of 1940 contrasted starkly with the survival of the Stalinist regime in Russia despite merciless battering by German armies and despite the ruin and loss of its richest farmlands and most productive industrial region. Even the lesser dictators—Franco in Spain, Peron in Argentina, and others—seemed to substantiate the view that authoritarian government could outplay the democracies upon the international stage.

This pessimistic conclusion was reflected in books and articles published before and during World War II. It was well summed up in 1947 in a pair of editorials in *The Economist* (London weekly newspaper of business and finance). These articles commented on the relative capacities of Britain, the United States, and the Soviet Union to play the "game of power politics" in the Cold War.†

Soviet leaders can be absolutely certain that no government which is in the Western sense democratic can suddenly declare aggressive war. It cannot secretly prepare defensive war. It cannot even face the possibility of hostilities without [public] discussion of the issue and the possible enemy. [In contrast, the Soviet government] need fear within the U.S.S.R. itself no organized criticism . . . no strikes, demonstrations, passive resistance or sabotage. In their use of police methods they are as far ahead of the British and Americans now as they were behind them in industrial methods twenty-five years ago. They have the power to direct movements of industry and population where strategy demands . . . whatever the cost in money, efficiency or human life. . . . They can control most of the information on the outside world which reaches the Russian public. They can therefore prepare the ground for any move that might be unpopular, or inconsistent,

---

* From pp. 194-5 of *The Conduct of Foreign Relations under Modern Democratic Conditions*, by D. C. Poole. Copyright 1924 by Yale University Press, New Haven; reproduced by permission.

† From "Russia's Strength" in *The Economist*, May 17, 1947, and "Imperialism or Indifference," May 24, 1947. Copyright 1947 by the Economist Newspaper, Ltd., London; reproduced by permission.

or unfamiliar. . . . What is more, Soviet statesmen can choose their own pace in policy; they need promise no quick results or neat compromises. [These considerations emphasize] some of the inherent weaknesses . . . from which any democracy, and still more a collection of democracies, suffers when it comes to the game of power politics. For that game demands patience, resolution, clear sight, a lack of illusions, a refusal to be frightened by tactical moves, a determination not to be taken in by appearances or to yield to emotions. . . .

In the second article, *The Economist* spoke bluntly of the weakness of American democracy, in particular in the field of foreign politics.

Perhaps the greatest single obstacle to the emergence in America of a sustained and positive foreign policy is the nature of its political system. The division of power between President and Congress, the possibility of different parties controlling the one and the other, the lack of a cabinet responsible to the legislature, the working of the party system, are all weighted against the present pursuit of long-term national or international objectives. So long as the essence of the political struggle in the country is the conciliation of minorities and the avoidance of controversial topics, the great issues of foreign policy cannot be fairly placed before the electorate and later confidently worked out. The spectacle . . . of the wool bloc in Congress, representing a minute fraction of American political life, pressing an increase in tariffs in the middle of the Administration's attempt to lead the world to freer trade and lower tariffs is a typical example of the pluralism of objectives and scattering of efforts which characterize American politics. The only way in which an administration in these circumstances can make its voice heard above the clamorous shouts of minorities, lobbyists, special interest groups, silver senators, cattle senators, and cotton senators is by dramatizing the issue at stake to ten times life size and compelling Congress by a species of shock treatment to pass the necessary appropriation. . . .

The thesis that dictatorships are inherently better adapted to cope with the contemporary international environment has failed to convince many astute observers of foreign affairs. The German, Italian, and Japanese defeats in World War II gave the victors access to abundant evidence to test this hotly debated proposition. The case of Nazi Germany has proved especially enlightening.

Post-mortem on the Third Reich

Hitler's Germany reached its high-water mark in the autumn of 1942. At that time Rommel's famed Afrika Korps stood deep inside Egypt awaiting reinforcements to crack the last line guarding the Suez Canal and the road to the Indian Ocean. Far to the north, Leningrad was cut off and subjented to incessant bombardment. German armies crowded the approaches to Moscow from the west. The Ukraine, the Donets Basin, and most of the Caucasus—the richest food and mineral-producing area of the Soviet Union —were in German hands. Hitler was confidently predicting the early fall of Stalingrad, key to future Soviet resistance and gateway to the Middle East.

In terms of increased military potentiality, the Nazi achievement was no less impressive. Axis Europe—Germany, the satellite states, and the occupied countries, not to mention the tribute-paying neutrals—covered two million square miles, two-thirds the area of the United States. The population under German domination or influence exceeded 300 millions at that time. The Wehrmacht numbered several million veteran troops, finely equipped, fanatically loyal to the Führer, and supported by the labor of possibly 50-60 million workers.

In the Ukraine Hitler possessed Europe's richest granary. He had a firm grip on the iron ores of Lorraine and Krivoi Rog, and seemingly indisputable access to the high-grade ores of Sweden in addition. He had the coal of the Donets Basin and the Ruhr, the manganese of Nikopol, the Maikop and Grozny oilfields, the bauxite of France, Hungary, and Yugoslavia, and other strategic minerals to make Axis Europe all but self-sufficient for a war of indefinite duration. In addition, German armies had captured more or less intact the industrial machinery of Western and Southern Europe, and with a little time the efficient Germans could restore the wrecked mines and ruined factories of occupied Russia.

Hitler's New Order that was to endure for a thousand years actually lasted less than three. By the spring of 1945 Germany's great industrial cities were smoking ruins, her transportation system a chaotic mass of wreckage. German armies, occupation forces, and their camp followers had all been driven back into the Fatherland, with huge losses in men and matériel. Hitler and his Nazi elite were either dead or fugitives or captives awaiting trial for their crimes against humanity. During May the last battered remnants of the once invincible Wehrmacht laid down their arms in unconditional surrender.

Never in modern times has so great a power suffered so crushing a defeat in so short a time. What is the explanation of this debacle? Is it simply that Germany was confronted with overwhelming odds? Or did the Nazi façade of power, like Mussolini's in Italy, and the military dictatorship in Tokyo, conceal grave structural weaknesses?

After the war official investigators probed deeply for answers to these questions. They studied captured records of the defunct Nazi government and interrogated most of its surviving officials. One of these investigations was the Strategic Bombing Survey carried out by the U. S. Air Force, under the direction of John K. Galbraith (professor of economics at Harvard, appointed American ambassador to India in 1961). Galbraith's conclusions are summarized in an article with the significant title: "Germany Was Badly Run." *

After describing the overconfidence with which the Nazi elite started the war in 1939, their failure to organize production on a sufficient scale or to allocate enough to the military forces, their failure to locate or to make effective use of top-grade generals and administrators, Galbraith continues:

> The most interesting question about German war management is the extent to which it suffered from Hitler—or from the circumstance that Germany was a dictatorship. . . . [Hitler] controlled not only those decisions that are the normal business of the chief of state but also an enormous number of decisions that in any ordinary government would be delegated to subordinates or to specialists.
>
> The German armies were run from Hitler's headquarters. . . . Once a day . . . Keitel and Jodl of the General Staff, the Supreme Commanders of the Army, Air Force and Navy, and their Chiefs of Staff, met with Hitler for a briefing on the day's operations of the Wehrmacht. . . . The orders issued after these briefings were not confined to broad strategy; they specified minute details of tactics. . . . Often they bore little relation to conditions on the battlefield. When the U.S. Third Army moved on Koblenz [for example], General Model got orders from the bunker [Hitler's headquarters in Berlin] to throw in two divisions to stem the attack. . . . According to arms minister Speer, who was on the front at the time, the divisions in question consisted of only a few hundred men, twenty-odd tanks, and no gasoline whatever.
>
> Hitler also master-minded the homefront decisions. He met with production officials at least once a week and would express a judgment on five to twenty questions presented to him and would issue a half dozen to a dozen orders of his own. Again these were not just policy decisions. When a new series of tanks was under consideration, Hitler gave the final word not only on the number to be produced but also on the kind of engine, the position of the armor, and the type of armament the tank should mount. . . .
>
> Whether Hitler's judgment was good or bad, it is clear that he made too many decisions, too many of which inevitably were snap decisions. And all the decisions were made with the egoist's certainty that they were infallible, so that right or wrong they could not be seriously debated, much less reversed. . . .
>
> Hitler's alert but undisciplined mind was peculiarly susceptible to

---

* Reprinted from the December 1945 issue of *Fortune* magazine by special permission of the editors and the author. Copyright 1945 by Time, Inc., New York.

doctrine. Since the Nazis invented most of their own doctrine, decisions were often based not on fact but on the official propaganda line.

Only a part of Germany's fantastic propaganda was a deliberate effort to mislead the German people. . . . Part and perhaps most of it was what Germany's leaders wanted to believe. The very theme of German wartime propaganda is an example. In contrast to the British theme of "Blood, sweat, and tears" or the American theme of "Avoid overconfidence," the German slogan was "Victory is certain."

Some such slogan may have been necessary to keep up the spirits of the long-suffering *Herrenvolk,* but it was also highly agreeable to Germany's leaders. Complete confidence in victory, in turn, was an important source of Germany's delayed and partial mobilization. Germany's leaders and a whole army of subordinate officials failed to recognize the need for all-out effort because they believed their own newspapers.

Distortions of the truth affected decisions even when the distortions were deliberate. Hitler in the last two years of the war became increasingly annoyed by American production figures as quite accurately reported by German intelligence. Finally he ordered that no American production figures were to be quoted to him—nor were they to be believed by German officials or even discussed in private conversations. . . . The enemy's production is an important datum for a country fighting a war. The German leaders preferred the comfortable fiction that the figures lied.

At the end even the Propaganda Ministry had to be curbed for telling unpleasant truths. Through a special section of the ministry a careful check was kept on the morale of the German people. This office, headed by one Schaffer, received and tabulated for the top officials reports from all parts of the Reich and it had access as well to the reports of the Gestapo. In the summer and autumn of 1944 the reports became more and more disturbing; they told of growing war weariness among the people, declining confidence in the leaders, and a popular conviction that the war was lost. In November the Nazis took decisive action. They fired Herr Schaffer.

If German war management was poor how did the German armies manage to fight so well and so long? The Wehrmacht, in the days of its great successes, occupied all Europe except for a few odd corners. It reached the Volga and almost reached the Nile. When it was finally thrown on the defensive it stood off the armed millions of Russia, the United States, and the British Empire for two and a half years.

The simple fact is that Germany should never have lost the war it started; the under-mobilization and overconfidence of the early years help to solve the very real mystery of why it did. . . . Had the Nazi leaders applied their own formula of total war from the beginning, they could hardly have avoided overwhelming the opposition they met before 1942.

Even after the tide turned at Moscow and Stalingrad, Germany's position was strong. There was the well-publicized advantage of

internal lines of communication that grew shorter and thicker as the communications of all Germany's enemies became longer and more tenuous. German weapons were of good quality, German scientists and technologists were ingenious, and because of the short pipelines new weapons could be quickly put into use. Most important of all, there is little doubt that Germans are durable and skillful fighters with a well-disciplined acceptance of the idea of getting killed. Except in the east they were well moated by the ocean and the Mediterranean. They should have been hard to defeat. That they were defeated is conclusive testimony to the inherent inefficiencies of dictatorship, the inherent efficiencies of freedom.

During the 1950's, debate over the relative capabilities of autocratic and democratic systems of government naturally focused on the United States and the Soviet Union. Much has been said on both sides. There is still no consensus among experts; there probably never will be. Among those who have written on this subject is Harrison E. Salisbury (formerly *New York Times* correspondent in Moscow). He speaks on "The Fatal Flaws of Dictatorship," an article published in 1955:

The fatal flaws of dictatorships *

Certainly democracy is not the most efficient kind of government. It bristles with checks and balances and internal controls. Often it succeeds in paralyzing itself, but, generally speaking, in times of crisis it proves flexible enough to act resolutely and forcefully.

A dictatorship can change policy overnight as Russia did when Stalin made his pact with Hitler [in August 1939], because policy is made by one man. But quick policy changes are not necessarily wise policy changes. The Nazi-Soviet pact merely set the stage for the Nazi assault on Russia in June, 1941, which almost cost Stalin his regime and inflicted incalculable losses on his country.

An equally dramatic policy switch was made by England early in this century when in 1907 it decided after nearly eighty years of conflict to sign an entente with Russia. But England's switch followed a decade of debate in the democratic fashion. It was a decision long in the making and typical of cumbersome democratic procedures. But unlike Stalin's cheap and almost fatal deal with Hitler the Anglo-Russian accord laid the foundation for British victory and German defeat in World War I. . . .

It is sometimes suggested that dictatorships are better at waging wars than democracies. And it is pointed out that in time of war a democracy starts slowly by comparison with a dictatorship and

* From *The New York Times Magazine*, Feb. 20, 1955, p. 12. Copyright 1955 by the New York Times Company, New York; reproduced by permission.

generally ends up by granting virtually dictatorial powers to its leaders for purposes of waging the war.

While it is true that a major collective national effort like war requires a concentration of power and authority, it remains to be proved that dictatorship can accomplish this task more effectively than democracy. Part of the genius of democracy consists of its ability to adapt itself to the exigencies of the moment. Democracy can vest in itself the virtues of dictatorship in wartime. But dictators can seldom avail themselves of the reverse privilege. A democracy can shift generals at will and change prime ministers until a winning combination is evolved. Chamberlain can yield to Churchill and the system goes on. Foch replaces Pétain, Grant succeeds McClellan, and democracy forges ahead to victory.

But the Great Dictator cannot shuffle and experiment. He cannot step down and let the leader of the opposition take over because, as in Stalin's example, Trotsky and all the rest of the opposition had been exterminated. His choice of generals is limited. Even his choice of tactics and strategy may be restricted. For he cannot lose. Even when his people retreat, it is a "strategic withdrawal." With Hitler this factor of "face" was such an acute problem that he literally forbade commanders to withdraw or take a backward step. The famous Stalingrad encirclement was achieved by the Russians largely because Hitler's commanders had no freedom to obey the ordinary laws of military necessity.

With dictators there can only be victories. Every act of government is personified as the dictator's act. It is a "Stalinist" army—hence it has to win. It uses "Stalinist" tactics—hence they must succeed.

The same principle carries over into peacetime. There can be no failures. Or if there are they must be blamed on the treachery of enemies. In the absence of enemies, enemies must be created. Because the dictator can take no blame.

Thus, the supposed "freedom of action" of the dictator, his ease in meeting problems, the absence of controls over his acts become in reality a straitjacket which is often more constricting than the checks and balances of democracy. The dictator must walk a narrow path leading only upward. He is limited by the dialectic of Communism or National Socialism in his choice of techniques and only too often is even more sharply restricted by the urgencies of his presumed infallibility. He must reveal no mortal flaw in his divine apparatus. Thus, considerations of prestige often do not permit him to utilize the men whose brains and ability he and his country badly need. And there is no parliament to compel him.

A dictatorship is a thirsty god. The dictator must constantly sacrifice his underlings lest he himself become a sacrifice. If the harvest is bad, Andreyev is sacked. If it is even worse, peasants must be shot and people uprooted from the soil. If the train is wrecked—shoot the engineer. If the blast furnace breaks down—send the director to Siberia.

Every dictatorship by its very nature must be a police state. Only police can provide the terror which is necessary to make people work and accept such conditions. But once the population is intimidated the police themselves become a problem, for in the absence of threats to the state threats must be created. It is only in an atmosphere of threat and terror that the wheels of the mechanism can be made to turn over. Ordinary motivations are destroyed or paralyzed by the terror.

The closer you look at dictatorship the more you are surprised, not at its surface "efficiency" but that the system can be made to run at all. The sheer effort which a man like Stalin had to mobilize just to make his clumsy dictatorship work would have produced miracles if applied to our supposedly cumbersome democratic apparatus.

In no field do the fatal flaws of dictatorship emerge more strikingly than in relation to people—both individuals and in the mass. For no system is more wasteful of human materials. Stalin purged and sacked one generation of colleagues and advisers after another. He wreaked havoc among millions of plain people. Only a country with inexhaustible resources of humanity could even survive such wastage. No wonder dictatorship in Russia moved from crisis to crisis like a terrified goat among the Caucasian peaks. Each time a crisis was "solved" it merely lighted the fuse to another one.

But no crisis in dictatorship is so sharp and severe as that of the dictator's death. For a dictatorship without a dictator is a contradiction in terms. And in the inherent nature of one-man rule it cannot produce a reliable and waiting successor. . . .

One of the most complex features of democracy is its system for insuring the continuity of government, of making certain that, regardless of whether a certain man lives or dies, government will go on. . . .

The earlier monarchical form of government paid even greater attention to continuity. In fact, one of the clear virtues of the monarchical principle over rule by a tribal chieftain or a council of elders was that it tended to relieve a country of periodic crises and the anarchy arising from contests over the succession.

It took many years to establish the principle of monarchical succession firmly, as English history clearly shows. And in some countries, notably Russia, it never took hold too well. Even before the Bolshevik Revolution one of the Russian Grand Dukes frankly said, "In Russia the throne descends according to the principle of usurpation rather than by inheritance or election." Commissars replaced the Czars but the Grand Duke's principle still held.

Modern dictatorships differ in detail but each of them has insisted on order and plan. In so far as possible Hitler did not allow matters to be decided by chance. He himself might govern, thanks to his famous "intuition." But he insisted on planning in government down to the last item of business. Mussolini was the same. . . .

Each of these dictators was a man of ability, outstanding force and considerable intellect. Yet none could devise a method of passing on the mantle of authority to a successor. . . .

The imposing and granite fact which emerges is that the so-called "system" of dictatorship simply provides no method for the continuation of power except by resort to the cruel and primitive law of the jungle—the survival of the strongest and most rapacious. . . .

Salisbury's delineation of the "flaws of dictatorships" was matched in the same year, 1955, by an equally forceful and candid description of the handicaps which democratic governments suffer in the sphere of foreign affairs. The author of this indictment is another well-known American journalist, Walter Lippmann. In a book entitled *The Public Philosophy*, Lippmann presents his case under the heading—

The Democratic malady *

Experience since 1917 indicates that in matters of war and peace the popular answer in the democracies is likely to be No. For everything connected with war has become dangerous, painful, disagreeable and exhausting to very nearly everyone. The rule to which there are few exceptions—the acceptance of the Marshall Plan is one of them—is that at the critical junctures, when the stakes are high, the prevailing mass of opinion will impose what amounts to a veto upon changing the course on which the government is at the time proceeding. Prepare for war in time of peace? No. It is bad to raise taxes, to unbalance the budget, to take men away from their schools or their jobs, to provoke the enemy. Intervene in a developing conflict? No. Avoid the risk of war. Withdraw from the area of conflict? No. The adversary must not be appeased. Reduce your claims on that area? No. Righteousness cannot be compromised. Negotiate a compromise peace as soon as the opportunity presents itself? No. The aggressor must be punished. Remain armed to enforce the dictated settlement? No. The war is over.

The unhappy truth is that the prevailing public opinion has been destructively wrong at the critical junctures. The people have imposed a veto upon the judgments of informed and responsible officials. They have compelled the governments, which usually knew what would have been wiser, or was necessary, or was more expedient, to be too late with too little, or too long with too much, too pacifist in peace and too bellicose in war, too neutralist or appeasing in negotiations or too intransigent. Mass opinion has acquired mounting power in this century. It has shown itself to be a dangerous master of decisions when the stakes are life and death. . . .

Between the critical junctures, when public opinion has been inattentive or not vehemently aroused, responsible officials have often been able to circumvent extremist public opinions and to wheedle their way towards moderation and good sense. In the crises, however, democratic officials—over and above their own human propensity to err—have been compelled to make the big mistakes that public opinion has insisted upon. Even the greatest men have not been able to turn back the massive tides of opinion and sentiment.

There is no mystery about why there is such a tendency for popular opinion to be wrong in judging war and peace. Strategic and diplomatic decisions call for a kind of knowledge—not to speak of an experience and a seasoned judgment—which cannot be had by glancing at newspapers, listening to snatches of radio comment, watching politicians perform on television, hearing occasional lectures, and reading a few books. It would not be enough to make a man competent to decide whether to amputate a leg, and it is not enough to qualify him to choose war or peace, to arm or not to arm, to intervene or to withdraw, to fight on or to negotiate.

Usually, moreover, when the decision is critical and urgent, the public will not be told the whole truth. What can be told to the great public it will not hear in the complicated and qualified concreteness that is needed for a practical decision. When distant and unfamiliar and complex things are communicated to great masses of people, the truth suffers a considerable and often a radical distortion. The complex is made over into the simple, the hypothetical into the dogmatic, and the relative into an absolute. Even when there is no deliberate distortion by censorship and propaganda, which is unlikely in time of war, the public opinion of masses cannot be counted upon to apprehend regularly and promptly the reality of things. There is an inherent tendency in opinion to feed upon rumors excited by our own wishes and fears.

At the critical moments in this sad history, there have been men, worth listening to, who warned the people against their mistakes. Always, too, there have been men inside the governments who judged correctly, because they were permitted to know in time, the uncensored and unvarnished truth. But the climate of modern democracy does not usually inspire them to speak out. For what Churchill did in the 'thirties before Munich was exceptional: the general rule is that a democratic politician had better not be right too soon. Very often the penalty is political death. It is much safer to keep in step with the parade of opinion than to try to keep up with the swifter movement of events.

In government offices which are sensitive to the vehemence and passion of mass sentiment public men have no secure tenure. They are in effect perpetual office seekers, always on trial for their political lives, always required to court their restless constituents. They are deprived of their independence. Democratic politicians rarely feel they can afford the luxury of telling the whole truth to the people. And since not telling it, though prudent, is uncomfortable, they find it easier if they themselves do not have to hear too often too much of the sour truth. The men under them who report and collect the news come to realize in their turn that it is safer to be wrong before it has become fashionable to be right.

With exceptions so rare that they are regarded as miracles and freaks of nature, successful democratic politicians are insecure and intimidated men. They advance politically only as they placate, appease, bribe, seduce, bamboozle, or otherwise manage to manipulate the demanding and threatening elements in their constituencies. The decisive consideration is not whether the proposition is good but whether it is popular—not whether it will work and prove itself but whether the active talking constituents like it immediately. Politicians rationalize this servitude by saying that in a democracy public men are the servants of the people.

This devitalization of the governing power is the malady of democratic states. As the malady grows the executives become highly susceptible to encroachment and usurpation by elected assemblies; they are pressed and harassed by the higgling of parties, by the agents of organized interests, and by the spokesmen of sectarians and ideologues. The malady can be fatal. It can be deadly to the very survival of the state as a free society if, when the great and hard issues of war and peace, of security and solvency, of revolution and order are up for decision, the executive and judicial departments, with their civil servants and technicians, have lost their power to decide.

The theses argued in the foregoing readings may seem at first sight to be utterly contradictory and irreconcilable. Hermens contended that the fear, distrust, and violence which characterize the domestic political struggles in a highly authoritarian system are bound to carry over and introduce rigidities in such a government's external policies and operations. Moore found that the Soviet dictatorship has displayed realism and flexibility in adjusting its strategies to changing external conditions. De Tocqueville argued that management of foreign affairs requires qualities of knowledge, secrecy, judgment, planning, and perseverance, in which autocratic systems are inherently superior to democratic systems. Bryce and Poole admitted the follies to which public opinion in democracies may be addicted, and the resulting weaknesses of democratic control, but held that autocratic systems had done no better on the whole, and had displayed crippling weaknesses of their own in addition. The editor of *The Economist* presented a modernized version of De Tocqueville's thesis, contending that the perils of the nuclear age magnify the weaknesses of democracy. Galbraith found one specific modern dictatorship, Nazi Germany, to have been grossly mismanaged for reasons at least partly inherent in its form of government. Salisbury delineates "fatal flaws of dictatorships," especially their built-in reliance on police methods, waste of manpower and physical resources, lack of blunder-correcting mechanisms, and inability to change leadership without throwing the whole system into crisis. Lippmann dwells pessimistically on the "malady" of democratic government, stressing public ignorance, preference for affluence at the expense of vital national interests, aversion to sacrifice, the vindictiveness and irrationality of an aroused public, and the timidity and sycophancy of politicians and officials in democratic countries.

Careful study of these writings indicates that they may not be as contradictory as first appears. The strengths and weaknesses attributed to democratic and nondemocratic systems are different, at least in degree. Moreover, the strengths attributed to one type are not uniformly matched by the weaknesses attributed to the other, and vice versa. They all reflect a conviction supported by cogent arguments, that operational differences and contrasts are attributable, in significant degree, to differences in the format of government. But when all is said, there remains a hard core of disagreements as to what forms of government are best, or least, adapted to cope with the ever more complicated problems which confront governments everywhere these days.

CHAPTER SEVEN

★ ★ ★

The Revolution in Science
and Technology

THE EXTRAORDINARY advance of scientific knowledge and its engineering applications was stated in the Introduction to be the key to our revolutionary age. Applied science has transformed and is still transforming every feature of the environment in which international politics is conducted. For this reason, the scientific and technological revolution provides the logical starting point in our examination of the foundations of international politics.

Technology is a term with many shades of meaning. The essence of most definitions is: the application of techniques to accomplish human purposes. The purpose may be production of goods and services, treatment of disease, or any other. Technology is sometimes called applied science. The term is also used rather loosely as a synonym for engineering. .

Technology is embodied, figuratively speaking, in every man-made structure, be it simple or complex, temporary or enduring. Technology is represented in the design of processed foodstuffs and raw materials, in houses and household equipment, in farms and factories, in monuments and skyscrapers, in medicines and medical apparatus, in libraries and laboratories, in books and maps, hand tools and machine tools, military equipment and every other man-made structure. These objects compose, in the aggregate, a large part of the physical environment of modern man. The larger and more complex this component of a society's environment, the higher generally is the level of its technological advance.

But it is not with the products of technology *per se* that we, as students of international politics, are concerned. The structures acquire political meaning and significance only in the context of the human beings who make and use them. An early-warning radar apparatus, for example, has not the slightest intrinsic political interest or significance. It acquires significance, in part as evidence of the knowledge and skills operative in the society which produced it. More particularly, its significance derives from the military uses to which it is put and the operational results presumably achievable with it.

With respect both to the undertakings (policies, strategies) and to the accomplishments (results, capabilities) of nations, the importance of technological factors has become so great as almost to justify regarding them as the master variables in any political analysis. Such a view would command much support these days. At least a great many statements could be quoted to this effect. Here are three samples, picked more or less at random:

> Throughout history the progress of science and technology has been reshaping the geographical, economic, and military premises of foreign policy.*
>
> Technological advance tends to make states powerful and dangerous.†
>
> Power in the world of tomorrow will fall to those who are technologically the most competent.‡

Such statements have a familiar ring in the 1960's, but it is well to remember how recently technological factors were all but ignored in the study of international politics. Leading American textbooks of the 1920's and 1930's, for example, include no index entries for such items as science, engineering, technology, inventions, and the like. One finds in most of these books only cursory reference—often no reference at all—to the political implications of the swelling stream of new scientific knowledge and the inventions which have given people in all but the most primitive societies an increasing control over their environment.

The turning point on this issue came during World War II. That war drove home the lesson that scholars, engineers, universities, and research laboratories are vital adjuncts of statecraft in the modern age. Unfortunately the bombs that wrecked Hiroshima and Nagasaki catapulted us all into the nuclear age before we had halfway assimilated the political consequences of prenuclear technology. This holds true not merely for

* From "Science and Foreign Policy," by E. M. Friedwald, a journalist, in *Impact of Science on Society*, Spring 1952, p. 21. Published by Unesco.

† From p. 381 of *The Study of International Relations*, by Quincy Wright, leading authority on international law and politics. Appleton-Century-Crofts, New York, 1955.

‡ From "A Scientist in Russia," by Fred Hoyle, British mathematician, in *The Observer*, London, September 7, 1958.

military machines, but also for nonmilitary machines of many kinds as well. We have only commenced, for example, to explore and understand the international implications of printing, photography, radio, television, and other nonmilitary media for influencing the behavior of people.

Since 1945 scientific and engineering feats have become headline news. Tens of millions of words are now being written about these every year. In the chilly atmosphere of the Cold War, news about weapons generally commands the most attention. But, we repeat, the technological revolution pervades every nook and cranny of international politics, not just the military. Hence the decision to follow up the discussion of national political systems with an examination of the scientific, engineering, and technological developments which are profoundly affecting the meaning and significance of all the other foundations of international politics, to be considered in the remaining chapters of Part III.

We shall begin by reviewing briefly certain salient characteristics of scientific and technological advance in general. We shall then review in historical and poliitcal perspective certain specific features of the scientific and technological revolution. Third, we shall consider some of the broader international consequences of these events. Finally, we shall go to some of the leading scientists for a speculative look into the crystal ball of the future. In Chapter 8 we shall take up in further detail some of the implications of recent developments in military technology; and in subsequent chapters the impacts of the scientific and technological revolution on other facets of the environment in which international politics is conducted.

Characteristics of scientific and technological advance

In order to appreciate the international significance of the technological revolution, it is necessary to keep in mind certain characteristics of scientific and technological advance in the modern world. These include the tendency of scientific discoveries and their engineering applications (1) to be cumulative, (2) to be accelerative, (3) to be irreversible, and (4) to diffuse widely and quite rapidly from the country of origin.

To an extent far exceeding anything in the social sciences and humanities, scientific and engineering knowledge is cumulative. Most of the important discoveries and inventions of the past 300 years appear, in retrospect, as links in a more or less continuous chain of interrelated events. There have been many false starts and dead-end streets. But previous discoveries and inventions have gone on preparing the ground for new ones. The same experiments or observations may be repeated, but nearly always in order to confirm or refute previous hypotheses. Simultaneous and independent discoveries and inventions are not uncommon. But the physical and engineering sciences have achieved a common body of concepts, theories, techniques, and modes of communication, which tends to reduce duplicative effort and to maximize accumulation of knowledge.

For various reasons the advance of science and technology tends also to be accelerative. This has been more apparent in some environments than in others. In general, this accelerative tendency becomes more marked as we approach the present. New knowledge and engineering firsts are now piling up faster than individuals and nations can adjust to them. This is what is meant by such expressions as the "technological revolution" and "runaway technology."

An error prevalent in our time, and in past times too, has been the assumption that future technological advances will be less radical and unsettling than those that have gone before. This assumption underlies a great many of the predictions that the huge area of the Soviet Union, its northerly location, short growing season, generally scanty rainfall, geographical dispersion of mineral resources, and other physical obstacles would prevent the Soviet government from ever wielding the political potential of a World Power. Similar predictions are being made today about Communist China and other underdeveloped countries. Such assertions should always be treated with scepticism. On the present record there is no basis for assuming that the process of technological advance is slowing down or that it will level out in the foreseeable future.

Technological advances, once achieved, may be regulated and (to some degree) controlled, but rarely can they be eradicated. People may yearn for the good old days before H-bombs and ballistic missiles, but mankind is stuck with these and thousands of other machines. Technological advance, in short, is not only cumulative and accelerative; it tends also to be irreversible, barring totally disruptive social catastrophe.

This qualification is very important. Social catastrophe and disorganization may not only wreck man's physical works; catastrophe might be so overwhelming as to destroy the knowledge necessary for recovery. This has happened more than once in the collapse of earlier civilizations. Something like this may have been in the mind of Sir Edward Grey, British Foreign Minister, when he said (as the armies began to march in August 1914): "The lamps are going out all over Europe; we shall not see them lit again in our lifetime." The same grim idea underlies the parody on Grey's historic words, in a recent book on (of all things) the history of bathing. Speaking of the physical breakdown of Roman civilization, the author writes: "The taps were being turned off all over Europe; they would not be turned on again for nearly 1,000 years."* We shall encounter this idea later, in Harrison Brown's profoundly disturbing thesis that our complex industrial civilization probably could not recover from the catastrophe of a third world war fought with H-bombs, ballistic missiles, and other weapons of mass destruction.

The fourth characteristic of scientific and technological advancement is its tendency to diffuse. Knowledge of scientific discoveries, new theories, and their engineering applications tend to spread from their country of origin. Much of this knowledge can be expressed and communicated in the universal language of mathematics. Hence its diffusion is not impeded by linguistic barriers to anything like the degree that it is the case with knowledge communicable mainly through verbal languages. Obstacles to diffusion exist, but they tend to be political rather than linguistic.

Security-minded politicians and military planners have tried diligently in recent years to prevent the diffusion of scientific, and especially of engineering, knowledge that might give aid to potential enemies. But diffusion continues despite tight security rules. Professional journals in mathematics, physics, chemistry, and other sciences, as well as in various branches of engineering, generally enable sophisticated specialists to keep fairly abreast of every nation's achievements in pure and applied science.

One extremely important aspect of the diffusion of scientific and engineering knowledge is the ability of the industrial late-starters to take short cuts. It is unnecessary for today's underdeveloped nations to explore all the alternative processes (many of which turned out to be dead-end streets) which characterized the slower advance of technology in the last century and earlier. The late-starters can take advantage of the mistakes as well as the triumphs of those who blazed the earlier trails. Thus it becomes possible to shorten the timetable of technological advancement. We have seen this occur with spectacular results in the Soviet Union. It is now occurring in India, China, and other nations climbing the industrial ladder. This industrial speed-up is being accelerated by intense Soviet-American rivalry to assist, and thereby to influence, the course of modernization in the underdeveloped countries.

Technological diffusion is not an isolated phenomenon. Rather it is but one of many facets of the spread of values and knowledge. The total effect of this diffusion has been to hasten the social transformation of the "traditional" societies of Asia and Africa, frequently in a manner repugnant to Western observers. We shall return later on to these broader aspects

* Quoted in *The Spectator*, London, February 26, 1960, p. 300.

of the diffusion of knowledge, for they constitute one of the inescapable givens of the environment of international politics today and in the years ahead.

The technological revolution in historical perspective

Down to about 1450 most of the tools, machines, and skills available anywhere in the world resembled rather closely those that had prevailed in the same localities a thousand years earlier. Knowledge regarding the nature and processes of the physical universe was increasing, but slowly and unevenly. Likewise uneven and infrequent had been applications of new knowledge to practical human activities such as growing food, providing clothing and shelter, transporting goods, waging war, etc. Communication of new knowledge between distant regions, and even within smaller areas was generally slow, fragmentary, and uncertain.

The nations of Western Europe were the first to break out of this scientific and technological stagnation. In Europe the rate of discovery and invention quickened around 1200 and again around 1450. Thereafter the rate of advance sharply accelerated. With some fluctuation, this acceleration has continued to the present. The sociologist P. A. Sorokin has attempted to identify and enumerate the scientific and technological advances in the Western world at various periods. Any such effort suffers from imprecision. But different orders of magnitude can be readily demonstrated and compared. Table 7.1, based upon Sorokin's data, shows very clearly the acceleration which began about 1450. Though his data come down only to 1900, the rate of scientific and technological advance is probably still rising. It should be noted that Sorokin's data relate only to the Western world, in which he includes only European and American countries. A comparable investigation of non-Western countries would probably confirm that scientific and technological stagnation persisted in most of those countries until they were subjected in the nineteenth and twentieth centuries to various intrusions and other shocks at the hands of the better-equipped Western nations.

Going behind the bare statistics of Table 7.1, one discovers technological advances in numerous directions. Without attempting a complete description, we would note the following. (1) Western peoples learned to grow more and better food per worker per unit of land. (2) They learned how to make many other kinds of labor-saving machines with which to manufacture better clothing, houses, and other amenities of what we moderns call civilized living. (3) They developed more capacious, faster, and longer-range carriers of goods, people, and messages. (4) They

TABLE 7.1   SCIENTIFIC DISCOVERIES AND TECHNOLOGICAL
ADVANCES, 700-1900 [a]

DATES	LENGTH OF PERIOD (YEARS)	SCIENTIFIC DISCOVERIES, NUMBER IN PERIOD	IMPORTANT INVENTIONS, NUMBER IN PERIOD	TOTAL NUMBER OF DISCOVERIES AND INVENTIONS IN PERIOD
701-1200	500	12	21	33
1201-1450	150	82	51	133
1451-1600	150	278	153	431
1601-1750	150	852	306	1,158
1751-1900	150	5,611	3,859	9,470

[a] Data from pp. 134-5 of *Social and Cultural Dynamics,* Vol. II, by Pitirim A. Sorokin. Copyright 1937 by American Book Co., New York.

learned how to control some of the diseases which had been rapid or gradual killers from time immemorial. (5) They invented increasingly destructive, more mobile, and longer-range instruments with which to coerce and destroy their fellow men.

A satisfactory explanation of the development of modern urban-industrial societies would have to take into account many factors, broadly social as well as specifically scientific and technological. Among the latter we would emphasize three sets of factors, in the absence of which modern industrial civilization could not have developed as it did: (1) advances in the utilization of energy, (2) improvements in structural materials, and (3) increase of scientific knowledge.

The first heading covers the basic and subsidiary inventions which record man's progressive mastery over more potent substitutes for human and animal muscles. In the aggregate this group of inventions might well be called the "energy revolution." Writers on the energy revolution have resorted to many comparisons to illustrate what has happened during the past 200 years. One engineer puts it this way:

> The four sources of labor which man has so far put to practical use are: *the muscular strength of men and animals;* the kinetic and potential mechanical *energy* of wind and water, which is released by certain changes in the distribution of molecules; the *molecular* or chemical energy stored up in matter which is released by certain changes in the structure of the molecules; the *nuclear energy* stored up in the atom, which is released by certain changes in the structure of the atom.
>
> Each stage in this advance has been matched by a change of scale in the quantity of labor power which the new robot has been able to furnish its masters. A waterfall may take the place of a whole army of slaves. And if: 1 kilogram of water, in falling 1 meter, releases

1/427 calorie; 1 kilogram of gunpowder, in combustion, releases 800 calories; 1 kilogram of petrol [motor fuel], releases 12,000 calories; 1 kilogram of uranium-235, in fission, might release some 15,000,000,000 calories.*

It was estimated a few years ago that the electrical power consumed daily in New York City was equivalent roughly to the work of three million horses, or thirty million men. Put in economic terms, "animal energy probably costs thirty to a hundred times as much as mineral energy, and human energy from three hundred to a thousand times as much."†

There can be no doubt that per capita consumption of energy, derived from other than human or animal muscles, indicates a good deal about the stage of a nation's technological advancement. A country with a high per capital consumption is one in which power-driven tools and other machines do much of the work formerly done by men and animals or not done at all. Low per capita consumption is *prima facie* evidence of technological backwardness. Table 7.2 shows the rank-order in terms of energy consumption of the twelve most populous nations, to which have been added a few other high energy-consumers. Those near the top of the list represent advanced stages of technology. Those near the bottom are still in the early stages of industrialization. They include some of the most talked-about underdeveloped countries. These low energy-consumers are typical of most of the countries of Asia, Africa, and Latin America. By comparing per capita energy consumption in any country at different dates (five dates are included in Table 7.2), one can learn something of the trend of technological advance during the period covered.

Utilization of progressively more potent forms of energy has followed the development of structural materials capable of being fashioned into more intricate shapes and capable also of withstanding higher and higher heat and greater and greater pressures, impacts, and other stresses. In the main, wood and natural stone, the principal structural materials of many preindustrial societies, fail to meet the more rigorous requirements of modern technology. Hence advances in energy utilization have depended upon developments in structural maetrials—especially metals and reinforced concrete, but also to increasing degree a variety of synthetic plastics. These, in turn, have made it possible to produce energy more efficiently: to drill deeper oil wells, to refine more useful fuels from crude oil, to generate more electricity, etc.

* From "Energy as the Key to Social Evolution," by W. Tiraspolsky, in *Impact of Science on Society,* Spring 1952, p. 5. Published by UNESCO.

† From page 65 of *World Resources and Industries,* rev. ed., by E. W. Zimmermann. Copyright 1951 by Harper & Brothers, New York; reproduced by permission.

TABLE 7.2   PER CAPITA CONSUMPTION OF ENERGY IN
SELECTED COUNTRIES [a]

POLITICAL UNIT	POPULATION 1959 (MILLIONS)	PER CAPITA ENERGY CONSUMPTION IN METRIC-TONS COAL EQUIVALENTS				
		1959	1955	1950	1937	1929
U.S.A.	177.7	7.83	7.77	7.51	5.89	6.57
Canada	17.4	5.60	5.28	6.47	4.83	5.42
United Kingdom	52.1	4.59	4.99	4.42	4.28	4.11
Australia	10.0	3.68	3.54	3.12	2.27	1.86
W. Germany [c]	52.8	3.27	3.26	2.55	....	....
U.S.S.R.	210.5	2.94	2.24	....	1.14	....
France	45.0	2.36	2.17	2.03	2.12	2.42
Italy	49.0	.99	.72	.63	.66	.61
Japan	92.7	.96	.74	.78	.93	.74
Mexico	33.3	.82	.64	.60	.44	.30
Colombia	14.1	.46	.41	.27 [b]	.14 [b]	.07
Brazil	65.7	.33	.33	.22	.13	.10
China [d]	669.0	.51	.16	....	.07	.06
Turkey	27.0	.24	.22	.26	.13	.09
Egypt	25.4	.23	.24	.15	.13	.15
India [e]	402.8	.14	.11	.10	.09	.07
Indonesia [f]	90.3	.13	.12	.06	.05	.05
Ghana	4.9	.09	.12	.09	.06	.04
Paraguay	1.7	.07	.06	.02	.01	....
Angola	4.5	.07	.04	.02	.01	.00 [b]
Pakistan	86.8	.05	.04	.04 [b]	....	....
Nigeria	33.6	.04	.03	.04	.02	.02

[a] The table covers consumption of energy derived from coal, lignite, petroleum, natural gas, and hydroelectricity, expressed in units of metric-tons coal equivalent. Countries are listed in rank-order of magnitude of energy consumption as of 1958. Energy consumpton figures, except for Soviet consumption for 1937, are from United Nations, *Statistical Papers,* Series J, nos. 1 (1952), 3 (1960), and 4 (1961). Population figures are from United Nations, *Demographic Yearbook, 1960.* Numbers are rounded to nearest tenth or hundredth.

[b] Estimated.

[c] Not including West Berlin.

[d] The statistics for China for the years 1959 and 1955 exclude Taiwan but include North Korea, North Vietnam, and Mongolian People's Republic.

[e] The statistics for India for 1950, 1937, and 1929 include what is now Pakistan.

[f] Pre-1950 statistics for Indonesia are for the Dutch East Indies.

One can trace the interrelationship of energy utilization and structural materials in any sector of industrial development. A good example is the evolution of the modern ocean-going steamship. The first steam engines were bulky primitive machines. They operated on low steam pressure; their weight-to-power ratio was high. Early steamships burned so much coal that little space was left for cargo or passengers, even with frequent stops for refueling. In order to make the power plant more efficient, higher steam pressure was required. In order to withstand higher pressure in cast- or wrought-iron boilers, more massive structures were necessary. Beyond a certain point, wooden hulls could not carry the added weight and stresses involved. Thus the development of useful ocean-going steamships lagged until stronger and lighter materials became available for hulls and engines. These came with the invention of practical steel-making processes about the middle of the nineteenth century. Invention of the steam turbine further stepped up the ratio of power to weight. But the advantages of turbine design could not be fully exploited until still stronger steels became available. Modern steel alloys enabled designers to raise steam pressures to levels inconceivable a few decades earlier. With high-pressure turbines, weight-to-power ratio was progressively reduced, less fuel per horsepower was consumed, speed was increased, and the modern highly efficient ocean-going cargo and passenger carrier reached the form in which we know it today.

The foregoing example suggests the close correlation between energy consumption and the technology of steel. Per capita steel production is, in fact, frequently used as a basis for comparing the technological advance of different economies. Steel in its simplest form is an alloy of iron and carbon. During the past century, however, metallurgists have developed scores of other alloys in which steel is combined with manganese or nickel or chromium or other metals to produce structural materials of greater hardness or toughness or tensile strength or resistance to corrosion or other superior properties. These steel alloys have made possible not only the modern ocean-going steamship but also today's railway and highway vehicles, aircraft, machine tools, skyscrapers, agricultural machinery, military weapons, and many other kinds of structures and machines. The steel-alloy complex is manifestly a most useful indicator of technological advance.

Production of basic steel and its more complicated alloys consumes huge quantities of energy, chiefly in the forms of coal and electrical power. Except for aircraft, steel is the most widely used material in machines—powered by steam turbines, internal-combustion engines, and electric motors—which are in turn large energy consumers. Hence comparative statistics of steel production will generally be found to correlate more or less closely with energy consumption.

A third useful indicator of technological advance is the proportion of a nation's workers employed in agriculture and related occupations. In preindustrial societies this proportion is invariably high—generally around

75 percent. As late as 1870, agriculture, forestry and fishing occupied over half of all American workers. Today the farm population of the United States is less than 10 percent and is still declining. This trend indicates, among other things, the degree to which power-driven machines have taken the place of men and animals in the production of food and natural fibers.

A fourth indicator is per capita gross national product—that is, the per capita value of all goods and services which an economy produces. Since the productivity of labor tends to vary in proportion to the degree to which mineral fuels and hydroelectricity take the place of human and animal muscles, per capita GNP tends likewise to correlate more or less closely with energy consumption per capita.

One should take care, however, not to assume too specific and immediate a relation between scientific discoveries and their engineering applications, at least not until quite recently. In the words of a recent government report, prepared by the Research Institute of Stanford University for the Senate Committee on foreign Relations:* "Until modern times technology consisted of the slowly accumulated lore of the practitioners of the various arts and crafts; it had comparatively little direct relation to science."

Moving towards the present, however, one finds the process of invention becoming more and more closely related to new observations and theories in pure science. In our own time, the Stanford Report continues, "the technologist who designs a new space probe or a new hormone medicine or a new insecticide bases his work very directly on quite sophisticated theories which have been tested by the scientific method."

Though many important inventions are not easily connected with specific scientific theories, it is safe to conclude that the military weapons, non-military machinery, roads and buildings, medicines and most of the other man-made features of our modern environment would never have come into existence but for the upsurge of scientific inquiry and knowledge during the past three or four centuries.

Table 7.3, taken from the Stanford Report cited just above, illustrates schematically the sequence of events that may be triggered off by a new scientific discovery. Commenting on this diagram, the report continues:

> The main sequence . . . moves from top to bottom . . . that is, from scientific progress (discovery) through new technology (inventions) through practical adoption and spread of the new ideas and techniques (innovation and diffusion) to economic, social, and political adjustments

* From "Possible Nonmilitary Scientific Developments and Their Potential Impact on Foreign Policy Problems of the United States," prepared pursuant to S. Res. 336, 85th Congress, and S. Res. 31, 86th Cong. Government Printing Office, Washington, D.C., 1959.

(social change) to impacts on foreign policy. The sequence, however, is really circular, for social, economic, and political considerations exert a powerful influence on the direction of discovery and invention. . . . Various kinds of social change may encourage or retard scientific discovery. Invention sometimes precedes [scientific discovery]. . . . More and more, however, the main sequence is coming to be from progress in scientific understanding to achievement of desired technological applications, to their practical introduction and spread. This is the normal method of work in organized scientific research and development today.

TABLE 7.3　SEQUENCES WHICH LINK SCIENCE TO FOREIGN POLICY [a]

		MEANING OF TERM	FURTHER EXPLANATION
	DISCOVERY (SCIENCE)	Acquiring new knowledge	Interplay between theory and observation
	INVENTION (TECHNOLOGY)	Creating new ways for accomplishing purposes	Applied science and development engineering
	INNOVATION	Launching an invention	Introduction of a new product, process, or social technique; entrepreneurship, industrial leadership, social pioneering
	DIFFUSION	Spreading science and technology to new places or groups	Education, training, selling, extension work, international technical assistance
	SOCIAL CHANGE	Modifying customs, institutions, ways of thinking	New policies, new legislation, new social habits, new education
	FOREIGN POLICY	Responses to international conditions, in the light of national aims	Influenced by scientific developments and also influences them

(Left margin labels: MAIN SEQUENCE, FEEDBACKS)

[a] There are many interrelations and feedbacks. Scientific discovery may directly induce social changes and foreign policy changes by altering the climate of ideas. Various kinds of social change encourage or retard scientific discovery or turn the attention of scientists to new fields. Invention sometimes precedes discovery. For example, in animal husbandry the fact that mixing minute quantities of antibiotics in feedstuffs substantially increases the growth rate of poultry and pigs was observed and widely used before scientists could explain why it worked. More and more, however, the main sequence is coming to be from progress in scientific understanding to achievement of desired technological applications, to their practical introduction and spread. This is the normal method of work in organized scientific research and development today.

International politics in technological perspective

Table 7.4 presents in parallel columns some of the major technological advances and events and trends in international politics during the past 300 years. Are these two sets of events significantly related? Today probably most people would answer yes. But what does such an answer imply? Are technological advances to be conceived as the "cause" of international events and of changes in the political relationships of states? Statements to this effect certainly are common enough.

Take, for example, a sentence from one of the standard works on resources and technology: that the invention of the basic steel-making furnace (which made it possible to produce good steel from the acidic ores of Alsace-Lorraine) *"led inevitably* to Germany's industrial hegemony on the continent" of Europe during the last quarter of the nineteenth century. Construed literally, this statement ascribes a deterministic causal relationship between a technological advance (invention of basic steel furnace) and an industrial development which had important political implications. We doubt whether that is what the author intended to convey. Our interpretation of the statement would be as follows:

The invention of the basic steel furnace *made it possible* to produce good steel out of acidic ores. A lot of such ores *were present* inside Germany. German industrialists *took advantage* of the new process to expand their steel production. Thus a change in one environmental factor (steel-making process) enabled German industrialists to make use of another environmental factor (acidic iron ore) and thereby to outstrip the steel production of other European nations and achieve the "industrial hegemony" which they did, in fact, achieve.

Now let us try to state in general terms the principle involved. New tools and machines alter the range of opportunities and limitations, with respect to the objectives and strategies of interacting nations. The same invention may expand or contract the opportunities of both sides. Or more typically the invention may serve the purposes of one to the disadvantage of the other. With this principle in mind, let us proceed to examine the relations of technological advances to (1) the formation and defensibility of territorial-nation-states, (2) the historic expansion of Europe overseas, (3) the subsequent contraction and break-up of European colonial empires, (4) the bipolarization of political potentials in the society of nations in our time, and (5) new patterns in the conduct of international statecraft.

The European States System—from which today's international political system is derived—is conventionally dated from the Peace of Westphalia

TABLE 7.4   TECHNOLOGICAL ADVANCE IN THE CONTEXT OF
INTERNATIONAL POLITICS

PERIOD	INTERNATIONAL CONTEXT	INVENTIONS BROUGHT INTO GENERAL USE
AS OF 1650	Close of Thirty Years War; Peace of Westphalia; Formation of modern European States System	Navigating instruments (compass, and primitive latitude-calculating instruments); ships capable of trans-oceanic voyages, and able to sail fairly "close to the wind"; printing with movable type; relatively immobile cannon firing solid projectiles; primitive small arms
1650-1815	Intermittent wars in Europe; American Revolution; French Revolutionary and Napoleonic Wars; Peace of Vienna	Steam engine, applied to pumping out mines, textile manufacture, and to primitive steamboats; mobile "horse artillery"; standard smooth-bore musket; primitive rifled small arms and explosive artillery shells
1815-1914	Industrialization of Western Europe; spread of industrialization to U.S.A. and Japan, and beginning elsewhere; expansion of European colonial empires in Asia and Africa; recognition of U.S.A. and Japan as Great Powers; several local but no general wars	Progress in metallurgy, especially in steel-making; application of steam power to overland transport, with development of extensive railroad systems in Europe, N. America, and elsewhere; progressive displacement of sail by steam at sea; development of steam turbine and introduction of oil-fired boilers Improved agricultural techniques, resulting in increased production of food and fiber. Rapid growth of chemical industries late in period, including process for "fixing" atmospheric nitrogen, and development of high-yield chemical explosives; electric telegraph, telephone, generator, motor, light, wireless telegraph; internal combustion engine; many applications: automobiles, submarine, aircraft, etc.; great increase in military firepower: marine mines and torpedoes, rapid-firing guns, and artillery
1914 TO DATE	World War I; Russian Revolution; recurrent crises provoked by aggressive actions of Fascist Italy, Nazi Germany, and Japan; World War II; breakup of colonial empires;	Further progress in metallurgy, especially in ferro-alloys and light metals; high octane motor fuels; synthetic substitutes for natural materials: fibers, polymers, plastics, etc.; "miracle" drugs: sulfa, antibiotics; antivirus vaccines, etc.; hard-surfaced highways and large-capacity motor vehicles, radio, radar, and television; mobile armored military

PERIOD	INTERNATIONAL CONTEXT	INVENTIONS BROUGHT INTO GENERAL USE
1914 TO DATE (cont.)	spread of Communism; radical redistribution of political potentials in society of nations; Cold War between Communist Camp and Anti-Communist Coalition; massive political, economic, and social changes in Asia, Africa, and Latin America	equipment: tanks, etc.; rocket artillery; poison-gas and (still unused) bacteriological weapons; military airpower: manned craft and missiles; nuclear fission and fusion; atomic bombs, hydrogen bombs, nuclear powered ships, etc.; artificial satellites; air-mass analysis and other advances in meteorology

(1648-50), which terminated the religious wars that followed the Protestant Reformation. In actuality, the system was in process of formation much earlier, and its evolution was not completed until much later. This period of formation coincided with the introduction of a military technology utilizing the explosive properties of gunpowder (a mixture of carbon, sulfur, and a nitrate called saltpeter).

The invention and improvement of firearms, especially cannon, made castles and walled towns increasingly difficult to defend. The walls could be knocked down and the defenders overwhelmed. As artillery became more powerful, and as more mobile gun-carriages were developed, it became possible to defend larger geographical areas. More powerful weapons, together with some improvement in roads, likewise enlarged the area which could be policed and administered from a central capital. Thus the modern territorial state supplanted in due course the castle and fortified town as the basic political unit in Europe.

The predominant concern of the rulers of these states was to make their territory as secure (that is, as impenetrable to military attack) as possible. In pursuit of this objective, much attention was devoted to establishing strong frontiers. Among the coveted kinds of naturally strong frontiers seacoasts ranked high. A state that was wholly insular, like Great Britain, enjoyed an especially strong strategical position. Other types of strong natural boundaries included mountain ranges, other rough terrain, rivers, jungles and deserts.

National wealth, in materials and labor, was allocated to strengthening a country's borders, to make it more "impenetrable" to invasion. Elaborate systems of frontier fortifications were built. Roads and railways were designed to serve military purposes first, and commercial purposes second.

The large-scale development of railways rendered it possible to defend and administer huge countries such as the United States and the Russian Empire.

Geographical space—between the state's borders and its vital centers of habitation and economic production—was likewise considered a strategic asset. Where space was deemed inadequate to provide security, a buffer zone of dependent states—satellites in the idiom of today—could sometimes be created to absorb the initial shock of military invasion.

By the end of World War I (1918) it was apparent that increases in the mobility and firepower of weapons were seriously undermining the military security of all but the very largest and strongest countries. A long sequence of inventions had multiplied the per capita fire power of military forces. Development of mines, torpedoes, and submarines provided new and effective weapons with which to attack shipping, especially essential to insular states. Aircraft, though still in their infancy, provided more than a hint of the possibility of overleaping even the most strongly fortified frontiers.

Subsequent development of airpower transformed this hint into fearsome reality. In World War II, it became possible for the first time in history to lay waste industrial installations and crowded cities deep inside a country's interior, without blasting a path across fortified land frontiers or storming ashore on strongly defended open beaches. The effect was reminiscent of the destructive impact of artillery on medieval castles and walled towns.

Down through World War II, however, geographical space still counted heavily as a defensive cushion against military attack, even against aerial bombardment. But no country in western Europe proved large enough to absorb the shock of modern mobile warfare. None possessed sufficient geographical space for protective dispersal of vital economic activities. In Russia, on the contrary, armies could retreat for hundreds of miles, and factories could migrate to the comparative security of inner Asia.

Post-1945 increases in the destructiveness and range of airborne weapons systems have progressively depreciated this asset, even for the states with the greatest geographical depth. Today no country, however large, could hope to escape devastation, probably crippling devastation, if attacked with the most destructive weapons now available. There is literally no place to hide. In the historic seesaw struggle between offensive and defensive weapons systems, the offensive has decisively outrun the defensive. Some experts optimistically hope that the defense will eventually catch up, as it has always done in the past. There are rumors of anti-missile missiles and other defensive innovations that might restore in some measure the impenetrability of territorial states, at least states of continental or subcontinental size. But it is noteworthy that some of the most knowledgeable and imaginative scientists and engineers are generally less optimistic on this issue than are the politicians and professional military experts.

The possible irrecoverable loss of territorial impenetrability—the inability with any known means to prevent deep and devastating penetration of any country's geographical space—is one of the inescapable givens of the transnational environment today. This consequence of weapons development poses an unprecedented and very likely insoluble military problem for strategists and planners.

We shall return to this military problem in Chapter 8 which deals with recent developments in weapons technology. Here it will suffice to say that if it should turn out that no effective *military* defense can be perfected to protect nations against devastating airborne attacks, future historians, from the perspective of the twenty-first century (if somehow irretrievable catastrophe is avoided, or if, in case catastrophe occurs there are any historians left to interpret the past), may well conclude that the combination of thermonuclear explosives, chemical and bacteriological weapons, and long-range airborne and ballistic carriers made the territorial state as unviable as a unit for providing security as the medieval castle and walled town became after the development of artillery.

Turning to the second issue—the historic expansion of European power and influence overseas—the significance of technology is immediately apparent. This significance can be dated from the notable inventions which set the stage and progressively facilitated the voyages of discovery and exploration which preceded and accompanied the earlier stages of European empire-building. These inventions included improvements in sailing-ship design which enabled the vessel to sail closer to the wind, and navigating instruments which reduced the perils of venturing far out onto the oceans. Without compass, various instruments for taking latitude, and clocks to keep track of longitude, the Americas and most of Asia and Africa might have remained *terra incognita*.

These developments in navigation coincided with the introduction of firearms in Europe. The explorers took cannon and primitive hand arms with them. Superiority in weapons enabled small parties of Europeans to overwhelm non-European populations nearly everywhere. In addition, the European conquerors wielded a comparably decisive superiority in transport and communications, in agricultural and industrial equipment and techniques, and in still other spheres of activity. The technological differential, moreover, greatly increased during the centuries of European empire-building. The American demographer Dudley Kirk sums up the cumulative impact as follows:

> The quantitative expansion of Europeans cannot be disassociated from the process of industrialization and modernization that made it possible. The growth of the European population at home and the settlement of large overseas areas by Europeans was, of course, dependent on the material power placed in their hands by technological advance. For generations Europeans enjoyed a monopoly of those military and economic skills that give power in the modern world. These flourish today only in strong industrial civilizations broadly based on healthy, literate, and urbanized populations indoctrinated with strong material aspirations and with national loyalties transcending familial and local ties. The world hegemony of European and especially Western European countries has been founded on the material advance of her population.*

The geographical extent of European expansion overseas is well known. By the end of the nineteenth century (to recapitulate what was said in Chapter 3), nearly all of Africa, much of Asia, and the islands of the Pacific and Indian oceans had been partitioned among the empires of Britain, France, Germany, Netherlands, Italy, Portugal and Spain. China, the largest and most populous country of Asia, remained nominally independent, but was in fact divided into Russian, German, Japanese, British, and French "spheres of special interest." Only Japan, throughout the Afro-Asian Realm, proved able to meet European empire-builders on their own terms, largely, it would appear, because Japan's rulers succeeded in carrying through a program of forced-draft industrialization and militarization after 1870.

If the expansion of Europe can be regarded as the predominant feature of world politics from the seventeenth to the end of the nineteenth century, the steep decline of European power and influence overseas is clearly one of the principal developments of the first half of the twentieth century. This decline, it would appear, derives from two sets of events among others: (1) the break-up of European colonial empires and (2) the rise of the continental-size Superpowers, the United States and the Soviet Union. Both of these shifts in the world structure of political potential appear to have significant technological aspects.

By the end of the nineteenth century, European colonial authority had come to rest upon a combination of visible military force on the scene and a less tangible reputation of invincibility. Because of this reputation, which rested in turn upon technological superiority, it was gener-

---

* From p. 254 of *Europe's Population in the Interwar Years*, by Dudley Kirk. Published in 1946, by the Economic and Financial Department of the League of Nations.

ally unnecessary to maintain large bodies of troops in the colonies to sustain the civil authority of imperial administrators.

The world wars of 1919 and 1939 fatally undermined these regimes. Europeans turned their superior weapons and technological skills against each other with deadly efficacy. In the process they destroyed or weakened the human and material resources which had previously sustained their political potential overseas. The two wars, especially the second, also dealt a body blow to the myths of European invincibility and the white man's special aptitude for technological advance. Japanese conquests demonstrated, to the humiliation of the West in general and of Britain and America in particular, the ability of an Asian people to learn the skills and to use the machines of Western technological civilization. Later in the war, Americans (and to a lesser degree Europeans too) taught Chinese, Indians, and other Asian peoples to use and maintain motor vehicles, modern military weapons, electronic equipment, and other complicated apparatus. Colonial subjects increasingly rejected the myth that non-European races were incapable of absorbing advanced technology. At the end of World War II, Americans and Europeans were admitting what should have been evident decades earlier: that Chinese, Indians, Indonesians, Africans, or any other preindustrial population were probably as capable of achieving and operating an urban-industrial civilization as anyone else.

In the words of Dudley Kirk, the American demographer quoted above,

> non-European peoples have been slow in achieving the material advance of the West, not because of any inherent incapacity but because its achievement rests in a very wide complex of factors involving a fundamental cultural revolution and a sharp break with old patterns of thought and custom pervading every phase of life. This cultural revolution takes time, but it is occurring and with increasing rapidity and explosive force as advances in communication have brought non-European peoples into closer contact with the West. Everywhere contact with the physical power and comforts of European civilization have stimulated imitation. . . .

The second aspect of the relative decline of European political potential —the development of greater capabilities in the United States and the Soviet Union—appears also to derive in part from technological developments. Railroads, improved highways, motor vehicles, aircraft, and still other advances gradually provided systems of inland transport and communications upon which to build effective political communities on a continental scale. Increased military mobility and striking power on land.

and the development of airborne weapons of ever-increasing range and destructiveness, made it more and more difficult to provide effective defense systems in the relatively small countries of western Europe. The ever-increasing scale and cost of military weapons gave an advantage (which tended to grow) to large states based upon the resources and labor of compact continental areas. Developments in naval weapons, coincident with the progressive breakdown of European imperial systems, reduced the probability that the former imperial sovereigns could continue to count on the labor and resources of rich colonial areas overseas in case of war.

Turning to the impacts of the technological revolution on the conduct of international statecraft, one can identify effects of varying significance. These effects cover the whole range of instruments and techniques described in Chapter 3. We have singled out a few of them for special comment here.

Most people these days take modern rapid communications for granted. Yet television became a going concern less than twenty years ago. Radio broadcasting on a significant scale is less than forty years old. Wireless telegraphy in code dates from the early years of this century. Commercial airlines did not exist before World War I and became important only in the later 1930's. Telephones did not come into general use until near the end of the nineteenth century. In short, millions of people alive today can remember a time when rapid communications meant railroads, telegraphs, and a few telephone lines—and nothing more.

Before the era of rapid communications, physical distance imposed severe limitations on the conduct of international statecraft. When, with the establishment of the United States in the 1780's, the society of nations began to spread beyond the European subcontinent, these limitations had some remarkable effects. The early years of American diplomacy provide many instances when it took months to send a minister to his foreign post or to bring him home, weeks or months to receive his dispatches or to send him new instructions.

Increased mobility and more rapid communications changed all that. On the one hand, ambassadors are more strictly controlled from the foreign office; on the other, they can bring their first-hand observations and judgments more quickly and effectively to bear on policy-making processes. Top officials of different states confront each other face to face more frequently. In recent years diplomatic junketing has added a new dimension. The travels of an American President or Secretary of State, a British Prime Minister, a Soviet Premier, and other heads of government and foreign ministers, as well as scores and hundreds of legislators, lesser civil servants, military officials, and others, performs a symbolic function formerly reserved to naval ships. This is the function known as *showing the flag.*

The increasing substitution of diplomats for gunboats in the performance of this symbolic function may have greater significance than is generally appreciated. Complaints that state visits rarely settle anything, and hence are a waste of time, human energy, and the taxpayers' money, miss the whole point. This new mode of showing the flag emphasizes the upgrading of nonmilitary techniques of statecraft, and the relative decline of gunboat diplomacy. Not that display of military force has lost its significance. Far from it! But nonmilitary public relations have gained in importance and may play a steadying role in the volatile and changing atmosphere in which international statecraft is carried on in our time.

State visits may or may not resolve specific conflicts ot national interests and policies. The most important function of summit conferences and the like may be simply to keep the talk going, in the hope (sometimes justified by events) that time will soften seemingly irreconcilable attitudes and policies. Periodical meetings of heads of government and other high-ranking officials provide public gestures of amity and good will, even when no resolution of conflicting interests is immediately within reach. Much of what goes on in the Security Council and in the Assembly of the United Nations, and in the public conferences of other international organizations, has this kind of symbolic significance. These activities, carried on more or less in public view, can provide a sort of lubricant for the gears and bearings of the international political system, though (as exemplified by the summit conference debacle of 1960) such beneficial effects are not always achieved.

Without modern rapid communications these symbolic activities and their impacts on public opinion in the various countries would be severely curtailed. Imagine state visits on the present-day scale, or the current functioning of international organizations, under the conditions of transport and communication prevailing before the days of planes and radio!

Development of rapid printing processes, cheap paper, regular mail delivery, railroads, all-weather highways, motorized highway vehicles, planes, telegraph and radio, movies and television, *and increasingly literate populations,* have brought the "public"—the whole people, or large masses of them—into the process of statecraft. When Thomas Jefferson justified the American Declaration of Independence as a manifesto required by a "decent respect to the opinions of mankind," he was speaking metaphorically. Today, however, thanks to the so-called mass media, the opinions of mankind have a bearing on national and international decisions to a degree inconceivable only a few decades ago.

This transformation can be graphically illustrated by the diagram presented on page 142. This model depicts a greatly oversimplified international political system consisting of only two states. In the model g stands for "government"; and c, for "constituency," or public, as follows:

STATE 1   STATE 2

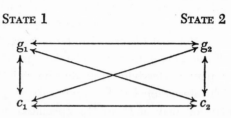

Before the era of modern rapid communications and mass media, the relative importance of the different channels of communication was very different from the state of affairs today. The transnational channels g_1——c_2, g_2——c_1, by use of which governments seek to build fires in the rear of their diplomatic or military adversaries, have become much more heavily utilized. Increase in tourism, letter correspondence, educational exchange, and other people-to-people contacts and transactions (c_1——c_2), have likewise radically altered the environment in which statecraft is carried on.

One could cite many examples of the greatly increased sensitivity of governments to foreign attitudes and opinions. Here are a few selected from a few days in early 1960. The Department of State intervened to secure further reprieve for Caryl Chessman, under sentence of death in California, on the ground that execution of this globally controversial criminal at that juncture might evoke embarrassing demonstrations during President Eisenhower's trip to South America. The United States took no punitive actions against Castro's violently anti-American policies in Cuba—again, lest such steps evoke hostile demonstrations elsewhere in Latin America and provide more grist for the Communist propaganda mills. The savage racial struggle in South Africa evoked a wave of protests in every continent. Finally, in the same short period, President Eisenhower decided (apparently contrary to technical advice) to offer the Russians a continuation of the ban on nuclear-weapons testing. Commenting on this last decision, Arthur Krock asserted bluntly (in *The New York Times*, March 31, 1960): "Once again in the making of United States high policy the controlling factor is world opinion, the approval of which is the common goal of the East-West contestants in the 'cold war.' " * Can anyone imagine governments paying so much attention to "world opinion" during the Napoleonic Wars?

Modern "message carriers" may produce unintended as well as intended effects abroad. Take, for example, the repeated Soviet outbursts of aggressive vilification and threats which at critical junctures have re-solidified the Atlantic Alliance. Or consider the effects of American movies abroad. There may be disagreement among Americans as to whether Hollywood projects the image of the good life that is predominant within the United States these days. But no one who has observed the impacts of American movies on European and other foreign audiences can have much doubt as to the damaging effect which these culture bearers have inflicted on American prestige abroad.

Technological advances in transport and communications have radically altered the methods of collecting and processing intelligence. Cameras of various kinds in planes and in space satellites, seismographs and Geiger counters, and electronic warning devices are but a few of the newer mechanisms (many of them ultrasecret) which enable intelligence agencies to penetrate the frontiers of other states and keep track of activities beyond reach by direct observation. Public astonishment over the almost incredible detail of pictures taken by a camera in the U-2 plane, from an altitude of thirteen miles, merely highlighted (in the spring of 1960) the time lag between technological achievements and public appreciation thereof in the swiftly moving currents of the continuing technological revolution.

Perhaps the most important of all the impacts of the technological revolution on the conduct of statecraft may turn out, in the long run, to be the upgrading of nonmilitary instruments and techniques of statecraft. Three sets of events (to be taken up more fully in the next chapter) have fundamentally altered the utility of large-scale military action as a technique of statecraft. One of these is the enormous increase of fire power which has occurred in this century, and in particular since 1945. In the same category is the much less publicized advance in techniques for paralyzing a nation by means of epidemic diseases and bacteriological and chemical poisons. The second set of events is the still increasing (now almost global) range of airborne and ballistic carriers of nuclear bombs and other instruments of mass destruction. The third and most decisive set of events is the lag which has occurred in the development of defensive means against the weapons of mass destruction. Not the least important

---

* From "The Controlling Factor in High Nuclear Policy." Copyright 1960 by New York Times Co.; reproduced by permission.

aspect of this lag in the technology of defense is the apparent inability to control the geographical diffusion of radioactive fallout following nuclear explosions.

As long as two or more nations possess the means of long-range crippling attack, and no nation has any effective means of defense against such attack, military stalemate seems likely to continue. Even if antimissile missiles or other fairly effective defensive means are perfected, the danger of atmospheric contamination from even the most distant nuclear explosions may stay the hands at the push buttons. In the meantime, the more imaginative statesmen in every country are experimenting with new variants of less dangerous modes of action—diplomacy, public relations, propaganda and subversion, economic pressures and inducements, economic aid and technical assistance—as described in Chapter 4.

Technological objectives in national strategy

Scientific and technological advance has become more and more important as an objective of national strategy closely linked to the external relations of states. This objective finds expression in various contexts. One is the desire to make _political_ independence more effective and meaningful by reducing a nation's _technological_ dependence on other nations. Closely associated with this objective have been the more or less constant efforts of the Great Powers to overmatch the military capabilities of nations regarded as potential enemies. In our time, scientific and technological advance has become in itself a symbol of national prestige, an indicator of status and rank in the international political system.

Desire to reduce economic dependence on other nations is, at its roots, essentially a problem of technological advance. This desire has been historically associated with protective tariffs and other policies designed to stimulate diversified economic growth. Throughout most of the nineteenth century, Western European nations, Britain in particular, were the leading producers of manufactured goods of most kinds—clothing, household furnishings, industrial machinery, railway equipment, etc. Until well into the twentieth century, the predominant pattern of international commerce was the exchange of European manufactures for foodstuffs, industrial fibers, minerals and other primary materials produced in the main under conditions of poverty and near-slavery in Asia, Africa, and parts of Latin America.

Much has been written about the _political_ leverages latent in this pattern: latent, that is to say, in the ability of the technologically advanced nations to provide or to withhold on their own terms the manufactures desired by the primary producers overseas. A broadly political-economic as well as a narrowly military conception of national security has underlain nearly all the arguments for protective tariffs, import quotas, manufacturing subsidies, and other devices designed to promote diversified economic development.

In nonsocialistic economies, such protective policies have also generally worked to the advantage of private business interests. Such interests have carried on a great deal of hypocritical propaganda about protecting the national interests of the country. But one should not allow the self-seeking pressures of private groups to obscure the larger *political* motivations, without which the private pressures might in most instances have been much less successful.

In recent years rapid technological advance to stimulate economic diversification has become a key objective of the new nations of Asia and Africa for *political* reasons, and also of some of the older but still economically retarded countries of Latin America. Most of the underdeveloped countries were formerly colonies of European empires or at least economic vassals of the older industrialized economies. Most of these former political colonies and economic vassals were heavily dependent upon imported manufactures. They were influenced—one is almost justified in saying compelled—by the policies of the industrial Powers to remain producers chiefly of primary materials.

Classical economists justified this division of labor on the principle of comparative advantage. They argued that it was economically advantageous for many of the producers of primary materials to continue to depend on the older industrial economies for most of their manufactures, transport, and business services. But this argument has rarely carried much appeal in the underdeveloped countries. The United States, within a few years of their secession from the British Empire, took a position which is now almost universally held throughout Asia, Africa, and Latin America: that a diversified economy is a necessary precondition of effective political independence. Hence the widespread demands in these countries for rapid and diversified industrialization, and the technological know-how to make this possible, regardless of economic costs and the dogmas of classical economists. The basic premise of many Asian, African, and Latin American political leaders seems to be: It is better to be poor and free, if the price of affluence is continued dependence upon former colonial or quasi-colonial masters.

Closely linked with this demand is the not always consistent demand to conquer poverty and misery as well as to be free. The British scientist, civil servant, and novelist C. P. Snow has caught this mood in the following eloquent passage:

> Through luck we got in first with the scientific-industrial revolution; as a result, our lives became, on the average, healthier, longer, more comfortable to an extent that had never been imagined; it doesn't become us to tell our Chinese and Indian friends that that kind of progress is not worth having.
>
> We know what it is like to live among the shops, the cars, the radios, of Leicester, and Orebro, and Des Moines. We know what it is like to ask the point of it all, and to feel the Swedish sadness or the American disappointment or the English Welfare State discontent. But the Chinese and Indians would like the chance of being well-fed enough to ask the point of it all. They are in search of what Leicester, Orebro and Des Moines take for granted, food, extra years of life, modest comforts. . . . *Their determination to get these things is likely in the next thirty years to prove the strongest social force on earth.** [Italics added.]

The military incentive for technological advancement is well known. American naval expansion in the 1890's provided strong incentive for improving the techniques of American steel making. The desire to escape from the crippling vulnerability to naval blockade was an even stronger incentive for the forced-draft growth of German chemical industries in the generation before World War I. The aviation industries in numerous countries owed their rapid growth during the 1930's in considerable degree to the rather general movement to rearm in the face of deteriorating international relations. Mobilization of American, British, and Canadian scientists to beat the Germans in the race to produce the first atomic bombs will long remain the classic example of technological achievement under military pressure. Military incentives have accelerated technological advance in many fields. These range from basic metallurgy to synthetic substitutes for scarce materials and the most complicated electronic and other machines. It has become axiomatic in our time that neglect of science and engineering can produce swift and disastrous repercussion on the state's military capabilities.

We come finally to a related but much more complex and subtle conception. That is the idea that scientific and technological leadership *per se* is a symbol of national prestige, and hence of superior political potential in the international system. Competition for scientific "beats" and "firsts," often with no evident or immediate military applications in

---

* From "Man in Society," by C. P. Snow, in *The Observer*, July 13, 1958. Copyright by The Observer Ltd.; reproduced by permission of publisher and author.

sight, has become part of the apparatus of the Cold War. It is widely accepted today that being the first to put a dog or a monkey or a man into outer space, for example, profoundly affects a nation's ability to command respect and deference and generally to make its policies prevail.

Klaus Knorr (director of the Center of International Studies at Princeton University and very knowledgeable regarding military factors in international politics) has expressed doubt that outer-space research is likely, "during the next twenty-five years . . . to produce revolutionary changes in world affairs." But he has this to say about the prestige value of scientific and engineering achievements on this new frontier:

> Scientific and technological prestige will be a major objective motivating nations to participate in and, indeed, try to excel in space activities. In the present age, scientific and technological achievement is valued highly. . . . Such achievement is taken as a sign of national "vigor" and—because of the exceedingly close (actual or assumed) relationship between such achievements and military potential, if not military capability—also as the symbol, if not the substance, of military power. Space activities being especially glamorous, consider-able advantages of international prestige are likely to accrue to the nation which assumes leadership in this enterprise. The Soviet Union has understood this and derived great propaganda benefits from its early space successes, thus rendering world public opinion still more sensitive to spectacular space activities. Although some American officials . . . have affirmed that in outer space activities we should not engage in a prestige race with the Soviet Union, it is clear to others that we are so engaged. Thus Mr. George V. Allen, director of the United States Information Agency [in the Eisenhower Administration], declared to the House Science and Astronautics Committee: ". . . our space program has an importance far beyond the field of the activity itself, in that it bears on almost every aspect of our relations with people in other countries and on their view of us as compared with the U.S.S.R. Our space program may be con-sidered as a measure of our vitality and our ability to compete with a formidable rival, and as a criterion of our ability to maintain technological eminence worthy of emulation by other peoples." . . .
> The prestige effects may indeed turn out to be the major con-sequence of outer space activities in the international system. One has only to imagine the impact if Communist China appeared suddenly as the third space power, and countries that are now "neutral" in the East-West conflict were disposed to generalize from Communist space successes about the superiority of Communist technology and of the social and economic system which achieved such competence in one generation. Preoccupation with the prestige effect would be greatly reinforced if leadership in space exploration were widely equated with preponderant military strength, and outerspace obviously lends itself to the demonstration of military capabilities. Space success

might thus stiffen the negotiating attitudes of governments even though this were not warranted by the hard military facts. The U.S.S.R. and the United States, and perhaps some other countries as well, may for these reasons continue to vie for outer space supremacy even though doing so constitutes a net drain on economic resources and is of insignificant or marginal worth in terms of real military strength.*

The continuing technological revolution

A good many people these days, intelligent people, and well educated, appear to experience the greatest difficulty imagining a future dominated by continuing technological advance. They may appreciate more or less the social consequences of what has already occurred. But inability to imagine a future radically different from the present is as prevalent in this sphere as in others. For this reason we bring this chapter to a close with two previews of the continuing technological revolution that the scientists and engineers have in store for us. The first is by Dr. J. D. Williams, chief of the mathematical division of the RAND Corporation, research subsidiary of the United States Air Force.†

Many discoveries may rank with—or outrank—the steam engine and the lathe as key elements in the story of human technological development. Synthetic materials may have this importance. The nuclear chain reaction certainly does. Thanks to the confluence of the explosion of knowledge with our advanced technical position and our wealth, we are in a position to develop and exploit many of these keys. Unfortunately we cannot do so indefinitely without regard to the consequences. The nuclear chain reaction in a world of political anarchy will always be the textbook example. Another example is the case of the general-purpose antibiotics in the presence of the biological explosion [to be discussed later in chapter 13 on demographic factors and trends]. On the other hand, some developments will be essential. For example, it is time to stop talking about the weather and, instead, attend to it. Recent evidence suggests that the next ice age may be about to close in.

Another recent technological development of great significance is the feedback loop—the servomechanism—built largely of cheap, reliable electronic parts. This device permits a machine to engage in a limited way in self-criticism, to examine its own work and to make small improvements in its output. Significantly, machines may now become sophisticated at a moderate increase in cost. As a consequence

---

it is now feasible to design machines, for example, to do some tasks which are repeated only ten thousand times, rather than tasks which are repeated millions of times.

We had scarcely begun to exploit the improved feedback loop when the electronic computer appeared. This new machine already reaches speeds of thousands of operations per second with high reliability and can carry within its memory the instructions needed for an almost endlessly long and complex sequence of operations. This computer can be used to control the behavior of another machine. Now, rather than use a costly special-purpose machine to perform some phase of a manufacturing process, we can use a more versatile machine, controlled by a computer, to perform more of it. And, by changing the instructions in the computer, we can use the same machine to make a different product. Elaborate as well as simple operations can be performed, and the machine can be used for quite short production runs. It can even construct prototypes. Thus the impetus toward mechanization has increased tremendously, presenting another complex and challenging set of problems with tantalizing potentialities.

The concept of an economic paradise-on-earth may be no idle dream. It is possible that we could reach a stage where any given set of goods within our resources, from food to H-bombs, could be created with ease. The productive effort might involve a fraction of our labor force, or we might have our entire labor force work for a fraction of the time. But there are difficulties on both paths.

In order to operate with a fractional labor force, for instance, we must discover how to provide goods for those who do not toil. To employ the fractional-time labor force, on the other hand, we must as a people achieve a new level of intellectual competence; for the balance between manual and intellectual workers in a predominantly automated economy would doubtless be very different from the present balance. Yet we have recently placed most of our school system in the hands of people preoccupied with physical culture, togetherness and intellectually trivial curricula.

I have mentioned only the technical and economic feasibility of automation, from which one would infer that an explosive development is at hand. But any such development will undoubtedly encounter massive inertia from the vested interests of labor and capital—a resistance which will appreciably retard the process. It may, in fact, seem desirable to proceed slowly, to reduce the pains of adaptation. But this course also has its peculiar dangers. For example, more primitive populations, less cumbered by vested interests, may let the explosion run free and soon outdistance us technologically. That this would drive us out of the world's markets could be the least serious effect. It could also alienate those peoples who now think it well to stand with us because we are technologically strong. Almost certainly a technologically superior foe would sooner or later overwhelm us. . . .

Clearly, on both a global and national scale, we must make important, difficult and sometimes unpalatable decisions. We will be wise to make them deliberately while there are real alternatives, rather than make them by default when there are none. The prospect for just bumbling through are poor. Rome looked good to the ancient world for about ten life-spans, but . . . the pace of life has quickened frighteningly since then. Vitally significant changes can now occur in a tenth of a life-span. For instance, the United States was, between one and two tenths of a life-span ago, the most powerful nation in history, both absolutely and relatively. Today its relative power has so diminished that we do not know to what extent it can control its own future —and this despite our conscious desire not to bumble, despite our effort toward specific technical improvements in our strength and posture, despite our day-to-day amelioration of international crises. . . .

Dr. Williams speaks for many nonscientists as well as scientists when he emphasizes the difficulties experienced in adapting political strategies to the swiftly moving advance of technology. In the sphere of military technology this time lag is notorious. It is summed up in the oft-quoted maxim that generals prepare for the last war instead of the next. We need not labor the life-and-death importance of looking forward, not backward, in this period of revolutionary change. And this applies as certainly to nonmilitary as well as military techniques of statecraft. What will scientists and engineers have achieved by the time the present generation of students have taken over the responsibilities of their elders? Dr. Williams, in the passage just quoted, hints at some of the possibilities. These and others are sketched in an arresting discussion by the late Dr. John von Neumann, one of the most gifted and imaginative scientists of our century. Von Neumann was professor of mathematics at the Institute for Advanced Study and (at the time of his death) was a member of the Atomic Energy Commission. Shortly before his untimely death he addressed himself to some of the possibilities of future technological advance and their implications for international politics. We reproduce here his discussion of the question:

"Can we survive technology?" *

. . . In the first half of this century the accelerating industrial revolution encountered an absolute limitation—not on technological progress as such but on an essential safety factor. This safety factor, which had permitted the industrial revolution to roll on from the mid-eighteenth to the early twentieth century, was essentially a matter of geographical and political Lebensraum: an ever broader geographical scope for technological activities, combined with an ever broader political inte-

* From Fortune, June 1955, p. 106 ff. Copyright 1955 by Time, Inc., New York; reproduced by permission of the publisher of Fortune and Mrs. Klara von Neumann-Eckart.

gration of the world. Within this expanding framework it was possible to accommodate the major tensions created by technological progress.

Now this safety mechanism is being sharply inhibited; literally and figuratively, we are running out of room. At long last, we begin to feel the effects of the finite, actual size of the earth in a critical way.

Thus the crisis does not arise from accidental events or human errors. It is inherent in technology's relation to geography on the one hand and to political organization on the other. The crisis was developing visibly in the 1940's, and some phases can be traced back to 1914. In the years between now and 1980 the crisis will probably develop far beyond all earlier patterns. When or how it will end—or to what state of affairs it will yield—nobody can say.

In all its stages the industrial revolution consisted of making available more and cheaper energy, more and easier controls of human actions and reactions, and more and faster communications. Each development increased the effectiveness of the other two. All three factors increased the speed of performing large-scale operations—industrial, mercantile, political, and migratory. But throughout the development, increased speed did not so much shorten time requirements of processes as extend the areas of the earth affected by them. The reason is clear. Since most *time* scales are fixed by human reaction times, habits, and other physiological and psychological factors, the effect of the increased speed of technological processes was to enlarge the *size* of units—political, organizational, economic, and cultural—affected by technological operations. That is, instead of performing the same operations as before in less time, now larger-scale operations were performed in the same time. This important evolution has a natural limit, that of the earth's actual size. The limit is now being reached, or at least closely approached.

Indications of this appeared early and with dramatic force in the military sphere. By 1940 even the larger countries of continental Western Europe were inadequate as military units. Only Russia could sustain a major military reverse without collapsing. Since 1945, improved aeronautics and communications alone might have sufficed to make any geographical unit, including Russia, inadequate in a future war. The advent of nuclear weapons merely climaxes the development. Now the effectiveness of offensive weapons is such as to stultify all plausible defensive time scales. As early as World War I, it was observed that the admiral commanding the battle field could "lose the British Empire in one afternoon." Yet navies of that epoch were relatively stable entities, tolerably safe against technological surprises. Today there is every reason to fear that even minor inventions and feints in the field of nuclear weapons can be decisive in less time than would be required to devise specific countermeasures. Soon existing nations will be as unstable in war as a nation the size of Manhattan Island would have been in a contest fought with the weapons of 1900.

Such military instability has already found its political expression.

Two superpowers, the U.S. and U.S.S.R., represent such enormous destructive potentials as to afford little chance of a purely passive equilibrium. Other countries, including possible "neutrals," are militarily defenseless in the ordinary sense. At best they will acquire destructive capabilities of their own. . . . Consequently, the "concert of powers"—or its equivalent international organization—rests on a basis much more fragile than ever before. The situation is further embroiled by the newly achieved political effectiveness of non-European nationalisms.

These factors would "normally"—that is, in any recent century—have led to war. Will they lead to war before 1980? Or soon thereafter? It would be presumptuous to try to answer such a question firmly. In any case, the present and the near future are both dangerous. While the immediate problem is to cope with the actual danger, it is also essential to envisage how the problem is going to evolve in the 1955-80 period, even assuming that all will go reasonably well for the moment. This does not mean belittling immediate problems of weaponry, of U.S.-U.S.S.R. tensions, of the evolution and revolutions of Asia. These first things must come first. But we must be ready for the follow-up, lest possible immediate successes prove futile. We must think beyond the present forms of problems to those of later decades.

Technological evolution is still accelerating. Technologies are always constructive and beneficial, directly or indirectly. Yet their consequences tend to increase instability—a point that will get closer attention after we have had a look at certain aspects of continuing technological evolution.

First of all, there is a rapidly expanding supply of energy. It is generally agreed that even conventional, chemical fuel—coal or oil—will be available in increased quantity in the next two decades. Increasing demand tends to keep fuel prices high, yet improvements in methods of generation seem to bring the price of power down. There is little doubt that the most significant event affecting energy is the advent of nuclear power. Its only available controlled source today is the nuclear-fission reactor. Reactor techniques appear to be approaching a condition in which they will be competitive with conventional (chemical) power sources within the U.S.; however, because of generally higher fuel prices abroad, they could already be more than competitive in many important foreign areas. Yet reactor technology is but a decade and a half old, during most of which period effort has been directed primarily not toward power but toward plutonium production. Given a decade of really large-scale industrial effort, the economic characteristics of reactors will undoubtedly surpass those of the present by far.

Moreover, it is not a law of nature that all controlled release of nuclear energy should be tied to fission reactions as it has been thus far. It is true that nuclear energy appears to be the primary source of practically all energy now visible in nature. Furthermore, it is not surprising that the first break into the intranuclear domain occurred at the unstable "high end" of the system of nuclei (that is, by fission). Yet fission is not nature's normal way of releasing nuclear energy. In the long run, systematic industrial exploitation of nuclear energy may shift reliance onto other and still more abundant modes. Again, reactors have been bound thus far to the traditional heat-steam-generator-electricity cycle, just as automobiles were at first constructed to look like buggies. It is likely that we shall gradually develop procedures more naturally and effectively adjusted to the new source of energy, abandoning the conventional kinks and detours inherited from chemical-fuel processes. Consequently, a few decades hence energy may be free—just like the unmetered air—with coal and oil used mainly as raw materials for organic chemical synthesis, to which, as experience has shown, their properties are best suited.

It is worth emphasizing that the main trend will be systematic exploration of nuclear reactions—that is, the transmutation of elements, or alchemy rather than chemistry. The main point in developing the industrial use of nuclear processes is to make them suitable for large-scale exploitation on the relatively small site that is the earth or, rather, any plausible terrestrial industrial establishment. Nature has, of course, been operating nuclear processes all along, well and massively, but her "natural" sites for this industry are entire stars. There is reason to believe that the minimum space requirements for her way of operating are the minimum sizes of stars. Forced by the limitations of our real estate, we must in this respect do much better than nature. That this may not be impossible has been demonstrated in the somewhat extreme and unnatural instance of fission, that remarkable breakthrough of the past decade.

What massive transmutation of elements will do to technology in general is hard to imagine, but the effects will be radical indeed. This can already be sensed in related fields. The general revolution clearly under way in the military sphere, and its already realized special aspect, the terrible possibilities of mass destruction, should not be viewed as typical of what the nuclear revolution stands for. Yet they may well be typical of how deeply that revolution will transform whatever it touches. And the revolution will probably touch most things technological.

Also likely to evolve fast—and quite apart from nuclear evolution—is automation. Interesting analyses of recent developments in this field, and of near-future potentialities, have appeared in the last few years. Automatic control, of course, is as old as the industrial revolution, for the decisive new feature of Watt's steam engine was its automatic valve control, including speed control by a "governor." In our century, however, small electric amplifying and switching devices put automation on an entirely new footing. This development began with the electromechanical (telephone) relay, continued and unfolded with the vacuum tube, and appears to accelerate with various solid-state devices (semi-conductor crystals, ferromagnetic cores, etc.). The last decade or two has also witnessed an increasing ability to control and "discipline" large numbers of such devices within one machine. Even in an airplane the number of vacuum tubes now approaches or exceeds a thousand. Other machines, containing up to 10,000 vacuum tubes, up to five times more crystals, and possibly more than 100,000 cores, now operate faultlessly over long periods, performing many millions of regulated, preplanned actions per second, with an expectation of only a few errors per day or week.

Many such machines have been built to perform complicated scientific and engineering calculations and large-scale accounting and logistical surveys. There is no doubt that they will be used for elaborate industrial process control, logistical, economic, and other planning, and many other purposes heretofore lying entirely outside the compass of quantitative and automatic control and preplanning. Thanks to simplified forms of automatic or semi-automatic control, the efficiency of important branches of industry has increased considerably during recent decades. It is therefore to be expected that the considerably elaborated newer forms, now becoming increasingly available, will effect much more along these lines.

Fundamentally, improvements in control are really improvements in communicating information within an organization or mechanism. The sum total of progress in this sphere is explosive. Improvements in communication in its direct, physical sense—transportation—while less dramatic, have been considerable and steady. If nuclear developments make energy unrestrictedly available, transportation developments are likely to accelerate even more. But even "normal" progress in sea, land, and air media is extremely important. Just such "normal" progress molded the world's economic development, producing the present global ideas in politics and economics.

Let us now consider a thoroughly "abnormal" industry and its potentialities—that is, an industry as yet without a place in any list of major activities: the control of weather or, to use a more ambitious but justified term, climate. One phase of this activity that has received a good deal of public attention is "rain making." . . .

But weather control and climate control are really much broader than rain making. All major weather phenomena, as well as climate as such, are ultimately controlled by the solar energy that falls on the earth. To modify the amount of solar energy, is, of course, beyond human power. But what really matters is not the amount that hits the earth, but the fraction retained by the earth, since that reflected back into space is no more useful than if it had never arrived. Now, the amount absorbed by the solid earth, the sea, or the atmosphere seems to be subject to delicate influences. True, none of these has so far been substantially controlled by human will, but there are strong indications of control possibilities.

The carbon dioxide released into the atmosphere by industry's burning of coal and oil—more than half of it during the last generation —may have changed the atmosphere's composition sufficiently to account for a general warming of the world by about one degree

Fahrenheit. The volcano Krakatao erupted in 1883 and released an amount of energy by no means exorbitant. Had the dust of the eruption stayed in the stratosphere for fifteen years, reflecting sunlight away from the earth, it might have sufficed to lower the world's temperature by six degrees (in fact, it stayed for about three years, and five such eruptions would probably have achieved the result mentioned). This would have been a substantial cooling; the last Ice Age, when half of North America and all of northern and western Europe were under an ice cap like that of Greenland or Antarctica, was only fifteen degrees colder than the present age. On the other hand, another fifteen degrees of warming would probably melt the ice of Greenland and Antarctica and produce worldwide tropical to semi-tropical climate.

Furthermore, it is known that the persistence of large ice fields is due to the fact that ice both reflects sunlight energy and radiates away terrestrial energy at an even higher rate than ordinary soil. Microscopic layers of colored matter spread on an icy surface, or in the atmosphere above one, could inhibit the reflection-radiation process, melt the ice, and change the local climate. Measures that would effect such changes are technically possible, and the amount of investment required would be only of the order of magnitude that sufficed to develop rail systems and other major industries. The main difficulty lies in predicting in detail the effects of any such drastic intervention. But our knowledge of the dynamics and the controlling processes in the atmosphere is rapidly approaching a level that would permit such prediction. Probably intervention in atmospheric and climatic matters will come in a few decades, and will unfold on a scale difficult to imagine at present.

What could be done, of course, is no index to what should be done; to make a new ice age in order to annoy others, or a new tropical, "interglacial" age in order to please everybody, is not necessarily a rational program. In fact, to evaluate the ultimate consequences of either a general cooling or a general heating would be a complex matter. Changes would affect the level of the seas, and hence the habitability of the continental coastal shelves; the evaporation of the seas, and hence general precipitation and glaciation levels; and so on. What would be harmful and what beneficial—and to which regions of the earth—is not immediately obvious. But there is little doubt that one *could* carry out analyses needed to predict results, intervene on any desired scale, and ultimately achieve rather fantastic effects. The climate of specific regions and levels of precipitation might be altered. For example, temporary disturbances—including invasions of cold (polar) air that constitute the typical winter of the middle latitudes, and tropical storms (hurricanes)—might be corrected or at least depressed.

There is no need to detail what such things would mean to agriculture or, indeed, to all phases of human, animal, and plant ecology. What power over our environment, over all nature, is implied!

Such actions would be more directly and truly worldwide than recent or, presumably, future wars, or than the economy at any time. Extensive human intervention would deeply affect the atmosphere's general circulation, which depends on the earth's rotation and intensive solar heating of the tropics. Measures in the arctic may control the weather in temperate regions, or measures in one temperate region critically affect one another, one-quarter around the globe. All this will merge each nation's affairs with those of every other, more thoroughly than the threat of a nuclear or any other war may already have done.

Such developments as free energy, greater automation, improved communications, partial or total climate control have common traits deserving special mention. First, though all are intrinsically useful, they can lend themselves to destruction. Even the most formidable tools of nuclear destruction are only extreme members of a genus that includes useful methods of energy release or element transmutation. The most constructive schemes for climate control would have to be based on insights and techniques that would also lend themselves to forms of climatic warfare as yet unimagined. Technology—like science —is neutral all through, providing only means of control applicable to any purpose, indifferent to all.

Second, there is in most of these developments a trend toward affecting the earth as a whole, or to be more exact, toward producing effects that can be projected from any one to any other point on the earth. There is an intrinsic conflict with geography—and institutions based thereon—as understood today. Of course, any technology interacts with geography, and each imposes its own geographical rules and modalities. The technology that is now developing and that will dominate the next decades seems to be in total conflict with traditional and, in the main, momentarily still valid, geographical and political units and concepts. This is the maturing crisis of technology.

What kind of action does this situation call for? *Whatever* one feels inclined to do, one decisive trait must be considered: the very techniques that create the dangers and the instabilities are in themselves useful, or closely related to the useful. In fact, the more useful they could be, the more unstabilizing their effects can also be. It is not a particular perverse destructiveness of one particular invention that creates danger. Technological power, technological efficiency as such, is an ambivalent achievement. Its danger is intrinsic.

In looking for a solution, it is well to exclude one pseudosolution at the start. The crisis will not be resolved by inhibiting this or that apparently particularly obnoxious form of technology. For one thing, the parts of technology, as well as of the underlying sciences, are so intertwined that in the long run nothing less than a total elimination of all technological progress would suffice for inhibition. Also, on a more pedestrian and immediate basis, useful and harmful techniques lie everywhere so close together that it is never possible to separate the lions from the lambs. This is known to all who have so laboriously tried to separate secret, "classified" science or technology (military) from the "open" kind; success is never more—nor intended to be more

—than transient, lasting perhaps half a decade. Similarly, a separation into useful and harmful subjects in any technological sphere would probably diffuse into nothing in a decade.

Moreover, in this case successful separation would have to be enduring (unlike the case of military "classification," in which even a few years' gain may be important). Also, the proximity of useful techniques to harmful ones, and the possibility of putting the harmful ones to military use, puts a competitive premium on infringement. Hence the banning of particular technologies would have to be enforced on a worldwide basis. But the only authority that could do this effectively would have to be of such scope and perfection as to signal the *resolution* of international problems rather than the discovery of a *means* to resolve them. . . .

What safeguard remains? Apparently only day-to-day—or perhaps year-to-year—opportunistic measures, a long sequence of small, correct decisions. And this is not surprising. After all, the crisis is due to the rapidity of progress, to the probable further acceleration thereof, and to the reaching of certain critical relationships. Specifically, the effects that we are now beginning to produce are of the same order of magnitude as that of "the great globe itself." Indeed, they affect the earth as an entity. Hence further acceleration can no longer be absorbed as in the past by an extension of the area of operations. Under present conditions it is unreasonable to expect a novel cure-all.

For progress there is no cure. Any attempt to find automatically safe channels for the present explosive variety of progress must lead to frustration. The only safety possible is relative, and it lies in an intelligent exercise of day-to-day judgment.

The problems created by the combination of the presently possible forms of nuclear warfare and the rather unusually unstable international situation are formidable and not to be solved easily. Those of the next decades are likely to be similarly vexing, "only more so." The U.S.-U.S.S.R. tension is bad, but when other nations begin to make felt their full offensive potential weight, things will not become simpler.

Present awful possibilities of nuclear warfare may give way to others even more awful. After global climate control becomes possible, perhaps all our present involvements will seem simple. We should not deceive ourselves: once such possibilities become actual, they will be exploited. It will, therefore, be necessary to develop suitable new political forms and procedures. All experience shows that even smaller technological changes than those now in the cards profoundly transform political and social relationships. Experience also shows that these transformations are not *a priori* predictable and that most contemporary "first guesses" concerning them are wrong. For all these reasons, one should take neither present difficulties nor presently proposed reforms too seriously.

The one solid fact is that the difficulties are due to an evolution that, while useful and constructive, is also dangerous. Can we produce the required adjustments with the necessary speed? The most hopeful answer is that the human species has been subjected to similar tests before and seems to have a congenital ability to come through, after varying amounts of trouble. To ask in advance for a complete recipe would be unreasonable. We can specify only the human qualities required: patience, flexibility, intelligence.

CHAPTER EIGHT

★ ★ ★

New Dimensions of Violence:
Military Technology Since 1945

SINCE 1939—A tiny interval in time, even in the perspective of the modern Society of Nations—a sequence of scientific and technological events has given to the political relations of states a new dimension which reduces to antiquarian interest most of what was said about this subject before 1945 and a good deal of what is still being said today. We refer, of course, to the enormous, unprecedented, and largely unanticipated increase in man's capacity to destroy. The most dramatic and publicized aspects of this development—those relating to the atomic and hydrogen bombs and ballistic rocket missiles—are generally well known. A much less publicized set of events, though possibly no less lethal potentially, relate to the development of weapons based on the destructive properties of viruses, bacteria, and chemical poisons. The following timetable may help to put into sharper focus this new dimension of international politics:

> 1939: Experimental work in scientific laboratories in several countries established the practicability of splitting the uranium atom, with enormous accompanying release of energy.
> 1942: A self-sustaining chain reaction was established in an experimental nuclear reactor at the University of Chicago.
> 1945: The first atomic (nuclear-fission) bomb, with an explosive power estimated to equal 20,000 tons of TNT, was dropped on the Japanese city of Hiroshima, killing or injuring over 35 per cent of its 350,000 inhabitants.
> 1949: Successful testing of a Soviet atomic bomb ended the short-lived American monopoly of nuclear weapons.
> 1952: The United States exploded its first hydrogen (nuclear-fusion) bomb, the explosive power of which was estimated to be equivalent to 4,000,000 tons of TNT.

1953: The Soviet government exploded its first hydrogen bomb.

1954: The United States government tested a more powerful H-bomb, of explosive power equivalent to 8,000,000 tons of TNT, and lethal radioactive fallout covering some 7,000 square miles.

1957: The Soviet government announced successful testing of an intercontinental ballistic missile (ICBM), and later in the same year successfully fired two rocket-powered satellites (Sputnik I and II) into orbit around the earth.

1958: First U.S. earth satellites successfully fired into orbit.

1959: U.S. Office of Civil and Defense Mobilization published an estimate that an attack on 224 strategic targets in the United States, with 263 H-bombs of a total yield equivalent to 1,446,000,000 tons of TNT, would result on the first day of the attack in over 50,000,000 casualties, a large majority of whom would be killed or fatally injured.

1959: Also in 1959, Dr. Brock Chisholm, former Director-General of the World Health Organization, told the press that "any country which can afford one good biologist can render any other country incapable of war in a single night . . . as a result of the research into germ warfare carried on since the end of World War II."

1960: A public-opinion poll carried on through a period of three years for the Joint Commission on Mental Illness and Health disclosed that only about 4 percent of the Americans polled, expressed concern over world tensions and the possibility of a war of annihilation.

Extending the panorama through a longer time-span reveals the same speed-up in military technology as in other aspects of the technological revolution. This is strikingly presented in a table prepared by Hornell Hart (an American sociologist who has specialized in the conquest of geographic space). Taking the range of projectiles as "the most reliable index of destructive power," Hart's table (reproduced as Table 8.1) shows the progressive increase of maximum range in miles and killing area in square miles.

This rise in destructive capabilities is one of the inescapable realities—one of the "givens" or "datum points"—of international politics in the 1960's. Policy-makers and their constituents may react in different ways to this pervasive reality. Some, figuratively speaking, may try to sweep the whole dirty business under the rug, or, to change the metaphor, bury their heads in the sand and try to forget it all. But no one can escape the consequences of man's unprecedented rise in ability to destroy. The dimensions and implications of this factor are the focus of discussion throughout this chapter.

Military technology in our time presents many faces. Our point of departure is a brief review of the rising costs—human as well as material—of military wars in our century. We shall next examine some expert opinions regarding the consequences of a major war fought with nuclear explosives

TABLE 8.1 [a]   WORLD-RECORD-BREAKING RANGES OF PROJECTILE
1,000,000 B.C. to 1954 A.D.

DATE	TYPE OF PROJECTILE	MAXIMUM RANGE IN MILES [b]	KILLING AREA IN SQUARE MILES [c]
From before 1,000,000 B.C. to at least 200,000 B.C., nothing better than rock missile, thrown club, or simple javelin		0.01	0.0003
Period between javelin and arrow		0.03	0.005
Starting somewhere between 75,000 B.C. and 10,000 B.C. bow and arrow		0.10	0.09
From about 500 B.C. to 1453, catapult and ballista		0.35	0.8
1453	Cannon	1.0	3.
1670	Cannon	1.1	4.
1807	Rocket	2.0	13.
1830	Coast artillery	3.0	28.
1859	Breech-loading rifle gun	5.0	78.
1900	Coast artillery	6.3	125.
1910	Coast artillery	10.2	326.
1912	Coast artillery	11.4	408.
1915	Zeppelin raid on London	200.	126,000.
1918	Bombing plane	280.	246,000.
1938	Av. European bombing formation	750.	1,761,000.
1943	Bombing plane	1,200.	4,480,000.
1944	Bombing plane	2,050.	12,900,000.
1945	Bombing plane	2,500.	19,000,000.
1948	Bombing plane	3,900.	45,000,000.
1949	Bombing plane	5,000.	69,000,000.
1954	Bombing plane refueled in flight	12,500.	197,000,000.

[a] Data from "Acceleration in Social Change," p. 36 of *Technology and Social Change*, by F. R. Allen et al. Copyright 1957 by Appleton-Century-Crofts, Inc., New York; reproduced by permission.

[b] Record-breaking range of projectiles (maximum range in miles) defined as "longest nonstop distance, from base to target, over which a missile intended to destroy life or demolish structures has been hurled or piloted through the air."

[c] "Killing area" (in square miles) defined as "maximum area within which lives and property may be destroyed by such projectiles."

and biological and chemical weapons. Third, we shall note briefly the impacts of nuclear weapons on the military strategies of those who do and those who do not yet possess them. Fourth, we shall attempt to identify some of the more important positions that have emerged in the arguments and counterarguments over the implications of nuclear weapons.

Finally, we shall suggest, by way of anticipating points to be more fully examined in the final group of chapters, what appears to be some of the effects of our runaway military technology on the overall configuration of international politics.

Costs of modern wars

It is not easy to compute the costs of the two world wars of our century, and of the lesser wars which preceded and followed them. These costs have not been merely material, to be totted up in units of money. Even that presents great difficulty. But it is vastly less difficult than to estimate the intangible social or human costs. How is one to measure the misery inflicted on scores of millions of human beings caught up in the savage destructive fury of their rulers? How is one to calculate the indirect consequences of total war: its stimulus to the spread of revolutionary communism, its degradation of human dignity, and other imponderable costs? Formidable as these difficulties may be, and impressionistic as any-one's conclusions must inevitably be, the effort should nevertheless be made. It should be made if for no other reason than to counteract the propensity of military planners, politicians, and academic scholars to behave as if nations were collections of puppets on strings instead of flesh-and-blood human beings.

One of the more sober attempts to get at both the material and the human consequences of World War II was made some years ago by a free-lance journalist, C. Hartley Grattan. We reproduce here his findings and conclusions.*

> No earthquake, no hurricane, no flood known to the record has matched World War II in destructiveness. No previous war—the incursions of Attila and his Huns, the pillagings of the barbarians in the declining years of the Roman Empire, the frightful scourgings of men and cities during the Thirty Years War—did anywhere near so much damage. Even World War I was only one-seventh as destructive. . . .
>
> The life-cost of World War II fell far more heavily on civilians than on the men in uniform. The sardonic joke about the front line being the safest place in wartime became in many places the unvarnished truth. In no war in modern times have so many civilians suffered death in so many different ways as in World War II. There were the deaths by bombing (three hundred times more numerous than in World War I); the planned killings of civilians by the hundreds

* The following selection is from "What the War Cost," by C. H. Grattan, in *Harper's Magazine*, April 1949. Copyright 1949 by Harper & Brothers, New York; reproduced by permission of the author.

of thousands in extermination and concentration camps; the losses in underground movements (which in some countries were three or four times bigger than the losses in the regular armies); and the further deaths when people were turned out of their homes onto the roads to wander about looking without real hope for a haven, or were herded like cattle into freight cars and taken to labor for the enemy as slaves, with thousands of them inevitably dying long before their time. Taking all these into account, we may safely conclude that at least three times as many civilians died because of the war as died in the armed forces.

What, then, were the losses in the armed forces? General George C. Marshall has estimated that the principal belligerents lost 15 million dead and missing. It is likely that the smaller countries lost another 1½ million in the same way. Most of the missing later turned up as prisoners of war, but as there was protracted and illegal delay in repatriating Axis prisoners . . . some of these must have lost their lives. At any rate it would seem conservative, bearing all these figures in mind, to say that in all at least ten million members of the armed services came to their deaths.

Add three civilian deaths for every one of these, and we add thirty million to ten million—arriving at forty million as a total for deaths in World War II. That is just about equivalent to all the children in the United States under nineteen years of age.

Of the material costs, the largest by all odds came from that most appalling innovation of ruthless destruction, air bombardment—especially area raids which were indiscriminate in that no specific target was aimed at. Aside from air bombardment, the chief causes of destruction in World War II were undersea and surface warfare against both merchant and naval ships, and warfare on land, including underground activities and the scorched-earth techniques used by nations retreating out of their own territory and also used by an enemy when driven from occupied territory. These various kinds of destruction cannot be exactly differentiated from one another. For instance, ships were sunk from the air as well as by surface ships and submarines, and ground operations were usually preceded and accompanied by air bombardment. Nevertheless we are reasonably sure that air bombardment, whether carried on behind the enemy's lines as in the raids on Britain and Germany, or as a phase of frontline operations, caused by far the greatest proportion of the damage.

Air bombardment was intended to destroy the ability to manufacture munitions. But munitions production today involves in one way or another practically the whole economy of a nation; a campaign against munitions production is an effort to destroy a nation's economic life. Of the bomb tonnage dropped on Europe, over half fell on Germany, about one-fifth on France, about one-eighth on Italy; the rest was scattered. Germany, of course, was the principal source of munitions on the Continent as well as leader of the Axis. If we divide up the bomb tonnage another way, we find that three quarters of it was dropped to destroy the ability to produce, while the rest fell on more narrowly defined military targets. As practiced in World War II, air bombardment represents the most systematic effort ever made to destroy the economic underpinnings of nations. In destroying a nation's power to make war, one destroys a nation's ability to keep its citizens alive. This paradox will plague us as long as war exists. This is why it is taking so long to "restore" Europe.

To destroy an enemy's ability to produce, one does not have to destroy literally everything. The job can be very efficiently done by smashing up the transportation system, especially the railroads but also the roads (particularly the bridges) and the canals. No modern nation can function for long without rapid and certain circulation of freight. Out of every 100 tons of bombs dropped on Europe, 31 were aimed at inland transport, chiefly railroads.

At one time or another special efforts were made to knock out factories making oil from coal, aluminum, airplane engines and frames, and submarines. (It was discovered that the effects of bombing on industries vary enormously. For instance, the heavy equipment of steel works is exceedingly difficult to damage, but the works can be slowed down, though not finally stopped, if the water and gas lines serving them are broken. On the other hand, plants producing oil from coal are highly vulnerable, as are most chemical plants, and can be sufficiently damaged by bombs to be knocked out permanently.) But it was not until well into 1943 that the effects of bombing on German production became noticeable and not until another year had passed, when the railroads began to fall apart, and the final, fatal decline began. In proportion as the railroads were battered, the decline accelerated. When the war ended, maps showing the condition of Europe's railroads resembled nothing so much as those pictures of germs seen through a microscope—merely disconnected dashes. The men who planned the wrecking of Europe's transportation knew precisely what they were doing. They smashed what any economist or technologist would tell them was the basic service of any economy.

The same lesson was learned with regard to transportation by sea. The critical phase of the battle to keep Britain in the war was the effort to keep supplies moving in from overseas. On the other side of the world the same lesson was enforced. Japan was well on the way to final industrial decline even before the United States captured bases from which bombers could operate against factories. This was because Japanese factories could not operate without a steady flow of supplies from across the sea, and the immensely successful American campaign against Japanese cargo shipping had halted this flow.

The planned destruction of a nation's capacity to make war is one thing; the planned destruction of people's houses is quite another. The assault on dwellings ranks as one of the great horrors of the war. Cities heavily bombed often lost half their dwellings, and in areas bitterly fought over on the ground and from the air, like vast portions of Russia, the number of people left homeless ran into millions. Terror and obliteration air-raids were considered successful almost in proportion to the number of people who lost their homes; for homeless people cannot work well, and production falls toward zero. It was for these reasons that 20 out of every 100 residential buildings in Germany were destroyed, that every fifth Greek was left homeless, that 28,000 houses in Rotterdam alone were knocked down, that the British had 460,000 houses destroyed and the Japanese two and a quarter million. Even in New Guinea numerous native villages were flattened to the ground.

What this wholesale destruction of dwelling space meant in human terms it is impossible even for people with highly developed imaginations to grasp. And with the "space" went the furniture and other equipment and possessions of the millions of human beings who occupied it, often things painfully gathered after hard toil over many years. That man did all this to himself only adds the final touch of irony.

To the costs of waging the war and the costs of the destruction of railroads, roads, canals, ships, docks, factories, and dwelling houses must be added others which seldom appear in published totals because they occur only to the minds of specialists. Among these are such things as the cost of raw materials, manufactured articles, and food-stuffs carried off by invaders to help sustain their production for war; the worth of the labor power carried away from invaded countries to provide "hands" for the industries of the enemy; the cost of running down equipment by neglecting maintenance during a war; the cost of the reckless use of natural resources; the eventual cost of having, on the one hand, sold off foreign investments and, on the other, run up the nation's debts owed abroad; the disorganization of established systems of trade and finance; and the cost of depressing the standard of living of the people by diverting more and more of total national production from consumption for well-being to expenditure on war. These, too, are among the things which leave nations at the end of a war in such desperate straits; these, too, are part of the cost of a war, however difficult it may be to place a dollar value on them.

It was these various kinds of costs which, when piled one on top of the other, reduced Europe and the Far East to such low levels at the war's end. It was clear that the world had suffered a catastrophic blow. In Europe the blow appeared mortal. The continent which was the homeland from which Western civilization had spread over the entire globe was teetering on the edge of final collapse.

What, then, was the grand total of the cost of achieving this frightening end? Let us try to add the figures up.

The military expenditures recorded in national budgets—let us assume that they are accurate—come to a total of over one trillion dollars, or $1,117,000,000,000. Let us further assume that the cost of destruction came to at least twice that figure; this is a very modest assumption indeed, for in some countries it was much more than twice, though in others it was less. This would give us a figure of a little less than two and a quarter trillions, or $2,234,000,000,000. Toss in an additional $650,000,000,000 for the sort of losses which I have said above tend to elude even the most industrious figure-makers. Then add up these monstrous sums, and you get a grand total of just about four trillion dollars. Or, if a trillion is difficult to comprehend, say four thousand thousand million dollars.

Forty million people and four trillion dollars. Look hard at those figures and you begin dimly to see what World War II cost. And even so, you have left out the *moral* cost of what man so systematically and purposefully did to man. . . .

What price World War III?

In estimating the nature and probable magnitude of the price of World War III, it will help to clarify the issues if one distinguishes between the immediate physical effects—buildings and other structures destroyed, people killed and injured, services disrupted, etc.—and the longer-term biological and social effects.

With respect to the immediate human and material damage that might result from a large-scale attack with nuclear weapons, estimates vary considerably. We cited, in the timetable of events with which this chapter opened, the 1959 estimate prepared by the Office of Civil and Defense Mobilization. This estimate has been characterized by Ralph E. Lapp (a respected popular interpreter of nuclear science and weapons technology) as neither "light" nor "heavy," but rather as "modest."

This estimate, which formed the basis of a Congressional investigation in 1959 (by the so-called Holifield Subcommittee) assumed attacks on 224 cities, military installations, and other targets in the United States with 263 megaton bombs equivalent in aggregate explosive power to *one and one-half billion tons of TNT*. Such an attack, it was estimated, would result on the first day in about 50 million deaths and 20 million additional casualties. About 12 million homes would be destroyed, and another 10 million damaged. That is to say, about one-third of the population would be killed or fatally injured, and one-half of all homes obliterated or rendered unusable.

It is almost impossible for Americans to visualize so massive a catastrophe. Suppose, for example, only ten to twenty of the largest cities and transportation centers in the United States were smashed as completely as Hiroshima was smashed with a single atomic bomb of less than 1 percent of the explosive power of the superbombs now stockpiled by the thousands. (Such a catastrophe, be it noted, would be very much smaller than the one assumed in the official estimate, which Lapp characterized as a "modest"-scale attack.) What would living conditions be like for the survivors of such a disaster? How would they bury the dead, or care for the injured? With water supplies polluted and transport disrupted if not completely paralyzed, what would the survivors eat and how would they cope with the epidemics that would surely follow the bombs? What would happen to even the most tightly disciplined society under such conditions?

The fact that Germany, Russia, Japan, and Britain did in fact carry on in World War II, despite heavy and widespread damage is sometimes cited as evidence of the shock-absorbing capacity of modern industrial nations. But the scale of destruction in World War II—except for the atomic bombing of Hiroshima and Nagasaki—was trivial in comparison to the scale postulated above, characterized as a "modest" attack. Moreover, one should never forget, the German and Japanese economies were progressively paralyzed and brought to a virtual standstill—with TNT, before nuclear weapons came on the scene. It should likewise be remembered that the most productive economy of all—that of the United States—remained throughout the war beyond reach of enemy attack. Massive infusions of aid from this undamaged source helped—probably decisively—to keep Britain going under the rain of Nazi bombs. Furthermore, a combination of timely American aid and German inability to reach the Soviet Union's more remote industrial regions just barely saved the Russians from irreversible disaster. In short, the hundredfold or greater increase in the capacity to destroy since 1945 dwarfs into utter insignificance the events of World War II.

Manifestly there is for every nation some point of no return, the point where catastrophe becomes irreversible, where morale and discipline collapse, where an organized society is transformed into a dazed mob. Nations undoubtedly differ in their respective capacities to carry on in the face of disaster. In predicting the probable behavior of any nation under such extreme stress, one would clearly take into account its past record of morale and discipline, capacity for improvisation, etc. One would also take into account the nature and extent of its preparations for coping with disaster. At the same time, it should be recognized that, with weapons systems now available, destruction might well be inflicted far beyond the capacity of any nation to absorb and still carry on.

The unprecedented destructiveness of today's weapons has been driven home in scores and hundreds of scientific and popular books and articles. Jonathan N. Leonard, science writer on *The New York Times*, opens a review of a recent book on the aftereffects of nuclear explosions, with these words:

A century from now, if all goes well, scholars may take from the Library of Congress a dusty book titled "Fallout," run through its yellowed pages and wonder how it felt to live in the 1960's under the threat of nuclear war. If all does not go well and nuclear war really happens, the Library of Congress will not be serving scholars a century from now. Perhaps its building will still exist as a crumbling ruin which the primitive farmers of the neighborhood have little reason to explore.

The gloomy speculation above is not to be found in "Fallout," which is a reserved, careful and unemotional symposium on nuclear weapons and their consequences. But no one who reads the book with attention can escape having such speculations form in his mind. . . .

The chapters on nuclear war by physicist Ralph E. Lapp and on national survival by Mr. Fowler [physicist, of Washington University] make clear that the lives of even sheltered survivors of full-fledged nuclear war will be hardly worth living. After a month or so of cowering underground, they will emerge into a shattered and sickly world. Most of their countrymen will be dead, and a large part of the living can count on developing cancer or other diseases caused by radiation. Staying alive will be difficult and seldom accomplished for long. Even the soil will be poisoned and will grow poisoned food.

The above will happen if only 3,000 megatons of nuclear weapons are exploded over United States or Soviet territory. Real "saturation" attacks will do worse. Mr. Lapp calculates that 20,000 megatons will kill 95 percent of the United-States or 90 percent of the Soviet population. Such attacks are easily possible. "Present stockpiles," says Mr. Lapp, "are more than adequate to spread radioactive lethality over an entire continental land mass." *

Not everyone takes so pessimistic a view of the consequences of nuclear warfare. One of the more important dissenters is physicist Herman Kahn, formerly with the RAND Corporation, director of the Hudson Institute. Kahn says:

Many biologists and geneticists are worried about the genetic effects of even the peacetime testing of nuclear weapons, and some imply that the future of the human race is being jeopardized by exploding a few bombs in the Pacific Ocean or the Soviet Arctic. One must grant that a lot of bombs exploded inside a country would be far more dangerous than a few exploded farther away. But would it be cataclysmic?

Calculations in this field are inherently uncertain, and experimental evidence is insufficient to be conclusive about some important effects. One study indicates that if, in a country that was hit by hundreds of bombs, the survivors of the attack took modest precautions they might average about 200 or 300 roentgens of radiation to their reproductive organs before age thirty. This is an enormous amount of radiation—one or two thousand times as much as people in the United States would receive as a by-product of the test program. It is fifty to a hundred times as much as they would normally get from natural sources. It is a large and frightening dose. It would result in much damage, but there is no evidence that it would be annihilating.

If present beliefs are correct, the most serious genetic effect of this amount of radiation would be to raise by 25 per cent the number of children born seriously defective; that is, the rate would increase from the current 4 per cent of the total to a new level of 5 per cent. This is a high penalty to pay for a war, and more horrible still, one might have to continue to pay a similar though smaller price for twenty or thirty or forty generations. But it is still far from annihilation. . . .

There are medical problems other than the genetic ones: the bone cancers and leukemias that might be caused by strontium-90 and the other life-shortening effects of the internal and external radiation from fission products. Here again, analysis indicates that while the problems are horrible, they may well be within the range to which we are accustomed. . . .

The situation devolves to this: Even if it were true that every time a megaton explodes a thousand people die prematurely from the effects of the world-wide fallout—which would mean that testing a single 10-MT bomb in the Pacific would kill 10,000 people—this does not necessarily mean that the backlash from war would deter a determined decisionmaker. Assume, for example, that the Soviets dropped 5000 MT on the United States (a fairly large attack). This would mean that world-wide, 5 million people would die just as a result of the backlash. Less than half a million of these deaths would occur in the Soviet Union, however, and even those half million deaths would be spread over fifty years or so. The impact of these deaths would be less significant than, say, that of the annual number of deaths due to automobile accidents in the United States. So far as the object of the attack—the United States—is concerned, the effect of the fallout would be much more serious, but it might not be a total catastrophe. More and closer bombs cause more trouble than fewer and more distant ones—but not necessarily that much more. If the country is hit as hard as is assumed, but people take advantage of the moderate protection that is available in existing buildings and take other simple measures . . . , both the long- and short-term effects of fallout are mitigated. With such preparations and some advance warning (the more preparation, the less need for warning) most people can survive the short-term fallout effects even though the long-term effects are less avoidable. The war might shorten by one or two years the life expectancy of those who were lucky or protected, and by five or ten years the life expectancy of those survivors who were not so lucky or well protected. In any case, life would go on.*

* From "The Nature and Feasibility of War and Deterrence," RAND Publication No. P-1888-RC, January 20, 1960; reproduced by permission of Dr. Herman Kahn.

"The preoccupation of military strategists and disarmament planners with nuclear weapons has often excluded the consideration of the reduction and control of other armaments." With these words Senator Hubert H. Humphrey introduced a study, carried out for the Senate Foreign Relations Committee, on chemical and biological warfare. There has been some tendency to brush aside as inconsequential the military potentialities of bacteria, viruses, and chemical poisons. One reason for this attitude is probably the tight official secrecy which, until recently, has kept this subject pretty much out of the news. Yet available evidence indicates that all major Powers and probably many of the lesser ones too, are conducting extensive experiments on B-C (biological and chemical) weapons.

This aspect of military technology is as sinister as nuclear weaponry, possibly more so. B-C weapons add still another dimension of frightfulness to man's capacity to destroy his fellowmen. A conference of scientific and medical experts who met to examine B-C warfare came to the conclusion:

> Biological weapons—microbes, viruses, and their toxic products—can be delivered and dispersed in such a way that fatal or incapacitating diseases might be produced over large areas. They can be produced cheaply on a significant scale, even in a country whose technological development is not highly advanced. Such weapons could be used alone or together with others. The attack could be local or massive or could consist of individual acts of sabotage. The agent could be selected to cause a great many casualties or to initiate epidemics.*

Recently there have been numerous breaches in the conspiracy of silence which has cloaked research in B-C weaponry. It has been revealed that British scientists, for example, have been "producing botulinus toxin and experimenting with forty other deadly germs . . . Botulinus is so deadly that eight and one-half ounces of it properly distributed could kill everyone in the world." †

In the United States, the former head of the Army Chemical Corps told a Congressional committee, of

> chemicals that could "set you Congressmen dancing on the desks and shouting Communist speeches," or else kill almost instantly.

A scientist directly involved in government research in this field warned in a public address, of the fearful potentialities of chemical and biological warfare. These range, he said, from weapons that would only briefly immobilize to others that would bring instant death with just one breath of contaminated air. A single aircraft would be capable of delivering such a weapon, which could affect an area of thousands of square miles, he said.*

Speaking before the American Chemical Society in 1960, Dr. Harold B. Leuth (of the Council of National Security of the American Medical Association) stated that

chemical agents that might be used in warfare, either openly or through sabotage, include the mustard gas that was used in World War I, the nerve gases that were developed but not used during World War II, and the so-called "psychochemicals," discovered only six years ago. . . . [These psychochemicals were described as] incapacitating agents that fall into two groups, both of which appear to have broad implications as future weapons. The agents of one group are physically disabling, causing temporary blindness, paralysis, deafness and nausea. The other group consist of emotionally disabling agents that might be used to reduce the will of people to repel an enemy.

At the same conference another expert, directly involved in government research, reported that "the greatest threat" from biological and chemical warfare,

may not lie in its capacity to kill people, but rather in the destruction of the economy through the incapacitation of the working force and the reduction of crops and domestic animals.†

These activities by no means exhaust the range of future technological developments in the military field. Any scientist could list additional destructive possibilities. No one yet knows precisely what may be the military potentialities of the stratosphere and outer space. Another line of possible future development is control of climate for destructive as well as constructive purposes, as described by the late John von Neumann (see pp. 246 ff above).

If, as now seems quite possible, techniques are perfected for modifying the reflection of solar energy from polar icefields or for controlling radiation into space of the earth's stored heat, man would have in his hands the capacity to shift climatic zones, to raise or lower the levels of the oceans, and to produce other fantastic changes in the physical environment. It takes no great effort, for example, to imagine the dire consequences of

* As reported in *The New York Times*, June 17, 1959, p. 8, and December 3, 1959, p. 10.

† From *The New York Times*, April 9, 1960, p. 8. Copyright by New York Times Co.; reproduced by permission.

inundating the world's great seaports—New York, Philadelphia, New Orleans, London, Rotterdam, Shanghai, to mention but a few of them. The potentialities of such a capability either for international blackmail or for destruction would be formidable.

Turning from the problem of destruction *per se* to the longer-term problem of recovery, one encounters a wide range of opinions. The one that has evoked the most controversy in recent years is the pessimistic thesis advanced by Professor Harrison Brown, of the California Institute of Technology. Brown's thesis, most fully developed in his widely read book, *The Challenge of Man's Future*, is more concisely outlined in the magazine article from which the following selection is quoted:*

Industrial civilization consists today of a vast interlocking network of mines, factories, and transportation systems. It feeds on huge quantities of raw materials such as ores of iron, copper, aluminum, phosphate rock, sulfur, and water. Huge quantities of energy in the form of fuels such as coal, natural gas, and petroleum are necessary for its functioning.

As per capita demands for goods continue to grow, as population increases, and as industrialization spreads to other regions of the world, the demands for raw materials will surge upwards. Each decade we must produce more metals than were produced the decade before, we must produce more fertilizers, insecticides, machines, and medicines. Correspondingly, we must consume more ores, more coal, more petroleum, and we must tap new sources of energy.

In terms of the changes which are being brought about by the spread of industrial civilization, we are much closer to the beginning of the revolution in which we now find ourselves than we are to its end. The problems which will confront us will increase in complexity as time goes by.

Today we are confronted by diminishing grades of raw materials in many areas of industrial activity. For example, only a few decades ago copper ores were being mined that contained five percent copper. Today our average copper ore contains only 0.6 percent of the metal. Undoubtedly in the years ahead we shall be mining ores that contain even smaller concentrations of the element. From the point of view of technology, this is something well within the realm of technological feasibility—but at a price. In order to extract copper from ores of still lower grade, we must pour more technology into the system; we must move and process larger quantities of ore per unit of production; we must use more machines and consume more energy. In short, extrac-

---

* From "Science, Technology, and World Development," by Harrison Brown, in *Bulletin of the Atomic Scientists*, December 1958, pp. 409, 410-12. Copyright 1958 by the Educational Foundation for Nuclear Science, Inc., Chicago; reproduced by permission of publisher and author.

tion of metals from lower grades of ore requires using more steel and other metals and consuming more energy.

No matter how we look at the situation, we must conclude that consumption of energy and raw materials, even in the presently industrialized societies, must continue to increase with time. When we couple this with the fact that per capita demands for goods are still increasing, population is increasing, and industrialization is spreading, it seems inevitable that world-wide demands for raw materials in the years ahead will pale those of today into insignificance. . . .

So long as there is an ample supply of energy, we shall be able to process extremely low-grade substances in order to obtain the raw materials we need. As grades move downward, increasing emphasis will be placed on the isolation of by-products and co-products, and eventually we may reach the time when as many as twenty to thirty products are obtained from the single operation of "mining" ordinary rock. As grade goes down, energy costs per unit of output will of course go up, but given adequate energy, industry can be fed for a very long time from the leanest of substances.

Fortunately, nature has placed at our disposal huge reservoirs of energy. We know that, if necessary, the sun's rays can be harnessed directly to produce mechanical power. We know that useful power can be produced from uranium and thorium, and we know that sufficient quantities of these substances are available in the earth's minerals and rocks to keep a world civilization operating at a high level of productivity for many millennia. We know that it is possible to generate eventually thermonuclear power in almost infinite quantities. We know that in some regions of the world there are large quantities of coal and petroleum that have not yet been tapped. It seems clear that given the trained manpower, imagination, and the collaborative research, man has at his disposal ample supplies of energy.

However, Professor Brown goes on to demonstrate, all these potentialities rest upon one essential condition: the avoidance of catastrophe that disrupts the increasingly complex processes involved in producing energy, raw materials, and fabricated goods of all kinds. He continues:

The vast network of mines, factories, and communication systems, upon which the industrialized part of the world has become dependent, is extremely sensitive to disruption. So interdependent are the components of the network that the sudden failure of but a relatively small section of it could result in a breakdown of the entire system. It is for this reason that machine civilization is probably far more vulnerable to disruption from nuclear attack than most persons suspect. For example, not many well-placed hydrogen bombs would be required to destroy the productive capacities of the larger world powers. Indeed it is quite possible that far more persons would die in the chaotic aftermath of a nuclear war as a result of the breakdown of the industrial network than would be killed directly by explosions.

As industrialization spreads, the world as a whole will become more vulnerable in this respect. At the same time as the years pass, increasing numbers of nations will find themselves in a position to wage large-scale nuclear war. Hand in hand with industrialization goes the power of manufacturing the tools of war, including nuclear armaments. Thus it would appear that the likelihood of disruption will increase steadily in the future—at least in the absence of some semblance of international order.

If industrial civilization were destroyed on a world-wide basis, there would be a very real question as to whether it could ever be started again. Our own civilization was made possible by an abundance of ores and other resources which could be easily tapped. As we have seen, these resources are disappearing and will one day vanish. As long as we maintain a high level of technology and an intact industrial network we can keep going for an indefinitely long period of time. But if there were a catastrophe, the technological requirements of getting started again might prove to be impossible to surmount. We are indeed approaching a "point of no return"—a point in time beyond which the machines of the world must continue to function, or industrial civilization will perish, possibly never to reappear.

Disagreement with Brown's thesis rests mainly upon two grounds. It is contended that he underestimates human capacity for improvisation in the face of disaster. It is further contended that some industrial regions would remain undamaged or be less severely damaged than others, and that the still operable regions would be able to start the process of recovery. The post-1945 rebuilding of Germany, Japan, Western Europe, and the scorched areas of western Russia is cited in support of this counter-thesis. But does this evidence really rebut Brown's argument?

Recovery of Western Europe, Britain, Germany, and Japan was made possible—or, at the very least, greatly expedited—by massive aid from the United States; and Soviet recovery, by the existence of productive undamaged industrial regions elsewhere in the huge area of the Soviet Union. In a future war fought with nuclear airborne weapons, with or without bacteria, viruses, and chemical poisons, the magnitude of destruction would be incalculably greater—at the very least, on the scale of Hiroshima. Furthermore, if all went according to plan, there would be no undamaged highly productive industrial countries or regions from which to initiate and support the recovery process. Finally, as Brown strongly emphasizes, the depletion of high-grade mineral fuels and raw materials has accelerated inexorably during the period of feverish industrial activity since 1945. This process continues to accelerate so that every passing year adds cogency to Brown's pessimistic thesis.

A corollary implicit in this thesis is that there is likely to be a rather consistent correlation between stage of economic-technological development and vulnerability to nuclear war. The higher the level of a nation's scientific and engineering achievements, the more complex and interdependent become its farms, mines, factories, and transportation systems. For this reason, there is some basis for predicting that nuclear war would probably disable countries roughly in proportion to their level of industrialization and the geographical concentration of their industries.

In the United States industrial concentration is very high on the east coast, around the Great Lakes, in California, and in one or two other regions. American industrial regions east of the Rocky Mountains, moreover, are heavily dependent on each other. Schemes for relocating industries as a means of reducing the American economy's vulnerability to nuclear attack, have repeatedly encountered resistance from labor unions, real-estate associations, and other groups who would suffer thereby. Moreover, estimates of what it would cost to carry out a really significant relocation of American industries run into astronomical figures. Such projects, it scarcely needs to be emphasized, are difficult if not impossible to accomplish in a democratic political system in which local interests can wield a strong influence in the national legislature.

In Britain nearly all major industries are crowded into three or four dense conurbations, as the British call their densely populated urban-industrial regions. The small size of the island of Britain makes any significant dispersion geographically impossible. The Rhine Valley holds another crowded industrial constellation which has to stay put because that is where the iron and coal are located.

Before World War II most of the major industries of the Soviet Union were similarly crowded into several closely interlinked areas around Moscow, Leningrad, and in the Ukraine. Two of these regions were shattered and the third heavily damaged by bombing, artillery fire, and other demolitions. Meanwhile, the Russians carried out a massive migration of factories and workers to safer locations in the Ural Mountain area and farther east. One goal of postwar Soviet planning seems to have been to develop new and widely separated industrial regions, each as self-sufficient and autonomous as possible. The geographical location of mineral and other resources within the Soviet Union has facilitated this project. Experts differ as to how much has been achieved. But prudence requires the assumption that the Soviet economy is certainly less vulnerable to crippling nuclear attack than is Britain or Western Europe, and probably less vulnerable than the United States.

It would further appear that nations at a lower level of technological development may also be less vulnerable to the consequences of industrial destruction. Take the situation of China, for example. Because of the smaller scale and the more primitive and less easily dislocated character of Chinese industries, China would probably be far more difficult to reduce by nuclear bombardment than the Soviet Union or any of the industrialized countries of the West. Chinese Communist leaders have openly boasted of China's ability to absorb devastation and still carry on. All this is consistent with Harrison Brown's thesis and supporting evidence.

These possibilities should give little comfort to the military planners in Washington and Moscow or to their respective constituencies. A fair inference from Brown's argument is that large-scale nuclear war within the next decade or so would probably wipe out the geographically concentrated and highly urbanized economies of Western Europe, damage the United States and Soviet Union perhaps beyond recovery, and turn over the management of a shattered world to the Chinese Communists and other emergent nations of Asia and Africa, which, because of their relatively lower level of technological advancement, would be better able to withstand and recover from the catastrophe. One may hope that this hypothesis may never be put to test. But the possibility, even probability, that vulnerability to military catastrophe varies with level of technological advance constitutes one of the datum points in any realistic discussion of international politics in the 1960's.

Nuclear weapons and military strategies

There is a large element of speculation in every estimate of the costs and consequences of a third world war. The destructiveness of existing weapons has been established by repeated testing. But no one can predict with certainty the future course of weapons development. Nor can anyone *know* in advance how much ruin a given nation could absorb without cracking up, what its recuperative capacities would be, or where destruction would pass the point of no return. Uncertainty is all the greater because the unprecedented rate of technological advance in the military sphere renders irrelevant so much of the historical experience upon which predictions are implicitly if not explicitly based. In any case, estimates and speculations regarding the *consequences* of a third world war represent only half of the picture.

The other half—and in the short run at least, an equally important aspect—is the human reactions to this newly acquired capacity for destruction and homicide en masse. In examining this aspect, it is essential to distinguish between the official strategies and counterstrategies of governments, on the one hand, and the opinions and sentiments of individuals and groups who form the respective constituencies of those governments. With respect to the former, states can be classified into four classes as follows:

(1) Those which control significant capabilities in nuclear weapons
(2) Those which control relatively insignificant nuclear capabilities
(3) Those which have or are presumed to have definite nuclear development programs in hand
(4) All other states

To date only two states qualify for Class 1: the United States and the Soviet Union. The impact of nuclear weapons on their strategies will be considered in a moment.

By the early 1960's two states had qualified for Class 2: Great Britain and France. Neither the British nor the French government has been able—or, at least, willing—to pay the high price of developing a militarily significant nuclear capability. For both, possession of some nuclear capability—even a token capability—has been regarded as a prestige item necessary to sustain the international role which these states have traditionally played, and which their ruling elites desire to continue to play.

Class 3 includes states definitely on the way to acquiring some nuclear capability. Reliable information on this subject is extremely difficult to acquire. Sweden is frequently cited. Though little firm information is available, all indications point to Chinese determination to become a nuclear power at the earliest possible moment.

Either the American or the Soviet government could speed up the development of nuclear capabilities in other countries. In general, both have displayed reluctance to do so, and an even stronger reluctance to supply nuclear arms without restrictions even to their closest allies. There are indications that the prospect of the diffusion of nuclear capabilities is regarded with anxiety if not with dismay both in Moscow and in Washington.

There is only one way in which such diffusion can be indefinitely prevented. That way is concerted international action to abolish or to limit nuclear weapons. It is generally agreed that such an agreement, to be effective, would require some system of inspection of industries and military installations. Such inspection would necessarily have to apply to the United States and the Soviet Union along with all the others. Neither of these two major nuclear powers has been able to formulate a scheme acceptable to the other, and in the meantime, the diffusion of destructive capabilities continues unchecked, with additional states knocking on the door of the Nuclear Club each year.

Turning specifically to strategic concepts and planning, the initial reactions to the atomic bomb (1945, and immediately thereafter) varied somewhat from country to country. Scientists who had worked on the atomic-bomb project tended to regard 1945 as a decisive turning point, or watershed, in the history of weapons. Professional military men and most politicians and civil servants were generally slower than the scientists to appreciate the A-bomb's revolutionary implications. Officials everywhere were prone to take the bomb in stride, and to regard it simply as "another weapon," for which suitable counterweapons would come along in due course. A sentence in the British Government's Statement on Defense for 1948 probably sums up an attitude widely held in many countries: "New scientific developments do not modify the basic principles of defense policy, but the advent of weapons of mass destruction must profoundly influence both the preparations for and the conduct of war."

The initial policy of the United States was to guard the secret of the A-bomb. This policy rested upon the assumption—mistaken as it turned out—that the Soviet government commanded neither the scientific knowledge nor the engineering skills and industrial resources necessary to produce atomic bombs within the near future. It was hoped, and rather generally and confidently expected, that the American monopoly of nuclear weapons would continue for a decade, perhaps for a generation or more; and that our long head-start would assume decisive superiority indefinitely. This expectation was shattered when the Russians exploded their first atomic device in the summer of 1949. This event occurred against a background of Russian moves, consolidating their hold on the satellite countries of eastern Europe, and their first determined but unsuccessful attempt to force Western troops out of Berlin. This combination of events evoked reconsideration of American military strategy all along the line. The subsequent evolution of American and Soviet military strategy is described in the following excerpt from a report prepared for the Senate Committee on Foreign Relations, by the Washington Center of Foreign Policy Research of the Johns Hopkins University: *

> In the period since World War II the United States has developed and pursued a national military strategy . . . [which] has come to be almost exclusively one of nuclear deterrence. . . . The strategy of nuclear deterrence evolved in response to the very specific threat of a nuclear attack on this country that was implicit in the August 1949

* "Developments in Military Technology and Their Impact on United States Strategy and Foreign Policy," by J. R. King, P. H. Nitze, Arnold Wolfers, et al., all of the staff of the Washington Center of Foreign Policy Research of the John Hopkins University. Committee print, December 6, 1959, pursuant to S. R. 336, 85th Cong., and S. R. 31, 86th Cong. Government Printing Office, Washington, D. C., 1959.

explosion of the first Soviet nuclear device. . . . As the pressures of Soviet expansionism [in Europe and the Middle East] continued to mount, the U. S. strategic response was . . . a rebirth of those concepts that had proved valid in World War II. . . . [These included] "stockpiling of strategic materials" . . . [plans] for "war mobilization" . . . a proposal for universal military training. . . heavy reliance on airpower . . . superior naval power, and the ability to mobilize both manpower and economy in any crisis carrying the threat of war. . . . The American response to the [Berlin blockade in 1948] was renewed emphasis on collective defense which led to the formation of the North Atlantic Treaty Organization and the deployment of U.S. strategic airpower abroad.

The strategic priorities of this period [1945-49] were . . . first . . . our ability to deliver the bomb, followed, in this order, by the capability of Western fleets to keep the sealanes open for transport of war materiel, a hard core of defensive allied ground forces-in-being on the Continent and, finally, the provision of air defense and tactical airpower by England and France. This was a strategy of collective defense clearly aimed at deterrence of the potential aggressor from Europe and in Europe.

Announcement of the Soviet atomic explosion [in August 1949] presaged a considerable revision of these concepts. The Soviet achievement meant not only that the Soviet threat to our allies and overseas outposts would soon be gravely increased, but that, within the span of a few years, the security of the continental United States itself would be endangered as it had not been for more than a century. It was this latter threat, coupled with the low esteem in which active air defense systems were held at the time, that made creation of a strong strategic air arm the first defense priority. Its purpose was to establish a counterthreat of nuclear retaliation capable of deterring the Soviets from ever deciding to strike at the United States.

"Deterrence" now acquired a new significance. It had previously meant such support for the ground defenses of NATO members that an aggressor, denied the opportunity of achieving a quick and easy victory, would be deterred from attack by the fear of intervention by U.S. strategic air forces and allied reserve components. Now the deterrent mission was enlarged to include dissuasion of an all-out nuclear attack upon the United States itself. It was assumed this task required a strategic retaliatory force superior in size to its Soviet counterpart. The result was a national commitment to the achievement of superiority in nuclear striking force, and it was the vast strategic force resulting from this commitment that was eventually to shape American strategy in areas distinct from its initial role of deterring a direct attack on the United States.

The immediate change, however, was one of emphasis rather than of direction. It remained the policy of the United States "to build the balanced collective forces in Europe that will continue to deter aggression after our atomic advantage has diminished," as the Secretary

"I'M WORKING ON A DETERRENT TO DETER DETERRENTS."

of State stated in 1951. The conviction also remained that our forces could prove effectively deterrent only if the West could confront the Communist bloc with balanced military capabilities ranging from a strategic retaliatory force at one extreme to forces at lower levels that could be expected to deter or defeat aggression in Europe and Asia without the support of strategic nuclear retaliation that was threatening to become self-destructive. Events in Korea in the summer of 1950 emphasized the importance of non-nuclear ground and tactical air forces to the containment of communism and that the U.S. military power was seriously deficient in this regard.

It was at this strategic picture that a "new look" was taken in 1953 and 1954. By then the striking power of the Strategic Air Command . . . had reached impressive levels. Congress and the public had in addition grown restive over the cost in blood and treasure of the Korean war and weary of a conventional [that is, non-nuclear] military effort that seemed to offer no chance of success or victory.

[The resulting change of strategy was publicly announced in January 1954 by the Secretary of State, John Foster Dulles. The United States would depend henceforth] "primarily upon the capacity to retaliate, instantly, by means and at places of our own choosing." This implied that the military had now been authorized to plan on the assumption that, should deterrence fail, nuclear weapons of the U.S. strategic force would be utilized rather than held in reserve as a last resort to be avoided if at all possible.

. . . the new strategy . . . was not a defensive strategy in the common meaning of this term. The Secretary of State himself pointed out the contrast between "deterrent power" and "local defensive power." Reliance on local defensive forces was to give way to dependence on the threat and, if necessary, the employment of the strategic nuclear counteroffensive that became known as "massive retaliation." Now a potential aggressor, whether or not he was contemplating the use of nuclear weapons, was to be faced by the power and the will to furnish so massive a response that he could not hope to gain more than he was sure to lose.

Announcement of this "new look" also signaled a change in this country's attitude toward collective defense. The nature of the security guarantee given our allies changed from a promise to reinforce threatened allies with forces appropriate to local defense to the pledge to punish an aggressor with nuclear weapons at places of our own choosing. The new strategy did not eliminate the need for local defenses, whose purpose, as was later explained in relation to NATO, was now to compel the enemy to commit sufficiently clear-cut aggression as to trigger the nuclear response and, hopefully, to prevent occupation of the allied nations before the U.S. nuclear attack could take effect. It was noteworthy that the speech announcing the new strategy did not contain any reference to the existence or the potential of Soviet nuclear power. This omission was perhaps due to the Secretary's immediate concern with the Far East, where the Chinese Communists, who possessed no nuclear weapons, were adding to the troubles of the French in Indochina. It must also be said that, as its advocates made clear, the purposes of the new look were as much economic as military [that is to say, to reduce or at least to prevent increase of the U.S. military budget].

The consequences of the new strategy soon became evident. . . . In December 1954, NATO members were authorized to plan wartime operations on the assumption that atomic weapons would be used from the outset; NATO forces would now balance those of the presumptive opponent only insofar as nuclear weapons compensated for numerical weakness. At the time such weapons were strategic, and their employment, or nonemployment, was outside NATO's control. The assumption was that U.S. strategic power, rather than localized NATO defenses, would suffice to deter Soviet military aggression in Europe.

It was thus that the national military strategy changed from one committed, at least in principle, to a reliance on local defensive forces to deter an aggressor by denying him the opportunity of a quick and easy victory, to a strategy of deterrence based primarily upon nuclear-armed strategic forces. In terms of deterring a direct attack on the United States there was no alternative to the threat of nuclear retaliation once the Soviets had acquired weapons against which there was no defense in the traditional meaning of resistance to attack. This new strategy was then extended to cover the older threat of conventional military aggression on the erroneous assumption that what would deter the Communists from the one would deter them equally well from the other. But it also reflected a desire to build and support the requisite strategic force with assets diverted from the creation of those tactical forces which could have given substance to a strategy of local defense.

[From the American viewpoint] it is . . . unfortunate that the capacity to retaliate instantly at places of our own choosing, which had emerged as a byproduct of the strategic deterrent force, was to prove no more a Western monopoly than had the nuclear weapons themselves. . . . [Evidence quickly accumulated] to signify a major advance in Soviet capability to strike at targets within the United States . . . [and it was predicted] that the Soviets would soon be producing jet bombers at a rate twice that of the United States.

Now the very ability of SAC to deter a direct attack on the United States was believed to be at issue; its commander . . . argued that, being barred from striking first himself, he must have a strategic force several times that of the Soviets in order to have sufficient retaliatory force left after a Soviet first strike. This objective, which was soon to receive national acceptance, called for sufficient bombers to accomplish on a second strike what the Soviets might accomplish by striking first.

To create a force of this size required an extraordinary increase in SAC's power to deliver a first or a second strike, thereby adding to the attractiveness and apparent feasibility of applying the strategy of nuclear deterrence to the threat of Communist aggression in Eurasia [as well as the continental United States]. But the growth of the Soviet nuclear force was bound to restrict SAC's freedom of action in this regard and consequently to downgrade the deterrent value of threatening to employ SAC against any aggression that falls below the strategic nuclear level. Such a restraining influence might be called "counterdeterrence" from the Soviet viewpoint. Its influence was reflected [in a statement in which the Secretary of State] referred to the possibility of localized Communist aggressions and stated "we and our allies should, between us, have the capacity to deal with these without our actions provoking a general nuclear war."

It must be remembered that the opportunity to discourage all forms of Communist military aggression by the strategy of nuclear deterrence was, in many ways, the byproduct of our efforts to deter a direct attack on the United States—a bonus, in essence, of a military posture. It should not have surprised us that the Soviets also received a "bonus" from the creation of their own strategic force, one which the Soviet Premier used to advantage during the 1956 Suez crisis when rattling his rockets against our NATO allies. . . .

The distinction between a "deterrent" and a "counterdeterrent" force or strategy depends on which adversary is credited with having the military initiative. The purpose of U.S. military power is deterrent in terms of the American conviction that it is the Soviets who wish to act aggressively and that it is therefore the mission of U.S. forces to convince them that doing so would not be to their advantage. The Soviet purpose [according to the above American assumption] is to discourage the employment of American military power and, presumably, to preserve their own freedom to act aggressively despite the threat of nuclear retaliation posed by the United States.

A solution of at least one of their military problems would be to acquire strategic forces of such strength and character that the retaliatory threat posed by SAC would no longer be credible when applied to nonstrategic aggression. Should they achieve such a force and be convinced that the United States would refrain from irrational or self-destructive use of its strategic nuclear power, they would have countered the U.S. extended deterrence strategy and regained considerable freedom to act militarily in Eurasia.

It is possible that such counterdeterrence has been, since the late 1940's, the mission of the Soviet strategic force. Recently published studies of Soviet strategy reveal no clear evidence to the contrary. Even today the Soviet concept of a third world war is said to be one of grinding attrition that is to be finally decided on the ground; their military strategists appear to be placing an increasing emphasis on the importance of surprise attack but to be not yet convinced, as are their American counterparts, that a first strike could decide the conflict. Their thinking on this point must be considered traditional, however, and it would, moreover, be most unwise to assume that published information on Soviet strategy is up to date or even that adequate knowledge of their intentions is attainable. What one can say is that the postwar evolution of Soviet strategy appears to have followed, belatedly, a path similar to that taken by our own.

While Stalin lived there was apparently no basic change in Soviet strategy; his object was to win a ground war in Europe and he remained convinced that the way to do so was by mobilizing and relying upon large and modernized but essentially "conventional" [that is, nonnuclear] ground forces. Soviet development of strategic airpower began with a bomber of medium range copied from us . . . and was later notable for the mass production of a medium-range jet bomber . . . clearly useful for attack on targets in Western Europe and North Africa. There appeared, in this transitional period, no Soviet counterpart of the U.S. B-36 intercontinental bomber, although it is difficult to tell whether they lacked the capability or the intention to produce such a weapons system. Indoctrination of their own armed forces during this period was heavily larded with propaganda on "capitalist encirclement" and paranoic attributions of hostile intent to the non-Communist world. There was an emphasis, in short, on "defense" in the same sense, but not in the same degree, that Western preparations were defensive in the early stages of the cold war. Such strategies and corresponding capabilities were for the West, but even more for the

Soviet Union, insufficient for the deterrence of an opposing nuclear force or for its destruction in a first strike.

By 1954 the effects of nuclear weapons were being taken with increasing seriousness by the Soviet military and a reassessment began of the importance of surprise attack. Soviet estimates of the situation may be assumed to have begun, as ours began, with an appraisal of the threat presented by the opposing strategic force. Whether they looked at U.S. capabilities, in the form of a burgeoning force of strategic bombers well capable of reaching targets in the Soviet Union, or at the intentions so freely expressed in support of the U.S. strategy of extended deterrence, the future may not have appeared promising for the further expansion of the Soviet domain or even for the national security of the Soviet Union.

The Soviet response was a buildup of previous neglected air defense systems, gradually intensified programs of civil defense training, an attempt to disperse or conceal key industrial and military installations and an increased emphasis on the development of strategic weapons capable of reaching targets within the United States. One result was the creation of an impressive strategic air force, albeit one that remained remarkably inferior to SAC in size and capability and was thus more appropriate to the neutralization of our strategic air arm by posing the threat of retaliation, than to its actual destruction by a massive counterforce strike.

Soviet counterdeterrence began to affect the actions of the United States and its allies at possibly the same moment at which the Soviets themselves became aware of their capacity to deter the United States from employing its strategic force against peripheral aggression, or of making it credible that the United States would so employ it. Britain and France appear to have taken Khrushchev's Suez "bomb rattling" seriously, and the United States might not have disavowed any intention of intervening in the Hungarian revolt as categorically as it did had Soviet nuclear strength remained at its 1953 level. Faced with the damage this Nation might suffer in the course of a "punitive" strike against an opponent who was himself capable of massive retaliation, the U.S. strategy of nuclear deterrence began to disclose its limitations.

The nuclear guarantee was now at least implicitly withdrawn from certain peripheral areas in recognition of the fact that their security was no longer worth the risks of nuclear war. The problem remained of what to do for deterrence of or defense against more provocative forms of aggression that would affect vital American interests. Here, particularly in the case of the NATO countries, no satisfactory alternative to an increasingly unwarranted dependence on strategic nuclear deterrence has yet been developed. This is partly because the past reliance on the threat of nuclear retaliation was so great as to discourage the development of other military capabilities and partly because the growth of strategic nuclear power has, for the United States at least, been accompanied by a matching decline in those forces appropriate to the deterrence and countering of less than total aggression.

This lack of a viable alternative to the strategy of extended nuclear deterrence emphasizes the serious limitations and weaknesses of both U.S. military capabilities and the strategy that has hitherto guided their development and employment. . . .

From the foregoing discussion it is manifest that the United States— and presumably the Soviet Union too—entered the 1960's with baffling unsolved problems of military defense. The ultimate issue confronting both was how to achieve desired goals—in particular how to defend the territory and life of the nation—without provoking a train of events that would end in mutual ruin. From the specific standpoint of the United States, the paramount issue was the patent insufficiency of the doctrine of massive retaliation under the altered conditions prevailing in the 1960's. Quoting further from the above report:

> If the American nuclear monopoly, coupled with an ample supply of nuclear warheads and delivery vehicles, had continued to exist, the reliability of the American nuclear deterrent would not now be open to question. The United States and its allies could have remained confident that the threat of massive retaliation against Soviet cities in response to any serious Soviet aggression would have been both credible and effective. As a nuclear monopolist, the United States would not have had to fear the self-mutilating consequences that could follow a strike on an opponent able to retaliate in kind.
>
> With the advent of Soviet nuclear striking power, the situation radically changed. Now, neither side, if it initiates the use of strategic force, can be certain that it would avoid being struck itself by nuclear weapons, unless it can predict with assurance that its first-strike blow against its opponent's strategic forces will be almost totally effective. If one side should achieve such an overwhelming counterforce ability, it could gain or regain the position of a monopolist by employing its strategic power against the strategic forces of its adversary.
>
> Development of the capabilities required for such a knockout blow by either the United States or the Soviet Union is not now likely, although it cannot be ruled out as a future possibility in view of the rapid pace and uncertain predictability of technological developments. . . ."

According to one hypothesis, the spectacular rise of Soviet nuclear capabilities in the 1950's has not increased but rather has lessened the probability of a third world war. A leading exponent of this thesis is Arthur L. Burns, of the Australian National University. Mutual strategies of nuclear deterrence lead to international stability, according to Burns, "whenever the development of military technology makes (i) the physical destruction of all of an opponent's forces impossible, and (ii) the physical destruction of his economy easy." These conditions, Burns contends, now exist; and as long as they continue to exist, he foresees "much disturbance" in the relations of the greater states, "but none of it turning into world war."

Burns also rejects the prevalent arguments that deterrent strategies necessarily lead to an endless spiral of increasing armaments or that such strategies must eventually culminate in a third world war or that partial disarmament is the only way to combat these tendencies.

> The arms race, given weapons-systems of a certain type and capacity [he contends], sometimes ceases of itself, each side acquiring and maintaining just that quantity of armaments which would enable it to retaliate after a "first strike" by the other, since no possible further increase would put it in a position to launch a successful first strike itself.*

The implication of this hypothesis is that the nuclear stalemate has largely taken the function of decision making out of the hands of politicians and generals. In place of fallible human decisions and interactions, in which some element of uncertainty is always a factor, mutual strategies of nuclear deterrence have produced an international system, functioning semiautomatically, and promising to postpone catastrophe indefinitely.

Other experts have doubts about the semiautomatic functioning of mutual deterrence. Strategies of deterrence, they contend, must satisfy certain conditions in order to be effective; and these conditions may or may not prevail in the environment of the Society of Nations today. William W. Kaufmann (of the RAND Corporation) has composed one of the more lucid statements of the "requirements of deterrence," from which the following passage is taken.†

> Essentially, deterrence means preventing certain types of contingencies from arising. To achieve this objective it becomes necessary to communicate in some way to a prospective antagonist what is likely to happen to him should he create the contingency in question. The expectation is that, confronted with this prospect, he will be deterred from moving in directions that are regarded as inimical, at least so long as other less intolerable alternatives are open to him.
> A deterrence policy thus constitutes a special kind of forecast: a forecast about the costs and risks that will be run by the party to be deterred, if certain actions are taken, and about the advantages that he will gain if those actions are avoided. . . .

---

* From "From Balance to Deterrence," by A. L. Burns, in *World Politics*, July, 1957, pp. 524, 528; and "Disarmament or the Balance of Terror?", by A. L. Burns, in *World Politics*, October 1959, p. 133. Copyright 1957 and 1959 by World Politics; reproduced by permission.

† From pp. 17-20 of *Military Policy and National Security*, by W. W. Kaufmann et al. Copyright 1956 by Princeton Unversity Press, Princeton, New Jersey; reproduced by permission.

The statement of intentions can be meant in all seriousness or it can be in the nature of a bluff. Whichever it is will determine to a considerable extent the formulation and communication of the policy. Presumably the precision of the forecast and the manner in which it is communicated will vary with the willingness to live up to the expressed intentions. But whether the forecast is intended or is a bluff, a very real risk and some serious potential costs are attached to a policy of deterrence. The risk is that, despite our best efforts, the antagonist will challenge us to make good on our threat. If we do so, we will have to accept the consequences of executing our threatened action. If we back down and let the challenge go unheeded, we will suffer losses of prestige, we will decrease our capacity for instituting effective deterrence policies in the future, and we will encourage the opponent to take further actions of a detrimental character. This kind of cost can be as serious as the cost attached to fulfillment of the forecast.

In order to minimize this risk, with its attached costs, and at the same time preserve the effectiveness of the policy, it becomes necessary to surround the proposal with an air of credibility. In this connection it must be remembered that a large and varied audience will be observing our behavior and that the reactions of this audience will be crucial to the success or failure of the policy. For the purposes of this discussion, the audience may be broken down very simply into enemy, domestic, and allied categories.

Dealing first with the enemy audience, it is quite obvious that we must know specifically who the opponent is in order to make our policy meaningful to him. . . . Assuming a knowledge of the antagonist's identity, there are three main areas in which credibility must be established: the areas of capability, cost, and intentions. The enemy must be persuaded that we have the capability to act; that, in acting, we could inflict costs greater than the advantages to be won from attaining his objective; and that we really would act as specified in the stated contingency.

Potential as against actual capability cannot be regarded as a convincing instrument of deterrence in the present state of affairs. Nor is it enough simply to have a certain number of planes supplied with fission and fusion bombs. The enemy must be persuaded not only that the instrument exists but also that its power is operational—in the case of SAC, for example, that it can get through to its targets and inflict a most burdensome cost upon him.

Even if capability and cost requirements can be fulfilled, there remains the difficult and delicate problem of making intentions credible. An intelligent opponent—and it would be dangerous indeed to postulate a stupid one in dealing with the Communist world—may be expected to use three main sources of information about the intentions of a country such as the United States: its record of performance in comparable contingencies during the recent past; the statements and behavior of its government; and the attitudes of public opinion, both domestic and allied. A policy of deterrence consistent with the country's recent behavior in the international arena is likely to seem much more plausible than one which constitutes a sharp break with tradition. Similarly, the credibility of the policy will vary with the degree of consistency in the speech and action of the government and its executive agencies. Nothing can be more crippling to a policy of deterrence than to have the statements of the Secretary of State contradicted or reinterpreted by other officials of national standing. Nor will official statements seem convincing if actions are being taken simultaneously to nullify the statements, or if nothing concrete is being done to support them.

Finally, and perhaps most importantly in the realm of intentions, a policy of deterrence will seem credible only to the extent that important segments of public opinion in domestic and allied countries support it. In democratic nations, especially, the process of formulating policy is much more than the enunication of intentions by governmental leaders. Before these intentions can be regarded as policy, there must be genuine evidence of popular support for them from the country at large. This consideration suggests a rather crucial and specific requirement that a policy of deterrence must fulfill. Its potential costs must seem worth incurring. In other words, there must be some relationship between the value of the objective sought and and the costs involved in its attainment. A policy of deterrence which does not fulfill this requirement is likely to result only in deterring the deterrer. . . .

Examination of the "credibility" of a strategy of deterrence inescapably opens up the question: whether it is reasonable to assume that such a strategy will in fact deter an adversary. In plain English, will a nation's rulers accept the risk of damaging counterattack under certain conditions? This issue is bluntly posed in the Report by the Washington Center of Foreign Policy Research, from which we have already quoted at length:

> Neither the United States nor the Soviet Union can ignore the possibility that its adversary might someday settle for less than a knockout blow and, rationally or irrationally, be content with a strike at its adversary's retaliatory forces sufficiently crippling to make tolerable the damage it might suffer in return. Conceivably, for instance, one side or the other might consider even very grave damage more tolerable than the risks of allowing its adversary to strike the first blow, should such a strike appear imminent.

This disturbing possibility (which may or may not rest upon sound psychological grounds) has inspired certain experts to play down the destructive consequences of nuclear war. One of these is Herman Kahn, whose optimism about survival and recovery from a nuclear war was noted earlier in this chapter. Kahn argues that the United States strategy of deterrence by threat of massive reprisal will actually deter (that is, be "credible") only if the other side is convinced that the American people are physically and psychologically prepared to "accept" the consequences of war with nuclear weapons. Kahn continues:

> The critical point is whether the Soviets and the Europeans believe we can keep our casualties to a level we would find acceptable, whatever that level may be. In such an eventuality the Soviets would be deterred from very provocative acts, such as a ground attack on Europe or evacuating their cities and presenting us with an ultimatum. But if they do not believe we can keep casualties to a level we would find acceptable, the Soviets may feel safe in undertaking these extremely provocative military adventures. Or at least the Europeans may believe that the Soviets will feel safe, and this in itself creates an extremely dangerous situation for pressure and blackmail.*

Such speculations, implying the possibility of pre-emptive attack as a way out of the nuclear impasse, highlight another of the psychological fruits of our runaway technology: namely, the dehumanizing effect which seems to come from prolonged concentration on the apparatus of destruction unlimited. International politics comes to be conceived as a game—a dangerous game, but all the more exciting because dangerous. In this game, simulated in the seclusion of military conference rooms and research institutes, flesh-and-blood human beings, the ultimate units of all politics, come to be regarded as puppets on strings, and international politics as a sort of macabre Punch and Judy show.

Evidence of this dehumanizing trend can be culled from newspapers and magazines, from Congressional hearings, and from the reports and recommendations of experts. This is not an entirely new phenomenon in military thinking. War games have long been a standard device of advanced military training and planning. What is new—and perhaps highly significant—is the cold-blooded dehumanized proposal to *accept* massive destruction and human misery in *one's own country* as part of a deliberate strategy of international statecraft.

It is certainly significant that the attempt to reinstate the use of unlimited violence as an acceptable technique of statecraft comes after the upsurge of Soviet science and military technology has evoked doubts as to who is deterring whom in the East-West struggle. It is also notable that this development occurs after the passage of time has begun to dull the most acute memories of the physical destruction, human misery, and political consequences of the last (though far less destructive) total war.

---

* From "The Nature and Feasibility of War and Deterrence," RAND Publication No. P-1888-R.C., January 20, 1960; reproduced by permission of Dr. Herman Kahn.

If international politics is simply puppetry on a grand scale, a game in which the blue chips are megaton bombs, it is perfectly logical for gamesters to experiment and define the conditions under which military attacks of various magnitudes would be "acceptable."

This trend of thought has evoked some strong reactions. One of these is embodied in a letter to *The New York Times* by Lewis Mumford, the well-known American architect, historian, and commentator on public affairs. Mumford addresses himself to the testimony of certain scientific experts in a Congressional hearing in 1959 on the probable scale of destruction in a nuclear war. Noting the experts' generally optimistic opinions regarding the long-range effects, he continues:

> . . . They have no scientific means of predicting the ecological pattern that will emerge. What is quite as serious, they make no mention of the fatal effects of both kinds of damage [short-term and long-term] on human society. Hence the favorable estimate is gratuitous and unsupported by evidence. . . .
>
> Even if we push the cold war into a nuclear catastrophe by clinging to our now impotent strategy, some mutilated stump of our country, they tell us, will survive. . . .
>
> By what standard of prudence do we commit our lives and the lives of future generations to such demonstrably fallible and imprudent "authorities"? Why do we permit the specialists who favor the fullest use of nuclear energy to sit in judgment on the human consequences of their own work? Their unqualified commitment to nuclear technology is one of the present dangers that must be scrutinized and weighed.
>
> The apparent willingness of our fellow citizens to leave life-and-death decisions to specialists is an abdication of their human responsibility. The lives our Air Force strategists are so ready to sacrifice by the tens of millions are our own.
>
> It is not for military or scientific experts to tell us how many deaths per million from leukemia and bone cancer are "permissible," or how many monsters may be born, so that our Government may stubbornly cling to its original mistakes in exploiting nuclear energies and nuclear weapons. Still less is it for Executive decision to determine what gross fraction of the country is expendable, provided we are able to use our own varied instruments of collective extermination on equally large populations in Russia.
>
> That we share these insane plans with Russia is a fact that doubles our danger but does not halve our guilt. There is no "permissible" or tolerable sacrifice of human life in a conflict whose method nullifies every rational object and makes the victor indistinguishable from the victim.
>
> The fact is that those scientific advisers our Government chooses to listen to, and the politicians who accept their judgment, live in an underdimensioned and distorted world. Having meticulously eliminated

the "human element" from their thought, they are equally capable of sanctioning its elimination from this planet. Their limited methodology has driven out the feelings, anxieties and hopes that alone could bring us to our senses.

As a nation we have, I submit, been subjugated and enslaved by our commitment to nuclear weapons. We still vainly try to find mechanical, electronic, and radioactive answers to problems that can be solved only by human proposals addressed to a human end—mankind's survival.

Neither rocket weapons nor planetary sorties nor underground shelters will save us. We must rather deliver ourselves from our faith in weapons of annihilation and in the sick fantasies that would prompt us in the last extremity to use them.

If we are destroyed it will not be in the first instance by Russia, but by our original delusions of nuclear omnipotence, and our self-induced later fears of Russia's equal powers, which are now leading us steadily to the very goal which we profess to abhor. . . .*

This is a strong indictment. But Mumford's attitude is not unique. On the contrary, it appears to be quite typical of those who face the Kahns across the seemingly unbridgeable chasm which nuclear weapons have opened up in American public opinion or, more precisely, among that tiny fraction of Americans who appear to give any serious and sustained attention to the subject at all. The positions of the Kahns and the Mumfords are irreconcilable, and thus far the Kahns appear to come much closer to representing official opinion and policies than do the Mumfords.

These positions are irreconcilable because they rest upon irreconcilable assumptions. These irreconcilable assumptions cover a wide range of issues. But they all relate to Soviet and American capabilities and intentions, and in particular to the conditions that must prevail in order to convince Soviet statesmen that American statesmen mean what they say when they threaten to counter any serious aggression with nuclear bombs and rockets.

Taking the American people as a whole, no such clear-cut division has been observed. One characteristic of a good deal of American talk about world affairs is marked compartmentation of intellectual and emotional responses to the perils of the nuclear age. One hears people talk glibly, even flippantly, of the "inevitable" war that is going to incinerate everybody. But the same people go about their private affairs—rearing children, building homes, buying life insurance, investing in stocks and bonds, and making all sorts of other long-term commitments, which, in most instances manifestly reflect a deepseated faith that Providence takes care of women, children—and the United States.

* From *The New York Times*, July 6, 1959. Copyright 1959 by The New York Times Co.; reproduced by permission of the author.

Alongside this compartmentation, and apparently associated with it, one notes a widespread American tendency to ignore the threat of World War III altogether. Specific evidence of this tendency came to light in a recent nation-wide survey of sources of happiness, unhappiness, and anxiety. In this survey it was discovered that

> international tensions, fear of atomic extinction, and the anxious atmosphere of a troubled world do not figure importantly among the things the American people say trouble them. Fewer than one in ten expressed an outstanding concern for community, national, or world problems.

The analysts could find no satisfactory simple explanation for this apathy. They speculated that it

> may be due partly to the fact that most of us are concerned with the realities of our immediate environments, and that the extent to which sources of worry and tension affect us decreases in proportion to their remoteness. It may also reflect a retreat from the realities of the larger world, a sense of helplessness in the face of events that the individual feels are beyond his ability to control. Or it could be a symptom of political immaturity combined with a persistent undercurrent of isolationism, resulting in a renunciation of social responsibility.*

One might speculate a little further, that American indifference to the military perils of our time is a little like the behavior of people who live upon the slopes of a temporarily dormant volcano. They know that the volcano has periodically erupted, destroying everything within range. Reason tells them the volcano will erupt again, with comparable devastating results. But the land is fertile—and who knows when the disaster will strike? It has been observed repeatedly that people who live in the shadow of possible disaster come to terms with it by putting the whole dirty business out of their minds.

Moreover, World War II is rapidly receding into the past. College students in the 1960's have no personal recollections of Pearl Harbor, the bombing of London, the scorching of western Russia, the massive fire-raids on Berlin and Tokyo, and scores of other horrors of that war. Of the men and women old enough to recall those events, only some of those who served overseas—a tiny fraction of the American population—ever had any close-up experience of what modern war is like. To the vast majority of Americans, World War II and the subsequent smaller war in Korea

---

* From p. xiii of *Americans View Their Mental Health*, by Gerald Gurin et al. Published for the Joint Commission on Mental Illness and Health. Copyright 1960 by Basic Books, Inc., 1960, New York; reproduced by permission.

brought full employment and a prosperity such as they had never known before.

Very few Americans came to grips with the realities of catastrophe during World War II, and few appear to give much thought to the dimensions of possible future catastrophes. Fewer still, it would appear, can imagine what it would be like if New York or Chicago or any other American metropolis were smashed into rubble the way Berlin, Tokyo, Hiroshima, Stalingrad, and scores of other European and Asian cities were smashed. For this reason, among others, Americans contemplate the fruits of modern war from a radically different perspective than do Britons, Germans, Russians, Japanese, and all the other peoples, among whom millions still living bear the psychological as well as the physical scars of the catastrophes which swept over them.

Even in countries which suffered heavy damage in World War II, the memory of disaster is fading as the years slip by; and the postwar children apparently learn relatively little about it from their parents. At least that was the authors' impression in the middle 1950's as they conversed with Europeans and watched little boys playing cops and robbers in the rubble of some of Europe's worst devastated cities. If time blunts the memories even of those who lived through overwhelming catastrophes, how much more difficult it is for Americans (most of whom have had no such experience) to envisage the frightfulness of modern war!

Within the United States one discovers remarkably little overt protest against the strategy of defense by deterrence through threat of nuclear reprisal. The Mumfords, as suggested above, appear to have a very small following. One may assume, though proof is largely lacking, that comparable public acquiescence prevails throughout the Soviet Union. One may assume further, again without much definite evidence, that the Chinese government will experience no difficulty in mobilizing whatever public support it might deem necessary for its military policies. Finally, there is evidence that many influential persons and groups in the leading European countries regard national possession of nuclear weapons as an important symbol of prestige and status that will enable them to deal on more nearly equal terms with the Superpowers.

All these attitudes stand in marked contrast to the neutralism which prevails in certain countries and seems to be latent in many others. The essence of mid-century neutralism is the desire to avoid becoming either participant or pawn in the power struggles of Moscow and Washington. Neutralism in this sense is the avowed policy of numerous states in Asia and Africa. In Western Europe neutralism is nearly everywhere rejected at the level of official policy. But neutralist sentiment exists in Britain and on the Continent, probably in much greater strength than our own government and press are willing to admit. Whether this sentiment will continue to grow, and whether it would significantly influence the behavior of these nations if East-West relations should deteriorate to the brink of nuclear war, one can only speculate. But one of the givens of the international environment of the 1960's is clearly a massive groundswell of human yearning in Europe, Asia, and Africa to have no part in the potentially lethal strategies and counterstrategies emanating from Moscow, Washington, and Peking.

CHAPTER NINE

The Geographic Setting: Images and Realities

THE EARTH'S SURFACE is the human habitat. With the aid of mechanical equipment men can fly through the air and tunnel beneath the surface. Experimental probings into more distant space, and the certainty of greater achievements on this new frontier, do not alter the fact that most human activities occur upon or relatively close to the earth's surface.

The oceans and connecting seas, continents and islands, lakes and rivers, mountains and plains, deserts and verdant landscapes which comprise the earth's surface have often been likened to a theatrical stage. Upon this stage from time immemorial the human race has enacted many plays. For centuries men have speculated regarding relationships between the properties of this earthly stage and human projects and accomplishments.

These relationships evoke a special interest in the student of international politics. Every political community (though not necessarily every political system) has a territorial basis. From a geographer's viewpoint, a state is "organized space." Territory is, by definition, one of the absolute requisites of statehood (see page 81). In nearly all transactions between nation-states, including those in which some conflict of purpose or interest is involved, factors of location, space, and distance are nearly always significant variables. This sense of significance is embodied in the maxim: "Power is local."

Political demands are projected through space from one location to another. Such operations involve expenditure of energy and consumption of other resources. A state's access to essential physical resources may affect decisively its ability to impose its demands, and conversely its ability to resist demands, pressures, and attacks by other nations. In ways both obvious and not so obvious, the factors of climate appear to have affected both directly and indirectly the distribution of political potential over the earth. Awareness of these various nonhuman factors, and notions as to their limiting effects, have commonly entered into the deliberations of statesmen and appear to have affected significantly on many occasions the substance of their policies.

Today the relations between man and his nonhuman environment are very much in flux. As a result of revolutionary advances in technology and other social changes scarcely less revolutionary, these relationships are probably more unstable than in any previous era. There are indications that recent huge strides in science and engineering may be altering in fundamental ways all the patterns of human occupancy of the earth.

In thinking about the relations of politics and the earth, it is essential to keep constantly in mind the distinction between image and reality. As we have said before and shall emphasize again, what matters in making policies and in explaining policies is how the policy-maker imagines his environment to be, not how it actually is. Conversely outcomes, accomplishments, the operational results of policy decisions, depend on conditions as these actually are, not as someone imagines them to be. This distinction is basic to an understanding of the bearings of the geographic setting on the actions and potentials of nations.

The earth as an image in men's minds

An important corollary flows from the distinction between image and reality. It is that, with reference to the attitudes and decisions of statesmen and their constituents, erroneous geographical ideas may be just as influential as ideas which correspond to the facts of the real world.

Any number of examples could be cited to illustrate this proposition. Recently one of the authors stopped in a Western Union Office to send a cablegram to Brussels, *Belgium*. The clerk checked the message, and said: "Belgium, that's in Holland, isn't it?" Professor Stephen B. Jones (geographer, of Yale University) tells of the "book-club clerk who filed letters from Brussels, Brazil, and Syria under 'miscellaneous islands.'" Then there was the American tourist who stepped into the postoffice of a small French town, to mail a parcel to Boston, Massachusetts. The postmistress, however, refused his parcel, saying: "Boston, Angleterre oui; Boston, États-Unis, cela n'existe pas!"

Various maps have appeared from time to time caricaturing the geographical perspective of different American regions. In one of these, entitled "A New Yorker's Idea of the United States of America," the most conspicuous features are Manhattan, Long Island, and Florida. Cape Cod appears as an enormous peninsula, Great Salt Lake is one of the Great Lakes, Nebraska is a town in Illinois, and the remainder is comparably and fantastically jumbled. In another of these caricature maps, entitled "A Texan's Map of the U.S.A.," Texas appears larger than all the other States combined, with most of the northern and eastern parts of the country labeled "unexplored territory."

Turning to some rather more notable historic examples, there is the decision of the Queen of Spain to finance Columbus to sail westward across the Atlantic to Asia, in ignorance of the geographic layout that rendered the undertaking impossible as planned. For centuries thereafter men imagined the existence of a Terra Australia Incognita somewhere in the distant ocean where they would discover the gold mines of King Solomon. Until nearly the end of the fifteenth century most men imagined that the Atlantic and Indian oceans were separate and unconnected bodies of water. In a recent book, a sequence of maps depicting the West Indies and adjacent mainland as conceived through several centuries following the voyages of Columbus, shows how slow and halting was the accumulation of reasonably accurate geographical knowledge.* As originally drawn, the boundary between the United States and Canada failed to conform in several places with the actual geographic layout. On early American maps the territory west of the Missouri River was frequently labeled "Great American Desert" and was long imagined to be unfit for civilized habitation.

How many oil wells have been driven where no oil existed? How many farmers have tried to grow crops unsuited to particular soils and climates? How many ships have been wrecked on reefs and shoals incorrectly marked on navigational charts? How many military campaigns have failed because of erroneous notions of topographic, climatic, or other physical obstacles to be overcome?

Frequently misconceptions arise not so much from ignorance of the geographic layout *per se,* as from ignorance or neglect of its political or other significance. For example, the great British naval base upon the island of Singapore is said to have been designed on the mistaken assumption that swamps, jungles, and other natural obstacles would prevent any hostile approach across the nearby mainland of Malaya. Englishmen still speak of "going to Europe," as if the crossing of the Channel took days or weeks instead of a few hours (by ferry) or a few minutes (by plane). Many Americans still behave as if the wide oceans protect their country as in the early years of the Republic, even though every American city lies within range of Russian planes and missiles. Discrepancies between the earth as

* The book cited is *The Southeast in Early Maps,* by W. P. Cumming, Princeton University Press, 1958.

it is and as men have imagined it to be are characteristic of all peoples in all ages.

Cumulative geographic knowledge results in fewer gross misconceptions these days than in earlier times. Nevertheless, the knowledge and perspectives of individuals vary enormously. If anyone doubts this, we suggest that he perform the following experiment: Distribute to any group (excluding professional geographers, of course) a blank outline map of the world, and ask them to draw in the boundaries of the Soviet Union, the principal rivers of Africa, and the more important mountain ranges of Asia; and to locate the capitals of the greater states, the world's most productive oilfields, and the leading industrial regions.

Geographical perspective and terminology

Many of the geographical terms in the vocabulary to which we are accustomed are derived from the viewpoint and perspective of Western Europe, especially Britain. From Europe the most heavily used routes to Asia run to the east. This was so in ancient and medieval times, and continued to be so even after explorers in the sixteenth century demonstrated the westerly route to Asia via the Strait of Magellan and Cape Horn. Hence Asia early became the East in European parlance.

In the course of time the Balkan lands of southeastern Europe and the Moslem lands of southwestern Asia came to be called the *Near East*. The more distant Asian countries came to be called the *Far East*. In the traditional usage of our own Department of State, the Near East includes a larger area also designated as the *Middle East*. This latter term, rarely used very precisely, has come to embrace the non-European parts of the Near East, plus several additional countries of southern Asia, in particular, Iran and Afghanistan, and (less commonly) Pakistan, India, and Burma.

Beyond the Middle East from the geographical perspective of Western Europe, lies the Far East. That term came rather early to embrace the countries of eastern Asia which front on the Pacific Ocean and its connecting seas and also the islands in the southwestern Pacific. These islands became, in the European idiom, the *East Indies*, the islands east of India. The partially enclosed arm of the Pacific Ocean, bounded by the China coast, the island of Taiwan, and the Japanese archipelago, was called the *East* China Sea, or simply the *Eastern* Sea. Sometimes the Indian Ocean, the western reaches of the Pacific, and all their connecting waterways, were referred to as the *Eastern* Seas.

The same perspective is discernible in the Atlantic. This ocean came to be rather generally called the *Western* Ocean: that is, the ocean west of Europe. The islands of the Caribbean Sea (erroneously regarded for a long time as part of the Asiatic Indies) came to be known as the *West Indies*; that is, one went there by sailing west from Europe.

If the interregional history of the past thousand years or so had been written from a different geographical perspective, our vocabulary might be considerably different. From the viewpoint of North America, for example, the Atlantic might have been the Eastern (instead of the Western) Ocean; Europe might have been the Near East; the Near East might have been the Far East; the Far East might have been the Far West; and the East Indies, the West Indies. If one shifts the viewpoint to China, the perspective is still different. The Pacific becomes the Eastern Ocean; America, the Far East; and Europe, the Far West.

In short, we start our study of international politics with a geographical vocabulary and a set of geographical ideas inherited from the era when European peoples dominated most of the interregional communication, traffic, and political relations of the earth. This vocabulary affects not only our mode of speaking. It also affects in subtle ways our mode of thinking about places and peoples and about the links which bind them together into a global international system.

Maps as a source of geographic ideas

One can scarcely hope to understand the foreign policies and interactions of states without recourse to maps; and yet maps have long been a prolific source of confused and even mischievous thinking about international politics.

Putting cameras and men into space ships that orbit the earth has added a new dimension to geographical exploration. It is now possible, from a single viewpoint, to photograph or observe a large area of the earth's surface. But that is not how most of our present knowledge of the earth's surface was accumulated. Such knowledge has been built up piece by piece from accounts of earthbound explorers, navigators, and others, supplemented in more recent times by measurements taken with compass, sextant, chronometer, transit, barometer, and other instruments.

In our own century, aircraft equipped with cameras have added details to our knowledge of the earth's surface. More is likewise known of the location and magnitude of subsurface mineral bodies and the distribution of climatic phenomena. At long last, real progress is being made in mapping the floor of the oceans. But the process to date still remains one of fitting together bits and pieces of information, and with these data constructing models of the earth's surface, subsurface, and atmosphere.

Such models, as is well known, are of two kinds: globes and flat maps. Globes come closer to being replicas of the earth.

They are often (erroneously) called scale models of the earth. We say erroneously because even the largest and most detailed globes involve gross oversimplification of the earth's intricate design of lands and seas, mountains and rivers, and other features. Because of their cost and bulk, moreover, people have come to rely mainly on flat maps for their visual concepts of the layout of our human habitat.

Flat maps, like all models, are indispensable but tricky tools. Used with knowledge of their properties and limitations, maps can illuminate almost every international problem. Without them the statesman, the military planner, the teacher, his students, and everyone else would be as helpless as a mariner without chart and compass. (Nevertheless, there is abundant evidence that a survey of our schools, colleges, and universities would reveal the shocking state of affairs, that a relatively small minority of teachers make any continuous and imaginative use of maps in their classes and lectures).

A map to be effective, and not merely misleading, must fit the job in hand, or at least be used with explicit awareness of its properties and limitations. This is elementary common sense to any geographer. It is evidently not so obvious to many teachers of international subjects, to college and university administrators, and to the editors of books, magazines, and newspapers. Undiscriminating use of "any old map" (if indeed any map is used at all) has been and continues to be a common source of geographical misconceptions. These, in turn, appear to have been responsible —at least in some degree—for many illusions regarding the political relations of nations. Hence the very great importance of acquiring some knowledge of the qualities of maps most frequently encountered, as well as a clear understanding of the geographical realities which they are intended to portray.

Various methods have been devised for drawing flat maps. All involve the technically insoluble problem of transferring to or projecting upon a flat surface a design from the surface of a sphere. Methods of doing this are called projections. Most projections involve mathematical concepts and technical procedures which need not concern us here. But we do need to concern ourselves with the distinguishing features that characterize the more common projections.

Most maps in common use are derived by projecting the design of lands and seas from a globe onto a cylinder, or a cone, or a plane. Actually this way of describing "projections" is somewhat metaphorical. In practice, maps are drawn, not projected. However, the concept of projection may help us understand certain principles of cartography.

MERCATOR WORLD MAP

The Mercator map of the world was designed nearly 300 years ago by the Flemish geographer, Gerhard Mercator. It is popularly characterized as a cylindrical projection. From an imaginary viewing point at the center of the globe, the geographical design is, metaphorically speaking, "projected" onto a cylinder tangent at the equator. A rough approximation of this projection is depicted in Figure 9.A. In actual practice, the map is not produced in this manner, but is drawn according to certain technical mathematical formulae.

The continents can be centered in various ways on the Mercator map, or the map can be continued horizontally so as to show certain areas more than once. By placing Europe in the center (Figure 9.B) the Pacific Ocean is divided. By placing the United States in the center (see pp. 612 f.) a divided Eurasia appears on the right and left margins. By placing the Soviet Union in the center, the United States appears divided. Thus depending on how one manipulates the map, Europe, the United States, the Soviet Union, or any other country or region can be given the "central position."

In a strict geographical sense, the concept of central position is pure illusion. No country, and every country, occupies a central position on the globe. It all depends on one's perspective and viewing point. The strategic military or commercial properties of any country's position depends not only on its geographical location, but even more on the state of technology, the political geography of the Society of Nations, the prevailing patterns of alliances and other relationships, and the kinds of operational contingencies that one is thinking about.

The Mercator map includes the following technical characteristics. Meridians of longitude, those imaginary lines which converge to a point at each pole, appear as parallel vertical lines. Parallels of latitude are parallel as upon the globe, but, as a result of the mode of projection, degrees of latitude increase progressively from the equator to the poles. Thus both east-west and north-south distances appear increasingly too long the farther one moves from the equator. Each pole is transformed from a point, as it is on the globe, to a line of infinite length.

Because of these features the Mercator world map does not distort shapes too seriously; but this quality is purchased at the price of gross distortion of areas, and hence also distances, especially in the higher latitudes. Greenland, for example, *appears* about the same size as South

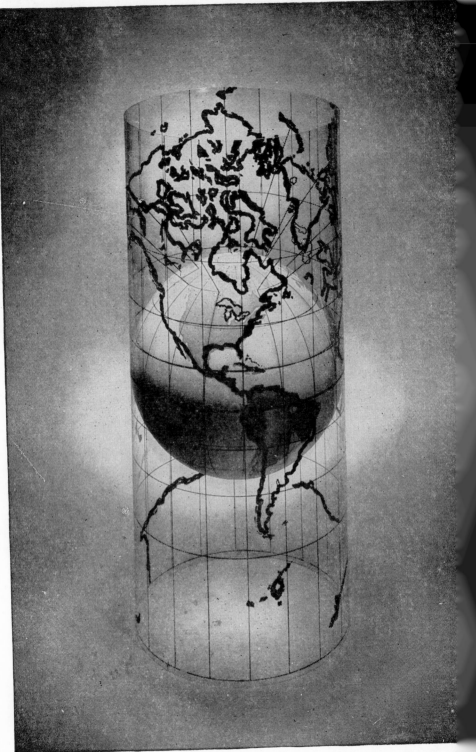

FIG. 9.A. PRINCIPLE OF THE MERCATOR PROJECTION
Courtesy Herbert Gehr, Life Magazine. Models by Norman Bel Geddes.

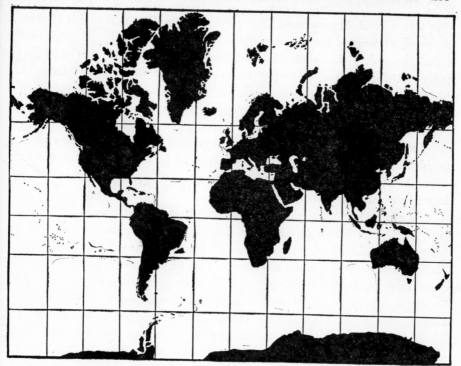

FIG. 9.B.   EUROPE-CENTERED MERCATOR WORLD MAP IN SILHOUETTE
A world map with the United States at the midline is shown in Fig 21.A, pp. 612 f. From
N. J. Spykman, *Geography of the Peace*. Copyright 1944 by Harcourt, Brace & Co., New
York; reproduced by permission.

America, but is in fact (as every geographer and some nongeographers
know) only about one-tenth as large. Canada, Alaska, the British Isles,
Northern Europe, and the Soviet Union all appear relatively larger than
they are in reality.

The Mercator projection was designed as a chart for mariners. Since
meridians and parallels on this grid intersect at right angles, as they do
on the globe, it follows that a straight line connecting any two points on the
map shows the same compass bearing at every point on the line. But such
lines, with certain minor exceptions, do not represent the shortest distances
between the points in question. These shortest distances, known as *great
circles* on the globe, appear (except along the equator and the central
vertical axis) as curved and sometimes discontinuous lines on the Mercator
map. A good idea of these features can be visualized by studying the maps
which accompany the article "This Hemisphere" by S. W. Boggs, beginning
on page 307 of this chapter.

As a chart for navigating ships across the oceans, the Mercator projection was a great improvement over earlier charts. It is still useful for this purpose. As long as European states dominated the world, and ships provided the only links connecting continents, the Mercator map was also fairly satisfactory for depicting commercial and military problems. A Mercator map, placed with its central north-south axis on the longitude of London, illustrated quite well the geographic structure of British sea power in the nineteenth century.

Experts often disagree as to what projection is best suited for a given problem. But there is little or no disagreement on one point—that the familiar Mercator map of the world is ill suited to portraying most of the larger international problems of our time.

As a map to portray the intercontinental relations of the Soviet Union and the United States in an age of jet planes and ballistic missiles, the Mercator world map (however centered) has serious and manifest defects. No Mercator map can depict the clustering of Canada and the Soviet Union around the Arctic Ocean (Figure 9.F). Viewed upon this map, the elaborate system of American air defenses in northern Canada and Greenland makes no sense whatever. Likewise the Mercator map exaggerates the width of the northern reaches of both Atlantic and Pacific oceans, thereby contributing to the historic American illusion of political and military isolation from the Old World.

The impact of the traditionally ubiquitous Mercator map (which still hangs in thousands of classrooms, government offices, and business establishments) is easily exemplified. At the end of the last century, it was widely believed to be essential for the United States to acquire a naval port in the Samoan Islands, far out in the South Pacific. The reason most commonly given was the need for a naval outpost to protect the western approaches to the projected Panama Canal. Even on a Mercator map, the distance from Samoa to Panama looks rather long. But on a globe, the project is shown to have been roughly equivalent to acquiring a naval port in the Baltic Sea to protect the port of New York.

Hawaii and Guam, annexed in 1898, were visualized then and for many years thereafter, as stepping stones on the direct route to the Philippine Islands. And so they do appear on the Mercator map. But the short route to Asia, by steamship as well as by plane, lies approximately 2,000 miles to the north of these mid-Pacific islands. Alaska (which includes the westward reaching chain of Aleutian islands) lies much closer to this great-circle route. But Alaska, purchased from Russia in 1867 mainly through the efforts of Secretary of State Seward, was characterized then and for many years afterwards, as "Seward's folly."

Perhaps the most extreme example of the spell cast by Mercator's world map comes from the autobiography of George Frisbie Hoar, Senator from Massachusetts around the turn of the last century. Let him tell it in his own words: "Hawaii is 2,100 miles from our Pacific coast. Yet if a line be drawn from the point of our territory nearest Asia to the southern boundary of California, that line being the chord of which our Pacific coast is the bow, Hawaii will fall this side of it." We suggest that the reader try this one upon a Mercator map, and check his result on a globe. We think he will agree that Hoar out-Mercatored Mercator!

CONIC PROJECTIONS

For mapping small areas and certain larger ones as well, several varieties of conic projections are in common use. In its simplest form, the hypothetical viewpoint is the center of the earth. The geographical design is projected, as from that viewpoint, onto a cone superimposed upon the globe, as shown in Figure 9.C. The cone, figuratively speaking, is then unrolled and becomes the flat surface of the map.

A simple conic map displays the following features among others. If cone and globe are tangent along a parallel of latitude (as is normal practice), the parallel of tangency and all other parallels appear on the map as arcs of concentric circles. All meridians are straight lines crossing the parallels at right angles as on the globe, and radiating from the pole like spokes of a wheel. Close to the parallel of tangency, shapes, distances, and areas approximate their counterparts on the globe. The farther one departs from the parallel of tangency, however, the greater becomes the distortion of all three properties.

Simple conic projections are useful to portray small areas—a city, a harbor, a county, even a small country as a whole. For larger areas in relatively high latitudes—for example, Canada, the United States, Europe, or the Soviet Union—various modified conic projections have been developed. For still larger areas, up to about a quarter-sphere, still other projections have also been designed. These are described in most good atlases, and the details need not concern us here.

The most difficult problems arise (as we have seen in connection with the Mercator projection) when the need is for a map that portrays all or most of the earth's surface without interrupting either land or water areas. Such a map is required if we are to visualize many of the political relations of the United States and the Soviet Union. World War II stimulated cartographers to design maps that would portray more effectively the intercontinental military operations and global political commitments which the War thrust onto the American people.

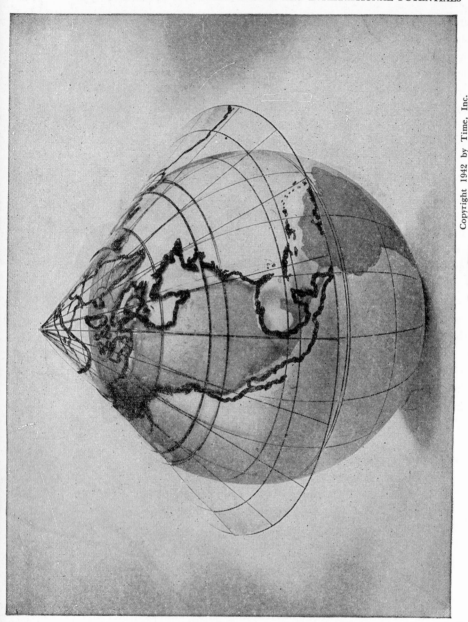

FIG. 9.C.   THE PRINCIPLE OF THE CONIC PROJECTION
Courtesy Herbert Gehr, *Life* Magazine. Models by Norman Bel Geddes.

AZIMUTHAL PROJECTIONS

One group of alternatives to the traditional maps has been sought in the various azimuthal projections. These differ in detail, but all are based on the principle of projecting onto a plane tangent at one point on the surface of the globe, from a hypothetical viewpoint somewhere inside or outside the globe. The point of tangency can be anywhere on the globe's surface.

On one of this group, the *gnomonic projection,* all straight lines are equivalent to great circles on the globe. This feature is important in long distance air navigation. But the feature is achieved at heavy cost in conformality. Shapes are so distorted that gnomonic maps of large areas are scarcely recognizable to the layman. For this reason, gnomonic maps have limited utility as graphic aids in the study of global political relations.

Another type of azimuthal map, one that achieved great temporary popularity during World War II, is the *orthographic projection.* Rather imprecisely one can liken an orthographic hemispheric map to a photograph of the earth taken from outer space. Orthographic maps are roughly analogous to photographs of the moon taken through a telescope. The visual effect is similar to the appearance of a twelve-inch globe viewed at a distance of ten feet or more.

Orthographic maps were popularized by the cartographer Richard Edes Harrison as a device for helping people not expert in map reading to visualize a global war and future international politics in the air age. To this end Harrison drew many interesting, suggestive, startling maps. By centering the map on different points of the globe, and by drawing quasi-orthographic maps from oblique hypothetical viewpoints in outer space, he attempted to suggest how differently geographic layouts and relationships must appear to Americans, Russians, West Europeans, East Asians, and others.[*]

An example of an orthodox orthographic map centered on mid-Atlantic is shown in Figure 9.D. For the purpose of emphasizing geopolitical perspective, as this example indicates, orthographic maps can be quite effective. For almost every other purpose, the orthographic projection is unsatisfactory. Neither shapes nor areas nor distances nor directions are faithfully represented.

Perhaps the most familiar map in this group is the *equidistant azimuthal.* As in all azimuthal-type projections, all straight lines radiating from the point of tangency are great circles. Near the center of the map, shapes, areas, distances, and directions are rendered quite well, though distortion increases progressively towards the margin of the hemisphere depicted. The area can be extended beyond a single hemisphere, though at the price of still greater distortion of all properties. (Figure 9.E).

During and following World War II, azimuthal maps centered on the

---

[*] A collection of Harrison's maps was published in the atlas, *Look at the World* (Knopf, 1944). This atlas, available in most libraries, is well worth an hour or more of careful study.

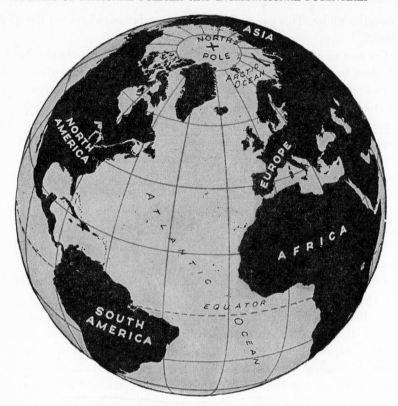

FIG. 9.D. ORTHOGRAPHIC PROJECTION
Centered on the mid-Atlantic. From R. E. Harrison and R. Strausz-Hupe, "Maps, Strategy, and World Politics," in *The Smithsonian Institution Report for 1943*.

North Pole acquired a vogue that has now somewhat subsided. This polar perspective was advocated mainly on the related grounds: (1) that all the Great Powers are located well north of the equator, and (2) that their future connections, commercial as well as military, will depend increasingly upon air routes that follow great circles across the arctic region. This argument is graphically illustrated by two cartograms in a little book on *Air Geography*, published in 1951, and reproduced here as Figure 9.F.

The force of this argument has been weakened somewhat by the recent rapid rise of Chinese political potential, by the slightly less rapid development of India, and by the increasing international importance of southern Asia, Sub-Saharan Africa, and South America. If these trends continue, the problem of cartographic portrayal of international politics will become still more difficult.

Harrison also has led an attack on the cartographic convention which puts north at the top of the map sheet. He argues convincingly that looking

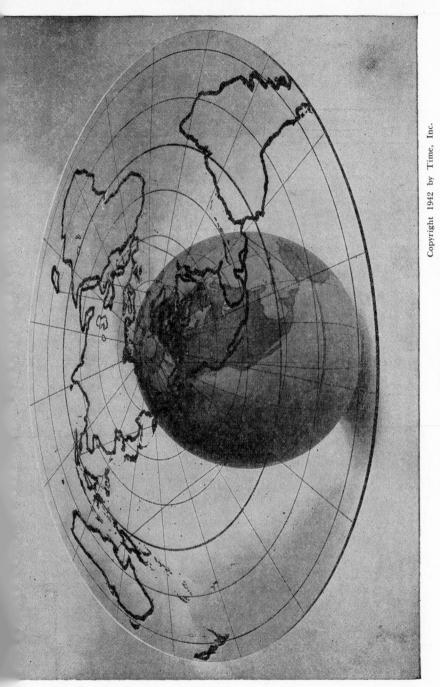

FIG. 9.E.   PRINCIPLE OF THE AZIMUTHAL EQUIDISTANT PROJECTION

Courtesy Herbert Gehr, *Life* Magazine. Models by Norman Bel Geddes.

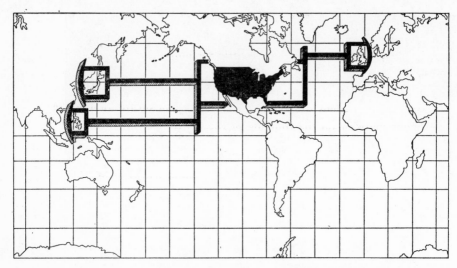

PUSHING BACK THE ENEMY—ON A MERCATOR MAP

THE BACK DOOR IS OPEN—TOWARD THE NORTH

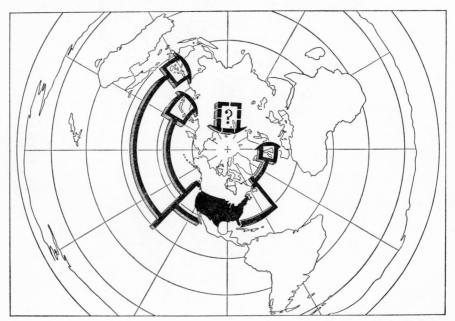

From *Air Geography*, by T. C. Lyn

FIG. 9.F.

at maps in one position subtly affects people's ideas of geographical relationships. On this he is undoubtedly correct. If the reader has any doubt about it, we suggest that he experiment a little for himself. So strong, however, is the north-south convention that all of Harrison's crusading zeal, backed up by the immense circulation of the Luce magazines which printed many of Harrison's maps, seems to have left scarcely a dent on the practice of those who make maps or on the thinking of those who look at them.

JOINED-HEMISPHERES MAPS

Though never as popular as the Mercator world map, atlases have long featured a double-hemispheric map, joined at some point on the equator. The usual point of juncture is at 20 degrees west longitude. This centers the land masses of Eurasia-Africa in the so-called Eastern Hemisphere, and North and South America in the Western Hemisphere, and divides the Atlantic and Pacific oceans.

The joined-hemispheres map seems to have exerted a subtle influence on American political thinking throughout our history. American political discourse, from the days of the Revolution onward, is replete with references to the Western Hemisphere, the American Hemisphere, our hemisphere, this hemisphere, the two spheres, etc. This vocabulary, and the concepts which underlie it, greatly interested the late Dr. S. W. Boggs who served for many years as chief geographer of the Department of State. He dealt imaginatively with this problem in an article entitled "This Hemisphere," published in the *United States Department of State Bulletin,* of May 6, 1945. The substance of this article is reproduced later in this chapter.

Misuse of maps

There is an old saying that "figures don't lie, but liars will figure." This applies to maps as to many other media of communication in our era of deceptive advertising. The late Dr. Boggs (cited just above) turned his attention also to the booby traps which cartographic propagandists can set for the unwary. He called this trick "cartohypnosis." In the following article he summed up these and other misuses to which maps are commonly put.*

> . . . Maps are often deliberately employed to sell ideas to individuals and nations. In every continent maps . . . are now being used to disseminate mischievous half-truths and to obfuscate the thinking of men. They are employed as graphic devices—subtly to suggest an idea, to inculcate a prejudice, or to instill a patriotic fervor. Such

* From "Cartohypnosis," by S. W. Boggs, in *U. S. Department of State Bulletin,* December 12, 1946.

maps may be true in every detail, but in their omissions and their perverse emphasis they may be socially poisonous. . . .

In an article entitled "Magic Cartography," relating to the uses of maps in propaganda, Hans Speier observes: ". . . [Maps] may make certain traits and properties of the world they depict more intelligible —or may distort or deny them. . . . They may give information, but they may also plead. Maps can be symbols of conquest or tokens of revenge, instruments for airing grievances or expressions of pride. Indeed, maps are so widely used in propaganda and for such different purposes that it is difficult to understand why propaganda analysts have paid so little attention to them. . . ."

The private cartographic industry [in Nazi Germany] was declared to bear a very heavy responsibility as a mediator between science and the people, and between the policies of the government and the people. Every map had to be submitted before publication to all government departments that might have an interest in it. An obligatory organization of several large publishers of school atlases was created in order that unified school atlases would be published for the whole Reich.

Special symbols and devices, adapted to a minimum of mass education in reading maps, were developed and standardized by frenetic propagandists, in order to convey ideas of threatening forces, attack and resistance to attack, hostile encirclement, and the like. Posters in railway stations and other public places utilized maps that had a powerful effect upon the uncritical mass of the population.

In Italy cartography was employed by Mussolini to stimulate an urge for territorial expansion. Most striking, perhaps, was the series of maps on a wall in Rome, erected on the Via Imperiale, a new boulevard cut through from the National Monument to the restored Forum. On these maps, which were executed in choice marbles of selected colors, the growth of Rome from a city-state to the empires of Augustus and Trajan was artistically depicted. The purpose was obvious; the method artful. The dominions of Rome once encircled the Mediterranean. Modern Italy's destiny seemed manifest; *mare nostrum* was again used with the present tense. No critical appraisal of the lack of pertinence of the extent of Trajan's conquests to the role that can or should be played by Italians in the twentieth century world was ever tolerated. . . .

In a distraught world whose teeming millions sometimes hesitatingly follow their leaders and would-be leaders . . . honest and critical thinking about maps is important. Men, women, and even children should all be more critical of the maps they see in daily papers and periodical publications, in books and atlases, and on the screen. They need to be taught to *read* maps (an art in itself), and not merely to *consult* maps (frequently only for location of a single city or point, or regarding a route of travel). Economists, historians, political scientists, and others need to cultivate a keener sense of earth distributions of resources and of peoples and their activities—which necessitates development of ability to read distributional maps. . . .

The map user who desires to guard against becoming the victim of cartohypnosis should keep in mind three things:

(a) That it is the actual situation on the earth that is significant;

(b) That maps have definite limitations as well as certain unique capabilities; and

(c) That map makers are human.

It is what one would find on the ground, in all its complexity, and not simply what one finds on a map that is significant. In looking at a map one may well ask, "What the map shows may be perfectly true, but what is the whole truth? What is on the ground—including peoples, and their customs, their ideas and prejudices? What other types of information are pertinent to the subject?" . . .

Like an aerial photograph that reveals a pattern, perhaps of archeological origin, almost erased by time and imperceptible on the ground— or like an X-ray photograph—a map may disclose patterns of great significance which are not discernible on surface inspection. Many maps based on statistical data thus reveal pertinent invisible transitions which, if even suspected, would be only vaguely perceived on visiting the area.

A map is unique in its capacity to represent with fidelity literally millions of observed facts, accurately generalized and artistically presented, conveying to the mind a vivid, true picture of the distribution of certain phenomena on the earth's surface that could not be obtained in any other manner. Large-scale topographic maps, for example, if they are highly accurate, belong to this category.

But the limitations of a map should be borne in mind. One of the most important is that a map cannot be more accurate and reliable than the data upon which it is based. A map printed in beautiful colors may be of little value and may mislead the uncritical if it is a work of art. On the other hand, a crudely executed map compilation may be highly accurate and of the greatest importance.

People seldom consider that a map is like a single chapter in an encyclopedic compendium; one map cannot present the result of an inventory of geology, natural vegetation, and water resources. Any map that attempts to show too much is of little use. . . .

In this so-called "air age" in which men glibly talk of global relations—which are misleadingly visualized on all world maps, polar and otherwise—one ventures to suggest that the phrase global geography should be restricted to those aspects of world relations which can be rationally comprehended, without geometrical acrobatics, only with the aid of globes. The writer finds that transparent plastic hemispheres, some with geographical patterns and others with geometrical patterns imprinted, which can be moved into any position upon a globe resting only in a cup or ring, provide the best means of comparisons between one part of the globe and another. Map projection distortions and differences of scale are completely eliminated. After a situation is clearly seen on the globe itself, a map projection may be selected which is adapted to the special requirements of visualizing that particular set of data. There are, to be sure, many types of data which may be grasped even better when presented on maps than on globes. But there are other categories of highly significant relationships, notably the longer ocean trade routes, air routes and distances, radio and other wave propagations in the field of electronics, and problems relating to the peaceful development of atomic energy for the benefit of all mankind, which require the use of globes and certain types of accessories, and actually deserve the appellation *global geography*. . . .

One of the most important uses to which maps can be put is to dehypnotize people, to wake them up to the facts and phenomena of the mid-twentieth-century world, and to educate them to world understanding. Where words utterly fail, maps can sometimes portray, vividly and memorably, some of the freshly and sharply etched but as yet dimly perceived lines of interplay between peoples in a world which in many areas is scarcely reminiscent of the conditions upon which our thinking is largely premised. We should bear in mind that, until the nineteenth century, there were no "world problems." . . .

The world needs maps that visualize economic interdependence of countries and regions; that locate the principal natural resources and their volume of production; that correlate the volume of commerce with decreasing costs of production and transport and that reveal the increases of trade over both short and great distances; that reflect trade balances and international balance of payments; that depict the rapidly expanding patterns of communication in terms of both total and per capita volume; that record the rapidly changing levels of living; that trace migrations of peoples in all parts of the world in recent decades; that disclose the areas in which disease constitutes a threat to health in distant lands—and many other types of maps. . . .

The earth as pervasive reality

In the preceding pages we have been stressing the importance of discovering how people in different periods and places have conceived and visualized their earthly habitat. We have also emphasized the importance of understanding the properties of the graphic models which record men's evolving concepts of the earth and help to shape their thinking about it. Much more could be said on these subjects. The main point is simply that people's attitudes and decisions, their projects and undertakings, are based on their ideas of what the earth is like, and these in turn appear to depend considerably on the kinds of maps to which they are accustomed.

Important as it is to appreciate how people have imagined the earth to be and how they have reacted to these images, that is clearly only half of the picture. The earth is not merely a concept in men's minds. It is also a pervasive reality which sets limits to human accomplishment, limits which may be operative regardless of whether or how these limits are perceived by the human actors upon the earthly stage.

What are the salient features of this pervasive reality? Which of these features are especially relevant to an understanding of international politics?

The planet earth is an approximate sphere about 8,000 miles in diameter and about 25,000 miles in circumference. The total area of the earth's surface is nearly 200 million square miles—more than 50 times the size of the United States. About 70 percent of the total area is covered with water. Land and water are very unevenly distributed. These distributions—the layout of lands and seas—are described and graphically illustrated in Dr. Bogg's article, "This Hemisphere," cited a few paragraphs back.*

. . . Americans frequently speak of "this hemisphere," meaning *the* hemisphere in which the United States finds itself. They will better grasp the "global" relationships of the United States if they get a true mental picture of some of the many hemispheres in which the United States is located.

Hemispheres are infinite in number. Rest a transparent glass or plastic geographical globe on its south pole, half fill it with water exactly to the line of the equator, and seal it shut. Roll it into any position whatever; the bottom hemisphere will be filled with water and the top with air. The water level will always be a plane passing through the center of the globe. The visible water-line will invariably be a "great circle"—a circle greater than any that can be described on the globe with a radius either less or more than the interval between one of the poles and the equator. Any two points on the earth's surface lie on one of these great circles—which constitutes the shortest route between them. Therefore, with surface features and weather permitting, great-circle routes between ports are naturally preferred by both steamships and airplanes.

The Northern Hemisphere. Any hemisphere may be identified and distinguished from all other hemispheres by its center point. Conversely, any point on the earth's surface is the center of a hemisphere which somewhat differs from all other hemispheres.

The United States is in the Northern Hemisphere, nearly half way between the Equator and the North Pole, the 45th parallel of latitude coinciding with the northern boundary of New York State and with the Montana-Wyoming boundary.

The northern and southern hemispheres are the only hemispheres whose common boundary has any geographic significance. The seasons

* From "This Hemisphere," by S. W. Boggs, in *U. S. Department of State Bulletin,* May 6, 1945.

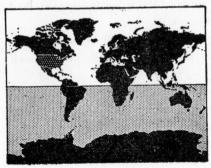

FIG. 9.G.

THE NORTHERN HEMISPHERE

The center is the North Pole, and the limiting great circle is the equator. The unshaded portion of the world map on the Miller projection corresponds to the hemisphere map below.

on opposite sides of the Equator are antipodal, since it is summer in one when it is winter in the other.

Approximately 37,570,000 square miles (74 per cent of the world's 50,973,000 square miles of land area, exclusive of the icecaps in Greenland and Antarctica), with . . . approximately . . . 91 per cent of the world's population . . . are to be found in the northern hemisphere. This hemisphere includes all of North America, Europe and continental Asia, part of South America (17 per cent of its area and 15 per cent of its population), and part of Africa (67 per cent of its area and 68 per cent of its population).

The so-called "Western Hemisphere." The concept of the "Western Hemisphere" or New World, comprising the American continents and islands, is very important, both historically and politically. But this so-called "Western Hemisphere" is inadvisedly called "western" and does not deserve the appellation "hemisphere." . . .

The Americas comprise only about 30 per cent of the world's land area and contain about 13 per cent of its population. As may be seen in Figure 9.H, the American continents and islands, including Greenland, lie wholly within one half of a certain hemisphere, and in that quartersphere there is twice as much water as land. The Americas therefore scarcely deserve to be called a "hemisphere."

"Western" Hemisphere suggests limiting lines running due north and south, namely meridians. Now it happens that map-makers make many maps of the Americas within circular limits which embrace, therefore, a hemisphere. Merely for convenience and economy, they utilize limiting lines, a pair of meridians 180° apart, that would appear on the map anyway. So they take a meridian between Africa and South America,

FIG. 9.H.

THE MAP-MAKER'S CONVENTIONAL "WESTERN HEMISPHERE"

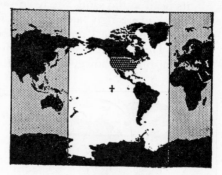

The meridians 30° W and 160° E of Greenwich constitute the conventional limit of this hemisphere. The center is a point in the Pacific Ocean, on the Equator, in 110° west longitude, about 1250 statute miles from the nearest point on the American continents, near Acapulco, Mexico, and more than 2000 miles from the Panama Canal. The unshaded portion of the world map comprises this conventional "Western Hemisphere," and the shaded portion is the "Eastern Hemisphere." The letters around the circular hemisphere map signify: N, North Pole; I, Iceland; A, Azores; C, Canary Islands; S, South Pole; NZ, New Zealand; and G, Guadalcanal Island in the Solomon group.

usually 20° west of Greenwich (if that is used as the prime meridian for the map), and then necessarily employ its anti-meridian, 160° east longitude.

The center of this conventional hemisphere is in the Pacific Ocean, on the Equator, in 110° W longitude. It is about 1,250 statute miles from the nearest point on the American mainland, west of Acapulco, Mexico, and 1,850 miles from the nearest point in the United States, near Brownsville, Texas. Clearly this center point is without geographic significance.

The limiting meridians of this so-called "Western Hemisphere" have no political, historic, geographic, or economic significance. If we were to follow the ancient custom of "beating the bounds" . . . we would traverse open ocean most of the time. Going north on the 20th meridian we would cross part of Antarctica, Iceland, and a mere northeastern tip of Greenland; going south on the 160th meridian we would cross the eastern tip of Siberia including the Kamchatka peninsula, the island of Guadalcanal in the Solomons, and part of Antarctica. Within this hemisphere are found the Cape Verde Islands, the Azores, the western third of Iceland with its capital city, almost all of Greenland, eastern Siberia, thousands of Pacific islands, all of New Zealand, and a large part of the Antarctic continent—in addition to North and South America. The Atlantic and Pacific islands and the eastern portion of Asia within this hemisphere comprise only 1.1 per cent of the world's land area, with 0.5 per cent of its population.

This hemisphere, mapped by itself, induces complacency in Americans. It embraces almost the maximum area of ocean in any hemisphere which contains all of North and South America. Like an ostrich with its head in the sand, we avoid seeing the other half of the world, much of it surprisingly near. .

People in the United States sometimes identify this so-called "Western Hemisphere" with the Monroe Doctrine. The term "Western Hemisphere," however, was not employed in the message of President

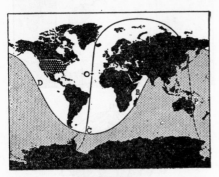

FIG. 9.I. HEMISPHERE
CENTERED AT 28° N 31° W

The straight line AOC through the center divides it into quater-spheres. The western quarter-sphere contains all of North and South America, including Greenland, and a portion of Siberia. The eastern quater-sphere comprises all of Europe and Africa (except a small part of Madagascar) and about 42 percent of the area of Asia. The limit of the hemisphere, ABCDA on both maps, is a complete great circle (like the equator or any meridian circle) while the line AOC which divides it into halves is half of such a great circle, the other half being APC as shown in a dotted line on the world map.

Monroe to the Congress in 1823. The terms "the American continents" and "this hemisphere" were used, evidently synonymously; Russia was in mind at that time and certainly no part of Siberia was thought of as part of "this hemisphere." Neither were New Zealand, part of the Solomon Islands, Samoa, the Fijis, and other Pacific islands, nor was any part of Antarctica (of which they knew almost nothing) contemplated when men spoke of "the American continents" and "this hemisphere" in 1823. . . .

A more significant hemisphere for Americans. A hemisphere centered in the north Atlantic Ocean, at 28° N and 31° W, is much more significant for all people in North and South America than is the mapmaker's "Western Hemisphere" centered in the Pacific on the Equator. This hemisphere, illustrated in Figure 9.I, includes all of the Americas except the westernmost Aleutian Islands, and all of Europe and Africa and more than 40 per cent of Asia. Altogether it comprises 76 per cent of the world's land area, with fully 50 per cent of its population.

This might be called a "Western-civilization hemisphere," since it embraces Europe and the Americas (but with all of Africa and much of Asia besides). Only Australia and New Zealand are outside its bounds. Both history and geography make this hemisphere important to peoples on both sides of the Atlantic.

The land hemisphere. Geographers have made careful determinations to ascertain which hemisphere contains a larger percentage of land area than any other. It has been found to have its center in western France, near Nantes, in about 47°13′ north latitude, 1°32′ west longitude. On its 44,904,000 square miles of land (88 per cent of the world's land area) live about . . . 94 per cent of the world's population. In addition to all of Europe and Africa and North America, the land hemisphere includes nearly 88 per cent of Asia's territory and nearly 92 per cent of its population (the Philippines, Netherlands Indies,

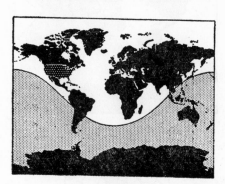

FIG. 9.J. THE LAND HEMISPHERE

The hemisphere with the maximum land area (45.6 percent land, 53.7 percent water, 0.7 percent Greenland icecap). About 94 percent of the world's population lives here on 88 percent of the world's land area. On the world map, the shaded area is the water hemisphere.

British Malaya, and parts of French Indo-China and Thailand being excluded); the land hemisphere also embraces about 79 per cent of the area of South America with 73 per cent of its population.

This hemisphere includes all of the United States and all of its noncontiguous territories except those in the Pacific. The United States is located near the edge of the hemisphere. Considering the vast area and the enormous population, the resources and the industrial development, the land hemisphere may be regarded as the most important hemisphere. The advantages of central location, particularly in a military sense, have not been overlooked in Germany. Commercially the situation is different, in part because ocean transport costs roughly only a tenth as much a ton-mile as railroad transport.

From the center of the land hemisphere, in Western Europe, one can account for the origin of major regional terms which Americans have inherited and still use. [See p. 290 above.]

Hemisphere centered within the United States. In all four hemispheres just described (Figures 9.G to J) the United States is found somewhere near the edge, or at least the center of the United States lies about half way between the center and the edge of the hemisphere. A hemisphere centered near the middle of the United States, in 40° north latitude, 100° west longitude (near Beaver City, Nebraska, and Norton, Kansas), is illustrated in Figure 9.K.

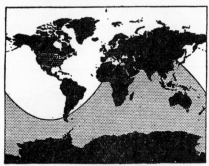

FIG. 9.K.   HEMISPHERE CENTERED NEAR THE CENTER OF THE UNITED STATES

A hemisphere centered at 40° N 100° W is shown here. Although it does not include the southern tip of South America, it does include all of Europe, part of Africa, and, in Asia, part of Turkey, most of Russian Asia, most of Manchuria and Japan.

This hemisphere fails to embrace the southern end of South America, but it includes all of Europe except the island of Crete, about 30 per cent of the area of Africa, and more than 10 per cent of the area of Asia; it includes all of the Arctic Ocean, a very large portion of the Atlantic Ocean, and an even greater area in the Pacific. Asia and Africa are nearer to the United States than most Americans realize. Dakar, Moscow, and northern Manchuria are nearer to the center of the United States than is Buenos Aires. The actual "global" relations of the United States, which are remarkably different from the conceptions many people cherish, based on Mercator maps, have suddenly acquired heightened importance in these days of airplanes and radio. . . .

The global relations of the United States are disclosed in a rather remarkable way by a series of hemispheres such as those shown above. When a person speaks of "this hemisphere" as the one in which the United States of America is located, one may well inquire, "Which hemisphere?"

In terms of human occupancy, and especially economic and political development and stature, ours is definitely a northern-hemisphere world (see Figure 9.G above). All of North America, all of Europe, and virtually all of Asia lie north of the equator. Of the twelve most populous countries, ten are located in the Northern Hemisphere. Of the three most productive food-growing regions, two (United States-Canada and the Soviet Union) are in this hemisphere; only the Argentine prairie is in the Southern Hemisphere. Mineral fuels are more abundant in the Northern Hemisphere. Raw materials too are generally more abundant and, on the whole, more favorably located in relation to fuels than in the Southern Hemisphere (see Chapter 12). All the major industrial regions so far developed lie north of the equator (see Chapter 14). To date no political community in the Southern Hemisphere has attained economic or military stature comparable to the Great Powers of the Northern Hemisphere. The geographical distribution of climates strongly favors the northern lands (see Chapter 11). While many nations south of the equator are rising, some of them rapidly, it seems likely that the greater centers of political potential will remain in Eurasia and North America.

Geography and technology

The limitations implicit in the physical earth change through time, in part because of changes in the earth's physical structure, in part because of other events which widen or restrict the range of fruitful human choice.

Some of the changes in the earth's structure result from physical processes of nature: earth slipping, volcanoes erupting, rocks falling, water flowing and freezing, wind blowing, plants, animals and micro-organisms proliferating, etc. Sometimes these natural processes cause human catastrophes—earthquakes, floods, famines, epidemics, etc.

Alongside these natural phenomena—and probably more important for the study of international politics—are changes in the earth wrought by the hand of man. With advancing knowledge, more efficient tools and greater skills, men have produced ever greater changes in the physical structure of the earth. They have dug canals and changed the courses of rivers. They have built harbors and tunneled through mountains. They have cut down forests and planted new ones. They have depleted the soil and sometimes restored its fertility. They have made deserts bloom and have turned verdant landscapes into deserts. They have pumped oil and water from underground reservoirs, moved bodies of soil and rock, and used up irreplaceable minerals. They have smashed atoms and fused them, creating new elements and transmuting matter into energy. In these and in many other ways, men have altered the structure of their physical habitat. Such basic structural changes have affected in varying degree the economic and political capabilities of nations and their political relations in peace and in war.

A good example is the building of the Suez Canal, opened in 1869. That engineering feat created a shipway across the narrow isthmus which separates the Mediterranean Sea from the Red Sea and Indian Ocean. The canal cut several thousand miles from voyages between European ports and southern and eastern Asia. It soon became one of the most heavily used trunklines of international commerce. But the canal also became a strategic link in the world-wide communication system of the British Empire. This led within a few years to British occupation of Egypt and military domination of the canal. The existence of the canal also affected Britain's political relations with every country fronting on the Mediterranean; it tightened Britain's grip on the Indian Ocean and its borderlands; and in subtle ways it also affected political relations in more distant parts of the world.

As another example, consider the international implications of the heavy and progressive depletion of North American forests, soils, mineral fuels, and other natural resources. This depletion has been going on for well over a century. The rate of depletion has accelerated sharply in the present century. Consumption of natural resources reached record levels during World War II. It is climbing to still higher peaks in our time. These alterations of the physical geography of North America have various political implications. Not the least of these is the increasing dependence of the United States on imported iron ore and other basic raw materials in a period of continuing instability in the political relations of all states and regions.

The international consequences of man-made changes in the earth's surface and subsurface have been great in the past and seem likely to be even greater in the future. But great as these changes have been, they are overshadowed in their political effect by other changes—especially advances in basic science and in engineering—which, while not actually altering the earth's physical structure substantially, have given new meanings and new values to such geographical properties as location, distance, terrain, climate, and natural resources.

Consider, for example, the changes which have taken place in the military properties of oceanic space during the past sixty or seventy years. Theories of sea power which appeared, in 1900, to be as permanent as the oceans themselves have become progressively obsolescent during the intervening years. The oceans and seas (one set of environmental factors) have remained approximately constant in terms of this particular problem. Their size and shape have not changed significantly. But the activities which men can carry out upon the oceans and seas have changed profoundly. Ships have been designed to cruise greater distances without refueling. Methods for refueling at sea have been perfected. Submarines armed with automotive torpedoes have become formidable weapons with which to challenge the passage of ships upon the surface. Special ships have been designed for landing troops and heavy military equipment on hostile open beaches. Aircraft have become powerful factors in the control of the sea and of lands beyond the seas. Submarines propelled by nuclear engines can remain beneath the surface for months at a time. Rockets with nuclear warheads can be launched from beneath the water's surface. These and other technological advances have radically modified and continue to modify the military properties of oceanic space.

It would be difficult to overstress the importance of the giant and ever-lengthening strides with which modern science and technology are conquering space, time, and matter. These achievements affect on all sides the range of fruitful choices open to the statesman. Sometimes the effect has been broadening, sometimes narrowing. To understand and appreciate the impact of these developments, the political properties and meanings of geographic facts have to be reconsidered in the light of technological and other social change. If attention is directed to one set of environmental factors—oceanic space, in the example above—the change in the range of possible activities appears as an adaptation to a stable environment. But such adaptation appears, from a different perspective, to consist of alterations in another set of environmental factors—modes of transportation and design of weapons, in the example—alterations which change the social meaning or properties or implications of environmental factors which themselves may not have undergone significant structural change.

This interaction between human activities and the nonhuman environment has been going on ever since man emerged as a tool-inventing and tool-using agent. But until a century or so ago, the rate of technological advance was slow. Today the rate is rapid and still accelerating. The unsettling effects of new tools and new techniques on the political, military, and economic meaning of geographic layouts and configuration, climatic variation, and the distribution of useful earth materials have great and varied significance in the study of international politics.

CHAPTER TEN

★ ★ ★

Some Geopolitical Interpretations

MEN HAVE SPECULATED from time immemorial on causal relationships between the nonhuman environment and human behavior and accomplishments. This record of speculation includes many attempts to explain and to predict political behavior and relationships by reference to geographical factors. Such interpretations have come in our century to be rather generally called geopolitics; or more precisely, geopolitical interpretations and hypotheses.

One can sort these geopolitical interpretations into two main categories: those which purport to explain or to predict the behavior of a particular nation; and those which purport to explain or to predict larger political patterns, regional or global. Many, though not all, geopolitical interpretations can also be classified on the basis of some limited set of geographical factors hypothesized to be determinative or at least especially influential. Thus one finds interpretations in terms of geographical configuration, in terms of climate, in terms of natural resources, or some other set of geographical variables.

Certain general considerations apply to all geopolitical theorizing and speculation. Geopolitical hypotheses may serve various purposes. The purpose may be simply to explain certain political behavior or distributions at different historical periods, or to predict possible or probable future behavior and distributions. Or the purpose may be to discover what alterations of a given status quo it is possible to achieve with certain opportunities and means available, or to estimate what would have to be done in order to bring about a desired change. Or the purpose may be to influence policy-makers and their constituents in favor of some course of action. Geopolitical speculation, in short, may serve either the purposes of pure analysis or the purposes of propaganda and policy making.

Most geopolitical discourse, whatever the avowed intent of its author, has tended to serve both kinds of purposes. More often than not, one can detect some mixture of pure analysis *and* propaganda. That is to say, most geopolitical writings, even those which purport to be scientific and politically neutral, are found to embody some element of polemical argument, justifying or attacking a particular state of affairs or proposing ways to change it.

All geopolitical discussion, furthermore, is carried on with reference to some set of ideas regarding the layout of things in space and their movements and changes through time. The geopolitical theorizer makes assumptions or reaches conclusions on the basis of evidence as to which factors of the environment are most significant and which are undergoing or are likely to undergo significant change during the time span with which he is dealing.

The fruitfulness of geopolitical theorizing may depend on these initial assumptions. Yet those who make use of such theories for policy making or for polemical purposes often overlook or disregard the assumptions built into them. This practice fosters uncritical acceptance of geopolitical propositions long after events have falsified some or all of their underlying premises.

Finally, nearly all geopolitical theorizing, however repugnant or untenable one may judge it to be, can contribute something towards a better understanding of past and present trends in the behavior and relations of nations. The men who formulated these interpretations and propositions were rarely either fools or lunatics; they were in the main serious and astute observers. None of their interpretations explains everything to everyone's satisfaction. Some have become patently obsolete. But any one of them provides a fruitful starting point, a first approximation to be qualified and modified by taking into consideration additional factors of the environment. For this reason, we have selected some of the more interesting geopolitical hypotheses for critical scrutiny in this and succeeding chapters.

In Chapter 11 we shall examine some of the bearings of climate on human affairs; in Chapter 12, some geopolitical speculation based on the distribution of natural resources. In the present chapter, the focus will be on two famous geopolitical interpretations derived mainly from the physical layout of lands and seas.

The underlying premise of these interpretations is that the configuration of lands and seas provides opportunities and sets limits within which the political relations of nations have evolved and will continue to evolve. The schemes to be considered—those by Captain Alfred Thayer Mahan and by Sir Halford Mackinder—are built upon pretty much the same set of geographic features. Some of these have already been mentioned in the preceding chapter. These salient features of the earth's surface should be kept clearly in view. It may help if one reads this chapter with a globe and one or several world maps at hand for ready reference.

Mahan and Mackinder

Mahan and Mackinder were contemporaries, though Mahan's career began and ended earlier than Mackinder's. Mahan's creative years extended from 1890 to about 1910; Mackinder's from about 1900 to World War II. They came from totally different backgrounds. Mahan pursued until middle age the routine career of an officer in the American Navy, which in those days was conspicuously going nowhere. He was forty-four years old when, in the 1880's, he forsook the quarterdeck of an obsolete man-of-war for the lecture platform of the still embryonic War College of the United States Navy at Newport, Rhode Island. Mahan had nothing remotely resembling a university education. He started almost from scratch; he taught himself, with no significant guidance and with access to remarkably few books. Yet within six years he produced a book—*The Influence of Sea Power upon History, 1660-1783*—which made him famous and has strongly influenced the currents of political and military thinking in many countries to this day.

Mahan set out to prepare a course of lectures on naval history. His reading came gradually to a focus on the seventeenth and eighteenth centuries. He was deeply impressed by the political-economic doctrines known as mercantilism which flourished in those centuries. Hence, from the perspective of today, important aspects of Mahan's thought are not merely sixty years but more nearly two hundred years out of date.

Mackinder, twenty-one years junior to Mahan, brought to his career a very different preparation and perspective. He had the best university education obtainable in the Britain of his day. He was trained both in science and in history. He brought to his work the methodical procedures of academic scholarship.

These differences in background are reflected in the writings of the two men. Mahan's consist entirely of rambling histories of naval warfare and popular magazine articles on current topics. One who plods through his massive literary output will find historical narratives, technical analyses of battles, discussions of strategy, tactics and weapons, homilies on ethics and on the white man's destiny to rule the world, odd mixtures of current events and political prophecy, interpretations of history, and a great deal of gratuitous advice to the makers of history.

One will search in vain, however, for any neat exposition of Mahan's geopolitical ideas. One has to reconstruct his philosophy of history and statecraft from bits and pieces, plucked from hastily written books and articles. This we have attempted to do in the following section.

Mackinder's geopolitical writings are less voluminous than Mahan's, but much more orderly. Mackinder had a gift for epigrammatic expression. He presented bold and imaginative generalizations. He addressed himself to many audiences: professional geographers, teachers, students, statesmen. Some of his most interesting ideas were first presented in textbooks for elementary school children. His best known book, *Democratic Ideals and Reality*, originated as a tract for the peace conference after World War I (1919).

Both Mahan and Mackinder were highly sensitive to the march of events. Their interpretations and policy prescriptions underwent change through time. In their old age, both were arguing positions almost the reverse of some they had advanced earlier.

One finds a large element of propaganda in both Mahan and Mackinder. The former was from beginning to end a tireless crusader for a bigger American merchant marine, for a greater navy, and for more aggressive American participation in world politics. Mackinder spoke from the perspective of a successful but threatened imperial system. He sought in geography and in history the ingredients of a national policy for preserving Britain's world position. Neither Mackinder nor Mahan appeared to experience any difficulty in believing that what seemed good for his own country must also be good for mankind as a whole. It would be difficult to discover more nationalistic-minded commentators on events.

Comparison reveals still other common perspectives. Despite their dissimilar backgrounds, both men were much alike in their emphasis on the military values of space and on the strategic principles to be derived from the layout of lands and seas. Both of them—though Mackinder less than Mahan—appear to have undervalued economic resources in their concept of power. Both virtually ignored the factor of climatic variation in space and through time. Both used history to buttress their geopolitical arguments, but for both the study of history was purely a means, never an end in itself. Their main interest was in the future.

Mahan and Mackinder seem to have reasoned from substantially similar conceptions of international politics. Each regarded conflict as the normal condition. Each betrayed almost fatalistic belief in the inevitable recurrence of war among the greater states. Each regarded military force as the decisive instrument of statecraft. Both of them stressed the relativity of power in space and through time. Under these conditions neither Mahan nor Mackinder hoped for anything more than an uneasy equilibrium requiring frequent reappraisal and adjustment to counteract differential changes in the capacities of the Great Powers.

Finally, the geopolitical concepts and hypotheses for which Mahan and Mackinder are studied today are by no means as far apart as often asserted. They have been repeatedly contrasted as the exponents of sea power and land power respectively. This is a false antithesis. Indeed, their basic propositions are in certain respects so similar as to evoke at once the conjecture that Mahan and Mackinder must have avidly read each other's books and magazine articles. Mackinder probably borrowed more from Mahan than he contributed in return. But it was Mackinder rather than Mahan who methodically ordered the concepts and hypotheses, propounded an interpretation of history in the grand style, and drew a geopolitical blueprint of the future which for better or for worse still grips the imagination of men in many lands.

Mahan: seapower is world power

Mahan's major thesis, from which he never deviated or retreated, is that command of the sea is the dominant form of political power and the decisive factor in the political relations of national states. When he applied this thesis to the world as he conceived it, Mahan displayed bold and imaginative thinking.*

Four geopolitical concepts underlie Mahan's thinking about international politics: (1) a continuous and unbroken ocean and connecting seas; (2) a vast transcontinental, nearly landlocked state—the Russian Empire—extending without a break from the ice-bound Arctic to the rugged desert-mountain belt of inner Asia, and from eastern Europe to a point farther eastward than Japan; (3) the maritime states of continental Europe and maritime borderlands of southern and eastern Asia; and (4) the insular states—Great Britain and Japan, with which he also grouped the United States—all wholly disconnected from the mainland of Eurasia.

The Russian Empire typified for Mahan the strength and the weakness of landpower. Within the vast Russian realm, Mahan observed a profound urge to expand towards the seas. This was manifest in wedgelike thrusts towards the Indian Ocean and the Yellow Sea. Two sets of obstacles stood in the way of this Russian expansion: obstacles imposed by Russian geography, and by the policies and capabilities of the maritime states.

---

* The excerpts from Mahan's writings quoted in this section are from *The Influence of Sea Power upon History* (1890), *The Interest of America in Sea Power* (1897), *The Problem of Asia* (1900), and *The Interest of America in International Conditions* (1910).

Regarding the former, Mahan wrote: "Hindrances . . . imposed by natural conditions, place checks upon her freedom of movement." "Huge distances" and "inadequate internal communications" severely limited the mobility of "disposable strength." Russia fronted only on "enclosed seas, liable to be definitely shut by a hostile power." Russian coasts, moreover, were far distant from the productive centers in the interior. "Natural conditions" thus rendered it improbable, in Mahan's judgment, that Russia could expand against resistance into the oceanic realm. If the Russian "center" could "not be broken," if the Russian Empire could not be brought down by seapower, it could nevertheless be contained.

The instrument of containment, the second obstacle to Russian expansion, was seapower—to date (1900) the seapower of Great Britain. This conclusion followed, in Mahan's thought, from the historical record. By the end of the Napoleonic Wars (1815), the British Navy had demonstrated its ability to drive enemy fleets and merchant shipping from the open seas, to cover the movements of British armies to oversea battlefields, to maintain the flow of essential supplies into Britain, and to prevent invasion both of the British Isles and of Britain's widely scattered colonies.

These achievements Mahan attributed in part to the British policy of supporting a powerful navy, in part to the strategy of concentrating British naval units into massive fleets and employing these fleets to seek out and destroy or drive to cover the naval forces that might otherwise protect enemy merchant shipping. However, Mahan recognized that in performing these functions, Britain enjoyed significant, perhaps decisive, advantages derived from geography.

Britain alone among the European Powers was an insular nation. Hence the British homeland could be made secure without heavy outlays for defense of land frontiers. This left more men and money for the navy. British ships also enjoyed secure havens overseas. Through a remarkable combination of muddling and foresight, Britain had come into possession of most of the best naval ports in every ocean and in most of the connecting seas. Almost without exception, those outlying stations resembled the British Isles in their natural defensive strength under operational conditions prevailing in the nineteenth century.

In this global layout, the island of Britain itself was the master position. It lies between northern Europe and the open Atlantic. The deep-sea commerce of all European ports, from the farthest reaches of the Baltic to the Low Countries and northern France, either had to pass through the narrow English Channel or had to take the long detour to the north around Scotland. British squadrons within easy reach of their protected anchorages could blockade the Atlantic and Channel ports of France, close Dover Strait, patrol the North Sea, and even make sweeps into the more distant Baltic.

By concentrating superior forces in these narrow seas, Britain could prevent the rendezvous of hostile forces from northern and western Europe, and could disrupt the flow of seaborne traffic to and from Continental ports all the way from St. Petersburg (now Leningrad) to Brest. And with unrivalled economy of effort, the same forces which performed these offensive missions simultaneously shielded British shipping in the Atlantic and the British insular homeland from counter-attacks by Continental enemies.

The Rock of Gibraltar dominated even more completely the narrow strait which provided the only marine exit from the Mediterranean before the Suez Canal was opened in 1869. All seaborne traffic to and from eastern Spain, southern France, the whole of Italy, the Balkan peninsula, the Levant, and the entire Black Sea hinterland of Russia, had to pass through this bottleneck under the guns of the British Navy. The island of Malta provided a similar operating station at the central narrows of the Mediterranean.

The opening of the Suez Canal placed a heavier burden on the Royal Navy, but did not weaken Britain's grip on the waterways of southern Europe. The British Navy already possessed a station at Aden near the passage from the Red Sea into the Indian Ocean. Alexandria on the Mediterranean coast of Egypt was later developed into a naval base near the northern terminus of the canal. These two positions, together with Malta and Gibraltar, commanded every narrow passage along the new short cut to India and the Far East. Though legally an international thoroughfare, the sea route to India was actually, in a military sense, a British waterway under exclusive British control.

Through its hold on four narrow seas—Suez Canal, Gibraltar Strait, English Channel, and North Sea—British seapower could virtually dictate the terms of Europe's access to the lands beyond the Atlantic and the Mediterranean. Under conditions prevailing until almost the end of the nineteenth century, control of these narrow seas had political as well as purely military effects felt around the world. As long as no important naval power existed outside Europe, British control of the ocean portals of the Continent constituted in effect a global command of the sea.

Besides the leverages that could be exerted from the narrow seas encompassing Europe, Britain also held the essentials of a local naval dominance in some of the more distant seas. Of these the most important was the Indian Ocean. After British occupation of India and the establishment of British colonies at numerous places along the borderlands of the

Indian Ocean, that ocean became in effect a closed British sea all the way from the Cape of Good Hope to Australia, closed in the sense that British naval forces could presumably deny its use to the shipping of any combination of Powers at war with Britain.

The colonies of Singapore and Hong Kong extended the long arm of the British Navy to the coast of China. In the Falkland Islands, Britain possessed a commanding naval station vis-à-vis the Strait of Magellan and Cape Horn. In Nova Scotia and in Puget Sound, British naval stations flanked the great-circle routes from the United States to Europe and to Eastern Asia. In the West Indies, Britain held comparable flanking positions along the approaches to the American isthmus. Only by the narrowest of margins did American statesmen in 1850 thwart British ambition to control a future transisthmian canal.

Mahan early grasped the essential features of Britain's world-wide seapower. In particular, he emphasized the importance of Britain's main positions flanking all exits from northern Europe, and the obstacles which Britain's position in the waters and borderlands of Asia presented to the expansion of the Russian Empire.

Writing in 1900, Mahan gave priority to the situation in Asia. Russian strategy, as Mahan conceived it, was to drive a great wedge between Afghanistan and Persia clear to the shore of the Indian Ocean, and in the Far East to push southeastwards through Manchuria to the narrow seas opening onto the Pacific. "Alike in the Far East and in the Far West [of Asia]," he noted "the same characteristic of remorseless energy." Russia "in obedience to natural law and race instinct," as he put it, was working geographically to the southwards in Asia by both flanks, her center covered by the mountains of Afghanistan and the deserts of eastern Turkestan and Mongolia.

Against this Russian advance, the martitime Powers, depending primarily on naval force and sea communications, could make an effective stand only on the periphery of the Russian Empire. No frontal assault on the inland citadels of Russian strength should even be contemplated. "The Russian center [Mahan was positive] cannot be broken." The arenas of struggle with Russia should therefore be confined mainly to the southern and eastern borderlands of Asia. "The land power will try to reach the sea and to utilize it for its own ends, while the seapower must obtain support on land" through the inducements and pressures it can bring to bear upon the inhabitants" of the coastal borderlands of Asia. Equilibrium would be reached along a line where the contending forces of land and sea power could advance no further against the resistance of the other.

Mahan in 1900 contended that a grand strategy of blocking Russian expansion was in the interest not only of the insular nations but also of the maritime nations of continental Europe. That such an oceanic coalition could achieve its objective of containing Russian expansion he had not the slightest doubt. The combined resources of Britain, Japan, Germany, and the United States, he argued, "outweigh . . . in foundation and in superstructure" the potentialities of Russia, even in alliance with France.

Events did not work out, however, as Mahan anticipated. After the Russo-Japanese War and the abortive revolution in Russia (in 1905), that empire seemed considerably less menacing than previously. Simultaneously the rapid growth of German military and naval strength accompanied by aggressive diplomacy and commercial rivalry, impelled Mahan to reconsider the alignment that had previously seemed so necessary and natural to him. He ceased to envisage Germany as a natural partner in an oceanic coalition to contain the land power of Russia. He began to regard Germany itself as the most dangerous threat to the insular nations. By 1910 he was seriously contemplating the possibility that Germany would come to wield dominant power on the Continent and dominant power upon the oceans—an achievement which he had previously dismissed as impossible.

Mahan reasoned his way to this contradictory conclusion as follows: Germany had achieved "political unity," a "huge industrial system," and a large and growing navy and merchant marine. Population was increasing more rapidly in Germany than in other European countries. In alliance with Austria-Hungary, the German government dominated a solid bloc of territories extending from the Baltic to the Black Sea. Railways, located with a view to military as well as commercial needs, had largely overcome earlier obstacles to overland movement, thereby giving Germany an effective central position with internal lines of communication. Germany, moreover, was demonstrating superior capacity for organizing "all departments of life" and bending them to the purposes of national power. Finallly, while a disciplined German nation was forging ahead, the Russian Empire was prostrated by internal disorder, and Britain and France showed alarming symptoms of the lack of purpose and will which Mahan found distressingly characteristic of all democratic states.

Germany, he recognized, operated under geographical handicaps. As he had previously emphasized, Germany's only seaboard fronted the North Sea. German ships could reach the Atlantic only through narrow seas hitherto firmly controlled by the British Navy. Only by defeating Britain could Germany establish more than a strictly local predominance in the North Sea. That Britain might be thus defeated or at least neutralized by the German threat Mahan by 1910 had come reluctantly to admit. If that should happen, he grimly predicted, Germany would not only dominate Europe but command the seas as well.

This prospect was abhorrent to Mahan. Previously he had conceived of the United States as remaining more or less outside the power struggles of the Old World, playing an active but uncommitted role in international politics. Now he saw no viable alternative but for the United States to enter into alliance with Britain, an alliance in which he contemplated the United States as eventually becoming the dominant partner.

From time to time Mahan speculated on the possibility of the United States itself becoming the world's dominant sea Power. America, in his view, had the essential requisites: continental insularity from Eurasia, a secure industrial base, frontage on both the Atlantic and Pacific, a strategically central position from which to threaten all the coasts of Eurasia.

Mahan recognized only dimly the handicap which the United States suffered from lack of colonial bases close to Eurasia. The mutual rivalries of the European Powers had limited their capacity to oppose the United States in American waters, and the ancillary rivalries of the same states and Japan had imposed a similar restraint in the Pacific. All these conditions contributed to the defensive strength of the United States, but provided relatively limited opportunities for the exercise of American seapower across the wide oceans. Britain held such positions at all the vital sea portals of the Old World. An Anglo-American coalition could exercise a decisive leverage almost anywhere on the maritime fronts of Eurasia and Africa. But the point that Mahan apparently missed was that the layout of lands and seas and the political geography of the American "empire," *given the types of ships and weapons available in the early 1900's,* interposed obstacles to a *Pax Americana* that could have been surmounted only with an outlay of manpower and wealth far beyond anything even Mahan would have regarded as politically feasible for the United States.

After making due allowance for this and other shortcomings in Mahan's geopolitical theses and arguments, one can still be impressed by the scope of his imagination and insight. Some of his most striking concepts and perspectives are still current today. He clearly anticipated Mackinder's concept of the Eurasian "Heartland." His strategy vis-à-vis the Russian Empire closely resembled in geopolitical conception the strategy for containing the Soviet Union actually pursued by the United States during the later 1940's and 1950's, nearly half a century after Mahan's death in 1914.

We have said virtually nothing about the principles of fleet organization and naval strategy and tactics, on which Mahan had a great deal to say. Those ideas have little relevance in our age of mechanized land forces, jet planes, ballistic missiles and thermonuclear warheads. Whether Mahan's geopolitical ideas are as obsolete as his technical principles still remains to be considered. We shall return to this issue after a brief scrutiny of the geopolitical ideas of Mahan's great contemporary, Sir Halford Mackinder.

Mackinder: geography and the pattern of power

Mackinder's geopolitical theorizing went through two phases, somewhat comparable to Mahan's. In the first, extending from the early 1900's until the end of World War I, his main concern (like Mahan's) was the rapid growth and aggresive tendencies of the German Empire of Wilhelm II; his major premise, that "the great wars of history . . . are the outcome, direct or indirect, of the unequal growth of nations, and that unequal growth is not wholly due to the greater genius and energy of some nations as compared with others," but is in large degree "the result of the uneven distribution of fertility and strategical opportunity upon the face of the globe"; his main thesis, that "the grouping of lands and seas, and of fertility and natural pathways, is such as to lend itself to the growth of empires, and in the end of a single world empire."*

The second phase extended from the 1920's until Mackinder's death in 1946. During this period his concern shifted gradually to the developing potential of the Soviet Union; and he revised his geopolitical thesis radically. In the revised thesis he contended that the grouping of lands and seas and of economic resources favored not one but two ultimate centers of great political potential: the "Heartland" of Eurasia, occupied by the Soviet Union, and the grouping of nations facing the North Atlantic Ocean.

For Mackinder, as for Mahan, the march of events provided the stimulus for geopolitical speculation. As he himself recalled in his old age, three events in particular set him to thinking about the bearings of geography on international politics. One of these events, rather a cluster of events, was the rapid rise of German naval power around the turn of the century. To Mackinder, as to Mahan, this meant the possibility of the nation "already possessing the greatest organized land power and occupying the central strategical position in Europe" now acquiring a navy "strong enough to neutralize British seapower."

The other two events to which Mackinder attributed his early geopolitical thinking were the Boer War (1899-1902) and the Russo-Japanese

---

* From pp. 1 and 2 of *Democratic Ideals and Reality*, by H. J. Mackinder. Copyright 1919 and 1942, by Henry Holt & Co., New York; reproduced by permission.

War (1904-1905). The first was fought by Britain at the end of a 6,000-mile supply line by sea. The other was "fought by Russia at a comparable distance across the land expanse of Asia." These events set in motion the train of thought which led Mackinder to seek a "correlation between the larger geographical and the larger historical generalizations."*

Mackinder's starting point was the same as Mahan's: the supreme importance of seapower, capable of producing global political effects because of the global continuity of the oceans which envelop the "divided and insular lands." †

The rediscovery in the fifteenth century

> of the ocean road to the Indies . . . and . . . to the New World . . . altered the whole course of history by changing our geographical ideas. . . . It was soon realized that all the lands however vast are merely islands, and that although we may give names Atlantic, Indian, and Pacific to different parts of the ocean, there is in reality only one ocean . . .—a continuous water plain covering three-quarters of the globe.‡

From the global continuity of the oceans and connecting seas, Mackinder (still following in the footsteps of Mahan) developed the implications of seapower.

> Owing to the continuity of the ocean and the mobility of ships, a decisive battle at sea has immediate and far-reaching effects. Caesar beat Antony at Actium, and Caesar's orders were enforceable forthwith on every shore of the Mediterranean. Britain won her culminating victory at Trafalgar, and could deny all the ocean to the fleets of her enemies, could transport her armies to whatsoever coast she would and remove them again, could carry supplies home from foreign sources, could exert pressure in negotiation on whatsoever offending state had a sea-front. . . . So impressive have been the results of British seapower that there has perhaps been a tendency to neglect the warnings of history and to regard seapower in general as inevitably having, because of the unity of the ocean, the last word in the rivalry with land power.§

Seapower, Mackinder warned, could be no stronger in the long run than the land base which sustained it. The fertility and the coal mines of the British Isles had enabled a vigorous and adventurous people to

---

* From "The Round World and the Winning of the Peace" in *Foreign Affairs*, July 1943, pp. 595-6. Copyright 1943 by the Council on Foreign Relations, Inc., New York; reproduced by permission.

† From "The Geographical Pivot of History," in *The Geographical Journal* (London), April 1904.

‡ From p. 126 of *Distant Lands*, George Philip & Son, Ltd., London, 1910; reproduced by permission.

§ From pp. 58-59 of *Democratic Ideals and Reality*. Reproduced by permission.

build a world-wide empire and global seapower during a period of some three hundred years. But Britain in the twentieth century was, in Mackinder's view, the legatee of a depreciating estate. In 1902 on the final page of his book, *Britain and the British Seas,** he warned that: "in the presence of vast powers broad-based on the resources of half-continents, Britain could not again become mistress of the seas."

As early as 1904, Mackinder definitely envisaged the possibility that the Great Continent of "Euro-Asia" might become the land base of an invincible global seapower.

Eurasia, with Africa added, covers about a sixth of the earth's surface. It is by far the largest continuous land mass. One of the predominant features of this supercontinent is a thousand-mile-wide belt of deserts and mountains. This desert-mountain barrier extends from the western extremity of Africa to the northeastern extremity of Asia. To the north and northwest of the barrier lie a vast interior plain and the irregular promontory known as the "Continent" of Europe. To the south and southeast of the barrier lie the "monsoon lands" of which the largest and most populous are India and China.

The east-European and Siberian plains coincide, in the main, with the pre-1917 Russian Empire and the Soviet Union of today. Most of this area (which is more than twice the size of the United States) was in the early 1900's very sparsely populated. A great deal of it is either too dry or too frosty for general farming. The distances are vast. Until the end of the nineteenth century, most of the area was totally without modern overland transport.

Nevertheless, Mackinder predicted, in 1904 (in the paper quoted above), that this region (which he later called the Heartland) would become the "pivot area" of world politics. The Russian government had just completed the trans-Siberian railway. Mackinder predicted that the twentieth century

> will not be old before all Asia is covered with railways. The spaces within the Russian Empire and Mongolia are so vast, and their potentialities in populations, wheat, cotton, fuel, and metals so incalculably great, that it is inevitable that a vast economic world . . . will there develop inaccessible to ocean commerce

and hence invulnerable to pressures exerted by seapower.

But this "pivot area," Mackinder argued, contained within itself the requisites for a great seapower.

---

* D. Appleton & Co., New York, 1902, p. 358.

In the world at large [the Russian Empire] occupies the central strategical position. . . . The full development of her mobility is merely a matter of time. Nor is it likely that any possible social revolution will alter her essential relations to the geographical limits of her existence. [If the pivot state should expand] over the marginal [that is, maritime] lands of Euro-Asia, [it would then come into possession of all the requisites for a world empire:] vast continental resources for fleet-building, [a country whose vital centers of production would lie beyond the reach of hostile seapower; and with naval ports on every ocean].

This hypothesis, advanced first in 1904, lay more or less dormant for a few years. The Russo-Japanese War demonstrated that vast overland distances and disconnected seaboards severely limited Russian military mobility. The abortive Revolution of 1905 emphasized the Russian Empire's crippling internal weaknesses. Under these conditions, Mackinder apparently ceased to regard Russia as the nucleus of a transcontinental Eurasian empire, at least in the near future.

After 1906 Mackinder (like Mahan) appears to have transferred his anxieties to Germany: In 1911, with Germany obviously in mind, he wrote:

If one of the states of Europe were to become great out of all proportion to the others, it might use the surplus of its vast resources to outbuild the British fleet.*

This state of affairs came close to fruition in World War I (1914-18). In 1917 the Russian Empire collapsed in revolution. The Communists, who took over in 1918, quickly made peace with Germany—on German terms. If the Western Allies had suffered defeat (as they very nearly did in 1918), Germany's rulers might have gained effective control over the population and physical resources of much of Eurasia. Writing in 1919, Mackinder said:

We have conquered, but had Germany conquered she would have established her seapower on a wider base than any in history, and in fact on the widest possible base.†

This "widest possible base" was the Great Continent of Eurasia, with which Mackinder now grouped Africa. To Afro-Eurasia as a whole he gave the name "World Island"; and its great northern plain, formerly called the "pivot area," he now renamed "Heartland." Surrounded by water, Afro-Eurasia exhibited the properties "both of insularity and of incomparably great resources." In comparison, all other lands were mere

* From Vol. 1, p. 290, of *Nations of the Modern World*. George Philip & Son, Ltd., London, 1911; reproduced by permission.

† From page 62 of *Democratic Ideals and Reality*. Reproduced by permission.

insular appendages. Into this category he lumped not only the obviously insular countries of Britain and Japan but also North and South America and Australia. These "three so-called new continents are in point of area [he argued] merely satellites" of the Great Continent of Eurasia-Africa. Even "North America is no longer . . . a continent; in this twentieth century it is shrinking to be an island."

Addressing himself to the peace conference of 1919, Mackinder asked:

> What if the Great Continent, the whole World Island, or a large part of it, were at some future time to become a single united base of seapower? Would not the other insular bases be outbuilt as regards ships and outmanned as regards seamen? . . . If we would take the long view, must we not still reckon with the possibility that a large part of the Great Continent might some day be united under a single sway, and that an invincible seapower might be based upon it? *

Of Russia, Mackinder in 1919 had little fear. The greater danger, as he visualized it, was that a vengeful Germany would rise from defeat, to bid again for sway over the vast Eurasian spaces and the immense human and material resources of the Russian heartland. Against such an empire, the insular nations (among which, be it remembered, he included the United States) would stand little chance.

Mackinder's image of the possible, if not highly probable, future is summed up in the formula which has been quoted endlessly by men both wise and foolish:

> Who rules East Europe commands the Heartland;
> Who rules the Heartland commands the World Island;
> Who rules the World Island commands the World.

As World War I faded into the past, Mackinder began to reconsider this grand geopolitical hypothesis. He reached a more optimistic view of the capacities of the insular nations and the maritime nations on the European mainland. The concept of a strategic Atlantic community began to take shape.

He first outlined this concept in 1924.

> Western Europe and North America [he said] now constitute for many purposes a single community of nations. . . . The victory of the oceanic nations [in the recent war] has brought it about that the line between east and west, between the continental and the oceanic nations, runs today along the Rhine and not through mid-Atlantic. In the United States the most abundant rainfall and the most productive coalfields are to be found in the east, but in Europe they are in

* From pp. 64, 65, 70 of *Democratic Ideals and Reality.* Reproduced by permission

the west. Thus the west of Europe and the east of North America are physical complements to one another and are rapidly becoming the balanced halves of a single great community.*

By 1930 Mackinder had extended and further developed this concept of the Atlantic community. He now put its eastern boundary at the Volga instead of the Rhine, suggesting that he was beginning to think of the Soviet Union rather than Germany as the future nation to watch in Eurasia. Europe west of the Volga and North America east of the Mississippi comprise some two million square miles of land. This area, Mackinder noted, is equivalent to the "group of regions which constitutes the East." Adding three million square miles of oceans and connecting seas which linked North America and Europe together, he reached a

> total of four per cent of the globe surface, and . . . the main geographical habitat of Western civilization. Within this area are 600 million people . . . Notwithstanding the oceanic break it may be regarded as a single area . . .†

By mid-1943, with Nazi Germany on the road to shattering defeat, Mackinder had definitely accepted the probability that

> if the Soviet Union emerges from this war as conqueror of Germany, she must rank as the greatest land power on the globe. Moreover, she will be the power in the strategically strongest defensive position. The Heartland is the greatest natural fortress on earth. For the first time in history, it is manned by a garrison sufficient both in number and quality.

But in 1943, Mackinder hedged once again, this time on the implication of Soviet primacy in Eastern Europe and inner Asia. He no longer contended that "who rules the Heartland commands the World Island; and who rules the World Island commands the World." Why? Apparently because he now recognized, as he had failed to recognize twenty-five years earlier, the enormous industrial strength of the United States and Western Europe combined and the military potentiality of a coalition of Atlantic states, bound together by mutually supporting links of sea and air power.

This area of strength, which he had first begun to visualize back in 1924, he now described as the "Midland Ocean—the North Atlantic—and its dependent seas and river basins." He emphasized, in particular, three geographic elements of this strategic North Atlantic region:

---

* From Vol. 2, pp. 251-2, of *Nations of the Modern World*. Copyright by George Philip & Son, Ltd., London, 1924; reproduced by permission.

† From "The Human Habitat," in *The Scottish Geographical Magazine*, Jan. 1931, pp. 321, 329. Copyright by the Royal Scottish Geographical Society; reproduced by permission.

a bridgehead in France, a moated aerodrome in Britain, and a reserve of trained manpower, agriculture, and industries, in eastern United States and Canada.

He conceived this community of nations—strong in the essential ingredients of modern military power, and held together both by a common cultural tradition and by strategic opportunities and dangers in common—as an effective counterbalance to the emerging political potential of the Soviet Union in Eurasia.*

Mackinder was an aged man, in his eighty-fifth year, when the first atomic bombs were exploded in 1945. One will never know how this revolutionary event might have affected his geopolitical thinking. His last substantial public utterance, in 1943, two years previously, reflected radical revision of his earlier pessimistic prediction that the future belonged to the rulers of the vast open spaces of Eurasia. It seems likely that his fertile mind would have continued to adapt his geopolitical ideas to the dawning era of nuclear explosives and ballistic missiles.

New perspectives on geographical configuration

Many have speculated and theorized about the effects of the geographical configuration of the earth on the political potential of nations and on the larger patterns of international politics. Most of these have been simply geopolitical castles in the air which have enjoyed a deservedly short and usually quite local vogue. A few have lasted beyond their day. Mahan and Mackinder, perhaps more than any others, continue to live in the minds of men in many countries. Mackinder especially has left a deep imprint.

Critics have approached his geopolitical ideas with various purposes and from various national perspectives. Some have pointed to flaws in his historical analogies and generalizations. Others have debated his predictions regarding future international trends and patterns. Still others have denounced his views as vicious or have found in his ideas a prescription useful for their own national purposes.

The late Nicholas J. Spykman (professor of international relations at Yale) exemplifies the first and second types of criticism. Unfortunately his commentary is too long to reproduce in full. In concluding, he said:

The Mackinder study represented a picture of the constellation of forces which existed at a particular time and within a particular frame of reference. It was first elaborated in 1904 before the conclusion of

* From "The Round World and the Winning of the Peace," in *Foreign Affairs*, July 1943, p. 595. Copyright by the Council on Foreign Relations, Inc., New York; reproduced by permission.

the British-Russian Entente of 1907 and was strongly influenced by the previous century of conflict between Russia and Great Britain. When, in 1919, his book *Democratic Ideals and Reality* was published, the conception of an inevitable historical opposition between Russian land power and British sea power was reemphasized. The fallacy of this blanket application of a theory of history is seen when we realize that the opposition between these two states has never, in fact, been inevitable. Actually, in the three great world wars of the nineteenth and twentieth centuries, the Napoleonic Wars, the first World War, and the second World War, the British and Russian Empires have lined up together against an intervening Rimland Power as led by Napoleon, Wilhelm II, and Hitler.

In other words, there has never really been a simple land power–sea power opposition. The historical alignment has always been in terms of some members of the Rimland with Great Britain against some members of the Rimland with Russia, or Great Britain and Russia together against a dominating Rimland Power. The Mackinder dictum: "Who controls eastern Europe rules the Heartland; who rules the Heartland rules the World Island; and who rules the World Island rules the World" is false. If there is to be a slogan for the power politics of the Old World, it must be: "Who controls the Rimland rules Eurasia; who rules Eurasia controls the destinies of the world." *

Hans Weigert (professor of geography at Georgetown University) is another critic of Mackinder. The following excerpts from one of his papers make several additional well-conceived points:

Any attempt at a critique of Mackinder's powerful generalizations should begin with the acknowledgment of our indebtedness to the man who did more in our time than anybody else to enlist geography as an aid to statecraft and strategy. The fundamentals of his closed-space concept [see the quoted passage on page 98, Chapter 2] stand so firmly today that we almost forget how revolutionary the concept was when first formulated [in 1904] . . . The same observation applies to Mackinder's land power thesis which, appearing at what seemed to be the height of the Victorian sea power age, seemed shocking and fantastic to many in the English-speaking world. But in reviewing his thesis today, we should remember that it is the concept of a man who viewed the world from England. . . . Only a Britisher could have written as Mackinder did. Recognizing this and taking account of the technological changes which have surpassed even Mackinder's imagination, we should have sufficient perspective today to speak critically of the theory of the Heartland.

It is perhaps not incidental that the logic of Mackinder's Heartland seems to reveal itself best on a Mercator world map (such as Mackinder used when he first laid out his blueprint). Here the Heart-

* From p. 43 of *The Geography of the Peace*, by N. J. Spykman. Copyright 1944 by Harcourt, Brace & World, Inc., New York; reproduced with their permission.

land lives up to its name. We see it surrounded by a huge arc forming an inner crescent which includes Germany, Turkey, India, and China. Beyond the crescent of peripheral states, Mackinder envisaged an outer crescent which embraced Britain, South Africa, Australia, the United States, Canada, and Japan. Again the Mercator projection lent a helpful hand in constructing what seemed to Mackinder a "wholly oceanic" and "insular" crescent.

However, we find it difficult, if not impossible to visualize this relation of the Heartland to a surrounding inner and outer crescent if we exchange the Mercator map for the globe or any azimuthal-equidistant map. The North America which seemingly was a part of a chain of insular powers distant from the Heartland now becomes a geographical myth. Instead . . . we see the Heartland over the top of the world as a politico-geographical reality, as the result of the lessons of a new geography of world air transport. We have a different view of the Heartland than Mackinder, who plotted it from Britain and with the destinies of Britain foremost in his mind. While time has verified Mackinder's concept of Russia's growing importance as a land power in a pivotal area, the skyways of the Arctic Mediterranean give validity to a new way of regarding the geographical relations of North America and the U.S.S.R. . . .

Mackinder's citadel of land power still stands—and mightier than ever. And it is not merely the Heartland quality of its land-mass that accounts for its leading role in today's world theater. Equally important are the wealth of its resources and the human intangibles which make a nation great. In the political and economic geography of a shrinking world, location is not a static element. Its value changes constantly. . . .*

Quite a different approach to Mackinder is revealed in the writings of Karl Haushofer, the leading spirit of the so-called German school of geopolitics which flourished just before and during the Nazi period in Germany. Mackinder had outlined his early geopolitical theorems as a warning to his own nation, Great Britain. Between 1904 and 1919, he was saying in effect: disaster is likely to overwhelm us unless we take steps in time to prevent it. Haushofer, from the perspective of a German elite smarting from defeat in World War I, grasped Mackinder's formulas, saying in effect: Mackinder has something for Germany; let us try it out. That is to say, Mackinder's main thesis (as it stood in 1919) was that the geographical layout of lands and seas favored an East European state gaining control of the Eurasian Heartland and from that position acquiring dominance over Eurasia as a whole and eventually over most of the oversea continents and islands as well. This was a formula tailor-made to the appetites of imperial-minded post-1919 Germans. Thus, unintentionally and to his acute embarrassment, Mackinder became in the 1920's and 1930's a part of the intellectual apparatus by which Haushofer and others blueprinted the strategy of aggression and conquest which Hitler carried so far towards execution.

Within the United States, Mackinder remained virtually unknown until after the German invasion of Russia in 1941. A year or two earlier some spot checks had seemed to indicate that scarcely one teacher of international relations in ten had ever heard of Mackinder, much less read his books and shorter essays.

The man most responsible for the "discovery" of Mackinder in America was the late Edward M. Earle (professor at the Institute for Advanced Study in Princeton). Largely due to his efforts, *Democratic Ideals and Reality*, first published in 1919, was reissued in 1942. In an introduction to the new printing, Earle wrote as follows:

> This little volume by Sir Halford Mackinder has the rare quality of timelessness. Although it was written in 1919 with special reference to the then impending settlement with Germany, there is no better statement anywhere of the facts of geography which condition the destiny of our world. . . .
>
> Forty years ago—when Mahan's theories concerning the supremacy of seapower were at the height of their prestige—Mackinder told his countrymen that Britain had no "indefeasible title to maritime supremacy," that seapower could be outflanked by land power, that the rise of great industrial states in Europe . . . could undermine the foundations of British economic and strategic security, that it was no longer possible for England to pursue a policy of limited liabilities. Furthermore, he warned that, should Britain once surrender the long lead which she then held over her competitors, she probably would have lost for all time both her naval supremacy and her position as a Great Power.
>
> He saw that Germany and Russia were so situated on the continent of Europe that, should they combine or should either acquire control of the other, they would rule the world. He understood that modern transportation was reducing continents to islands. Europe, Asia, and Africa constituted not three continents but one—the "World Island." This World Island is the true center of gravity of world power, the Western Hemisphere being only an island of lesser proportions, lesser manpower, and lesser natural resources. The "Heartland" of this World Island is central and eastern Europe, so situated geographically and strategically that it could dominate the World Island as a whole. . . .
>
> [Earle concluded: this book] should be read by soldiers charged with the prosecution of the war [that is, World War II]; by statesmen concerned with the formulation of grand strategy; by diplomatists

who deal with international affairs; by journalists who are concerned with the underlying facts of the last war, the last peace, and the present struggle; and certainly by citizens who are consecrated to victory and ponder the principles which must govern a postwar settlement.*

Two things should be noted about the passage just quoted. First, it introduced into American thinking a version of Mackinder which was then (in 1942) already twenty years out of date. It was a version, be it remembered, which Mackinder himself had drastically revised in 1924 and 1930. Second, this discarded geopolitical formula caught on in the United States. Mackinder—the Mackinder of 1919—was widely quoted and rather generally endorsed by American educators, news commentators, military experts, and postwar planners. Mackinder's Heartland concept made a deep imprint on American thinking that lingers to this day.

Was Mackinder right? And which version, the earlier or the later? No dogmatic answer can be given to these questions. So much has happened in recent years that judgments expressed even as late as 1950 are certainly debatable today. For example, writing in that year for the second edition of *Foundations of National Power*, we said on this issue:

> The meteoric rise of Soviet prestige and influence has brought the problem down from the clouds to the levels of serious public discussion and practical statecraft. We are no longer dealing with mere theory, but with the stubborn trend of disquieting facts.
>
> The first stage of Mackinder's (1919) hypothesis is now fulfilled, if not quite in the manner its author originally anticipated. The vast bloc of territory, reaching from Central Europe to the Pacific, and from the Arctic to the desert-mountain belt of inner Asia, has been brought under one rule. Its immense resources—physical and human—are being integrated and organized to support a gigantic political power. . . .
>
> We now face the second stage envisaged by Mackinder's formula— the struggle for the World Island. So far the Russians have made alarming progress. Despite heavy losses and devastation, the Soviet Union emerged from the war by far the strongest power in the Eastern Hemisphere. No state or combination of states in Europe or in Asia could stand unaided at present against the Soviet colossus.
>
> With Soviet military power firmly established in eastern Germany and in the Danube valley, all Western Europe is a potential hostage in the sense that Soviet forces could probably move westward to the Atlantic if ordered to do so. The same condition exists with qualifications in the Middle East and in Eastern Asia.

* From pp. xxii f. of the Introduction of the second edition of *Democratic Ideals and Reality.* Copyright by Henry Holt & Co., New York; reproduced by permission.

Only the presence of American forces in Japan and in the islands of the western Pacific has prevented the Soviet Union from wielding virtually unopposed power in the Far East. The danger of full-scale resistance by the United States is likewise a powerful deterrent in the Middle East and in Europe. Only the United States possesses the necessary surplus of economic capital and the added military weight necessary to offer a viable alternative to progressive Soviet expansion towards the "rimlands" of Europe and Asia.

Should Moscow achieve that goal—assuming that it is a goal—it would give to the Soviet Union a strategical position with greater opportunities even than those which Hitler won and lost. It would largely or completely wipe out the strategical handicaps that now stand in the way of the Soviet Union projecting its power beyond the oceans by means of ships. It would put in Russian hands a combination of natural resources, manpower, and economic plant exceeding that of the United States. Such a result, in short, would go far toward realizing Mackinder's third and final prediction [of 1919], that one-power domination of the Old World would lead inexorably to one-power domination of the whole world.

Assuming—from our point of view—a less disastrous sequence of events, specifically some stabilization of power relationships in Europe and in Asia, one must still ask whether recent and prospective developments in military technology will not enormously enlarge the striking range of the Soviet Union. We have noted the growing vulnerability of the Soviet Union itself to devastating attack by air. Will not the converse become true? To ask the question is to answer it, for no city in Europe, in Asia, in Africa, or even in North America, will lie beyond the future range of airborne attack that might originate at some point inside the huge bloc of real estate which comprises the Soviet Union and its surrounding zone of satellite states.

Trends that were dimly perceived in 1950 have passed into history, along with much else besides. The Korean War (1950-53) temporarily checked the advance of Communist power in eastern Asia. European economic recovery, NATO, the American H-bomb, and the U.S. Strategic Air Command stabilized the frontiers of Central Europe and the Near East. Much more quickly than generally anticipated, the Russians overtook the commanding American lead in military rocketry and thermonuclear explosives. The result has been an appalling rise in the destructive potentialities of any direct confrontation of American and Soviet military power. Deterrence has become the watchword of military planning.

None of these developments refute *per se* Mackinder's early thesis regarding the long-term concentration of world power and influence in Eurasia. Nor do these events necessarily confirm his later concept of a durable equipoise between East and West, though the present balance of terror comes closer to fitting the later than the earlier Mackinder formula. What the events of the 1950's more forcefully suggest is that geographical configuration—the global layout of lands and seas—has become very much less politically significant today than formerly. When ballistic rockets armed with thermonuclear warheads can be fired from nearly any point upon the earth's surface, either from land or from ships at sea, with a range and accuracy that enable them to devastate whole cities at nearly every other point upon the earth's surface, we shall have reached the end of the line for geopolitical concepts and theories which purport to explain and to forecast the overall design of international politics by reference to the configuration of lands and seas.

In retrospect, this appears not as a sudden transformation, but rather the logical outcome of trends long in evidence. At the close of the lecture to the Royal Geographical Society in 1904, the lecture in which Mackinder outlined his original geopolitical interpretation of history and the future, one member of his audience rose to challenge the whole scheme. That man was Leopold S. Amery, a name virtually unknown to most Americans today. Amery argued that a "great deal of this geographical distribution must lose its importance" with future advances in the means of transportation on land, upon the sea, and in the air. "The successful Powers" of the future, he predicted, would be "those which have the greatest industrial basis." It would "not matter whether they are in the center of a continent or on an island; those people who have the industrial power and the power of invention and science will be able to defeat all others."*

Events of the past half century have gone some way towards confirming Amery's prophecy. Naval forces can refuel and carry out even major repairs at sea. Nuclear-powered submarines can remain at sea for months at a time. These developments have reduced the military value of permanent oversea bases, which figured so importantly in Mahan's geopolitical universe. Submarines, bombing planes, and ballistic missiles have eroded the former defensive strength of islands, peninsulas, promontories, and remote ports on coasts protected by mountains, deserts or jungles. Pipelines, motor vehicles, railways, and still expanding highway grids have enormously increased the mobility and capacity of overland movement. Airplanes have shrunk the widest oceans and continents and have surmounted refractory barriers of terrain and distance. These and other changes in weapons and communications have profoundly altered the relative military value of heartlands, marginal lands, rimlands, and islands.

Other far-reaching changes cast even more doubt on the fruitfulness of old-style geopolitical thinking. Mahan and Mackinder, and most of their critics as well as their disciples have proceeded from the assumption that

---

* The *Geographical Journal*, London, April 1904, p. 441.

military wars determine, in the final reckoning, the ordering of influence and deference in the Society of Nations. In our time, as emphasized in Chapter 4 and elsewhere, the patterns of international political potential are increasingly affected by social changes and by paramilitary and non-military forms of political interaction. We shall return again and again to these critically important new dimensions of international politics. We simply note here that, for these as well as for strictly military reasons, all geopolitical thinking of the Mahan-Mackinder type requires careful reassessment.

The physical dimensions of our planet remain the same as ever. The geographic layout of lands and seas has not changed significantly during the past generation. What has changed, and changed almost beyond recognition, is the political value and significance of these geographic realities. This is not to argue that geographic variables no longer have political significance. In many situations the mountains, deserts, oceans, and other geographic realities still present obstacles to political undertakings, both military and nonmilitary. Certain recent investigations suggest that distance —the ultimate geographic variable—still has a bearing on the patterns of political influence and deference among nations, an issue to which we shall return in Chapter 13. What is being questioned here is whether geographic shapes and layouts any longer provide a basis as fruitful as formerly for grand hypotheses intended to explain and to forecast the larger distributions of political potential in the Society of Nations.

CHAPTER ELEVEN

★ ★ ★

"Climate and the Energy of Nations"

W E HAVE ENCLOSED the title of this chapter in quotation marks because it is also the title of a well-known book on a subject which has attracted a great many inquiring minds from time immemorial.* The proposition that climate—by which we mean simply the recurring patterns of weather—affects human behavior and performance, has a long and respectable lineage. A partial list of those who have expounded this hypothesis in one form or another through the centuries would include the Greek physician Hippocrates (about 400 B.C.), the Greek philosopher Aristotle (about 350 B.C.), the Roman historian Pliny (about 60 A.D.), the Arab historian Ibn Khaldun (about 1300 A.D.), the French political philosophers Bodin (1530-96) and Montesquieu (1689-1755), the British physician Arbuthnot (1667-1735), the French naturalist Buffon (1707-88), the French geographer Reclus (1830-1905), the Scottish historian Ferguson (1725-1816), the British historian Buckle (1821-62), the Swiss-American geographer Guyot (1807-84), and many others. In our century, Americans who have discovered significant correlations between climate and human behavior and accomplishment include Ellsworth Huntington and Stephen Visher (geographers), Raymond H. Wheeler (psychologist), and Clarence A. Mills (medical-research scientist).

It has become fashionable in recent years to deride and make jokes about those who have emphasized these relationships. Huntington has been a favorite target. His critics have branded him an environmental determinist and hurled even more unpleasant epithets. All this needling and mudslinging has drawn from Wheeler (cited above) the following retort:

> Were all these investigators wrong? Were they crazy? Obviously not. It is patent to any intelligent person that different climates

---

* The book is by S. F. Markham and was published by Oxford University Press, New York, 1944.

produce different fauna and flora. Why should they not produce different kinds of people? Yet broach the subject today to many a scientist and one will immediately elicit a blank look of incomprehension, or one will be regarded as a crackpot fit only for the company of astrologers.*

Such doctrinal controversies need not disturb us. As we have emphasized repeatedly, environmental factors of any kind can affect human affairs (1) by being perceived and taken into account in making choices and decisions, and (2) by putting a ceiling on performance. With respect to recurring patterns of atmospheric temperature, relative humidity, barometric pressure, and air circulation—the principal aspects of climate—the issue is simply stated as follows: (a) Have these factors entered significantly into the calculations of political decision-makers? and (b) Have these factors affected significantly the operational results of decisions? At a more general level, the second question can be restated: Are climatic variations in space and through time significantly related (and if so, how) to the geographical distribution of political potentials in the Society of Nations?

The first question has not received as much attention as it deserves. But one can note a few datum points with regard to it. A great many political decisions appear to have been taken on the assumption that tropical and Arctic peoples cannot compete on equal terms in political and economic struggles with inhabitants of the so-called temperate zones. Temperate-zone empire builders have repeatedly justified their projects in terms of the white man's burden—a self-assumed duty to confer the benefits of temperate-zone civilization on the handicapped natives of the frozen Arctic and the Asian, African, and American tropics. With certain more or less fixed notions about the enervating effects of humid heat, white men in the tropics have historically cast themselves mainly in roles which required as little physical exercise as possible, leaving most of the hard manual labor to the natives. At the same time, be it noted parenthetically, business corporations and governments alike have only recently begun to show much interest in accumulating knowledge of the direct effects of climatic conditions on the human organism and the possibilities of countering adverse effects by means of diet, clothing, exercise, and other adaptations.

Most of the controversy over climatic effects on human affairs has centered on more general hypotheses regarding the impact of weather on performance and accomplishment. We shall present some of these argu-

* From "Climate and Human Behavior," by R. H. Wheeler, in *The Encyclopaedia of Psychology*, p. 80. Copyright 1946 by The Philosophical Library, Inc., New York; reproduced by permission.

ments later on, but first a few words on the principal climatic patterns of the earth.

Only within the last hundred years or so has knowledge about climate evolved from subjective personal impressions to increasingly exact measurements. Even today large parts of the earth are not covered by systematic weather records. The principal categories of climatic data include atmospheric temperature, relative humidity, air circulation, and barometric pressure.

Atmospheric temperature is recorded on either the Fahrenheit or the centigrade scale—generally °F in North America and Britain, and °C nearly everywhere else. Weather observations at a given station usually include maximum and minimum temperature readings during each 24-hour period. The *daily mean* temperature is the mathematical average of maximum and minimum. The *normal mean* for a given date is the average of the daily mean during the historical period that records have been kept at a given station. *Monthly mean* and *annual mean* statistics may also be kept; they are simply the average of the daily mean for the stated period. Departures from the daily norms are derived by comparing the actual high, low, and mean temperature for a given date with the long-term averages. Such departures are recorded as so many degrees *plus* or *minus*. The daily plus and minus statistics may be aggregated for a month or a year as so many *cumulative* degrees plus or minus the norm. The following table illustrates the use of these data in a sample daily weather report from the Weather Bureau's New York City station.

TEMPERATURE DATA
Highest yesterday, 71 at 3:40 P.M.
Lowest yesterday, 58 at 7:50 P.M.
Mean yesterday, 65
Normal on this date, 67
Departure from normal, −2
Departure this month, −40
Departure since Jan. 1st, −95

Atmospheric temperature at a given station varies, of course, from day to day. These day-night patterns vary from season to season. Daily and seasonal patterns differ more or less widely from place to place.

Relative humidity is the amount of water vapor present in the atmosphere expressed as a percentage of saturation at the place of observation. Relative humidity varies of course from place to place and from time to time in the same place. In any given place there are averaged patterns, or norms, of relative humidity for daily, seasonal, and longer periods.

For *air circulation*—wind, in plain English—daily, seasonal, and annual norms or long-term averages are computed in precisely the same manner.

A related concept is *sensible temperature*, which is a function of the interaction of the human organism to particular combinations of atmospheric temperature, relative humidity, and air circulation. Sensible temperature is reflected in the sense of warmth or chill experienced by individuals. Above a certain temperature, around 80°F, but varying somewhat from person to person, increase in relative humidity makes the air seem warmer than it actually is. At lower temperatures, just the reverse occurs. Air circulation, as is well known, makes warm air seem cooler, and cold air positively frigid. These effects are all related to the physiological mechanisms and processes by which the human body gets rid of surplus internal heat.

Barometric pressure represents the weight of the air pressing on a column of mercury or some equivalent. It varies with the elevation or altitude above sea level of the recording station. It also varies with changes in weather patterns. Warm air is capable of holding more water vapor in suspension. Given certain other conditions, a falling barometer is associated with stormy weather, and a rising barometer with settled weather. The effects of barometric pressure on human behavior are controversial and appear to vary considerably from person to person, depending on individual differences in bodily metabolism and other physiological factors.

Climatic patterns, by definition, involve generalizations derived by averaging weather records in a given place over periods of time. Descriptions of the climate of a country or of a smaller or a larger geographical area involve still further generalizations derived by averaging the averages of a few or many local weather stations, often supplemented by the personal impressions of individual observers. Thus, any description of the climate of a large region—for example, western Europe or equatorial Africa—represents a very high level of abstraction. But, as the above paragraphs indicate, climatic patterns do have an empirical basis; and it is possible to make a number of general statements more or less descriptive of the type of climate likely to be observed in the area in question. But one should always keep in mind that climate is an abstraction, and that weather alone is what any specific person enjoys or endures. What follows is a very generalized picture of the climatic patterns of a number of geographical regions which figure importantly in international politics.

Until quite recently, prevailing ideas regarding the impacts of climate on man came predominantly from Europeans or from their descendants in other parts of the world. Many of these ideas appear to have originated simply as extensions of European ways of thinking and reacting. For example, the climate of the North American Atlantic seaboard from New York to Florida resembles the climate of coastal China more than that of western Europe. But it was mainly Europeans, not Chinese, who settled eastern North America; and from Europe they brought their folklore about climate and how to cope with it. It is interesting to speculate how different these adaptations might have been if Chinese instead of Europeans had settled this area.

One typical idea of European origin is that the middle latitudes in the northern hemisphere make up the temperate zone. These latitudes can be generally so characterized with respect to Europe. But numerous climatic regions in the same latitudes in North America and in Asia are anything but temperate. Indeed, within this belt one finds some of the most disagreeable and even savage climates in the world. But however fallacious, it is part of our European cultural heritage to imagine that latitude is the chief determinant of climate; that the middle latitudes constitute the temperate zone; and that this zone is the natural habitat of the white race.

Speaking generally, and subject to many intraregional qualifications and local variations, the predominant quality of weather in Britain and western Europe (with the exception of Spain and Portugal) is its lack of extremes. European summers are generally cool, somewhat comparable to the San Francisco Bay and Puget Sound regions. American visitors to Britain frequently complain that the climate is cold and nasty; but palms and other tropical plants grow outdoors the year round in southwestern England.

West European weather is rather damp on the whole, with the dampness distributed rather uniformly through the year. Relative humidity is comparatively high most of the time, and rains occur frequently—sometimes almost daily for months at a time in the lands facing the North Sea. But total rainfall is relatively low. In New York, for example, the average annual rainfall is nearly twice that of London. It rains frequently but rarely very hard or very long at a stretch.

The wind blows a good deal in western Europe, but almost never with the violence that characterizes the destructive cyclonic storms of our eastern seaboard and Middle West, and even more the eastern marginal lands of Asia. The farther inland one goes in Europe (in southern Germany, for example) the more the climate resembles the mid-continental climate of North America—greater extremes of temperature, in particular.

The lands fronting the Mediterranean exhibit a different climatic pattern. The salient features of Mediterranean-type climates include: a winter rainy season (though not *very* rainy as a rule), a long dry summer (often six to eight months without appreciable rainfall), and considerably higher summer temperatures and lower relative humidity than in western Europe. Somewhat similar patterns occur in central and southern California, in northern Chile, near the Cape of Good Hope in Africa, and along the southwest coast of Australia.

Eastern China and Japan exhibit still another climatic pattern, sometimes called humid semitropical. Its characteristics are cool to cold winters, hot damp summers, violent cyclonic storms (called typhoons in Asia, and similar to the hurricanes in eastern North America). Versions of this climatic pattern occur along the Atlantic and Gulf coasts of North America from New York to Galveston, throughout most of the lower Mississippi Valley, in southern Brazil, Uruguay, and northern Argentina, in northern India, and in northeastern Australia.

Humid subtropical patterns merge into mid-continental patterns farther north in the United States, in southern Canada, and in eastern Europe and western Siberia. These regions experience cold winters, hot summers, and generally sparse rainfall. In the American Middle West, the absence of east-west mountain ranges enables polar and tropical air masses to interact in tornadoes, severe thunderstorms, blizzards, and sudden temperature changes, with a violence rarely encountered in other continents.

Much of the earth's surface is either too dry or too frosty for the needs of man. Either the growing season between frosts is too short, or natural rainfall is too scarce for the needs of a settled society. This is true of well over half of the Soviet Union, western China, much of Canada, western United States, and Mexico, the whole interior of the subcontinent of Australia, large areas in southern Africa, and a huge belt of deserts and arid plains averaging about 1,000 miles in width and reaching from southwest to northeast with scarcely any interruptions from the western bulge of Africa to Bering strait on the opposite side of the earth.

Finally, there are the warm to hot intertropical climates found mainly between twenty degrees north and twenty degrees south of the equator. These may be very rainy, as in parts of the interior of Brazil, Central Africa, southern Asia and southwestern Pacific. Or they may exhibit alternating rainy and relatively dry seasons, as in eastern Brazil, a belt across Africa between the Sahara desert and the equator, most of southern Africa, and parts of India and southeast Asia.

No climatologist would find these generalities satisfactory; but they will suffice for our purposes. In any case, one conclusion emerges from any classification of climates. In most parts of the world, from time immemorial, climate has constituted an obstacle, sometimes negligible, more often considerable, and in a few places nearly insuperable, to the higher levels of human achievement.

In our century the most prolific and probably the most influential investigator of the effects of climate on human affairs has been the late Ellsworth Huntington (long of Yale University). He confirmed that climatic factors—temperature and all the rest—have varied everywhere not merely from day to day and from season to season but also in cyclic patterns through decades, centuries, and millennia. He was a pioneer in developing methods for discovering the historical and prehistorical patterns of climatic fluctuation in some of the regions which the human race has inhabited the longest.

Huntington collected a vast array of evidence convincing to him and to a great many who read his books and articles that the human organism functions more efficiently in certain climatic conditions than in others. He derived, by observation and experiment, the concept of optimum climate: the combination of temperature, relative humidity, windiness, storminess, etc., most conducive to energetic effort and accomplishment. The optimum varied somewhat with the level of technology, according to Huntington; in general he favored an average temperature in the 65–70-degree range (Fahrenheit), with moderate variation between day and night, with frequent changes of weather and considerable storminess, and with substantial variation from season to season.

Huntington also emphasized the indirect effects of climate—on food production, incidence of disease, water supply, and many other factors related to human existence and well-being. These he considered to be nearly as important as the direct effects on the human organism.

Finally, he reiterated that both direct and indirect effects varied with the state of technology: that is, with the level of knowledge regarding architecture, domestic heating, clothing materials and design, nutrition, sanitation and medicine, water control, plant and animal biology, and many other kinds of knowledge involved in coping with different patterns of weather.

Huntington's theses regarding the relation of climate to human advancement and accomplishment evoked a great deal of controversy. His propositions are summed up in the following sentences quoted from two of his earlier books:

> A certain peculiar type of climate prevails wherever civilization is high. In the past the same type seems to have prevailed wherever a great civilization arose. Therefore, such a climate seems to be a necessary condition of great progress.*

Applying this premise to international politics, Huntington contended that

* From p. 9 of *Civilization and Climate*, by Ellsworth Huntington. Copyright 1915 by Yale University Press, New Haven; reproduced by permission.

the expansion of the great nations of the world is to a large extent determined by climatic conditions. . . . Every nation that has been stimulated by an energizing climate has apparently spread its power over neighboring regions either by land or by sea.[*]

Support for Huntington's theses has come from, among others, an American psychologist, Raymond H. Wheeler. His interest in climatic cycles and in their larger social effects originated as a by-product of research in the history of psychological doctrines. He discovered certain rhythmic cycles in a wide range of human activities through several thousand years of history.

Following in the footsteps of Huntington, Wheeler has amassed an enormous amount of evidence that seems to confirm the hypothesis that there has been throughout history a remarkable correlation between—

Climatic cycles and human behavior and accomplishment [†]

A culture pattern representing all important phases of human activity was fluctuating back and forth in rhythmic fashion as a vast, complex, but integrated whole or Gestalt, each detail of which related logically with the others in so intimate and clear a manner that, knowing one of them, the others could be predicted. The major rhythms average about one hundred years in length, but clustered into groups of five, beginning with the middle of the sixth century B.C. The termination of the 500-year rhythms occurred near the death of Caesar and the turning point in the vitality of the Roman Empire; in the fifth century (fall of Rome and its contemporary ancient empires); the tenth century (ending the first half of the Middle Ages); and the fifteenth (the fall of the second half of the Middle Ages). The termination of the present 500-year period is due around 1980.

The manner in which climate came to be involved was another accident. While inspecting the culture curve a colleague remarked that it resembled the California sequoia tree ring curve which goes back to 1350 B.C. . . . On investigation it was found that the two curves resembled one another in a manner that could not possibly have been explained by chance. This led to the assumption that the culture fluctuations could have been climatically determined, but the culture curve represented practically all of the civilizations of the world, past and present. Was there such a thing as a fluctuating world climate? Huntington had suggested an affirmative answer, but no exhaustive work had ever been done in an effort to trace the history of climate over the

[*] From p. 24 of *World Power and Evolution*, by Ellsworth Huntington. Copyright 1919 by Yale University Press; reproduced by permission.

[†] From "Climate and Human Behavior," by R. H. Wheeler, in *The Encyclopaedia of Psychology*. Copyright 1946 by the Philosophical Library, Inc., New York; reproduced by permission.

world as a whole. . . . No one had even made a complete comparative study of temperature and rainfall curves as far back as they go for the world as a whole. . . . The data are [now] complete enough to justify the statement that unless the cultural fluctuations are climatically conditioned, the coincidences violate all the laws of chance and are utterly inexplicable in the light of our present knowledge.

The data warrant the conclusion that there is a world climate, although never completely homogeneous in character; that this world climate has fluctuated in rhythms within rhythms which tend to follow the multiples of the sunspot cycle of 11.3 years; that these rhythms whether long or short tend to follow a similar pattern of phase sequences, the phases being cold-dry, warm-wet, warm-dry, cold-wet, then cold-dry again, in that order. The 100-year and 500-year climatic rhythms correspond with the culture rhythms already mentioned. Shorter climatic and cultural rhythms superimposed on the longer ones also correspond, frequently down to the single sunspot cycle.

Space does not permit explaining in detail the sources of information regarding the history of climate prior to measured temperature and rainfall. A partial list must suffice: tree rings, lake levels, river levels, drought and flood chronologies from different localities; famines, crop failures, harvesting dates, ice-forming and ice-breaking dates, early and late frosts, reports of excessive heat, cold, storms, snow; clay varves; travel through mountain passes; the receding and advancing of glaciers; formation of bogs; pollen analysis; expansion and contraction of arid regions; data from military posts, monasteries, government records and numerous diaries; data from accounts of campaigns that ran into extreme weather; locust plagues, types of vines and other vegetation; sunspots large enough to see with the naked eye and aurora (both known to be associated with drops in temperature or with cold periods); lengthening and shortening of the sunspot cycle, etc.

Even though individual items run into the tens of thousands, there is no way of telling what the average temperature or rainfall was during a given period, but it is possible to locate the phases of the 100-year cycle beyond much question, and in many instances the phases of shorter fluctuations.

Assuming this picture to be reasonably correct, there is no question but that nations or empires rise and fall on tides of climatic change. Dated international and civil war battles from over the known world since 600 B.C. . . . plotted against the curve, fall so consistently during the warm and cold phases, respectively, or overlap on the transition from warm to cold or cold to warm, that these battles alone would have located the warm and cold phases of the 100-year rhythms as well as most of the interruptions (smaller superimposed rhythms), if the interruptions were as long as ten years.

The so-called Golden Ages of history generally occur on the transition from the cold to the warm phase of a 100-year cycle which has all of the appearances of being a high energy-level time in history. Occasionally a Golden Age will occur on the transition from warm to cold, but evidently only under certain special circumstances which cannot be discussed here. Never do they occur during the hot-dry or cold-dry phases. Out of fifty-five sovereigns who come down through history with the title, The Great, forty-eight have ruled on this transition. Of 650 rulers, about half of whom the historians characterize as good and half poor, 80 per cent of the good, in the world as a whole, have ruled at the close of a cold and opening of a warm phase. Over 90 per cent of the poor rulers divide almost equally between the hot-dry and cold-dry phases of the cycle. The transition from cold to warm is nation-building time the world over; and the transition from warm to cold is nation- or government-falling time. These correlations hold even for the warrior states of Africa and the East Indies. They hold for the Orient as well as for the Occident, and for the Indian civilizations of the Western world in so far as data are available. It should be kept in mind that we are discussing world trends. From time to time there have been lags and leads both in the climate of particular regions and in the shifting of the culture patterns. No known exceptions of any consequence have yet been found, although there are instances in which the data are incomplete. Where nothing is known of the prevailing climate in a particular country at a particular time, the chances of that country not following the general trend of the 100-year cycle are practically nil. But the summation of all possible exceptions would not materially change the nature of the correlations. . . .

The highly integrated character of the culture pattern loses its mysterious character when it is seen that the atomistic or cold-phase pattern in every respect emphasizes the part of anything at the expense of the whole, while the warm-phase, organismic pattern emphasizes the whole of anything at the expense of the part. . . .

[Thus] the hot drought phase is the typical season for despots, dictators, communism, totalitarianism, Gestapos, pogroms, fascism, and decadence in general. And what more logical explanation could there be than that through devitalization from the effect of temperatures much higher than those to which they have been accustomed, people have become irritable and unstable or lethargic and indifferent, depending upon circumstances. Similarly it would seem obvious that the Golden Age period occurs where both temperature and rainfall and sufficient variability in humidity and temperature following a revitalizing cold period have raised the human energy level to its maximum, along with conditions adequate for economic prosperity. . . .

World leaders of today should be cognizant of the fact that an intensive study of the climate of the past will ultimately lead to accurate predictions of trends far ahead into the future, and that the climatic phases of the future will probably produce the same types of cultural and behavior problems as they seemed to have produced in the past, over and over again, by controlling man's vitality or energy level. . . .

Further support for Huntington's climatic hypotheses has come from Dr. Clarence A. Mills (professor emeritus of experimental medicine at the University of Cincinnati). From a wealth of personal observations of human behavior in various climates, supplemented by experiments with laboratory animals, Mills has found evidence which convinces him of the essential validity of Huntington's ideas.

Mills, however, has gone a step further than Huntington and Wheeler. He has propounded a sweeping geopolitical hypothesis with reference to future trends in international politics. Mills' experiments and his general hypothesis were described in the journal of the American Association for the Advancement of Science. The following selection is reproduced from that article entitled—

Temperature dominance over human life *

Temperature bears an importance to man far beyond the mere matter of his hour-to-hour comfort. In some places it lays a heavy, stagnating hand over his life and holds him to a vegetative existence; in others, it generates an energy and progressiveness which drives him forward with irresistible impetus. Its effects begin even before he is conceived, for the metabolic vigor of parental germ cells at the time of their union exerts a potent influence over the entire course of the new life. Without favorable temperatures, neither individual nor nation can develop innate potentialities to the full.

The hand of temperature is being felt over the world today, much as Ellsworth Huntington so ably pictured its course through past centuries. We are now caught in one of the long cycles of climatic change that alter the courses of nations and of world trends. Man thus has urgent need to understand the mechanism of this temperature dominance over him as an individual and over mankind as a whole. The answer lies in a close study of human dynamics.

The human body is essentially a combustion machine that functions only as its cells release energy by burning the foodstuffs taken in. True, this combustion in the cells is a very complicated affair, carried on at low temperature and in numerous independent steps through the aid of special catalysts. Although it is far less violent than the gasoline explosions in an automobile motor, its over-all efficiency is no greater, and it is even more dependent upon rapid dissipation of its waste heat. The working efficiency of men, horses, and dogs ranges between 20 and 25 percent, but the Diesel engine designed by present-day engineers performs at over 40 percent efficiency.

For every unit of combustion energy transformed into work-output by our bodies, three or four similar units must be dissipated as waste heat. Failure of such dissipation to keep pace with heat production in the body may mean heat stroke and death within a few hours. The waste heat of combustion thus becomes one of the body's most important excretory products.

Sudden changes in external temperatures, or in the rate of heat production within the body, are quickly countered by the movement of more blood into, or away from, the skin and by the activity of the sweat glands. The body can thus meet short-term emergencies with only slight changes in its internal temperature or behavior characteristics. External heat or cold, prolonged through many weeks or months, however, induces basic and important changes in the body economy. . . . .

Climatic temperature differences, whether brought about by latitude or altitude, are potent factors in human life, and so also are the wide seasonal temperature swings of the earth's middle latitudes. The fortunate nations of the earth are those located where the body's waste heat can be lost readily. Many other factors of life are also of great importance, of course, but this article is devoted to the basic role of temperature. Due recognition must be given to the part that improved nutrition may play in minimizing the depressive effects of external heat. Natural resources may thus exert a marked and beneficial effect on a given population group by making possible a better dietary intake, but dietary improvement will still be conditioned on the exercise of mass intelligence in food selection and on the willingness to work for the better food, no matter how great the natural resources. We thus come back to [human] energy as the mainspring of life, with all its potentialities and handicaps. . . .

Up through the millenniums since the last Ice Age, the crest of human civilization has shifted farther and farther poleward, with irregularly rising earth temperatures and melting ice caps. Improved housing and greater protection against winter cold have been considerable factors in this poleward shift, but probably of greater importance has been the expanding region of tropical heat. . . .

Through the last 10,000 years of the earth's history, cyclic changes in temperatures have left fairly clear records. A millennium of rapidly receding glaciers and polar ice caps was succeeded by one of stability or advance. Five such cycles are in evidence over the last 10,000 years of rapid Ice Age regression. The next-to-last cold millennium fell in the days of early Greek and Roman glory and was followed by the thousand years of Dark Age warmth, when cereal grains could be ripened in Iceland and grapes in England.

The peak of Dark Age warmth occurred about A.D. 850, when optimal temperatures in far northern Scandinavia activated the Norsemen and Vikings into a century of exploration and settlement. The gradual return of benumbing cold to their homeland and to the Greenland and Iceland settlements from the tenth to the fourteenth centuries dimmed their glory. Central Europe was at the same time relieved of her enervating warmth and entered the Renaissance and the period of industrialization. The miracles of this Western mechanistic civilization have reached a peak in America during the century just passed.

Once again earth temperatures are surging irregularly upward, reaching levels in 1930 about as high as prevailed a thousand years earlier. During the warmth of the early thirties soil thawing in Greenland allowed excavation of Viking bodies that had lain in solidly frozen earth for a thousand years. All records available indicate that earth temperatures have been rising for a full century, bringing definitely milder winters and the long summers of depressive heat that sap human energy and change the course of nations. . . .

Retarded by the benumbing winter cold of past centuries, much of Russia today enjoys temperatures which are near the optimal for human endeavor. Freer flow of her energies and the heady successes of war and postwar years have given her a self-confidence that considers nothing impossible. Hers is now the early American frontier reaction of bubbling enthusiasm and nigh irresistible impetuosity. In the warm centuries ahead she may gain the sought-for place-in-the-sun, along with the lesser northern nations of Scandinavia and Canada. To appreciate that Russia is really a far-northern nation, one should bear in mind that the city of Stalingrad lies close to the latitude of Winnipeg.

The effects of temperature will go far beyond their present influence over individual life and national trends. The present millennium of warmth may witness complete melting of the polar ice caps and consequent profound changes in the climates of present polar and temperate zones. The earth has experienced long eons of freedom from polar cold during the past periods of interglacial warmth, and Brooks, in his book, *Climate through the Ages*, pictures the present ice caps as being down to the critically small diameter that makes them susceptible to rapid disappearance. Anyone desiring to make use of this information for long-term investment in northern real estate should buy high land, however, for the ocean level will rise roughly 150 feet as the ice caps disappear.

Present-day international interest in the mineral and fuel deposits of Antarctica may prove to be well based, in view of these temperature trends. Also, the broad, fertile, but still frozen reaches of northern Siberia and Canada may someday support the earth's most energetic populations, if the present outward expansion of semitropical lethargy continues. It takes only a few degrees of change in mean annual temperature to produce striking climatic alterations; Dark Age temperatures of Scandinavia, Britain, Iceland, and Greenland, for instance, were probably only 4–5 degrees higher than those prevailing through the colder centuries since the time of the Renaissance. . . .

Today we pride ourselves upon our scientific achievements and the conquest of disease by men of medicine; yet months or years of unseasonable warmth bring devastating economic downturns against which we have found no defense, and at such times sickness and death rates decline, even while our physicians are least busy. Statistically, one might say that people are better off the less they see of a doctor, but in reality, it is the lessened storminess and reduction in bodily stress that account for the health betterment in hard times.

Man is in reality a pawn of the environmental forces encompassing him, being pushed forward to a vantage point at one time or held in lethargic bondage at another. Here is a challenge of the first magnitude—can human intelligence find an effective answer? If not an answer, then it should at least comprehend the forces at work and the major significance of their effects.

By no means all experts on climate and human affairs accept the Huntington thesis and its political extensions by Wheeler, Mills, and others. One of the strongest dissenters is Earl Parker Hanson (professor of geography at the University of Delaware).

Hanson's experience appears to contradict at least some of the claims of Huntington and his disciples. That experience has taken Hanson to the arctic and to the equatorial tropics. Part of his field work was concerned with adapting American military forces for service in those regions during World War II. The Japanese attack on Pearl Harbor confronted American politicians, civil servants, military commanders, and their technical experts with the problem of fighting a war in some of the nastiest tropical and arctic climates in the world. Hanson's conclusions are buttressed by the experience of many others, from whom he cites liberally in his exciting book *New Worlds Emerging*. This book is as timely today as when it was published in 1949. If Hanson's rejection of the Huntington-Wheeler-Mills theses is well grounded, it puts into entirely different perspective the future of the emerging nations of Asia and Africa and the older but still underdeveloped countries of Middle America and northern South America. Space does not permit as long a selection as one would like to include from this work. But in the following section we have summarized with liberal quotations the main thesis, some of the supporting evidence, and the flavor of Hanson's—

Revolt against climatic determinism *

Many scholars . . . claim that no real civilization can arise or thrive in the tropics. . . . Some seem to take it for granted that the term *civilization* is synonymous with the white man's culture, from which it follows that the former cannot thrive where the latter cannot. Others start with the premise that the colored races are inferior to the white and hence incapable of building a civilization. Still others may grudg-

---

* The quotations in this section are from pp. 80-100 of *New Worlds Emerging*, by E. P. Hanson. Copyright 1949 by E. P. Hansen; published by Duell, Sloan & Pearce, New York; reproduced by permission of Duell, Sloan & Pearce, an affiliate of the Meredith Press, New York.

ingly grant the colored peoples at least potential equality with the whites, but insist that the tropical climate reacts on the former as on the latter, and so prevents any effective attempts at civilization-building. No matter what the causes, the clinching argument of the anti-tropical school of thought is usually the claim that no great civilization has ever arisen in the hot countries—which leads naturally to the conclusion that none ever can. . . . When confronted by ancient India and Egypt, with their stupendous civilizations, Huntington and his followers insist that in former times the climates of those countries were cooler than they are today. . . .

The idea that the white man can live in the tropics only temporarily as a sojourner seems to have grown largely out of the experience of those who did and do live there only as sojourners—most of whom add the eloquent voice of personal testimony to scientific reasoning. When a man goes to some tropical outpost for a few years as a planter, engineer, or government official, he goes under special circumstances that may themselves be enervating. . . . Too many things that are done normally at home cannot be done abroad. . . .

Whether or not climate stimulates man is a debatable question; there is no debate, however, over the fact that men stimulate each other in the normal course of human existence. Those who don't, those who bore each other, can stay apart. But they have no choice in the artificial life of the tropics [that still prevails in the remaining colonial and semicolonial areas]. . . . The white man's traditional life in the tropics, where custom demands that he stay aloof from well over 99 percent of the population with its many human problems, is above all an excessively boring one. Boredom is known to produce its own debilitating lassitude.

Consciously and effectively, those who live in the tropics by the orthodox [colonial] rules form small "back pockets" of culture which are isolated from the immediate world around them. . . .

Hanson attacks the dietary habits of white sojourners in the humid tropics—in particular the notion that intake of meat and animal fats should be reduced. He cites evidence from the West Indies, South America, and Africa, that the most healthy communities are those which are able to consume large quantities of animal fat and protein. To emphasize the traditional European-American phobia on this issue, he cites the amusing incident of an American medical missionary

who had lived healthfully in Liberia for twenty-five years and was distressed when he visited Washington and a restaurant waitress told him he couldn't have pork sausages for breakfast because the weather was too hot.

In the light of such evidence [Hanson concludes], it seems possible that the white man's avoidance of fat meats in warm weather may well be a contributing factor to his debilitation in the tropics. . . .

Hanson finds other contributing factors in the clothing habits and ideas of northern peoples who go to the tropics. He makes derisive comments about the cork helmets that white men formerly thought necessary to protect them against the tropical sun. The cork helmet, he insists, was really worn as a status symbol to set apart the ruling race from their colonial serfs and servants.

Hanson is severely critical of the body clothing worn traditionally by Americans and Europeans in the tropics. He notes that the scourge of "prickly heat and athelete's foot" among American military forces in tropical areas "during World War II led to much physiological research in those ailments. As a result it became recognized that they are always caused by insufficient ventilation of the body, and that it is all but impossible to be infected by them if one goes barefoot or naked." As wartime and other experience has abundantly demonstrated, "loosely woven clothing, so cut as to provide maximum ventilation" is a requisite of "comfort as well as health" in the humid tropics. He likens the practice of wearing cool-climate clothes in hot climates to covering most of a car's radiator-surface on a warm day and then blaming the overheating of the engine on the temperature of the air.

Another myth which Hanson attacks is the notion that physical work is harmful for white people in the tropics. He notes that

> soldiers usually get along much better in the tropics than do civilians, apparently because their life demands a greater amount of exercise. . . . White men have lived on the Dutch tropical island of Saba [in the West Indies] for many generations with no sign of deterioration and no colored people to do their work for them. They are excellent sailors and fishermen, which means that they spend large parts of their lives in healthful activity in the tropical sun. . . .
>
> During World War II a million ordinary GI's in the Southwest Pacific could not afford to avoid the sun and have colored people to do all their work for them. By the same token they became guinea pigs in a vast physiological experiment in which the tropics were themselves the laboratory. The main conclusions reached from that far flung experiment were reported in *Time* on April 21, 1947, to the effect that the war had proved that the white man has nothing to fear from the tropical climate provided he eats and dresses properly, takes adequate medical and prophylactic precautions, and otherwise leads a normal and healthful life. . . .

Turning to tropical diseases, malaria and hookworm in particular, Hanson stresses the cumulative evidence of correlation between living standards and health. Given modern medical technology, adequate nutrition, properly ventilated housing and clothing, and plenty of physical activity, these diseases are no more intractable than they formerly were in eastern and southeastern United States.

Turning to the relation of temperature to human health and energy (the relationship, it will be recalled, on which Mills built his geopolitical hypothesis quoted in the preceding section), Hanson starts by noting that the average minimum monthly temperature of the tropics is, by definition, 64.4°F.

> Contrary to prevailing popular impressions, the maximum in such regions as equatorial West Africa and the Amazon lowlands seldom rises above 95 degrees. . . . Summer visitors from the tropics to such cities as New York, Washington, and Kansas City usually complain loudly about heat as well as humidity and wish they were home again.
>
> Some years ago the American Society of Heating and Ventilating Engineers sponsored a series of elaborate investigations to determine the "comfort zone" of temperatures, within which people feel best. Similar investigations were made by other people in various parts of the world, tropical and non-tropical, and when all the results were in it was found that man feels most comfortable at temperatures that range from a minimum of about 63 degrees to a maximum of some 95. Variations within that range depend on circumstances. For instance, at any one temperature out of doors comfort varies with humidity, while the indoor "comfort zone" ranges with individual preference and seasons from about 65 to 85 degrees. . . .
>
> The range of temperatures encountered in the tropics is very close to that beyond which, granting normal housing conditions, the American tenant will start to pound on his radiator, complain to the city health department, and begin to look for a new landlord.
>
> When the tenant goes outdoors for any length of time he uses clothing instead of walls and mechanical equipment for the purpose of surrounding himself artificially with a tropical climate. Layer after layer of such clothing is put on or taken off for no other purpose—besides adornment—than that his torso shall be encased by a temperature within the required range.
>
> Vast industries are maintained for the purpose of making those things possible. Limestone is quarried to make cement with which to build houses within which the climate can be controlled; bricks are made, and forest areas are stripped of trees for the same purpose. Coal is mined and transported hundreds of miles to provide heat in those homes; oil and gas are piped equal or longer distances. Millions of men earn their livings in mines, steel plants, and factories, turning out furnaces and air-conditioning equipment. Sheep ranches in Patagonia and Australia provide wool for warm clothing; spinning and weaving mills, and thousands of tailoring establishments cooperate with the miners of iron and coal to provide conditions under which man can surround himself artificially with a temperature that does not range above or below that of the humid tropics.

While writing scholarly books to prove that the tropical climate is bad for us, we also invest millions of dollars to be able to surround ourselves artificially with such a climate. Indeed, when we examine our way of life in the temperate regions we begin to realize that the natural climates of places like New York, Chicago, and Washington are actually uninhabitable except as improved by man. . . .

Man not only started in the tropics when he began to spread all over the world, but he is still an equatorial animal and cannot live in any climate but the tropical—provided either by nature or artificially by man himself.

Perspective on climatic interpretations

The reader who has reached this point may wonder how it is possible for experts to disagree so widely on the effects of climate on human activities and capacities. Actually, the theses of those who assert and of those who deny the political and social significance of climatic variation may not be as irreconcilable as seems at first glance. In any case, locating specific points of disagreement and weighing the evidence marshaled in support of conflicting hypotheses should help anyone to reach more fruitful conclusions regarding the international significance of climatic variations. And now as never before it is crucial to reach tenable conclusions—what with the break-up of the colonial empires, modernizing drives of the new nations, and the unrelenting competition between East and West to participate in the modernizing process.

Discussion of the interrelations of climate and human affairs began with speculations by intellectuals. Their speculations were derived in part from their own observations, but in the main from unverified tales told by travelers to distant lands in an era when very few people did any traveling at all. Down to the present century this hearsay evidence was subjected to scarcely any rigorous testing.

Wheeler's contribution (see pages 347-9 above) lies in part in marshaling the subjective impressions of thousands of observers through several thousand years. His work represents a long step forward in the comparison of climatic cycles and the correlation of climatic data with human events. The correlations which he discovered certainly command serious attention from students of international politics.

Huntington's investigations, in which he discovered rather consistent correlations between certain indices of civilization and climatic distributions, tended on the whole to confirm earlier, more speculative conclusions. Some critics have objected to his criteria of "civilization." One may agree or disagree with Huntington's thesis that "civilization" can be "measured" by the number of entries in Who's Who, the percentage

TABLE 11.1 EFFECTS OF VARIATIONS OF FACTORS OF CLIMATE ON HUMAN DECISIONS AND ACHIEVEMENTS

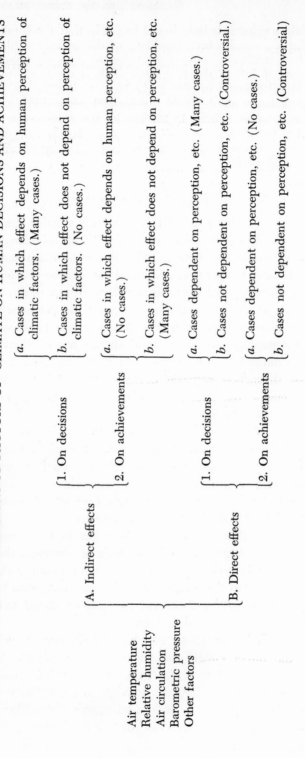

Air temperature
Relative humidity
Air circulation
Barometric pressure
Other factors

A. Indirect effects
  1. On decisions
    a. Cases in which effect depends on human perception of climatic factors. (Many cases.)
    b. Cases in which effect does not depend on perception of climatic factors. (No cases.)
  2. On achievements
    a. Cases in which effect depends on human perception, etc. (No cases.)
    b. Cases in which effect does not depend on perception, etc. (Many cases.)

B. Direct effects
  1. On decisions
    a. Cases dependent on perception, etc. (Many cases.)
    b. Cases not dependent on perception, etc. (Controversial.)
  2. On achievements
    a. Cases dependent on perception, etc. (No cases.)
    b. Cases not dependent on perception, etc. (Controversial)

of a population possessing motor cars and telephones, the relative volume of bank clearings, and similar data. Clearly such data do indicate something about relative levels of material accomplishment in various countries. On the whole, controversy does not center so much on the data—both climatological and social—which Huntington assembled, as on the hypotheses which he formulated to account for the observed correlations.

It will help bring order into the present-day controversies on this subject if one proceeds with the aid of some conceptual scheme designed to identify systematically all possible relationships between climate and human affairs. Table 11.1 is such a scheme. It is built upon the basic distinction between indirect and direct effects. The essence of this distinction is the presence or absence of some intermediate agent or instrumentality (such as plants, subhuman animals, micro-organisms, or other nonhuman structures) between the climatic and human variables under consideration. This distinction underlies all the selections reproduced above. It is, on the whole, a fruitful distinction in the sense that it helps to locate and pin down the issues in controversy. As we shall see, controversy centers mainly on the nature and significance of direct effects.

Also built into Table 11.1 are two distinctions which we deem to be especially significant in the context of international politics. The first is the familiar distinction between decisions and performance (the latter defined to include the operational results of decisions). The second is the distinction between events in which perception by the actor is a requisite to occurrence and events which may occur irrespective of his perception. These two distinctions, it will be remembered, differentiate the intellectual operations called respectively policy analysis and capabilities analysis.

Let us begin with the indirect effects, since these are less controversial. With respect to decisions, it is common knowledge that people frequently take into account the indirect effects of climate. A farmer moves from a semiarid steppe to a well-watered prairie—and immediately switches from cattle to corn. The captain of a ship observes the barometer falling—and prepares his ship to withstand a storm. A prudent householder in a warm damp climate takes steps to safeguard his furniture, clothing, leather goods, and other property from the ravages of mildew. In each case and in countless others, the decision involves application of knowledge regarding the direct effect of climate on some intermediate agent or instrument and (through it) the indirect effect on human affairs.

It is likewise accepted that failure to take into account the direct effects of climate on intermediate agents and instruments can lead to indirect adverse effects on man himself. No one would be surprised, for example, to read of the bankruptcy of a farmer who persisted in trying to raise avocados and lemons in Alaska. Nor would anyone be surprised to learn that automobile radiators freeze and burst in subfreezing weather unless adequately protected by antifreeze.

It is well understood that certain combinations of temperature and moisture are more favorable than others to the proliferation of micro-organisms and chemical processes that attack human beings and their equipment. We have already noted the example of mildew. Damp air promotes oxidation (rust and corrosion) of many metals. Food spoils more quickly when exposed to warm damp air. Parasites and bacteria of many kinds thrive under such conditions.

In all these and similar cases, the climatic factors operate directly on some intermediate agent or instrumentality and thereby indirectly on human performance and achievement. Depending on the level of knowledge attained in the society in question, these phenomena are more (or less) adequately understood. At the more advanced levels one finds well confirmed explicit propositions regarding the environmental requisites of plants, micro-organisms, mechanical equipment, etc.

No one denies that a motorist is capable of neglecting his automobile radiator. It is not the choice that is limited. Rather it is the operational results or the level of performance and achievement which are indirectly limited by factors of climate, as by other factors of environment.

These indirect limits vary, of course, with advances in technology. Antifreeze, for example, is required to operate water-cooled engines in subfreezing weather. But general adoption of air-cooled engines would put antifreeze out of business.

None of this is controversial. There may be some disagreement as to what are *in fact* the environmental requisites of wheat or other plants or of domestic animals or of micro-organisms or of various kinds of mechanical equipment and other materials. But the principle at issue—that environmental limitations exist and that these will directly effect intermediate agents and instruments, and thereby indirectly affect human achievements, irrespective of whether the human actors perceive and understand these effects—all this, we repeat, is almost universally taken for granted.

It is likewise well understood and rarely disputed that the indirect effects of climate may have political and other social significance. These effects help to account for differences in the economic patterns of countries and regions. In the past, weather conditions have halted military campaigns, delayed diplomatic dispatches, frustrated empire builders in the tropics, and otherwise affected political events. The spectacular advances of engineering in the past century have progressively surmounted these barriers. Today, as we shall see in a moment, the issue becomes increasingly, not man's technical ability to conquer nature, but his economic ability and his willingness to pay what it costs.

Some of the direct effects of climate on man—those that occur in the absence of any intermediate agent or instrument—are likewise non-controversial. It is well understood that people make choices and take decisions in response to their perception of environmental stimuli. A person feels uncomfortably cool; he reacts by shutting the window or turning up the heat or putting on a wrap or starting to exercise, etc. There are countless responses of this kind. But one may query whether such responses, by themselves, have much significance for the student of politics.

When we move on to Category B.1.*b* (Table 11.1), we enter much more controversial ground. There is evidence, plenty of it, that the moods of people—or at least, some people—vary with changes in combinations of air temperature, relative humidity, barometric pressure, air circulation, and perhaps still other climatic factors. Such responses may take the form of a sense of depression or a sense of well-being. Such personal states may demonstrably affect an individual's inclination to make or postpone decisions, as well as the *quality* of his decisions. The effect thus falls within the border zone between decision and performance. Controversy here tends to focus less on the facts than on their interpretation and social significance.

With respect to Category B.2.*a*, anyone can think of instances in which a person attributes his level of achievement to the stimulating or depressing effect of the weather. However, it is debatable whether the effect, whatever it is, depends on the subject's *explanation* or rationalization of his mood, or on *autonomic responses* (that is, changes in rate of heart-beat, level of body temperature, blood pressure, basal metabolism, and other responses over which the individual can exert no conscious control). To the extent that one classifies such reactions as autonomic responses, the cases fall within the next category, B.2.*b*.

Category B.2.*b* seems to be the main focus of controversy. Controversy centers on three issues. The first is an issue of fact: What are the physiological responses of the human organism to various combinations of climatic stimuli? And how wide is the range of response among individuals to the same sets of stimuli? The second is an engineering issue: What can be done to produce better adaptation or a more favorable environment? The third issue is one of interpretation: What is the social (including political) significance of such physiological effects as may occur?

The first issue—the issue of fact—is less controversial than formerly.

The human body's need to get rid of surplus heat generated in the process of transforming food into energy is now well understood. The mechanisms by which this is accomplished—chiefly radiation, convection, and evaporation—have been repeatedly demonstrated in the laboratory. Hanson (see pp. 353 ff.) who disagrees with the political conclusions of Huntington and Mills, would agree with them regarding the physiological necessity and process of dissipating waste heat from the body.

Where these experts mainly disagree is on the possibility of improving physiological and cultural adaptation to wider extremes of climatic variation. Specifically, the issue is whether modern knowledge of diet and exercise, heating and cooling of spaces enclosed by clothing and by buildings, and control of air circulation and humidity in enclosed spaces is sufficient to enable people of all races to carry on substantially similiar activities with substantially similar levels of achievement under a wide range of climatic variation.

This problem has two sets of variables: the climatic and the human. Changing these variables is essentially an engineering operation. One line of attack has been to change the climatic factors: within the space enclosed by clothing and by larger man-built structures called the microclimate. When one changes from woolen winter clothing to cotton shorts, he changes the microclimate which envelops most of his body. Chimneys, fireplaces, stoves, furnaces, fans (manual and electric), insulated walls, and more recently air cooling and dehumidifying machines are all engineering devices for controlling the climate in the enclosed spaces within which one lives and works. Scientists in various countries are working on projects which envisage eventual control of climate on a much larger, possibly even a global scale.

Changing the human variables has also received attention, especially in recent years. One approach is manifestly to alter the amount of heat to be dissipated from the body. Another is to take steps to facilitate the process of heat dissipation. Hanson indicates how these ends can be achieved in some degree by altering diet, exercise, clothing, etc.

One aspect of the human side of the problem that is still rather obscure is the differential range of adaptability among individuals. Individuals differ much more than has been commonly assumed, with respect to rate of "normal" metabolism, "normal" blood pressure, "normal" pulse rate, "normal" body temperature, ability to sweat, and in other respects. Some combinations of individual "norms" appear to be much more adaptable than others to extremes of temperature, humidity, air circulation, and other climatic variations. Hanson's position is tenable only if most individuals are physiologically capable of adapting without serious reduction of efficiency to a wide range of climatic conditions. On this point the student of politics needs further enlightenment from the physiologists.

However, in the technically more advanced civilizations at least, the problem of adaptation becomes more and more economic and less and less physiological. Sufficient technical know-how exists to heat buildings and cool them, to control humidity and air circulation in enclosed spaces, to adjust clothing and exercise to a wide range of climatic conditions, to combat climate-related diseases, etc. As the late Isaiah Bowman (American geographer and statesman) repeatedly emphasized, modern man has sufficient technical knowledge to build and maintain a "comfortable and well-lighted city and provide education, opera, and games at the South Pole, or build an artificial rain-compelling mountain range in the Sahara" desert—at a price! To do these things as well as to carry out various large-scale projects of economic and political development in arctic and equatorial environments, requires capital—money, if you will—huge quantities of it.

The capital and operating costs of heating buildings through long severe winters and cooling them in hot damp summers can be paid in economies which show relatively high per capita productivity. To provide these and all the other defenses against unfavorable climatic conditions consumes substantial percentages of even the richest nations' economic product. These percentages, moreover, vary from one environment to another. The per capita cost of domestic heating and cooling alone, for example, is many times greater for the United States, with its large areas of savage mid-continental weather, winter and summer, than it is for any of the larger countries in the more gentle climates of western Europe.

Thus the issue is not only whether it is technically possible to control the impacts of climate on man. Increasingly the issues are economic costs and who pays. These issues cannot be dodged. They are and seem likely to remain for some time highly relevant aspects of the relative capabilities of nations and of the patterns of interaction between the richer and more technically advanced nations and those which are now fighting their way up the ladder of modernization.

That climatic variations affect the allocation of a nation's resources is indisputable. That effort expended in keeping warm or keeping cool or combating climate-related disease and other climate-related handicaps cannot be expended on military force, education, or something else is equally evident. That the conquest of climate—if the capital and operating costs can somehow be met—may more than pay for itself in increased productivity is manifestly possible. Whether the controversies of such men as Mills and Hanson rest ultimately on grounds of economic cost or on grounds of physiological adaptive potentiality is obscure. In any case, it appears that climatic variation—whether for economic or ecological reasons or both together—has been and will continue to be a politically significant source of differences in the political potential of nations.

CHAPTER TWELVE

★ ★ ★

Natural Resources: Shrinking Assets

IN THIS CHAPTER we take up a third set of geopolitical hypotheses: those based on the uneven geographical distribution of natural resources. It will be necessary a little later to examine the concept of natural resources. For the moment it will suffice to define natural resources as *useful* materials and processes found in nature and to note that what is useful depends both on what people want to accomplish and on the level of their technology.

No one has advanced the thesis, so far as we are aware, that a nation whose territory is richly endowed with natural resources is thereby predestined to play an important role upon the international stage. Nor does the argument run to the effect that natural resources are the only environmental factors that really matter. As generally stated, the proposition is rather that a government's capacity to provide military and other instrumentalities of statecraft and to keep on providing them even if its country is subjected to military or economic blockade is a necessary condition of becoming and remaining a Great Power. A corollary of this thesis is that governments which aspire to Great Power stature are nearly certain to give high priority to gaining control over or secure access to adequate supplies of natural resources essential to maintain a desired level and pattern of military power in relation to other nations envisaged as possible enemies.

In the political idiom of the 1930's, nations endowed abundantly with natural resources constituted the "haves"; all the others were "have-nots." To those who regarded international politics as fundamentally a military or potentially military struggle for power—more precisely a struggle for domination—it seemed obvious that *control* over large and varied sources of essential raw materials would be a prime objective of national policy. To persons oriented this way, it was only a short step to the thesis that the aggressive international behavior of certain nations—in the 1930's these were chiefly Germany, Italy, and Japan—was *caused* by the desire of their rulers to control a larger share of the world's natural resources.

The uneven geographical distribution of land, minerals, water power, and other natural resources also provided the basis for explanations not only of national policies but also of the international potentials of nations: that is, the power and influence which they exerted on other nations. According to this second hypothesis, secure *access to* adequate natural resources was a necessary condition of a nation becoming and remaining a Great Power. We have italicized *access* because, under certain conditions, the ability to command resources produced abroad was deemed to provide as firm a basis for national power as resources produced within a state's own territory.

One of the earlier exponents of the resources-as-a-basis-of-power thesis was Brooks Emeny, an early American specialist on international politics. In 1934, he argued that

> capacity for industrialization [is the key to a state's future power position]. And since large-scale industrialization presupposes the possession or ready availability of vast quantities of the basic industrial raw materials, nature, through her unequal distribution of these, has rigidly set a limit to the number of states capable of achieving the status of Great Powers.*

Another book, published during World War II and entitled *World Minerals and World Peace* opens with the statement that

> potential world control is not necessarily afforded by control of any of the great land masses [as Mahan and Mackinder had contended], but it lies in the control of mineral resources, wherever they are, backed up by control of the air and the sea.

Proceeding on the assumption that that United States and Great Britain would continue indefinitely, through their concerted naval and airpower, to control the oceans and most of the connecting seas, the authors contended further

> that the combined mineral resources controlled by the United States and the British Empire far outweigh the mineral resources of the World Island [which they erroneously called a "German geopolitical

---

* From p. 1 of *The Strategy of Raw Materials*, by Brooks Emeny. Copyright 1934 by the Bureau of International Research, Harvard University and Radcliffe College; published by the Macmillan Company, New York; reproduced by permission of the author.

concept"] and afford a much broader and more powerful base for for world control both for peace and war.*

Just as World War II was drawing to a close in 1945 Robert Strausz-Hupé (professor of international relations at the University of Pennsylvania) restated the resources hypothesis as follows:

> Political and military power is largely based on industrial power. Industrialization calls for an unlimited supply of raw materials, chiefly minerals. . . . Today there is hardly one of the host of raw materials modern man extracts and consumes which is not used for making tools of war. Hence the attainment of power involves the control of raw materials. All other things being equal, those countries are the most powerful which possess an adequate supply of all "essential," "strategic," and "critical" materials or which are able, by virtue of their mastery over transportation routes, to import in time of war, materials inadequately supplied at home.†

Partly on the basis of sovereignty over or estimated security of access to essential ores and fuels, Strausz-Hupé predicted that the United States would continue, until 1970 at least, to be the foremost industrial nation. The Soviet Union was ranked second—or third, depending on whether the West European industrial complex was treated as a congeries of separate national industries or as a single industrial region. Smaller industrial developments were considered possible for China, Japan, and India on the basis of natural resources located in eastern and southern Asia.

In 1952 a special Materials Policy Commission, appointed by the President to evaluate the raw-materials situation of the United States and to formulate policies for strengthening it, based a set of recommendations on the premise that

> materials strength is a prime ingredient of general economic strength and growth, which in turn is the foundation of rising living standards in peace and of military strength in war. . . . Military security depends heavily on a vigorous and expanding economy to produce the overwhelming quantities of the equipment, machinery, and supplies necessary for modern military strength. On the other hand, healthy economic growth depends importantly on military security to maintain that climate of confidence in the future in which private enterprise flourishes. Neither military nor economic strength can be raised to its highest potential without an abundant and varied flow of materials.‡

* From p. 4 of *World Minerals and World Peace*, by C. K. Leith et al. Copyright 1943 by The Brookings Institution, Washington, D. C.; reproduced by permission.
† From p. 119 of *The Balance of Tomorrow*. Copyright 1945 by Robert Strausz-Hupé; published by G. P. Putnam's Sons, New York; reproduced by permission.
‡ From pages 3 and 153, of *Resources for Freedom*, Vol. 1 of the Report of the President's Materials Policy Commission. Government Printing Office, Washington, 1952.

The foregoing quotations exhibit a core of basic agreement. They also reflect certain widely shared presuppositions regarding the nature and conduct of international politics. In particular, their authors appear to accept the classic thesis that a nation's place in the international hierarchy of power depends upon its war-making capability; and that this depends heavily upon the security of its access to many kinds and adequate quantities of foodstuffs and industrial raw materials. Reading further in the books from which these passages are taken, one finds relatively little on other bearings of material resources on the policies and political potentials of nations.

It is not surprising that books and articles written before and during World War II should be so preoccupied with the problem of total war. It is more surprising to find the President's Materials Policy Commission reasoning, as late as 1952, as if war waged with nuclear weapons would be essentially similar to prenuclear wars, and as if ability to provide raw materials for a long-drawn-out total war would continue to be one of the more significant measures of a nation's stature in international politics.

As will become increasingly apparent in the following pages, advances in military technology since 1945 may have rendered such presuppositions dangerously obsolete. The development of nuclear weapons, their stockpiling in the quantities indicated in Chapter 8, and the parallel development of chemical-biological weapons of incalculable destructiveness, all require a fresh approach to the problem of assessing the functions of natural resources and the raw materials derived therefrom in the international politics of today and the future.

Other aspects of the scientific and technological revolution reinforce this need for new perspective on natural resources. An especially important aspect is the progressive depletion of the higher grades of nearly all nonrenewable earth materials. The resources problem also needs reexamination in the light of social change in the underdeveloped countries, the so-called population explosion, and the strategy of the Cold War.

All these issues will receive attention in the following pages, but first some preliminary consideration to certain basic concepts and principles. What is a natural resource? How does it become a raw material? What determines priorities among raw materials? How and why do these change through time? These questions were dealt with in an essay written over twenty years ago, but as relevant today as then. The author was the economist Karl Brandt (of Stanford University), to whom we now go for a discussion of the concepts of—

Natural resources and raw materials *

The question of raw materials with reference to peace and war leads straight into a confusing jungle of problems in international relations and political economics.

The maze begins with the very conception of what constitutes a raw material. It is true that superficially we pretend to know what this group name covers. The large catalogue of raw materials contains commodities of vegetable and animal origin as well as minerals. It includes the sources of man's food, clothing, shelter, of the feed for his animals, of heat, light and power, and of all sorts of industrial goods. Thus raw materials embrace, first, vegetable and animal products carrying carbohydrates, proteins, fats and vitamins; second, wood, vegetable and animal fibers, rubber, hides and skins; third, stored fuels like peat, lignite, coal, oil and natural gas; fourth, other ferrous and non-ferrous minerals. The activities they entail are equally various: collecting, fishing and hunting, mining, forestry, agriculture, horticulture and synthetic production.

The situation becomes even more complex if we search for characteristics that would determine whether a specific commodity is a raw material, or that determine whether it is an essential, an optional or merely a luxury good. We soon discover that we can do no more than simply list those commodities which, often enough for heterogeneous reasons, are considered somewhere as raw materials, adding perhaps one or several question marks in the column denoting the necessity of their use. There are no objective measurements of necessity. It is an evaluation, determined ultimately by manifold social, technological and economic standards as they are followed by a specific civilization or social group at a specific time. . . . The majority of the world's population lives on a more or less vegetarian diet; if all peoples should prefer to obtain a large part of their nutritional energies from animal products, as the leading occidental nations do now, the world would be faced with an insoluble maldistribution of food. Fortunately peoples have developed their diets through the ages in conformity with their environment and their ability to secure supplies. And yet their habits and thereby their demands are changing as time passes.

The determination of what is and what is not a necessary raw material is even more functional with reference to fibers, fuels and other minerals. During the sixteenth and seventeenth centuries wood was almost the only fuel used in industry. In the beginning of the nineteenth century oil did not mean much; nor was the significance of waterpower sites or lignite deposits recognized, because the hydroturbine, the steam turbine and the electric generator had not been invented. In 1850 Chilean saltpeter as fertilizer was practically worthless; in 1900 it was an invaluable treasure of international importance; by

1920 it was on its way to oblivion. In 1880 the "man-made" metal aluminum was not known for technical use, while in 1930 it ranked as one of the first-grade metals for general application in industry and the household. Its substitute, magnesium, also "invented" and man-made, was of no importance in 1920, whereas today it is a serious competitor. Such examples could be multiplied.

Human wants are continuously shaped and reshaped by civilization, its technical and social standards and its progress. Some of man's greatest achievements lie in his successful adaptation to the available raw materials, in his rendering more of them accessible and with his genius discovering new ones.

Except for wild fruits and the products of hunting and fishing, raw materials are not readily available. What really exist and are potentially available in abundance or scarcity, either near by or in the distance, are the so-called "natural resources." . . .

Whether a certain situation in the environment is considered as a "natural resource" depends on a multiplicity of conditions: on whether the specific society has already developed a demand for the raw material that may be made available; on whether a sufficient standard of technology and skill has been built up to launch the attack upon the resource; on the availability of sufficient skilled labor and on the presence of sufficient capital, if only in the form of equipment and food supplies for the labor force. And yet with all these conditions fulfilled it may be found that the efforts to exploit the resource are comparatively too great. In this case it may relapse into a potential reserve or may be discarded and forgotten as such.

If the exploitation should prove profitable from the standpoint of the social group as a whole, the yield in raw materials may be exceedingly different under the application of different principles. How long the resource will continue to yield depends partly on the speed of exploitation, but even more on its intensity and efficiency. Petroleum, for instance, can be mined by drilling a well in which natural gas pressure spits the oil above the surface. When the gas is exhausted the well stops producing, and may then be abandoned. The oil of the gusher can be made available for use in the crude manner of skimming off the small percentage of gasoline, leaving the rest of the oil to be used instead of coal as a fuel. With an advanced technique the yielding capacity of the same well may be multiplied by more efficient drilling, by maintaining or recreating the gas pressure, by proceeding later on with pumping out the oil, and especially by fractional distillation, cracking and refining. Similarly the duration of the resource may be prolonged by thrift and greater efficiency in consumption. This example is typical for practically every one of the known resources. At the same time it illustrates a logical historical sequence of increasing intensity in production and utilization.

Enough has been said to indicate how relative is the whole question of raw materials and natural resources. There is no objective measurement by which we can ascertain, for a particular country, the potential necessity of known resources or even the existence of resources we are yet unaware of; and in regard to international relations we are equally at a loss if we try to form an absolute judgment on the distribution or maldistribution of "natural resources."

It appears utterly impossible to measure political phenomena which are described by such misconceived concepts as "population pressure" or "resource-man ratio." With these suggestive terms it is often attempted to interpret a complex situation in simplified pseudo-physical terms. The most popular form of this fallacy is the specifically American idea that this country's relatively high standard of living depends on its favorable "land-man ratio." If that were correct the Argentine ought to have the highest standard of living and the greatest wealth per capita among the nations; and, if the land-man ratio referred to minerals as well as land, Mexico would probably have the title to the most luxurious economic status, while Belgium and Switzerland would rank among the poorest countries in the world.

The assumptions that a specific piece of land as such has a certain "absorptive power" for population, and that land as such can be classified as profitable or "submarginal," are modern fancies which cause more harm than the notion that the machine impoverishes human society. Land, like all natural resources, is no more than an opportunity for man to apply his inventiveness, management, labor and capital. Each of these factors may contribute in varying degree to the yield. Consequently poor land may yield highly, while rich land may yield nothing or carry the most impoverished farm population. Ten thousand acres of land may not be worth a penny, in spite of sufficient rainfall and a high content of plant nutrients. Its "absorptive power for population" may be zero. It begins to have a social value only when it is cleared of woods or brush, developed with roads and public utilities, drained or irrigated, tilled and planted either in part or as a whole—in short, when it is developed by men, animals and machines. It may be farmed by one man with the aid of ten laborers or sharecroppers and provide him and his crew with so small an output that all of them are condemned to poverty. Or it may be farmed by fifty or a hundred families and offer a satisfactory livelihood to several hundred people. It all depends on the use of capital and skill. Land which is thus useless and may nevertheless be given a value is to be found in every country, even in those with the supposedly highest "population pressure," though in smaller amounts than in thinly populated areas.

In attempts to appraise natural resources we face the dilemma that every possible measuring rod involves imponderable philosophical or ethical axioms like justice or duty. Shall we measure the natural resources of a country by geologists' estimates of total deposits, or by the capacity of the existing industry, or by the actual output? Shall a nation be considered to have the moral duty to invent devices for the full utilization of its own resources, or shall it be considered to have a claim on those of its neighbors?

In 1914 Germany as a highly industrialized country produced 75 per cent of her food at home. As a consequence of the [first] world war she lost fertile surplus-producing agrarian provinces in the East. [By 1939, nevertheless, she] . . . attained a domestic food production of 87 per cent of her needs, . . . The use of minerals as fertilizers, taken from the underground and from the air, as well as improvements on the land and better farming methods, combined with a shift of consumption toward synthetic substances, [worked toward this] . . . end. Denmark . . . increased her exclusively domestic agricultural production (excluding conversion of foreign raw materials) by 200 per cent within fifty years. . . .

In discussing the international distribution of natural resources it is often admitted that a particular "have-not" nation has, indeed, the resource in question but that it is "sub-marginal." Sub-marginality is an appraisal of the profitability of exploiting a natural resource at a specific time on a specific soil, with consideration of all the factors affecting net profits. Hence such a term is inappropriate in discussing the international problems of natural resources. According to prevailing American ideas about farming, three-fourths of all European agriculture must be operating on "sub-marginal" land. At the same time, hundreds of thousands of American farmers live on fertile land the life of rural proletarians. The complexity of the cost structure for the total production of a commodity within a national economic system, and the lack of any international basis of comparison for the items involved, render the whole discussion of international cost comparisons highly academic.

This preliminary reconnaissance of some of the problems underlying the question of raw materials and natural resources makes it possible to draw several conclusions.

First, the utmost caution should be observed in applying to this subject concepts and measuring rods which are either too ambiguous to mean much or, worse than that, basically deceptive. "Population pressure," "density of population per square mile," "sub-marginality of existing resources," are such terms. International raw material problems should be approached not with the static assumptions of any *status quo* or with moral postulates but with expert knowledge and with awareness of contemporary trends in economic and technical development.

Second, man has considerably more freedom of action in adapting himself and adjusting the particular civilization of his society to a given environment than an uncritical survey suggests or than certain propagandists would have us believe. Technical progress and science have made it more possible for man to substitute for non-available raw materials and resources those that are accessible, thus making him less dependent on specific resources. For the commonwealth of nations as a whole the earlier scarcity of raw materials has changed more and more into an abundance which, significantly enough, is often called from the point of view of price a "surplus" situation.

Third, the raw material problem of nations cannot be solved permanently within their narrow political boundaries, because the conception of what constitutes an essential raw material changes continuously with technical progress in the pursuit of peace and national defense.

Fourth, the use of crude gauges for measuring the adequacy of a nation's natural resources or domestic supply of raw materials leads to calling the most inventive and industrious nations saturated and the skimming exploiters and rugged primitives the "have-nots."

It is within man's capacity to make adjustments and to invent new solutions. For a more adequate production of foodstuffs it is possible to intensify agriculture and horticulture; for power and fuel it is possible to shift from "deposit resources" to "flow resources" and harness the latent energies of lakes, rivers and tidal sites; for metals synthetic products can be substituted; and in general consumption it is possible to promote thrift and an intensified utilization of available materials. Thus nothing can be more misleading than to assume that there is something like a natural law which by the force of economic gravitation makes nations inevitably dependent on foreign raw materials. It all depends on a large number of factors, many of which are subject to modification by man. . . .

Natural resources and economic development

In the most primitive societies man himself is the beast of burden and the primary source of work-energy. As he ascends the technological ladder, he has impressed animals to work for him—to pull the plow, to carry loads, and to perform other tasks which he previously performed with his own muscles or left undone. With further advances in tools and skills, he begins to tap inanimate sources of energy—wind, fuel wood, falling water, etc. Economic history is, to a considerable degree, the story of mankind's increasing utilization of inanimate energy: to bring water to arid land, to break heavy sod, to smelt mineral ores, to grow more and better food, to build better houses, to produce more clothing with less labor, to fabricate all sorts of useful tools and machines, to make more lethal weapons, to transport goods and people longer distances, and eventually to re-form natural materials into an ever widening array of synthetics which do not exist in nature at all.

In modern times there has been a surprising correlation between utilization of work-energy and political potential in the Society of Nations. According to one estimate, the seven Great Powers of the mid-1930's were consuming over 70 percent of the world total of available inanimate work-energy. The United States then led the field, with nearly 38 percent, with the other six in the remaining order: Great Britain, 9 percent; Germany, 8 percent, the Soviet Union, 8 percent; France, 4 percent; Japan, 3 percent; and Italy, 1 percent. Italy's low consumption of work-energy was frequently cited as the crippling weakness which explained Mussolini's "feet of clay," a weakness that persisted despite the impressive façade of military power and civic grandeur built up during the Fascist regime's existence.

By the early 1960's changes in gross consumption of energy from inanimate sources again showed interesting correlations with observed changes in the distribution of political potential among the greater nations. An estimate published in 1961 ranked the ten top gross consumers of energy in the following order: United States, Soviet Union, United Kingdom, China, West Germany, India, France, Canada, Japan, and Poland.*

Gross consumption of work energy may or may not correlate with a society's standard of living. Political communities differ widely in their allocation of goods and services: who gets how much and for what purposes (questions which will be taken up in Chapter 14). Moreover, even a very low consumption of energy per capita may yield a relatively high gross if, as in the case of China and India, the total population is immense. Nevertheless, the fact remains that gross consumption of energy does correlate in some degree with the observed political potential which a state exerts in the Society of Nations.

Since the nineteenth century industrial revolution, coal has been by far the most important source of work energy. Directly and indirectly, Britain's world primacy in that century rested heavily upon a long lead in the utilization of good quality, abundant, and relatively accessible coal. Coal was the bedrock upon which was built the imposing industrial structure of modern Germany. Huge coal production has been one of the keys to American industrial leadership. Without abundant coal the industrialization of the Soviet Union would have been a slower and more difficult process. Large reserves of coal are among the prime assets of China today. Japan has suffered from comparative poverty in this essential resource. Shortage of coal has been Italy's most serious material handicap.

The supreme importance of coal arises from its varied and high-priority utilities. It is the primary fuel for reduction of mineral ores. It is one of the main sources of domestic heating. It is still widely used to raise steam to propel ships and railway locomotives. Coal-fired boilers generate a large part of the world's electricity. In addition to its importance as a fuel, coal also figures as a key raw material in a wide range of chemical industries. From derivatives of coal come synthetic nitrates, synthetic rubber, synthetic motor fuel, and a long list of drugs, plastics, and other products. It seems likely that coal will become even more important in the technology of the years to come.

The geographical distribution of coal is very uneven. By far the

* From *Atlas of Economic Development,* by Norton Ginsburg et al., University of Chicago Press, 1961, p. 78.

greater part of known reserves are located in the Northern Hemisphere. According to one estimate, the total coal reserves of South America probably amount to less than 0.05 percent of the world total. The same estimate gives Oceania (mainly Australia) about 0.8 percent, and Africa (mainly South Africa) about 3 percent. In contrast the estimate for North America is around 50 percent, of which over 45 percent represent United States reserves. Next in rank come China and the U.S.S.R., each with nearly 20 percent of the world total; then Germany (about 5 percent), Britain (about 3 percent), and Poland and India (around 1 percent each).*

These and other estimates represent far from complete knowledge. They tell nothing about accessibility or about relative qualities. But they do indicate that the coal-energy-rich countries are the United States, China, the U.S.S.R., Canada, Germany, Britain, Poland, India, in about that order.

Coal, of course, is only one of numerous sources of work energy. Likewise important are hydroelectricity and (in the shorter run) petroleum and natural gas. A recent estimate, which combines all these sources with all grades of coal, puts the United States and Soviet Union far out ahead of all other countries, followed in order by China, West Germany, United Kingdom, Poland, Canada, India, Union of South Africa, Australia, and Japan.†

These or other estimates may prove to be inaccurate in detail, but nevertheless indicate probable orders of magnitude. And these orders of magnitude may become increasingly important if, as is widely predicted, the continuing advance of technology is accompanied by ever larger demands for energy.

Developments in nuclear science and engineering suggest the possibility of tapping for industrial use a vast new source of energy. But experts seem thus far to doubt that nuclear energy will soon supersede the existing energy sources. It seems more likely that nuclear energy will simply add one more supplement to coal, which promises to remain the most abundant as well as the most versatile energy-producer in the foreseeable future.

Next to coal, iron has been the most important resource of modern industry. Lighter metals, chiefly aluminum, and plastics are displacing iron to an increasing extent. But it seems likely that iron will continue to hold a high place in the hierarchy of raw materials.

Mineral iron exists in many forms and in many degrees of richness. Certain compounds of iron are more easily smelted than others. Like coal,

---

* From W. S. and E. S. Woytinsky, *World Population and Production,* Twentieth Century Fund, 1953, p. 855.

† From Norton Ginsburg, *Atlas of Economic Development,* University of Chicago Press, 1961, p. 56.

large bodies of iron are widely but unevenly distributed in the earth's subsurface. Before World War II, five fields were producing 75 percent of the total world output. These were in order: The Lake Superior region in the United States, Lorraine in eastern France, Krivoi Rog in southwestern Russia, the Kiruna field of northern Sweden, and the Birmingham district in Alabama. Large high-grade ore bodies exist also in Brazil and India. Smaller but nevertheless important deposits are widely distributed: in Newfoundland, Cuba, Philippine Islands, Spain, England, China, elsewhere in the United States and Soviet Union, and in numerous other countries.

Estimating iron reserves for the long-range future is even more tricky than in the case of coal. This is so because iron is a minor ingredient of a great many minerals. Future value of these low-grade sources depends on advances in metallurgy and on the rate at which higher-grade ores are exhausted. Estimates vary widely depending on the estimater's assumptions regarding the future. One estimate, published by the United Nations in 1950, indicated the possibility that Africa might contain the largest potential reserves, followed in order by North America, Middle and South America, non-Soviet Asia, Europe, and the U.S.S.R. The rank order of specific countries, in terms of estimated iron content ultimately recoverable, was Southern Rhodesia, United States, Brazil, India, Cuba, Union of South Africa, U.S.S.R., and France, plus a wide scattering of smaller units.

Regions where good grades of coal and iron ore lie close together constitute naturally advantageous sites for heavy industry. Perhaps the most ideal of these is the frontier zone between France and Germany. Iron may travel long distances to coal where bulk transportation is cheap. A great fleet of ore vessels has annually floated huge quantities of Lake Superior ore to Gary, Detroit, and other industrial cities along the southern shores of the Great Lakes. With the progressive depletion of high-grade ores in Minnesota, new steel plants have risen along the Atlantic seaboard to smelt iron ore shipped in from Canada, Liberia, and elsewhere overseas.

Less frequently, and invariably at higher cost, coal and iron ore are hauled long distances overland. In the Soviet Union, for example, where some of the most productive coal and iron fields are a thousand miles or more apart, trains shuttle back and forth on costly overland hauls, bringing iron to the coal and vice versa.

Almost never has a strong steel industry taken root in a country lacking good-grade coal. At present numerous ambitious projects are under way or envisaged for overcoming this handicap by use of electric furnaces or other methods. If heavy industries do develop successfully in Central Africa, South America, and other coal-poor areas, they will come mainly via the route of new and more complicated technology. Energy requirements per unit of output will be as high as or higher than those in the more favorable locations. For the shorter future at least, the principal centers of heavy industry seem likely to remain pretty much where they are now located or in process of active development: in North America, Western Europe, U.S.S.R., and (with certain reservations) in China and India.

Pure steel, an alloy of iron and carbon, is no longer sufficient for the needs of modern technology. Other metals must be combined with steel to yield special qualities of hardness, toughness, resiliency, strength, etc. These metals are called ferroalloys. The principal ones include manganese, chromium, nickel, tungsten, molybdenum, and vanadium. There is a certain amount of interchangeability among these and other ferroalloys.

Like coal and iron, the ferroalloy metals are widely and unevenly distributed over the earth. In the main, however, the required quantities are extremely small compared with coal and iron. Hence scarce items can be stockpiled to escape pressures that might otherwise be brought to bear by other states.

Besides coal, iron, and ferroalloys, modern industry consumes huge quantities of nonferrous minerals. These include a long list of metals headed by copper, aluminum, tin, and lead. Equally important are many nonmetallic substances: sulfur, potash, nitrates (also made synthetically), chlorides, and other ingredients of the widely spreading chemical industries which produce a vast array of commodities from munitions to fertilizers, from drugs to plastics.

Finally, there are the products of the soil, derived from forestry, agriculture, and animal husbandry; and the products of the sea derived from fishing and related industries.

Products of the soil and sea include a wide variety of foodstuffs, industrial fibers, natural rubber, crude drugs, and other materials. At the present stage of technology, there is considerable and increasing interchangeability between raw materials of vegetable and animal origin on the one hand, and those derived from mineral sources on the other. Motor fuel, for instance, can be made from grain as well as from petroleum and coal. Rubber can be grown naturally or produced synthetically. Certain food elements have even been synthesized from inorganic materials. The time may come when science and engineering will relieve the human race of its historic dependence upon the products of the soil and seas. But that time is not yet in sight.

As long as people remain heavily dependent upon plants and animals for subsistence, the land and its encompassing waters will retain high priority in any assessment of national assets and liabilities. What and how much can be produced upon the land and how much can be derived from the seas vary widely from country to country.

Much of the earth's land surface is too rough or too dry or too frosty or too infertile or otherwise unsuitable for cultivation in its natural state. According to one estimate, no more than 7 percent of the world total has all these factors of environment in favorable combination. By continents, Europe leads with 37 percent, followed in order by North and Middle America, 10.4 percent; Asia, 5.8 percent; South America, 4.8 percent; Africa, 3.3 percent; Oceania (mainly Australia), 2.9 percent.

These percentages can be increased by various applications of technology: by applying nitrates, phosphates, and potash to infertile soil; by irrigating arid land; by breeding plants that will mature in a shorter season or grow on dryer land or bear heavier crops, etc.; and, finally, by careful management to prevent erosion and otherwise to improve the soil. Most of these expedients require large outlays of capital; and all of them require a higher level of technical knowledge than prevails generally in many parts of the world, especially in Asia, Africa, and Latin America, where living standards are lowest and ignorance is highest.

The productivity of the land and the seas is receiving rather more attention these days than it did only a few years ago. Some nations are already in trouble with respect to food; and trouble, grave trouble, is in store for many others. Population, for reasons to be examined in Chapter 13, is virtually everywhere on the rise, posing problems of subsistence of a magnitude scarcely dreamed of a generation ago. It is estimated, for example, that the underfed people of India eat less well than before World War II. Crop failures have been blamed for serious dislocation of Communist China's ambitious modernization schemes. Getting enough food produced has been a recurrently refractory problem in the Soviet economy. For a people living as close to the subsistence margin as do the Indians or the Chinese, and many other peoples too, a single crop failure can be a major catastrophe. Living in a land of agricultural surpluses, Americans can scarcely imagine how critically close may be the relation between a nation's food supply and its overall economic development.

Natural resources in international politics

To the degree that uneven geographical distribution of natural resources affects differentially the cost and rate of economic development from country to country, and to the degree that level of economic development affects a national government's policies and capabilities vis-à-vis other nations, there is a manifest relationship between resources and international politics.

In the geopolitical statements quoted in the opening paragraphs of this chapter, two propositions were advanced: (1) that uneven distribution of essential resources inspires corrective policies on the part of the "have-nots"; and (2) that a nation's resource-endowment affects its war-making ability, and thereby its international political position.

The first proposition is easily substantiated. Secure access to sources of food and raw materials has long been a major concern of governments. But the basis of this concern has broadened during recent years. Most of the new nations, as well as many of the older ones now in process of modernization, are confronted with serious shortages of food and raw materials. In some cases—Somalia, for example—the national territory (for Somalia, an arid region in eastern Africa south of the Red Sea) contains few of the bare essentials of a viable independent economy. In other cases —India, for example—the land is incapable of providing even a minimum adequate food supply without control of population increase and large capital outlays to improve the soil and to modernize agricultural methods. The older industrial nations, despite flexibilities introduced by advanced technology, are depleting their higher-grade ores, resulting—as in the case of the United States steel industry—in enforced use of lower-grade ores *and* increasing dependence upon foreign sources of supply. And this rising dependence upon imports parallels developments in military technology which render it increasingly doubtful whether overseas sources could be defended in case even of a nonnuclear war.

The second proposition—the bearing of resources on war-making ability—requires more detailed examination. The Industrial Revolution, as we have seen, affected in many ways the practice of statecraft and the political configuration of the Society of Nations. The impact of progressive and ever widening industrialization was especially heavy on the conduct and scale of war. Rapid-firing guns consumed vastly more ammunition. More equipment was destroyed and had to be replaced. Power-driven transport—railroads, ships, road vehicles, and eventually planes—enabled belligerents to maintain large military forces in the field and to keep them supplied. Advances in sanitation and in the medical arts made possible larger-scale and more continuous operations over longer periods. The scale of military operations, in short, increased all along the line, with corresponding increase in the kinds and quantities of raw materials required.

Every war between 1815 and 1914 exhibited this consequence of the Industrial Revolution. World War I provided impressive additional evidence that a government's military capabilities depended not only upon its productive plant but also upon secure access to huge quantities and many kinds of raw materials.

Nations varied widely in their ability to adjust to rising materials requirements. They differed, first, in the degree to which enough of the bulky basic essentials—food, fibers, coal, iron, etc.—could be produced inside their own territorial boundaries. They differed, second, in the ease or difficulty of making domestic sources secure against enemy action. They differed, third, in their capacity to supplement domestic deficiencies from foreign sources; and, finally, in their ability in time of war to bring home supplies procurable abroad.

Great Britain illustrates all these conditions. The British Isles were endowed with large quantities of coal, smaller deposits of iron ore, and a few other essential resources. But Britain after the Industrial Revolution became heavily dependent upon imported foodstuffs, industrial fibers, and a growing list of critically important materials. Britain in the nineteenth century was able financially to command the resources of every continent to make good domestic deficiencies and was also capable of protecting the ships which brought these materials to the British Isles. Before the development of submarines and airplanes into formidable commerce-destroying weapons, the capabilities of Britain rested upon a virtually world-wide command of foodstuffs and raw materials. After introduction of these and other ship-destroying weapons, Britain's dependence upon overseas resources became increasingly precarious. And the British situation was further weakened when the development of airpower brought the British Isles themselves within range of devastating air attack.

In France the insecurity of domestic sources of basic essentials—especially iron ore—became evident at a much earlier date. Realistic appraisal of French military capabilities from 1870 onwards had always to take into account the location of France's iron mines close to the country's eastern border, the vulnerable frontier crossed by German armies three times between 1870 and 1940.

In contrast, under conditions prevailing until recently, the United States represented a degree of resources security unapproached by any other Power, with the possible exception of Russia. Most of the basic resources, nearly all of the bulky ones, were available either within American territory or in nearby countries. The nickel ores in Canada were as available and secure as if located in Illinois. Coffee and manganese from Brazil, sugar from Cuba, and other essentials from the Caribbean area, Middle America, and the west coast of South America were only slightly less accessible and secure than if produced in Michigan or Louisiana. Only in rubber, tin, antimalarial cinchona bark, and a few other essentials drawn mainly from southeast Asia could the United States, prior to World War II, be severely pinched by enemy action.

The environment in which experience of these kinds accumulated was an environment in which war was a recurring and generally accepted technique of statecraft. During the 1920's and especially during the 1930's, it was widely assumed that general wars, more or less like World War I, would continue to recur in the future. It was further assumed that a nation's role and stature in international politics, the deference which other nations paid to its demands, would continue to vary in proportion to its presumed ability to back up its demands by resort to war. It was also recognized that the list of essential raw materials was still lengthening, and that the consumption of basic fuels, ores, and other bulky essentials was still rising. Given these expectations, it was logical to postulate that secure access to varied and abundant material resources, whether domestic or foreign in origin, would constitute in the future as in the past a major variable in determining the patterns of power and influence in the Society of Nations. This, it will be recalled, was precisely the conclusion reached in the statements quoted earlier from Emeny, Leith, and Strausz-Hupé.

The initial impact of World War II seemed to reinforce the conviction of many experts that capacity to sustain enormous matériel demands in a protracted war was still one of the basic determinants of any nation's international stature. The destructive bombing of Germany, Japan, Britain, and other countries did not immediately shake this conviction. Nor did the glimpse of the enormously greater destructiveness of nuclear explosives offered by the destruction of Hiroshima and Nagasaki with a single atomic bomb apiece. It was still widely assumed that future general wars would recur, and that these would more or less closely resemble, in matériel requirements and in other respects, the war just concluded.

In that war, as in the earlier war of 1914, victory, even survival, had depended upon a government's ability to meet both the minimum needs of its civilian population and the nearly insatiable demands of huge combat forces, frequently operating simultaneously in widely separated regions. It was manifestly this experience and the lessons which many analysts drew from it which led the Policy Materials Commission to conclude in 1952 that secure access to abundant and varied material resources was a continuing basic condition of the national political potential to which the United States aspired. And the same reasoning led the Commission to the conclusion that nations could be realistically rated on the basis of their estimated capacity to meet these requirements under conditions of protracted total war.

The development of nuclear explosives in massive quantities—first the fission type, and then the enormously more destructive fusion type—and the parallel development of airborne carriers capable of delivering these explosives to targets halfway around the globe, have manifestly added new dimensions to the problem of raw materials. On the one hand, the quantities of energy and other raw materials required are greater than ever before. On the other hand, it is difficult to imagine how any war fought with these superweapons could last long enough for blockade to become significant. Furthermore, the destructiveness of the new weapons has convinced many experts that no nation so attacked could survive as a going concern. In consequence, the emphasis is shifting somewhat from estimation of presumptive ability to maintain the flow of essential materials during a protracted war, to the problem of providing at continuously rising cost the materials required to maintain a huge military establishment constantly ready to strike with maximum strength from the outset.

But this is not the only aspect of the problem; it may not even be the most important one in the future. Raw materials are also weapons in the Cold War. During the 1950's, for example, the United States pursued a deliberate policy of withholding so-called strategic raw materials from the Soviet Union, the Communist countries of eastern Europe, and, above all, Communist China. The rationale of this strategy is evident. It proceeded from the assumption that depriving the Communist nations of certain essential materials would slow down their industrial development and thereby impede significantly their weapons programs.

The actual results of these raw-materials embargoes and other forms of denial are difficult to assess. Applied to countries heavily dependent upon foreign sources of supply, concerted action on the part of the principal suppliers may have significant retarding effects. Applied to countries with abundant latent resources, policies of denial may merely hasten the opening of new mines, new oil wells, and other projects to expand production from domestic sources. In the specific case above, the embargo of strategic materials to the Communist countries has showed an incurable tendency to develop leaks; and it appears to have yielded scarcely any of the results intended. On the contrary, it has probably stimulated rapid development and diversification of the Communist economies and tightened the economic links which bind those economies together and render them less vulnerable to economic pressures from outside the Communist Realm.

Ability to supply essential resources may be as important politically as ability to deny them. Aid in the form of foodstuffs may strengthen political ties with friendly regimes in countries subject to periodic famines or less severe shortages—like India, for example. Subsidies in the form of raw materials may produce similar effects in relation to countries in the early stages of industrial modernization. During the next generation at least, it seems likely that foodstuffs and raw materials will continue to figure importantly in that aspect of the Cold War which relates to the East-West competition to guide the modernizing process in Asia, Africa, and Latin America.

Another dimension of the raw-materials problem in international politics today derives from the continuing rapid advance of science and engineering. Industrialization invariably increases the demand for raw materials, both in quantity and in variety. The higher the level of economic development, the greater and the more diverse these requirements have tended to become. However, the growth of scientific knowledge and engineering technique, which have made industrialization possible, have eventually tended also to make industrialized societies *less* vulnerable to blockades and embargoes. This counteractive effect arises from increased ability at higher levels of technology to provide (at a price) synthetic substitutes for scarce materials, and frequently to make products with similar properties by more than one method and with alternative substitute materials.

This characteristic of *advanced* technology became dramatically evident during World War I. Nitrogen salts (especially potassium nitrate, popularly known as saltpeter) have long been an essential ingredient of chemical explosives. In the early 1900's nitrates were derived chiefly from the west coast of South America where these water-soluble chemicals had accumulated over the centuries in a virtually rainless desert. The Allied blockade imposed from the outbreak of the war in 1914 cut Germany off from this source of nitrates. Under conditions existing previously, German military forces would have suffered nitrogen starvation within a few months. However, German chemists had been developing a process for taking, or "fixing," nitrogen from the atmosphere. This invention, known as the Haber process, was put into production just in time to enable Germany to hold out for four years instead of a problematical six months or so.

Another example is the case of synthetic rubber in World War II. The Allied blockade again cut Germany off from overseas supplies. This time one of the crucial shortages was natural rubber from the plantations of southeast Asia. Two years later the Japanese conquest of that region deprived the United States and its Allies of this same source of natural rubber. But in Germany, and somewhat belatedly in the United States, industrial chemists and engineers met the rubber crisis by intricate processes for transmuting petroleum and coal into synthetic rubber.

Synthetic substitutes may be more costly to produce than their natural equivalents. They may be less efficient in use, though this is by no means always the case. But the experience of World War II, and of the continuing Cold War that has followed, seems to indicate that denial of particular materials becomes less crippling as scientists and engineers contrive more and more ways to circumvent shortages of natural materials, and that the more advanced a nation's technology, the less vulnerable *politically* it becomes to blockades and embargoes.

This general conclusion requires certain qualifications. The first arises from the changing character of war. In the wars of 1914 and 1939 it was possible to convert or build plants to produce synthetic substitutes after enemy blockade or conquest cut off the flow of natural materials. It may be doubted whether that experience has much relevance for the future. It seems unrealistic to assume that any highly industrialized nation, subjected to devastating attack with nuclear explosives, would be able after the attack to develop latent strength by building the complex installations involved in nearly every branch of the synthetic industries. Even if such an economy should survive the initial attack at all, which may be doubted, its devastated and crippled industrial plants would almost certainly be reduced to more primitive levels of technology.

A second qualification arises from the fact that synthetic substitutes themselves are made of raw materials—ultimately from natural resources, though different from the natural materials replaced: for example, synthetic rubber from coal as described above. To date, the most important resources involved in making synthetics include coal and petroleum, as well as sulfuric acid and other chemicals. In general, production of synthetics consumes larger quantities of energy, again in the form of coal or oil, supplemented increasingly by hydroelectricity. Thus, in World War II, Japan (poor in domestic sources of energy) was much less able than Germany (with abundant coal) to cope with the blockade by substituting synthetics for scarce natural materials.

The usually larger energy requirements of synthetic industries anticipate a more general problem that is associated with the accelerating rate of depletion of reserves of higher-grade mineral ores and other nonrenewable resources. National economies represent widely different stages of economic development. The higher the level of development, the more rapidly they consume the higher grades and more easily accessible natural resources. In general, the earlier a country experiences the industrial revolution, and the larger the scale and more productive its output, the more quickly does it pass from a condition of comparative resources-abundance to a condition of increasing domestic scarcities of high-quality natural materials. As the older industrial economies of Western Europe, and now the United States too, have moved into this condition, they have turned increasingly to raw materials imported from the underdeveloped countries. But the drive for industrialization in the latter implies that they too will be consuming resources at rising rates. Thus the demands of the older industrial economies and of the newer industrializing economies converge to produce soaring demands for shrinking reserves of natural resources. As high-yield reserves of these materials become depleted, men will have to fall back on lower-yield materials. These include the oceans and most widely distributed common rocks. This trend is already discernible in numerous industries here and abroad. It will continue to spread as demands increase and high-yield resources are exhausted.

The further this trend continues, the smaller will grow the differential between the mineral-rich and the mineral-poor countries. The ability to exploit low-yield materials for purposes either of power or of human welfare will depend increasingly on the level of a nation's science and technology. If this hypothesis is tenable, the conclusion follows that the geographical distribution of natural resources (which, in the past, has meant high-yield resources) may become, like the physical layout of lands and seas, considerably less significant than formerly in relation to the geographical distribution of political potential in the society of nations. This sequence and some of its consequences are examined in an article by Harrison Brown (professor of geophysics at the California Institute of Technology). The process which Brown describes may not have immediate effects on the policies and potentials of nations. But any middle-range or long-range forecast must take into account the international political consequences of—

Technological denudation of the earth [*]

In order to produce the multiplicity of goods consumed by society, we mine iron ore, convert it into pig iron, and then mill it into steel. We produce copper, lead, zinc, aluminum, and a variety of metals from their ores and blend and shape them to suit our needs. We mine phosphate rock, fix the nitrogen of the atmosphere, evaporate sea water, and quarry rock. We transport vast quantities of sand, gravel and clay; manufacture cement; and mine sulfur, gypsum, and pyrites. For every person who lives in a highly industrialized society, many tons of material must be moved, mined, and processed each year.

From the time that coal was first linked to iron, the per capita flow of goods in the industrialized part of the world has steadily increased; associated with that increasing flow we see an increasing per capita demand for raw materials. By 1950 the yearly per capita demand for

[*] From pp. 1023-1032 in "Technological Denudation," by Harrison Brown in *Man's Role in Changing the Face of the Earth*, edited by W. L. Thomas, Jr. Copyright 1956 by University of Chicago Press; reproduced by permission.

steel in the United States had reached 1,260 pounds; demand for copper had reached 23 pounds; demand for stone, sand, and gravel had reached 7,300 pounds; and demand for cement had reached 520 pounds. In order to power the industrial network, energy demands had risen to the equivalent of over 8 tons of coal per person per year. It must be stressed that these per capita demands are still rising.

In addition to the rise in per capita demands, we must consider the fact that machine civilization is spreading throughout the world. The Soviet Union and Japan are the most recent additions to the roster of industrialized nations, and enormous efforts aimed at industrialization are now being made by India and China. Further, the human population of the world is increasing rapidly and is apparently destined to continue to increase for some time in the future. . . .

It is the declared intention of Asian leaders to stimulate the industrialization of their countries to levels which approach existing Western levels. Whether or not they are able to accomplish this will depend upon a variety of factors: resources, population, rate of capital formation, rate of population growth, extent of help from the outside, etc. However, for the purpose of our discussion, let us assume that India is able to carry out successfully an industrialization program and that it is able to double its consumption of metals every ten years—a rate somewhat less than that achieved by the U.S.S.R. and Japan for rather lengthy periods. Starting with a pig-iron production of 1.8 million tons in 1951, production would reach 10 million tons by 1976 and 100 million tons by 2009. By 2021 production would reach 235 million tons, and a total of 1,400 million tons of pig iron would have been produced since 1951. By that time the population of India will almost certainly have doubled once again, and, when we take into account the losses of iron in use and in the steel cycle, the amount of steel in use would correspond to about a ton per person—a value considerably lower than the 8 tons per person in use in the United States at the present time.

Were pig-iron production to double every ten years, coal production would probably do likewise and might reach 4,000 million tons annually by 2021. By that time, 27,000 million tons of coal would have been removed from the ground, an amount approximately equal to the estimated reserves of all grades of coal *in situ* in India down to a depth of 2,000 feet (excluding lignite). The amount actually susceptible to mechanized mining operations may be only a small fraction of this.

India possesses some of the richest and most extensive iron-ore deposits in the world, and, in the absence of exports either of the ore or of pig iron, its reserves would probably permit India to build up an amount of iron in use equivalent to existing Western per capita levels. With a doubling time of ten years nearly a century would be required. However, it might well turn out to be necessary for India to export pig iron or iron ore in order to help finance the considerable capital outlay which would be required for such an industrial development. In such an eventuality it might be necessary for India to utilize low-grade deposits in order to approach existing Western levels of industrialization.

On the basis of considerations such as those outlined above, the industrialization of India would necessarily follow a pattern markedly different from the pattern observed thus far in the history of industrialization. India's existing resources would enable it to obtain a reasonable start toward industrialization; but, long before existing Western levels of productivity could be achieved, supplies of metallurgical coal would have disappeared, and India would be forced to produce pig iron by utilizing low-grade coals, perhaps by the sponge-iron process or by a process similar to the Swedish electrometal process. Again, long before existing Western levels are achieved, coal itself will be in very short supply, and pig iron will have to be produced by utilizing some other energy source, quite possibly atomic energy. Again, it is quite possible that, before India achieves existing Western levels of production, it will be forced to utilize ores of lower grade. This would create still greater needs for energy and for metals.

When we examine India's long-range requirements for other metals, we encounter similar difficulties. Local high-grade deposits of most ores are completely inadequate sources of metals in the quantities which are required. Clearly, the industrialization of India will require either the importation of huge quantities of metals, many of which are becoming scarce elsewhere in the world, or the satisfying of the demand internally by the extraction of the needed metals from very low-grade deposits, utilizing processes which are at present undeveloped but nevertheless conceivable.

There are those who maintain that areas such as India will not attempt to emulate the industrialized West with its high per capita level of productivity. Persons subscribing to this view maintain that the average Indian or Chinese does not desire large quantities of material possessions—that he desires only to live at a consumption level where life is not quite so difficult as at present. He would be happy, it is maintained, with an adequate food supply and adequate clothing, medical care, schooling, and housing—but divorced from the luxuries to which we have become accustomed in the West. Proponents of this general view believe that the bulk of Western productivity is aimed at the production of luxuries and that the production of life's necessities would require relatively little industrialization.

However, most persons, both Asian and non-Asian, agree that one of the better features of industrial civilization is that it has increased the length of the average human life-span, and most persons believe that each human being should have the right to live out that normal life-span. Indeed, the desire to live for as long a time as possible is one of the strongest of human desires and one which has contributed substantially to the formulation of existing development efforts.

When we enumerate all the facilities which are necessary in order to make it possible for the average person to live for a span of seventy years or thereabouts, we find that the list is surprisingly long. First, we require adequate food production, and this in turn requires irrigation and fertilizers. Elaborate transportation facilities are required to insure adequate distribution of fertilizers and food and to insure distribution of raw materials to the fertilizer factories. Construction of fertilizer factories, hospitals, and plants for the production of antibiotics requires steel, concrete, power, and a variety of raw materials. And, indeed, when we carry to completion our list of essentials which are necessary in order to permit the average man to avoid premature death, we find that we are not far removed from the per capita flow of goods which exists in the West today. To be sure, it is not necessary to have 8 tons of steel in use for every person, but it would be very difficult to get by with fewer than 1 or 2 tons.

Thus we see that the underdeveloped areas of the world are enormous potential consumers of the earth's resources. It is of course possible that war, political difficulties, social upheavals, or technological barriers will effectively prevent the industrialization of these areas. But if industrialization continues to spread over the surface of our globe, as seems likely, there will be consumption of resources on a scale difficult even for Americans to imagine.

It is clear that, as material desires and needs increase, as more and more areas become industrialized, and as the population of the earth increases further, ever greater demands will be placed upon the earth's mineral resources. Although only a small fraction of the world is at present industrialized, we have already been confronted with diminishing concentrations of needed elements. And whereas man once found abundant high-grade ores at the surface of the earth, he must now frequently follow the seams deep underground. The time must inevitably come when ores as such no longer exist, and machine civilization, if it survives, will feed on the leanest of substances—the rocks which make up the surface of our planet, the waters of the seas, and the gases of the atmosphere.

As time goes by, we will see mineral grades diminish, but with each step downward in grade there will be an enormous step upward in tonnage. As grades move downward, increasing emphasis will be placed upon the isolation of by-products and co-products, and eventually we may reach the time when as many as twenty to thirty products are obtained from a single rock-mining operation. As grade goes down, energy costs per units of output will of course go up; but, given adequate supplies of energy, it will be possible for industry to be fed for a very long time from the leanest of substances.

One hundred tons of average igneous rock contain, in addition to other useful elements, 16,000 pounds of aluminum, 10,000 pounds of iron, 1,200 pounds of titanium, 180 pounds of manganese, 70 pounds of chromium, 40 pounds of nickel, 30 pounds of vanadium, 20 pounds of copper, 10 pounds of tungsten, and 4 pounds of lead. Given adequate supplies of energy, these elements could be extracted from the rock, and it appears likely that the rock itself contains the requisite amount of energy in the form of uranium and thorium.

One ton of average granite contains about 4 grams of uranium and about 12 grams of thorium. The energy content of this amount of uranium and thorium, assuming nuclear breeding, is equivalent to the energy released on burning approximately 50 tons of coal. It seems likely that the actual processing of the rock can be accomplished at an energy expenditure considerably smaller than 50 tons of coal, with the result that it seems possible to obtain a net profit from average rock and at the same time obtain a variety of metals which are essential to the operation of an industrial society.

There are large beds of rocks of various types which are intermediate in richness between existing low-grade ores and the average rocks discussed above. Before man processes average rock on a large scale, he will process higher-than-average rock. He will isolate iron from taconites, aluminum from anorthosites and clays, produce sulfuric acid from calcium sulfate, and isolate copper, tin, lead, nickel, and germanium from a variety of very low-grade deposits. But, eventually, man will learn to process ordinary rock and, with practically infinite amounts of this lowest common denominator available, he will be able to build and power his machines for a very long time. . . .

If there is a world catastrophe, or if civilization regresses to an agrarian existence, technological denudation will be halted. However, let us assume for the purpose of discussion that industrialization spreads during the course of the next century to India, to the rest of Southeast Asia, to China, to Africa and to South America. Let us assume further that world population continues to rise and that per capita demands for goods in existing industrialized areas continue to increase. Clearly in such an eventuality denudation will take place on a scale which is difficult for us to comprehend.

Let us now examine some of the patterns of consumption of raw materials which might be expected, during the decades and centuries to come, on the basis of these assumptions. In order to do this, we must let our imaginations run free and recognize that almost anything is possible from the technological point of view which does not violate the fundamental physical and biological laws which govern our world.

As time goes by, and the earth's resources of fossil fuels are consumed and deposits of high-grade ores are exhausted, we will approach asymptotically the condition wherein machine civilization is fed entirely by the processing of lowest common denominators—air, sea water, ordinary rock, and sunlight. By this time, population densities will have risen to the point where a great deal of water will be distilled from the sea for agricultural and industrial purposes, and most food will be grown by using artificial fertilizers. Metals such as iron, aluminum, titanium, manganese, copper, tungsten, and lead will be obtained from rock, which raw material will also provide the major source of phosphorus. The waters of the seas will provide magnesium, chlorine, bromine, iodine, and sulfur. Energy will be provided by the uranium and thorium of rocks, by the rays of the sun, and conceivably by controlled thermonuclear reactions utilizing deuterium extracted from the oceans. Liquid fuels and the whole complex of organic chemicals and plastics will be produced from the carbon of limestone, utilizing either atomic energy or controlled photosynthesis—probably both.

Let us assume that, by the time this point is reached, the technological complexities of extracting the necessary raw materials and of producing and transporting the requisite finished products necessitate that about 100 tons of iron and other metals be in use for every person alive. Under this circumstance the bulk of the necessary metals could be obtained under steady-state conditions by processing something on the order of 50 tons of rock per person per year. An amount of energy would be available from the rock which, depending upon the efficiency of extraction, might amount to the equivalent of about 1,000 tons of coal per person. Making due allowance for the efficiency of utilization of atomic energy under circumstances where nuclear "breeding" must be accomplished, at least this amount of energy will probably be necessary for powering the diverse extractive and manufacturing operations and for the processing of the sea water.

The total rate of denudation in this hypothetical world of the future will depend upon the level of population which has been reached by that time. On the basis of what we now know concerning the rates at which population growth can be slowed down, it is difficult to see how the population of the world can be stabilized at a level of much less than 7 billion (again, in the absence of a world catastrophe). On the basis of what we know about the potentialities of technology, a population of perhaps 100 billion could be supported, although, even with the high level of technology described above, the task of supporting this number might prove to be extremely difficult. For the purpose of our discussion let us assume that world population reaches a level intermediate between these two extremes—about 30 billion, corresponding to a twelvefold increase over the existing population level.

A population of 30 billion persons would consume rock at a rate of about 1,500 billion tons per year. If we were to assume that all the land areas of the world were available for such processing, then, on the average, man would "eat" his way downward at a rate of 3.3 millimeters per year, or over 3 meters a millennium. This figure gives us some idea of the denudation rates which might be approached in the centuries ahead. And it gives us an idea of the powers for denudation which lie in mankind's hands.

The approach to the condition above is, for obvious reasons, difficult to put in time perspective. However, certain probable patterns of future raw-material consumption emerge which can be discussed.

If we assume that pig-iron production outside the industrialized West doubles every decade, we can expect that, by the turn of the next century, a substantial fraction of the world will depend upon low-grade iron ore such as taconite. As supplies of metallurgical coal dwindle, an ever increasing fraction of our iron will be produced by utilizing processes which minimize or avoid the use of coke.

As supplies of elemental bauxite dwindle, the aluminum industry will shift over to the processing of anorthosites and clays. Consumption of magnesium will increase, in part due to the ready availability of the element in sea water.

As supplies of elemental sulfur dwindle, increasing quantities of sulfuric acid will be manufactured from pyrites. As pyrites in turn disappear, sulfuric acid will be manufactured from calcium sulfate. These developments in turn will result in increasing emphasis being placed on the utilization of nitric and hydrochloric acids in chemical processing.

As the higher-grade deposits of other minor metals such as copper, lead, zinc, tin, germanium, and nickel dwindle, increasing emphasis will be placed upon the processing of low-grade deposits and upon the isolation of by-products and co-products. The mining industries as we know them today will gradually be transformed into enormous chemical industries.

As petroleum and oil shales dwindle, liquid fuels will be produced by coal hydrogenation. As coal in turn dwindles, its use will be confined to premium functions such as the production of chemicals.

These various changes, from one type of technology to another, will take place irregularly in the various regions of the world. Anorthosites will be processed in one region, while bauxite is still being processed in another. The use of atomic energy will become widespread in some regions, while others are still obtaining their energy from coal. But gradually, the leveling effects of denudation will result in convergence of techniques and of raw materials—and mineral resources as we now know them will cease to play a major role in world economy and politics.

CHAPTER THIRTEEN

★ ★ ★

Malthus in the Twentieth Century

THE FUNCTION OF this chapter is to provide a framework for thinking about population in the context of international politics. A population may be defined, for our purposes, as the total number of human persons who inhabit a given area. The aggregates with which we are primarily concerned here are *national* populations: the people who constitute the inhabitants of independent political communities which, in turn, are the units of international politics and the international political system.

National populations may be viewed from various perspectives. They are aggregates of human beings who consume food and other goods and services. They are also producers of goods and services. From still another perspective, human beings appear as the building blocks of all kinds of social systems, including, of course, the nation-state.

Acts of states, to repeat a truism stressed in Chapter 2, are always acts of human persons, though this is too often disguised by the verbal usage which attributes personality to the state itself. The nonhuman apparatus of statecraft—instruments of communication and transport, foodstuffs and raw materials, productive equipment and military weapons, and all the rest— are products of *human* imagination, *human* organization, and *human* labor. A national population can also be likened to a reservoir from which come politicians, soldiers, civil servants, scientists, engineers, managers, factory workers, farmers, and all the other kinds of performers who carry on the work of an organized political community.

The relative size and qualities of a nation's population are usually of high-priority concern to its rulers and a source of limitations on what they can accomplish vis-à-vis other nations. For these reasons the geographical distribution of population and the characteristics of national populations have come generally to be regarded as important foundations of national policies and potentials.

Special interest attaches to these demographic factors in our time. This interest arises in part from radical changes taking place in the relative size, composition, and capacities of particular national populations. Special interest derives also from changing attitudes within the United States and elsewhere as to what should be done with regard to the rapid increase of population, especially in the underdeveloped countries, an increase which is characterized by such expressions as "crisis," "time bomb," and "explosion."

As indicated above, the student of international politics has a general comparative interest in population and population trends. But we are also especially interested in the more populous units of the Society of Nations. Let us begin, therefore, by comparing some basic demographic facts regarding the twelve most populous nation-states, Table 13.1.

TABLE 13.1   THE TWELVE MOST POPULOUS STATES

STATES	TOTAL POPULATION AS OF 1959 (MILLIONS)	BIRTH RATE PER 1000 POPULATION	DEATH RATE PER 1000 POPULATION	INFANT MORTALITY PER 1000 LIVE BIRTHS	APPROXI- MATE RATE OF ANNUAL INCREASE (%)
China	640	41 [a]	17	n.a.	2.4
India	412 [a]	43 [a]	24 [a]	185	1.9
U.S.S.R.	210	26	8	45	1.8
U.S.A.	175	24	9	26	1.8
Japan	92	17	8	40	1.2
Indonesia	87	40	20	150	1.7
Pakistan	85	20	12	n.a.	1.4
Brazil	63	43	21	170	2.4
W. Germany	54	17	11	36	1.2
U. Kingdom	51	16	11	24	0.4
Italy	48	18	10	50	0.5
France	44	18	12	34	0.8

[a] Figure supplied by the Office of Population Research on the basis of intercensal increase 1951-1961.

With respect to the data displayed in Table 13.1, the following explanatory and cautionary comments should be noted.

1. All items are given in round numbers.

2. The three columns of vital rates are no better than the reporting and recording procedures from which these data are derived. Recording of births and deaths in most countries is more or less incomplete. In most of the non-European countries (except U.S.A.), vital statistics are fragmentary and (in some instances) possibly falsified substantially. Demographers general believe, for example, that the rates given for China and India are considerably lower than complete recording would show.

3. The last column (annual rate of increase) is the average of five years, 1953-1957.

4. Most of the data in Table 13.1 are derived from the *Demographic Yearbook* of the United Nations.

The data in Table 13.1 reveal disparities of size, rate of increase, and regional variations of possibly great political significance. Of the seven most populous states, six are located wholly or partly in Asia. Of the remaining five, four are European states. The combined populations of these four total less than any one of the top three, and only slightly more than the United States. The combined populations of China and India exceed all the other ten combined (and these ten, be it remembered, include both the Soviet Union and the United States).

Among the largest eight in Table 13.1, all but Japan and the United States show a birth rate above 25 per 1000, and a death rate ranging from 24 in India (perhaps actually higher) down to 8 per 1000 in the U.S.S.R. and Japan. In every one of these eight countries, excepting the United States and to a lesser degree the Soviet Union and Japan, infant mortality runs very high. Because of high fertility the average age is much lower than in the countries which industrialized during the nineteenth century.

As we shall consider more fully later, the combination of high birth rate, high death rate, and in particular, high infant mortality sets the stage for very rapid population increase. Substantial improvements in nutrition, medical care, and other aspects of a higher standard of living, bring down a high death rate, sometimes as much as 50% or more within a decade. Unless there is a simultaneous and comparable drop in the birth rate (which generally declines much later and more slowly), the result is an explosive rate of population increase.

This so-called population explosion is imminent or already occurring throughout most of Asia, Africa, and Latin America. It is a side effect almost everywhere of the industrial revolution which is belatedly taking place in the underdeveloped countries of those continents. Moreover, the industrializing process that triggers off rapid population increase also brings within reach of these massive populations the military and other instrumentalities of statecraft which have in the past given such an overwhelming advantage to the smaller but highly industrialized nations of Europe and America.

This suggests the importance of viewing population qualitatively as well as quantitatively and of noting the distribution of these factors through time. As students of international politics we should be particularly alert to differential changes (that is, changes at different rates in different countries) in these demographic factors. Table 13.2 indicates some of the principal categories of information which may be significant for our purposes.

Table 13.2 displays the important distinction between factors that are more and those that are less, easily quantified. Categories 1-15 can be defined precisely and are potentially quantifiable. It may or may not prove

TABLE 13.2   DEMOGRAPHIC FACTORS IN SPACE AND THROUGH TIME

UNITS TO BE COMPARED:	State A	State B	State C
TIMES TO WHICH COMPARISONS REFER:	$t_1 t_2 t_3$	$t_1 t_2 t_3$	$t_1 t_2 t_3$

ASPECTS TO BE COMPARED (below):

1. Size (total population)
2. Fertility (birth rate per 1,000 per year)
3. Mortality (death rate per 1,000 per year)
4. Natural increase (or decline)
5. Rate of natural increase (or decline, as percent of total population)
6. Immigration
7. Emigration
8. Net change in size of population
9. Expectation of life at birth
10. Average age of population
11. Distribution by age, 0-14 years

12. Distribution by age, 15-34 years
13. Distribution by age, 35-59 years
14. Distribution by age, 60 and over
15. Distribution by sex
16. Proportion of total fit for military service
17. Proportion of total fit for non-military employment
18. Proportion of total partially disabled
19. Proportion of total unfit for any employment
20. Proportion of total who are literate
21. Distribution of other skills (see Table 13.3 below)

possible to obtain the data necessary to fill these categories. That will depend on the scope and reliability of the statistics kept by the states under consideration. Items 16-21 represent aspects which are more difficult to define precisely, and hence are more controversial. What constitutes fitness for military service or for various kinds of nonmilitary work? One standard prevails in the United States, another in the Soviet Union, still another in China. How well does a person have to read in order to be classified as literate? Again criteria vary widely from country to country. These are issues on which even the experts may disagree hopelessly. When we come (in Table 13.3) to compare the distribution of other skills, still greater difficulties of definition and classification will become manifest.

Table 13.2 emphasizes the dimensions both of space and of time. The structure and capabilities of two or more populations can be compared at time$_1$, or at time$_1$ and time$_2$, or at still more points in time. Even with inadequate data, demographers have devised methods for plotting trends through shorter or longer historical periods. Later we shall exhibit one of the standard models used to portray demographic development through relatively long periods (see Figure 13.A page 102).

Demographic trends can be extrapolated, or projected from the historical past into the unknown future. Such projections, like all rational human predictions, rest upon assumptions regarding future conditions of the environment and regarding normally expectable human behavior. No respectable demographer would predict, for example, that the population of China *will* reach such and such a total twenty-five years hence. What he might predict is that *if* certain specified environmental conditions and behavioral patterns develop as he assumes will occur, *then* the population will vary within such and such limits. In the example of China, a twenty-five year projection would almost certainly include assumptions (1) as to occurrence or nonoccurrence of natural or man-made catastrophes—famines, epidemics, wars, etc.; (2) as to the rate of economic development; (3) as to future attitudes regarding desirable family size; (4) as to developments in techniques of birth control; etc. Population projections, we repeat, are predictions within a framework or matrix of assumptions as to future environmental conditions and patterns of human behavior. Such projections can never rise above the assumptions upon which they are founded.

Since population trends can be modified within rather broad physiological and environmental limits, demographic projections themselves tend to evoke political actions to increase or decrease fertility, to encourage or restrict migration, etc. We shall return to this point later in the chapter.

Returning now to Table 13.2, the first fifteen items refer to purely objective features—number of people, their sex, their ages, their movements into or out of the political communities under consideration. Items 16-21, however, refer not merely to people as objects upon the landscape, but more especially to their capacities to perform various kinds of work. Viewed from this second perspective, population appears not only as a mass of manpower, but as individual persons carrying out defined functions, less well than, as well as, or better than comparable persons in other countries. Table 13.3 suggests one way of thinking functionally about human capacities in the context of international politics.

The distribution of specialized functional skills manifestly varies widely from country to country and within any given country through time. Moreover, the political significance of particular distributions and combinations of skills varies with other changes taking place simultaneously inside a particular country and in the Society of Nations as a whole. Furthermore, judgments differ as to the significance of these distributions, as will become more apparent later in the chapter. Superior numbers of manual laborers—both soldiers and civilians—were a much more reliable index of a state's international power and influence during the centuries when the ratio of human muscles to nonhuman forms of energy was much higher than it has become in the more advanced industrial nations today. The seventeenth century maxim that "God is always on the side of the big battalions" clearly made more sense when the ratio of firepower to manpower was a trifling fraction of what it has become in the nuclear age. Some experts contend that percentage of literacy has become the most important aspect of population in the present state of technological advancement.

TABLE 13.3 DISTRIBUTION OF SPECIALIZED FUNCTIONAL SKILLS

UNITS TO BE COMPARED:	State A	State B	State C
TIMES TO WHICH COMPARISONS REFER:	$t_1 t_2 t_3$	$t_1 t_2 t_3$	$t_1 t_2 t_3$

SPECIALIZED SKILLS TO BE COMPARED (below):

A. People as instruments of statecraft
  1. Nonpolitical heads of state
  2. Politicians (heads of government, cabinet ministers, certain diplomatic officers, members of legislative bodies, politicians out of office, etc.)
  3. Nonpolitical civil servants (diplomatic officers, departmental staffs, technical administrators, etc.)
  4. Military personnel (officers, enlisted men, specialists, women as military personnel, etc.
B. People as producers of goods and nonpolitical services
  1. Executives (managers of banks, industrial corporations, agricultural enterprises, transport and communication units, research laboratories, etc.)
  2. Engineers (civil, mechanical, electrical, aeronautical, etc.)
  3. Physicians, nurses, social workers, etc.
  4. Secretaries, clerks and technicians
  5. Manual workers of all kinds (industrial, agricultural, etc.)
C. People as conservators of national culture
  1. Teachers
  2. Clergymen
  3. Lawyers
  4. Historians
  5. Some artists and men of letters
D. People as creators of new knowledge
  1. Mathematicians
  2. Physical and biological scientists
  3. Social scientists
  4. Philosophers
  5. Creative artists and men of letters

Population trends in space and time

No one knows how many human beings inhabited the earth in the remote past, and there is no way to find out. Systematic and periodic counting of heads and recording of births and deaths are relatively recent innovations. The oldest trustworthy records reach back only into the late eighteenth century. Even today reliable census returns and vital statistics are lacking in many countries, notably in Asia, Africa, and Latin America. Much of the data in the United Nations *Demographic Yearbook* and in atlases, encyclopaedias, and other reference works represents scarcely more than rough approximations based on scanty and often untrustworthy records. However, experts on population (called demographers) are all in accord on one point at least: after thousands of years, during which population stagnated for long periods, recurrently suffered catastrophic declines in particular regions, and increased very slowly in the long run, the human species is today multiplying at an unprecedented and still accelerating rate.

According to one estimate, the total number of people in the world early in the Christian era may have been as high as 250 millions. Everything known about ancient peoples and preindustrial modern countries, in which people subsist precariously by hunting, food gathering, or primitive tillage, indicates that the birth rate was probably close to the biological maximum: somewhere between forty to sixty per thousand people per year. It is probable, further, that the death rate was nearly everywhere correspondingly high on the average, and that it fluctuated widely. In some years in some localities births would have exceeded deaths; in other years, there would have been more deaths than births. Such fluctuations would occur as a result of famines, epidemics, floods, or other disasters with which primitive peoples were unable to cope. In the long run we may infer that the good years outnumbered the bad ones; otherwise the human race would not have survived. But the net increase in numbers was slow, and the average rate of increase over long periods was low.

The turning point came apparently about the middle of the seventeenth century. By 1650, according to the most generally accepted estimate, the world total had reached about 545 millions, with a geographical distribution about as follows:

Asia	330 millions
Europe	100 millions
Africa	100 millions
Middle America	6 millions
South America	6 millions
Oceania	2 millions
North America	1 million

Since 1650 the world total is estimated to have increased about as follows:

1650	545 millions
1700	623 millions
1750	728 millions
1800	906 millions
1850	1,171 millions
1900	1,608 millions
1950	2,400 millions
1960	3,000 millions

More significant than the increase in total number is the accelerating rate of increase. For example, on the basis of the above estimates, world population increased nearly as much between 1950 and 1958 as in the sixteen centuries from 50 to 1650 A.D. In terms of percentages the *average decennial increase* by half-centuries is estimated as follows:

1650-1700	2.7%
1700-1750	3.2%
1750-1800	4.5%
1800-1850	5.3%
1850-1900	6.5%
1900-1950	8.3%

By the end of the eighteenth century it was apparent to at least one contemporary observer that European countries were filling up. This observer was a British economist named Malthus. Without benefit of census returns or vital statistics, Malthus formulated a hypothesis of population growth. The essence of this hypothesis is that population tends to increase faster than the means of subsistence and that this increase is checked by wars, diseases, and famines, to which Malthus subsequently added "moral restraint," meaning deferred marriage and sexual abstinence.

For a century and more, events seemed to refute Malthus' hypothesis. Between 1800 and 1900, the estimated population of the earth increased by some 80 percent. In the same period the population of Europe (which formed the basis of Malthus' hypothesis) more than doubled. Between 1800 and 1950, it is estimated, populations of European origin increased more than fourfold. What is more, most of these 800-odd millions of European stock were eating more and better food. Settlement of sparsely occupied lands in the Americas and elsewhere, and vastly improved tools and transport, created the illusion of endless vistas of increasing population and a rising standard of living. Only within the past twenty years or so have many people begun to doubt seriously whether this confidence is justified.

Since about 1945, doubt has mushroomed into alarm in many circles as demographers have repeatedly revised upwards their estimate of probable future increase of population. Tables 13.4, 13.5, and 13.6 indicate what has happened since 1900, and what may happen between now and the year 2000 if events confirm projections derived from "medium" (that is, fairly conservative) assumptions, by demographers working under the auspices of the United Nations.

What has happened to bring about this explosive population increase? In a word: falling death rates. Birth rates have increased in several countries recently, but such increases are insignificant in comparison with the

TABLE 13.4   POPULATION TRENDS; 1900-2000 (MILLIONS)

Dates	World	Asia (excl. USSR)	Europe (incl. USSR)	Africa	Anglo-America	Latin America	Oceania
1900	1,550	857	423	120	81	63	6
1925	1,907	1,020	505	147	126	99	10
1950	2,497	1,380	574	199	168	163	13
1975	3,828	2,210	751	303	240	303	21
2000	6,267	3,870	947	517	312	592	29

TABLE 13.5   ESTIMATED PERCENTAGE POPULATION INCREASE PER QUARTER-CENTURY 1900-2000

1900-1925	23	19	19	22	56	57	57
1925-1950	31	35	14	35	33	65	36
1950-1975	53	60	31	52	43	86	59
1975-2000	64	75	26	71	30	95	40

TABLE 13.6   PERCENTAGE OF TOTAL WORLD POPULATION IN EACH CONTINENT 1900-2000

Dates	Asia	Europe	Africa	North America	South America
1900	55.3	27.3	7.7	5.2	4.1
1925	53.5	26.5	7.7	6.6	5.2
1950	55.2	23.0	8.0	6.7	6.5
1975	57.2	19.6	7.9	6.3	7.9
2000	61.8	15.1	8.2	5.0	9.4

From Population Studies, No. 28 (1958): *The Future Growth of World Population.* Prepared in the Department of Economic and Social Affairs, Of the United Nations.

Figures for 1900, 1925, and 1950 are factual estimates; figures for 1975 and 2000 are based on United Nations projections, using the middle, or medium, set of assumptions regarding birth and death rates during the projection period.

spectacular reduction of mortality in recent years. With the development of insecticides (such as DDT) and drugs (sulfa, penicillin, and many others), it has become possible within the past twenty years or so to bring down high death rates in any country with dramatic suddenness and at remarkably low cost.

Post-1945 events in Japan and Ceylon illustrate how dramatic such results can be. In 1946 the death rate in Japan was between 17 and 18 per thousand, about the same as before the war. Public health measures, begun under the American occupation, reduced mortality by five points within three years. Today it stands at about 8 per thousand. In Ceylon, the death rate in 1946 was about 21 per thousand. Mainly as a result of wiping out malaria-bearing mosquitoes, mortality was reduced by 50 percent within ten years. Comparably spectacular reductions in mortality are taking place in many countries and are potentially achievable wherever annual mortality runs to 15 or more per thousand.

The phenomenon of falling death rates occurred *gradually* in the nineteenth and early twentieth centuries in most European countries and in non-European countries with populations of predominantly European origin. Today's *rapidly* falling death rates are mainly in underdeveloped countries in Asia, Africa, and Latin America. With very few exceptions these countries have very high birth rates, and some of them very large populations already. Five of the eight largest population aggregates in the world—China, India, Pakistan, Indonesia, and Brazil—fall into this category. Their present combined populations make up nearly half of the world total. This, in a word, is why total world population is growing so rapidly these days.

Where mortality has declined in the past, the birth rate has followed downwards too—but only after a time lag. This is what happened generally throughout Western Europe and the European-settled countries of North America and elsewhere, which have experienced the industrial revolution. The process can be visualized by a diagram which divides a population's development into three stages, as indicated in Figure 13.A. The first or pre-industrial-agrarian stage is characterized by a high, rather constant birth rate, and a slightly lower, somewhat fluctuating death rate. In the second or industrializing stage, the death rate shows less fluctuation and turns decisively downwards, the birth rate following downwards after a time lag. In the third or advanced industrialization stage, the death rate stabilizes at around 8 to 10 per thousand, while the birth rate fluctuates on a considerably higher plateau, generally somewhere between 15 and 25 per thousand. At every stage in the process, population tends to increase, most rapidly in the second stage, least rapidly in the first. And, be it remembered, the two largest populations in the world, China and India, are now entering the critical second stage, with many other large populations in the same or similar stage of development.

Falling death rates in the past have been the result of rising standards of living: more food, better food, more sanitary conditions, improved facilities for transporting and storing food, and the like. The spectacular reduction of mortality that is taking place in many of the underdeveloped

Figure 13-A   STAGES OF DEMOGRAPHIC DEVELOPMENT

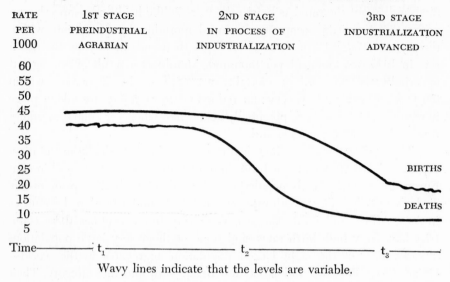

Wavy lines indicate that the levels are variable.

countries today is more specifically the result of rapid technological advances in pesticides, chemotherapy, and antibiotics. Introduction of these new weapons against insects, parasites, bacteria, and other causes of illness and premature death can bring down a high death rate with dramatic suddenness.

When birth rates decline, the means has everywhere been pretty much the same: increasingly widespread practice of some or all of the known methods of deliberately limiting the size of families. Such means are brought into use when changing values in a society make it seem desirable to enough people to have fewer children. Conversely, as in the United States since about 1940, greater affluence, fuller employment, and other shifts in values can (within physiological limits) reverse a trend towards smaller families.

The time lag between decline of mortality and the subsequent decline of fertility in a modernizing society may be a few years, several decades, or a century or more. The temporary, and often not-so-temporary, gap between a falling death rate and a continuing high birth rate determines the amount of natural increase per thousand in the country in question. The larger the population base and the wider the gap, the greater will be the annual increase. In the case of China, for example, a base estimated to exceed 600 millions, and a gap claimed to be as high as 20 points, yields a current annual increase exceeding 12 millions. In comparison, the annual increase in the United States is about 3 millions.

If the gap remains more or less constant through a considerable period, and if there is comparatively little emigration from the country, each annual increment enlarges the base from which future population is derived. Under such conditions total numbers show a tendency to rise at an accelerating rate, in a manner analogous to compound interest.

With mortality generally declining, especially in the populous underdeveloped countries, and with the birth rate nearly everywhere higher than the death rate by 5 to 30 points, the time required to double the population of particular countries and of the earth as a whole grows progressively shorter. In the early 1960's, natural increase in Taiwan, Malaya, Singapore, Ceylon, Mexico, and some other Latin American countries was exceeding 3 percent per year—a rate that would double a population every 23 years or less. If prevailing estimates for the world as a whole be accepted, the earth's total population approximately doubled between the first century A.D. and 1650. It approximately doubled again in the following 200 years. It more than doubled during the next 100 years (1850-1950). According to one conservative estimate, the rate of increase prevailing in 1950 would double the world total again in 64 years. At the average rate between 1950-1960, the doubling time would be cut to 40 years. By 1961, the doubling time was down to 35 years. And the end of the acceleration is not in sight!

This trend could be slowed or reversed by one or both of two kinds of change—(1) higher death rates, and/or (2) lower birth rates. In populations with a high birth rate, reduction of mortality has been greatest among infants and children. Hence the initial effect of a declining death rate is to increase the number of children and very young adults. But young adults eventually become elderly adults. To date there has been little progress in lengthening the total life span. Unless there are radical breakthroughs in the attack on diseases of middle and later life, there must in the long run be an upturn in mortality as a result of the general aging of the population as a whole.

In the shorter term, other positive forces may also increase mortality. A third world war fought with nuclear weapons might solve the whole problem. But if, as seems likely, the immediate human as well as property damage of such a war should fall most heavily on the more advanced industrial countries, the demographic effect on the populous and less developed countries—China, India, Indonesia, Pakistan, and Brazil, for example —might be relatively inconsequential. In any event, it seems improbable that this solution to the problem of population increase will appeal to very many people anywhere.

Another possibility, it would appear, is that food production may not keep pace with population growth. Note well that we do not say "cannot," for it is by no means certain that any such creeping disaster will occur. But it has to be said that in some of the most populous countries—India, for example—the ratio of available food calories to the number of mouths to be fed, a ratio already grossly inadequate by Western standards, has been either constant, or actually deteriorating in recent years. That is to say, increase in economic productivity may be either barely sufficient or even insufficient to sustain an already marginal level of subsistence. This state of affairs presents the possibility of more deaths resulting directly from famine or (more likely) indirectly from malnutrition. In other words, DDT and antibiotics may be keeping more infants and young people from dying of dysenteries, malaria, tuberculosis, and other infectious diseases in order that they may die from the pathological effects of malnutrition.

The other line of attack on population increase—reduction of birth rates—presents greater promise but also greater difficulties. Dr. Frank W. Notestein (president of the Population Council of America) explains as follows why it is universally easier to reduce death rates than birth rates:

> More than half of the world's people live in densely settled agrarian economies. They are disease-ridden, poverty-stricken, illiterate. Becoming aware of their unfortunate lot, they are beginning to aspire to better things. . . .
>
> Because information about the control of disease is easy to communicate, and because the motivation for its acceptance is already present, there is little difficulty in the early stages of modernization in bringing elementary knowledge of the control of disease to the level of social action. On the whole, death rates fall responsively to new knowledge. . . .
>
> But the case of the birth rate is far different. . . . The attitudes, loyalties, and beliefs governing marriage and reproductive behavior have grown up during thousands of years in which high birth rates were an essential for survival. These attitudes and beliefs, governing as they do the most intimate aspects of human behavior, are held with deep emotion and ramify throughout society. They govern the means by which the individual gains status among his fellows, are deeply involved in the economic institutions of agrarian societies, and they pervade the moral codes and religious teachings—ingeniously coercing the people to "be fruitful and multiply." The fact that such high levels of reproduction are no longer essential for survival, or indeed may threaten the very existence of societies under modern conditions, has little immediate result in social action. By now, beliefs, loyalties, and customary ways of living have become good and proper in their own right and not merely for the ends that they serve. In this situation we would not expect that a miracle contraceptive, even if it were available, would bring the sort of spectacular drop in birth rates that the miracle drugs have produced in the case of death rates.

The result is that death rates are declining rapidly wherever even rudimentary programs of public health have been undertaken, while birth rates tend, if anything, to rise somewhat—simply as a result of improved health. . . .

The epoch of rapid population growth will not go on indefinitely. If birth rates should remain high for two or three generations, the economic and political situation would probably deteriorate until death rates rose to check growth. If there were the resources needed to support a leisurely change, development might well parallel the course it took in the Western world. Here, the new ways of living, forced by an urban-industrial society, gradually corroded old loyalties and generated a new set of beliefs which emphasized the desirability of small families with better opportunities for health, education and advancement. With such beliefs the population, as a whole, turned slowly to the rational control of fertility, and birth rates began to fall.

But in today's densely settled agrarian populations, on the threshold of modernization, there are two drawbacks. On the one hand, the new efficiency with which mortality can be reduced would produce a much more rapid and sustained growth than that encountered in the Western world; and on the other hand, the base populations from which the transitions start are so large that it is difficult to see how they could stand the more than four-fold multiplication that the West experienced. . . .

Precisely because the matter is so clearly tied to moral and religious values, there is little the Westerner can do *directly* to create a better understanding of the implications of population trends in the under-developed countries. National, racial, and cultural sensitivities are far too high, and there has been too much talk of rising tides of color to permit the opinion of Westerners to be taken as disinterested. The most acceptable help the Westerner can give is technical, and in general the most acceptable auspices for such help is the United Nations which can give the sense of collaborative operation. . . . *

Population as a source of national policies

Demographic facts, trends, and projections become subjects of political action in the same way as any other phenomena: by being perceived and taken into account by the policy-makers. Connections between population data and national policies must be sought, therefore, in the attitudes of those who make policy decisions and in the discourse of those who contribute to the formation of such attitudes.

Political attitudes respecting population appear to have been derived mainly from reactions to (1) the size and composition of the state's population in comparison with other states; (2) trends in birth and death rates; (3) various aspects of emigration and immigration; (4) the presence of

* From "Knowledge, Action, People," by F. W. Notestein, in *Princeton Alumni Weekly,* September 25, 1959; reproduced by permission of Dr. F. W. Notestein.

more or less "unassimilated" ethnic or other minorities; (5) the density of settlement in relation to desired living standards; and (6) predictions as to future population trends and distributions.

Population policies may reflect a wide range of purposes: desire to increase the state's military manpower and to deny such increase to other states; desire to bring in cheap labor, and also to keep out cheap labor; desire to achieve greater national unity; and to raise living standards at home or abroad.

One set of population policies has dealt with migration. For various reasons, chiefly military it would appear, governments have repeatedly prohibited their citizens from deserting their country. Depending on conditions—economic, military, or other—governments have either encouraged or restricted immigration. Throughout the nineteenth century, for example, the United States encouraged or at least put few obstacles in the way of immigration—with certain notorious exceptions aimed mainly at immigrants of Asian origin. Today Canada, Australia, various South American republics, and certain other states encourage immigration—again with racial or other qualifications.

Restrictions may apply impartially to all applicants; more frequently restrictions are selective and discriminatory. Discrimination tends to be based, overtly or covertly, on ethnic or economic grounds. The United States maintains a quota system designed to curtail immigration from Asia, southern Europe, and other regions, and to encourage immigration from western and northern Europe. The Australian government overtly follows a policy designed to keep Australia white. Immigration restrictions everywhere tend to be flavored with the almost universal dislike of foreigners in general.

Another set of policies has dealt with ethnic minorities. In the extreme case, a government may undertake to liquidate such a minority by wholesale massacre, and persecution. For centuries Jewish minorities in European countries have been victims of such persecution. The Nazi attempt to wipe out the Jewish population of central Europe is the most notorious modern example. It is also a case of special interest in this context because the policy was explicitly based on a racist doctrine and was designed to "purify," and thereby to "strengthen" the Teutonic German "race." Scarcely less drastic have been large-scale exchanges of ethnic and religious minorities. The most recent of these was the largely unplanned exchange of several million people, involving incalculable hardship and misery, that followed the establishment of India and Pakistan as separate independent states.

A variant of the minorities problem is the case of the Arab refugees.

Several hundred thousand Arabs fled or were driven from Palestine when that country became the state of Israel. Many if not most of these exiles have remained unassimilated refugees, herded into virtual concentration camps in neighboring countries. The failure of the Arab states to cope with this problem has been widely attributed to the cold war which they have waged relentlessly against Israel.

Slogans of "overpopulation" and "population pressure" have been invoked repeatedly in the past to justify territorial conquest and other aggressive policies. This was one of the themes of German, Italian, and Japanese imperialism before World War II. The Nazi intellectual and propagandist General Karl Haushofer put this argument in classic form in defense of the German demand for more living space (*Lebensraum*):

> Every nation is primarily concerned with the task of maintaining itself in a hostile environment, and since its very existence depends on the possession of an adequate space, the preservation and protection of that space must determine all its policies. If the space is too small, it has to be expanded. . . . Two of the world's great nations (Germany and Japan) can prove irrefutably by the pressure of their population on their living space that these spaces, exploited to the highest degree, are unable to feed the masses crowded into them. . . .*

Since a large population, increasing more rapidly than the populations of rival states, has been traditionally considered to confer military advantages, policies of territorial expansion justified in terms of population pressure have normally been accompanied by other policies designed to encourage more rapid population increase. Thus, for example, Mussolini argued during the 1920's and 1930's, that Italy was overpopulated; that Italy needed colonies in which to settle its surplus population; that colonies "could be won only" by big armies; and that Italy needed more manpower to provide the armies to conquer the colonies to relieve population pressure!

The exclamation point, which concludes the sentence just above, is intended to emphasize a cynicism which many Americans felt regarding the population policies of Nazi Germany, Fascist Italy, and Imperialist Japan. A less cynical attitude was reflected in the prewar text, *The Great Powers in World Politics*, by F. H. Simonds and Brooks Emeny, who said in this book, written in the middle 1930's,

> Second among the basic factors of national policy is the economic, the primary elements of which, land and people, must be considered respectively from the point of view of production and numbers. . . .
> Population pressure, of course, is determined primarily neither by

* Quoted by Andreas Dorpalen, in *The World of General Haushofer*, pp. 38-39. Copyright 1942 by Andreas Dorpalen; published by Farrar & Rinehart; reproduced by permission.

the size nor by the density of population, but by the relation existing between these and national productivity. The situation will manifestly be affected also by the rate of the annual increase in numbers of people in relation to the expansion in production. The fact that Great Britain and Germany are far more densely populated than the United States or Russia is not, in itself, significant. But when . . . population has passed the saturation point, regard being had to the capacity of the territories of . . . [the country under consideration] to maintain the present standard of living, then the effect upon national policy of this condition of density must be immediate and far-reaching. For each country will, as at least one solution of the problem, seek lands abroad on which to establish its surplus population, and in order to retain that surplus as an element of national power it will also strive to include those lands within its own empire.

Exactly the same results will be discoverable, but in an even greater degree, when, the population of a state having actually reached or passed the point of saturation, every year sees a further increase due to a surplus of births over deaths. The rate of natural increase, too, will have a direct influence upon the energy with which the national policy pursues the primary objective of acquiring lands suitable for colonization. In this circumstance it is possible, for example, to discover an explanation for the familiar insistence on the part of various Italian and German statesmen upon a redivision of the earth's surface. . . .

The desire to acquire markets and to possess new lands rich in natural resources, to insure the prosperity of larger populations at home quite as much as to obtain territories abroad suitable for colonization, was one of the compelling motives of national policy in the case of certain of the Great Powers of Europe in the closing quarter of the nineteenth century, and in fact to the very eve of the [first] World War itself. And this motive has again been revealed in the case of Japan in Manchuria [occupied by Japanese military forces in 1931, and transformed into a satellite state], where the underlying cause is discoverable in a deliberate attempt to counteract the effect of population pressure. The population of Japan has already passed the point of saturation, while the rate of annual increase is still [middle 1930's] relatively very high indeed. Hence . . . Japan has undertaken to control territories whose markets and resources appear in her eyes sufficient to make it possible for her to maintain her great and growing population at home. . . .

Density and the rate of increase of the population, as these produce population pressures, must therefore profoundly affect the national policy of Great Powers. [These conditions] . . . will drive the nations subjected to such pressure to seek changes in the territorial status quo of the world and thus bring them into collision with the states whose interest lies in maintaining the status quo both of their own territories and of those of other states.*

* From pp. 61, 90-95 of *The Great Powers in World Politics*, rev. ed. Copyright 1939 by M. G. Simonds and B. Emeny; published by American Book Company, New York; reproduced by permission.

The concept of "saturation" in the above passage is metaphorical rather than analytically precise. But the underlying idea is clear enough. A sense of population pressure, however derived, may lead a government in either of two directions: to foster further population increase, or to take steps to check further increase. We have noted the pro-natalist policies of Germany, Italy, and Japan during the 1930's and the reasoning upon which they were founded. The opposite response is exemplified in the post-1945 policies of India and Japan. Any governmental attack on the birth rate presents formidable political difficulties, as shown earlier in this chapter. India and post-war Japan are among the very few states in the world today which are making a major effort to cope with population increase.

Red China, and Communist states generally, present an intermediate and oddly contradictory position on this issue. A Chinese official spokesman stated in 1956, that

> there are still some people in China who believe the preposterous "theory of overpopulation" of Malthus. The collapse of the so-called law of diminishing returns of the fertility of soil is . . . a proof of the nonsense of the Malthusian population theory. . . . There is no sign of overpopulation in China. The truth is that China's agricultural productive power was seriously damaged by the reactionary rule of foreign capitalists, feudal landlords, and the Kuomintang before China was liberated. . . . Of course we do not deny the importance of the food question to our work of Socialist construction. The way to solve this question is to change agriculture from the system of individual economy to the system of cooperation. . . . China can provide room for at least another 600 million people. . . .

Commenting on this and other Chinese Communist utterances, Dr. Irene Taeuber (of the Office of Population Research of Princeton University) observes:

> Marxian orthodoxy with its refusal to admit overpopulation, surplus population, the pressure of population on resources, or demographic deterrents to capital formation bars many of the arguments for birth control that have been prevalent in the West and in Japan.*

Marxian dogma, however, has not completely inhibited Chinese Communist leaders from sanctioning and even encouraging a variety of measures designed to curtail a rate of population increase that would frustrate all their efforts to bring China rapidly up the ladder of industrialization.

American responses to the accelerating rate of population growth in the underdeveloped countries have ranged all the way from proposals to do a great deal to opposition to doing anything. In a controversial book

* From "Population Policies in Communist China," in *Population Index*, October 1956. Reproduced by permission of the Office of Population Research, Princeton University.

entitled *Road to Survival*, William Vogt, an American conservationist, drew protests from many quarters in 1948 by proposing that

> any [economic] aid we give [to foreign countries] should be contingent on national programs leading toward population stabilization through *voluntary* action of the people. We should insist on freedom of contraception as we insist on freedom of the press; it is just as important. And as we pour in hundreds of millions of the American taxpayers' dollars we should make certain that substantial proportions make available educational and functional contraceptive material. Quite as important as the Four Freedoms, which we have made a shibboleth, is a Fifth Freedom—from excessive numbers of children. Far more than much of the world realizes, even the partial achievement of the first four is dependent upon this last. . . .*

In 1959 this issue suddenly blew up into a major political issue in the United States. A report prepared for the Senate Committee on Foreign Relations by a group of experts at the Stanford Research Institute emphasized that

> the world-wide consequences of the population problem are greatly complicated by the diverging cultural, ideological, and religious attitudes in many countries. In fact, as pointed out in [the March 1959] issue of the United Nations *Population Bulletin,* any multilateral approach to population problems has not been possible within the United Nations because of a "three-way split in thinking concerning policy formulation" between the Communist countries, the predominantly Roman Catholic countries, and those countries where Victorian taboos make the subject matter undesirable political or social publicity.†

The Stanford Report continued:

> World hunger and population control present major long-term international policy problems to the United States and to the other nations of the world.
> In a finite world some means of controlling population growth are inescapable. The traditional means have been disease, famine, and war. If other means are to be substituted, conscious national and international policies will be required.
> Population pressures can become significant causes of social unrest and war. In certain parts of the world overpopulation is already prevalent, and new approaches to the problem are urgently required. While some $30 million are spent each year on the worldwide attack

---

* From p. 211 of *Road to Survival.* Copyright 1948 by William Vogt; published by William Sloane Associates, New York; reproduced by permission of the author.

† From p. 39 of *Possible Non-military Scientific Developments and their Potential Impact on Foreign Policy Problems of the United States.* A report prepared for the Senate Committee on Foreign Relations, 86th Cong., 1st Sess., September 1959. Government Printing Office, Washington, D. C.

on mortality, only a few million dollars are allocated to programs which affect birth rates. A possible approach would be for the United States government to study (with the governments of other nations, through the United Nations or bilaterally) the possibility of providing research funds to certain foreign agencies and laboratories (for example, in Japan and in India) for the large-scale human testing of devices, which is so necessary but difficult to conduct without adequate cooperation and funds. In this way those governments and people that feel the problem to be acute would be enabled to speed up their quest for the physical, biological, and social knowledge needed to check population growth by means other than disease, famine, and war.

Almost simultaneously another committee appointed by the President to "study the United States Military Assistance Program" presented a similar recommendation. The report of this Committee, headed by William H. Draper, Jr., noted that population increase in the underdeveloped countries threatened to nullify the purposes of American economic and technical assistance. The committee therefore

> strongly support studies and appropriate research as a part of the [American] Mutual Security Program, within the United Nations and elsewhere, leading to the availability of relevant information in a form most useful to individual countries in the formulation of practical programs to meet the serious challenge posed by rapidly expanding populations.*

These mild recommendations—which amounted merely to putting the United States in a posture to help nations which desired to be helped —evoked strong protests, especially from the higher Roman Catholic clergy in the United States, and counterstatements from influential Protestant clergymen and others. Government spokesmen hastily disavowed any intention to do anything. But numerous observers predicted that this incident was a portent of things to come. The world-wide acceleration of population increase and the differential growth potentialities of Western and Afro-Asian populations might result in progressively less food available per capita in the most populous, fastest growing and least affluent nations. These conditions presented a problem that neither the United States nor any other nation could sweep under the rug indefinitely. Unchecked population increase, it was predicted, would produce ever heavier demands on food supplies and other raw materials; it might well lead to more bitter attacks on the restrictive immigration and commercial policies of the United States and other Western nations; it might even tip the scale in

---

* From p. 97 of *Composite Report of the President's Committee to Study the United States Military Assistance Program*, August 17, 1959, Washington, D. C.

favor of Communism in some of the more populous underdeveloped countries. Whatever the course of events, it appeared that the accelerating
increase of population, which policy-makers could ignore only at great peril,
had become and would remain for the rest of the twentieth century one
of the more dangerous and potentially explosive problems of international
politics.

Early in 1960, *The New York Times* posed this issue bluntly with reference to the Indian State of Kerala. Even though the Communist Party
had just suffered defeat in an election there, the *Times* found "little reason
for jubilance." Kerala is India's "most overpopulated" State, having "nearly
1,000 inhabitants to a square mile." Kerala also

has the highest literacy rate in India (50 percent). This means that a
high level of unemployment and poverty coincide with an educated
youth. Every time and everywhere one has found that combination
in the twentieth century, there has been a strong bias either to the
extreme right of fascism or the extreme left of communism.*

Finally, we should not close this section without noting the impact of
demographic projections *per se* on political attitudes and national policies.
Speaking generally, all policies are derived (1) from images of what the
future will be like, and (2) from belief that the future can be altered within
limits in accord with the policy-maker's desires. The mushroom growth of
demographic forecasting in recent years has brought more sharply into focus
both of these aspects of policy-making.

Models of future population trends are said to have entered into the
German decision to attack Russia in 1941. The argument ran somewhat as
follows: Russian population was expanding rapidly; the German birthrate
had dropped radically; within a few years Germany would have decidedly
fewer men of military age; never again would the balance of manpower
be as favorable to Germany as in the early 1940's.

Demographic projections have been widely reported and discussed in
newspapers and magazines, and over the air, since 1945. There is reason to
believe that these forecasts have influenced American thinking on most
of the issues reviewed in this section. It seems likewise probable that politicians, officials, editors and others in London, Paris, Moscow and elsewhere
are following the demographic projections of the United Nations and other
agencies just as closely as we are in the United States. And it may be safely
assumed that both here and abroad, these forecasts are influencing popu-

* From *The New York Times*, February 4, 1960. Copyright 1960 by the New
York Times Company; reproduced by permission.

lation policies, military planning, foreign aid programs, and other aspects of national policy.

Population as manpower

The term *manpower,* so familiar today, did not come into general popular use until World War II. Some dictionaries published as late as the 1930's do not contain the term at all. Others of that or earlier vintage define manpower as units of human energy applied to any kind of work, a concept analogous to horsepower.

Military departments made rough comparisons of populations, but almost exclusively from the standpoint of men available in the young-adult age group preferred for military service. Some old-line military professionals professed to believe that this was the most acceptable criterion of national power. Most people simply took it for granted that God is always, or nearly always, on the side of the biggest battalions. The concept of manpower as the entire human resources of a state, economic and intellectual as well as strictly military, scarcely existed before World War II.

During the 1930's at least two research institutes and numerous individual scholars were systematically investigating the patterns of population growth and distribution. But remarkably few government officials and teachers of international politics even knew about this pioneering research in demography. Suddenly, about 1943, the War Department, the Department of State, and numerous other government agencies discovered demography. Simultaneously the word spread through the colleges and universities that population trends had something to do with the policies and potentials of nations. Almost overnight, so to speak, demographic terms and models got into circulation and became the vogue in government and university circles. But when generals and professors moved in on demography, they continued to regard population mainly as manpower, and manpower mainly as people engaged directly (in the military services) or indirectly (in industry, agriculture, etc.) in activities which affected the military power of the state. To this day the concept of manpower, at least in American usage, continues to carry the same military overtones that we noted (in Chapter 4) with reference to the general political concept of power.

Two theses appear to underlie most discussions of population in books on international politics. One is that a state's total power and influence (what we prefer to call its political potential) vary in proportion to its ability to impose its demands on other nations, and in the final test to back up its demands with dominant military force. The second thesis is that relatively larger numbers—both in the military forces and on the labor front—are one of the necessary conditions of achieving a commanding power position in the Society of Nations.

That "God is always on the side of the biggest battalions" is not a new idea. Indeed, it is as old as politics. One can trace it through history from ancient times. Today it is rarely argued that there is a one-to-one correspondence between population size and a state's power and influence. A *ceteris paribus* is nearly always inserted. That is to say, other things being equal, superior numbers are likely to be decisive. The generally prevailing position can be summed up in a sentence: A large population does not guarantee that a state will be a Great Power, but no state can become a Great Power without a relatively large population. Lurking in most discussions is the assumption that population contributes to the so-called power stature of a state mainly by providing manpower for its armed forces and for the economic plant which keeps the armed forces supplied with food, transport, and munitions.

Experience in World War II, especially the campaigns on the Russian front, seemed to confirm this thesis. It was demonstrated that numbers still counted heavily upon the battlefields. It was further demonstrated that huge quantities of labor were required to keep large combat forces supplied with food, clothing, transport, munitions, and all the other paraphernalia of war. To the argument that quality counted more than ever against sheer mass, it was replied that technical skills are readily teachable and could be expected to spread rapidly in the future to even the more backward countries. If all this is so, then we do come back to the proposition that political potential in the Society of Nations tends to vary with population.

Much of the discussion of manpower, as of other foundations of international politics, rests upon the premises, more often implicit than explicit, that international politics consists mainly of wars and preparations for war, that the political relations of states are determined in the main by their respective military capacities, and that improving the state's military capabilities is the primary concern of soldiers and politicians alike.

Even if one accepts this view of international politics, it does not follow that comparative size and composition of national populations is as politically significant as formerly. Other things are never equal; and as repeatedly emphasized throughout this book, the technological variables become ever more important. In short, even within the narrow concept of military capability, national differences in population remain significant today only as between nations of roughly similar technological capacities.

This conclusion follows from the enormous increase in per capita ability to destroy, either by means of nuclear explosives or by means of chemical-biological weapons.

Military capacity, however, is not the only level on which population factors may affect national political potential. One of the major theses of this book is that the appalling increase in the destructiveness of military weapons has had the side effect of upgrading less violent and dangerous instruments of statecraft. If this thesis is accepted, then it may be necessary to take another look at the international implications of population distributions and trends.

Population is more than manpower

National political communities affect each other's behavior in various ways and through numerous channels. The display and use of military force are clearly part of the picture, but they are by no means the whole picture; and, contrary to superficial appearances, gross military manpower (even when supported by a high level of technology) may actually play a less determinative role today than in any recent historical period. If this is so, or even if the evidence is inconclusive, it will be fruitful to establish a more general concept to express both the military *and the nonmilitary* political significance of population trends and distributions.

For such a concept we turn to the collaborative work of John Q. Stewart (professor of astrophysics at Princeton University) and William Warntz (also of Princeton, as well as research associate of the American Geographical Society). Stewart and Warntz have developed the concept of *population potential*, derived from the concept of potential in physics. The reader will immediately recognize that our own concept of *political* potential, denoting the total effective power and influence of a state, is derived from the same source. But the Stewart-Warntz concept relates to a much wider range of human responses, Political responses fall within this wider range, but they are only one set among others.

An early statement of the concept of population potential is in a book written by Stewart in connection with World War II, from which the following passage is quoted:

> The . . . influences of 100,000 people are not confined to the immediate neighborhood of the city blocks where they live. In all sorts of ways, points at a distance are affected. Twenty miles away, highways, railways, suburban developments, gasoline stations, produce gardens, restaurants, tourist camps, and the like evidence the existence of the 100,000. In correspondingly less degree their influence can be traced still farther away by material evidence. . . .

Common sense indicates that the influence of many people is more than the influence of a few, and that their influence at a great distance is less than near at hand. The easiest mathematical embodiment of this common-sense expectation is: The influence is proportional to the number of people, divided by their distance away from the point where their influence is measured. . . .

In place of representing a person as a dot [upon a map showing distribution of population] . . . think of him as surrounded by a great sand pile. Suppose that the sand is piled, around a ring of a mile radius about the individual's residence. Around wider rings let the height decrease in proportion as the radius increases, so that at two miles the sand is 0.5 foot high, and around the 1,000-mile ring it is only 0.001 foot high. Then the height of the hypothetical sand pile anywhere in the country symbolizes that person's "influence" there, on the basis of the assumed inverse-distance rule.

Around the place of residence of each individual in the country suppose that there is a similarly constructed sand pile. Then suppose that all this sand is superposed. At any point the total height of the sand will be the sum of all the heights of the sand piles of the separate citizens at that point. Let a contour map be made of the elevations of the resultant terrain. . . .

Where the influence of people sums up to large values we have "highlands" and "peaks" of influence. Such points are nearer to more people, and all sorts of sociological activities are expected to be at a high level there. Where few people are near at hand, there are "lowlands" of influence—areas which appeal to hermits. . . .

Consider the summed-up value, at any point in the country, of the coefficient number of people divided by distance from the point (that is, the total height of sand there, in our illustration). Give to this sum the name *population potential*. It is measured in units of persons per mile. The name is suggested by a mathematical similarity with electrostatic potential, which equals electric charge divided by distance. In our analogy the number of people plays the role of a charge.*

Stewart and Warntz have tested the rule (that the influence of an aggregate of people is proportional to their number, divided by their distance away from the point where their influence is measured), and have found it to hold with remarkable regularity for a wide variety of activities. Their results tend to confirm conclusions reached by other methods, and to suggest new and previously unsuspected manifestations of influence.

Stewart recognizes (in a later article) that the potential (influential or attractive effect) of a population aggregate on another may derive

---

* From pp. 163-5 of *Coasts, Waves and Weather*. Copyright 1945 by Ginn & Company, Boston and New York; reproduced by permission.

from variables other than mere numbers of people. Different levels of technology and economic development, for example, may modify this influential effect.

> When different sorts of people are compared in the formula for potential, each population must be multiplied by an appropriate weighting factor. . . .

Stewart mentions three such factors, the principal one being what he calls "social mass," which he defines as "the tonnage of material moved or fabricated for social purposes" per capita in a unit of time. Social mass depends in part on the work energy available per capita, and in part on the

> amount of information at hand to be communicated from one person to another, or incorporated into the patterns of mechanical or intellectual tools.
>
> It seems likely [Stewart continues] that the per capita amount of the social mass indicates the size of the weighting factor just mentioned. This would mean that the formula for influence turns into just the actual physical formula for "gravitational potential"—which every physical mass sets up in a "field" surrounding it. Newton discovered the force of gravitation, varying as the inverse square of the distance, but it was not until a hundred years later that the French analyst, Lagrange, found the usefulness of the gravitational potential, which is likewise proportional to the mass which sets up the field of force, but falls off less rapidly with distance, as the inverse of the first power. It measures energy instead of force. . . .
>
> Because Asia exhibits much less social mass per capita, the people there not having raised themselves as yet above an ancient poverty, the fraction of total population potential over vast areas of the globe which is ascribable to the Atlantic powers is greater than that of the Asiatic peoples and Russia. The latter fraction predominates only close to the territory those nations actually inhabit. [One may query whether this conclusion holds as strongly today as when it was first published in 1954.]
>
> There is an extreme range in social masses per capita as estimated for various peoples and countries. Australian Bushmen have little more than the few score pounds of their body weights, while we in the United States share in a total which is estimated as perhaps some three thousand tons per person. In any culture, other than the most primitive, the social mass includes a relatively small fraction of highly fabricated stuff, which comprises the material treasure of the culture. There is a much bigger fraction of weight in the form of mere gravel and sand moved into foundations for roads and buildings, of water pumped in aqueducts, and above all of the fertile tilled soil which farmers must stir a few feet at different seasons of every year.
>
> When a primitive people advance to agriculture, after having been hunters and collectors, the increase in their social mass is by a con-

siderable factor, correlated with an advance in other aspects of their culture. . . .

Between primitive people and residents of the United States and Canada, the tonnage of the social mass per capita rises in a long sequence. . . . In the United States there are several acres of arable land per person, but in China there are several persons per acre. China away from the coast has few roads, and little pumping of water supply, and may average one hundred tons per capita of material moved or fabricated for social purposes.

Natural resources are not social mass, but are necessary for producing or maintaining it. Where resources are large, social mass is likely to be large also—although not necessarily large per capita, because population has grown excessively in nonindustrial countries like China and India. Great Britain in the heyday of its Empire, and now the United States, have drawn in special necessary components of their social mass from distant quarters. Such is the complexity of the material requirements of modern technological civilization that a flux of interchange of such components is needed to sustain the living of the people in advanced countries—and not just to provide luxuries for the well-to-do as the trade routes did in old times.

Correlated with the social mass per capital is the use of mechanical power. A humorously named but seriously intended unit of the latter has been put forward recently. . . . This is the "enerjoe," and is the amount of usefully applicable mechanical work produced each year by the average laboring man. This amount is estimated as, nearly enough, one hundred horsepower-hours, or seventy-five kilowatt-hours per year [for the world as a whole].

The Australian aborigines, who have no beasts of burden, can apply —after we allow for dilution from women and children—even less than one enerjoe per person. In Canada and the United States people luxuriate in several hundred enerjoes apiece.

Yet we should not be too scornful of the single enerjoe. Building of the New Jersey Turnpike required moving ten tons of earth per inhabitant of the Garden State. If New Jersey boasted a big enough mountain, and if the weak minds of its residents suggested nothing better to do with their strong backs, they could in a year carry that much material a mile up into the air. If the world's underprivileged peoples ever come to be freed from the continuous labor required for their mere survival, the power of their own muscles, if directed by enough brains, will accomplish not-too-slow increases in their social mass.

One aspect of brain-power already lends itself to objective estimation, namely, the amount of information people have at their command. . . . That is to say, what is comprised in the designs and shape of mechanical, thermal, electrical, chemical, and intellectual tools and equipment. . . .*

---

* From "Natural Law Factors in United States Foreign Policy," in *Social Science*, June 1954, pp. 127-34. Copyright by Social Science Publishing Co., Winfield, Kansas; reproduced by permission.

What light does all this cast on the widely held idea of international politics as a game in which military force is directly or indirectly the dominant variable, and in which military force tends, at least in the long run, to vary in proportion to population? Stewart and Warntz have demonstrated that numbers and distance are both significant dimensions of population potential (that is, the influence which aggregates of people exert on each other). Stewart has further shown how the concept of "social mass" can be utilized to provide a "weighting factor" to compensate for differences in the technological and economical levels of the interacting aggregates. Common sense tells us that demonstrated or reputed ability to coerce and destroy (an ability very definitely related to numbers plus social mass plus distance) contributes something to an explanation of the extent and distribution of a political community's "influence" beyond its own territorial borders. The proposition that ability to coerce diminishes with distance has long been recognized and accepted. That is to say, energy is expended in projecting instruments of coercion and destruction through space. And the corollary, that energy expenditure varies with distance, is probably as true with respect to airborne weapons systems as it ever was with respect to naval and overland operations. But is this all that the concept of population potential signifies for the study of international politics? Is population potential wholly or even predominantly a function of brute force, active or latent, in the relations of political communities?

This issue, first raised in Chapter 4 in our discussion of *political* potential, is perhaps the most fundamental question posed in this book. It is a question which every reader will have to answer for himself, in his own way. In answering it, however, it will perhaps be helpful to consider some further aspects and implications of the broader concept of *population* potential. Let us begin by comparing population potential within a single national community and in the Society of Nations as a whole.

Why, as Stewart and Warntz have shown to be the case, do great cities, New York in particular, exert a variety of influences (diminishing with distance) on smaller communities within the United States? Why does the metropolis influence buying habits, banking practices, and other economic activities? Why does the metropolis exert influence on style of dress, taste in entertainment, and other aspects of daily living? Why do these influences show a highly regular tendency to vary with the size of the metropolis and its distance from the point where influence is measured?

Clearly the impact of New York City on American society does not depend on the size or the weapons of the metropolitan police force. On the contrary, common sense suggests that this influence depends mainly on such considerations as, for example, economic benefit and convenience. The city is the locus of complex financial and other economic services. The city's population sets styles which outlanders emulate for reasons of social status, convenience, or other motives. There are also, no doubt, many subtle and not self-evident reasons for the pulls and pressures which the metropolis exerts on the behavior of other people at a distance.

When we shift from the domestic to the international scene, it is manifestly necessary to take into account important differences in the way power and influence are organized and exercised. In the absence of a system-wide international police force, the demonstrated or reputed coercive capabilities of the system's units (that is, nation-states) represent a source of "influence" which functions differently than in national political communities. Superior military force, nearby and available, unquestionably enhances Soviet *political* potential vis-à-vis the satellite communities of eastern Europe. The latent coercive ability of national military forces certainly contributes to an explanation of the influence of every Great Power and of many lesser Powers as well. And these forces do not always correlate positively with size of population.

But is that all? In the nineteenth century, for example, the British government wielded a world-wide influence which came rather commonly to be called the Pax Britannica. This Pax Britannica certainly was not unrelated to the past exploits and reputed capabilities of the Royal Navy. But British influence overseas rested also on Britain's capacity to consume huge quantities of imported food and raw materials, on British industry's ability to provide cheaper manufactures, and on London's superior ability to provide investment capital, banking and insurance services, and other necessities of economic development and commerce.

The abortive Suez War of 1956 supplies an impressive recent example. The Franco-British project to retake the Canal by force and to oust President Nasser in the process was abandoned in midstream, following imperative demands from the United States, the Soviet Union, the U.N. Assembly, and other sources. The Soviet demand was accompanied by a threat to bombard French and British cities with rocket missiles. But as subsequent revelations have rather convincingly demonstrated, it was not the threat of Soviet military attack which moved Sir Anthony Eden to quit Egypt, but financial pressure from the United States.

Russian influence, and increasingly Chinese influence too, in many of the underdeveloped countries of Asia, Africa, and Latin America cannot be satisfactorily explained wholly, or even primarily, in terms of the massive strength of the Soviet and Chinese armies or in terms of reputed Russian primacy in rocketry. It is widely recognized that Russian influence in these countries springs mainly from the impressive Russian example of a huge backward population raising themselves by disciplined effort to become within a single generation one of the leading industrial nations.

Why do foreign students flock to American, Soviet, British and other centers of higher learning? Is it because of the military prestige of these nations? Or is it solely because of their intellectual achievements and reputations? Or does sheer size, combined with impressive achievements of many kinds, constitute an important dimension of national political potential?

These examples and questions will suffice to emphasize once again the multiple sources of influence in international politics. Military force is manifestly one of these sources. In some situations and in some relationships, military force may be the predominant factor. But Stewart's concept of population potential and his suggestion for "weighting factors" to compensate for different levels of technological and economic development suggest the conclusion that influence is related to population, and that population is more than military manpower.

Population and political potential: the long view

If one accepts the thesis that, in the long run, the relative population size of political communities is a significant variable in international politics (whether for purely military or for a broader spectrum of reasons), then one must face up to another proposition: that we are destined to experience a profound redistribution of political potential (power plus influence) in the Society of Nations, with predominance passing ultimately out of the hands of the Western nations (Europe plus Anglo-American) and probably out of Soviet hands too.

This is not a new idea. It was repeatedly expressed as far back as the early years of this century. It was brightly reflected, for example, in the titles of two books, once widely read but now almost forgotten—*The Passing of the Great Race* by Madison Grant (published in 1916), and *The Rising Tide of Color* by Lothrop Stoddard (1920). These books swayed many readers in the 1920's; Stoddard's book went through six printings within ten months of publication. Here is the message that Stoddard drove home with fiery rhetoric:

> Before the war [World War I] I had hoped that the readjustments rendered inevitable by the renascence of the brown and yellow peoples of Asia would be gradual, and in the main a pacific, process, kept within evolutionary bounds by the white world's inherent strength and fundamental solidarity. The frightening weakening of the white world during the [first world] war, however, opened up revolutionary, even cataclysmic, possibilities.
>
> In saying this I do not refer solely to military "perils." The sub-

jugation of white lands by colored armies may, of course, occur, especially if the white world continues to rend itself with internecine wars. However, such colored triumphs of arms are less to be dreaded than more enduring conquests like migrations which would swamp whole populations and turn countries now white into colored man's lands irretrievably lost to the white world. Of course, these ominous possibilities existed even before 1914, but the war has rendered them much more probable.

In an introduction to *The Rising Tide of Color,* Madison Grant said:

If the predictions of Mr. Stoddard's book seem far-fetched, one has but to consider that four times since the fall of Rome, Asia has conquered to the very confines of Nordic Europe.*

The idea of a yellow peril receded and was largely forgotten during the 1930's. But the inner kernel of the idea has reappeared in our time in connection with the events of World War II, in the triumph of Communism in China, and, above all, in the radical change that is taking place in the geographical distribution of population.

In an article published during World War II, Dr. Dudley Kirk (then a research associate in the Office of Population Research at Princeton) argued the following thesis:

If the modernization of Asia follows the course that it took in Europe it will be accompanied by large population increase. Increase of population, and the very mass of the Asiatic population itself, could be ignored in the past as unimportant in the balance of world power. But with the prospect that the Asiatic masses will ultimately learn to forge the tools that will give them power, the differential population trends [that is, more rapid increase in Asia than in Europe and Anglo-America] may become of very great importance. Population increase has been part and parcel of the spread of European populations over much of the globe. In the past European populations have been growing very rapidly in a relatively slowly growing world. The present outlook is for relatively slowly growing populations among Western European peoples in a rapidly growing world. Western European peoples will almost certainly become a smaller part of the total population of the world. To the extent that numbers are a factor in the distribution of economic and political power, there will be some redistribution of power from old to new centers.

What all this means for the future is that we are not going to see again a world in which huge areas inhabited by non-European peoples may be casually regarded as the political playthings of Western European and American powers. The day is rapidly passing when a

handful of Europeans, equipped with superior weapons and a com-
placent and somehow contagious faith in white supremacy, can expect
indefinitely to dominate the half of the world that is occupied by the
colored peoples. . . .*

Since 1945, interest in population trends has focused increasingly on
the accelerating increase of non-European peoples. Much of the discussion
is decidedly alarmist; some of it is reminiscent of the yellow peril warnings
of half a century ago. A frequent and generally moderate contributor to
this discussion is the American demographer, Kingsley Davis (of the University of California). In an article in the Sunday *Magazine* of *The New
York Times,* Davis summarized, in 1959, the conservative United Nations
estimate which indicates a world population of nearly four billions by
1975, and over six billions by the year 2000, with most of this increase
coming from the underdeveloped poverty-ridden countries of Asia, Latin
America, and Africa. Davis continues as follows:

The central fact is that population growth will tend to be greatest
where people are poorest. In this desperate situation the less developed nations will hardly be squeamish about the means they adopt
to further their national goals. Caught in the predicament of having
an ever larger share of the world's people and an ever smaller share
of the world's resources, they will be driven to adopt revolutionary
policies. . . .

Not only is the glut of people in the poorer areas itself conducive
to communism, but in the past communism has made its gains by
conquest rather than by population growth. In 1920 it held less
than one-tenth of the world's people under its fist; today it holds
more than one-third. The lack of unity in the rest of the world
against communism suggests that Red expansion may continue. If this
happens, and if the conquests are made in the poorer countries,
superior population growth will join territorial expansion in increasing
communism's share of the world.

One of the questions of the future centers on China, whose sheer
size poses a major political problem for the world . . . At the moment
China is not quite in a position to challenge Russia or America. She
has more manpower than anything else; indeed, she has too many
people and too fast a rate of increase to realize her economic or
military potential. But she is apparently bent on converting her weakness into strength by radical economic methods. . . . By the tightest
of controls she is directing her masses into the most productive channels and trying to avoid the dissipation of scarce capital that would
result if the masses were allowed more than a subsistence
consumption. . . .

* From "Population Changes and the Postwar World," in *American Sociological
Review,* February 1944, pp. 28, 35. Copyright 1944 by American Sociological Society;
reproduced by permission of publisher and author.

If the venture succeeds, China, with a projected 1975 population almost double the expected figures for the United States and Russia combined, would be the strongest contender for world leadership. Such a mass, equipped with modern arms and disciplined by a dictatorship bent on conquest, could be stopped only by a united world outside. . . .*

Davis manifestly doubts that China is likely to attain any such political dominance, at least within any near future. In a discussion of "The Political Impact of New Population Trends," he notes how difficult it appears to be for people anywhere "to rise above the old elemental belief that numbers as such mean power, that multiplication and fruitfulness are identical." Davis continues:

> The rôle of population as a guarantee of national strength is waning while its rôle as an economic and military liability is increasing. The ever larger dependence of industry and warfare on scientific technology enhances the value of trained manpower; yet the unique rate of population growth now prevailing severely hinders an increase in the proportion of highly trained people, especially in the underdeveloped countries. It also hinders their employment when trained, because the capitalization of long-run industrial and developmental projects, which employ trained manpower is difficult in the face of rising consumption demands on the part of indigent but increasing millions.†

Dr. Notestein (already quoted) is another demographer who warns against selling the United States short because of differential population trends. In 1951, during the Korean War, he wrote as follows:

> The tense international situation and our experience in Korea seem to have fostered many misconceptions about the power position of the United States. We hear talk of our being hopelessly outnumbered in a struggle for survival with the rapidly increasing peoples of the Far East. This pessimistic account runs to the effect that our population is small, whereas the Far Eastern population is huge; that our numbers are not increasing, while unlimited reproduction is multiplying those in Asia; that our nation is no longer rich in young men, whereas China's population is heavily loaded with youths. From these notions many draw the inference that our power is waning while that of the Far East is rising rapidly. Actually there are several errors in this picture.
>
> [Noting that the United States has always constituted a very small part of the total world population, Notestein continues] But our

---

* From "The Other Scare: Too Many People," in *New York Times Magazine*, March 15, 1959. Copyright 1959 by the New York Times Company, New York; reproduced by permission of publisher and author.

† From "The Political Impact of New Population Trends," in *Foreign Affairs*, January 1958. Copyright 1958 by the Council on Foreign Relations, New York; reproduced by permission.

proportion . . . has been increasing, not falling . . . more rapidly than that of the world in general or of the Far East in particular . . .

Most important, we are much the healthiest and wealthiest of the world's great powers. Our influence and that of our friends in the Western world has never depended mainly on numbers; we always have been and shall remain, a rather small minority of the world's people. The prosperity, prestige and power of the United States have been based largely on the rich natural resources at our command, our excellent health, our high skills and our effective political and economic organization. Taken together, these spell large per capita production. . . . Whereas in Asia three or four out of every five workers work on the land and produce only a meager per capita supply of food and fiber, in the United States our people are fed and clothed better with only about one worker in every eight working on farms. This leaves the other seven of the eight available for nonagricultural pursuits. That circumstance, coupled with our high industrial efficiency, accounts for the fact that the United States, with only six percent of the world's population, produces almost one-half of the world's industrial goods.

The huge population of Asia . . . and its very high birth rates are not the threat to our leadership that they may seem. . . . For some decades to come the situation in Asia spells poverty and not power—except power to absorb suffering and punishment. . . .*

The issue is clear: how rapidly and how far, in the large and potentially much larger populations of the underdeveloped countries, China in particular, can the transformation of human mass into specialized skills and high per capita performance proceed? The superior political value of literate and trained people was recognized long before the atomic bombs exploded over Hiroshima and Nagasaki. Everything that has happened since 1945 confirms the premium on specialized knowledge and skills, manual as well as intellectual and managerial. Russian success seems to indicate that strong motivation coupled with despotic rule can modernize a backward, semiliterate population much more rapidly than we Westerners complacently imagined to be possible.

However, China is starting from a still lower standard of living, a less favorable ratio of natural resources to population, and a demographic situation in which future increase of population is more likely to obstruct rapid technological and economic development. What is true of China is also true, in greater or lesser degree, of India, Pakistan, Indonesia, Brazil, and many other underdeveloped countries. Whether the relatively greater handicaps in these countries can be surmounted as rapidly and as successfully as comparable but lesser ones have been in the Soviet Union remains at this time one of the "sixty-four dollar questions" of international politics.

* From "Population," by F. W. Notestein, in *Scientific American*, Sept. 1951, pp. 28-35. Copyright 1951 by Scientific American, Inc.; reproduced by permission.

CHAPTER FOURTEEN

★ ★ ★

National Economic Systems

OLITICAL POTENTIAL—the exercise of power and influence in international politics—is related at many points to a nation's economic system. As outlined in Chapter 4, goods and services—military equipment, industrial capital, foodstuffs and other consumers goods, transportation, financial services—are important instruments of statecraft. A government's ability to back up its demands on other nations, to attract and support allies, to bring pressure to bear on adversaries—these international operations involve the manipulation of goods and services of many kinds, quantities, and qualities. Even the intangible called national prestige may depend to some extent on the properties of a nation's economic system.

National policies and strategies too can have an important economic basis. Statesmen's ideas as to what undertakings are promising, even their concepts of national interest and purpose, may be associated with their judgments regarding the economic strengths and weaknesses of their own and other nations.

The magnitude and composition of a nation's economic output depend on a complex of variables: natural resources, labor, plant, technology, institutions and other social patterns. We have already dealt with some of these factors in preceding chapters, and we shall deal with others later on. The focus in the present chapter is on the integration of all the factors of production and distribution into a going concern called the *national economic system*.

In some countries the structure of political rule and the organization of production and distribution are merged into a single social system. This is one of the earmarks of totalitarianism. In other countries, the political government plays a much less active role in production and distribution. In every organized national community, one finds facilities (resources, labor, plant), some set of principles and working rules for integrating these into a going concern, and other rules governing allocation of what is produced. This is what we mean by an economic system. The bearings of national economic systems on the foreign policies and international capabilities of states is the main subject of this chapter.

The ingredients of a national economic system include natural resources (Chapter 12), manpower (Chapter 13), technology (Chapter 7). We have also examined aspects of the physical environment which indirectly affect economic operations: geographical configuration (Chapters 9-10) and climate (Chapter 11). All institutions function within a limiting matrix of social patterns—ideals, values, traditions, myths, desires, fears, expectations, discipline, morale and other patterns which differentiate the behavior of each national community from all others (Chapters 15 and 16).

Comparing economic systems

There is a tendency especially within the United States, to lump economic systems into two general categories: capitalist systems and socialist systems—with communism regarded as a particularly odious version of socialism. These terms—like democracy, dictatorship, and totalitarianism—are rarely defined precisely. They are heavily value-laden, and hence are likely to evoke more heat than light in discussion. There is also ground for doubt whether these ideological labels bear much relationship to the actual productive capacities of different systems. For these and other reasons, it is well to use sparingly such value-ridden labels as capitalism, socialism, and communism when comparing the functional properties of differently structured economic systems. And it is functional properties, after all, that count most heavily in analysis of the policies and capabilities of nations.

That is not to say that values and preferences here are negligible. On the contrary! Nor could one contend realistically that people's notions about their own and other systems are not profoundly colored by ideologies. Of course they are! Moreover, conflicting economic philosophies—especially those of private-enterprise capitalism and Marxian socialism—are instruments of international statecraft, weapons in the Cold War. Americans and West Europeans, on the one hand, and Russians and Chinese, on the other, are striving to export their economic principles along with material aid and technical assistance to the modernizing societies of Asia, Africa, and Latin America.

Each side in this struggle makes extravagant claims for its chosen economic principles. The Communists claim that modernization can be accomplished more quickly and efficiently under their kind of system.

They point to the spectacular transformation of the Soviet economy since 1930 and to China's giant steps towards modernization since 1949. Such claims are frustrating as well as alarming to spokesmen for the American system. They are alarming because there is accumulating evidence of the attractiveness of totalitarian socialism to the leaders of traditionalist societies bent on modernizing in a hurry. It is hard to convince such leaders that too much centralized planning and direction, heavily laced with coercion, may be wasteful of manpower and physical resources; that systems organized on these principles may, in the long run, prove less productive than systems characterized by more private initiative and greater pluralism; and that pluralistic systems are infinitely less destructive of human dignity and freedom.

Disputes over conflicting economic philosophies and the social values which they represent and tend to foster may serve various purposes. But disputation does not seem the best method for comparing the functional properties of different kinds of economic systems. For the student of international politics, concerned with the policies and potentials of nations, interest centers rather on such questions as: How do different forms of economic organization affect the quantity and quality of output? What are the magnitude and composition of various nations' economic plants, and of the output which comes from them? What portion of output is allocated to military and to other public purposes? What proportion is saved and invested in new capital designed to increase the system's future capacity? How much aid, and for what specific purposes, is being given to or received from other nations?

One encounters difficulties in answering these questions. Most of the hundred-odd nation-states do not keep even approximately complete or accurate economic records and national accounts. Some governments habitually conceal significant data or falsify statistics for publication. As noted earlier, comparisons of economic systems are often conducted in terms of ideology rather than statistics. It certainly cannot be stated dogmatically that the relative efficiency of economic systems is unrelated to their ideological premises. But this issue cannot be fruitfully discussed apart from underlying national purposes reflected in the allocation of what is produced. We shall return later to this problem of allocation, one of the most revealing categories of national economic data for the student of international politics.

Let us conclude this reconnaissance with brief notice of the ways in which physical conditions may affect both output and allocation regardless of ideological premises. In a large country a great deal of labor, fuel, and equipment have to be allocated to transportation. Compare, for example, the distances to be traversed within the Soviet Union, Brazil, Canada, the

United States, or China, on the one hand, and in Britain, Japan, West Germany, and France, on the other. Mineral resources may be more favorably distributed in some countries than in others. In some, heavy loads must be hauled over mountains; in others, across level plains. Countries vary widely with respect to climate, which in turn affects the allocation of resources for domestic heating and other purposes. Compare in this respect, for example, the heating requirements per capita in the savage winters of Canada and in the mild winters of Britain, countries in about the same latitude. Manifestly, energy expended to combat cold or heat or to reach inaccessible minerals or to traverse varying distances and terrain cannot be used for other purposes. Whatever their ideological premises, the performance of economic systems will always bear some relation to the magnitude of environmental limitations to be overcome, though such limitations tend to diminish with the advance of technology.

Comparing national outputs

Economists have devised various measuring devices for describing and comparing the outputs of national economies. None of these provides an ideal yardstick for the purposes of international political analysis. Probably the one most useful here is the concept of Gross National Product, GNP for short.

GNP is usually defined as the total value of a nation's annual output of goods and services. GNP is computed in money paid for goods and services, though this misses a good deal that may be quite important: for example, unpaid labor performed within family households. Such omissions generally exaggerate differences between poor and rich economies, especially between predominantly rural, family-oriented systems in which a great deal of unpaid work is done and highly industrialized systems in which unpaid labor forms a much smaller component. Thus, when one reads (in a recent Government report) that the per capita GNP of the United States in 1957 was $2,570, in comparison with $69 in India, it should be remembered that the disparity, though huge by any standard, is considerably less than the statistics indicate because of the much higher unpaid component in the Indian economy.

Another source of imprecision is the difficulty inherent in translating prices from one national currency to another. For example, the official ratio between the $ and the £ is 2.8 : 1. Yet it was estimated in 1961 that, in terms of goods and services, £1 would buy considerably more in Britain than $2.80 in the United States. Difficulty increases enormously when one undertakes to convert Soviet or Chinese prices, for example, into Western currencies. However, in spite of these various difficulties, one can gain general notions of the comparative magnitudes of different national outputs.

From the standpoint of international politics today, probably the most interesting and controversial comparisons are those between the American and Soviet systems. Khrushchev and other Russian leaders have repeatedly asserted what appear in the West to be exaggerated claims regarding the current productivity and growth rate of the Soviet economy. Various experts have attempted to evaluate these claims—and have reached conflicting conclusions.

One of numerous comparative analyses was carried out in 1959 by Gerhard Colm (of the National Planning Association) for the Congressional Joint Economic Committee. His conclusions are summarized in Table 14.1.

TABLE 14.1 COMPARISON OF UNITED STATES AND SOVIET GNP, 1950-70 [a]

	ACTUAL				PROJECTED		AVERAGE ANNUAL GROWTH RATE (PERCENT)	
	1950	1955	1957	1958	1965	1970	1950-57	1957-70
Soviet GNP (billions 1958 dollars)	117	158	179	190	286	378	6.3	6.0
U.S. GNP (billions 1958 dollars)	352	435	452	442	633	790	3.6	4.4
Ratio, USSR:USA (percent)	33	36	40	43	45	48		
Soviet population (millions)	182	198	204	207	233	250	1.6	1.5
U.S. population (millions)	152	165	171	174	196	214	1.7	1.6
Soviet GNP per capita (1958 dollars)	643	798	877	918	1,227	1,512	4.5	4.3
U.S. GNP per capita (1958 dollars)	2,316	2,636	2,643	2,540	3,230	3,692	1.9	2.6
Ratio, USSR:USA (percent)	28	30	33	36	38	41		

[a] Source: Gerhard Colm, "Evaluation of the Soviet Economic Threat," in *Comparisons of the United States and Soviet Economies*, Joint Economic Committee, 86 Cong., 1 Sess. Gov. Printing Office, 1959 p. 534.

In presenting his conclusions (summarized in Table 14.1), Colm reviewed the difficulties and warned that his analysis indicated no more than the comparative "general order of magnitude." But the "table serves to restore some perspective to United States–Soviet GNP comparisons." In particular, he contended,

> the figures lend scant support to Khrushchev's boast of Soviet equality in per capita production by 1970. Even equality in total production by 1970 would require, on the one hand, still higher rates of growth for the Soviet economy than those projected in the table, and, on the other, stagnation in the U.S. economy. Yet, little complacency is called for. For example, had our tabulation of recent growth rates taken 1955 and 1958 (instead of 1950 and 1957) as terminal years, the United States would show virtual stagnation in GNP. On the other hand, the rate for Soviet GNP would be high no matter what combination of years had been chosen. And the "erratic nature of capitalist growth," of course, comes in for its share of Communist propaganda.
>
> A similar point can be made for the years ahead. Projected data for U.S. GNP are based on reasonably full utilization of technology and manpower, and a pursuit of policies in support of economic growth. But suppose the actual rates of increase to 1970 averaged only about 3 percent. It would mean, should the Soviet Union be able to sustain its rate at about 6 percent, that annual increments to GNP would be as high in the U.S.S.R. by 1970 as in the United States. The impact of compound interest bears reckoning.

When one turns to Communist China, still greater difficulties and uncertainties are encountered. Experts voice skepticism as to whether China's rulers themselves have any precise and reliable information of the magnitude and productivity of the Chinese economy. Nevertheless, outsiders have attempted to reach some conclusions, however tentative, with regard to China's GNP. These outside estimates necessarily involve making many assumptions and working with extremely fragmentary, probably unreliable data. W. W. Hollister, who has analyzed all the data there are, concludes that in 1955 China's GNP was somewhere "between 6.8 and 22.5 per cent of that in the United States, and that per capita output in China was at least 1.8 percent and not more than 6.1 percent of that in the United States." [*]

Comparing economic allocations

One can examine a nation's GNP from two perspectives: from the perspective of production, or output; or from the perspective of consump-

[*] From p. 4 of *China's Gross National Product and Social Accounts, 1950-1957*, Free Press, Glencoe, Ill. Copyright 1958 by Massachusetts Institute of Technology; reproduced by permission.

tion, or allocation of output. From the second perspective, one investigates to see who gets how much of what is produced.

This second perspective is always important in the context of international politics. Some economic systems are oriented predominantly towards public welfare, towards attaining or maintaining a relatively high standard of living for the community as a whole. Other systems may be oriented towards increasing the system's productive capacity as rapidly as possible. Still others may be oriented towards maximizing the military or other capabilities of government. Differences in purpose will show up in the allocation of goods and services among different categories of consumers. Frequently, systems with lower total output may supply the nation's policy-makers with more abundant and effective instruments of statecraft than systems with higher productivity but different allocation. For example, the Soviet Union is believed to be spending about as much as the United States on military defense, though Soviet GNP is still much lower than American.

Economists classify allocation in various ways. The categories most generally in use (in non-Communist countries) are the following:

(1) Personal consumption
(2) Domestic investment
(3) Net foreign investment
(4) Government consumption

These categories are not quite parallel, and they overlap a little. Moreover, there are slight differences in terminology. Net foreign investment sometimes appears as foreign balance. Government consumption is also called government expenditure.

Let us begin with Category 4. Governments have always taken (by taxes or other means) some portion of the community's economic output. The percentage of GNP allocated to government has shown a nearly universal tendency to expand. In some countries the proportion of the government's take that goes for support of military forces, diplomatic missions, foreign-aid projects, and the like has risen more rapidly than governmental outlays for domestic civilian purposes. This is especially true of the larger nations with extensive foreign interests and projects to support.

It is always fruitful to compare the internal and external costs of government and to break down the external costs into military and non-military categories. Sometimes it is possible to do so. Unfortunately, however, many governments (especially Communist governments) do not make these details public. The analyst has to work out as best he can, often doing a lot of guessing in the process, what proportion of a nation's GNP is allocated to its military establishment, its foreign assistance projects, and other international operations.

The proportion flowing into the military establishment varies widely from country to country and from time to time within the same country. A report prepared for the Congressional Joint Economic Committee, for example, estimates that Soviet and American outlays for military purposes in 1955 represented 13 and 10.2 percent of GNP respectively. Another government estimate for the calendar year 1960 compared military expenditures of the European NATO members and the United States as follows:

United States	9.3% of GNP
United Kingdom	7.0% of GNP
France	6.8% of GNP
Turkey	5.6% of GNP
Greece	5.0% of GNP
Portugal	4.5% of GNP
West Germany	4.3% of GNP
Netherlands	4.1% of GNP
Italy	3.7% of GNP
Norway	3.3% of GNP
Belgium-Luxemburg	3.2% of GNP
Denmark	2.8% of GNP

Such statistics tell something about the level and intensity of a nation's military effort, but nothing, of course, about its quality and specific characteristics. For that information one must go to other sources. Nevertheless, information regarding the percentage of a nation's GNP allocated to military defense is nearly always a useful statistic, especially when examined in relation to other military variables.

A government's nonrepayable grants to other states—whether for specific military purposes, for civilian consumption, or for capital development—may or may not show up in GNP tables. As a rule such statistics, if obtainable at all, must be sought elsewhere. For example, a special report on this subject was prepared in 1959 for the Congressional Joint Economic Committee. This report compared economic and technical assistance given by the Communist Camp and by the United States to selected underdeveloped countries during the period 1954-1959. The results of this analysis are reproduced in Table 14.2.

Category 3 (foreign balance or net foreign investment) is derived from transfers of goods and services across a nation's customs frontier. This item is expressed as the difference between total exports and imports. Thus, if total exports of goods and services exceed imports by $1 billion,

TABLE 14.2 SINO-SOVIET AND UNITED STATES ECONOMIC
ASSISTANCE TO SELECTED UNDERDEVELOPED COUNTRIES,
1954-59, IN $ MILLION [a]

	SINO-SOVIET ECONOMIC ASSISTANCE	UNITED STATES ECONOMIC ASSISTANCE
Middle East and Africa (8 countries)	849	1,197
South and Southeast Asia (8 countries)	907	2,495
Europe (2 countries)	114	655
Latin America (2 countries)	106	962
Totals	1,975	5,309

[a] Source: H. A. Aubrey, "Sino-Soviet Economic Activities in Less Developed Countries," in *Comparisons of the United States and Soviet Economies.* Joint Economic Committee, 86th Cong., 1st Sess., Government Printing Office, 1959, p. 447.

the net foreign balance is $1 billion. If imports exceed exports by that amount, the net balance is –$1 billion. Since a positive balance indicates an increase of foreign indebtedness to the economy, and a negative balance an increase of indebtedness to foreigners, this category (as noted above) is frequently called net foreign investment. This item, like items in the other three categories, can be expressed either as a monetary value or as a percentage of GNP.

The foreign balance item, inspected for a period of several years or decades, provides information regarding the trend of the economy's international financial position: that is, whether it is gaining or losing monetary reserves. For example, the large and persistent deficit in the foreign trading balance of the United States during the 1950's shows up in this GNP category; likewise, the growing international financial strength of West Germany during the same period. Large monetary reserves and a trading balance which sustains them generally increase a government's ability to give economic assistance to allies or to underdeveloped countries or to exert financial pressures for political purposes.

Under certain conditions, paradoxically, the reverse may occur. The Nazi government in the 1930's, for example, purchased large quantities of primary materials on credit furnished by the weaker states of southeast Europe. In due course the latter acquired so large a financial stake in

Germany that they had no effective recourse but to go on supplying credit to the powerful and increasingly menacing debtor.

Category 3 by itself, reveals nothing with regard to the relative importance of exports and imports in a nation's economy. For this one goes to a table showing the economy's international accounts. Such a table is technically called a balance of payments. A balance-of-payments table shows the value of goods and services exported and imported, short- and long-term increases or decreases in the nation's foreign investments, and changes in its monetary reserves.

Taken together, balance-of-payments data and GNP data provide highly significant information regarding the degree to which a given economic system is linked with others. If the ratio of exports and imports to total GNP is high, it immediately suggests that the nation's economic life (in the words of a recent British report) "is linked with the outside world in many different ways," with the consequence, as a rule, that foreign economic events "can have a profound effect upon it." Such an economy is vulnerable to foreign commercial regulations (tariffs, import quotas, and others), to exchange fluctuations and controls, to foreign dumping (sales of goods at ruinous prices), to changes in world prices of commodities, especially differential changes in the prices of primary materials (foodstuffs and raw materials) and manufactures, and, in general, to all kinds of economic trends beyond the nation's own frontiers.

The degree of such a nation's political vulnerability to changes in economic conditions abroad was dramatically revealed by the British Government's ill-fated project to reoccupy the Suez Canal in 1956. Liquid fuels are an essential ingredient of modern economic life. Britain produces no oil in the home islands. Most of the oil consumed there comes from the region around the Persian Gulf. This oil is paid for in British currency (sterling) or in local Middle Eastern currencies with which the British government is adequately supplied. When (for reasons which we need not consider here) President Nasser of Egypt nationalized the Suez Canal (that is, dispossessed the canal's private owners) in the summer of 1956, leading Britons reacted violently. By this act, Nasser had put himself in a position to set the terms on which tankers could bring oil from the Persian Gulf to Britain. When British and French military forces invaded Egypt to take back the canal, Nasser blocked it by sinking ships in the channel. Immediately the British Government was compelled to buy oil elsewhere, chiefly in the Western Hemisphere. But American oil had to be paid for with dollars, and Britain was short of dollars in those days. Let John Appleby (writer for the *Daily Telegraph,* Conservative newspaper of London) describe the consequences:

1956 has shown us and the world the truth about Britain's economy. The beginning of the year found us still struggling with the balance of payments. . . . A balance of payments surplus of £144 millions in the first six months showed that some success had been achieved.

Seven days of not-immediately successful war and the blocking of the Canal showed the fundamental weakness of which we had been largely unaware. Petrol rationing and the increase in its price demonstrated how dependent the economy had become on Middle Eastern oil. The run on sterling, draining $100 millions in one month, showed how perilously low the reserves had been: an eighth vanished at a stroke. Without the International Monetary Fund loan there would have been disaster. . . .

A few weeks later, Appleby examined the Suez disaster in the context of British military expenditures. He wrote:

regardless of what kind of armaments the military planners wish to have, regardless of what kind of war they think we may have to fight, defense expenditure which produces tanks and airplanes at the expense of supplies of petrol is self-defeating. It buys the horse by selling the field.

This is precisely what has happened to us—though not quite so literally as the Suez war might suggest. Petrol stands for supplies of all kinds, or rather the means of buying them [from abroad]—that is the gold and dollar reserves. And the real question of the . . . [monetary] reserves is this:

1938................ £864 m. reserves.....could buy 12 months' imports;
1945................ £610 m. reserves.....could buy 6.5 months' imports;
1956 (June) £852 m. reserves.....could buy 2.5 months' imports.

The second column shows the real value of the reserves. Its meaning is that last summer (1956), even if we had imposed upon ourselves the restrictions of a siege economy, our power of independent action in self defense was only one-fifth of what it had been in 1938. . . .*

A high ratio of imports-exports to total output has not invariably rendered a nation so vulnerable to external events and pressures. Contrast the towering strength of Britain's position in the nineteenth century. For various reasons, the Industrial Revolution (characterized by the application of mechanical power to manufacturing and transportation) and the accumulation of capital for investment commenced earlier and proceeded more rapidly in Britain than in other countries during the first half of the nineteenth century. By mid-century British imports of food and raw materials and exports of manufactures and coal had come to constitute a considerable portion of the world's international commerce. London had become the business and financial center of an economic community which

* From London *Daily Telegraph*, Dec. 31, 1956, and Jan. 22, 1957. Copyright 1956 and 1957 by Daily Telegraph and Morning Post; reproduced by permission.

eventually embraced not only the British Empire but also many politically independent countries in several continents. British Governments appear to have made relatively little direct use of imports and exports and of financial services as a means of strengthening allies or bringing pressures to bear on foreign adversaries. But the strong commercial and financial links which tied so many foreign economies to Britain's, and widespread awareness abroad of dependence on the British market, seem to have been ever-present factors underneath (if not upon the surface of) the diplomatic tables across which statesmen conducted their negotiations.

But why was Britain's dependence on imports and exports a source of strength then and a source of weakness today? The answer, in large part, lies in a profound transformation of Britain's military position. Before the development of submarines, military planes, ballistic missiles, and nuclear warheads, the British Navy wielded a virtually world-wide command of the sea. In those days, the combined capabilities of fleets and finance enabled British statesmen to wield an influence abroad which approached, though it never quite attained, the dimensions of sovereignty and a world order. As long as Britain's military primacy lasted, the high ratio of foreign trade to total output was a source of strength. With the march of military technology, accompanied by profound changes in the political geography of the globe, Britain's economic interdependence with the outside world was gradually transformed from a position of strength to one of weakness and vulnerability.

The British example is most instructive. Relatively few economies approach self-sufficiency today. For various reasons the trend nearly everywhere is towards greater interdependence with the outside world. Even the United States, once more nearly self-sufficient than any other country, is becoming increasingly dependent on imported raw materials and exports of various kinds to pay for them. The same trend will overtake the Soviet Union in due course, and Communist China too. A nearly universal concomitant of economic growth—both in the new nations and in the older ones—is rapid increase of economic interdependence.

The political implication is clear. With increase of interdependence goes greater sensitivity to economic pressures and other changes in the international economic environment. Economic techniques of statecraft have gained in importance and seem likely to increase still more in the future. And few, if any, governments seem likely to be able to counter effectively by military threats or by war the pressures that can be exerted upon them through the manipulation of goods and services by other nations.

Returning to the subject of GNP allocations, Category 1 (personal consumption) always accounts for a large fraction of total output. This fraction covers food, clothing, housing, household equipment, transportation, recreation, and many other categories of personal expenditure. Personal consumption varies considerably from country to country. It rarely drops below 50 percent of GNP. It may reach as high as 80 percent.

There is some tendency for personal consumption to correlate with GNP per capita. This tendency is illustrated in Table 14.3 which compares per-capita GNP and percentage of GNP allocated to private consumption, during the calendar year 1960, in the European NATO countries and the United States.

TABLE 14.3   PER CAPITA GNP AND PERCENTAGE ALLOCATED TO PRIVATE CONSUMPTION IN NATO COUNTRIES, 1960 [a]

COUNTRY	GNP PER CAP.	RANK ORDER	PRIVATE CONSUMPTION AS % OF GNP	RANK ORDER
United States	$2,749	1	63	8
United Kingdom	1,317	2	65	7
Belgium-Luxemburg	1,293	3	69	4
Norway	1,244	4	58	12
Denmark	1,226	5	67	5
West Germany	1,218	6	58	11
France	1,196	7	60	9
Netherlands	957	8	56	13
Iceland	881	9	60	10
Italy	616	10	65	6
Greece	359	11	73	3
Portugal	243	12	77	2
Turkey	170	13	79	1

[a] Source: *Hearings on International Development and Security.* Senate Committee on Foreign Relations, May-June 1961. 87th Congress, 1st Sess., p. 713.

In Table 14.3 Greece, Portugal, and Turkey correlate as expected. Denmark and Belgium-Luxemburg show both a relatively high per capita GNP and a comparably high private consumption, a negative correlation explicable, at least in part, by the very low per capita allocations to military defense in those countries (see page 433 above). A high rate of domestic investment (savings) accounts, again at least in part, for the very low personal consumption with a relatively high per capita GNP in West Germany.

Broadly speaking, there is a tendency in all countries for personal consumption to absorb an increasing share of the nation's economic output. Since there are never enough goods and services to satisfy all demands, the demands of private consumers can have important implications for military defense, other government projects, and especially for economic growth.

Category 2 (domestic investment) provides important information regarding the trend of economic growth. In general, the higher the rate of investment, the higher the rate of increase in the nation's GNP. Investment provides new capital, of which new productive equipment is a very important component. New capital can be derived by cutting down military and other government expenditures, by denying goods to private consumers through high taxes, low wages, rationing, or other means, and also by loans or gifts from abroad.

With rare exceptions the most important source of new capital is savings—voluntary or involuntary—at the expense of personal consumption. Every economically advanced nation today industrialized largely on the more or less forced savings of its citizens. This holds for Britain, France, Germany, the United States, the Soviet Union, and all the rest.

Substantial inflows of goods and services from other economies, in the form either of private investments or government loans or gifts, can accelerate growth. In some instances, foreign infusions of new capital have provided a crucially important shot in the arm, so to speak. Such was the effect of the Canadian and United States loans to Britain in 1946, and the Marshall Plan grants for European economic recovery from World War II. Such has been the effect of foreign grants in accelerating somewhat the modernizing process in India and elsewhere. But the lesson of history is that new capital must come largely from savings within the community itself. Some new capital can often be derived by cutting down government expenditures for military or welfare purposes. But this source of capital is trivial in comparison with the consumer market, which accounts for a vastly larger share of the nation's GNP. In short, a nation obtains new capital mainly by denying goods and services to the very people who produce these—often making the deprivation more tolerable by assuring everybody that there will be more "pie in the sky by-and-by."

In many, if not most, of the underdeveloped countries of today, conditions are likely to get worse before they get better. This is because better times in the future can only be purchased by great austerity in the present. This is a cruel and unpalatable truth, wholly unacceptable to either the politicians or the masses in the poverty-ridden societies of Asia, Africa, and parts of Latin America. One by-product of the Cold War has been to encourage the leaders of those societies to believe that they can escape this historic price of modernization. This is so because Soviet and

American bidding for influence in the underdeveloped countries has taken the form, in part, of grants-in-aid, with implicit promises of more to come.

One way to visualize the relation of savings to consumption is to depict a nation's GNP by means of a pie chart. The pie is cut into wedges representing personal consumption, domestic investment, foreign balance, and government expenditures, military and nonmilitary. Figure 14.A illustrates this mode of graphic representation. It is a pie-chart indicating the allocations of GNP in the West German Republic in 1955.

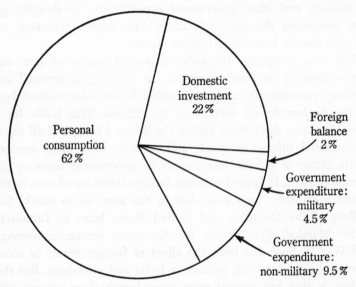

FIG. 14.A. ALLOCATION OF WEST GERMANY'S GROSS NATIONAL PRODUCT, 1955
Source: Central Intelligence Agency, *Comparison of the National Accounts of East and West Germany*. Washington, 1960.

The West German case is often cited as a model of rapid economic growth. Germany in 1945 was a heap of ruins, a landscape devastated beyond anything previously witnessed. Ten years later that part of the country which became the West German Republic was outproducing every economy of Western Europe. How was this "miracle" accomplished? Among other factors, the following were manifestly important: Beginning in the late 1940's, West Germany received massive infusions of new capital from abroad, chiefly from the United States. During most of the period, 1945-1955, German expenditures for military purposes were minimal, averaging for the decade probably no more than 2 percent of GNP. Finally, by means of various controls, personal consumption (especially for such expensive items as new houses, durable household equipment, motor cars, and the like) was held down to a level of spartan austerity.

Ability to curtail personal consumption drastically, we emphasize again, may spell the difference between a low or a high rate of economic growth and/or a low or a high level of military expenditure. Hitler told his fellow Germans in the 1930's that they would have to manage with less "butter" (personal consumption) in order to buy more "guns" (a bigger military establishment). The Soviet government has held down personal consumption for thirty years, in order to free goods and services for rapid economic growth *and* a huge military establishment. In China the Communist regime has squeezed large savings out of its half billion people already living on the margin of bare subsistence. In Britain, on the contrary, the Government has yielded to consumer demands at the price of a lower rate of economic growth and also some deterioration of the country's military defenses during recent years.

Americans are wont to imagine that we can have lots of butter and plenty of guns too. This notion, generally encouraged by American politicians throughout the 1950's, was tenable so long as our GNP was sufficiently larger than any of our rivals. As late as 1955, for example, American GNP was approximately ten times Britain's, and was estimated to be nearly three times the Soviet Union's.

There is, of course, a limit below which further savings for economic development or for military forces cannot be squeezed from personal consumption. Without sufficient food, clothing, and other necessaries of subsistence, people cannot subsist, and long before that point is reached malnutrition and disease will take a heavy toll of productive effort. But evidence on all sides indicates that most nations never approach the absolute limit of bare subsistence. Generally, the effective limit is set by social rather than physiological factors. Human tolerance for austerity varies widely. Tolerance may depend on past experience and expectations, on the degree of national unity and public sense of urgency or peril, on form of government and use of police power, and on other social conditions and circumstances. But whatever the operative factors, differences between nations in tolerance of austerity can have profound effects on the rate of economic growth and on the resources available for military or other governmental purposes. It is at this point that the structure of political authority may prove to be decisive. As already emphasized, there seems to be little doubt about the nearly universal demands of private consumers everywhere in our time, for more and better food, clothes, housing, welfare services, and other ingredients of higher living. Hence governmental policies designed to direct labor and resources into rapid economic growth (Category 2), or to foreign aid programs or larger military establishments (Category 4), require exercise of police power or other techniques of persuasion. The more rapid the economic growth desired, or the larger the foreign aid or military defense envisaged, the more the results are likely to depend on massive governmental interference in economic processes. In practice, the greater a government's autonomy from restrictive public demands and pressures, the greater is likely to be its capacity to manipulate the economic system for political purposes. Conversely, the greater the government's responsiveness to public demands and pressures, the more effective is likely to be public resistance to curtailing personal consumption in favor of faster economic growth or a larger government budget. The only apparent exception is the case of an economy in which the total GNP is expanding fast enough to absorb increases in Categories 2 and 4, without contraction of Category 1.

One of the most insistent and baffling questions confronting every nation today is: What are the relative capacities for rapid economic growth discernible in the Communist-bloc economies, on the one hand, and in the major Western economies, on the other. More specifically, what are likely to be the relative economic capabilities of the Soviet and American systems during the next decade or so? On this question depend many others, such as: What are likely to be the relative capabilities of East and West to extend the scientific and technological frontier, to explore outer space, to support advanced weapons systems, to maintain large conventional military establishments, to supply capital to underdeveloped countries, and to provide all the other paraphernalia of statecraft in the years to come?

Many experts have attempted to estimate the growth potentialities of the Soviet and American systems. All such estimates embody a good deal of speculation and guessing. One of the more lucid discussions was prepared by G. Warren Nutter (of the University of Virginia) for the Congressional Joint Economic Committee, in 1959. The following selection is from his report on—

Soviet and American capacities for future economic growth *

What can be said about Soviet industrial achievements? In the first place, they have been impressive. In terms of its ability to generate sheer growth in industrial output—the question of the

* From "The Structure and Growth of Soviet Industry in Comparison with the United States," in *Comparisons of the United States and Soviet Economies*, Joint Economic Committee, 86th Cong. 1st Sess., Government Printing Office, Washington, D. C., 1959.

structure of products and of how they are put to use being left aside —the Soviet system of centralized direction has proved itself to be more or less the peer of the market economy, as exemplified by the United States. This much seems beyond dispute even in the face of the questionable reliability of Soviet statistics.

Of course, the character of Soviet industrial growth has not been the same as in other Western economies. Enhancement of state power has been the primary objective, the consumer being treated essentially as a residual claimant. Investment goods and ordnance have been emphasized at the expense of consumer goods; and other important sectors of the economy—agriculture, construction, and consumer services—have been relatively neglected to help foster industrial expansion. At times, large groups of the population have been sacrificed or made to work in forced labor to promote internal economic policies. Leisure has shown little tendency to grow. This is all well known but deserves repetition to place Soviet industrial achievements in perspective. The character of industrial growth being so different from elsewhere in the West, there is a sense in which the two sets of achievements cannot be compared at all.

The last point should be underlined. The pattern of industrial growth observed in the Soviet Union would never be duplicated by a market economy. Sovereign consumers would not choose the paths of growth chosen by Soviet rulers. . . . If we bowed to the stern dictate of logic, we would be able to compare Soviet and American industrial growth only if both economies served either consumer welfare or state power. But that is ruled out by the very difference in social order whose influence on growth we wish to assess. This dilemma can be mastered only by admitting it—by avoiding the delusion that there is some single-dimensioned, neutral measure of growth, equally meaningful for all types of economies.

The question of economic waste is a related matter and equally difficult to treat. Growth is measured in terms of things "produced," not in terms of things usefully consumed. In a market economy, the two magnitudes are essentially similar but not at all identical: mistakes are made by both entrepreneurs and consumers, rendering some productive activity worthless. The same kinds of mistakes are made in the Soviet Union, probably on a larger scale since centralized planning is involved. In addition, because of the weak position of most buyers, substandard goods often pass for standard quality, goods are damaged and spoiled in transit beyond normal experience in a market economy, and so on. Although Soviet industry does not experience business cycles as they are known in market economies, it is periodically faced with the need to reallocate resources on a large scale, and the accompanying waste that would appear in the form of temporarily unemployed resources in a market economy will appear, at least in part, in the form of unwanted accumulation of inventories. It is difficult enough to say something sensible about which type of economy has the more waste inherent in it. It is even more difficult to say what all this has to do with the problems of measuring growth. Unless wastage has, in some meaningful sense, been growing at different rates in American and Soviet industry, there is nothing to be gained by taking account of this factor as far as comparing growth of industrial output is concerned.

These qualifications serve as warnings against careless comparisons of either the relative size or the relative growth of Soviet and American industry. In particular, broad aggregative measures of industrial output tell us nothing about capacities for specific tasks, such as waging war or promoting consumer welfare. While Soviet industrial output in 1955 may have been, in the aggregate, less than a quarter of the American level, production directly available for military purposes was undoubtedly a larger fraction, and production available for consumers a smaller one. Similarly, growth in the two areas has differed in the same way in the two countries.

It remains also to be noted that the quantitative achievements of Soviet industry have not been understated by Soviet authorities. The official Soviet index of industrial production embodies a myth that should be dispelled from the popular mind. On this matter, Western scholars speak as one, though they may disagree as to the gravity of the myth. The official Soviet index shows industrial output as multiplying 27 times between 1913 and 1955; the indexes presented here, based on official Soviet data on physical output and unit values and constructed according to conventional Western methods, show output as multiplying 5 or 6 times. If our indexes are taken as reasonably accurate, the official index contains a four- to five-fold exaggeration of growth over this period.

Somewhere in these generalizations and the mass of figures behind them lie lessons of history. The trick is to find them. The interesting lessons point to the future in one way or another, for the main purpose of history is as prolog: to help us to foresee what is likely to come if things continue developing as they have been; or, barring that—and it generally will be barred—at least to help us to understand why things are happening as they are. . . .

As one looks to the immediate future—the next five years, say—it seems reasonably certain that industrial growth will proceed more rapidly in the Soviet Union than in the United States, in the absence of radical institutional changes in either country. This conclusion does not seem to be in doubt even when due allowance is made for the shortcomings of Soviet data. It is more doubtful that industrial growth in the Soviet Union will be faster than in rapidly expanding Western economies, such as Western Germany, France, and Japan.

Over the more distant future—the next generation, say—the outlook is veiled, even if we might suppose there would be no important changes in the economic systems of either West or East, a most improbable assumption. There is no definitive evidence that the Soviet economic system has been able to generate more rapid industrial growth over the long run than the traditional private enterprise system of the West. Despite the fact that the Soviet Union was able to inherit an advanced Western technology at little cost, industrial growth over the entire Soviet period has been less rapid than in the United States over the 40 years bracketing the turn of the century, a period more or less comparable in other important respects. It has also been less rapid than growth in the last half century of the Tsarist era, a less comparable period.

On the other hand, if Soviet performance is best illustrated by achievements over the plan period [since 1928], the Soviet record of industrial growth appears more exceptional. Which period is more representative of longrun growth trends: 1913-55 or 1928-55? There are good arguments to be made for both, and inevitable differences of opinion will be finally resolved by the course of history alone. . . . In any case, the future will not be a simple reflection of the past.

Growth has not been a mechanical process in either the United States or the Soviet Union. The driving force within the American economy has been private initiative mobilized by the incentives inherent in a free society. The trend of the day is in the direction of choking off incentives. One foreboding economic symptom is the slackening speed at which resource productivity has been growing in American industry. Incentives are being strangled and nothing is being put in their place to drive the machinery of growth.

There is in fact only one thing to put in their place: the whiplash. The Soviet system has made clever use of both knout and honey, and the latter has been rapidly supplanting the former. If this evolution continues, the balance of economic growth will surely tip further in Russia's favor, since—fortunately, from the broader point of view— the West does not intend to take whip in hand.

Experts may differ as to the rates at which the Soviet and American economies are expanding. But there is substantial agreement as to the implications of different allocations of output. Who gets what, how much, and for what purposes, as already emphasized, affects not only a nation's rate of economic growth but also the policies and capabilities of its government. For a brutally frank statement of prevailing American attitudes towards the allocation problem, and for a provocative argument as to the international implications and probable consequences of these attitudes, we reproduce part of a report prepared in 1959 for the Congressional Joint Economic Committee by Walt W. Rostow (at that time professor of economics at the Massachusetts Institute of Technology, and more recently special adviser to the President of the United States).*

> Our dangers do not lie primarily in the size of the Soviet economy or its overall rate of growth. Our dangers lie in a particular allocation

* From W. W. Rostow, "Summary and Policy Conclusions," in *Comparisons of the United and Soviet Economies,* Joint Economic Committee, 86th Cong., 1st Sess., Government Printing Office, Washington, D. C., 1959, pp. 589 ff.

of Soviet resources; in particular Soviet policies; in the way we Americans now conceive of our problems on the world scene; and, consequently, in the way we allocate our resources, human and material. . . .

The root cause of our difficulty lies not in our income or our growth potential but in certain American habits of mind, carried over from earlier phases of our history, and in the workings of the political process, as they affect the allocation of resources. This .interplay of intellectual conception and conventional politics conspire to make it difficult for Americans to increase the scale of public outlays except at moments of acute crisis. Here lies a danger to the national interest as well as a threat to the quality of American society.

Specifically, the working concepts of modern economics encourage the view that public outlays should be accommodated to the natural ebb and flow of the private sector, perhaps to be expanded at times of recession but certainly to be restrained when the private sectors exhibit high momentum. This perspective, carried over inappropriately from the era of depression and peace to a time of chronic cold war and secular expansion, constitutes a powerful deterrent to outlays in the public sector, especially at a time of chronic prosperity; for it renders difficult a rational choice between marginal outlays in the public and private sectors, without extraordinary exertions of political leadership which have not been forthcoming [written in 1959]. Without such efforts, the calculation takes the form of a crude clash between the total claims of the state as against the individual family budget, in which the latter enjoys an evident prima facie advantage. The existing level of taxation acquires a degree of acceptability as citizens accommodate themselves to its burdens. . . . Lacking a concerted effort of political leadership to dramatize the meaning of marginal shifts from the private to the public sector, it is difficult to generate the political base for tax increases or other forms of restraint on private outlays; for example, checks on installment buying. This leads politicians, except under acute crisis circumstances, to work out the pattern of public outlays within ceilings determined by what the existing tax schedules—the arbitrary product of the last acute crisis—will yield at existing levels of income, if indeed it does not lead to inappropriate tax reductions.

It is essentially these two features of the American scene which have made our response to the changing directions of challenge in the cold war so sluggish on the one hand and convulsive on the other. Neither our concepts of political economy nor our notions of politics have made it possible to deal with threats to the national interest in a forehanded flexible way. We have shifted erratically from the moods and political economy of peace, to those of war. In the interval between, say, mid-1948 and the attack in Korea, for example, men in responsibility came to believe that a miiltary budget beyond $15 billion was a threat to the American way of life. After the convulsive reaction to the Korean war had lifted military outlays more than threefold, this new range became again accepted as a line to be defended with a quite irrational ideological fervor.

The heart of the Soviet challenge lies, then, in presenting us with a situation where our interests may be eroded away, without palpable crisis, to a point where a traditional convulsive American response will no longer suffice. Our conceptions and methods of allocation to the public sector are inappropriate to a world caught up in a technological arms race and a slow grinding struggle for power and ideological conception in the underdeveloped areas. It is not the Soviet growth rate we need fear but a mode of American allocation which tends to imprison us at a level of public outlays determined by our arbitrary response to the last major crisis. . . .

A high rate of growth in gross national product makes it possible to enlarge both private income per head and public outlays, at existing tax rates. . . . The higher the growth rate, the less the potential clash between the claims of the two sectors. But a high rate of growth, in itself, does not guarantee that the public sector will be adequately supplied with resources: for the American allocation system does not automatically maintain constant fixed percentage allocations to various purposes (assuming for a moment that such a system would yield increases adequate to the national interest at high rates of growth in GNP). Without purposeful efforts, the natural tendency of the American system is for public outlays to decline as a percentage of total resources, except at intervals of acknowledged crisis.

In fact, as a rough approximation, it is quite accurate to identify the Soviet advantage over the United States as consisting in a more stable percentage allocation to military and foreign policy sectors, starting from a high initial percentage base, at a time of rapid increase in Soviet GNP. Soviet allocations follow a regular path of expansion accommodated to the high rate of growth of GNP. American allocations follow a convulsive path, moving from plateau to (downward sloping) plateau, as crises dictate.

There is every reason for us to seek a higher American rate of growth, and notably an accelerated increase in productivity. Such an achievement could ease the problem of allocation and ease the problem of inflation. But it would not automatically remove from us the hard choices of allocation, nor would it remove the challenge to the democratic process represented by the need to control inflation without stagnation or damping the rate of growth. . . .

Between now and 1970 a decisive test will take place. . . . There is nothing in the structure or growth rates of the two economies that will automatically determine the outcome of this test. The answer lies in whether our political leadership mobilizes the evidently ample resources that lie to hand—resources of will, of skill, of talent, of commitment to the American heritage, as well as goods and services— to do the job.

Industrial mobilization in nuclear perspective

One aspect of the allocation problem which has received a great deal of attention in the past is capacity for industrial mobilization. This issue came to the forefront during World War I. It had been rather widely assumed before 1914 that no national economy could support modern war over a long period. No economy, it was contended, could provide ammunition as fast as the guns could shoot it away; and no economy could supply new equipment as fast as modern firepower could destroy it.

Events proved these forecasts to be much too conservative. It was discovered that a much higher proportion of an industrial nation's GNP could be allocated to military purposes; that many civilian plants could be converted to produce military goods; and that whole new industries could be built while the battles raged.

World War II confirmed and extended this experience. Between 1918 and 1939, advances in metallurgy and in other branches of technology tended to increase the adaptability of an industrial economy. Also during that period, improved machines considerably increased the efficiency of labor, thereby freeing more manpower for military service without disrupting the economic system on the home front.

All this experience focused attention as never before on the problems of industrial mobilization for total war. These problems continue to receive attention in military planning. But altered conditions raise serious doubts in many minds as to the continued relevance of past experience. These doubts spring from the thesis, widely accepted these days, that nuclear war would be furious, decisive, and short. In other words, there would be no time to convert and mobilize a national economy for a sustained total military effort.

This issue can be brought into sharper focus by considering the economic implications of several kinds of postulated military contingencies, as follows:

(1) Total war fought with all weapons available
(2) Total war fought with conventional weapons only
(3) Localized wars fought with "tactical" nuclear weapons
(4) Localized wars fought with conventional weapons only
(5) Continuing condition of cold war

Contingency 2 represents the type of war most comparable to World Wars I and II. In such a war, ability to convert an industrial economy through some period of time would still represent an important aspect of national capability. But what is the probability of a third world war of this kind? Opinions differ, but the weight of expert opinion appears to be that probability of such a war is remote—but perhaps not so remote as to justify responsible military planners from ignoring it altogether.

With respect to the other four contingencies, the main issue is not how massive a "convulsive effort" a nation could make after the fighting begins. The issue is rather what ratio of military outlay to total GNP a nation will support on a long-term continuing basis. And this is squarely the issue discussed by Professor Rostow in the statement quoted in the preceding section.

CHAPTER FIFTEEN

Change in the Underdeveloped Countries

THIS CHAPTER, as its title indicates, focuses on the social revolutions that are taking place in the underdeveloped countries. Nearly everywhere in Asia, in Africa, and in the less developed parts of Latin America ancient values and traditional ways of life are being uprooted as these peoples belatedly begin to experience the shocks and stresses of economic, psychological, and political modernization.

Modernization in the underdeveloped countries coincides with and is profoundly affected by changes simultaneously occurring in other sectors of human society: advances in science and technology (Chapter 7), increases in human mobility, in economic productivity, and in military destructiveness (Chapters 7, 8, 14), approaching scarcities of previously abundant natural resources (Chapter 12), progressive conquest of climatic obstacles (Chapter 11), explosive growth of population (Chapter 13), the bipolarization of great military power (Chapter 2), a military stalemate, however temporary, between the Soviet Union and the United States, which opens up unprecedented opportunities for weaker political communities to assert their demands and to play a role of some influence upon the international stage (Chapters 19, 22).

Under these conditions of rapid and differential change on so many human fronts, what is taking place in the underdeveloped countries acquires an international significance of the first magnitude. It is the thesis of many observers of the contemporary international scene that social, economic and political changes occurring nearly everywhere in Asia, Africa, and Latin America have a significant bearing (1) on the attitudes, demands, and strategies of the modernizing nations, (2) on the strategies of the greater Powers, (3) on the relative political potentials of all nations, and ultimately (4) on the structure and functioning of the international political system as a whole.

In the course of examining this thesis, one has to cope with such questions as: What is an underdeveloped country? What is meant by modernization? How does the modernizing process—a process often violent and disruptive—affect the behavior of the political communities in question? How do their spokesmen react to the Cold War and to other aspects of the East-West struggle? What are their capabilities to affect events beyond their own borders? What strategies do they employ? What roles are they playing in the United Nations and in other institutional settings? Conversely, how do the greater Powers—especially the Soviet Union, the United States, and the former colonial Powers of Western Europe— view the transformations taking place in the underdeveloped countries? How do political, economic, and other social changes in those countries affect the strategies and relations of the greater Powers with each other and with the modernizing nations themselves? In short, what is the cumulative impact of the underdeveloped nations on international politics?

The term *underdeveloped country* has become almost a cliché. Like most clichés it is used loosely and imprecisely. As late as twenty-five years ago the favored term was *backward* countries. Backwardness connoted inferiority: a people were backward presumably because they were stupid, or lazy, or improvident, or otherwise inferior. This connotation fitted another widely prevalent Western myth—the myth of white superiority. Associated with that myth was the correlative notion of a white man's burden—the self-appointed mission of the white race to rule and "civilize" the backward, inferior peoples of Africa, Asia, and the Pacific islands. So much has happened so swiftly in recent years that Europeans and Americans are prone to forget how prevalent these notions were right down to World War II.

The change of terminology—from backward to underdeveloped—seems to have been a response both to changing notions about race, and also to the exigencies of the Cold War. The notion of backwardness was deemed to play into the hands of Communist propagandists. Communist leaders boasted their rejection of racial prejudice or any idea of racial inequality. Moreover, the Soviet Union was not identified in Asia, Africa, or Latin America as a colonial Power. The Communist victory in China ended a long period of Western domination over that country. Chinese and Russian leaders could pose persuasively as champions of the new nations emerging from European colonial subjugation. Under these conditions, for Americans and Europeans to speak of Asians, Africans, and Latin

Americans as backward and (by implication) inferior was to play right into the hands of Communist propagandists.

As generally used today, the term *underdeveloped country* refers simply to any country in which most of the work is done by human and animal muscles, and in which most of the people suffer from severe chronic poverty. This definition will suffice, if one remembers that poverty may be the result not only of primitive and obsolete methods of producing goods and services but also of a scarcity of essential natural resources. In this latter respect, the underdeveloped countries vary enormously—all the way from the potentially rich resources endowment of China and the oil-rich lands of the Middle East to the sterile physical environment of Somalia in East Africa at the southern end of the Red Sea.

Underdeveloped countries generally exhibit social structures which have come to be called *traditional* or *traditionalistic,* in contrast to societies characterized as *modern.* Transition from the first to the second type involves progressive substitution of machines and inanimate forms of energy to do the work previously done by human and animal muscles or not done at all. This is, broadly speaking, the process called industrialization or the Industrial Revolution.

As already noted, most of the areas commonly designated as underdeveloped are located in Asia, the Pacific islands (generally included under the designation *Asia*), Africa, and in parts of Latin America. With few exceptions, those in Asia and Africa were until 1945 or later under the colonial rule, direct or indirect, of Britain, France, the Netherlands, Belgium, or Italy. In terms of socio-economic development, generally similar conditions prevail in most of the colonial areas still under French or British rule, as well as in the African dependencies of Portugal and Spain.

In the American hemisphere, political colonialism—with insignificant exceptions in the Caribbean region—has long since disappeared. But social and economic conditions in many Latin American countries are not very dissimilar to those in countries more recently subject to alien rule. In the eyes of many Latin Americans the Monroe Doctrine, American-owned plantations and other business enterprises, and recurrent American military interventions in the past have cast the United States in the image of a hated colonial sovereign. This image persists widely, in Latin America as in Asia and in Africa, despite progressive liquidation of the colonial empires and of paternalistic attitudes towards former colonial and semi-colonial peoples.

The majority of the population in most of the countries of Asia, Africa, and most parts of Latin America eke out a meager subsistence, in comparison to standards widely prevailing in Western Europe and North

America. In some of the underdeveloped countries there are modern mines and smelters, oil wells and refineries, plantations and other large-scale modern enterprises. These may provide handsome profits for a tiny fraction of the local population. But most of the profits from such undertakings have been traditionally siphoned away to absentee foreign stockholders. Local wages have generally been very low by European and American standards. Per capita income (always excluding the comparative affluence of a tiny elite) is almost nowhere adequate, often grossly inadequate, to provide even the bare essentials of decent subsistence.

Many observers have recorded the "sights and sounds and smells" * of the cities and countryside of Asian, African, and many Latin American countries: skinny, undernourished people; hungry, scabrous children; flies feeding on babies' eyes, vermin and dirt everywhere; evidence of chronic malaise on every hand; endemic tuberculosis, malaria, dysenteries, and parasites; periodic epidemics of plague, cholera, typhus, and other fast killers; people clothed in rags, men sleeping in the streets; high infant and childhood mortality but trending downward with the slightest improvements in medication and sanitation; high birth rates everywhere; population in many countries multiplying at the rate of compound interest; poor housing or none; primitive household equipment or none; illiteracy and ignorance, but a spreading awareness of the comparative affluence that is taken for granted nearly everywhere in Europe and North America.

There is evidence, moreover, that in several countries, including some of the most populous, the gap between the underprivileged nations and the affluent is widening. An Indian official asserted in 1960, for example, that India's per capita income, which by then had reached about $70, contrasted starkly with the $2700 per capita income prevailing on the average in the United States. During the previous ten years, he contended, India's per capita income had increased only as much as the American rose every fifteen days.

Until World War I, most of the peoples in most of Asia, Africa, and Latin America accepted their bleak existence as inevitable and inescapable. Very few had any image whatever of what it was like in the more favored countries of Europe and North America. The events of that war began to open their eyes to new possibilities. In 1937, Harold Butler (then director of the International Labor Organization) reported after visiting southern and eastern Asia:

> . . . a great change is stirring Eastern society to its depths. The consciousness of misery has been created by the growing realization that

* Title of an eloquent book of eye-witness impressions by the American journalist John Scott, of *Time* magazine.

it is not the inescapable lot of the poor and that chances of a better life now exist. The immemorial passivity and fatalism of the Orient are beginning to yield to the desire for higher standards and the determination to acquire them.*

World War II extended the opportunities for Asians, Africans, and Latin Americans too, to observe the comparative affluence of West Europeans and North Americans. Western military forces and civilian personnel —especially from the United States—were stationed by the thousands in the Southwest Pacific, southern Asia, China, the Near East, and elsewhere. Many Asians and Africans served alongside Europeans and North Americans in every theater of war. It was observed that even the lowliest privates in European and especially in American armies commanded amenities—food, clothing, transport, personal luxuries, etc.—available only to the privileged elites of Asia, Africa, and most parts of Latin America. There occurred—gradually at first, but with accelerating momentum—what has been called a "revolution of expectations." The age-old fatalistic assumption that no alternative to hardship and misery was possible began to give way to demands for some of the amenities which all but the poorest classes in the West have long taken for granted.

It is doubtless difficult for most Americans to conceive of their own culture as a force inspiring revolt and even fostering the spread of Communism. Yet a by-product, perhaps the most important by-product in the long run, of the display of American affluence abroad during and since World War II appears to have been precisely that. From this perspective Americans appear as the "terrible instigators of social change and revolution." †

World War II and its after-results also improved the opportunities of colonial populations to press their demands for a "new deal." The humiliating defeat inflicted in 1942 by the Japanese military forces on European and American defenders in the Far East shattered the myth of the white man's invincibility. Never again, despite the subsequent defeat of Japan, would it be possible for a few administrators and small well-armed police forces to hold in subjugation large colonial populations. After 1945 it became increasingly evident that the European colonial Powers lacked either the physical capability or the will that would be required to restore the colonial status quo in Asia and Africa.

The breakup of those empires has been more rapid and more complete than anyone anticipated in 1945. Between 1945 and 1960, the British Gov-

* From *Problems of Industry in the Far East*. Studies and Reports, Series B, No. 29, p. 65. International Labor Office, Geneva, 1938.
† From "World Revolution—American Plan," by I. C. Lundberg, in *Harper's Magazine*, December 1948.

ernment negotiated agreements for the orderly transfer of authority to most of its Asian and African colonies. It remained to be seen whether the British would be as successful in coping with the demands of the *African* populations of their remaining African dependencies, especially Kenya and the Rhodesia-Nyasaland Federation with their relatively larger permanent European minorities.

The French retreat from empire was less orderly and much more damaging to French prestige. Indochina (later to be partitioned into the independent states of North and South Vietnam, Laos, and Cambodia) was lost in 1954 after a humiliating military defeat inflicted with aid from nearby Communist China. French Guinea (in West Africa) was cast loose in 1958 to the accompaniment of mutual recriminations and the subsequent drift of Guinea into closer association with the Communist Camp. Morocco (in 1956) and Tunisia (in 1957) broke away from indirect French rule. Rather more successfully on the whole, the French have transformed their remaining colonies in western and central Africa into an association of independent states called the French Community. But in Algeria they met their nemesis. Legally Algeria was not a colony at all, but part of metropolitan France, with a large minority of permanent French residents. But in Asian and African eyes the Moslem majority in Algeria were colonial subjects. The bloody civil war which year after year pitted several hundred thousand French troops against the Algerian rebels not only eroded the prestige of France but did incalculable harm to the relations of France's allies (including the United States) with the Afro-Asian peoples.

World War II destroyed irretrievably the Dutch empire in the East Indies—since 1949, the independent Republic of Indonesia. Belgian rule in the Congo—frequently cited as a model of good colonial administration—came to a sudden disastrous end in 1960. Early in 1961 rumors of trouble began to trickle out of the tightly controlled African colonies of Portugal. Western imperialsm and colonialism, to paraphrase words previously quoted from *The New York Times,* are everywhere in precipitate retreat.

But this is not the whole story; indeed it is only background. One after another the emancipated colonies and protectorates have knocked at the door of the United Nations. With very few exceptions they have been promptly admitted, as indicated in Table 15.1. In consequence, the structure and functioning of the United Nations has been profoundly altered.

The United Nations Assembly provides for these new nations (and for the older underdeveloped nations too) a sounding board which carries their voices to the most remote corners of the earth. Before World War II, floods, famines, epidemics, or other spectacular catastrophes in Asia,

TABLE 15.1 NON-CHARTER MEMBERS OF THE UNITED NATIONS

DATE OF ADMISSION	NATION	DATE OF ADMISSION	NATION
1946	Afghanistan	1956	Sudan
	Iceland		Tunisia
	Sweden	1957	Ghana
	Thailand		Federation of Malaya
1947	Pakistan	1958	Guinea
	Yemen		United Arab Republic
1948	Burma	1960	Cameroun
1949	Israel		Central African Republic
1950	Indonesia		Chad
1955	Albania		Congo (Brazzaville)
	Austria		Congo (Leopoldville)
	Bulgaria		Cyprus
	Cambodia		Dahomey
	Ceylon		Gabon
	Finland		Ivory Coast
	Hungary		Madasgascar
	Ireland		Mali
	Italy		Niger
	Jordan		Nigeria
	Laos		Senegal
	Libya		Somalia
	Nepal		Togo
	Portugal		Upper Volta
	Rumania	1961	Mauretania
	Spain		Mongolia
1956	Japan		Sierra Leone
	Morocco		Tanganyika

Africa, or Latin America might reach the front pages of metropolitan newspapers. But chronic poverty in faraway colonies evoked slight interest, frequently none at all, in the foreign offices and parliaments of the Great Powers.

All this has changed. The needs and demands of the emerging nations have been caught up in the Cold War. East and West are competing for their support—with proffers of material aid and technical assistance, laced (especially on the Communist side) with plenty of propaganda.

The military stalemate at the level of nuclear armaments provides the emerging nations with unprecedented opportunities to bargain with both sides while rejecting dictation from either. Thus the political communities, which only yesterday were mere pawns in the calculations and strategies of the Great Powers, have become more significant and influential actors upon the international stage. But as already emphasized, most of these emerging communities are simultaneously undergoing social transformation, often accompanied by civil war or lesser violence. In order to appreciate their present and possible future impacts on international politics, it is necessary to visualize in greater detail the nature and magnitude of the modernizing processes which are disrupting traditional patterns of life in Asia, Africa, and Latin America. For this we shall depend heavily upon a report prepared for the Senate Committee on Foreign Relations by a group of scholars at the Center for International Studies of the Massachusetts Institute of Technology.

This MIT report describes the patterns of events which are reshaping the underdeveloped communities. Each one, the report emphasizes, has

> its own particular history, resource endowment, class structure, political system. . . . Yet generalization is essential if we wish to understand and to cope with the problems which the revolution of modernization presents. Events cannot be understood if they are taken one by one, at their face value alone; they must be regarded in the full context in which they occur and compared with similar events occurring elsewhere. . . .*

The MIT report is built around three models: (1) a model of the typical traditional-preindustrial-agrarian society; (2) a model of such a society undergoing modernization; and (3) a model of the typical modern-industrial-urban society. None of these models fits exactly the conditions prevailing in any particular country. But the fit may be close enough to evoke fruitful comparisons and insights and thereby enable one to gain an overview of what is taking place throughout much of Asia and Africa and in the less developed parts of Latin America.

The MIT report says very little about the modernization occurring in China and in other Communist-ruled countries. From the standpoint of international politics as a whole, this is a shortcoming which the authors of the report themselves appear tacitly to admit. At several points they iterate that leaders of modernizing movements in traditional societies have a choice between democratic and dictatorial methods. At the same time, one gains the impression from the report that Communist and other totalitarian recipes are regarded not only as degrading to human dignity but also likely to be less efficient and successful. Most Americans would plainly like to believe that this is so. Yet the evidence on this point is by no means conclusive. On the contrary, as we shall show later in the

---

* From p. 1 of "Economic, Social, and Political Change in the Underdeveloped Countries," a report prepared for and published pursuant to Sen. Res. 336, 85th Cong., and Sen. Res. 31, 86th Cong., March 1960; Government Printing Office, Washington, D. C.

chapter, there is some evidence that authoritarian recipes may prove more effective as a means of rapidly modernizing an economy, especially if (as in the case of China) the modernizing program envisages rapid development of heavy industry and military power.

The MIT report also takes the position that outsiders—in Washington, Moscow, or elsewhere—can exert considerable influence on the choices which African, Asian, and other modernizing communities may take. The international significance of such external influences may vary a good deal from country to country. In some instances they have virtually turned the underdeveloped country into a battlefield of the Cold War. We shall return to these and other international implications of the transformations in process in the Afro-Asian Realm and in parts of Latin America. But first we need a clearer image of the modernizing process itself. The MIT report opens with a description of conditions as they have widely existed before the process of modernization gets under way.

Traditional societies *

Traditional-preindustrial societies of the past—primitive tribes, classical empires, medieval Europe, etc.—and those surviving to the present in Africa, the Middle East, and elsewhere, all

> developed within a limited technology. They sometimes exhibited high proficiency in certain directions, but they were incapable of generating a regular flow of inventions and innovations and of moving into a sustained growth process. . . . The bulk of their economic activity was taken up with acquiring food. Typically some 75 percent of the working force was in agriculture.
>
> It followed from the preponderant role of agriculture that the ownership and control of land was a decisive factor in social prestige and, usually, in political influence. . . . In some, the bulk of the land was owned by a relatively small number of nobles and the king, and it was worked by peasants who stood in a feudal, hierarchical relationship to these owners. This condition still exists, for example, in parts of the Middle East. In other cases, landownership was quite widely spread, as . . . in China, resulting in an endless struggle by the peasants to acquire more land, to establish an economic position relatively independent of the luck of the harvests, and thus to rise in the society. In many of the African tribes, land was owned communally, with no concept of individual tenure and thus little incentive for systematic investment in improvements.
>
> In traditional societies, face-to-face relationships were extremely important, as were the ties to family and clan. Men tended to be

* From "Economic, Social and Political Change in the Underdeveloped Countries," previously cited, pp. 13-57.

bound together and be valued by one another in terms of such intimate connections rather than because of their ability to perform specifical functional tasks.

Although traditional societies sometimes provided a channel for able men of the lower economic classes to rise in power and prestige (often through the civil service and the military establishment), there was a tendency for people to assume that the status of their children and grandchildren would be similar to that of their parents and grandparents. A kind of longrun fatalism pervaded traditional societies despite the ebb and flow of family fortunes and despite the slow evolution of the society as a whole.

The cultural and religious life of traditional societies, and the values they elevated, varied widely. Generally, however, they formed a coherent pattern, giving men a reasonably orderly rationale for the relatively stable round of life they faced, at whatever level in the society they found themselves. They provided a set of relationships of men to one another and to the world about them which gave them a degree of security in facing their appointed destiny within the traditional structure.

Well before some traditional societies moved into an active phase of modernization, they began to develop men, institutions, and attitudes which helped prepare the way for modernization. The requirements of conducting war, for example, led the central government to enlarge the military caste, which in some cases proved to be more willing to face the consequences of modernization than the traditional landowners. . . . War also increased the requirements for credit and trade, tending to elevate somewhat the status of moneylenders and those who managed domestic and foreign commerce—men whose formal place in the traditional hierarchy was usually low. And in those traditional societies which assumed imperial responsibility, the management of empire itself strengthened the role and status of the civil servant and the technician.

Thus some traditional societies had undergone substantial changes toward modernization, out of their internal dynamics, before they were actually confronted with the shock of full scale intrusion by more advanced societies. In other cases, however, more advanced nations moved in on traditional societies which were extremely primitive, with virtually no elements initially prepared to deal with the values and methods of modern life.

Leaving aside the gradual evolutions of Great Britain, Western Europe, and the United States, what forces have in the past broken up traditional societies? The broad answer is that they have been disrupted, their cohesion and prestige shattered by contact with societies which were more advanced economically and as social and political units.

Disruptive impacts on traditional societies

The impact of more advanced societies took at least three distinguishable forms: physical intrusion, including in many instances colonial rule; economic example; and the communication of skills and ideas. . . . .

Intrusion. Intrusion by a more advanced society most commonly was accompanied by or followed by occupation and the setting up of colonial administrations, actions which had revolutionary effects on the traditional society in two ways.

First, in pursuit of its own interests (and often, too, in response to an impulse to spread the values and advantages of modern civilization) the colonial power executed specific policies which directly affected the economic, social, political, and cultural life of the traditional society. Ports, docks, roads, and, in some places, railroads were built. These were usually designed primarily for the economic or military advantage of the colonial power, but they had wider effects in creating national markets, commercializing agriculture, helping cities to grow, and bringing to backward areas contact with elements of modern life. Forms of central administration and centralized tax systems were usually set up, providing in some instances the initial framework for a modern government. Some colonials were drawn into the modern economic and administrative activities necessary to execute the purposes of the colonial power. Some modern goods and services were diffused, altering the conception of the level of life which men could regard as attainable. To at least a few colonials the opportunity for a Western education was opened. Perhaps most important the colonial power usually brought to the traditional society some version of the Western tradition of law, a version of those rules and procedures for the dispensation of justice which transcend and limit the powers of the individuals who exercise political authority.

In short, it was of the nature of the colonial experience that at every level of life it brought to the traditional society contact with some degree of modernization.

The character and extent of modernization varied with the concept of colonial rule that each power brought to its various colonies. In India, for example, the British made special efforts to train men for both the civil service and the army; the Moslems on the whole opted for military training, the Hindus for the civil service, reflecting in that choice underlying differences in the culture of the two groups in the Indian peninsula. In Burma, on the other hand, the British did relatively little to train either soldiers or civil servants. The French, in their empire, made great efforts to bring a thin top layer of the indigenous leaders as fully as possible into French cultural, intellectual, and political life. The Belgians in the Congo concentrated, for economic reasons, on literacy and vocational training for the lower levels of the labor force and did nothing to prepare an elite for leadership. The Dutch in Indonesia and the Portuguese in East Africa by and large adopted policies designed to limit the extent and pace of modernization.

But however colonial policy might vary, colonialism nevertheless had one first and universal direct effect. It set the static traditional societies in motion, so to speak, moving them into transitional status. . . .

As time passed, and an increasing number of men in the colonial society became acquainted with the methods and ideas of the West, they reacted against the human and collective humiliation that inevitably accompanied colonial rule, and they sought independence. Many, it is true, were drawn imitatively toward the manners and mores of the colonial power (for example, colonials who were educated abroad or who had positions of privilege within colonial rule), and others found their positions strengthened by colonial rule (for example, African tribal chiefs and the Indian princes). But in the end a reactive nationalism emerged, spreading through elements in the colonial elite, catching up the urban populations, and reaching back even into the countryside. Of all the forces which have helped bring about the modernization of traditional societies, this reactive nationalism has probably been the most powerful.

Colonial rule was not the only form of intrusion that helped unhinge traditional societies. The defeat of the traditional society in war against a more advanced power often played an important role. This was so, for example, in Germany after the Napoleonic occupation; in Russia after the Crimean War; in Japan after its imposed opening to trade by the West in the shadow of modern naval cannon; in Turkey after the First World War; in China after the defeats by the British in the 1840's and by the Japanese in the 1890's. The demonstration that the traditional form of organization was incapable of maintaining the physical integrity of the nation tended to lower the prestige of the traditional rulers, their values, and their institutions. And it tended to strengthen the hand of those groups in the traditional society— soldiers, intellectuals, men of commerce, civil servants, lesser nobility —who for various, often differing reasons were already interested in moving toward some form of modernization.

Economic Example. Quite aside from the multiple impacts of colonialism and superior military power, contact with more advanced societies sometimes led to a spreading awareness of what modernization could do in terms of human welfare. Such contact demonstrated, for example, that public health could be improved; that food output could be increased; and that cheaper textiles could be provided to the peasant and the worker. In the twentieth century the intimacy of communications, including the fact that modern armies have been based in many of these transitional societies, has peculiarly heightened an awareness of the gap between modern and traditional standards of life. Any awareness of this kind, creating as it does an increasing pressure for a rapid rise in popular welfare, undermines the traditional society.

The contrast between the traditional and the modern economy was not solely, or perhaps even most significantly, a contrast in standards of living and levels of consumption. The employment opportunities and the modes of life available in the new cities gave people new images of the roles they could play in society. . . . Modern economic activity, whether colonial or indigenous, has taken people out of their conventional roles and put them in new situations both of work and of life which have greatly broadened their perception of the range of alternative activities in which they might engage. This increased mobility and widened perception of alternatives has markedly weakened the most stabilizing elements in traditional society.

Communication of Skills and Ideas. Contact with the more modern societies has brought about, for some, a training in new skills. Those trained usually formed part of the transitional society's elite, with some access to instruments of political power. But until the local society was transformed in quite fundamental ways, these men found it difficult to exercise effectively their skills as, for example, doctors, engineers, economists, and soldiers. . . . A part of the force which has tended to disrupt the transitional societies has been the frustration of those with modern training who found that they lacked adequate scope for the exercise of their newly developed talents and opportunities to play newly perceived roles.

Moreover, the more advanced societies of the West communicated not only skills but also ideas. Among these ideas were the quite revolutionary Western notions that all men stood equal before the law, that they should have equal opportunity to develop their talents, and that policies should be determined and political leadership selected on a one-man, one-vote basis. *It is easy to forget how powerful and disruptive these long-accepted foundations of modern Western life still are in traditional or only partly modernized societies.* [Italics added.]

In addition to these democratic ideas, many of the new intellectuals from the transitional societies have been exposed during their formative years in the West to Marxist and other socialist notions. These have often had a great appeal because they purport to explain the forces at work in transitional societies. The theory of the class struggle, Lenin's theory of imperialism, and Communist doctrine on the organization of revolutionary movements have gained considerable currency and influence, and have helped generate dissatisfaction with traditional attitudes and values.

Although the traditional societies or those early in the transitional process were not technically prepared to install modern democratic processes, the disruption of the traditional society and the infusion of these new ideas sometimes led to strong movements toward increased popular participation in the political process. Among the peasants the spread of these ideas encouraged powerful movements for land reform, in which the peasant's ageless hunger for his own plot of land at last expressed itself. The modernization of Mexico,

for example, took its start with just such a primitive agrarian drive. . . .
From the French Revolution, through the Taiping Rebellion in China
and the Russian Revolution, down to the pressure for land reform
in contemporary Egypt and Iran, the spread of egalitarian ideas has
played a catalytic role of some importance. The impact of new
ideas, moreover, is vastly heightened today by the existence of the
mass media and the instrumentalities of mass organization. Revolutionary ideas can be diffused with extraordinary rapidity, reaching
groups throughout the society. . . .

Some requisites of modernization

Historical experience indicates that modernization does not require
the destruction of a traditional culture. On the contrary, the old
culture almost always leaves permanent and significant marks of
continuity on the fully modernized society. Nevertheless, the traditional
culture must undergo drastic alteration.

Psychologically, men must transform the old culture in ways which
make it compatible with modern activities and institutions. The face-
to-face relations and warm, powerful family ties of a traditional
society must give way to more impersonal systems of evaluation in
which men are judged by the way they perform specialized functions
in the society. In their links to the nation, to their professional colleagues, to their political parties, men must find a partial alternative
for the powerful, long-tested ties and symbols of the traditional life
centered on family, clan, and region. And new hierarchies, based on
function, must come to replace those rooted in land ownership and
tradition.

Politically, the people must come to accept new forms for the
organization of political power. The balance of social and political
power must shift from the village to the city, from the tasks and
virtues of agricultural life to those of commerce, industry, and modern
administration. And they must come to accept new forms for the
transfer of political power. They must begin—in a process with many
difficult stages—to judge politics and politicians in terms of policies
rather than merely inherited status or even personality; and they
must develop forms for transferring power by registering consent.

Economically, they must achieve a situation where the society
regularly saves and productively invests a sufficient volume of its
resources, and incorporates regularly new ways of doing things, so
that the growth of the national economy outpaces population increase
and continuing economic growth becomes the normal condition of
the society—a process which, in itself, involves every dimension of
the society and many sectors of the economy.

To achieve these conditions requires the passage of time: time for
the social structures to be altered; time for new political attitudes
and institutions to be created and consolidated; time for the creation
of the skills and habits and institutions on which capital formation

depends. Above all, time must pass for new generations to succeed one another, each finding the environment, techniques, and goals of modernization a bit more familiar and acceptable. . . .

The interplay between the new hopes and the old ways may yield bloody civil conflicts susceptible to exploitation by external powers; there may be efforts to channel the modernization process into disruptive foreign adventures; there may be a seizure of the society's politics by dictators who exploit popular frustrations and the inevitable looseness of the transitional period for their own or for other purposes.

Some obstacles to be overcome

There are four principal areas in which elements of resistance must be overcome if the modernization of a traditional society is to be carried through successfully: human attitudes, politics, economics, social structures. . . .

The Pull of the Past. The modernization process requires that fundamental human attitudes must change in such ways as to make the efficient operation of a modern society not only possible but also psychologically congenial; and it may well be that, especially in the first generations of the transition, the commitment of men to the goal of modernization is more apparent than real.

Modern man is psychically mobile, his distinctive characteristic being the ability to imagine himself performing all manner of tasks and roles. Traditional man was so inhibited by the barriers of status that he believed it wrong and dangerous even to move mentally out of his place in the social order. Transitional man can imagine and hope for change, but in his mind the exciting possibilities are balanced against old doubts and fears. And so the literate elite in transitional societies may be quite skilled, and they may talk the language of modernization with fluency and apparent conviction; but latent within them is a conflict between the modes of action and the values which modernization requires and the ingrained habits and attachments of the traditional society.

The latent power of the traditional society—the pull of the past— may take many forms. It may lead men to gather around them in authority not the most competent colleagues but those most personally loyal, often members of their family. It may lead them to talk of industrialization while in fact harboring a profound reluctance to engage in the homely pursuits of production and the marketplace, which in the traditional society enjoyed so low a status. It may prevent them—as in contemporary India—from treating cattle as part of the material stock of agricultural capital rather than as religious symbols. It may lead them to continue to concentrate their attention and emotions on old familiar issues and feuds—sanctioned by the values and history of the traditional society—rather than on the new issues and tasks of modernization.

No matter how passionately in one part of their beings men may want to see their societies and themselves enjoy the benefits of modernization, they are capable of sustaining, in tolerable psychological order, only a limited rate of change; and they may cling more tenaciously than they are aware to elements in the traditional society as a source of security in a transitional situation where much else about them is changing.

Political Resistance. A society freed from colonial rule or one which has overthrown a traditional government must create a minimally effective national government, a task which confronts such problems as these:

It is almost certain to be the case that much energy and attention must be devoted to overcoming the residues of political authority derived from the traditional society which cannot be harnessed constructively to the purposes of the new modern national government. Examples are the sects of southern Vietnam, the Indian princes, the Chinese war lords, the African tribal leaders.

The new government must also develop a minimum core of technically trained men capable of maintaining order, collecting taxes, and organizing the staff work required for the inevitably substantial role of the government in the economy and in the educational process.

Modernization develops aspirations in the minds of the various groups of citizens for progress toward many new goals, economic, educational, and cultural, which are not regarded by traditional governments as within their responsibilities. The new government must demonstrate effective leadership in establishing programs to promote these new objectives if it is to survive. Means of communication must be developed between the government and its citizens to convey to them a sense that the national goals being pursued are ones which they would sanction.

Political development thus must contend with vested power derived from the traditional society; the lack of trained men; the low literacy rate and the lack of other facilities permitting persuasive mass communication; and the absence of a widespread popular conviction that the new national government is an appropriate vehicle for furthering popular goals.

In the process of contention there are many occasions for frustration and backsliding, many ways in which political life may be diverted to sterile and disruptive goals. The Communist appeal to the underdeveloped areas is designed to exploit precisely these possibilities.

Lack of Basic Capital. The resistance to modernization also takes the form of certain basic initial economic weaknesses. A very considerable expansion must take place in the number of modern men and institutions, as well as in physical capital, before sustained growth is possible at rates which substantially outstrip population increase.

Regular growth requires that men learn to apply systematically and progressively to the production of goods and services [the techniques that] . . . modern science and technology have created. It is this ability to absorb and to apply modern technology (to agriculture and raw materials as well as industry) which distinguishes a modern growing economy from a traditional economy.

In one sense, the most basic economic change required is, therefore, psychological. Men must . . . learn that [the physical world] is capable of being understood and manipulated in terms of stable and logical rules which men can master. But such a change in attitude is not enough. Before a society's economic capabilities can grow regularly at a rate higher than its population increase, large numbers of men must be trained in specialized techniques; and the economic institutions of the society, public and private, must be effectively geared to the process of regular innovation. *The society must learn to mobilize and to use its surplus above minimum consumption not for high living for a few nor for war nor for traditional monuments but for productive investments.* [Italics added.] Moreover, the industrial process itself requires that important nonindustrial sectors be developed: notably, social overhead capital, agriculture, and foreign exchange earning sectors.

It will already be evident from this analysis that such wide-ranging economic change cannot occur unless there is prior or concurrent change in the social, political, and psychological dimensions of the society. But even on narrow economic grounds it is clear that a time interval will be required before the transitional society can acquire sufficient basic capital in human, institutional, and materials forms to gather momentum. . . .

Social Conflict. The small elite groups who dominate the political process in a transitional society will at first be united in motives and purpose only in opposition to some external power or threat. By their very nature they will be of many minds as to the evolution of their own society.

Some, in fact, may be primarily concerned not with modernization but with the maintenance of their own economic and social prerogatives, granted by the traditional society, the colonial powers, or both. Some may seek to divert the national sentiment and the energies of the new national government into external adventure in hope of redressing old humiliations or exploiting newly perceived opportunities for national aggrandizement. Still other groups may strive primarily to consolidate the power of the new central government as against contending regional authorities. Others may be interested primarily in seeing quickly installed the political and legal forms of modern democracy; and still others—initially usually a minority of the elite—may be anxious to get on with the concrete tasks of economic and technical modernization of the economy.

The confusions and cross-purposes which result from this diffusion of objectives inevitably retard the process of modernization. They may tempt men to seek escape from the frustrations of internal differences and to unite in aggressive attitudes or action toward the outside world. Or they may tempt men to accept in desperation the unity and discipline which Communist or other totalitarian forms hold out to them.

Although the small westernized and literate elites play a disproportionately powerful role in the early stages of the modernization process, in the end the mass of citizens must be brought into the mainstream of change. Each person must begin to assume new functions and new relations to the economic and political process.

The transition to modernization usually begins with more than 75 percent of the population in the countryside and less than 10 percent literate. The round of life is tied to the rhythm of the harvests and to the narrow local scene; to a traditional system of land tenure and the assumption that life for the children and grandchildren is likely to be much as it is and has been in living memory. Social life is built around a close family; traditional political and social relations, long sanctioned by custom, tend to be passively accepted. The government— and the nation itself—is likely to seem a remote and distant entity, associated with the extraction of taxes and the arbitrary recruitment of sons for military service.

In the end all this must alter. There must be a radical shift in balance to urban life; literacy must increase; agricultural methods must change; and the markets must widen and become increasingly commercial. Land tenure arrangements are likely to require alteration. . . . The government must come to be identified with activities and objectives which conform to popular interests. And in the end, if democracy is to emerge, the citizen must come to accept the responsibilities as well as the power to determine who shall rule and in what direction public policy shall go.

Merely to list this array of fundamental changes is to suggest the massiveness of what is involved in modernization for the many hundreds of millions of human beings whose lives now are caught up at various intermediate points between the traditional society and one version or another of modern society. The scale and profundity of change suggest also why time must pass . . . [and] why we must expect inner conflict, frustration, and outbursts of violent popular feeling as modernization proceeds.

As the traditional society loses its authority and sanctions, men are made both insecure and at the same time more hopeful that their lot may be improved. . . . But the process of modernization intrinsically requires a long time, even if the society's leaders give to its constructive dimensions all their energy and attention. It is not surprising, therefore, that popular moods may at times turn backward, in an effort to recapture some of the lost security and order of the traditional society . . . [or] that men and women caught up in the process of modernization can easily be led to turn their frustrations against foreigners. And it is not difficult to understand why, if frustration and chaos persist, communism may be accepted . . . as a promised resolution of these conflicts and dilemmas.

But there is also evidence from the distant and recent past that i\

the processes of modernization are steadily extended, if the loss of elements from the traditional life is balanced by evident, even if limited, progress, these multiple changes can take place without irreversible damage to the society and without its seizure by totalitarian dictatorship. . . .

Psychological aspects of modernization

A typical initial characteristic of a transitional society is the existence of a psychological gap; the society is overtly committed to modernization, but its people lack the psychological attitudes required to make modernization a reality. . . .

Planning is professional and attractive; but even the national leaders shy away from the problems of managing the enterprises which will bring progress because the practical problems of management are felt to be menial activities. Individuals may undertake the management of public enterprises only because they see them as means of benefiting their relatives and friends. What may seem like graft to us is the fulfillment of traditional family loyalties and moral obligations. Other individuals are earnest but lack initiative because they have proper respect for the opinions and ways of their elders. Or the individual wants progress but not at the cost of changing his relations with his relatives. He is immobilized by the conflict of purpose in his mind and his emotions.

This division of heart and purpose, which frustrates action, is especially great in some ex-colonial societies, where the people as a whole may be diverted from constructive effort by emotions surviving from the past. The colonial administrators were conquerors who often violated ancient family rights in land and other property, showed contempt for the indigenous religion, and treated the colonial people as an inferior race. For people who have emerged from such experiences with foreign rule, the questions of status, respect, and dignity, important values in all societies, can easily become central to their existence. Consequently they may favor projects that give the appearance of modern development, and reject policies that are less conspicuous but fundamentally more important for the development of the society.

Moreover, colonialism often created in the indigenous population an ambivalent attitude toward the West—the symbol of modernization. They respected the power of the Westerner and imitated his manner of living, but at the same time they resented his presence, hated his behavior, and determined to eject him and what he stood for, including his business enterprises. And so today in the transitional societies many people want and at the same time hate what the Westerner stands for. . . .

It is characteristic of all human beings that when their lives become rootless and insecure they cling to old values associated with "good old days" of emotional security and less anxiety. . . . It is also characteristically human in such a situation to seek a strong leader on whom to lean.

In societies whose traditional order has been disrupted by intrusion from without, these two tendencies converge toward the same effect. The good old days were days of hierarchical or patriarchal leadership; and so we see many newly independent nations turning to autocratic leaders, particularly after a short period of experiment with the democratic forms and after discovering that democratic institutions require a host of preconditions which do not yet exist. . . .

In African societies we find traditional relationships still existing under the surface of colonial rule or freshly won independence. The traditional tribal chieftains still exist and promptly take over, with only a thin veneer of modern forms covering the old arbitrary personal rule. The thin veneer is important; many of the desires of the people are new, and the old economic and educational conditions will not return; but the essence of political behavior may for a time be as of old.

The first modern leader in a transitional society is apt to be the man who led the independence movement. If he is half motivated by Western standards and half motivated by traditional values, he may be immobilized in some degree. However, his leadership may be a rallying point and preserve social order for a time; and if during this period there are strong forces for modernization at work, the society may gain sufficient momentum to save it from relapse. This happened under Ataturk [in Turkey after World War I], and it is to be hoped that it will prove true of India.

But if the forces for modernization are not strong, then, as the charisma of the independence leader wears off, people will seek some substitute for the traditional leadership which has been destroyed in the process of social disruption. At this stage the military is apt to take control. But the military leadership may not provide the emotional appeal and sense of communal unity needed. They may be too Western in their values or in their techniques, or too narrowly representative of the various forces at work in the society.

Psychologically, these are the circumstances when communism makes its strongest appeal. It appears to provide the needed leadership for unity and security. It offers an outlet for the resentments which have built up against the forces that have brought insecurity and anxiety. It ostensibly stands for modernity. . . .

The lesson of history and the contemporary scene is that, despite the psychological costs, human beings opt for modern life if the activities and institutions of modern life develop at a sufficient pace to absorb them in productive and stable activities.

But it is equally true that if the old is destroyed and the new does not grow up fast enough to absorb men's lives and justify the psychological costs of disruption, if there is no satisfying alternative to the traditional life but only the slogans of modernization and the enticing advantages of modernization enjoyed somewhere else—then men turn to disruptive or desperate or regressive courses of action. . . .

Political aspects of modernization

The political development of the transitional societies is clearly a critical factor shaping the world environment in which our own nation must function. The American national interest will be directly affected by the course taken by the transitional societies as they move to create national unity. Some may lead in promising directions, others may pose a threat to our national security. In this context general considerations apply to the overall process of political development in the newly emergent countries.

Our biggest problems are likely to stem from weak and divided societies. . . . Dictatorships can be strong and effective in the short run—and may indeed be a necessary stage through which some of the transitional societies will have to pass—but they are no permanent solution to the problem of national unity in the underdeveloped countries. . . . The heart of the problem of achieving national unity is that the people themselves, not merely their governments, must acquire a sense of responsibility for and sharing in the process of political as well as social modernization. . . .

There is obviously neither a single inevitable course which all countries must follow nor any set of political conditions applying identically to any two countries. Nevertheless, there are transitional societies which appear to share several common problems and to have at the present time similar political characteristics; and it is possible both to group such states and to envisage some common patterns of political development which may apply to each group. . . .

The Traditionalist Oligarchies. These are nations which have already felt the impact of the modernized world and have incorporated certain modern elements into their life but have not developed very far beyond their traditional forms.

Most of these countries are monarchies based upon an authoritarian structure of society . . . The national leaders . . . may even accept democratic symbols; but the test of participation in politics generally hinges upon questions of loyalty and allegiance rather than upon capability to perform modern tasks The typical examples of such countries are Ethiopia, Saudi Arabia, Jordan, Yemen, and Iran in the Middle East and Africa, and Cambodia and Laos in Asia.

The obstacles to developing more modernized structures of authority to replace the traditional ones are reflected in the basic indexes of development for these societies. The average literacy rate of the Asian and African societies we would classify as traditionalist oligarchies is slightly less than ten percent of the population . . . The per capita gross national product is less than $100 in all but two countries in which oil production gives a distorted figure. . . . The process of urbanization has hardly begun . . . The rate at which people are being prepared with new skills is extremely low . . .

These societies [are not likely to] remain for very long as they are today; change is certain, and it will be prompted by a desire to move forward into the modern world. The central question is whether the pattern of political development will be one of relatively gradual, peaceful change or of violent revolution.

Historically, peaceful transition from a traditional political structure has been the exception rather than the rule. The traditional oligarchy tends to suppress the forces of change, knowing that it is unlikely to be able to survive their onslaught; and the gap between the old ways and the new demands grows steadily greater and more dangerous. The threat of explosive and undemocratic developments is heightened today by the presence of the Communists, waiting in the wings to encourage and exploit any drift toward mob rule. . . .

The course of political development in what we have termed "the traditional oligarchies" depends centrally on the process by which power is transferred from the countryside to the city. Land-reform programs and agricultural development programs are fully as important politically as they are socially and economically. . . . If political change is to proceed without violence, the new urban elite must concern itself effectively with rural problems so as to begin to throw up political bridges between the cities and the countryside.

The Modernizing Oligarchies. In this second group we would include all the former colonial countries and a large number of the remaining transitional societies. For the most part, these countries have formally adopted Westernized institutions of government. At the one extreme are countries like many in Africa which have only a thin layer of modernized leadership and extremely fragile Western structures of government. At the other extreme are countries like Pakistan, Burma, Thailand, and Vietnam in which the dominant elite element is in full command of national power but faces tremendous problems in changing the rest of the society. Thus this group includes both newly emergent African countries with disturbingly few trained leaders and Asian countries in which there has been an overproduction of Westernized intellectuals.

These countries share a common goal—in a sense, a common mood. The leadership in each one of them seeks to develop a strong, prosperous state along modern lines and at the same time to preserve the unique qualities of the traditional society. Thus the basic issue is the adaptation of institutions of Western origin to local conditions. Moreover, they present a common picture of social tension. They have made an early commitment to representative institutions of government, but, in spite of apparent widespread support of nationalistic symbols, they have not yet created a genuinely national political process. Beneath the westernized leadership, parochial and sectional loyalties remain extremely strong. As a result, they tend to be extremely unstable societies in which the uneven process of change and disruption is dominant and where peoples' ambitions for a new life run far ahead of their ability to perform effectively in a modern world.

The Potentially Democratic Societies. These are the more advanced of the underdeveloped societies, where there may still be considerable numbers of traditionally oriented people but where the main focus is on maintaining and operating modern institutions. In these countries there is a broad enough leadership to provide some sense of stability and continuity, and in some of them elections have brought a transfer of power without undue violence.

Such countries as Turkey, Brazil, and Mexico seem to be well on their way to becoming modern societies. Others, such as Malaya, India, the Philippines, and Colombia are, so to speak, poised on the brink of sustained commitment to modern practices.

The central task in these countries is to maintain and accelerate the pace of economic and social development; to encourage the existing favorable trends and insure that physical limitations and resource shortages do not so impede development as to drastically disrupt the progress already under way toward modernization. . . .

Social aspects of modernization

In the early period of transition, when a society begins to break out of its traditional structure, the most powerful social class generally consists of the men who own or control the land, a group that is likely to be deeply conservative in every respect. . . . The basic shift to urban and industrial life, which is the core process of modernization, must spell the end of hegemony by landowners as a class. . . .

In the early stages of transition . . . the decisive challenge to the landlords' supremacy generally comes not from any one social class but from a coalition . . . whose leadership is almost invariably made up of men deeply affected by Western ways of thought and action. . . .

The balance of the social elements in such a coalition varies widely according to the initial structure of the traditional society and its experience during transition. In some instances the coalition has contained a large percentage of men from the military; in others (for example, the Congress Party in India) the military has played no significant role. . . . We can . . . make the general observation that the social basis for the modernizing coalition lies in the city and in the essentially urban skills of the elite, both military and intellectual, who have adopted Western attitudes. . . .

While the military are strong in their capacity to manage violence, in their commitment to rational institutions based on functional criteria and efficient performance, in their sense of nationhood as a supreme value, they are often weak in other skills and attitudes needed in a modernizing society. Consider, for example, the basic process of economic growth. Military men are not generally trained in economics. . . . In the Middle East, where military takeover has been virtually continuous over the past few decades, instances have multiplied in which new military regimes rapidly foundered on their own well-meant land reform programs. . . .

Military elites are liable to make dangerous errors in framing and administering laws, instituting and operating schools, devising and sustaining a communication network, unless they are guided by people with professional knowledge and experience in these activities. These people are the "secular intelligentsia"—the economists and engineers and agronomists, the lawyers and administrators, the doctors and public health officers, the deans and professsors, the "communicators" who manage the flow of public news and views that no modernizing polity can do without. They are an "intelligentsia" because it is they who acquire and apply modern knowledge to the manifold tasks of running an urban, industrial, participant society efficiently. They are "secular" because their public roles and social functions are independent of, and usually hostile to, the sacred symbols and institutions of the traditional society. . . .

The historical logic is clear. The military possess the coercive power needed to maintain stability; the secular intelligentsia have the knowledge needed to effect change. Military leadership alone usually has foundered because its perspective is too narrow to cope with the variety of problems that arise in modernizing societies; the secular intelligentsia alone usually has failed because its ideas outrun its capacity to develop institutions that are operational. Neither can manage the transition without the other. . . .

The coming to power of the modernizing coalition has direct effects on both the urban worker and the peasant. Their political role begins to change, for the new leadership feels impelled to make a direct appeal to the mass of citizens. The legitimacy of the new leadership, which has often won out by revolution against the colonial power or the old order, rests in large measure on a real or pretended commitment to advance the interests of the people as a whole and to achieve for all the citizens of the nation the fruits of modernization. . . .

Whatever the substantive accomplishments of the modernizing coalition in its early period of power, and however deep or shallow its commitment to furthering popular interests, its very existence will probably increase the demand for modernization and for an increasing degree of participation in the society's decisions.

This is a point of maximum danger for a developing society. The mass media, bringing news and views of the world to illiterates in their urban slums and remote villages, introduce a new element into the process of modernization. People learn for the first time about the world outside their immediate environs, and their sense of life's possibilities begins to expand. . . .

One danger is that people will learn the fashions of popular participation long before the institutions of representative government are properly functioning. Then "pseudo-participation" takes command, i.e., plebiscites that offer the form of public election without its substance, mob politics of the street in which "popular will" can destroy people and property without constructing better public policy. . . . The leadership is pressed to give radio propaganda primacy over political economy. . . .

To analyze such dangers is easier than to prescribe ways of overcoming them. What the new governments must do is to create institutions through which individual citizens can begin to take part in the decisions of the community. Fully as important as plebiscites, representative assemblies, and other instruments of participation on the national scale—indeed probably a vital prerequisite for the successful operation of national institutions—are local organizations of many sorts which can engage people actively in matters of immediate concern to them. . . .

Economic aspects of modernization

Economic development has tended to become the most obvious and best recognized dimension of modernization. To transform a relatively stagnant "traditional" economy into an economy of steady self-sustaining growth is one of the central objectives of all the modernizing societies.

The pattern of growth and the degree of difficulty involved will . . . vary markedly from one country to another. . . . Certain traditional cultures appear to adapt more easily to modern economic activity than do others; for example, modernization appears to have come more easily to Japan than to China, to Germany than to Italy.

Another and more tangible factor is the balance between population and natural resources. In some societies modernization is favored by a relatively ample supply of good land and natural resources in relation to population (parts of Latin America, Burma, Thailand). Such countries will have an easier time of it than areas such as the Indian peninsula, where the population-resources balance is most unfavorable. It should be noted, however, that some highly developed countries, notably Japan, have definitely been in the latter category and yet have managed to modernize.

Such factors as the adaptability of culture and the population-resource balance are particular to each country and are given—they must be taken into account, but not much can be done about them. Other factors, however, must be created if takeoff into sustained growth is to occur. . . .

Prerequisites of Cumulative Economic Growth. Development has generally required radical and early changes in . . . public utilities and agriculture. . . .

A buildup of public utilities (social overhead capital) such as communications, power, water, and transport is required both for new industrial activity and for a modernizing agriculture; to enlarge markets and lower costs; to permit more efficient exploitation of natural resources; and to provide the means whereby the national government can communicate with the countryside and thus influence the course of agricultural development. An insufficient expansion in public utility services—services which by their nature cannot be imported—is likely to slow down and perhaps frustrate expansion in other sectors by giving rise to bottlenecks and blunting incentives for private profit-motivated industrial expansion.

Second, a rapid expansion in agricultural output is necessary—and at an early stage in the process of growth—because people who are drawn off the land to build roads and canals and factories, and who are moving to fast-growing cities, must be fed. Moreover, the population is likely to grow faster as economic change gets under way. It may be that some of the increased demand for food can be satisfied by increased imports, paid for by new exports and by aid from abroad. But most countries are unlikely to succeed in maintaining growth unless they can produce more of their own food.

To produce more food where there is a plentiful supply of good underused land is relatively easy. In most contemporary low-income countries, however, where good land is scarce, nothing short of a revolutionary change in agricultural techniques will do. Without such a change, the increased demand for food—a consequence of rising income generated by increased activity in other sectors—will outrun the supply and food prices will rise. If accelerating inflation and severe shortages are to be avoided, scarce foreign exchange will have to be used to import food. Less foreign exchange will be available to pay for lathes, generators, and steel—things that in the early stages cannot be produced domestically at any cost and yet are needed if investment and growth are to be maintained. . . .

Capital resources from outside can promote significant improvements in agricultural productivity, can lead to aggressive building of social overhead capital. But the use of foreign aid to these ends, as opposed merely to keeping an essentially stagnant economy going, is sharply limited by another crucial factor: the availability of modern men and institutions.

To develop the kinds of men and organizations which modern economic activity requires is the third major precondition for initiating takeoff. No matter how much external aid in the form of foreign exchange may be available to a transitional society, there must be men on the spot in sufficient numbers to supply managerial, technical, and mechanical skills. And organizational forms must be created in which such men can effectively perform the many tasks without which development cannot occur. . . . Transitional societies need both first-rate civil servants and first-rate private managers, that is, effective entrepreneurs in both the public and the private spheres [of the economy]. . . .

The Takeoff. There arrives a time, however, when the groundwork has been laid for agricultural change, when considerable social overhead capital has been built, and when human resources and organization in many sectors of the economy are adequate to the tasks of modernization. The tempo of change can quicken at this point, as it began to quicken in India a few years ago, and the country may gather its forces for the critical attempt to break the vicious circle of poverty: lack of capital—low productivity—low income—little saving—lack of capital. Takeoff becomes possible.

For takeoff to occur the preconditions should have been established in enough different sectors of the economy so that simultaneous advance is possible on a number of interacting fronts. . . . Many efforts, each of which by itself would probably be abortive, so mutually reinforce each other that the economy as a whole rapidly gains momentum. At this point, precisely because many things must be done at once if each is to succeed, resources become the critical bottleneck—both resources in general and, in particular, command over foreign exchange.

With substantial external resource help, the economy can yield more output and income; this permits an increase in saving and investment, which leads to still more output. If all goes well . . . the economy crosses the threshold of self-sustaining growth; and expansion, though perhaps irregular expansion, becomes the norm.

It must not be thought, however, that an economy which has the capacity for initiating takeoff will necessarily do so. The process is not at all automatic. In most cases a considerable amount of central guidance and initiative is initially necessary to give the process its impetus and direction. At the same time the governmental environment must be such that individual producers, farmers, administrators, and lenders will respond well to the new opportunities with which they are confronted. . . .

In particular, institutional devices for tapping potentially available savings for purposes of investment must keep pace with the growth, diversity, and geographical spread of activity, and must channel savings into the most productive lines of investment. There must be a sufficient degree of coordination and synchronization of the rapidly increasing number and variety of interdependent activities—coordination that must become progressively more elaborate if the process of increasing specialization and diversification of function (which is central to expansion) is not to result in gross confusion, in plants standing idle for want of essential inputs, in the wrong goods being shipped to the wrong place, in machines falling apart for lack of skilled operators and maintenance, and the like. . . . Yet central planning likewise is ineffective without effective execution at all levels. . . .

The central problem of a country attempting takeoff is to achieve an effective balance . . . which will assure that centralization of decisions about the gross scale of various complementary activities does not frustrate the creation and operation of particular enterprises on a decentralized basis and the enlisting of private energies to achieve operating efficiency and imaginative innovation.

Clearly none of these conditions, all necessary if takeoff is to be achieved, can be taken for granted. Nonetheless—and despite all the difficulties—it is a defining feature of an economy on the threshold of takeoff that a large variety of previously vicious circles have become potentially "virtuous"; that the pervasive interactions between various facets of the economy and the polity which had previously reinforced stagnation tend, as the economy picks up speed, to reinforce expansion. It is at this point that there is a good chance for the process of growth to become cumulative. Economically, more output yields more capital which yields more output. Expansion of economic opportunities aids in the recruitment and development of people with organizational skills who in turn are instrumental in creating further opportunities. Workers learn by practice and then can teach their skills to other workers. The increased availability of public utility services stimulates demand for their services which permits high-volume, low-cost, low-price operation and hence stimulates still further demand. . . . Stimulated by the goal of profit and excellence, and by evidence that improvement is possible, producers start looking for new and better ways of doing things. Technical change in industry and agriculture begins to spread from factory to factory and from farm to farm, increasing productivity, releasing resources for new uses, creating demand for other resources. The result is cumulative growth.

The political and social climate will also change under the impact of rapid economic expansion. Successful takeoff will reinforce the social, political, and cultural power and prestige of those committed to modernizing the economy. . . . Yet the victory of the modernizers need not lead to the destruction of the traditional groups. Takeoff can create opportunities for the traditional elite to find new functions and thus can facilitate mutual accommodation, as it did in the case of the Junkers in nascent industrial Germany and in the Japan of the 1880's. . . .

The role of external capital will at this stage usually be critical. It is not impossible, of course, that a country which has arrived at a point of potential takeoff will be able to generate sufficient internal saving and investment to pick up steam virtually on its own. This has occurred in the past, as for instance in the case of Japan. But very unusual conditions must obtain. In most underdeveloped countries today the prospects of generating from a very low level of income the internal savings necessary for takeoff are very poor, especially if coercive totalitarian procedures are to be avoided. It is not an accident that the only known current attempt at unaided (or only skimpily aided) takeoff from low-income levels is that by Communist China. And as yet it is far from certain that China will make the grade without substantially more help from the Soviet Union. The fact is that it is not easy to squeeze much saving and investment out of $60 annual income per head.

Moreover, general poverty is not the only difficulty. Industrial growth, and, indeed, modernization of agriculture, require growing imports of equipment and material that literally cannot be produced domestically; it takes machines to build machines and steel to produce steel. Without aid, underdeveloped countries, with the exception of those few which possess a large endowment of a commodity with an unusually strong and steady export market, oil, for instance, are not likely to be able to pay for these things. . . . Initiating and sustaining growth in the early stages from very low levels of income is exceedingly difficult without substantial outside sources of foreign exchange even where governments are willing and able to use totalitarian coercion to repress consumption and push exports.

What if takeoff does not occur? In the short run the alternative is continued stagnation. But in the longer run, stagnation is not a real alternative. . . . Ultimately the pent-up frustrations in a society which fails to modernize its economy will destroy its chance for peaceful democratic growth.

The New Environment. Many of the problems of achieving takeoff in the mid-twentieth century are similar to those which countries faced in the past. The early economic tasks still center around social overhead capital and around technological change in agriculture and in the export industries. The necessary social and psychological transformations, too, are in many ways similar to those of the past. But in three critical respects—population pressure, technology, and politics—the current environment is quite unlike that in which the industrialized Western countries undertook takeoff. In fact, the importance of outside help and the need for a "big push" rather than gradual and piecemeal change are in part consequences of the differences.

Except in the United States and Russia, the rate of population increase in the early stages of growth in the past was typically less than 1.5 percent—often around one percent. In most though not all underdeveloped areas of the world today population is growing at rates of from two to three percent—due, in part, to the early impact of modern medical techniques on death rates. This would not pose serious difficulties if the countries in question possessed substantial reserves of good land. But in most of the world reserves of land such as those which the United States and Russia possessed during their periods of rapid growth do not exist. And to achieve takeoff without such reserves in the face of the rapid growth of population is likely to require substantially higher rates of investment and a substantially more elaborate organizational effort in agricultural production than has been the case in the past.

The second major difference has to do with the "pool" of available technological knowledge. By whatever measure, this is far greater than what was available to countries industrializing during the nineteenth and even the early twentieth century. . . . This circumstance on balance favors growth, though it is not an unmitigated blessing. It certainly offers the possibility of accelerating development. . . . But it also complicates the problem of growth. Technological change which has decreased the dependence of some countries on foreign raw material supplies has also reduced the ability of other countries to earn foreign exchange. Technological change which has increased the advantages of large-scale operation has also compounded the problem of organization and capital scarcity. Nowadays, first steps in many branches of industry and in utilities must be giant steps.

A third major change in the environment has to do with political structure and political and social attitudes. To cite the example of Japan as an instance of takeoff without substantial outside help in a context where natural resources were scarce and population plentiful is to ignore the fact that nowadays the attempt at takeoff in many countries is taking place in a context of general suffrage. *A small elite cannot readily impose sacrifices and privation when it must rely on popular support to maintain itself in office. All this is compounded by the fact that people's aspirations and expectations are qualitatively different from those of people a century or more ago.* Modern communications, like modern medicine, substantially complicate the problem of takeoff. . . . [italics added].

Modernization under Communism

The MIT report emphasizes the American interest in supporting democratic institutions and practices in the modernizing countries, but it says little about the alternative route—the route of authoritarian rule in general, and of Communist dictatorship in particular.

The Soviet Union in the 1930's, and again following the devastation suffered in World War II, exhibited the apparent potentialities of Communist-directed industrialization. Americans found it difficult to believe that a people so economically backward as most Russians were in 1918 or even in 1928 could lift themselves largely by their own efforts into the top rank of industrialized economies within a single generation. It was still more incredible, in American eyes, that this could be achieved under a rigorous socialist dictatorship. Americans in the 1950's showed similar scepticism towards reports of rapid modernization under Communist rule in China. This scepticism continues today. One reads, for example, that Chinese production claims are fantastically inflated, that the Chinese drive for greater food production is bogging down, that Chinese population increase will consume whatever rise in production is accomplished, and that it is doubtful whether China under Communism can achieve a successful industrial takeoff.

Such reactions tend to confuse two separable issues. The first is whether modernization under authoritarian rule—Communist or other—is likely to be more rapid than under democratic institutions and practices. The second is whether the undeniable achievements of Communist rule in Russia and the *apparent* achievements in China are likely to be so persuasive as to tip the scale in some or most of the underdeveloped countries embarking on programs of rapid modernization.

On the first issue, no conclusive answer is possible. In the first place, every political system represents a mixture of authoritarian and democratic principles and practices. At least in the short run, a predominantly authoritarian system may be able to cope with the basic problem of capital formation rather more effectively than a democratic system. It requires very inspiring leadership indeed, a quality of leadership rarely encountered, to persuade people who can vote their rulers out of office to forego more and better food, clothing, housing, and other amenities in order that more materials and labor may be allocated for production or purchase of new capital equipment. This point, it will be recalled, was made emphatically in the final paragraph quoted from the MIT report above.

This difficulty will be increased if, as in the Soviet Union a generation ago and in Communist China today, a nation is committed simultaneously to rapid industrialization and to massive outlays for armaments. Under such conditions, the apparent advantages of authoritarian rule may become decisive. If it is difficult for a government based upon popular elections to impose forced savings for economic development, it is manifestly a great deal more difficult to exact still heavier sacrifice for the additional burden of a big military establishment.

The problem of savings is further related to the prevailing standard of living. It is one thing to allocate, for example, 20 percent of the Gross National Product for investment when per capita income is $500 or more per year. It is a vastly more difficult operation to do this if per capita income is already at a bare subsistence level, say, from $50-$100, as in the case of China, India, and many other modernizing countries today.

Repugnant as the idea may be to democratic-minded humanitarians, authoritarian regimes have a generally more impressive record to date than democracies, when it comes to squeezing work out of people without giving them commensurately more goods and other benefits in return.

The relative potentialities of the democratic and dictatorial routes to modernization have been heatedly argued in comparative studies of recent Chinese and Indian accomplishments. Information on India is more accessible than information on China. It is extremely difficult to ascertain precisely what is happening in China. It is possible, as some authorities assert, that China's rulers themselves are not very well informed. Chinese statistics are certainly not to be taken at face value. But even after discounting Chinese claims substantially, the American economist Wilfred Malenbaum (professor of economics, University of Pennsylvania) finds China's achievements impressive in comparison to India's during the decade of the 1950's.

The relative progress in the devolpment of these two countries [Malenbaum writes] is of great significance. There were strong parallels in their preplan structure [as of about 1949] and strong contrasts between China's totalitarian and India's democratic programs. Their performance relative to one another may influence the programs adopted by other, now less advanced, countries. It will certainly bear upon Soviet and United States foreign policies. . . .

India achieved an annual rate of growth of real income of almost 3.5 percent in the period from April 1, 1950 through March 31, 1959. Over essentially the same period, the Chinese growth rate was at least three times as great. . . .

Gross investment ratios were close to the same level in 1950; thereafter they increased about three times as fast in China. Moreover, given the greater expansion in Chinese product, these ratios mean that in 1957 and 1958 the real level of gross investment in China was about five times what it was in 1950; in India, it was not quite twice the 1950 level. Can these differences be in any way attributed to differences in foreign capital inflows over these years? . . . If anything . . . China financed more of its investment program on the basis of domestic savings from current account. . . ."

Malenbaum found these differences reflected in various indices of production. Table 15.2, derived from a year-by-year comparison of production statistics, puts into sharp focus the much more rapid economic development of China between 1950 and 1958. (These statistics, at least in the case of China, manifestly represent no more than rough approximations; and they may, of course, involve deliberate exaggerations.) Malenbaum concludes:

The record of comparative performance . . . reveals that China has taken greater strides in investment, and this on the basis of

TABLE 15.2   CHINESE AND INDIAN ECONOMIC GROWTH, 1950-1958

		CHINA	INDIA
Overall production (in index numbers, using 1952 as 100)	1950	37.	85.
	1958	288.	137.
Steel production (in millions of tons)	1950	.4	1.01
	1958	5.	1.27
Cement production (in millions of tons)	1950	1.41	2.68
	1958	8.18	6.07
Electric power production (in kilowatt-hours)	1950	4,580.	5,112.
	1958	23,000.	12,198.
Coal production (in millions of tons)	1950	40.9	32.5
	1958	165.	44.8
Ammonium sulfate fertilizer (in thousands of tons)	1950	75.	47.3
	1958	700.	381.6
Textiles (in millions of yards)	1950	2,940.	3,650.
	1958	6,250.	4,925.

greater reliance upon domestic savings. Gross output per person actually increased more than twice as fast as India's. . . . The present analysis [1959] thus indicates economic developments overwhelmingly favorable to the Chinese effort, both with respect to actual performance and to potential for further growth. . . . The growing awareness of China's achievements relative to India's can have a profound influence upon world political and economic developments. . . .*

Other investigators have come to similar conclusions. A report, prepared for the Royal Institute of International Affairs (of London), found in 1959 that China,

a largely backward economy, with an extremely low volume of capitalization and poor in techniques both in industry and in agriculture, has already, within the space of nine years, been transformed into one capable of the production of aircraft, lorries, cargo ships, electric generators, locomotives, and automatic lathes, an economy in which a not inconsiderable and rapidly growing sector of modern industry has been built up, a very high rate of investment is being maintained, a knowledge of some of the most modern industrial techniques has been acquired and applied, and more advanced agricultural methods are beginning to be employed. The production of the main industrial commodities has grown several times over the highest previously obtained, and very big increases brought about in agricultural production. . . . There can be . . . little doubt that the industry and intelligence of the Chinese people, together with the overwhelming weight of their numbers, are likely to create in the Chinese economy a force that will have a rapidly increasing impact on the world in the years to come.†

The Chinese, like any other people industrializing their economy under forced draft, must overcome formidable psychological, economic, political, and other obstacles. One of the greatest difficulties—one that receives much attention these days—is the race between economic expansion and population increase. As explained in Chapter 13, both birth and death rates in preindustrial societies are nearly always very high. One of the first consequences of modernizing such societies is reduction of the death rate. Meanwhile, the birth rate responds much more slowly. These differential trends yield a rapid increase in the number of people to be fed, clothed, and housed. In China today this increase amounts to some ten millions per year. Unless economic production—especially food production—increases

* From "India and China: Contrasts in Development Performance," by Wilfred Malenbaum, in *American Economic Review*, June 1959, pp. 284 ff. Copyright 1959 by American Economic Association; reproduced by permission.

† From pp. 205, 207 of *The Economic Development of Communist China, 1949–1958*, by T. J. Hughes and D. E. Luard. Oxford University Press, London, 1959. Reproduced by permission.

faster than population, an economy cannot take off into sustained industrial growth. This rule holds just as rigorously, of course, for India or for any other modernizing people as for China. Here as in other sectors, authoritarian rule may prove more efficient in changing traditional values and habits.

The next issue is whether the advantages of authoritarian methods are likely to prove irresistibly persuasive to the leaders of other Asian, African, and Latin American countries, struggling to speed up the process of modernization. This question was dealt with in the MIT report,* as follows:

> Both historically and at present the appeal of communism has been strongest in societies caught up in the cross-currents of the transition from traditional to modern status. What communism has to offer such societies is a political and social method which promises these things: (1) a tight, unified organization of some of the elements of the elite who wish to modernize the society; (2) a domestic base of power capable of defeating those elements from the traditional society who would maintain regional authority or otherwise oppose the modernization process; (3) a technique for mobilizing the human and physical resources required to produce rapid industrial growth; (4) a psychological setting which gives a framework of security, discipline, and order to men cut adrift from the moorings of the traditional society. . . .
>
> It must not be overlooked, however, that the image of communism also has strongly negative aspects which have caused men to resist its adoption in the underveloped countries. First, communism has been unable to free itself, despite mammoth efforts, from its direct connection with Moscow, and, now, Peking; and, therefore, it encounters resistance from the spirit of nationalism and nationhood. Second, Communist parties are built on a relatively narrow segment of the modernizing elite and are therefore forced not only to struggle against elements from the traditional society but also to compete against those who would press toward modernization by other methods, under other banners. Third, there are deeper resistances than some Western observers would credit to the definitive violation of democratic hopes and commitments which the acceptance of communism involves. Put another way, the democratic vision is often more influential in transitional societies than a casual view of the low estate of democratic practice would suggest.
>
> Nevertheless, two things remain true in contemporary underdeveloped areas. First, communism is an active competing alternative to other methods of organizing the society for modernization—an alternative not only alive as a political party but also alive in the minds of non-Communists as they weigh the possibilities of progress against their frustrations. Second, a portion of the modernizing elite

* "Economic, Social and Political Changes in the Underdeveloped Countries," previously cited, pp. 64-65.

in most of the underdeveloped areas is committed to the Communist course and must be counted on to frustrate and complicate the efforts of others to move towards modernization by methods that hold open the possibility of a democratic evolution for their society. . . .

Moscow- or Peking-oriented Communism is not the only alternative to Western-style liberal democracy. One has also to reckon with the possibility that the governments of many, perhaps most, of the emerging nations will evolve into patterns quite different from either. This is the thesis of Kenneth T. Young, Jr., who has had long experience with this problem in the Departments of State and Defense, and in other positions of responsibility. We conclude this chapter with a short selection summarizing his views of the—

New politics in new states *

During the past few years "the erosion of democracy" has been spreading in many of the newly independent states of Asia, the Middle East and Africa. This weakening of Western-style representative government has baffled and alarmed many of us. We do not understand it, and we often condemn it too quickly. . . . For if we fail to understand the dilemmas and challenges of the new politics, American diplomacy will be even more ineffective than it has been so far in the huge segment of the world where over a billion people are experiencing the difficulties and trials of new nationhood. . . .

At the very time that the governments of these new states are struggling to get on their feet and set their own course, they are overwhelmed by competing ideas, people and organizations descending upon them from the Atlantic and Soviet worlds. They have little or no time to reflect upon the issues of national policy or to study new programs. Of course, the contest of which they are the object is advantageous to them. It gives them an importance out of proportion to their strength; they can play one side off against the other to get more aid and to increase their own freedom of maneuver in foreign and domestic policies. Nevertheless, this contest as to who shall aid them complicates their political development; they are compelled to make basic political decisions in conditions of tension and turmoil. And the hazards are increasing as Moscow and Peking now begin a new contest between themselves on how to win the new states over to Communism.

These alien and competing influences of the Atlantic, Soviet, and Sinic worlds reinforce those national voices which demand complete modernization. But they do not show the way. Nor can the new

* From "New Politics in New States," by K. T. Young, Jr., in *Foreign Affairs*, April 1961, pp. 494 ff. Copyright 1961 by the Council on Foreign Relations, New York; reproduced by permission.

states break away wholly from politics derived from traditional institutions. The new politics must seek to solve the problems arising out of the abrupt dislocation of ancient and static societies suddenly thrust into a turbulent, fast-changing world. . . .

Young identifies four sets of issues which bedevil the emerging nations: (1) the heritage of their colonial past, (2) pressures for rapid modernization, (3) lack of a unifying political culture, and (4) the limitations of charismatic leadership.

With very few exceptions, European colonial rule did not train enough executives and administrators, engineers and physicians, economists, teachers, and other specialists to operate an independent political community bent on rapid modernization. Furthermore, despite their revolt against colonialism, the elites of the new nations have tried rather generally at the outset to establish and operate Western-style representative governments. Yet these "facsimile" governments are not at all suited to communities where illiteracy is high. Nor are they likely to work well where extreme poverty is the rule, where expectations are rising fast, and where government must resist these demands in order to get on with the business of capital formation and other aspects of modernization. Confronted with these conditions, one after another the emerging nations are drastically modifying their Western-style constitutions or scrapping them altogether.

The second set of issues arises from the urge to modernize quickly. Here one encounters the whole range of psychological and social resistances so well described in the MIT report, complicated everywhere by explosive upsurge of population growth touched off by even slight improvements in living conditions.

The third cluster of issues center on the problem of national unity. The cement which transforms an aggregate of people into a community—shared values, myths, attitudes, fears, aspirations, etc.—do not come ready-made in most of the ex-colonial countries. Frequently, the geographical boundaries of these countries reflect merely decisions taken 50 to 100 years ago in distant European capitals without any regard to linguistic, tribal, or other ethnic considerations. At the outset, widely shared resentment against former colonial masters, and a fierce determination to be free of all that, may be about all that holds the new state together.

Finally, the emerging nations have been heavily dependent at the outset on some towering personality—a Nehru, Nkruma, Touré, Nasser, Sukarno. Without the compelling personal leadership of such men—the quality called charisma—most of the new nations would "collapse immediately."

Because of him [Young continues] the new states tend to combine all executive and legislative authority, and sometimes even judicial functions, in the hands of the one man and his regime. And to increase this authority he may bring to bear his personal will, his vision of destiny, his appetite for empire, or his greed for greatness. The result is not only the excessive concentration of power, but the erosion or overt destruction of the opposition.

Yet sooner or later, the regime runs into trouble. New men with new ideas appear. The old leader and his party have come to lean on their prestige and the glory of their past achievements to insure popular support. The leader is a national fixture—too indisputable to dislodge, too venerated to criticize, too hardened to change. No provision is made for a successor. The unitary party loses its revolutionary dynamism. It does not welcome the new approaches or the new faces. The dialogue between the older revolutionary generation and new political forces breaks down. Modernization and urbanization, however, are generating new associations which demand full expression of their points of view. Unions, faculties, business enterprises, professional societies, organized civil servants, the officer corps, cultural groups, and new voluntary associations of contemporary urban, suburban and even rural life all want a voice in the future.

As a result of the various pressures of the past and the present a political cycle is created, which typically appears to have six phases: the establishment of independence, the creation of modern institutions, the promotion of national unity and development, the appearance of contradictory factors, the collapse of leadership and political solidarity, the forming of new lines for the reestablishment of stability. . . .

With the completion of this cycle, the emerging nation reaches the stage which Young calls the "new politics":

While the new politics are still in the formative stage, it may be said that they are searching for a new ideological and cultural identity, an indigenous constitutionalism, a strong executive and a responsible legislature, a coherent system of representation, a modernized and democratic civil service, a flexible development of the economy and a regional diplomacy.

A visitor to Asia, the Middle East or Africa cannot but be impressed by the persistent search for an ideology and culture which are both indigenous and modern. Dissatisfied with an initial nationalism crossbred by so many alien strains, the younger leaders believe that a new synthesis is needed. . . . Not only a renaissance but a national discovery is taking place in many former colonial territories. Thus, the new politics take on more local coloration as the findings of the archeologist, anthropologist and historian begin to expose the heritage hidden by years of alien rule. Out of national consciousness may come national confidence and cohesion. The home-grown "ism" is strong because its roots are deep. But the new soil could breed a warped variety of impulsive, emotional, destructive ideology if badly treated. . . .

And finally, in economics and diplomacy, the new politics seem to be veering toward a more pragmatic approach. The economic dogmas concerning heavy industrialization and state ownership are being questioned, and in many parts of the world suspicion of private initiative and foreign investment is decreasing. Interest is growing in developing light industry, diversifying agricultural production, and improving village life. There is a more realistic attitude toward problems of economic growth, a willingness to extend timetables if need be, instead of rushing through impossibly rapid target dates, and an acceptance of partial planning in some sectors of the economy instead of total planning for the whole nation.

"In diplomacy, the new professionals [in the emerging nations] incline towards regional associations and avoidance of too close a political identification with East or West. In seeking to achieve an independent, or at least a complementary, diplomacy, they will try to strengthen bilateral relations with their neighbors, explore economic and cultural cooperation on a regional basis such as the Nagreb in North Africa or the Mekong Commission in Southeast Asia, and take common positions on issues before the United Nations. Such regional diplomacy does not necessarily mean "neutralism." It reflects the search in the new states for a national and cultural identity, the will to be on their own and the desire to be different. The new nationalists are likely to be very independent people to deal with, for both the West and the East. . . .

CHAPTER SIXTEEN

★ ★ ★

Public Opinion and National Character

FROM TIME TO TIME we have alluded to patterns of thinking, feeling, and doing which appears to be more or less prevalent within a given national community. Such patterns are many and varied. They may relate to particular current situations and events or to deeply rooted values and ideals, myths and traditions, customs and taboos, fears and hatreds, desires and expectations, discipline and morale, and other behavior. That is to say, these community patterns range from specific attitudes and demands, at one extreme, to imperfectly articulated moods and orientations at the other.

All such behavioral patterns are obviously manifestations of a nation's culture, as that term is generally understood these days. But culture connotes much else besides—formal institutions (governmental, economic, or other), equipment and skills (technology), and various other things. Hence the need for a special term of designation.

Public opinion is one such term. But we are concerned here not only with patterns of thinking and utterance, but also with patterns of feeling and doing. *National character* is the term most commonly used to designate this whole area of social behavior. But national character is a term with vices as well as virtues. This term tends to foster and perpetuate the mischievous idea of the community as an organism endowed with humanlike capacity to think, feel, and do. Most of the more impressionistic discussions of national character exhibit precisely this tendency. National character also suggests a degree of social conformity and uniformity never confirmed on close inspection of any national community.

Despite these objections we shall use national character as a term of general designation. But the reader is asked to keep firmly in mind that the

reference is *never* to the traits of a single personality, but rather to patterns
of thinking, feeling, and doing which appear to be quite widely prevalent
within the country in question.

A good deal of investigation and discussion of national character has
taken place *outside* the framework of politics. This is especially true of much
of the work of psychologists, sociologists, anthropologists, and geographers.
When these specialists apply their findings to *political* problems, they often
appear to assume that attitudes and other behavioral patterns observed in
particular national communities have an automatic or intrinsic political significance. "International tensions," or the absence thereof, are attributed
to widely held attitudes. And such attitudes are assumed to be significant
sources of official national policies.

The student of international politics cannot take these propositions for
granted. The reason he cannot do so derives from the nature of his frame of
reference. He is concerned with actions and interactions of governments.
Patterns of thinking, feeling, and doing, prevalent within a national community may or may not influence governmental action. As we have repeatedly emphasized, conditions and events outside the decision-making
apparatus of government can affect decisions in one way, *and one way only*:
by being perceived and taken into account by the decision-makers—a process which behavioral scientists call "internalization" in the personality of
the actor.

People in all but the most primitive and isolated communities do form
impressions and images of other nations and nationalities. They also have
notions of what their own national community is like, what it stands for,
what actions are right and proper, what perils confront it, etc. These images
show a universal tendency to harden and resist change—to become stereotypes, in the idiom of behavioral science. These stereotypes are likely to be
shared more or less by the community's rulers. To the extent that this
occurs, the prevailing stereotypes are quite likely to be reflected in their
preferences, judgments, and decisions. When this happens, or when the
rulers acquiesce in observed public attitudes and demands which they do
not personally share, *then and then only* do the behavioral patterns which
make up what in the aggregate is called national character become significant as a source of national policy.

There is no certainty that statesmen will share attitudes and beliefs
widely held within their country. Nor is there any certainty that they will
acquiesce in public demands in which they do not concur, even though
such demands appear to have widespread approval and support. Nations
differ widely in the degree of consensus among rulers and private citizens
as to what their own and other nations are like, and what courses are de-

sirable, feasible, and right. Governmental systems, as we have already observed (Chapter 6), differ also in the degree to which politicians feel compelled to pay attention to public opinions and moods.

In order to *prove* the *political* relevance of such opinions and moods in a specific instance, one has to demonstrate that these were actually taken into account in the policy-making process. In order to establish the *presumptive* relevance of these factors—whether for purposes of explanation or prediction—one has to establish that, in the governmental system under consideration, top-level decision-makers, the nation's leaders, do normally share widely prevalent constituency attitudes, or that the structure of the system renders leaders highly responsive to these attitudes.

In the light of these considerations, it is necessary not only to examine national character in the context of political processes but also to discover what kinds of personalities tend to become top-level political leaders in different systems and to find out what happens to their outlook and values as they rise to the top. Thorough study of this problem would require probing deeply into the modes and intensities of civic indoctrination and into the processes by which persons rise to positions of authority and responsibility in different societies.

We cannot hope to reach very firm conclusions on these issues in the present state of knowledge, but we can suggest a few questions for discussion. For example, would comparison of Communist and non-Communist systems tend to show that top-level leaders generally conform more closely to early indictrination in one than in the other? Specifically, is it safe to assume that the men who reach the top in the Soviet system will generally be more rigorously indoctrinated and less flexible in their world outlook than their counterparts in the American system?

If one answers this question in the affirmative, is it safe to take the next step, and assume that the Communist politician's purposes and reactions can be more confidently deduced from his cultural background? The answer one gives to this question will have a direct bearing on one's conclusions as to the priority of purposes—world revolution, old-fashioned imperialism, power for power's sake, defensive security, etc.—which underlie the international operations of the Soviet government.

Is it also reasonable to assume that rapid social changes are apt to be reflected in the substance and especially in the style of national policies? Is it to be expected, for example, that national leaders who are riding the tiger of violent social revolution—Mao-tse Tung in China or Castro in Cuba, for example—are likely to react more fanatically and aggressively than leaders of partially spent revolutions, as for example the Soviet Union? Are particular styles of foreign policy to be expected from nations newly liberated from colonial status? Or from those undergoing rapid modernization?

Would comparison of more stratified with less rigid social systems show that national leaders in the former tend to conform more closely to the outlook of the social class with which they are identified? Specifically, could one deduce a good deal about the presumptive behavior of British statesmen, simply by investigating what happens to a boy at Eton and other elite public (read "private") schools, and at Oxford and Cambridge, where the majority of them are educated? There is certainly some evidence to justify affirmative answers to all these questions, though one could also discover many exceptions.

Let us take the problem a step further: Soviet and American statesmen command greater destructive capacity these days than anyone imagined possible a mere generation ago. Each side has come to rely heavily on the threat of massive retaliatory attack to deter military aggression by the other. It may be assumed that the top-level leaders on each side are well aware of the devastation which could be accomplished by large-scale nuclear bombardment. Are there grounds for assuming that this knowledge inspires a degree of prudence and rationality in calculating consequences often conspicuously wanting in the statesmen of a less lethal age? Again, though evidence is by no means conclusive, there seems to be some basis for concluding that military technology imposes (figuratively speaking) a higher degree of rationality and caution than one might expect otherwise from the overall configuration of attitudes in the Soviet Union and in the United States.

In recent years, a good deal of attention has been devoted to ascertaining what set of conditions are necessary to make the threat of massive retaliation "credible" (that is, convincing, and hence effectively deterrent) to the other side? Is there ground for speculating that what is convincing to Americans may be less so to Russians, or vice versa? Implicit in this line of questions is the important issue discussed previously in several chapters: whether in the present configuration of international political relations, statesmen are likely to pay more attention to conditions and events beyond their frontiers than to attitudes, moods, and demands within their own national community.

So much for the bearing of national character and public opinion on policy making and the substance of national policies. But that is only half of the picture. Political decisions (projects, undertakings) generally have operational consequences. As previously emphasized, the physical and social environment sets limits to what is (or can be) accomplished. The patterns of thinking, feeling, and doing which, in the aggregate, are called national character form part of the social environment within which policies are executed, as well as conceived and initiated. Values and ideals, myths and traditions, customs and taboos, fears and hatreds, desires and expectations, morale and discipline, and other behavioral patterns which give distinctive character to a national community may set limits to performance and accomplishment. These, like other environmental limitations may be operative regardless of national political institutions and the perceptions of those who operate them.

Such limitations may have trivial or profoundly important consequences for the military defense, political prestige, and other manifestations of a nation's international political potential, its standing and stature in the Society of Nations. On the whole, the impacts of national character on a nation's political potential are no less important (and may be more important) than on its policy-making processes and its international projects and undertakings.

The remainder of this chapter should be read within the framework outlined in the foregoing pages. We shall deal first with impressionistic interpretations of national character, and then present a simple scheme for identifying more explicitly some of the types of behavioral patterns which appear to have special significance in the context of international politics.

Impressionistic images of national character

One could turn up thousands of impressionistic statements about national character. Bold generalizations about Americans, Britons, Russians, Chinese, and other nationalities are common currency in political discourse. It would be difficult to find anyone, at least in the older nations, who does not have rather definite notions of what his own and other nations are like.

The following examples are quoted, not because they necessarily fit reality, but simply because they are typical of impressionistic thinking about national character. The first is by a Frenchman and is about France:

> As for the national character, this is well enough known. France is lively of wit, generally prudent in its actions, mobile on the surface, but in its depths constant and unchanging. It neglects its traditions fairly easily and retains its habits; it is sagacious and flippant, penetrating yet abstracted, excessively mild and even infinitely too moderate in its real desires for an epoch in which enormous ambitions and monstrous appetites are almost normal conditions.*

The second example relates to the Germany of the early 1900's. The author is Harold Butler, a distinguished British statesman.

> The whole German soul was shot through with a megalomanic lust for power, dressed up in all the romantic trappings which appeal to it so irresistibly. The Nibelung saga was not just a gorgeous fantasy

---

* From p. 106 of *Reflections on the World Today* by Paul Valéry, translated by Francis Scarfe. Copyright 1948 by Pantheon Books, Inc., New York; reproduced by permission of the publisher and Thames and Hudson, Ltd., London.

of poetry and music. It was the call of the blood. In it the heroic and tragic destiny of the Teutonic race found its highest expression. When he listened to Siegfried's horn or the rushing music of the Valkyries' ride or to the devouring crackle of the fire music, the stolid German's visionary soul was filled with rhapsody. He dreamt dazzling dreams of mighty struggles and world-shaking cataclysms, in which he was cast for the role of the sublime warrior. He liked to think of his natural kindliness being transmuted into the ruthless stuff of which Attilas are made. His incurable romanticism was untamed by the hard common sense of the English or by the cold logic of the French. He was at the mercy of a leader who flashed the mirage of victory and conquest before his eyes.*

Our third example of impressionistic generalization is from a well-known American historian, Henry Steele Commager. We quote the summing-up paragraph of a long article on the "American Character," as it appeared to Commager in 1949.

What does all this add up to so far as the role of the United States in world affairs is concerned? What emerges most impressively are the positive traits. The American is optimistic, experimental, practical, intelligent, mature, generous, democratic and individualistic. He has heretofore fulfilled his responsibilities and can be expected to do so in the future. He has, in the last analysis, little confidence in other countries—except Britain—little confidence in their ability, their intelligence, or their goodwill. He is therefore inclined to think that the rest of the world will have to follow American leadership—not primarily because America is rich and powerful, but because the American way is the sensible, practical and right way.†

A few months before Professor Commager composed this image of American national character, a systematic survey was made to discover some of the widely prevailing stereotypes in eight different countries. Persons in Australia, Britain, France, West Germany, Italy, Netherlands, Norway, and the United States were asked to characterize various nationalities in terms of a set of given adjectives.

Any project of this kind faces formidable technical difficulties. Words carry different shades of meaning in different languages, even in the same language in different countries. One can never be sure that responses are strictly comparable. Findings also get out of date. A survey today would probably indicate some interesting changes in the patterns of responses: for example, one suspects there would be less disposition to characterize

---

* From Harold Butler, *The Lost Peace*, p. 93. Copyright 1942 by Harcourt, Brace & World, Inc., New York; reproduced with their permission.

† From "Analysis of the American Character," by H. S. Commager, in *New York Times Magazine*, January 2, 1949, p. 35. Copyright 1949 by the New York Times Company; reproduced by permission.

the Chinese as "peace-loving." This survey also suffered from lack of responses from behind the Iron Curtain. Despite these limitations, it is interesting to examine the response-patterns (summarized in Table 16.1), particularly those with reference to the nationalities for which we have quoted impressionistic images above.

TABLE 16.1 POPULAR STEREOTYPES OF OTHER NATIONALITIES

The six adjectives most frequently used to describe five nations
(braces indicate tie in percentages)

DESCRIPTION OF RUSSIANS BY—

AUSTRALIANS	BRITISH	FRENCH	GERMANS
domineering	hardworking	backward	cruel
hardworking	domineering	hardworking	backward
cruel	cruel	domineering	⎰hardworking
backward	backward	brave	⎱domineering
brave	brave	cruel	brave
progressive	⎰practical	progressive	practical
	⎱progressive		

ITALIANS	DUTCH	NORWEGIANS	AMERICANS (U.S.)
backward	cruel	hardworking	cruel
cruel	domineering	domineering	⎰hardworking
domineering	backward	backward	⎱domineering
⎰hardworking	hardworking	brave	backward
⎱brave	brave	cruel	⎰conceited
⎰intelligent	progressive	practical	⎱brave
⎱progressive			

DESCRIPTION OF AMERICANS (U.S.) BY—

AUSTRALIANS	BRITISH	FRENCH	GERMANS
progressive	progressive	practical	progressive
practical	⎰conceited	progressive	generous
intelligent	⎱generous	domineering	practical
conceited	peace-loving	⎰hardworking	intelligent
peace-loving	⎰intelligent	⎱intelligent	peace-loving
generous	⎱practical	⎰generous	hardworking
		⎱self-controlled	

ITALIANS	DUTCH	NORWEGIANS
generous	practical	hardworking
practical	progressive	practical
hardworking	hardworking	progressive
intelligent	⎰generous	generous
progressive	⎱peace-loving	peace-loving
peace-loving	intelligent	intelligent

DESCRIPTION OF BRITISH BY—

GERMANS	DUTCH	AMERICANS
intelligent	self-controlled	intelligent
self-controlled	peace-loving	⎰brave
conceited	⎰practical	⎱hardworking
domineering	⎱conceited	peace-loving
practical	hardworking	conceited
progressive	intelligent	self-controlled

DESCRIPTION OF FRENCH BY—

BRITISH	GERMANS	DUTCH
intelligent	intelligent	brave
conceited	conceited	generous
hardworking	⎰domineering	peace-loving
peace-loving	⎱peace-loving	⎰conceited
practical	⎰cruel	⎱progressive
⎰generous	⎱backward	⎰intelligent
⎰brave		⎱backward
⎱progressive		

DESCRIPTION OF CHINESE BY—

BRITISH	GERMANS	DUTCH
hardworking	hardworking	backward
backward	backward	⎰hardworking
peace-loving	⎰intelligent	⎱cruel
brave	⎰cruel	⎰brave
cruel	⎱brave	⎱self-controlled
intelligent	⎰self-controlled	⎱peace-loving
	⎱peace-loving	

Source: *How Nations See Each Other,* by William Buchanan and Hadley Cantril, pp. 51–52. Copyright 1953 by University of Illinois Press, Urbana; reproduced by permission.

The public mood

Impressionistic descriptions of national character often concentrate on the "public mood" or the "human climate" asserted to be discernible in a national community.

Many examples come to mind. Visitors to Mussolini's Italy in the 1920's and to Hitler's Germany in the 1930's came back with reports of startling transformation of the public mood. Apathy and inertia had given way to driving energy. Most Italians and Germans might not have much idea where they were headed, but millions had come to believe they were on their way, were "going places," in the idiom of American slang. That the destination was pillage and conquest did not diminish the international significance of this facet of the national character of Italy under Fascism and of Germany under National Socialism.

More recent examples are the reports brought back from Communist China. Impressions of foreign visitors vary widely, but there does seem to be a hard core of agreement that Communist rule has profoundly affected the mood of the Chinese people. This was the subject of a panel discussion programed in 1961 by the British Broadcasting Corporation, from which the following passage is quoted:

RICHARD HARRIS [a journalist with Chinese experience]: . . . I was in Shanghai when the Communists took over, and I had close contact with a lot of Chinese friends. The first thing that struck them was that they had an army which was disciplined, effective, and honest; and this was something they had never known before in China. What I observed in those first few weeks was a sudden sense of patriotism, which China had not had in the past. From that time onwards, the Chinese have been involved in their revolution.

NICHOLAS WOLLASTON [just returned from a visit to China]: I had never been in a Communist country before I went to China. I had no idea what to expect. But from what people told me in Hong Kong, I got the impression that I might be going into a country where the population was oppressed and slave-ridden and drab and colorless. I was very surprised when I got to Canton. I found that there were smiles on people's faces, and I had been told there wouldn't be. . . .

MRS. HUNG-YING BRYAN [Chinese wife of a former British Foreign Service Officer in China]: When I was in China recently I went back to my home-town in Fukien Province and visited the communes and villages which I had known before, and I did see what I wanted to see with no interference. The peasants, even now, are over 80 percent of the whole population; so what they are counts very much in China. The peasants in this part of the country were extremely backward from the point of view of science and technology. In my home-town there was no motor-road, no motor-car, and few bicycles. But the psychological change in the people was most revealing to me. For instance, my cousin's husband, who was a landlord, was often involved in banditry in the old days. After the liberation he was imprisoned by the People's Government for three years. My cousin used to smoke opium—she had nothing to do; they had plenty of money— but when her husband was imprisoned, she had to give up her servants, and her land was divided between the peasants who had no land, leaving enough for her and her family. When I saw her fifteen months ago, she was beaming with life, and she said: 'Look at my physique; I'm not smoking opium any more, because I'm doing things for my people; I'm learning from the peasants, and I'm now one of them." *

* From "Thinking About China: The Human Climate," in *The Listener*, March 2, 1961, p. 385. Reproduced by permission of the British Broadcasting Corporation, London, and of the panel participants.

The public mood in the United States has received a great deal of attention in recent years. There has been a spate of books on the moral consequences of our "affluent society." Noted commentators have repeatedly warned of the international consequences of the sense of drift and lack of national purpose which they observe in American society. Here are two samples. The first, quoted in part in our introduction, was written in 1959 by Walter Lippmann:

> The critical weakness of our society is that for the time being our people do not have great purposes which they are united in wanting to achieve. The public mood of the country is defensive, to hold on and to conserve, not to push forward and to create. We talk about ourselves these days as if we were a completed society, one which has achieved its purposes, and has no further great business to transact.
> The strength of the Soviet regime, which accounts for its harshness and its toughness and also for its cruelty, is that it is above all else a purposeful society in which all the main energies of the people are directed and dedicated to its purposes. This sense of purpose accounts for the astounding success of the regime in science and in technology both civilian and military. The Soviet nation has its energies and its resources focussed on purposes which its rulers define, and all else must make way for the achievement of these purposes.
> Thus in our encounter with the Soviet rulers, in the confrontation of the two social orders, the question is whether this country can recover what for the time being it does not have—a sense of great purpose of high destiny. This is the crucial point. For without a revival of American purpose, Mr. K. is likely to win the competitive race in which he is the challenger.*

The second commentary on the American mood is by George Kennan, lifelong diplomat and historian, and in 1961 appointed American Ambassador to Yugoslavia:

> If you ask me—as a historian, let us say—whether a country in the state . . . [of the American people] today, with no highly developed sense of national purpose, with the overwhelming accent of life on personal comfort and amusement, with a dearth of public services and a surfeit of privately sold gadgetry, with a chaotic transportation system, with its great urban areas being gradually disintegrated by the leading switch to motor transportation, with an educational system where quality has been extensively sacrificed to quantity, and with insufficient social discipline even to keep its major industries functioning without grievous interruptions—if you ask me whether such a country has, over the long run, good chances of competing with a purposeful, serious, and disciplined society such as that of the Soviet Union, I must say that the answer is "no." †

* From "Today and Tomorrow," Sept. 17, 1959. Reproduced by permission of Mr. Lippmann.
† From an address before the Woman's National Democratic Club, Oct. 22, 1959. Reproduced by permission of Mr. Kennan.

Self-criticism itself became in the late 1950's an important facet of the elite mood in America. A perceptive British journalist, Patrick O'Donovan, reported in 1960:

> If you listen to America, you will detect a persistent background noise. It is clearly audible behind the deafening small talk of practical politics and the noise of approval and happiness and self-congratulation. . . .
> It is a ferociously critical and very literate sort of noise. It is saying that there is something profoundly wrong in and with America.
> It is a fairly new sort of noise. It is made up of the voices and writing of university teachers, of theologians, of politically minded scientists, of perturbed generals, of most of the serious journalists, of almost all the artists and there are even a few politicians in the chorus.
> They express themselves in terms that even a dedicated European anti-American would hesitate to use. Their criticism sounds at times very close to despair. They talk of their own civilization and times as "dripping with fat," as "the age of the shrug," as one of "spiritual flabbiness." "We are breeding a new type of human being—a guy with a full belly, an empty mind and a hollow heart." Some, like the novelist John Steinbeck, return from abroad and sit in horror before a "creeping, all pervading nerve gas of immorality." All these things were said by the sort of men who in Britain might expect recognition from the Throne in their old age.
> There is nothing organized or unanimous about this disapproval. Its exponents may be Jesuits or a Presidential hopeful or a richly salaried California scientist. They all profoundly love the original idea of America. It is, en masse, quite different from the anger that comes echoing over here occasionally from England. . . .
> These wildly assorted Americans deplore a loss of morality and purpose in their society. They find an emptiness where a belief should be. . . . Almost invariably . . . there is the idea that their present society will be unable to compete morally and economically and, by implication, militarily, with the opposition, which, to put it bluntly, is Russian. . . .
> It fastens on the fact that few people choose to be perturbed and that few consider any real sort of sacrifice necessary for their own survival or the betterment of the world. It comes close to saying that America is going bad because it is so rich and intends to be richer. . . .*

Lippmann and Kennan were indicting the American mood as they perceived it in 1959. O'Donovan was viewing the American scene early in 1960. Whether these images fit the reality today, the reader may wish to decide for himself.

Plainly, impressions of the human climate, the public mood, in one's

* From "A Chorus Out of Tune," by Patrick O'Donovan, in *The Observer*, February 14, 1960. Copyright 1960 by The Observer, Ltd., London; reproduced by permission.

own country and in others, are data of prima facie relevance in any discussion of the foundations of international politics. So too, it would seem, are more comprehensive characterizations such as those quoted earlier. Whether generally accurate or grossly distorted, impressionistic images of national character provide, for good or for ill, much of the data upon which governmental policies are based, and upon which such policies are judged at home and abroad. We say for good or for ill, because distorted images can produce mischievous, even disastrous international consequences. On this subject the American psychologist, Alexander Leighton, has something important to say. With respect to

the images that other nations may have of us and we of them, there is the problem of discrepancy between reality and the images we have of ourselves as we move and act in relation to other nations. We have idealized pictures of ourselves and we have guilty pictures, and both are possibly as far from reality as are the distorted impressions other nations often have of us.

False images of ourselves as a nation produce barriers to understanding our position in relation to other nations and the consequences, particularly the indirect consequences, of our acts. Thus, we may think we are being cooperative when actually we appear weak. Or, on the other hand, what seems to us a demonstration of reasonable firmness may strike another country as an overt act of hostility requiring immediate retaliation. What we suppose is a generous effort to give support may be angrily treated as an attempt at exploitation. We are confident that we will never, without provocation, attack any nation with atomic bombs and so we discount the threat element in our possession of the weapons, while other nations with a different view of us never forget it.

When difficulties arise, we have a tendency to write off the behavior of another country as unreasonable, as due to peculiarities of its innate nature, or as the product of evil leaders with evil intentions. Other countries in their turn do the same regarding our behavior. Such conclusions may, at times, be just in terms of certain premises, but the trouble with them is that, just or not, they are a dead end. They do not lead to solving the problem. They lead to giving up, or to one of the well-established patterns of hitting back. There is no blindness like the blindness of self-righteousness. Inquiry and cool thinking with adequate perspective habitually cease to function at the time they are most necessary. In their place comes back talk, heightened emotions, hair-trigger readiness, misinterpretations and the taking of positions from which pride makes retreat impossible.*

* From pp. 105-6 of *Human Relations in a Changing World*, by A. H. Leighton. Copyright by A. H. Leighton; reproduced by permission of Russell & Volkening, Inc., on behalf of A. H. Leighton.

A functional approach to national character

Impressionistic images of national character may reflect keen observation and shrewd intuition. But such impressions, as Leighton says, are just as apt to reflect sheer bias and almost limitless capacity of people for self-deception about their own behavior and the behavior of other nationalities.

Impressionistic images, we repeat, have influenced policy-makers in the past. It would be unrealistic to suppose that such notions will not be just as influential in the future. But pure impressionism is an insecure basis upon which to build national policies or to estimate the international capabilities of nations. It would be highly desirable to put thinking about national character on a more trustworthy basis. One step in this direction is to establish an explicit frame of concepts within which to compare the behavioral patterns of different nations.

One can go about this task in various ways. Table 16.2 suggests one possible scheme for classifying those facets of national character which may be regarded as having special relevance in the context of international politics. Running through the categories of patterns identified in the table, one will find *normative* aspects (notions of what is right, proper, desirable, and vice versa), *cognitive* or *existential* aspects (notions of how things actually are in the real world), and *affective* aspects (emotional reactions or feelings—friendliness, hostility, fear, etc.).

A given pattern may be primarily normative: for example, notions as to what goals one's government should be trying to achieve. Or a pattern may be primarily cognitive: for example, notions as to the prestige and esteem one's nation actually commands abroad. Or a pattern may be primarily affective: for example, feelings of distrust towards certain nations. Normative, cognitive, and affective aspects may also be associated in the same pattern, as, for example, in the rather widespread American attitude towards China in the late 1940's, compounded of a generally kindly feeling towards Chinese, abhorrence of Communism, and expectation that somehow the anti-Communist forces in China would in the end prevail. The same three aspects are associated, to cite another example, in the rather prevalent American attitude towards female physicians: the notion that it is improper for female physicians to practice on adult male patients, the notion that female physicians are generally less competent than male physicians, and the reluctance of most men to consult female physicians no matter how competent they may be.

Finally, no matter how national behavioral patterns are classified, it should always be kept in mind that one is classifying personal images that are deemed to be more or less characteristic or typical (that is, prevalent) within a given national community; and that different observers, with different preconceptions and viewpoints, may reach different conclusions, sometimes startlingly different conclusions, regarding the behavioral characteristics of their own and other national communities. In short, one can systematize, and make them more explicit, but one cannot eliminate the factor of subjective personal judgment. Now, with these points in mind, let us examine Table 16.2.

TABLE 16.2 SELECTED INGREDIENTS OF NATIONAL CHARACTER

A. Behavioral patterns pertaining primarily to citizens' attitudes toward and relations with the national community of which they are members:
 1. Attitudes toward and relations with the community as a whole:
  a. Attitudes towards authority, obedience, loyalty, and the moral limits thereof
  b. Attitudes towards service to the state and towards those who serve the state
  c. Ideas, myths, and traditions regarding the nation's past
  d. Conceptions of national interest, purpose, and destiny
  e. Conceptions of and degree of commitment to intranation social goals
  f. Morale, discipline, and behavior under stress
  g. Other patterns
 2. Attitudes toward and relations with fellow members of the national community:
  a. Attitudes regarding role allocation: who should and should not do what
  b. Attitudes toward and relations with persons regarded as social equals, social inferiors, and social superiors
  c. Tolerance of values and attitudes antagonistic to one's own
  d. Other patterns
B. Behavioral patterns pertaining primarily to attitudes toward and relations with other national-states and the citizens thereof:
 1. Attitudes toward and opinions regarding other nation-states conceived as entities:
  a. Images regarding states identified as allies or potential allies
  b. Images regarding states identified as enemies or potential enemies
  c. Images regarding other states
 2. Attitudes toward and opinions regarding other nationalities:
  a. Images regarding nationalities toward which orientation is predominantly friendly and/or favorable
  b. Images regarding nationalities toward which orientation is predominantly hostile and/or unfavorable
  c. Other images
 3. Attitudes toward and relations with individual foreign persons:
  a. Patterns that prevail within our country
  b. Patterns that prevail when in foreigner's country

Most of the categories of Table 16.2 are self-explanatory, but a few comments and illustrations on them may be helpful. Attitudes towards authority, obedience, and loyalty (A.1.*a*) and towards service to the state and those who serve the state (A.1.*b*) should cast light on the measure of a nation's political solidarity and on its government's ability to command both loyal and dedicated service from its citizens—factors of manifest relevance in any calculation of a nation's international capabilities.

National myths and traditions (A.1.*c*) always contribute something to an understanding of current conceptions of national interest, purpose, and destiny (A.1.*d*). These, in turn, provide valuable indicators regarding the specific objectives and strategies to be expected from the governments under consideration. How, for example, could one make sense out of the United States government's refusal, throughout the 1950's, to accept the irreversibility of the Communist Revolution in China, without some knowledge of historic American myths and traditional American policies with regard to China? Very few Americans have visited China. But for several generations China was the scene of dedicated service by Christian missionaries of many faiths. American merchants never sold great quantities of goods in China. But the myth persisted that this most populous country was potentially the world's greatest market. When European imperialists moved in on the moribund Chinese empire in the waning years of the nineteenth century, the official voice of America was raised in protest. From that time on there was close to consensus among Americans who thought about foreign affairs at all that it was the duty of the United States to protect the political and territorial integrity of China until such time as a responsible and democratic Chinese government could assume effective responsibility for the country's future. The Communist victory was repugnant to everything Americans had stood for in China since the turn of the century, and the repugnance was heightened by the rather widely prevalent American fear and hatred of communism.

Commitment to particular intranation social goals (A.1.*e*) relates to public demands and expectations which may significantly limit the efforts and resources which politicians will venture to allocate for military defense, foreign aid, or other international projects. In the middle 1950's, for example, the British people had lived with austerity for some fifteen years—rationing, high taxes, and other policies that cramped the individual consumer's ability to purchase goods and services. During the same period, the British people had become accustomed to a range of publicly financed welfare services—of which the National Health Service became the symbol. By the mid-1950's public demands for an end to austerity and public expectations regarding the welfare services set highly inelastic limits on the proportion of the GNP which it was politically expedient to allocate to national defense—with consequent serious deterioration of the military establishment.

Patterns of morale, discipline, and especially behavior under stress (A.1.*f*) focus on the vitally important issue of how a national community is likely to react, not only to austerity and adversity, but especially to overwhelming disaster. For obvious reasons this aspect of national character obtrudes into any thorough examination of national capability, these days. As noted in Chapter 8, estimates of casualties in the initial hours or days of a full-scale nuclear war might run as high as 30 to 50 percent or more of a nation's civilian population. Buildings would be smashed; fires would become conflagrations; water systems would be wrecked; food and water would become contaminated; hospitals would be destroyed or rendered unusable by fallout. Transport would be so crippled as to render all but impossible any large-scale evacuation of survivors to safer places (if any).

How would the survivors of such a catastrophe behave? Would their routines and habits break down completely? At what point would a society cease to be a going concern, and become a hysterical mob? And (the sixty-four dollar question) are there grounds for believing that nations would react differently in such a catastrophe?

Official thinking and planning in the United States (and probably in some other countries as well) appears to rest upon optimistic assumptions regarding the nation's ability to carry on and recover from extreme catastrophe. Such optimism is frequently rationalized by reference to civilian behavior under bombing in World War II. That evidence, as we have emphasized already, has limited relevance because of the enormous rise in firepower since 1945. However, it is useful to recall the conclusions reached by the United States Strategic Bombing Survey, on the basis of on-the-ground investigations conducted immediately after the fighting ceased in Germany and in Japan.

Behavior in catastrophe: evidence from World War II

The report on Germany emphasized the severity of the effects of home-front destruction on civilian morale, and also the ability of a ruthless police to maintain some semblance of social order. In reading the following passage, the reader should remember that the bombs that rained on Germany were not armed with atomic or thermonuclear warheads, but with TNT and other pre-atomic explosives.*

* From the "Overall Report: European War," pp. 96-108, and the "Summary Report: Pacific War," pp. 21, 25, of the United States Strategic Bombing Survey. Government Printing Office, 1945 and 1946.

Members of the Nazi Party maintained their morale under bombing more firmly than persons not belonging to the party. People who accepted Nazi ideology likewise were stronger in their support of the regime under bombing than were the less zealous.

Civilians who had a vested interest in a German victory withstood bombing better than people who felt they had nothing to gain. Satisfaction with protective and relief measures was also associated with high morale. Where people felt the air-raid shelters were inadequate, morale was low.

Anticipation of the rigor of war and expectation of being bombed did not constitute the best preparation for the air war. Morale was higher among the people who had thought little about the war than among those mentally prepared. Whereas expectation should help to cushion the shock, it apparently has the opposite effect in many cases. . . .

Bombing achieved its depressing morale effects both through direct impact and through modifications in the civilian way of living. The indirect consequences . . . were crucial in affecting morale. The disruption of public utilities in a community did much to lower the will to resist. Especially significant was the disruption of transportation service; it was the most critical public utility for the morale of the civilian population. . . .

The German experience suggests that even a first-class military power—rugged and resilient as Germany was—cannot live long under full-scale and free exploitation of air weapons over the heart of its territory. . . .

The mental reaction of the German people to air attack is significant. Under ruthless Nazi control they showed surprising resistance to the terror and hardship of repeated air attack, to the destruction of their homes and belongings, and to the conditions under which they were reduced to live. Their morale, their belief in ultimate victory or satisfactory compromise, and their confidence in their leaders declined, but they continued to work efficiently as long as the physical means of production remained. The power of a police state over its people cannot be [that is, should not be] underestimated. . . .

The report on Japan states:

A striking aspect of the air attack was the pervasiveness with which its impact on morale blanketed Japan. Roughly one-quarter of all people in cities fled or were evacuated, and these evacuees, who themselves were of singularly low morale, helped spread discouragement and disaffection. . . .

Progressively lowered morale was characterized by loss of faith in both military and civilian leadership, loss of confidence in Japan's military might and increasing distrust of government news releases and propaganda. People became short-tempered and more outspoken in their criticism of the government, the war and affairs in general. Until the end, however, national traditions of obedience and conformity, reinforced by the police organization, remained effective in controlling the behavior of the population.

So much for TNT. But what about the effects of the atomic bombs dropped on Hiroshima and Nagasaki? which, it must be remembered, were mere birdshot compared with the thermonuclear monsters stockpiled in great quantities today:

> . . . the primary reaction of the populace to the bomb was fear, uncontrolled terror, strengthened by the sheer horror of the destruction and suffering witnessed and experienced by the survivors. Prior to the dropping of the atomic bombs, the people of the two cities had fewer misgivings about the war than people in other cities and their morale held up after it better than might have been expected. Twenty-nine percent of the survivors interrogated indicated that after the atomic bomb was dropped they were convinced that victory for Japan was impossible. Twenty-four percent stated that because of the bomb they felt personally unable to carry on with the war. Some forty percent testified to various degrees of defeatism. . . . In many cases the reaction was one of resignation. . . .

It is an open question whether the findings quoted above have much relevance to the scale of destruction manifestly achievable these days. Experts disagree as to the amount of ruin that would be required to smash any society beyond possibility of recovery. But ability to carry on under stress is a factor not only in total disaster but also in a wide range of lesser contingencies, *including the seemingly endless shocks and alarms of the Cold War.* With reference to such contingencies, it is highly relevant to compare the morale and discipline of different nations.

All the subcategories under A.2 of Table 16.2 apply to the issue of the bearing of interpersonal relationships on a nation's capabilities. Attitudes regarding who should and should not perform various social roles (A.2.a) manifestly bear on the extent to which a nation's human resources are efficiently utilized. A.2.b applies to the issue whether patterns of social stratification prevailing within a given society tend to lubricate or put sand in the gears of the nation's economic, governmental, and military institutions. The same relevance attaches to patterns of tolerance and intolerance (A.2.e).

Utilization of human resources

People constitute a nation's most valuable resource. This has been said many times. It bears repeating here because the rules governing utilization of human talents and skills have a profoundly important bearing on the relations of nations in this era of revolutionary technological advance and protracted cold war.

Nations differ widely in their patterns of human allocation. Such differences—as we have witnessed in recent years, for example, in the sphere of science and engineering—can have far-reaching consequences for a nation's military security and international prestige, as well as for its economic productivity and other achievements.

In every country one finds a more or less rigid set of rules as to who should and should not do what. Some rules may be embodied in formal laws: for example, regulations prescribing who is eligible for military service. More commonly such rules are expressed in more or less generally observed customs and attitudes, especially in socially approved taboos: for example, the American taboo against admitting women (except nurses) to roles of extreme military peril. In the idiom of sociology, these rules—formal and customary—determine the "role differentiation" prevailing in any given society.

Role differentiation can rest on either "universalistic" or "particularistic" criteria, to use two more technical terms. If a given position is filled on the basis of specified competence to do the work involved, universalistic criteria are said to prevail. If, however, the position is filled on some basis other than specific competence, particularistic criteria prevail.

In no society are all positions ever filled on the basis of the most competent person for each job. Persons may be excluded because they are women or Negroes or Jews or working class or too old, or for some other particularistic reason.

Traditionalistic preindustrial societies tend to be strongly particularistic. In such societies, family connections, social status, and similar criteria weigh heavily in who does and who does not fill certain roles. However, a high degree of particularism has not rendered societies incapable of survival so long as they rested primarily upon simple occupations such as primitive hunting, fishing, grazing animals, subsistence farming, etc.

Everywhere, as described in Chapter 15, the process of modernization has put traditionalistic societies under severe strain. Nearly always, one source of strain is role allocation. In order to modernize, a society has to acquire and make use of specialized skills of many kinds—mechanical, engineering, medical, administrative, managerial. The farther a society advances along the modernizing route, the greater becomes the need for assigning people to positions because of what they can do rather than because of who they are. Indeed, a relatively high degree of universalism in filling economic, administrative and other social roles has come to be generally recognized as one of the absolute requisites of achieving and operating any modern urban-industrial society.

No system ever scores one hundred percent on this requisite. In every society some roles continue to be assigned for particularistic reasons. Modern societies carry on in spite of these particularistic discriminations. Nevertheless, every society pays a price for its discriminations. The more complex and specialized a society becomes, the higher becomes the price. Such wastage of human resources has become in our advanced technological era an increasingly significant aspect of the relative capabilities of nations.

Table 13.3 (page 397, above) indicates something of the scope of this human allocation problem. The roles listed include only a fraction of the total in any complex modern society. Most of the categories could be divided into many subcategories. But even this selective and highly generalized list emphasizes the multiplicity of specialized skills required to operate a modern society.

A good deal has been said about the wastage of human resources in the Soviet Union and other Communist countries. There is evidence that many thousands of talented persons with specialized skills have fled into exile from the Communist terror. It is also known that the positions of greatest responsibility are reserved for trusted members of the Communist Party. Whatever the Communists have gained in submissive loyalty by such methods they have paid for in wastage of scarce human resources. But this truth provides no basis for complacency on our side of the Iron Curtain.

Western societies also have a poor record. In many countries religious faith operates, covertly if not overtly, to exclude or to limit the access of talented persons to certain professions. Hitler's ruthless anti-Semitic policies deprived Germany of many thousands of highly competent physicians, scientists, business executives, government administrators, and other talented specialists. Subtle—sometimes not so subtle—anti-Semitism produces serious, if less drastic, discriminations in every Western country. American Negroes are more or less excluded from many of the more important roles listed in Table 13.3. This has the effect of reducing from 180-odd millions to about 160 millions the population-base from which American society recruits most of its top-level politicians, civil servants, military officers, university scholars, physicians, engineers, lawyers, and others. Similar discrimination operates against other ethnic minorities: Filipinos, Mexicans, Indians, Chinese, Japanese, and still others. Altogether, ethnic discrimination in America constitutes a self-imposed handicap of at least 10 percent in terms of waste of human resources.

Prejudice, often amounting to a rigid taboo, against women in most nonhousehold roles continues to be an intangible but generally effective obstacle to full utilization of the brain power of a great many nations. This prejudice has prevailed in varying degrees in almost every society at one time or another. It is notorious in America, where most male scientists, engineers, physicians, lawyers, university professors, politicians, higher civil servants, and business executives bitterly resent intrusion of women into their respective professions. Most universities discriminate subtly against women in the higher faculty ranks. Social taboos virtually prohibit female physicians from practicing on male patients (except infants). Every conceivable obstacle is put in the way of women practicing the various branches of industrial engineering. These attitudes permeate not only the professions but also the student bodies of universities and colleges, and above all the family environment. They affect the career plans of most girls, no matter what their intellectual capacities and interests may be.

In contrast, according to an investigation carried out by an English educator, "in the Soviet Union no distinction is really made between the access of women and of men to the professions. Some 25 percent of engineers and 75 percent of doctors are women. There are women aviators, even generals." * Some of the leading Russian scientists are women. The American Educational Mission, which visited the Soviet Union in 1959, reported that "there seems to be complete equality between men and women" in Russian schools and universities.

Any nation may prefer to exclude one group or another from top positions in teaching, research, engineering, government, industry, or other professions. But for such discrimination, we repeat, a nation pays a price, the price of incomplete utilization of its intellectual resources. Under some sets of conditions this may not matter very much, at least not in terms of the nation's foreign relations. But in the intense struggle that has recently developed for scientific, technological, and industrial primacy, there is no use blinking the advantage which the Russians—and the Chinese too— derive from their fuller utilization of human resources.

Finally, racial discrimination is producing indirect effects which, in the long run, may prove to be no less damaging. Africans, Asians, and other non-European peoples are increasingly identifying with racial minorities in the Western countries. Africans may have very little in common with American Negroes, except a deep sense of bitterness and revolt against the historic discriminations associated with European colonial rule and with Negro life in the United States. But it is widely recognized that

* E. J. King, *Other Schools and Ours*, p. 167. Copyright 1955 by E. J. King; published by Rinehart & Co., New York; reproduced by permission.

national patterns of racial discrimination have international consequences, and that these consequences are generally adverse to the West and favorable to our Communist adversaries.

Attitudes toward education and learning

Attitudes toward education and learning deserve major attention in any discussion of the bearings of national character on international politics. It is evident that education is one of the keys required to unlock the intellectual resources latent in any community. It should be likewise evident that the educational requirements of a community increase rapidly with its technological, economic, and other aspects of social development.

The bearings of a nation's schools, universities, and research institutions, on its capacity to govern, to provide military defense, and to conduct foreign affairs have become increasingly apparent during the past generation. A modern military establishment depends heavily upon research scientists and industrial engineers as well as upon well-trained officers and enlisted personnel and capable civilian administrators. All the public services need more and better educated personnel. The same holds true for all but the most menial roles in farming, industry, transportation, communications, and every other economic enterprise. Social scientists as well as physical and biological scientists are coming to be recognized as having special expertise bearing on many problems of national interest. Distinguished works of philosophy, literature, and the fine arts contribute no less surely than do explorations of outer space to a nation's intellectual stature. The prestige which lends added authority to the voice of the statesman springs from intellectual achievements in many fields as well as from command of lethal weapons. The more advanced a nation's technology, the greater is its demand for scientists, engineers, and technicians of all kinds. The more complex a nation's social structure and the more extensive its foreign interests and projects, the greater becomes its need for expert social analysts and skilled administrators. In short, from whatever perspective one views the foreign policies and operations of a modern state, especially the greater Powers, the more evident it becomes that a nation's schools and universities, its teachers and students, educational policies and public attitudes toward education and learning, all have a critically important bearing on the nation's role in the Society of Nations.

National attitudes and policies with regard to education and learning vary widely. Such differences arise in part from the stage of a nation's economic and social development. For example, the overriding problem in most of the newer nations (and in some of the older ones as well) is to obtain even the bare minimum of educated men and women required to direct and sustain the modernizing process.

Education and higher learning present somewhat different but not less difficult problems to the nations which have experienced the industrial revolution. None of these nations has enough physical and social scientists, engineers and technicians, adequately educated politicians and administrators, to cope with the problems of this era of revolutionary change. In Western Europe and Britain, the central issue is how to overcome traditional attitudes and policies which have limited higher education to a tiny minority recruited predominantly from the more affluent social classes. In the Soviet Union, education is recognized as a requisite of rapid technological advance and as an important symbol of national prestige, and has been given high priority. In the United States the issue is more complex. The main problem here is not so much to provide more schools and universities (though more are and will be needed). The basic issue is rather to improve what we have, and to reorient American attitudes towards education and learning.

We in America have taken great pride in our country-wide system of state-supported schools and institutions of higher learning, supplemented by hundreds of private schools, colleges and universities. No other nation provides such educational opportunities for so large a proportion of its population. Yet there seems to be a growing conviction that American educational achievements and American attitudes toward education and learning fall far short of what is required to safeguard our future or to sustain the role which we have elected to play upon the international stage.

The plain truth, contend the critics, is that Americans have been slow to grasp the idea that libraries and laboratories, schools, colleges and universities, teachers and research scholars, all represent precious national resources. We do not yet seem to appreciate how heavily our future prosperity, influence, and even survival depend upon these intellectual resources. There has been tardy recognition that wars can be won or lost in scientific and engineering laboratories. There is growing awareness that the tools and skills of agriculture, industry, transportation, and other branches of the economy rest ultimately upon theoretical as well as applied science. But, it has been contended repeatedly, most Americans do not yet appreciate how vitally the liberal arts—the social sciences, philosophy, letters and the fine arts—can contribute to the statesman and to the private citizen who jointly face the baffling and often terrifying political problems of our age.

American scientists, social scientists, and humanistic scholars all played key roles in winning World War II. The organization and execution of the famous Manhattan (atomic bomb) Project was merely the most spectacular of the triumphs of American science and engineering. Less widely known were the contributions of economists, anthropologists, psychologists, and representatives of virtually every other branch of higher learning. These men helped to bring order out of chaos in bomb-target selection and in the conduct of economic and psychological warfare. They devised new methods for estimating enemy industrial capabilities, for evaluating enemy morale, for breaking enemy codes, for increasing American war production, for curbing inflation, for administering lend-lease aid to our allies, for educating American troops in the ways of foreign peoples, and for carrying out scores of other tasks essential to winning the war.

Americans may justly feel proud of those achievements. But we should not forget the effort and talent needlessly wasted in the process. Nor should we forget the risks and delays incurred because of prewar failure even to recognize the role and importance of academic knowledge and research in national defense and foreign relations.

The American people owe much to their wartime allies who held the lines while we belatedly mobilized our intellectual as well as our material resources. Spectacular achievements later in the war should not blind us to early blunders, described by one commentator in 1942, as "a forced evolution by progression from disaster to disaster."

In that struggle the needs of the military forces collided with all home-front activities—agriculture, industry, research and education. Agriculture wielded a sufficiently formidable club over Congress to secure liberal draft deferments for farm labor. Community sentiment impelled local draft boards to defer married men with families as long as possible. The result was a squeeze which progressively forced specialized workers from factories, offices, and laboratories. Colleges and universities, in particular, were all but stripped of able-bodied young men and most of their finest teachers and scholars.

Many public-spirited citizens apparently believe to this day that all this was as it should be. The military services wanted young men who made the best combat soldiers. Higher education was widely regarded as more or less a luxury that should be dispensed with in wartime. Besides, ran the argument, it was neither democratic nor fair to send one young man off to war and his next-door neighbor to college.

This pattern of thinking pervaded every influential group in the United States. A few voices were raised in protest, but no one in high authority paid the slightest attention. Only when the war was over did a few people begin to realize what had happened and to speculate on its implications and future consequences. After World War II, this facet of American character was characterized as follows by Raymond Fosdick (then president of the Rockefeller Foundation):

> Like any procedure which expends capital resources without providing means for replenishing them, the interruption of advanced training in the basic sciences seems to cost little at the moment, and it serves an emergency by releasing manpower. But it is a policy of desperation which places a crippling mortgage on the future. It grinds up the seed-corn of scientific progress in the next generation to make a day's feed for the war machine.
>
> The consequences of this unintelligent [wartime] policy are now upon us. There is a serious, even alarming shortage of adequate personnel in almost every field which requires advanced thinking. Whether in physics or chemistry or the biological and medical sciences, the situation is the same. In subjects like bacteriology, biochemistry, anatomy, biophysics and physiology, it is almost impossible to find younger men with adequate teaching and research qualifications.*

Results in the liberal arts were fully as disastrous as in the physical and biological sciences. Wartime diversion of talented youth from advanced training and research in the humanities and social sciences did not produce such spectacular deficiencies. It may be difficult to calculate so precisely the hidden damage done to America's ability to provide intelligent and human leadership in the years to come. But the shortage of top-quality middle-aged scholars and teachers today, in the 1960's, is as acute in the liberal arts as in the physical sciences. To the degree that superior leadership both in statecraft and in science and technology are elements of national strength, our World War II policy with respect to education and higher learning did indeed "grind up the seed-corn" of the next generation.

This brief review of wartime attitudes and policies provides essential background against which to compare present-day American attitudes and policies with those of our principal antagonist, the Soviet Union. For some twelve years following World War II, most American educators, and virtually everyone else, either ignored or derisively down-graded Soviet education and research. Those were also the days when the late Senator McCarthy and his cohorts were engaged in further weakening the American educational structure and the confidence of the American people in their teachers and scholars. Then, in 1957, the Russians put the first Sputniks into orbit. The reaction in America was incredulity and shock, followed by a long overdue examination of attitudes and policies. Since then there has been a spate of words, some of them hysterical, many of them ill informed, but all of them reflecting heightened awareness of the strategic political role which education and learning play in the world of today.

* From pp. 24-25 of The Rockefeller Foundation, *Annual Report 1946*.

The following paragraphs represent an attempt to summarize some of these currents of new thinking.

Broadly speaking, there are two ways to obtain personnel for any enterprise: by compulsion or by enticement. As a general rule, the more original and creative the work to be performed, the less effective is compulsion as a mode of recruitment. Soviet policies and experience are often cited as evidence to the contrary. A recent investigation of Soviet science and technology, by A. G. Korol (of the Center for International Studies of the Massachusetts Institute of Technology) concludes that the upsurge of Russian technology is in part attributable to ruthless allocation of human resources. "The individual is subordinated, fields of training are prescribed and limited, with quotas for each category, and the best possible facilities and resources are mobilized for training in the most crucially needed fields." *

The alternative mode of obtaining specialists is to make the role sufficiently attractive to win and hold enough talented performers. Broadly speaking, making a role attractive may involve pay, working conditions, social prestige, or any combination thereof. For a tiny minority, a very tiny one it would appear, the psychological rewards of research discovery, creative self-expression, and the sense of a job well done may be sufficient in themselves. But no nation could staff its university faculties, research institutes, laboratories, top-level engineering and administrative roles by means of psychological rewards alone. In addition, there must be relatively attractive pay, congenial working conditions, and social prestige.

Whatever degree of compulsion may remain in Soviet education and higher role-allocation, nearly every observer reports that Russian intellectuals are well paid, that they command steadily improving facilities, and that they stand high in the Soviet social hierarchy. Korol (quoted above) states (p. 403) that, "in terms of status, prestige, and economic advantage, there is no desirable alternative to professional education in the Soviet Union (aside from a purely Party career)."

The same certainly cannot be said of the United States, and probably not of any Western country. Regarding the United States, it is necessary at the outset to distinguish between careers in industry, in the universities, and in the public service. With rare exceptions, private industry pays better than government and much better than teaching institutions, *for comparable levels of talent*. The drift of American scientists and engineers, and to a lesser degree economists and other social scientists, away from university

---

* From p. 399 of *Soviet Education for Science and Technology*, by A. G. Korol. Copyright 1959 by the Massachusetts Institute of Technology, Cambridge; reproduced by permission.

teaching is frequently noted and deplored. Within the colleges and universities, scientists and engineers are generally paid more, often a great deal more, than teachers of history, philosophy, literature, and the fine arts. But academic salaries even of scientists and engineers, compare adversely with the financial rewards of business, medicine, and various other professions. Even more depressive is the relatively low esteem which teachers and scholars have generally commanded in American society. Also, except in a few of the richer universities, laboratories and libraries are usually inadequate and teaching conditions far from ideal. No well-run American business corporation would tolerate such waste of top-level talent as prevails in hundreds of American colleges and universities. These and other considerations are said to deter many youth from entering the American academic profession. These conditions also suggest a good deal with regard to the status of higher education in our predominantly business-oriented society.

Given attractive professional rewards, there remains the task of locating, supporting, and educating talented youth. Historically these functions everywhere were left mainly to private initiative and chance. Until quite recently, higher education everywhere was limited mainly to youth whose parents or patrons could pay the bills. In the United States a more flexible class structure and a tradition of self-help enabled a larger proportion of talented but impecunious youth to obtain college and university degrees. But systematic search for talent is still in its infancy in the Western world. And one has to admit that the principal stimulus to do anything at all about this has been the goad of Soviet competition.

The principle of educating talented youth irrespective of ability to pay involves subsidizing them through their higher education and professional training. In one country after another, government (at the local as well as national level) has accepted increasing responsibility for financing the education of future teachers, scholars, and other specialists. Here again the Soviet Union leads the field. According to various estimates, some 90 percent or more of Soviet students are subsidized, with the percentage still higher at the leading University in Moscow. In Britain over three-quarters of all university students are supported wholly or partially by some unit of government—a percentage which becomes rather less impressive when one notes that the university population constitutes only about one-fifth of 1 percent of the country's total population.

In the United States, family support and self-help have proved increasingly insufficient as higher education takes longer and longer and becomes ever more expensive. The State governments heavily subsidize higher education through relatively low fees in the State colleges and universities. Recently the Federal government has gotten into the act, with direct and indirect support, especially in the science and engineering fields. But total support, from all sources, falls far short of what will certainly be needed to sustain the international policies and prestige of the United States.

In spite of our long history of free public education, American society still suffers from other, still less favorable attitudes. We have alluded above to the rather low esteem which teachers have traditionally commanded in American society. This is but a facet of a more pervasive anti-intellectualism. One suspects that many business executives share Henry Ford's famous remark that "history is bunk"; and the cynical comment attributed to another leading business executive that "basic research is what scientists do when they don't know what they are doing"; and the widespread characterization of the social sciences as "various ideologies."

Given such attitudes, it is not surprising that in our strongly business-oriented society physical capital is generally more highly regarded than human expertise and imagination. Businessmen and politicians, as well as the vast majority of ordinary taxpayers, have traditionally given much higher priority to new machines than to better educated brains. The American economist Kenneth Galbraith contends that this characteristic American faith in machines, and the related notion that machines are more important than people, misses the point that "machines do not improve themselves; they are the product of improved men."

> And most technological advance [he continues] is now the result, not of the accident of inspiration or genius, but of highly purposeful effort. Once we had to wait for the Edisons and Wrights. Now, through education and organization, we get something approaching the same results from much more common clay.
>
> So it comes to this. We now get the larger part of our industrial growth not from more capital investment but from improvements in men and improvements brought about by improved men. And this process of technological advance has become fairly predictable. We get from men pretty much what we invest in them. . . . Investment in personal development is therefore at least as useful as an index of progress as investment in physical capital. This is the kind of change which solemn men of self-confessed soundness of judgment will continue to resist. . . .

But, Galbraith predicts, the Russians will goad us into it.

> The final reason for thinking that our arrangements for investing in personal development are deficient is that the Soviets have, technically speaking, superior ones. They begin with all resources under public control; hence there is no problem of transferring those to be devoted to personal development from private to public use. And

outlays for physical capital and those for personal development are items in the same huge budget. . . . There is no inherent reason why physical capital should have a preference, as in our case. The result is that the U.S.S.R., by our standards still a poor country, treats its schools, research and training institutes, universities, and adult education with a generosity which impresses all Western visitors. These outlays, not old-fashioned expansion of physical capital, were decisive in launching the Sputnik and landing its successor on the moon. . . .*

Given talented or at least capable students more or less adequately supported, their education will depend *partly* on what the colleges and universities provide, *but also* on what the students themselves are motivated to acquire. No college-university system is any better than its faculties. But no faculty, however excellent, can carry education to the higher professional levels effectively without first-class libraries, laboratories, *and* talented, strongly motivated students.

The total quantity of first-class educational equipment in America probably exceeds that of the Soviet Union or any other nation. In the United States as in other countries, non-Communist and Communist alike. the government provides most of the fantastically expensive equipment required for advanced teaching and research in the physical and biological sciences and engineering. In this respect the poorer countries are hopelessly handicapped. Even for a country as rich as Britain, the cost of scientific and technological leadership is becoming prohibitively high.

On this subject a scientific writer for *The Observer* (London) has stated:

> We [in Britain] are having to make a conscious effort to adjust ourselves to our new political and military position in the world; we are no longer a dominant Power. It will be equally important to make a correct appraisal of our proper size, so to speak, in science and technology. It is impossible to be top in everything—and being top in applied science and technology depends, in the long run, on the size of the resources available. Pre-eminence in a few such fields may be achieved by a smaller nation if the choice is made carefully, but it is impossible to be pre-eminent in all of them.†

The relative *intellectual* stature of a nation's university system is more difficult to appraise than its physical equipment. For example, a British mathematician writes:

---

* From "Men and Capital," by J. K. Galbraith, in *The Saturday Evening Post*, March 5, 1960, pp. 32, 98-99. Coyright 1960 by Curtis Publishing Co., Philadelphia; reproduced by permission of publisher and author.

† From "Science and Prestige," by John Davey, in *The Observer*, Sept. 14, 1958. Copyright 1958 by The Observer, Ltd., London; reproduced by permission.

Candor compels me to say that science in Britain is now at a low ebb. A generation ago Britain was full of men busily winning Nobel Prizes. Apart from rare exceptions, work of this high class is simply not being done [in Britain] today. Inferior laboratory equipment is in a considerable measure to blame, but the trouble appears to be partly psychological. The largeness of mind of former generations seems somehow to have been lost.*

After a tour of Soviet universities, an American physicist, Professor R. E. Marshak (of the University of Rochester), reported that the quality of Russian scientists and engineers is "generally high, and, in certain fields, superior to the United States." He found that the best talent was located in the academic institutes and universities "where basic research is carried on," rather than in purely industrial laboratories. He concluded:

> It is evident . . . that the Soviet Union is not only providing new up-to-date laboratories and the most modern experimental equipment for its scientists and engineers. It is also insisting on high educational standards and, by multitudinous devices, attracting persons of the highest intellectual caliber into the scientific and engineering fields.†

When one shifts the spotlight from faculty to students, comparisons have tended in recent years to be severely critical of attitudes prevailing widely in the United States. Americans are frequently accused of desiring higher degrees primarily as status symbols and of regarding college chiefly as a pleasant place to have a good time and make "contacts" before going to work. Too many American students, like their elders, it is often alleged, are indifferent when not actually hostile to learning in anything more than a purely perfunctory sense. College and university faculties constantly complain of the scarcity of really enthusiastic students, and of the anti-intellectualism which pervades so many American campuses.

A comparative study of American and foreign schools, colleges and universities, by the British educator E. J. King (already quoted) comes to these disturbing conclusions:

> Foreign professors often find American students too docile for their taste. . . . Undergraduates seldom show much independence in intellectual matters. Their whole training . . . has left them almost unschooled in criticism and often unprepared with the necessary facts. In extreme cases it is possible to get by with the professors'

* From "A Scientist in Russia," by Fred Hoyle, in *The Observer*, Sept. 7, 1958. Copyright by The Observer, Ltd., London; reproduced by permission of publisher and author.

† From "Nature of the Soviet Scientific Challenge," by R. E. Marshak, in *Bulletin of the Atomic Scientists*, Feb. 1958, pp. 83, 84. Copyright by Educational Foundation for Nuclear Science, Inc., Chicago; reproduced by permission of publisher and author.

handouts or the "book for the course," and one can hear idle or perversely able students swear that they "never cracked a book." [In contrast, King notes a] private as well as a public passion for education [which] possesses Soviet citizens, and is very noticeable even in young people. . . . Moreover, non-communist observers have frequently commented on the exhilaration often sensed in gatherings of Soviet youth. It seems they feel they are working together for a future which they can make for posterity if not for themselves.*

Such comparisons (and they could be multiplied) pose two questions: Are the observations accurate and typical? And if so, are they politically significant? Generalizations regarding attitudes are risky. One can always find plenty of exceptions. But testimony from numerous sources seems to confirm the contrasting attitude-patterns summarized above. The impact of these attitudes on national capabilities is likewise difficult to assess. But (to the extent that they prevail) frivolous, indifferent, and anti-intellectual attitudes towards learning and towards larger educational investment in people must be regarded as a major obstacle to rapid intellectual advance in general and to scientific and technological leadership and prestige in particular.

* From pp. 135, 150, and 151 of *Other Schools and Ours*. Reproduced by permission.

CHAPTER SEVENTEEN

★ ★ ★

Transnational Images, Movements, and Ideologies

THIS CHAPTER DEALS with the international significance of certain transnational phenomena. Reports of conditions and events occurring inside a national community's own geographical space circulate abroad and form images in the minds of foreign statesmen and their constituents. Organized social movements of many kinds communicate across national frontiers and operate simultaneously in several countries. Systems of ideas and beliefs—called ideologies—circulate without much regard for political geography.

Transnational carriers of information, projects, values, and beliefs are many and varied. The more obvious ones include persons traveling to foreign countries for diverse purposes; private letters and official communications; newspapers, magazines, books, and other reading matter; photographs and movies; telegraphs, telephones, radio and television. By these and other means, current information is transmitted across national frontiers; social movements are organized, extended, and operated; and ideologies are insinuated into the minds of men. All this communication flows across the most closely guarded frontiers. News and rumors, organizational directives, ideas and beliefs penetrate "iron curtains," "bamboo curtains," and any other kind of man-made barrier to communication.

Depending on conditions and circumstances, governments pay much or little attention to the transnational flow of news, ideas, and beliefs. They can influence the substance of what is communicated across national frontiers. News may be censored in ways both obvious and devious. Various kinds of reading matter may be intercepted and banned. Certain movements may be outlawed. Ideologies may be combatted. But even the most rigorous police measures rarely cut off the inflow and outflow of communication entirely. Nor can the most elaborate counterpropaganda completely neutralize the images that cross frontiers and infiltrate men's minds. Transnational communication, movements, and ideologies, in short, are givens of the international environment, "facts of life" which statesmen can modify and manipulate to some degree, but can by no means control completely.

These transnational givens may have considerable relevance and significance for the student of international politics. A few questions will indicate the possible scope of significance. To what extent do impressions and images of current conditions and events in one country or region—frequently distorted by biased reporting and interpretation, rumor and gossip—affect public attitudes and government policies in other countries. To what extent can such effects be linked with transnational movements, ranging from associations of scholars, Olympic games, and many other predominantly unofficial associative enterprises to various semiofficial movements such as Pan-Arabism, Pan-Africanism, or the world-wide Communist conspiracy? To what extent do widely disseminated systems of ideas and beliefs affect public behavior and policies? To what extent may any or all of these transnational phenomena affect the international capabilities of nations?

We shall devote most of this chapter to certain political ideologies, and organized movements associated with some of them; but first let us give a little more attention to the transnational impacts of domestic conditions, issues, and events.

A decent respect to the opinions of mankind

National communities go about their activities from day to day with very little concern, in the main, for the transnational repercussions and consequences of what is said and done within the community. Yet domestic conditions, issues, and events may profoundly affect a nation's international prestige and influence, as well as its own policies and the reactions of other nations thereto.

At the threshold of this subject, it is essential to distinguish explicitly between legal rights and political consequences. Governments and their constituents cling tenaciously to the principle of territorial sovereignty— the legal right of the national community to conduct its internal affairs as its rulers may decree. This principle is explicitly reaffirmed in the Charter of the United Nations, as follows:

Nothing in the present Charter shall authorize the United Nations to intervene in matters which are essentially within the domestic jurisdiction of any state or shall require the Members to submit such matters to settlement under the present Charter . . . (ARTICLE 2, SECTION 7)

In accordance with this principle, the French government insisted throughout that the long-drawn-out civil strife in Algeria during the 1950's was purely a "domestic question." Similarly the South African government has repeatedly invoked the doctrine of "domestic question" against foreign protests against its discriminatory racial policy. Likewise, the Portuguese government has stubbornly insisted that disorder and violence in its African colonies is a "domestic question." The United States too has invoked the doctrine of domestic question on many occasions—to counter foreign protests against discriminatory immigration laws, to justify tariff schedules, and other "domestic" policies.

In actual fact, treaties and other events have eroded considerably this historic legal barrier to extension of international jurisdiction into the internal affairs of "sovereign" national communities. But we are concerned here less with the legal principle than with the transnational political consequences of domestic conditions, issues, and actions.

The foreign repercussions of domestic conditions and events have long been recognized and often stressed. Hitler's persecution of the Jews within Germany reacted profoundly on the external relations of the Nazi Reich. Persecutions of scholars, civil servants, military officers, and even widely respected politicians during the McCarthy era shook confidence in the United States among all our allies. The onerous regulations imposed by Congress on foreigners desiring to visit the United States have shocked and offended even our best friends abroad. The painful and protracted struggle within the United States to achieve more tolerable interracial relations handicaps every agency of government which has to deal with Asian and African nations.

The ruthless racial policy of South Africa may be legally a purely domestic issue; but it has evoked waves of indignation, hostility, and reprisal in many countries. African *apartheid* has undoubtedly hampered the British Government's efforts to reach acceptable compromises between Europeans and Africans in Kenya, Rhodesia, and elsewhere in East Africa. In the perspective of history, South African behavior may appear as one of the more important influences working to produce a sense of solidarity among the many ethnic groupings of Sub-Saharan Africa.

Recurrent repressions and purges inside the Soviet Union have repeatedly affected foreign attitudes and policies. The great purge of the middle 1930's, in which tens of thousands of military officers, civil servants, industrial managers, and intellectuals were liquidated, lowered respect for Soviet military power in Europe and in America. The image of a nation honeycombed by subversion and ripe for revolt may have been grossly exaggerated; but such an image may well have influenced the fateful German decision to invade Russia in 1941.

Much more could be said about the transnational repercussions and consequences of what goes on inside national communities. But this will suffice to emphasize the political relevance of this facet of the international environment. Authoritarian systems enjoy certain advantages here. Internal conditions and activities inside the Soviet Union or Communist China, for example, are much less on public display than is the case with the United States or Great Britain or any other relatively open society. But a good deal of information leaks through the most rigorous censorship and tightly sealed frontier. Indeed, the very existence of censorship, restrictions on who may go and come, and other policies of concealment may in themselves erode the prestige of the nations who impose them.

Political ideologies

Ideologies, in the sense the term is being used here, are systems of ideas and beliefs. There are nonpolitical as well as political ideologies. Examples of the former are religious creeds, moral codes, and economic doctrines. Our interest, however, is primarily with belief systems oriented more specifically towards political institutions, forms of action, and goals. We shall examine four such systems: liberal (or constitutional) democracy, communism, nationalism, and internationalism.

The political impacts of these ideologies may be trivial or important, depending on conditions and events. In some instances the intrusion of new political ideas and beliefs into a society has been explosively disruptive. More often the effect is a subtle, gradual erosion of pre-existing beliefs and loyalties. In either case the intrusion may significantly affect the morale, sense of purpose, or other aspects of a nation's capabilities. Frequently a nation's rulers resort to harsh and oppressive measures to counteract these effects, and these measures may themselves be socially disruptive in the long run.

Largely for these reasons, most political ideologies have become instruments of statecraft. In general, those that stand for revolutionary change are the more effective: for example, liberal democracy in the nineteenth century; militant nationalism and communism in our time. Communism, in particular, has proved to be an especially dangerous weapon, for reasons that will be considered more fully later on.

The injection of ideologies into international statecraft on a significant scale dates from the later years of the eighteenth century. One of the early experiments in ideological propaganda was the American Declaration of Independence. The Continental Congress asserted in ringing words:

> We hold these truths to be self evident: that all men are created equal; that they are endowed by their Creator with certain inalienable rights; that to secure these rights, governments are instituted among men, deriving their just powers from the consent of the governed, etc.

This was dangerous, incendiary doctrine in the eyes of eighteenth-century monarchs and aristocrats. Even more dangerous and subversive were the slogans of the French Revolution. The doctrine of "liberty, equality, fraternity" assaulted the citadel of dynastic legitimacy and aristocratic privilege. It drew anguished protests from the frightened aristocrats of Europe, who ordered their soldiers into battle in a vain attempt to put out the fire.

However, until well into the nineteenth century, the opportunities for ideological warfare remained severely limited. Formidable obstacles confronted the purveyor of ideologies before the era of modern rapid communications. Travel was slow, uncomfortable, and expensive—a barrier to spreading ideas by word of mouth. Books, pamphlets, and newspapers circulated mainly among the upper classes, and not too widely even there. The biggest obstacle of all was nearly universal illiteracy. Inability to read blocked off the mass of humanity from easy access to the universe of ideas that existed beyond the local farm or village.

The industrial revolution started a transformation that continues to this day. The transition from hand labor to power-driven machinery was accompanied everywhere by human dislocation, exploitation, and misery. Such conditions evoked radical prescriptions for reform and various utopian and revolutionary social philosophies. These latter ranged from democratic socialism to Marxian communism. More efficient means for disseminating ideas—improved printing machinery, cheaper paper, faster ships and overland haulage, and eventually planes and the modern apparatus of electronic communication—progressively expanded the areas of circulation. The growth of literacy simultaneously enlarged the audience which could be reached.

The consequences of this transformation are well known. The circulation of people and ideas has doubled and redoubled many times. Contacts between national communities have become ever more varied and continuous. One has only to think of the millions of persons who cross national frontiers every year, to travel or to reside for short or long periods; or the huge quantities of personal letters, newspapers, magazines, books and other reading matter that circulate among countries; or the radio broadcasts which overleap every frontier, and international television already above the horizon.

Frightened politicians can obstruct the circulation of people and ideas. Governments can prohibit their citizens leaving the country; they can close their borders to unwelcome aliens; they can censor letters and other reading matter; they can jam radio broadcasts. But no government has ever succeeded in sealing off its citizens from "dangerous" foreign ideas. Radio and plane penetrate to the most remote and isolated localities. There are no longer any dark continents, though some are admittedly less brightly lighted than others.

This spread and circulation of knowledge and ideas is widely regarded as a significant source of the discontents which afflict not merely the underdeveloped countries but also the richest industrialized societies as well. The more widespread the discontents and frustrations, the more receptive a community seems to become to new prescriptions for reforms. That is to say, there seems to be a reciprocal relationship between discontents and ideologies. Hence the utility of the latter as an instrument of policy calculated to focus and channel frustrations, demands, and expectations, and otherwise to influence the behavior of whole populations.

A more baffling issue relates to the effects which political ideas and beliefs may have on the statesman's image of reality. To what extent do statesmen operate within an ideological jail? To what extent do the colored windows of these jails distort their perception of what the world outside is really like? It may be an exaggeration to say that statesmen before World War I generally shared a more or less common image of the international scene. But they certainly came closer to having a common view than their successors have since the Russian Revolution opened up the ideological gulf that divides the world today.

It requires training, discipline, and patience—especially patience, a commodity frequently in short supply—to communicate effectively across this ideological gulf. This was brought home in an account by Edward Crankshaw of an unofficial conference in 1961 attended by a mixed lot of Russian and British journalists and others. Crankshaw is a veteran British interpreter of Soviet ideology and behavior. Yet even he was astonished by the difficulty each side encountered in getting across to the other. "There are so many points at which we stare at each other in blank incomprehension." *

* From "Across the Gulf" in *The Observer*, March 5, 1961.

To the extent that ideology shapes the journalist's image of reality, it manifestly affects the way he reports events. In precisely the same manner, ideological blinders affect the statesman's judgments as to what projects and strategies are feasible and promising. To the extent that ideological bias obstructs communication, it inexorably restricts the diplomat's ability to negotiate and to anticipate reactions to his moves upon the international stage.

A still more controversial issue relates to the bearing of ideology on national systems of foreign policy. There has been endless unresolved disputation, for example, over the degree to which Russian politicians are dedicated to the mission of destroying noncommunist societies. It has long been the fashion, in certain circles, to scoff at the sincerity of European and American efforts to transplant democratic institutions to colonies and former colonies.

A great deal has been said on these and other aspects of ideological influence on the policies and capabilities of nations. One report, focused explicitly on these issues, was prepared in 1959 for the Senate Committee on Foreign Relations. Much of what is said in the rest of this chapter comes directly or indirectly from that report, in which a group of Harvard scholars undertook to assess the bearings of ideology on foreign affairs.*

Citing the developments mentioned above—improved means of communication, spread of literacy, popular discontents and frustrations in an era of rapid social change, and the nearly universal demand for a better standard of living—the Harvard Report declares:

> These conditions are fertile soil for political movements which depend on large-scale popular support. To mobilize it, leaders must be able to translate vague aspirations into political goals which can infuse in the masses a sense of purpose, a conviction of success and a readiness to sacrifice. In this effort to convert a restless mass into an organized political movement, ideology often serves to crystallize purposes, to bolster morale, and to justify obedience and discipline. And one common element [in nondemocratic as well as democratic ideologies] is the faith in social engineering . . .
>
> Any study centering mainly on a single facet of international affairs, like ideology, runs the risk of leaving a misleading impression. Obviously ideology is only one of many factors shaping events and policies and may be less central or controlling than others in many situations. . . . Moreover, ideologies are themselves affected by some of these other factors. . . .
>
> To be effective in the political arena, an ideology must be em-

* "Ideology and Foreign Affairs," a study prepared by the Center for International Affairs of Harvard University, for the Senate Committee on Foreign Relations, pursuant to S. Res. 336, 85th Cong., and S. Res. 31, 86th Cong. Government Printing Office, Washington, D. C., 1960.

braced by an organized movement or embodied by political institutions. A central feature of communism, for example, is the dominance of the party as the sole instrument for realizing the doctrine. Similarly, the nationalistic struggle for independence has always been carried on by dynamic leaders inspiring mass support and action. Constitutional democracy, as a more gradual growth, is the product of many such movements to advance specific ideas which have ultimately been absorbed into the bloodstream of the democratic faith and the institutions to which it has given rise. In all cases an ideology becomes a political force only as it inspires individuals to organize and make sacrifices to advance ideological goals. . . .

A second point is related. Any movement and its leaders struggle within a specific social and political environment. They face concrete obstacles and challenges in seeking to make the ideology prevail or to put its program into effect. Inevitably this poses hard choices at various points: some parts of the creed may have to be sacrificed or subordinated in order to advance or salvage others. Hence, again inevitably, the leaders must establish priorities among the various goals of the ideology and the means for attaining them. Their choice may take the form of postponing or projecting into the future the part of the program considered less urgent or less essential. But the effect may be to abandon that part as a practical goal. The history of the Communist movement is full of examples of this process.

Finally, the passage of time and changing conditions may reshape the content and priorities of the ideology. . . . Nationalist movements in Asia and Africa have experienced this with dramatic force after independence. In the case of the Soviet Union, one question is whether a prosperous and evolving Soviet society will tend to subordinate the expansive thrust of Communist ideology. . . .

Constitutional Democracy

Constitutional or liberal democracy is . . . the legitimate political heir of [Western culture and thought]. Its origins go back to both classical humanism and the Judeo-Christian heritage. Its concepts and institutions embody the struggles and insight of many generations. In its gradual, organic growth, it has drawn sustenance from many sources but especially from the experience and thought of England, and the United States, and France. By its nature, democracy cannot be a precise creed with prescribed content. Lacking an authoritative interpreter, it embraces variants differing in emphasis or specific detail. Nevertheless, the democratic tradition does rest on a common body of premises and political principles. . . . The basic elements of the democratic tradition, as expressed in American and European beliefs and practices, would include the following:

1. The human person and his unique worth stands at the center of the democratic doctrine. From this follows the deep concern for human liberty and dignity. Human welfare is the measure of social

and state action; the human being is looked on as an end in himself and not as a means or instrument to be manipulated by the society or state.

2. The idea of self-government is deeply rooted in this tradition. Government derives its just powers from the consent of the governed. A people is entitled to govern itself and to choose freely its form of government. The citizen has the right to share in the process of governing and hold the government responsible, through periodic elections of representatives.

3. The constitutional order must assure the rule of law and the safeguarding of certain fundamental rights of the individual. The institutions and methods differ in various democratic countries but they share a common purpose of protecting against arbitrary action.

4. The individual is entitled to the opportunity for a decent economic and social life. Constitutional democracy is compatible with many ways of organizing economic life, and with various mixtures of private and public activity. It has become an article of democratic faith that the conditions of human life can be steadily improved by technology and science and by the application of capital and investment. The growth of large cities and large industry has gradually led to greater reliance on state action for maintaining at least minimum standards of welfare. Public measures to protect working conditions and social security have come to be accepted as normal state functions.

5. Constitutional democracy presupposes tolerance of differing views, attitudes, and values. A vital feature of the system is the right of individuals and minorities to espouse unorthodox views and policies as long as they do not threaten the constitutional order itself, and to seek to change the system by procedures which do not involve violence or unconstitutional means. The social order is regarded as pluralistic in character; indeed the existence of many centers of social, political, and economic power is considered essential to the health and vitality of such a democratic order.

6. The democratic faith assumes that the system will continue to change and develop in order to realize more adequately its basic values and to adapt to new needs and changing conditions. It is dedicated, however, to evolutionary or gradual change by nonviolent means. It accepts the fact that society includes conflicting interests and purposes and conceives that the constitutional order should make it possible for these to exist and thrive without undue friction. Hence it places a high value on accommodating differing views or interests by compromise and adjustment.

7. Finally, the democratic values of the social order are looked on as universal. In other words, the rule of law and other basic features are considered as rights which should be available to human beings anywhere who desire to enjoy them.

The practice of democratic states falls short, of course, of these ideals and principles. In domestic affairs, for example, minority groups may not in fact enjoy full equality in social or political rights or privileges. Under conditions of crisis, the institutions or procedures may not be fully effective to safeguard against abuse or arbitrary action. Nevertheless, it would be fair to say that, where democracy is well established, the tendency of such societies is to keep open means for correction of abuses and improvement of performance.

In foreign relations the democratic states have faced some serious dilemmas in squaring their actions with the democratic creed. The colonial peoples, for example, could invoke the principles of Western democratic theory in claiming independence. The United States has repeatedly been faced with the difficult situation where one of its major allies resisted the demands for colonial independence and insisted that the United States support this position. In some cases one might conclude that the interests of the colonial people themselves would not genuinely be served by premature independence, that is, before they were in a position actually to govern themselves effectively. Yet was the metropolitan nation able to judge this capability objectively? Or even more basically, were these people entitled under democratic theory to make their own mistakes in governing themselves? Where the struggle for independence threatens to jeopardize basic security interests of the United States and a major ally, what becomes of democratic theory?

A similar issue arises when alliances for security interests are made with dictatorial regimes which suppress the rights of individuals. The benefits of the relation may assist the dictator to retain power.

Under such conditions, compromises which may well be unavoidable still have the effect of blurring the image of the United States and eroding its influence as the protagonist of the principles of democratic, constitutional order.

Communism

The rulers of the Soviet Union, Communist China and other Communist regimes constantly proclaim the primary role of Marxist-Leninist ideology as the basis of their policies and decisions. They ascribe to it a unique value as an infallible tool of analysis and guide to action in domestic and international affairs. To any student of Sino-Soviet policy, it is apparent that ideology is by no means the sole determinant of their purposes and courses of action. Their conduct also shows the influence, in various circumstances, of the historic drives of the nations they now control and of strategic and other considerations normally affecting the foreign policy of states.

Indeed, some observers would explain Sino-Soviet policy exclusively in traditional terms of "national interest," and deny that ideology plays any real role today in its direction. Strategic and similar factors, while influencing Soviet and Chinese policy, by no means suffice to explain its thrust and direction. In Sino-Soviet thinking, Communist doctrine directly affects conceptions of the scope and nature of their interests. National interest in traditional terms will hardly explain the worldwide scope of Soviet activities or its preoccupation with revolutionary change throughout the world. Those aspects of Soviet policy reflect their peculiar ideological perspective which inherently gives the Communists a global outlook focussing especially on such change. Turning to Eastern Europe, a Soviet quest for security could explain a national interest in the area. But only Communist ideology can explain Soviet dedication to transforming by force the social and economic structure of Eastern Europe, which only creates increased hostility toward the U.S.S.R. Their doctrine makes them distrust any non-Communist regime and drives them to recast it in the Communist mold. Again Soviet policy toward the Chinese revolution in the 1920's and after 1945 showed how their doctrine can influence their approach to problems. Soviet insistence on a proletarian revolution in China reflects ideological categories which in this particular case had little to do with Chinese reality. Indeed, as these examples show, the notion of "national interest" can be ambiguous when applied to Communist regimes. If "national interest" means whatever the Communist rulers say, the question still remains as to how far Communist conceptions distort the analysis of the Communist leaders even in assessing national interest.

Accordingly, this report reflects the conviction that the Communist creed does play a significant role in shaping the foreign policy of the Soviet Union and China. From this starting point, the first question then is: Which of the Communist tenets are currently relevant to foreign affairs (including relations among the Communist States themselves)?

Communist doctrine embraces, of course, a mass of material derived from the Marxian scriptures, the glosses of Lenin, Stalin, and others, and many other sources. The successive rulers have repeatedly reshaped the Marxist canon to reflect practical necessities and experience. . . .

[One can identify, however,] a number of concepts and tenets which seems important in molding the orientation of Communist leaders, especially in the realm of foreign affairs:

1. Communist ideology provides a conceptual framework for viewing the world. It looks on history as a continuous conflict in which "progressive" forces contend with "reactionary" forces and defeat them. In the present stage, communism claims to be a superior, a more advanced form of society. The Communist dictatorship and state ownership and operation of the means of production, it asserts, remove the sources of class conflict and the barriers to efficient use of the productive facilities inherent in capitalist society. . . . In short, the basic Communist faith is that capitalism is doomed, that communism is certain to replace it, and that this process must be vigorously abetted.

This does not mean that Khrushchev expects an imminent collapse of the United States, or that he does not know about many of the realities of American life. Doubtless he is aware of the American standard of living, the state of the American economy, and some of the social and economic changes in American life since the great depression. . . . Seen through his eyes, however, these facts do not invalidate his conviction that in the long run, capitalism will inevitably decline.

2. In the Communist view, this conflict between the two systems is inherently irreconcilable. It can be resolved only by the ultimate victory of the Communist order. Communist confidence in their ultimate triumph seems to have grown in recent years on the basis of Marxist-Leninist analysis. They now appear convinced that military conflict between communism and capitalism may no longer be necessary for final victory and that the military balance makes capitalism less likely to precipitate such a war as a last resort. Their analysis relies on two processes. First, in the newer nations they count on the struggle for economic growth to lay the basis for Communist takeover. This effort and its affects will disrupt the established social order and eventually force these nations to imitate the experience of the Communist States. Second, the Soviet leaders expect the rapid growth of the Soviet Union and the bloc to tip the balance of industrial might in favor of communism by 1975. Considering industrial development the key to modern power, the Communist leaders believe that this will be a turning point in modern history.

The Communist strategy seems to justify the assumption that they will strive to avoid a total global conflict with the West. An axiom of Communist strategy has been the injunction against risking a direct clash unless certain of Communist superiority. The tactic to be pursued when faced by a superior force is to engage in gradual envelopment and penetration and to destroy the enemy by a process of attrition. To undermine the morale of the superior force, to foster in the opponent an inclination toward ever-increasing compromise, then stage by stage to translate that compromise into capitulation—that is the way to victory whenever lacking the power to impose one's own solution.

The Communists have, however, frequently asserted that certain types of wars are in themselves progressive. . . . If the Soviet leadership should ever conclude that its military and technological superiority would assure victory in a total war without widespread destruction of the home base, it might well be prepared to engage in a so-called progressive war to effect the ultimate collapse of the capitalist world. . . . However, it seems unlikely that over the next decade the Soviet leaders would be able to reach such a conclusion with any degree of certainty. . . .

3. The Communist Party is the chosen instrument for achieving this millennium. . . . The Communist Party represents the proletariat for this purpose. This is one of the key ideas. The party is sanctified as the agent of history and is elevated into an absolute good in its own right. For this reason, each member must be disciplined to accept the party as the spokesman of history and the only true interpreter of the doctrine; and party unity becomes prima facie evidence of the correctness of its own historical course.

Since the party enjoys the exclusive title to this role, any effort to contest the course or control of the party identifies the individual or group as a class enemy. Thus the doctrine provides the justification for the monopoly of power by the party.

4. Communist ideology makes power central in its analysis of society and history and its own methods and goals. Indeed, the main focus of Communist writings in this century has been on the methods of acquiring and consolidating power. . . .

5. The creed itself allows for great tactical flexibility. In their practical decisions, the leaders of the party at any time enjoy a wide range of choice, especially since the ultimate goals are both vague and remote. Thus they are able to take account of the strategic and other factors often subsumed under national interest. And the Soviet Union, as the oldest and strongest Communist state, can easily identify its continued progress and security with the interests of the Communist cause as a whole.

These attitudes, plus the initial conspiratorial character of the movement, relieve the leaders from any qualms of conscience regarding the means used. Against non-Communists who oppose the ultimate Communist triumph, any methods are legitimate to achieve the historically inevitable outcome.

6. The ideology contemplates that Communist strategy will vary with the stage and circumstances. Within the Soviet Union, its main function is to justify the continued monopoly of the party and to certify the historical validity of its decisions and actions at home and abroad. Within the bloc, its role is somewhat more complex as an instrument of Soviet direction and control. In non-Communist areas, the movement recruits small numbers of local members with an ideological commitment to provide the hard-core apparatus in each country or area. In its effort to influence and manipulate mass opinion, however, it casts its appeals not in ideological terms but in those best calculated to cater to local discontents or aspirations. Thus at times, the policy may appear to run counter to basic tenets of the creed.

Nationalism

In essence, nationalism is the assertion by a people of its claim to a distinctive national identity, entitling it to live its own life in its own fashion. This finds its most characteristic political expression in the demand for a sovereign state whose prime purpose is to protect and promote the identity and interest of the nation in whose name it is brought into being.

The headlong drive for national self-realization has in successive waves embraced almost every people on the face of the earth. Since World War II the nationalist demands of the colonial and quasi-colonial countries have tended to monopolize public attention, but nationalism also still exercises a strong sway over governments and peoples in the advanced countries of the West where it found its first formulation. . . ,

Nationalism has, however, a peculiarly significant role to play in in the development of peoples undergoing the kind of physical, social, and psychological transformation which the West has thrust upon the rest of the world. The major immediate contributions of nationalism are a sense of independent worth and self-respect and a new social and political solidarity to replace the traditional bonds which have been shattered. For a dependent society to come to a sense of its own national existence is to make a substantial start along the road to equality with its alien rulers.

In the new countries, the nation constitutes a great potential widening of the social and political horizons of most of the people. Far from forcing men to live within restricted quarters, it opens new doors and windows to them. Where men's lives have traditionally been bounded by tribe or caste, village or petty principality, the emergence of nationalism creates pressures which force them into large communities. For many individuals and groups considerable time will surely elapse before their socio-political consciousness expands to the national limits, but the forces of the modern world all conspire to make man's age-old parochialism impossible. . . .

In many spheres of vital concern to the new countries, however, nationalism either offers no answers or answers so ambiguous as to be useless. Nationalism, indeed, rarely if ever represents a coherent and positive body of doctrine and belief reaching significantly beyond insistence on the establishment of an independent state as the political embodiment of the nation. . . . The fact that a people can launch an anticolonialist movement and for that purpose act as if it constituted a true nation conveys no assurance that it will be able to maintain political coherence once the impartial enemy has withdrawn.

Neither the political nor the economic institutions . . . of the new countries can be said to be determined by nationalism. . . . Nationalism offers no vantage ground from which to choose between the different types of systems and institutions which the modern West offers in relative profusion. . . . Nationalism is, of course, always the champion of self-government in the sense of national as opposed to alien rule; it is only accidentally self-government in the sense of rule by the many as opposed to rule by the few. The assertion of a sense of separate identity can by itself give no clue as to how the community may choose to manage its affairs. . . .

What is, in some sense, inherently democratic in nationalism is its mass character. . . . In the national era the state can no longer be seen as the ruler and his subjects (or an empire and its imperial domain) but becomes in principle the emanation and instrument of the nation, which is the people. . . .

Despite the inherent links between nationalism and democracy, it is open to grave doubt that many of the new countries will be able to make a success of the democratic constitutions which they have almost without exception adopted on attaining independence. . . . It is too much to expect that illiterate people living in poverty and inexperienced both in political life and in defending their own rights should be able to master the most difficult and precariously balanced of political systems. Great gaps divide the different elements of these societies, and both the new elites and the masses are inclined to operate on the age-old assumption that the few should govern and the many follow.

Nationalism itself contains ingredients which can with great ease be turned into undemocratic or antidemocratic directions. Wherever it is the main driving force, the temptation exists to give priority to the claims of national solidarity and strength over those of individual rights and democratic participation. In such circumstances the liberalism which is one of the faces of a democratic nationalism is likely to be forced to yield to the demand for unity put forward in the name of the nation. . . .

In the economic sphere as in the political, nationalism generally offers no firm ground on the basis of which choices might be made between different alternatives. As a means of achieving equality with the advanced peoples as well as for its more substantive contributions, economic development may be assumed to be embraced in any contemporary nationalist program. To such basic questions, however, as to whether development should be pursued within the framework of communism, socialism, capitalism, or some type of mixed economy, nationalism can by itself give no clear answer. . . .

In almost every instance, to hold up the concept of the national interest as the determinant of decision and action is to produce an empty symbol whose content is in dispute between different factions within the nation. Even in the realm of foreign affairs, where nationalism most evidently comes into play, it is likely to give no conclusive answer to questions concerning entry into this alliance or that, acceptance of a given treaty or of the proffer of foreign aid, or the adoption of a policy of neutralism or commitment. The danger is that nationalism may even serve as an impediment to advance, as, for example, in curtailing access to alien goods, skills, and capital, and, more generally, in inhibiting useful international contacts because of fear of alien intrusion.

Despite these and other negative aspects, the fact remains that nationalism has much to contribute to the new countries. The achievement of a sense of national unity, the breaking down of local and other barriers through the widening of social horizons, the dynamism and political activism which have been injected into the society, the sense of revolutionary élan, the new appreciation of the national worth and dignity, the devotion to the common cause—these are all matters of profound importance to the future of any people. . . . Nationalism opens the possibility of tapping sources of energy and participation which no alien or old-style autocratic ruler could hope to tap. The tasks of building a modern state, of putting through major social and economic reforms, and of requiring present sacrifice for future benefits enlist a new dimension of popular support if the national leaders can establish them as integral parts of the devotion which the nation expects from its members.

Nationalism, Communism, and Democracy

The Harvard Report presents numerous opinions regarding the interplay of nationalism, communism, and democracy in various parts of the world. These sections of the Report are too long to reproduce in full. The following excerpts summarize some of the conclusions reached in the omitted sections:

> . . . All three ideologies . . . are steadily interacting . . . This competition and conflict among them takes different forms according to the varied settings [in different countries and regions].
>
> The interplay is most apparent in the advanced democratic nations of the West. In these open societies, Communist parties and propaganda are able, by manipulating popular discontent, illusions and aspirations, to attract mass electoral support in several states and to confuse or divide public opinion in more. Yet not even the Communists seem to expect to extend their control into this area by force or threat in the near future. As has been said, they appear to count on the strategy of "encircling" the Western nations and suffocating them.
>
> In the West, nationalism is still a potent symbol which can be exploited by Communists or non-Communists for their own purposes. Even so, there are signs that, profiting by tragic experience, the Atlantic nations may now be working their way through nationalism to come out on the other side with a certain measure of maturity. There is reason to believe that they have come to enough awareness of the dangers and inadequacies of nationalism to lead them to seek greater regional and international integration and cooperation rather than to reemphasize their national separateness. . . .
>
> In the newer nations, the contest is more complex. In the struggle for independence, the nationalist torrent is fed from many streams of discontent. With the traditional social order in decay, the destitute, the dispossessed, the uprooted, tend to focus excessive hopes and expectations on the overthrow of colonialism and creation of a sovereign state. Yet the concept of the nation offers no pat formulas for their manifold political, economic, and social problems. Hence the leaders must look elsewhere for more explicit programs to meet the expectations aroused but not answered by the creation of the nation-state.
>
> In general the newer nations have inherited from the colonial past political institutions patterned on Western models, and their leaders and elites, usually trained in the West, ofttimes share much of the democratic creed, while sometimes rejecting the West for past "imperialism." Without essential social underpinnings, however, these

Western-style governments are likely to be too weak or ineffective to achieve the social cohesion and discipline necessary to modernize their societies at a rapid rate. And many, viewing the economic systems of the West in terms of exploitation and colonialism, are attracted by the ideas of socialism. Communism exploits all these attitudes and dilemmas, holding up the Soviet Union as a model for rapid industrial progress.

There are, however, underlying tensions between communism and nationalism. These are due, first of all, to the inherent conflict between national independence and efforts to promote the Communist subordination of national purposes to the interests of a particular state, namely the Soviet Union. Second, Communist contempt for human rights runs counter to nationalist efforts to gain human dignity through the quest for independence. The nationalist ideal of freedom is incompatible with the Communist view that national independence is merely a transitional phase on the way toward an inevitable international Communist society. . . .

The conflict among ideologies also penetrates the Communist bloc. As would be expected, the Communists are continuously concerned with the role of ideology within the bloc. They devote an enormous effort to indoctrinating the subjects of the Communist regimes in the Marxist-Leninist ideology and in justifying their policies and actions in its terms. At the same time, they expend major resources to sealing off the orbit and insulating its inhabitants from concepts and ideas which might create doubts regarding the Communist ideology or conduct. This policy is merely a special application of their concept of the two camps. Their orbit is regarded as a permanent Communist area from which no defection will be permitted and in which no outsider is entitled to interfere. The rest of the world, the other camp, is open country for Communist manipulation and infiltration for the purpose of bringing about the inevitable expansion of Communist control.

Despite this attitude and the efforts in its pursuit, the Communist bloc cannot escape the influence of other ideologies. For the bloc, nationalism may be a major force to challenge the Soviet hold in the satellite areas. Nationalism underlay Tito's breach with Stalin's Russia. The developments in Poland and Hungary made manifest the strong national allegiance still alive in the satellites. And the nationalism of one or both of the partners of the Soviet-Chinese alliance may in time create a barrier to further cooperation.

Within the Soviet Union there are also ferments which may well prove hard to control over an extended period. The development of an advanced urban society, the desire to learn more about the outside world, the urge for better living conditions, the effects of education: these and many other factors may tend to complicate maintenance of doctrinaire internal control. . . .

The Communist bloc [as a whole] is likely to face continued internal difficulties, and the Soviet leaders will find it increasingly hard to assert their unquestioned leadership. In maintaining unity, ideology is likely to be stressed as an important bond, although accompanied by continued reliance on Soviet power and mounting economic ties between the various units of the bloc. The revolutionary phase of the totalitarian development in China and elsewhere in Asia will probably result in increased aggressiveness on the part of these Communist states. The erosion of Communist ideology seems more likely to occur as a result of conflicts in applying it to differing national conditions among the bloc's various constituent units than through the impact of industrialization and urbanization within the individual states. . . . [But] this erosion is at best a long-range prospect and not to be expected in the immediate future. . . .

With regard to the new nations and Latin America, the Report concludes:

While both nationalism and communism, as revolutionary forces, challenge the status quo, there is a fundamental incompatibility between them, which is increasingly coming to the surface in many of the new nationalist states. On the other hand, despite inherent links between democracy and nationalism, it is open to grave doubt that many of the new countries will be able to make a success of the democratic institutions which they have almost without exception adopted on attaining independence.

The general trend in the new, economically developing nations and in Latin America is toward some form of socialism as a method for achieving social and economic betterment through rapid and planned development. In some cases, efforts to implement rapidly this objective are likely to result in considerable domestic instability and in a consequent quest for stability either through military regimes or through ideologically oriented movements. Many nationalists, seeing the United States as a capitalist power unduly interested in the status quo, rejected the relevance of American democracy to the problems facing them. Despite this, and despite the efforts of the Soviet Union to appear as a dynamic, socialist state, the Communist image has been tarnished lately, particularly in Asia. Communist reversals are due not only to the gradual consolidation of nationalist forces, but also to grievous errors of Communist policy itself . . . [for example, Chinese aggression in Tibet, and Indian reaction thereto].

In the Arab countries, the limited Communist gains have been largely due to the tactical association of the Communists with the local nationalist leaders and not to the appeal of communism as an ideology. . . .

Internationalism

Internationalism is a general term of designation for numerous systems of beliefs which postulate political values that transcend nationality. Internationalism takes various forms. But the common factor is belief that, for one reason or another, the geographical-nation-state can neither perform the essential functions of protection from external danger nor provide the environment most conducive to superior human achievement.

Arguments for internationalism may relate to military, economic, intellectual, or other social "facts of modern life."

The military case for internationalism has been most brilliantly stated by an American political scientist, John Herz (of the College of the City of New York).[*] The essence of his thesis is that past developments in military technology created a need for the geographical nation-state but that more recent technological advances have rendered the state strategically and tactically unviable. With nuclear and biological weapons systems now available, the geographical space of even the largest and strongest states can be penetrated with the fatal consequences which the early development of artillery posed for the medieval castle and walled town.

The economic case for internationalism rests upon several interrelated theses: The raw materials required to operate a modern industrial economy exceed the capacity of any nation-state to provide from its own geographical space. Technological advance plus the spread of industrialism are depleting at an accelerating rate the most accessible natural resources. Every economy grows more dependent on imported materials and on economic undertakings that extend far beyond the state's political jurisdiction. Every nation becomes more vulnerable to financial and commercial pressures from abroad. Increasing economic interdependence puts the national economy proportionately at the mercy of foreign Powers. The nation-state has thus become as vulnerable to economic pressure as to military attack.

The intellectual argument for internationalism stresses the global unity of knowledge. No nation these days has a monopoly, or even a near-monopoly, on scientific discovery or other advances in knowledge. Efforts by national governments to block the export of scientific knowledge or the import of "dangerous" ideas are scarcely ever very successful and are likely to hurt most severely the nation which resorts to them. In other words, national communities have become progressively more dependent on the higher learning of other communities, while simultaneously becoming more penetrable to ideological attack.

Finally, there is a broadly cultural argument that rests upon the theses: that the focusing of loyalty on the nation-state is only one step removed from the tribalism of primitive societies; and that nationalism fosters a parochial outlook, intolerance, and other destructive forms of behavior.

Despite the manifest and probably increasing vulnerability of even the

[*] "Rise and Demise of the Territorial State," in *World Politics*, July 1957.

largest and most powerful states, there are few signs that international values are likely in any foreseeable future to weaken seriously either the grip of national governments on their citizens or the loyalties of the citizens to the symbols of nationality. Of all the systems of political beliefs discussed in this chapter, internationalism remains the weakest.

This is substantially the position taken in the Harvard Report on "Ideology and Foreign Affairs."

> Internationalism is not a powerful ideology comparable to communism or nationalism. Indeed, it has never really been an ideology all by itself. It was part and parcel of most of the major ideologies of the nineteenth century, and took on as many facets as those ideologies themselves. Liberalism, putting its faith in the development of democracy and of industrialism, looked forward to a world of nation-states cooperating under law and brought together by the force of public opinion and world trade. Socialism stressed the solidarity of the workers as an international reality transcending national borders which would collapse along with the power of bourgeoisie. Even nationalism, in its liberal varieties, had an internationalist component; once every nation enjoyed the right of self-determination, there would be no more obstacle to the harmonious cooperation of states.
>
> The liberal dream of a world of nation-states willing to pool their power against any aggressor instead of resorting to traditional balancing policies, ready to settle their disputes by peaceful means and to work together within a league of sovereign nations—this dream which inspired Wilson survives only as a hope for the future rather than as a faith in the present. Nevertheless, internationalism remains an important feature of contemporary world politics. It appears today in varied guises. First, it is a component of the global outlook of both the West and the Soviets. Second, Asia, Africa, and Western Europe have seen the development of creeds and interests which are not exactly internationalist, if one equates internationalism and universalism, but which are certainly transnational. Third, the growth of universal and regional organizations represents the most impressive aspect of internationalism in the postwar world.

Like other political ideologies, internationalism is a significant political factor largely to the degree that its tenets become incorporated in organized movements and national policies. One of the strongest internationalist movements in the Western world is undoubtedly United World Federalism. This movement took form in the United States at the close of World War II. It has attracted many prominent citizens, including some leading intellectuals.

The early program of United World Federalism was founded upon two propositions: "Wars between groups of men forming social units always take place when these units exercise unrestricted sovereign power. Wars . . . cease the moment sovereign power is transferred from them to a larger or higher unit." One of the interpreters of United World Federalism says:

> Most world federalists today would probably point out that these statements oversimplify, failing to account for either the major phenomenon of civil war or for historical instances of concord between sovereign units. But the basic world federalist analysis remains unchanged, as well as the basic solution: a delegation of national governmental authority to form a new and higher level of government, a world federation.*

The realities of the Cold War and other events have considerably dampened the early hopes of most World Federalists. Despite widespread support among various elites, the movement seems to have had very slight impact on the actual course of international events.

Some optimists prior to World War I predicted that the international solidarity of working men everywhere in the Western world would impel them to lay down their tools if their governments resorted to war. Precisely because of the stronger contrary pull of national loyalty, backed up by the internal police power of the national state, socialist internationalism had no deterrent effect on World War I, nor did it lower significantly the capabilities of the principal belligerent nations.

As the Harvard Report suggests, the most impressive aspect of internationalism has been the growth in recent years of regional as well as universal institutions. Most of these institutions were created to cope with specific practical problems. Only to a limited extent do some of them also reflect explicit internationalist values and premises. International institutions supplement the norms of diplomatic procedure and ritual, and of international laws and morality. We turn next, in Chapter 18, to an examination of the international political consequences of these ritualistic, legal, ethical, and institutional norms.

---

* From "The Development of United Federalist Thought and Policy," by E. S. Lent, in *International Organization*, November 1955, pp. 486 ff. Copyright 1955 by the World Peace Foundation, Boston; reproduced by permission.

CHAPTER EIGHTEEN

★ ★ ★

Transnational Norms and Institutions

IN THIS CHAPTER we take up two other sets of transnational factors: the norms or standards of behavior which governments observe or are supposed to observe in their dealings with other nations; and the institutions of many kinds that cut across national frontiers.

"It is an observable fact that governments conduct much of their business with one another in regular patterns." With this statement, Percy Corbett (emeritus research professor of international law in Princeton University) opens a discussion of the functions of norms on the political interactions and relations of nations. Transnational norms are identified by various terms: diplomatic etiquette, comity of nations, international morality, international law, etc. These norms are transnational in the sense that, in the main, they are not products of any one national culture, but represent values and varying degrees of consensus among some or all members of the Society of Nations, as to what is proper, right, and legal in the policies and operations of governments.

Alongside, and closely related at many points to these transnational norms, there exists a large number of institutions which also cut across national frontiers. The *Yearbook of International Organizations* lists over 1200 such organizations. About 150 of these are intergovernmental; the rest are nongovernmental. Some—the International Court of Justice, for example—exist for the specific purpose of regulating international relations by the application of suitable norms. Others—the United Nations General Assembly, for example—contribute directly to the formation and modification of behavioral norms. A great many international organizations contribute incidentally, through research on special subjects, through meetings and other communications among specialists, and in other ways, to the growth of transnational social patterns.

Transnational norms and institutions are of interest in the context of international politics for precisely the same reasons that make other features of the environment relevant and significant. To the extent that behavioral norms and institutions are taken into account in the decision-making processes of government, they affect the form and substance of projects, undertakings, and operations. Like other environmental factors, norms and institutions may affect the operational results of undertakings, and, through these effects, raise or lower a government's international potential, its impacts on the behavior of other nations, in ways that may or may not be intended or even foreseen by its statesmen and diplomats.

The historic double standard

Perhaps the most pervasive effect of legal and moral norms on international politics derives from the double standard which for several centuries characterized the relations between peoples of European and of non-European civilization and culture. We refer to the two historic principles of European origin: (1) that the rules of European-made international law and Christian ethics were supposed to govern the relations of Europeans with each other, but did not bind Europeans in their relations with non-Europeans; and (2) that Europeans did not have to conform to norms prevailing in non-European societies. Non-Europeans, especially American Indians, Australian aborigines, and Africans, were simply beyond the pale so far as European law and morality were concerned; that is to say, they could invoke no rights which Europeans were bound to respect.

The consequences of this double standard were far reaching and long lived. Europeans could (legally in their own eyes) seize the lands of non-Europeans—and they did so in a big way in the Americas, in Asia, in Africa, and in the islands of the Pacific. Europeans could legally (by their own rules) herd non-European "natives" into "compounds" and "reservations," enslave them, compel them to labor for their foreign masters, or sell them as chattel property and transport them to distant markets overseas—and they did so. Europeans generally saw nothing wrong in mistreating non-Europeans and in subjecting them to all sorts of humiliating discriminations, when it suited their purposes to do so. When Europeans went among more primitive peoples to live, as in North and South America, Africa and Australia, they simply set up their own social apparatus and excluded the "natives" from participation therein—except in the role of slaves or servants. When Europeans resided in the older settled countries—China, Japan, Korea, Siam, the Moslem countries, and others—they insisted on taking their own laws and courts with them.

These principles—that only Europeans were entitled to the protection afforded by European norms, and that they should not be subjected to the "barbarous" rules and practices of the "heathen"—were enforced by the superior firepower, transport, and organization of European armed men. When the "natives" revolted against discriminations and exploitations, they were "punished"—and remarkably few voices in the Western world were raised in protest.

This double standard of law and morality sanctified much abuse and cruelty. American Indians were driven from their lands and shot down like wild animals. Australian aborigines were all but exterminated. Africans were sold into slavery by the hundreds of thousands. In the Congo and in many other European colonies, the avarice of absentee capitalists led to cruelties so notorious as to evoke protests in Europe and America, which eventually produced some measure of reform. In China and in many other non-European countries, Westerners evaded taxes, escaped punishment for serious as well as petty crimes against the "natives," monopolized many lucrative enterprises, and otherwise exploited their privileged "legal" status, sanctified by extraterritorial courts, and backed up when necessary by gunboats and marines.

The double standard left a deep and lasting imprint on both sides. It fostered in Europeans (both in those who stayed at home and in those who emigrated or served temporarily overseas) a feeling of racial superiority over the "lesser breeds," the "new-caught sullen peoples, half devil and half child," in the words of Rudyard Kipling, the poet of the "white man's burden." This one-time popular slogan reflected the sense of moral rectitude implicit in the white race's self-appointed mission to civilize the backward heathen, to convert them to Christianity, and to look out for them as one would for children and dumb animals. These themes run through much of the literature as well as the statecraft of the leading Western nations during the half-century culminating in World War I.

The impact of this double standard ramified in many ways in the Western world. When the Japanese, in the final quarter of the nineteenth century, broke free from Western chains and made good their demands to be treated as a full-fledged and important member of the Society of Nations, Captain Alfred T. Mahan (the American naval officer, whose geopolitical ideas were summarized in Chapter 10) rationalized this breach in the historic system by inventing the fanciful hypothesis that the Japanese, by adopting certain Western institutions and practices, had really become "Europeans" under the skin. When World War I and the Communist Revolution in Russia brought stirrings of incipient revolt throughout Asia, these events evoked warnings of a "yellow peril," and forebodings of the "passing of the great [European] race," as we have noted in Chapter 13.

The Nazi persecutions before and during World War II revealed still another facet of the historic double standard of law and morality. Men and women who had long averted their eyes, so to speak, from European abuses and cruelties inflicted on Africans, Australian aborigines, and other "natives" were shocked and outraged when Hitler inflicted similar cruelties and discriminations on other Europeans.

Much has been written in recent years of the long-range impacts of the double standard on Africans and Asians. In those continents the record has left bitter memories that seem likely to persist long after the hated colonialism has vanished. These resentments have fed disorder and violence, and inspired fear in the few remaining areas where European minorities still rule over much larger non-European populations, as in Kenya, Angola, South Africa, and a few other places.

The historic double standard is clearly on the way to extinction. Extraterritorial courts, exclusive clubs for Europeans only, and most of the other apparatus of discrimination have disappeared as one colony after another has made good its bid for political independence. But the psychological fruits of the double standard still frustrate Western relations with the African and Asian peoples. The psychological handicap on the West is all the greater because, for very human if quite illogical reasons, the Communist nations are not identified with discriminatory and abusive colonialism. The Russian Empire had relatively little part in the historic colonialism, and Russians today are not generally identified in African and Asian eyes with the double standard, even though Communist rule imposes its own, no less harsh double standard wherever it prevails. The psychological handicap on the West is heightened by the fact that China was one of the prime victims of the earlier double standard practiced by Westerners in the Far East. Thus, one confronts the paradoxical result that the legacy of the *historic* double standard of international law and morality tends to bias the emerging nations against the West, while it simultaneously blinds them to the *present* double standard implicit in the spread of Communism.

Legal and moral norms in today's international politics

On a more general view of the functions of norms in international politics, several aspects may be noted. Norms of intergovernmental behavior may embody slight or strong ethical connotations. Some norms are essentially procedural and ritualistic. They make up a sort of code, derived from decades and even centuries of diplomatic practice and precedents. On occasion, a government's success or failure may turn on the skill with which its representatives operate the diplomatic code. It is just as essential, therefore, for a member of a government's foreign service to know the patterns of standard diplomatic practice as it is for a lawyer to know the forms of legal documents and the rituals of the courts.

There is some tendency, in diplomacy as in the practice of law, to regard long-accepted forms and rituals as proper and right and to view deviations therefrom as improper and wrong. That is to say, rules that take form as norms of convenience may evolve into moral or even legal precepts.

This tendency is exemplified by recurrent complaints against the vituperative rhetoric and other vulgar behavior which has crept into diplomacy during the past two generations. It was standard practice before World War I for governments to observe a highly stylized diplomatic etiquette and to conduct their business with one another in restrained and generally courteous language. A retired British diplomat, Lord Vansittart, survivor from that era, is one of many who deplore what they regard as a vicious deterioration of diplomatic etiquette.

> Nowadays [he complains] our diplomats are booted around incontinent. The tone adopted to and about Western diplomatic and consular represenatives of all grades by all governments of the Iron Curtain is on the same level as the vituperations of their press. It is the style of an aggressive drunk.*

Vulgarity, deceit, and rapine often lurked behind the silken phrases of the old diplomacy, but certain amenities were punctiliously observed.

As Vansittart says, the Communists are the ones most responsible for this depreciation of the diplomatic currency. The early Bolsheviks, who took over Russia in 1918, were specialists in vituperation, vilification, and vulgar invective. The Fascists and the Nazis followed their lead. Even spokesmen of the liberal democracies indulge in rhetoric these days that would have been considered in bad taste and ineffective in the days before World War I. Nearly any sitting of the U.N. General Assembly or any Khrushchev press conference, for example, provides confirmation of the vulgarity which characterizes a great deal of diplomatic behavior these days.

Most of this resort to the language of the gutter is manifestly deliberate. It is calculated to arouse the masses, who with the spread of literacy,

---

* From "The Decline of Diplomacy," by Lord Vansittart, in *Foreign Affairs*, January 1950, p. 177. Copyright by the Council on Foreign Relations, Inc., New York; reproduced by permission.

newspapers, radio, and television have moved into ringside seats, so to speak. Increasingly, what passes for diplomacy consists of public declarations beamed at this wider audience. Sometimes vilification and invective appear to yield handsome dividends. But such tactics may also backfire, as they did when Khrushchev's pounding on his U.N. Assembly desk with his shoe and other disorderly behavior drew stern reproof from certain delegates of the new nations whom Khrushchev was apparently most anxious to impress.

Despite the frequent resort to *un*diplomatic rhetoric, and the recurrence of disorderly scenes in the United Nations and elsewhere, a great deal of intergovernmental business, probably most of it, is still conducted more or less in accordance with time-honored diplomatic forms and rituals. Governments maintain these in part because routines are necessary in any large-scale operations, in part because diplomatic bureaucracies (like all bureaucracies) become habituated to certain forms and rituals. As indicated above, ritualistic forms may acquire ethical values, but this is generally subsidiary to convenience and administrative efficiency.

When one turns to norms which relate not so much to the forms as to the substance of governmental action, the picture appears quite different. The essence of a *political* problem, it will be recalled, is conflict of purpose or interest. It will be recalled also that a political problem is transformed into an administrative problem when the conflict is resolved. One mode of resolving a conflict of interest or purpose is to apply an appropriate rule. This is one of the functions of domestic courts and governmental administrators. The same principle applies to international transactions.

If all parties to such a transaction recognize and comply with the same norms, the effect is to reduce the element of opposition or conflict. If they agree to the application of a suitable rule, such agreement may eliminate the element of conflict altogether, and thereby remove the business from the sphere of political controversy. This is the effect if the parties accept the jurisdiction of an international court of law or some less formal tribunal, and agree in advance to comply with the decision reached. More frequently there is dispute as to what the relevant norms are and whether particular norms apply to the issues in controversy.

Orderly application of transnational norms, either informally through simple compliance or direct negotiations, or more formally through international courts and other institutions, is confined in the main to situations in which governments recognize a clear advantage or, at least, no serious disadvantage in doing so. One can point to numerous types of situations in which legal rules, ethical precepts, or principles of comity are more or less consistently and faithfully observed.

For example, there is generally strict observance of rules designed to protect foreign diplomatic representatives. During the period when rules on this subject were taking shape, governments sometimes treated foreign diplomats like any other aliens: arresting them for violations of local law, trying them in local courts, and otherwise subjecting them to the authority of the state in whose territory the foreign diplomats were located. Such behavior, however, drew reprisals against one's own diplomats abroad. In due course it came to be recognized that special privileges and immunities for diplomats benefited everyone. Hence the development of such rules, which are followed generally, though not invariably, by governments regardless of their ideological complexion or the level of their political potential.

Much the same is true of rules and practices regarding jurisdiction over territory and territorial waters. Every state is legally entitled to exclude foreign persons from its territory, foreign goods from its markets, foreign ships from its ports and other territorial waters, and foreign planes from its airports and the airspace over its territory. This principle of jurisdiction is universally recognized, and quite generally (though, again, by no means universally) respected. Relative capacity to resist violations of national jurisdiction affects expectations of compliance in some degree. Great Powers do, on occasion, impose demands on weaker nations that could not be imposed on other Great Powers. But, in general, the overall configuration of relationships among nations makes it advantageous for the strong to recognize the legal sovereignty of the weak over national territory and adjacent waters.

National governments, especially those of the greater Powers, have stubbornly resisted rules designed to define aggressive behavior and the limits of legitimate defensive actions. They have resisted just as stubbornly all attempts to regulate the use of violence and, to a lesser degree, the use of propaganda, subversion, espionage, embargoes, boycotts, and other techniques of statecraft. However, there are some indications that the advance of technology may be gradually eroding such resistances. Some international lawyers expect rather confidently to see significant changes in national policies in this area within the not too distant future.

Governments may or may not conform to particular norms. They may deny that the norm exists as claimed by others. Or they may contend that it does not apply to the case in hand. Or they may justify noncompliance because of grave peril to vital national interests, sudden emergency, or for other reasons. But there is abundant evidence that most statesmen in most countries put a generally high value on appearing to comply with high moral and legal standards. There is likewise abundant evidence that a reputation for adherence to such standards tends, on the whole, to enhance a nation's political potential, its influence on other nations.

This is so, it would appear, because acting legally and in accord with high moral standards is regarded nearly everywhere as a virtue. A government may argue the legality of its claims and supporting actions, with a view to winning support by an ostentatious display of its own virtue. Or it may seek to weaken an antagonist's cause, or to injure its reputation and prestige, by arguments designed to demonstrate the latter's disregard of established law and morality. When a government recognizes that its legal position is dubious or untenable, the nearly universal tactic is to invoke the higher moral right to do whatever is deemed necessary to counter a "clear and present danger."

Such forensics are usually carried on with maximum publicity these days. The aim is to reach the largest possible audience. As with other aspects of public relations and propaganda, the spread of literacy, together with the development of world-wide news reporting, radio, and television and forums like the General Assembly of the United Nations, has probably raised the political value attached to ostensible conformity to legal and moral norms. In other words, such norms are highly prized instruments in the conduct of foreign affairs.

A few excerpts from the proceedings in the U.N. Assembly in the affairs of Suez and Hungary in the autumn of 1956 exemplify very clearly such manipulation of legal and moral norms.

The Suez case arose out of Israeli, British, and French responses to the action by President Nasser of Egypt nationalizing the privately owned canal company. Weeks of demands, threats, and fruitless negotiations ensued. Then an Israeli force invaded Egypt, and the fighting threatened to disrupt traffic through the canal. At this juncture an Anglo-French military force also attacked Egypt with a view to occupying the canal. Under a combination of pressures, including denunciation by resolution of the U.N. Assembly, the invading forces were withdrawn without achieving their announced purpose.

The U.N. action challenged the legality of the British and French operation, which had been undertaken for the avowed purpose of stopping the Israeli-Egyptian fighting and protecting the canal. But the Anglo-French action was widely interpreted as designed also to liquidate (or at least to humiliate) Nasser, who, in the estimation of the French and British governments, was a dangerous troublemaker, a threat to their vital interests in the Near East, and likely to align his regime on the Communist side in the Cold War.

The Hungarian case, which arose simultaneously, involved the legality of Soviet military operations to reestablish a compliant Communist regime in Hungary, following a rapidly spreading anti-Communist revolt in that country. The Soviet government had brought in heavy military equipment at the request of the Communist faction, which the Russians regarded as the legitimate government, and had ruthlessly stamped out the revolt.

In both cases the legal issues involved were (1) whether under traditional international law a government had a right to intervene in another country to protect what the intervener regarded as a vital interest (in the Suez case it was dependence on Middle Eastern oil plus right of transit through the canal, threatened by Nasser's posture; in the Hungarian case it was Russian fear of the consequences of establishing an anti-Communist regime in the U.S.S.R.'s western security zone); and (2) whether such intervention was illegal under the Charter of the United Nations, to which the intervening Powers had all subscribed.

The French and British Governments defended their attack on Egypt at length; their case boils down to these words by the British delegate, Sir Pierson Dixon:

> Our intervention was swift because the emergency brooked no delay. It has been drastic because drastic action was evidently required. It is an emergency police action. [It] . . . is not dissimilar to that which obtained at the time of the North Korean invasion [of 1950]. . . . Our aim is to re-establish the rule of law, not to violate it; to protect, and not to destroy. What we have undertaken is a temporary police action necessitated by the turn of events in the Middle East and occasioned by the imperative need not only to protect the vital interests of my own and many other countries, but also to take immediate measures for the restoration of order.

Now, for a sampling of the responses to the Anglo-French argument:

LODGE (U.S.A.): . . . the violent armed attack by three members of the United Nations upon a fourth cannot be treated as anything but a grave error inconsistent with the principles and purposes of the Charter . . .

SOBOLEV (U.S.S.R.): . . . those governments are hurling a challenge at the United Nations, at the fundamental principles of international law and at the conscience and honor of peoples.

LALL (India): There has been released over Egypt a manifestation of the law of the jungle instead of the law of peace and the law of nations as enshrined in our [U.N.] Charter.

JOJA (Rumania): In condemning the tripartite aggression against Egypt we shall, at the same time, be paying tribute to the principles of justice and international law. . . .

VITETTI (Italy): . . . we are convinced that we have to act in a direction which will lead us to affirm the fundamental rules of international conduct, the obligation of every state under the United Nations Charter. . . .

AZIZ (Afghanistan): The civilized world must not, and indeed cannot, accept the rule of brute force. In a world in which international law is not respected and the principles of ethics and decency lose their practical value, surely no one can feel secure.

TRUJILLO (Ecuador): . . . they violated the Charter, as well as the fundamental rights and guarantees of peoples. . . .

DEJANY (Saudi Arabia): What shocked the world was not only the shooting, but the actual trampling on the principles of international justice and moral values and the Charter of the United Nations.

The Soviet government which had uncompromisingly demanded compliance with international law and the U.N. Charter in the Suez case, just as strongly defended its own intervention in Hungary: partly on the ground that the whole affair was a purely domestic question outside the jurisdiction of any international organization; also on the ground that Soviet intervention had been in response to a specific request for help from the rightful government of Hungary; and finally on the ground that—

A victory of reactionary forces in Hungary would have converted that country into a new jumping-off ground for an aggressive war not only against the Soviet Union but also against the other countries of Eastern Europe.

Again, we quote from the record of the General Assembly a few of the responses to these Communist arguments:

IKRAMULLAH (Pakistan): Today an individual, even if right is on his side, does not take the law into his own hands, but has recourse to courts for a decision. The peace-loving peoples of the world have been trying to bring this state of affairs to prevail among the sovereign nations as well.

URQUIA (El Salvador): There can be no doubt but that the Soviet Union is violating the principles and purposes of the Charter, the obligations laid down by the Charter, the provisions of the Convention on the Prevention and Punishment of the Crime of Genocide and the provisions of the Treaty of Peace with Hungary. The intervention of Soviet armed forces in the brutal stifling of the liberation movement . . . the mass slaughter . . . the forcible deportation of men, women and children from Hungarian territory, undeniably constitute criminal acts in international law. . . .

ORTIZ (Bolivia): My delegation regards the Hungarian question as a case of flagrant violation by the Soviet Union of the principle of nonintervention in the internal affairs of a sovereign state.

CASSIMATIS (Greece): The attitude of Greece is based on its deep respect for the principles of the Charter, and is not influenced either by its friendships or its alliances. Greece sets the ideal of human freedom and of dignity of the human person above blocs and alliances.

PORTUONDO (Cuba: pre-Castro!): We, as free peoples, must oppose this invasion, which is contrary to the rule of law and to international law, carried out by the bloodthirsty troops of the Soviet Union. . . .

VITETTI (Italy): The contention of the Soviet delegation that the Hungarian affair is purely an internal matter has been firmly rejected by the Assembly, by the indignation of public opinion in Asia as well as America, and by Europe as well as Africa . . . the moral judgment of the world has been cast, the U.S.S.R. can ignore this moral judgment . . . it cannot contend that it has not been passed. And the fact that the Soviet Union remains indifferent to it does not detract anything from this judgment; it detracts only from the position of the Soviet Union in the community of nations. . . . The Soviet Union has rejected and offended this moral standard of the civilized world. . . .

Effects of legal and moral norms

Vitetti's words, quoted just above, pose the sixty-four dollar question: How much deterrent effect do legal and moral norms and arguments have on the behavior of governments?

One legal scholar who has attempted to answer this questions is the Harvard law professor Roger Fisher. He contends that governments, in both their domestic and foreign operations, are under heavy pressure from various sources to conform, or appear to conform, to accepted standards of behavior. He identified four such sources: (1) threats of retaliation by other governments directly affected; (2) less threatening but none the less adverse criticism from allies or other governments less closely involved in the issue in hand; (3) criticism from a government's own constituents; and (4) the deeply rooted and widely prevalent habit of obeying rules. On this final point, Fisher says:

> Man is by and large a moral creature who is usually anxious to believe that what he does is not only practical but right. Individual moral standards may differ, but it is nonetheless true that each of us is influenced by his idea of what he ought to do. An individual will frequently respect a rule simply because he believes that the rule ought to be respected, without appraising his chances of being caught and without a Machiavellian weighing of pros and cons.*

Whether domestic opinion exerts much pressure on a government to conform to international norms may be doubted. It is difficult to see how pressure from this source can operate at all in highly authoritarian

* From "Bringing Law to Bear on Governments," by Roger Fisher, in *Harvard Law Review*, April 1961, pp. 1135-6. Copyright 1961 by Harvard Law Review Association, Cambridge; reproduced by permission of publisher and author.

systems in which press, radio, and other media of communication are tightly controlled by the government. There is also plenty of evidence that, even in systems with generally free speech and a relatively free press and radio, a government's constituents will support almost any action taken in the name of national security. The popularity of Sir Anthony Eden rose steadily during the Suez crisis and was apparently affected scarcely at all by adverse foreign criticism. Very few Americans denounced their government's espionage flights over the Soviet Union (the U-2 affair) because these were illegal. Some foreign observers in the United States were shocked by the public's attitude toward the Central Intelligence Agency's role in the abortive anti-Castro intervention in 1961. As the Washington correspondent of *The Observer* (of London) put it:

> No one resigned from the Administration though there were certainly some members who disapproved of the invasion. No one has yet been dismissed though there are certainly some who deserve to be. There has been no public debate in Congress at all though a sub-committee of the Senate is investigating what happened in secret. The American press has dug up the bones with its usual thoroughness, but this post-mortem has been almost entirely concerned with the details. Why did the operation fail? Whose fault was it? Were the Chiefs of Staff more to blame than the Central Intelligence Agency? Hardly anyone has asked the basic questions. Was it right? Was it legal? Was it necessary? . . .*

Whether Fisher's faith in the moral nature of man, the "law habit," as it has been called, is as pervasive and effective at the supranational level as he seems to believe, is likewise debatable. If such doubts are well founded, one comes down finally to the deterrent effects that may come from the threats and/or criticism of other governments. On what kinds of issues, for example, would the Soviet government or the United States government be deterred, by threat of legal or moral obloquy, from pressing a claim against a weaker nation or actually intervening in its internal affairs? How much loss of prestige, and consequent shrinkage of political potential in the world community, can be inflicted on a government by branding its purposes and its operations as illegal or immoral? Specifically, how much damage did Britain and France suffer as a result of United Nations censure for their abortive Suez project? How much loss of influence did the Soviet Union suffer as a result of the legal and moral battle over its harsh and highly successful intervention in Hungary? How much loss of prestige did the United States suffer from its clearly illegal

---

* From "Behind the Cuban Fiasco," by J. D. Pringle, in *The Observer*, May 21, 1961. Copyright by the Observer, Ltd., London; reproduced by permission.

espionage flights over the Soviet Union? Or as a result of its less clearly illegal role in supporting counterrevolutionary operations against Castro's regime in Cuba?

These questions pose two quite different issues. The first is: Under what conditions, and to what degree, may legal and moral considerations deter a government from certain undertakings? The second issue is: To what extent, and under what conditions, may legal and moral disapproval have adverse longer-range effects on a government's political potential, its prestige and influence, either within a limited geopolitical region or in the world community as a whole? Different observers will give different answers to these questions, both the two posed just above and those raised earlier in this chapter. One scholar who has given much attention to them is Percy Corbett (emeritus research professor of international law at Princeton), and to his work we now go for a discussion of—

Legal and moral norms in the rhetoric of statecraft *

. . . Governments carry on legal arguments with one another. They employ legal ideas and terminology in defending their own case and in seeking to break down that of the other party. This occurs even when substantial interests are at stake. Often, when the issue is not one of the first magnitude, the argument leads to an agreed settlement. The ideas invoked in such discussions are drawn from two main sources. One source is the [internal] law of nation-states, technically known in this context as "municipal law," which is transferred by analogies often of doubtful relevance from the national to the international sphere. The other is the practice of states in their external relations—the patterns referred to . . . [in the quotation on page 540]. The analogies from municipal law are usually presented on one side as "general principles of law" . . . and this character is frequently denied on the other. The practice invoked is represented as corresponding to a general consensus, as being a rule of law established by the consent of nations, and these allegations are contested by the other party. Such contradiction is a normal feature of legal argument, the unique feature in the international sphere being the absence of an organ with authority, independent of the will of one party or the other, to end the dispute.

States do, however, join voluntarily in *ad hoc* and standing arrangements for adjudication. When a dispute is submitted to them, the tribunals so established draw upon the same funds of norms to justify the decision which they wish to render. At this stage, as also in direct discussions between governments, great use is made of famous treatises. The opinions of revered writers [on international law] are cited, theoretically as evidence of rule or practice, but often because such opin-

* From pp. 8-10 of *Law and Society in the Relations of States*, by P. E. Corbett. Copyright 1951 by Harcourt, Brace & World, Inc., New York; reproduced with their permission.

ions, quite apart from any relation to rule or practice, afford a respectable *ratio decidendi* [basis of decision].

Both in direct negotiation and in voluntary adjudication, then, the materials and the literature of what is known as international law or law of nations serve a useful purpose. They are used as instruments of national policy. Their invocation is one of the forms or stages of diplomacy. They assist in the relatively smooth dispatch of much international business, and it is probably true that in so doing they reduce the occasions of recourse to violence. . . .

In routine business involving no issues likely to develop into *casus belli*, it is extremely useful to have established norms by which questions in dispute can be settled. But where considerable interests are at stake the norms of international behavior exercise much less influence upon governments than does municipal law upon individuals and groups within the state. The reason for the difference is not far to seek. It is known to the man in the street, is indeed the burden of his frequent contemptuous assessment of international law. Law exercises its decisive influence within the state-society because under the machinery of government lies a foundation of strong community feeling and behind the abstract rules stands a complex of organs and procedures of compulsory interpretation and enforcement. In the international sphere there is little but the abstract rule. Only slowly, and with immense difficulties arising out of the value which governments and peoples continue to attach to the sovereignty of their states, are we beginning to construct some prototypes of the organization usually associated with the term *law*. The preliminary condition of such organization, which is a sense of community, of shared values, is present in the international sphere only in a highly rarified form.

On another occasion, Professor Corbett extended the focus to include moral norms, notions of what is right and proper, which no one pretends carry the sanction of law.*

The average man who expresses opinions on foreign policy appears to take it for granted that the conduct of governments in their external relations is a proper subject for moral judgment. He condemns governments, usually foreign, but sometimes even his own, for acts which he describes as immoral, unjust, wrong, evil, barbarous; and he commends governments, usually his own but sometimes even foreign, for acts which he describes as good, just, upright. In this use of language and categories he is encouraged by a constant flow of official communication cast in the same terms. . . .

How far do moral considerations in fact go to determine foreign policy? You will probably say at once that the answer depends upon what country's foreign policy is under consideration and what kind of government is directing it. Yet if you have the tolerance that is

* From pp. 2-14 of *Morals, Law, and Power in International Relations*, by P. E. Corbett. Copyright 1956 by The John Randolph Haynes and Dora Haynes Foundation, Los Angeles; reproduced by permission.

especially mandatory in international relations, and some capacity to look at matters from the other side of the fence, the differences may not appear so certain or so great. You may even be prepared to admit the possibility of systems of morals not on all fours with ours. To eliminate this complicating factor, however, suppose we select British and American foreign policy as our field of enquiry. Here there is a fairly broad background of agreement on morals.

The President of the United States and the Prime Minister of Great Britain met for policy talks in January 1955. On February 2, they published a Joint Declaration. The document is replete with moral principles stated as "truths," "aims" or "beliefs." These begin with the principle that "the state should exist for the benefit of the individual, and not the individual for the benefit of the state," and the derived "basic right of peoples to governments of their own choice." Recent achievements in this direction, affecting "six hundred million men and women in nearly a score of lands," are cited as proof of British and American sincerity in promulgating and implementing this principle and right.

But political independence is not enough to ensure that men can "pursue happiness" and realize their best potentialities. They may need material assistance, and this must come from those who have to those who have not. The Joint Declaration affirms that the United States and Britain are giving such aid with no thought to extend either "economic or political power. The purpose is not to dilute, but to enrich and secure their freedom."

Force is repudiated as a means of resolving the existing conflicts with the Soviet bloc. "We shall never initiate violence." Peaceful means will always be sought and supported. "We shall persevere in seeking a just and lasting peace and a universal and effectively controlled disarmament which will relieve mankind of the burden and terror of modern weapons." And, though the society of free nations must retain the power to deter aggression, it is recognized that "such power should never serve as a means of national aggrandizement, but only as an essential shield for every member of the community of nations."

"We are determined to make the conquest of the atom a pathway to peaceful progress, not a road to doom."

". . . we shall help ourselves and others to peace, freedom and social progress, maintaining human rights where they are already secure, defending them when they are in peril and restoring them where they have temporarily been lost."

In this pronouncement we can find most of the imperatives of what we are pleased to call the Christian ethic, which is also the ethic of countless non-Christians. Here are mercy and generosity, the will not to treat others as means, but to regard them as ends, the will to abstain from doing unto others what we would not have them do unto us, to succor the needy, to share goods and knowledge.

But of course these are words. Scores of similar declarations have been washed down the drain of history. The entire content of this noble-sounding proclamation can be paralleled in the utterances of Lenin, Stalin, Bulganin, and Khrushchev. And what right have we to assume that an absolute intelligence, looking with total objectivity at the multitudinous contradictions of our troubled world, would find a higher congruity of word and act on one side than on the other?

This is not a lecture upon the comparative morality of the Western and Soviet Powers. Yet I would not have given to the Eisenhower-Eden declaration the attention I have if I did not believe (a) that the leaders who made it were speaking with a reasonably high measure of sincerity; and (b) that their foreign policy—their attitude and action in international relations—is really influenced (note that I do not say totally determined) by the principles set forth. I also accept the evidence which they adduce as definite proof, not that all our foreign aid is extended in a spirit of pure altruism, but that it springs from a mixture of ideals, that is to say moral standards, and an enlightened view of national interests. . . .

Yet we may well ask—What is the value of a declaration by a government or a pair of governments that they will pursue a just peace and social progress and never use force as an instrument of national aggrandizement, "but only as an essential shield for every member of the community of nations?" Will the peace that they deem just be just for the other nations affected? Will they and their antagonists agree on social progress? Will it be clear that force used for the alleged protection of another nation has not been used to increase the user's influence and thus aggrandize his power?

No one familiar with the fate of election promises needs to be told how little commitment to specific action is involved in proclamations of high moral intent. In the case of election promises, moreover, there is something operating which hardly exists in the international field. That is a social organization which brings a variety of pressures to bear to check gross discrepancies between announced programs and actual conduct. But even in the international field such declarations cannot be totally ignored in the formation and execution of policy. The present distribution of power in the world involves something like organized opposition to every program of international action, and the eagerness of the opposition to score points is some deterrent to the transgressor. International organizations such as the United Nations provide a forum in which, as we have often seen, even the Great Powers may be embarrassed by charges that they are violating legal or moral obligations. But the debates in the General Assembly also reveal numerous cases of compromise between moral principle and political expedience, as for example when France is brought back into the session by an indulgent agreement not to discuss the application to Algiers of the principle of self-determination so solemnly proclaimed by the President and Prime Minister.

Actually, the best guarantee of substantive effect for international declarations lies in the character of the men making them. Our habit of talking about international relations as the interaction of abstract entities like states carries with it the risk of a good deal of error as to what actually goes on. We begin to think of the actors on the international stage as disembodied essences without conscience or feeling. In fact, though they act in a public capacity, subject to imperatives which they would not always regard as valid in their private affairs, statesmen are quite often idealists making an honest effort, amid all the compromises they may find necessary, to secure some advance towards their ideals. . . .

Within the state we commonly distinguish legal from moral obligations by the fact that the former are enforced by official compulsions while the latter are not. In the international sphere there is in general no such distinction, and the innumerable unofficial compulsions which reinforce the merely moral obligations are also largely absent. It takes a strong community spirit to make a moral code effective, as it takes well-structured organization to discipline human conduct by law. Both factors are still in their infancy in the aggregate of states.

Consensus and norms in the society of nations

The importance of a sense of community as a necessary condition of a public order based upon legal and moral norms is stressed twice in the selections which we have quoted from Corbett. In this stand Corbett would be joined by many social scientists who contend that enforcement of legal and moral rules depends heavily on existence of a public consensus, or agreement, as to what behavior is right and proper, and what is improper and wrong. It is claimed, for example, that no police force could enforce traffic regulations unless a large majority of drivers and pedestrians habitually observe most of the rules. The "law habit," according to this thesis, is a by-product of widely shared values among the members of the society in question.

It used to be imagined that such a consensus prevailed among the monarchs and their ministers and diplomats, who operated the European States System in the seventeenth, eighteenth, and nineteenth centuries. The classical writers on international law made much of the principles of proper conduct which were claimed to prevail rather generally among the ruling elites of the various European nations. The establishment of European communities in North America and elsewhere eventually enlarged the European system in a geographical sense, but without altering significantly the prevailing concepts of international law and morality. Even the recognition that Japan was a rising Power to be reckoned with on a basis of equality (during the 1890's and early 1900's) did not affect immediately the image of an international political system governed by Christian ethics (often called the "law of nature") and the principles and usages which had evolved through the centuries in the leading countries of Europe. Japan was assimilated into the Society of Nations under the fiction that Japan had become a European-type state—by adopting the legal and moral codes of Europe. Non-European cultures—represented by the Ottoman Empire, Imperial China, and the few others which escaped absorption into European colonial empires—were regarded as barbarisms beyond the moral and political pale. Europeans demanded, and exacted by superior force, the right of extraterritoriality for their citizens in such countries—that is, the right to take their own laws with them and to be exempt from the jurisdiction and processes of Turkish, Chinese, or other barbarous systems.

The Western-oriented international system suffered its first real shock in 1917 as the Russian Empire moved swiftly towards communism. The Empire of the Czars had always been on the legal and moral as well as the geographical periphery of the West. Many of its principles and practices violated European standards of propriety and legality. The grafting of Marxian ideology upon traditional Russian ideas of morality and law produced a system of public order which was, and remains, utterly repugnant to most people in the Western cultural tradition.

The breakup of European colonial empires administered further shocks to Western ideas of public order, morality, and law. The new nations of Asia and Africa have a veneer of Western civilization, imposed or at least provided by the soldiers, civil servants, businessmen, and Christian missionaries who dominated those countries during the period of Western colonial rule. But the indigenous cultures rest upon ethical and legal foundations which Europeans in the nineteenth century largely bypassed by imposing their own values to the degree required by commerce and colonial administration.

The political emancipation of Asian and African colonies has focused interest anew on their histories and philosophies. One of the leading authorities on this subject, Professor Adda B. Bozeman (of Sarah Lawrence College), has identified important differences between traditional Byzantine, Islamic, Indian, Chinese, and other non-European systems of values, on the one hand, and those derived from European experience on the other.

In Byzantine ideas, for example, she finds important antecedents of *Communist* Russian disregard for "humanity" and "human dignity." In Byzantine thought, she notes, "no intrinsic value inhered in peace and conciliation, and no moral opprobrium attached to war."

Bozeman finds little in the traditional Islamic or the traditional Indian ethics to sustain modern Western concepts of a "family" or society of sovereign nations, or, indeed, of a "body of international law." With respect to India, she quotes the Indian political scientist K. M. Panikkar, as follows:

> The textbooks which are taught in our [Indian] universities and the doctrines that are expounded by our teachers and studied by our students are unrelated to our social order, and are generally speaking foreign to our experience, so that I have often wondered whether as at present constituted these studies serve any purpose at all. To study Aristotle, Bodin, Hobbes, Rousseau, Green and others may be an intellectual discipline . . . to be concerned with such imprecise terms as democracy, dictatorship, will of the people and social contract, may not be less useful than being engaged in perpetual discussions on metaphysical problems, but no one could pretend that they teach the hard core of power in society.

With respect to China, Bozeman finds even less in traditional culture to support the concepts of a society of sovereign nations and a system of international law applying equally to all. She notes that in traditional Chinese doctrine, two kinds of legal relationships were recognized: those between the ruler and his subjects, and those between China and inferior nations.

> As read by the Chinese [she continues], China's history had established their state as the pivot of all earthly affairs and the exclusive domain of world culture. It was therefore the Middle Kingdom's primary responsibility—so the argument ran—to radiate civilization into less privileged adjoining areas in order to prepare all barbarians for their ultimate inclusion in the world state. And this task, it was felt, could be undertaken in a methodical way only after the "backward" nations had been brought to a full understanding and acceptance of the entire concept of "government through benevolence." While China's statesmen were well aware of the need to adapt their sinification policy to the degree of culture that they found in each instance, they did not, as a rule, depart from the basic Confucian family theme: in educating lesser peoples, the Middle Kingdom pretended to act either as a father in relation to his son, or as an elder brother in relation to his younger brother. (The relationships of friend to friend did not suggest its equivalent in the world of international politics.) The Chinese created, in this fashion, a Great-Power orbit and a system of conducting relations with their hedge-guarding satellites that was to prove enduring and successful. China's relations with Korea are a case in point. Before the seventeenth century they were patterned on the family relationship of father and son. Under the Manchu dynasty China's attitude was more appropriately described as that of an elder brother. These arrangements proved most perplexing to Western observers. When the United States showed an interest, toward the close of the nineteenth century, in opening up Korea, the

issue was raised as to which, if any, extent Western concepts were applicable. One document in the diplomatic correspondence then exchanged on this subject discusses the relevance of Vattel's [one of the classical writers on international law] views on the status of dependent states with reference to foreign Powers, and sets forth that: "the text has little application to countries which in their history antedate international law, of which, also, they never had any knowledge. What unwritten law or tradition controls the relations of China with her dependencies remains unknown." *

This picture of cultural diversity in attitudes toward legal and moral norms contrasts markedly with even the relatively primitive consensus upon which Europeans, in the seventeenth to early twentieth centuries, built up the conception of a universal system of international law and morality. This cultural diversity has become one of the ineluctable facts of today's Society of Nations. It raises fundamental issues as to how widely the system of Western, or European-derived, norms (which we have been wont to conceive as a universal system) is in fact accepted by or acceptable to the ancient and diverse societies which have now come to occupy so important a position in the United Nations and other international institutions. Also central to any discussion of the bearing of transnational norms on the political behavior and relations of states is the impact of Communist values and principles.

Absence of legal and moral consensus in the international sphere, as already noted, became sharply delineated following the Bolshevik Revolution of 1917-18. Communist ideas of international law and morality differ considerably from those historically associated with the Western tradition. Whether the cleavage is too wide and too deep to be bridged by operable rules of comity, ethics, and law is an issue on which the experts are notoriously divided.

On the one hand, it is contended, social values as incompatible as those of communism and liberal democracy, and political systems as antagonistic as those of the Communist bloc and those of Western Europe and North America, prevent international politics from rising above a savage and lawless struggle for dominance. According to this widely held thesis, there may be a system of rules within the Communist bloc, and another or others outside it, but there is no universal set of norms, either legal or ethical, that is recognized and applied across the ideological gulf.

* From "Representative Systems of Public Order Today," by A. B. Bozeman, in *Proceedings of the American Society of International Law, 1959*, pp. 13-19. Copyright 1959 by American Society of International Law, Washington, D. C.; reproduced by permission.

Against this pessimistic thesis, there are numerous dissenting voices, though these seem to be in a minority these days. The dissenters contend that one should compare actual behavior, not merely ideological premises and arguments; and that the actual conduct of diplomacy both by Communist and non-Communist governments reveals a considerable area in which similar norms are quite consistently applied and faithfully observed.

Writing on this issue is overlain with the corrosive film of ideological bias and distrust which characterizes so much of the discussion these days about Soviet and Western behaviors. The following selections are no more than representative samples of a running debate. They indicate certain positions taken and conclusions reached in recent American discussion of the bearings of legal and moral norms on the relations of East and West.

Western and Soviet perspectives on international law

Corbett (already quoted) finds considerable ambivalence in Soviet attitudes toward international law. Soviet legal theorists, he notes, have experienced perpetual difficulty in reconciling the Marxist concept of an international community based on class with the stubborn reality of national sovereign authority capable, in the main, of commanding the allegiance and obedience of citizens irrespective of class.

To the question: "Is there such a thing as an international society divided, across national lines, into exploiting and exploited classes?", Corbett answers:

To us who do not live in the Soviet Union, China, or their orbits, the answer seems clearly in the negative. We of course observe at times a measure of solidarity, transcending national boundaries, among ruling and employing classes, and, especially in the recent years of international unions, among employed classes. But we also observe not only how swiftly and completely this relatively frail sense of common interest has broken down when national groups have gone to war, but also how the executive, legislative, and judicial mechanisms of modern states are used to protect and enhance the interest of national groups of governors, employers, or workers against their counterparts abroad. The norms of international law so called, in so far as they operate at all, bear upon the conduct of persons acting for states regardless of their class provenance, and change only very gradually and indirectly with changes in the class affiliation of governing groups.

Since the 1920's, Soviet jurists have never ceased to worry about the twin problems of a community of diametrically opposed social orders and a class origin for the law of such a community. . . .

In most of the Soviet literature on the subject, the emphasis is sharply upon international law as a tool rather than as an objective system of control. It is a weapon in the struggle between different states or different groups and kinds of states. . . . In the hands of the [Communist states] . . . described as the "really democratic states and governments," it is a "weapon for strengthening the democratic principles of law and peace in international relations." In the hands of the [capitalist states], described as the "antidemocratic and reactionary governments," it is a "means of deceiving the peoples, of concealing imperialist designs of expansion and aggression." Apart from its complete denial of the community without which an objective system of legal controls cannot exist, this commonplace of the [Soviet legal] treatises stretches the elasticity of legal systems beyond the breaking point. How can one body of norms implement such diametrically opposed purposes?

Only in 1956 do we find an attempt at reconciliation . . . [In an article entitled 'Peaceful Coexistence and International Law', a leading Soviet legal theorist, T. I. Tunkin, says] "International law, besides being a fund of principles and norms binding upon states, is, like all law, an instrument of policy, and is so used in some measure by socialist and capitalist states in execution of their foreign policy. The generally recognized principles and norms, being democratic in essence, can only be used as an instrument of policy within limits determined by the content of these norms."

[Tunkin's argument, Corbett notes,] is remarkable for its moderation. . . . The author largely omits the folklore of capitalist aggression and imperialist conspiracy, and moves a long way towards traditional Western views about the basis and nature of international law. In doing so he firmly rejects the more advanced thesis, ascribed to a list of recent Western writers on the subject, that the system can emerge from its inchoate and primitive condition and become real law only with the development of world government. This, he says, is contrary to the laws of social development in our epoch. He sees no possibility of creating general international organizations, embracing the States of the two opposed world social systems, with any substantial supranational powers. The conception of a world state is, he insists, not only utopian; it is reactionary, since it reduces the significance of sovereignty and nonintervention and facilitates in the strong imperialist Powers a policy of dictation and intervention in internal affairs.

The relative restraint of these last words does not conceal the fact that Soviet writers must still maintain the diabolistic explanation of Western policy. And, though Tunkin concedes that international law, as an increasingly universal system, cannot consist of socialist norms, since on that basis agreement is impossible between the two orders of states, he admits no doubt as to the direction in which the content of the system is moving or the source of recent improvements. The contemporary development, he says, proceeds under the increasingly marked influence of the socialist camp. It moves towards the liquidation of reactionary institutions and the recognition of principles and norms guaranteeing peace, cooperation, and free national development. The two greatest advances in the last decade he attributes to Soviet initiative. These are the prohibition of aggressive war and the reinforcement and extension of the principle of national self-determination. The capitalist world, . . . [Tunkin] says, limited self-determination to the "civilized states," but Soviet stimulation has made it universal.*

Another authority on Soviet law, John N. Hazard (of the Russian Institute of Columbia University), finds "examination of practice" to indicate, at first sight, that the Soviet Union accepts a "system of rules having close similarity with the conventional rules known" as international law in the Western world. But, he contends, attitudes toward law should be judged not merely by the verbal content of the rules invoked but rather by the purposes which the rules are intended to advance. If one follows this approach, Hazard concludes, he will see that

norms of international law, no matter how familiar they may be in the non-Soviet world, change their content when utilized to further the aims of what Soviet policy-makers call the socialist camp. . . .†

Oliver J. Lissitzyn (of the Columbia University School of Law) reaches a somewhat similar conclusion in a comparative analysis of Soviet and Western perspectives on international law:

In the West, Soviet and Western attitudes . . . are often contrasted in terms of the measure of compliance by the official decision-makers of the two systems with the prescriptions of international law and particularly with . . . treaties. It is widely felt that in the West these prescriptions are taken more seriously and observed more faithfully than they are in the Communist governments of the Soviet bloc. . . .

But it is well to remember that charges of violations of recognized standards of inter-group behavior are as old as history. . . . Even in our own century, and in the relations of basically like-minded nations, mutual accusations of treaty violations and bad faith have not been unknown. . . . Not infrequently, international law is used not as a guide to conduct, but as a symbol of rectitude, and its norms are converted into slogans with which an elite belabors its opponents and endeavors to create or strengthen an image and a consensus favorable to its own policies. This use of international law is particularly evident in time of war. . . .

---

* From pp. 90, 101-103, of *Law in Diplomacy*, by P. E. Corbett. Copyright 1959 by Princeton University Press; reproduced by permission.

† From "Soviet Socialism as a Public Order System," by H. N. Hazard, in *Proceedings of American Society of International Law, 1959*, p. 39. Copyright 1959 by The American Society of International Law, Washington, D. C.; reproduced by permission.

Whether a government chooses to disregard the law openly, depends on the weighing and balancing of the objectives it is pursuing. The observance of international law is itself a policy by which governing elites seek to attain certain goals. No rational decision-maker can be expected to attach absolute or overriding value to this policy to the exclusion of other and possibly conflicting values and goals. It is particularly in times of great crises, when the very fate of nations and of preferred ways of life seem to be at stake, that decision-makers of even the most highly respected states may deliberately choose to disregard the norms of international law. A few examples will suffice.

In 1939, Churchill, who was then First Lord of the Admiralty, recommended that the Royal Navy plant mines in the territorial waters of Norway, a neutral state, in order to prevent the transportation of Swedish iron ore to Germany. Recognizing that this action would be a "technical" violation of international law, he said: "The letter of the law must not in supreme emergency obstruct those who are charged with its preservation and enforcement. . . . Humanity, rather than legality, must be our guide." . . .

The Nuremberg Tribunal, which can hardly be suspected of anti-Allied bias, held by clear implication that both Great Britain and the United States, as well as Germany, violated in the Second World War the 1936 Protocol on Submarine Warfare. The United States Navy, in public statements after the end of the hostilities, sought to justify its violation of the Protocol as an act of "moral courage of the highest order" which avoided an "inevitable increase in the length of the war and . . . the longer casualty lists that would have resulted" from waging the war in accordance with international treaties. . . .

The sense of moral obligation can hardly be relied upon as a firm basis for the continued observance of treaties. It is the task of diplomacy, now as ever, to arrive at international agreements whose observance rests on the continuing self-interest of the parties and not merely on moral sentiment. In this task, diplomacy has by no means failed. If the files of foreign offices are full of disregarded treaties, they are even fuller of treaties that continue to be substantially observed because they continue to serve the mutual interests of the parties. It is not to be denied that morality and what has been aptly called the "law habit" play a part in the observance of international law and enter into the very definitions of the goals sought to be achieved by the decision-makers; but we must beware of the naive assumption that they can be normally expected to prevail over all other considerations.

If we must reject as naive and unfounded the notion that in the Western system of public order the prescriptions of international law are universally honored and moral duty always triumphs over material interest, must we come to the conclusion that there is no significant difference between Soviet and Western perspectives on international law? Such a conclusion is unwarranted. For the ideology to which the Soviet governing elite subscribes and the system of public order which it administers have characteristics which distinguish them profoundly from the ideology which normally prevails in the West and from the Western system of public order. These characteristics cannot but be reflected in the Soviet attitude toward international law and the place assigned to the latter in Soviet policy. Differences in the degree of respect shown by the decision-makers of the two systems, respectively, for the prescriptions of international law are but surface manifestations of a deep-seated conflict of values, goals and expectations.

History is interpreted by Communist writers in terms of the class struggle between the exploiters and the exploited. In our time, the two classes whose struggle is regarded in Communist doctrine as decisively shaping the future of the world are . . . the capitalists, who still rule the non-Communist states, and the workers, led by the Communist Party, who have already triumphed in the countries of the Soviet bloc. Our time is regarded as a period of transition, a period of "the general crisis of capitalism." The conflict between the two antagonistic classes is believed to admit of no compromise solution and is expected to result in a worldwide victory of the workers. This victory is to bring about the eventual realization of the proclaimed Communist goal—the establishment of a universal classless society in which all forms of coercion, including law and the state, will disappear and human dignity will be maximized. For a good Communist, the supreme moral value is the attainment of this goal. The state and law are regarded as mere instruments of the will of the ruling class and as weapons in the class struggle.

There is no convincing evidence that these doctrines have been modified in any significant respect. Soviet leaders continue to speak with confidence of the ultimate triumph of Communism as a way of life; and, indeed, the evident failure of the West to keep up with the Soviet rate of economic and technological growth cannot but strengthen their belief in such triumph. "Peaceful co-existence" is envisaged as a period of struggle by other than military means—a period in which the economic advantages of the Soviet system will play an increasingly important role. Soviet writers, while often referring to "prolonged peaceful co-existence," are careful not to say or imply that "peaceful co-existence" between the capitalist and the Communist-ruled states can be a permanent state of affairs. . . .

Communist ideology, if it is taken seriously by the Soviet elite, means that the Soviet Union regards all the non-Soviet states as basically its enemies with which it can have no deep or lasting community of interest. Cooperation is bound to be temporary and for limited purposes only. It is expected that eventually Communism will prevail. It is this sense of basic hostility to non-Communist states and of the temporary nature of any accommodation with them that distinguishes most profoundly the underlying Soviet attitude toward international relations, including international law, from that which normally prevails within the Western system. In the West, no such feeling of pre-ordained hostility normally enters into relations between states. In fact, most of the states of the world have an expectation of friendly and lasting co-existence with most of the other states. This is often true even when they go to war with each other—the war is regarded as a temporary condition which does not necessarily mean undying hostility between the two nations. In the relations between non-Communist states, therefore, even though self-interest or expediency be the underlying principle of conduct, the value put on reasonably faithful observance of international law as a condition of stability and orderly co-existence is likely to be greater than that attached to it by Soviet decision-makers. The long-range value of good faith is likely to be better appreciated. Among states friendly to each other, consciousness of shared interests and expectations of stability engender a measure of mutual trust which is lacking in the relations of the Soviet world with the West. In recent years, hostile pressure from the Soviet bloc has served to intensify the sense of solidarity among Western states. The continual reinterpretation of legal norms, taking place in a framework of shared interests, generally does not provoke determined opposition or cause intolerable strain. Ways to compromise differences are found. Violations of the law do occur, but for the most part they are not felt to threaten the very existence of the system. Despite violations, the large and complex pattern of international law norms, customary and conventional, continues to exist and to grow because it continues to reflect many shared interests and expectations.

Communist ideology, moreover, leaves no room for the sense of moral obligation as a distinct factor in the observance of international law. As already suggested, even in the West this factor is probably less important than that of rational self-interest. But rational self-interest in the observance of law tends in the long run to be transformed into a moral imperative. In the pluralistic Western system, side by side with the idea that observance of law is a matter of expedience, there has always been another idea—that keeping the law is morally good, that law and morality have objective validity, and that they lie at the very foundation of civilized existence. There is a tradition of respect for law that carries over into international affairs. The over-all Western attitude toward international law is a composite, a blend in varying proportions, of these two principles—the principle of expediency and the principle of moral obligation—reenforced by the "law habit."

In the monolithic Soviet system, on the other hand, there is no room for public disagreement with the official ideology, which makes the advancement of Communism the supreme criterion of right and wrong and explicitly denies the objective validity of law. On the surface, at least, the ideology of expediency in the relations with a hostile non-Soviet world reigns supreme. A good Communist must not allow moral scruples to interfere with his struggle against the class enemy. . . .*

Maxwell Cohen (of McGill University) takes a more pragmatic and generally more optimistic view of the possibility of a system of norms that bridge the ideological chasm between East and West. His conclusions on this issue are presented in a discussion of—

International law in a bipolar world †

It is, I suppose, not difficult to make a case for the breakdown of universality in view of the profound differences between the Communist and non-Communist worlds, not only politically but in their view of law and its functions in a "society." It is possible also to make a good case for the fact that the idea of universality was only a workable fiction useful for West European international lawyers as the empires of Europe spread outward to all the continents. And, finally, it is almost a cliché to recognize that there can be no general system of law without an underlying social order, and such a unified social order internationally, globally, may be said, by definition, not yet to exist.

While all of this may be true, it seems to me to be protesting too much. A legal order can be extensive and effective even though there may be a quite inadequate degree of communication with respect to the existence or meaning of rules and the legal persons to be regulated by such rules. . . . What I mean by this is to suggest that, tyrannies apart, there is no necessary need for a highly integrated society antedating the legal orders, and indeed many legal orders conceivably could run ahead of the degree of social integration extant in the particular region concerned.

For these reasons it is almost a banality to insist on this need for intensive international integration ideologically, culturally, and otherwise, before "world law" or a common law of mankind of some durability is possible. Indeed, I would suggest that the division between the Communist and non-Communist world, far from having impeded the rate of the development of that common or world law, may in fact accelerate certain aspects of its growth simply because legal techniques become bridges which otherwise it might be very difficult to build between opposing cultural, ideological, or economic bases. The formulae, for example, that may eventually be used to

---

* From "Western and Soviet Perspectives on International Law," by O. J. Lissitzyn, in *Proceedings of the American Society of International Law, 1959*, pp. 26-27. Copyright 1959 by American Society of International Law, Washington, D. C.; reproduced by permission.

† From "Diversity to Unity: International Law in a Bipolar World," in *Proceedings, American Society of International Law, 1959*, pp. 101-7. Copyrght 1959 by American Society of International Law, Washington, D. C.; reproduced by permission.

help solve the present Berlin crisis will doubtless have a high degree of pure legal technique about them; and, indeed, to put it in a cruel way, the law is often a useful plaster to cover the cracks in an otherwise divisive social order until time helps fuse the parts socially more closely together.

The main difficulty with universality in my opinion . . . is a premature reliance upon law to deal with what are essentially power—and very often capricious or arbitrary power—decisions and situations. In trials of strength between the "super-Powers" what matters is not the search for norms having the highest universal validity and binding upon them, but, rather, for methods of accommodation between the titans in a generation in which a radical reformation is taking place in the structure of states and international relations generally. Indeed, the search for concepts of international law which truly increase the universal element of that law may be both premature and too late. It is premature in the sense that the urgent issues to which the lawyers and statesmen must devote themselves are not these criteria of universality but modes of accommodation. It is too late in the sense that we have gone beyond the classical notions of state self-limitation by customary law at least insofar as those notions today apply to the super-Powers when their deepest interests are at stake.

Finally, universality in rules seems reasonably assured where there is a high degree of inter-state reciprocity. I suspect that, to take the simplest example, the rules of diplomatic privileges and immunities remain persistently effective doctrine universally because they are so severely reciprocal in their effects and operation. At the other end of the spectrum, doctrines of "responsibility of states" and "denial of justice" are less satisfactory from the point of view of universal application because the sanctions of reciprocity are absent in so many cases.

If we wish to increase the movement toward universality or the return to universality, whichever way you look at it, the effort in my opinion should be toward searching for techniques of reciprocity rather than criteria for common values to provide a metaphysical unity upon which to build a viable legal structure. . . .

It seems to me an exercise in futility to beat our breasts about the failure of international law to regulate the great abuses of state power we have known not only in recent years but, indeed, throughout the history of international law from its beginnings. . . .

The world may be a desperate, miserable place in many ways, and some states and leaders have behaved abominably to their own people and to strangers all within our own lifetime. But this is a very old story for mankind, and what we have to ask ourselves is whether the quotient of immorality or illegality is greater today than at any earlier period. Here we face a paradox. On the one hand, German and Japanese aggression (and to some extent Russian Satellite policy) are evidence of highly organized state violence and an almost pathological disregard for international law in some areas.

Equally, the gas chambers, the concentration and slave labor camps are expressions of a kind of deep indifference to the moral and legal climate that the Western world had assumed to be applicable at least within the framework of its own civilization and region—although not necessarily always applicable to its overseas possessions. Yet despite man's inhumanity to man, there has grown, alongside, man's support of man to a degree financially, institutionally, and technically that no one could have foreseen two or three generations ago.

The juridical framework of international, technical, capital and social assistance, cultural exchanges, etc., and the development of regional systems of military security—at least within our "camp"—have led to a burgeoning of the conventional legal order and many significant experiments in new types of agreement . . . for example . . . the United Nations agreement with Egypt with respect to the clearance of the Suez Canal and the establishment of the United Nations Emergency Force [in 1956].

To that extent, therefore, it is possible to argue that law, far from disappearing or playing a lesser role, now plays a much more extensive role in security and welfare matters, in providing a network of formal relationships between people of all races, and the older and newer states, than anyone could have imagined a few years ago. . . .

There are already emerging some ideas suggesting the impropriety of any state polluting the common air of mankind with nuclear testing. If to this is added the stalemate of terror that now binds the super-Powers to a rigid posture of frightened military inactivity, it is possible we may emerge in the next decade or more with a system of multilateral rules either dealing with atomic weapons by outlawing them or, at the very least, limiting their future testing.

In a sense the breakdown of law, under previous conditions of non-nuclear warfare, except for the various reciprocal rules dealing with prisoners of war which remained in some cases reasonably effective in World War II, becomes an even more horrendous possibility for the conditions of nuclear warfare. Thus the gap between law and non-law has widened without there being a bridge, called the Laws of War, over which men and states could move to the march of ancient decencies. The pressure for reformulation here is a function of the fear of non-law and may push us faster than we realize, unless our prejudices and the antique doctrines that hold some leaders back delay us for a longer time.

It is more than likely that most of the newer states now emerging from various degrees of tutelage will not only inherit the classical and United Nations systems as they find them, but, on the whole, will play the game according to these rules, with one or two important but not dangerous exceptions. . . .

[One category of such exceptions is violation of traditional rules designed to protect owners of property in foreign countries against arbitrary seizures and confiscations. But even here, despite some notorious cases. Cohen finds the outlook] by no means as acute in the matter of protection . . . as it was thought to be a few years ago. Here again the problem of legal reformulation is less a question of finding a common value structure [between capital-rich and capital-hungry nations] than of solving urgent regional needs within a framework of political immaturity, where the law is an educator as well as a bridge to other peoples and their standards. . . .

Similarly, reformulation may be urgent for the problems produced by the population explosion. Here, of course, the most obvious questions are those that have to deal with the right of immigration and emigration and, in turn, this problem is linked, of course, to the . . . attitude of the less developed parts of the world toward the more advanced areas—with the former determined to have a taste of wealth and well-being, and possibly power in some cases, within the lifetime of their present leadership.

In this connection new concepts of international law, expressed either in customary or conventional forms, may be emerging in order to assure a more equitable employment or sharing of resources so as to aid in this process of improving living standards. . . .

Finally, it may be said . . . that a kind of standing international legal obligation now almost exists to require support for the destitute, the ill-fed and the socially retarded. Refugee problems, capital assistance to underdeveloped areas, the Children's Emergency Fund, the United Nations expanded technical assistance program and Special Fund, the various United States funds, and even the Soviet assistance schemes, are all of immense significance in the emergence of a kind of fixed duty to the capital- and technique-hungry peoples of the world. . . .

[The task of reformulating international law in universal terms involves] the search for new areas of reciprocity in law where the two great camps of our passing day are united in a common functional need, where diverse systems of order are likely to yield to a common hope for the avoidance of disorder, when disorder is costly or threatens the national interest. For even the idea of the national interest itself is changing under the twin drives of fear of the atom and the hope of taming nature to relieve the ancient burdens of men, a hope more widely shared than even before.

Normative Effects of Institutions

People's attitudes toward the United Nations and other international organizations tend to be associated with their beliefs (1) as to the extent to which such organizations affect their own and other nations, and (2) whether the observed or imagined effects are "good" or "bad."

The second question has evoked heated arguments in the United States, in Western Europe, and elsewhere. Some people favor the United Nations because it puts some restraint on national governments (chiefly other than their own); others oppose the U.N. for precisely the same reason. There is a running debate which reflects disagreement both as to values and as to the facts. It is the latter with which we are primarily concerned here. Putting the issue more explicitly: In what respects would the international scene be different if the United Nations, the Organization of American States, the North Atlantic Treaty Organization, and other international organizations should suddenly be snuffed out of existence?

As stated early in this chapter, the number of transnational organizations of all kinds exceeds 1200. Over a thousand are nongovernmental. Most of these latter affect the political relations of nations only slightly if at all. Of the approximately 150 intergovernmental organizations, a majority deal with matters which involve little or no serious conflict of national interests. The Universal Postal Union is such an organization. There is close to world-wide consensus that letters and other mail matter dispatched to foreign addressees should reach their destination.

A number of well-known international organizations deal with technical problems that have politically explosive aspects. Examples of these are the Food and Agriculture Organization, the World Health Organization, the International Labor Organization. Others could be added. In our modern interdependent world, prevention and cure of diseases, food supply and population increase, labor standards, pollution of the seas and atmosphere, and a great many other conditions and events pose problems of vital concern to many nations, but beyond the capacity of any one nation to cope with effectively by itself. On many of these social and economic problems, there is considerable agreement among nations as to goals, but often wide disagreement as to ways and means. Hence international organizations like FAO, WHO, and ILO, though primarily technical and nonpolitical in their approaches and functions, may nevertheless become forums of political controversy and sources of new standards of political behavior in their respective fields.

One can imagine, for example, how this might work out with respect to radioactive pollution. Suppose *technical* studies carried on under the auspices of the WHO should indicate beyond reasonable doubt that nuclear-weapons testing in Siberia, in interior China, in the Sahara Desert, and in the Western Pacific was seriously endangering human health and food supplies all the way from Africa to Japan to New Zealand. Suppose further that the Soviet, Chinese, French, and United States governments insisted that such testing operations were necessary to strengthen their respective defense systems. Suppose finally that widespread publicity given to the WHO findings should evoke a rising demand for a permanent ban on nuclear-weapons testing, from Japan, and from the new nations of Africa and southern Asia. Without speculating on the outcome, the point is obvious: that what begins as a technical study in this subject (and the same would hold for many others) can easily become transformed into an international political issue of the first magnitude.

Another category of international organizations includes those which appear to manifest the beginnings of supranationality; that is to say, organizations which encroach significantly on the time-honored sovereignty of their member states. This is possibly taking place more perceptibly in Western Europe than anywhere else as yet. The European Coal and Steel Community is perhaps the most clear-cut example of this supranational trend. In the ECSC, the member-states—West Germany, France, Italy, Belgium, Luxemburg, and the Netherlands—have in effect relinquished to a central board the authority to make important decisions regarding production and marketing of certain basic industrial commodities. Similar potentialities may be latent in the European Economic Community (Common Market organization) and in other European organizations.

No such trend is as yet clearly discernible in the relatively fewer international organizations which exist for the express purpose, among others, of promoting and maintaining public order in the international community. The most important organization in this category is, of course, the United Nations. Regional organizations dedicated to this purpose include the Organization of American States, NATO, and a few others. None of these primarily political organizations constitutes a government in the generally accepted sense of the term. None of them exhibits or even remotely approaches that essential attribute of a government: namely, a legitimized monopoly of organized violence over its members or within the geographical area of its operations. In no instance has it been possible to mobilize military force under the flag of the United Nations to prevent or to check resort to violence by the Superpowers. In only one instance— the Suez action in 1956—have the latter been sufficiently in accord to bring effective pressure to bear on nations in the second tier of power. Nevertheless, events seem to indicate that international political organizations have affected in important ways the interactions resulting from conflicts of national purposes and interests.

First, such organizations may have some restraining effect on those who make national policies. It is arguable, for example, that OAS has played an important role during the past twenty years or so in making more effective the stamp of illegality on outside interventions in the internal affairs of Latin American nations. It is likewise arguable that most governments today will try to shape their strategies so as to avoid public denunciation in the United Nations Assembly. It has been asserted that the United Nations' most significant political achievement has been to prevent direct confrontation of the Superpowers in the Middle East and in Central Africa, a confrontation that would almost certainly have occurred under former diplomatic conditions.

One should certainly be careful not to exaggerate this restraining effect on the Great Powers. The governments of these nations have demonstrated repeatedly that they may choose to incur moral obloquy in the United Nations rather than relinquish certain diplomatic postures and strategies: for example, Britain and France in Egypt, France in Algeria, the Soviet Union in Hungary, and other cases.

Second, international political organizations may serve as positive instruments of national policy. The most dramatic example in the 1950's was, of course, the intervention in Korea, in which (thanks to a temporary boycott of the Security Council by the Soviet government) the American strategy of resisting the spread of Communism in Asia was transmuted for a time into a military operation under the aegis of the United Nations. It has been repeatedly asserted, and seems to be substantiated by events, that Soviet projects to reform the structure of the Secretariat represent a determined effort to destroy the pre-existing Western predominance in the whole organization.

Roger Fisher, the Harvard professor already quoted, has made the suggestion that the International Court of Justice (a branch of the United Nations organization) could serve in quite a different way as a useful instrument of national policy.

> The judicial process [Fisher says] may enable a government to lose an argument gracefully and according to principle. Responsibility for an unpopular but necessary action can often be passed to the courts and immunized from partisan attack. A judicial decision may provide the executive with a good excuse for doing what it would have to do anyway.
>
> These considerations might well apply to decisions of an international court. The international interests of a government may be advanced more by having a matter decided fairly than by refusing to concede the point involved. If the status of China in the United Nations could be submitted to the International Court [note that this was written in 1961], a sensible solution might be achieved with far less disadvantage to the United States than would be involved either in abandoning a tenaciously held position under political pressure or in indefinitely prolonging an unsatisfactory situation.
>
> Similarly, although the Guantanamo Naval Base may be secure for the present, it is clear that the United States could not insist

forever on maintaining a military base against the wishes of the local government. Eventually this country might be better served by abandoning its Cuban base pursuant to an order of an international tribunal, which might provide for the removal of property and payments by the Cuban government, than by lingering on until pushed out by other means. Thus, internationally as well as domestically, situations may raise in which compliance with law is not coerced but proceeds directly from self-interest.[*]

A third evident consequence of the growth of international political organizations is greatly increased opportunity for weaker nations to bring moral and legal arguments to bear on the greater Powers. The United Nations Assembly, in particular, has come to provide an ideal forum for this purpose. Never before could nations which command so little military force exert so much political influence as they can today. Their activities in the United Nations and in other organizations have undoubtedly hastened the liquidation of European colonial empires. And, with the reservations indicated earlier, it is at least arguable that moral disapproval voiced in the United Nations Assembly has had considerable deterrent effect on the behavior of the greater Powers.

It seems probable that this deterrent effect, such as it may be, is related also to the nuclear stalemate, often referred to as the "delicate balance of terror." This state of affairs, as long as it continues, greatly enhances the ability of the weak to defy the strong with comparative impunity. But without a platform and a sounding board, such as the United Nations provides, it might be much more difficult for the voices of the weak to make themselves heard so clearly in their protests and denunciations of the strong.

This is manifestly part of what the editor of *The New Statesman* (British weekly magazine) had in mind when he wrote, at the height of the Congo crisis in 1960:

> Ever since the Cold War froze the world in the late 1940's, men of good-will have searched for a physical grouping of states which could act as some kind of barrier against the clash of the two committed power-blocs. The concept was christened the Third Force, and men as diverse as Tito, Nenni, Aneurin Bevan and Nehru worked to transform it into reality.
>
> They failed. For the one major power which was prepared to embrace the idea—India—lacked the physical means to make it effective, while the power which could have supplied these means—

[*] From "Bringing Law to Bear on Governments," by Roger Fisher, in *Harvard Law Review*, April 1961, p. 1138. Copyright 1961 by the Harvard Law Review Association, Cambridge; reproduced by permission of publisher and author.

Britain—has remained obstinately committed to one of the rival blocs. Yet, curiously enough, the embryo of a Third Force has existed all the time: the United Nations. And today—thanks, ironically, to the tragic chaos in the Congo—its true role is at last emerging.

The U.N. was created to be the symbol and instrument of Great-Power unanimity, expressed through the Security Council. As such, it could not function in the Cold War. Instead, by a series of fortunate precedents, it has become the instrument of the desire of the small powers—who by sheer numbers now control the General Assembly—not only to avoid commitment to the two major blocs, but to prevent them from coming into contact in sensitive areas.

Suez gave the U.N. its first opportunity. There, despite a great deal of ridicule and disbelief, a force provided by the smaller nations interposed itself between the rival antagonisms of the great powers and succeeded in stabilizing a situation which might well have led to a world war. . . .

The underdeveloped areas are universally and desperately in need of help from the advanced countries, not only in money and machines but, even more important, in doctors, engineers, scientists and teachers. Until now, they have been forced to turn either to the West—whose technicians were tainted with the stigma of colonialism—or to Russia —whose help can only be obtained at an unknown political price.

Now the U.N. offers a third and acceptable choice. The colored races who look with suspicion on a British, American, or Russian expert are willing to accept a Swede or an Irishman with U.N. credentials. For the U.N., they are beginning to understand, is not interested in bases or raw materials. It actually practices what all the colonial powers, old and new, have always preached. It is the missionary without a dogma. Nor is this the only virtue of the U.N.'s new role. By conferring new and important responsibilities on the Afro-Asian powers it accelerates their own progress to maturity. Indeed, provided world opinion recognizes the significance of the U.N.'s work in the Congo, and gives Mr. Hammerskjold the backing which he so desperately needs, we may perhaps one day see Congolese soldiers and technicians taking part in a rescue operation.*

Numerous experts have analyzed the larger political consequences of the evolution of the United Nations since its creation in 1946. One of these, Inis Claude, Jr. (of the University of Michigan), reaches the following conclusions: †

In the final analysis . . . the effort to control the use of force in international relations since World War II has been expressed in the

---

* From "The Missionary Without a Dogma," in *The New Statesman*, Aug. 13, 1960. Reproduced by permission of The Statesman and Nation Publishing Co., Ltd., London.
† From "The Management of Power in the Changing United Nations," in *International Organization*, Spring 1961, pp. 234-5. Copyright 1961 by the World Peace Foundation, Boston; reproduced by permission.

form of a balance of power system. What has emerged is a balance system modified by a number of factors, most significantly . . . the existence of a general international organization. It would be too much to say that the United Nations "presides over" the operation of the balance of power system, but its functioning does have considerable relevance to the working of that system.

The real question for our time is not whether the United Nations is likely to develop a collective security system—or, more remotely, to institute a scheme for the management of power which would deserve the name of world government—to replace the balance of power system. The real question relates to the manner in which, and the degree to which, the United Nations can and will modify the operation of the balance system and contribute to its success as a device for preventing war. In facilitating diplomatic confrontation, fostering serious and meaningful negotiation, and providing assistance to the pacific settlement of disputes, the Organization plays a role which may be useful in mitigating the dangers of failure. In putting moral and political pressure upon states to conform to the principles of international conduct which the Charter prescribes, the United Nations may help to limit the abusive aspects of state behavior which balance of power operations may otherwise entail. In carrying out its wide-ranging activities within the economic and social sectors, the Organization may contribute to a long-term transformation of the global situation which will create new possibilities for the effective management of the power problem.

Finally, it should be noted that a role for the United Nations, more immediately and directly related to the issue of military violence, has been for some time in the process of development. In a number of instances, the Organization has secured and provided military personnel for supervising truce arrangements, patrolling armistice lines, observing developments in zones of particular instability, and otherwise contributing to the maintenance of precariously peaceful relationships. Against this background, an act of creative political ingenuity occurred in 1956, when the Organization was given the mission of mobilizing a United Nations Emergency Force, composed exclusively of military elements from states other than great Powers, to function as stabilizer of the dangerously tense situation in the Middle East. When a somewhat analogous, albeit infinitely more complex situation arose in the Congo in 1960, the machinery of the United Nations was again used to organize and carry out a military operation. There were basic differences in the tasks required of the United Nations in these two situations, and it may be that those differences will produce different outcomes for the two ventures; at this writing [early in 1961], there seems grave danger that the Congo operation will fail as clearly as the Middle Eastern operation succeeded.

What is important for this analysis, however, is the element of similarity in the two cases. In both instances, the United Nations was used as a device for bringing into a troubled situation military contingents contributed voluntarily by smaller states and placed under the direction of the Secretary-General, for the purpose of preventing the eruption of disorder that might result in the competitive intervention of the rival Great-Power blocs. This is a far cry from the original notion of a United Nations enforcement system which would depend upon the unanimous participation of the Great Powers; it expresses the notion of a United Nations stabilization system dependent upon the unanimous abstention of the Great Powers. Such a system cannot be forced upon unwilling Great Powers. It can function successfully only with their acquiescence, derived from the recognition that they have a stake in the avoidance of conflicts that might precipitate war.

Intervention by the United Nations in the Middle East and in the Congo represents the experimental development of a significant role for the Organization in the balance of power system, that of assisting in its orderly operation by undertaking to insulate particular troublespots from the impact of the rivalry which dominates the relationships of the major Powers. This experimentation, whatever its outcome . . . points to the general recognition . . . that the potential contribution of the United Nations in our time to the management of international power relationships lies not in implementing collective security or instituting world government, but in helping to improve and stabilize the working of the balance of power system which is, for better or for worse, the operative mechanism of contemporary international politics.

PART IV: INTERNATIONAL POLITICS IN TRANSITION

CHAPTER NINETEEN

★ ★ ★

International Politics in Transition

IN CHAPTER 2 we described how modern international politics evolved from a system of interaction among European monarchies into a Europe-dominated global system, and how the latter was transformed during the second quarter of the twentieth century into a Washington- and Moscow-oriented bipolar system. Chapter 2 closed with the query: After bipolarism, what? The issue more specifically was whether bipolarism, perhaps an even tighter and more inclusive clustering of nations into the political orbits of Moscow and Washington, was likely to be the predominant pattern of the foreseeable future, or whether bipolarism would turn out to be merely another transient phase of a continuing evolution; and if the latter, what new patterns of international politics might be emerging in the third quarter of the twentieth century?

The intervening chapters have not provided specific answers to these questions. They were not intended to do so. Indeed, no firm answers can be given. But the conditions and events examined in those chapters offer some of the raw materials, the basic data, from which tentative, *very tentative* answers can be formulated.

Let us approach this task by reviewing a little history. Within the memory of living people, international politics could be meaningfully conceived in terms of three major political regions. We have called these the European Realm of the Great Powers, the Afro-Asian Realm of Rival Imperialisms, and the American Realm of Political Isolationism.

The historic European Realm extended beyond the geographic area of Europe proper. It included the coastal margin of North Africa and also the vast Siberian plain of Russia. The European Realm thus embraced most of the lands and narrow seas located to the north and northwest of the Afro-Asian desert-mountain belt, described in Chapter 10.

As late as the fourth quarter of the nineteenth century, every national political community which exerted large influence on distant lands and peoples was located within this European Realm. In those days a study of international politics would have centered on the interactions of the European Great Powers and on their competitive projects and operations in Asia, in Africa, and (to a lesser degree) in the Americas.

The Asian and African lands, to the south and southeast of the desert-mountain barrier, differed in almost every respect from those of the European Realm. From the standpoint of international politics, they differed, above all, with respect to their status in the international political system. The Afro-Asian Realm was predominantly an arena of rival European imperialisms. By 1900 Europeans had staked out claims to nearly all of Africa and Asia and ruled directly or controlled indirectly the inhabitants of those lands. We say nearly all, because the Japanese had shaken loose from European domination. They also held a bridgehead upon the Asiatic mainland. And the United States had just conquered and annexed the Philippine Islands and Guam in the western Pacific and was exerting a growing influence in eastern Asia.

Nevertheless, most of the decisions which vitally affected the lives of Asians, Africans, and (to a much lesser degree) Americans too, were taken in the governmental and business offices of Europe. Nearly everywhere in the Afro-Asian Realm the avarice and brutality of the local managers of European business enterprises and the behavior of European colonial administrators contrasted starkly with the humanitarian teachings of Christian missionaries and the self-assumed civilizing mission of Europe's ruling classes.

The successes of European empire-builders were widely attributed to their self-imagined innate superiority over the "colored races." Not until the European empires were well on the way to collapse and extinction was much attention paid to the historical conditions which gave Europeans—for a time—such a decisive advantage in their dealings with all non-European peoples: superior weapons, the principal instrument for subjugating less technically advanced peoples; and swifter and more capacious ships and overland transport which gave to European merchants, administrators and their supporting military forces a mobility denied to non-European peoples in the centuries of European empire building.

The third historic region of international politics—the American Realm—started along the same road to colonialism. By the time of the American Revolution (1775), virtually all the habitable areas of North and South America had been divided among the eighteenth-century empires of Spain, Portugal, Russia, France, and Britain. A century later, however, only vestigial traces of those empires remained, chiefly in the offshore islands of the western Atlantic and along the mainland coasts of Central America and northern South America.

The Americas were still heavily in debt to European capitalists. Most American countries carried on more commerce with Europe than with each other. European decisions still affected in varying degrees the lives of Americans. But European political influence had long since passed its peak and in the final quarter of the nineteenth century was on the wane nearly everywhere in the Americas.

It is unnecessary here to probe deeply into the many conditions and events which produced in the Americas a history so different from the simultaneous histories of Asia and Africa. In the long view of history the decisive turning point seems to have been the successful revolt of the Thirteen Colonies from the rule of George III and his ministers, a revolt incalculably aided by the greater power struggle then engaging Frenchmen and Britons in many parts of the world. The collapse of Spanish and Portuguese power, likewise hastened by events in Europe, similarly contributed to the early winning of political independence in Latin America. Also significant, in historical retrospect, was the posture of political isolationism—it would be called nonalignment today—which the Founders of the United States adopted in order to buy time in which to consolidate economically and politically their hard-won independence. To this should be added the corollary strategy, expressed in the Monroe Doctrine, of opposing any European political re-entries into the Western Hemisphere. For these and other reasons, the Americas developed largely on the periphery of the main arenas of Great-Power international politics. In a very real sense, the American Realm became politically a world apart, a Realm of Political Isolationism, relatively detached from the Old World except for periodic alarms heard faintly across the wide intervening oceans.

Two world wars and the social upheavals which accompanied them radically altered the geopolitical map of 1900. During World War II and for a few months thereafter, European and American elites—politicians, civil servants, military leaders, academic scholars, spokesmen for big business and finance, and others—clung to the hope that the wartime coalition of the United States, Britain, France, Nationalist China, and the Soviet Union would survive and provide an irresistible concert of power to enforce a new international order. The United Nations Charter was built explicitly upon this hope, which for many was a firm expectation. The Security Council, dominated by the Great Powers, was planned to be the primary instrument of the new world order. The General Assembly (in which all members would be represented) was conceived mainly as a device for making Great Power rule more palatable to the weaker and less influential members of the United Nations.

As everyone knows, the hoped-for concert of the Great Powers failed to survive. The manner of its failure forged the transition to the next phase of the international political system. From the American and West European perspectives (and one should always remember that the Russians and others interpret events from different perspectives), the grand coalition was progressively eroded by a series of Russian projects designed to surround the Soviet Union with a glacis, or defense zone, of Communist-ruled subservient allies. The East-West coalition was shattered beyond repair by Russian efforts to terminate by blockade the four-Power occupation of Berlin (1948-49), by the Communist North Korean attack on South Korea in 1950, and by mounting evidence of presumably Russian-inspired subversive activities inside many non-Communist countries. Within the United States, and to a lesser degree in West European and other non-Communist countries, these events were widely interpreted as moves in a global strategy to extend indefinitely the area of Soviet-supported Communist rule.

The response of the West, under leadership and pressure from the United States, was a series of policy declarations, military alliances, economic aid projects, propaganda, and other steps, designed to deter the Soviet Union or its satellites from further military attacks, to combat Communist subversion of non-Communist nations, and by these and other means to block any further geographical extension of the area of Communist rule.

The consequence of these moves and countermoves was the emergence of a state of affairs that was neither peace nor war in the traditional meaning of those terms. It was a state of affairs in which the most destructive weapons held the ring, so to speak, while less violent if scarcely less hostile offensives and counteroffensives were conducted across national frontiers and inside national political communities. These operations, carried on with the whole array of nonviolent instruments and techniques described in Chapter 4 and supplemented recurrently by limited violence, became known as the Cold War.

Virtually all countries, including those not yet committed either to Moscow or to Washington, became actual or potential battlefields of this Cold War. The underdeveloped countries, especially those in process of winning political independence, and those suffering the social stresses of modernization, were all expected sooner or later to succumb to the inducements and pressures of either Washington or Moscow. It was widely believed, in short, that the loose bipolar pattern which international politics exhibited in the late 1940's would expand and tighten until it came to dominate the Society of Nations completely.

As indicated in Chapter 2, this outcome has not occurred. Washington and Moscow have labored persistently to draw additional nations into their respective orbits. They have succeeded to a degree, but only to a degree. They have encountered stubborn resistance to the satellite role throughout most of non-Communist Asia and Africa. There have also been indications of incipient disaffection within the anti-Communist orbit, and even inside the more tightly organized Communist realm as well. Instead of the uncommitted nations being drawn irresistibly into either the Communist or the anti-Communist alignment, most of them have declared their intention to remain uncommitted, and thus far made it good. Thus in the 1960's there has come to be superimposed upon the bipolar pattern the still rather vague outline of a more complex grouping of nations. If the trend towards neutralism and nonalignment continues, and especially if significant fissures should open up in either the Communist or the anti-Communist coalitions, these events will confirm that bipolarism, contrary to widespread earlier expectations, is indeed but a transient phase in a continuing transformation of the international political system.

It is difficult to see one's way through the verbal smog which blankets the international scene these days. The meaning of events is frequently not what it seems to be. But certain datum points can be established, or at least conflicting theses and interpretations can be compared. One approach, the one employed here is to examine the structure and other characteristics of the major groupings which are now discernible in the Society of Nations and appear to be setting the larger patterns of international politics.

One of these groupings is, of course, the states under Communist rule, variously called the Communist Camp, orbit, or bloc. At least one Communist-ruled state, Yugoslavia, occupies an ambiguous position in this grouping. It is neither a satellite nor any longer a fully committed member of the Communist Camp, a term which we shall use to designate the international coalition of Communist states. To denote simply the area to which communist ideology provides the organizing principle of society and government, we shall use the term *Communist Realm*.

The second major grouping includes all the states associated in various ways for the primary purpose of opposing further spread of the area of Communist rule. Americans and (to a much lesser extent) West Europeans are wont to call this grouping the Free World. But since Free World, in this context, means simply free from Communist rule, and since the anti-Communist coalition includes numerous states which by no definition could be called democratic in the Western sense, and since a good many national communities free from Communist rule refuse to be identified with the crusade against Communism, a more descriptive label is the Anti-Communist Coalition, or simply Anti-Communist Realm when referring to the geographical area occupied by the national communities politically associated for the purpose of opposing the spread of Communist rule.

The remaining units of the Society of Nations have refrained from identifying formally with either the Communist Camp or the Anti-Communist Coalition. The elites in some of these uncommitted nations are ideologically attracted more or less towards Communist ideology; in others the orientation is more towards Western-style democracy. Still others exhibit no strong orientation either way. But with few exceptions, they manifest a common determination to avoid becoming satellites of either Moscow or Washington. In calling this grouping of states simply the Uncommitted Realm, one should remember that noncommitment embraces quite a variety of attitudes, strategies, and international relationships.

The emergence of the Uncommitted Realm as congeries of nations, exhibiting at least the beginnings of several intrarealm structures and a widely shared determination to play independent roles in international politics subordinate to neither East nor West, has checked at least temporarily the trend towards a tighter and more inclusive bipolarism. Soviet and American statesmen still devote a good deal of effort to extending their respective political orbits. But the spirit and method, as well as the results, of these efforts seem to have changed subtly in recent years. Moreover, it is becoming apparent that neither Moscow nor Washington is able, under conditions existing in the early 1960's, to impose its more rigorous demands on most of the uncommitted nations—except at suicidal risk of involving each other in a mutually destructive war of annihilation.

The bipolar model, in short, may still explain many of the interactions of the Soviet Union and the United States. It may also account (though less satisfactorily) for interactions between the Communist Camp and the Anti-Communist Coalition as a whole. The bipolar model may also explain the respective approaches of Moscow and Washington to the uncommitted nations, in the main. But the bipolar model no longer fits the realities of the global international system as a whole.

The three-realm model provides an alternative overview of international politics in our time. Into this model one can fit the interactions of the Superpowers, their respective approaches to and interactions with the uncommitted nations, and also a number of developments that appear to be taking shape within each of the three major groupings. In anticipation of what is to be said in the next three chapters, the following landmarks may be briefly noted here.

First, accumulating evidence indicates that the Communist Camp is becoming internally bipolar in its political configuration. It is no longer the monolithic structure it appeared to be in the days of Stalin. China is contesting ever more aggressively and apparently with considerable success the Soviet claim to exclusive hegemony over the Communist world. Further, there are indications that the Chinese challenge to exclusive Russian direction of the Communist international system has loosened, at least slightly, the bonds which have hitherto tied the Communist satellite states tightly to the Soviet Union. If these trends—towards a Soviet-Chinese bipolarism and a loosening of satellite relationships to the Soviet Union—should continue, they would open up vistas of possibly immense significance, not only for the future of the Communist Camp as a regional international system, but also for the relations of the Soviet Union, China, and the lesser Communist states with the non-Communist nations, both with those associated in the Anti-Communist Coalition and with those committed in varying degrees to nonalignment with either side in the Cold War.

Second, there are still clearer indications that the Anti-Communist Coalition is less solid and may be less enduring than American politicians and military strategists have labored to make it. Solidarity within the Anti-Communist Realm has varied roughly with the intensity of the perceived threat of Communist aggression. Solidarity has been weakest when the danger has appeared to be dormant. There has been a persistent tendency outside the United States to view the actions of the Communist Powers as less menacing than these have generally appeared to most people in America. For this and other reasons the European and Asian members of the Anti-Communist alliances have most of the time contributed less to the common defense, in proportion to their available resources, than has the United States. Furthermore, the competitive development of ever more destructive weapons systems by the Soviet Union and the United States appears to have fostered in many of the allied nations both a tendency to depend upon this balance of terror, to which they contribute little or nothing, and a desire to contract out of the East-West struggle altogether. This latter sentiment—discernible in Canada, in Britain, in Western Europe, and elsewhere—does not appear to have affected significantly the official policies of the allied Powers; but a continuing trend towards neutralism would clearly erode in some degree the foundations of the Anti-Communist Coalition. It is also possible that the more presumably effective the United States strategy of nuclear deterrence appears to our allies, the less sense of compulsion they will feel to make heavy sacrifices for the common defense at lower levels of military effort.

Third, the Uncommitted Realm has as yet no recognizable core or nucleus. No single state has become and none seems likely soon to become the recognized spokesman for the uncommitted nations. Nevertheless, the Uncommitted Realm exhibits numerous aspirants to such a role, though these have thus far been individuals rather than national communities as a whole. It is Nehru, not India; Nasser, not Egypt; Nkruma, not Ghana; and the same holds for other aspirants to leadership of the uncommitted nations. But these are straws in the wind, possibly foreshadowing emergence both of principles and organizations which might give to the Uncommitted Realm a more definite political structure and greater political potential in the international system as a whole.

The main point of the preceding paragraphs is that there is no ground for expecting that either the Communist Camp or the Anti-Communist Coalition or the Uncommitted Realm will exhibit stable relationships either internally or with each other in the years immediately ahead. Nevertheless, the three-realm concept or model provides a basis for investigating the present state of the international political system and for speculating on changes that are certain to come. This approach seems fruitful because so many of the major patterns of international politics today are meaningfully related to the three groupings described above.

The three-realm concept, one hastens to add, is not the same thing as tripolarism. Nor could one realistically describe the emerging overall pattern as tricentric. Rather, the reader is urged to think of the present trend as being towards a new polycentric pattern: a system with numerous centers of significant political potential, operating within a global three-realm grouping of nations. We say *new* because, as will be recalled, polycentrism within a three-realm grouping, but with quite different systemic features, characterized the international system which went to pieces in World War II. Certain essential differences between the earlier system and today's are already evident, and others will become so in the following chapters.

The new polycentrism may prove to be as transitory as the bipolarism that preceded it. Radical new developments in weapons, for example, might transform the international system or destroy it altogether. So likewise might the acquisition of enormously destructive weapons by a considerable number of national governments. There are numerous other possibilities. One of these, so important as to merit the most careful and critical scrutiny, has been expounded by George Modelski of the Australian

National University. Modelski's thesis (which will be presented in Chapter 20) is that the Communist Camp contains the necessary properties which could enable it, under favorable conditions, to expand progressively until it should become itself the universal or nearly universal international system.

Whatever the odds of these or other transformations, our own working hypothesis is that the major foreign policies and operations of nations, and the larger patterns of international power and influence during the third quarter of the twentieth century, are likely to develop within the three-realm grouping of nations as outlined above and to be related to reciprocal impacts of these political groupings on each other.

Essential data have already been presented and analyzed in the chapters of Part III, to which frequent reference should be made as one reads the remaining chapters. The task in these final chapters is to focus these data, these *foundations* of international politics, more specifically on the fluid patterns of contemporary interaction upon the international stage: in short to draw comparisons, necesarily general in the main, with respect to the geopolitical structure of the three realms, their economic stature and potentalities, the dynamic (and, in some instances, not so dynamic) social forces, military strengths and vulnerabilities, and the projects and undertakings, apparatus and techniques, by which ruling elites in each realm are striving to accomplish their respective national and transnational purposes.

CHAPTER TWENTY

★ ★ ★

The Communist Camp

THE COMMUNIST REALM, the area ruled by Communist-party dictatorships, appears upon a map as a contiguous bloc of territory in Eurasia. It extends from the Iron Curtain boundary of Central Europe to the Pacific coastline of Asia, and from the Soviet Arctic to the borders of Turkey, Iran, Afghanistan, Pakistan, India, Nepal, Burma, and Thailand.

In the early 1960's the Communist Camp, as Khrushchev and other Communist leaders are fond of calling the interlocked system of Communist political communities, included twelve full-fledged constituent units. These twelve countries comprise about 25 percent of the earth's land surface, and their combined population is about 36 percent of the world total. The Communist Camp includes the world's largest country, the Soviet Union, and the most populous one, China. The remaining ten fall into two geographical groups: those in eastern Europe and those in eastern and southeastern Asia.

The East European units are: Poland, Czechoslovakia, East Germany, Hungary, Rumania, Bulgaria, and Albania. Except perhaps in Albania, these Communist regimes rule by the grace of the overshadowing presence of the Soviet Army. Again excepting Albania, in which there have been some indications of a pro-Chinese orientation, these East European countries provide a military glacis, or defense zone, between Soviet territory and non-Communist Europe.

The East Asian satellites are more difficult to classify. Mongolia, a generally arid and sparsely populated country wedged between the Soviet Union and China, has long operated under Russian tutelage, but seems likely to become increasingly a pressure-zone between the two giants of the Communist Realm. North Korea and North Vietnam are the Communist parts of divided countries: the former at the base of the peninsula facing Japan; the latter at the base of the great promontory of Southeast

Asia. Both, especially North Vietnam, serve the Communist Camp as advanced salients of the highly unstable frontier between the Communist Camp and the Anti-Communist Coalition in eastern Asia.

The Communist Realm also includes Tibet in the mountain-girded plateau between China and India, Nepal, and Burma. Tibet was occupied in 1959 by Chinese military forces and is administered virtually as a Chinese dependency.

Yugoslavia, though indubitably a Communist-ruled state, has been since 1948 on the periphery of the Communist Camp. For the time being at least, it is probably realistic to classify Yugoslavia as a recurrently Moscow-oriented member of the Uncommitted Realm.

The Communist Camp has three kinds of footholds outside Eurasia. The Castro regime in Cuba represents the first. This regime has moved steadily towards affiliation with the Communist Camp and has come to be widely regarded as part of the Communist international apparatus. The second type includes more or less Communist-oriented regimes (chiefly in Africa) which strenuously assert their neutralism towards the East-West struggle. The third and probably most important type of Communist foothold beyond the Communist Realm is the world-wide congeries of non-governing national Communist parties.

Each of these parties constitutes

> the nucleus of a new Communist state. Several of the non-governing parties—and among them the French, the Italian, the Indian, and the Indonesian—are powerful organizations constituting key political forces in their respective countries. Sixty-three parties existed in the non-Communist world in 1958, with a membership that may be estimated at between eight and nine millions.[*]

The number of potential converts to Communism among the populations of the non-Communist countries is manifestly incalculable. But the number is widely believed to be very great, especially within the countries of Asia, Africa, and Latin America which are engaged in a desperate race between population increase and modernization.

The internal organization of the Communist Camp has, in the words of Zbigniew K. Brzezinski (Director of the Research Institute of Communist Studies and professor of Public Law and Government, in Columbia University), both "formal institutional aspects" and "dynamic aspects." The apparatus includes multilateral treaties, bilateral political treaties, bi-

---

[*] From p. 20 of *The Communist International System*, by George Modelski, Research Monograph No. 9, Center of International Studies, Princeton University. Copyright 1961 by Center of International Studies; this and subsequent quotations from this work are reproduced by permission of the Center and the author.

lateral economic agreements, and cultural pacts, supplemented by transnational associations of the many national Communist parties.*

In 1919, the newly founded revolutionary regime in Moscow organized an international association or league of Communist parties called the Comintern. This Communist International as it was also called, was dissolved in 1943 during the brief period of Soviet military collaboration with the West in World War II. In 1947 an international Communist Information Bureau called the Cominform was created. The Cominform lasted until 1956, when it was scrapped ostentatiously in the process of cleansing the Communist system of Stalinism. Since then there have been frequent *ad hoc* meetings of Communist party leaders, but no formal multilateral system-wide institution, charter, or treaty in the Communist Camp. The nearest approach to intergovernmental system-wide institutions are the Warsaw Treaty Organization (WTO) and the Council for Economic Mutual Assistance (CEMA).

Brzezinski characterizes the WTO as

> both a political and a military organization. Established formally . . . [in 1955], it is composed of eight of the twelve Communist states, with China "associated" but not a member, and North Korea, North Vietnam, and Mongolia remaining outside of the pact. It is thus primarily a European organization, serving externally as a counter to NATO, internally as the formal device for the perpetuation of close ties between the Soviet Union and its European satellites. . . .
>
> The political importance of the WTO is that (1) it provides a formal framework binding the various [European] states together, (2) supplies the juridical basis for limiting the exercise of their sovereignty [by prohibiting their participation in non-Communist alliance systems], and (3) serves as a useful forum for the articulation of unanimity, expressing ritualistically the bloc's support of Soviet foreign policy initiatives. . . .
>
> The original agreement provided for a Unified Command of the armed forces of the signatories. . . . [But] the international command has not been set up. . . . In this case, the Soviet Union's fear of arousing new anti-Soviet sentiments was combined with its desire not to share Soviet military secrets with its allies. . . .
>
> A much more active, positive role is played by the multilateral Council for Economic Mutual Assistance (CEMA). . . . The founding members were the USSR, Poland, Czechoslovakia, Hungary, Rumania, and Bulgaria. Subsequently they were joined by East Germany and Albania. These states together have about 300 million inhabitants, or

---

* In the following description of the internal structure of the Communist Camp we have depended heavily upon Brzezinski's paper entitled "The Organization of the Communist Camp," in *World Politics*, Jan. 1961, pp. 175 ff. Copyright 1961 by Princeton University Press; passages quoted from this paper are reproduced by permission of the Princeton Center of International Studies and the author.

11 percent of the world's population. They cover about 17 percent of the world's surface and produce nearly 30 percent of the world's industrial output. Although not members, China, Mongolia, North Korea, and North Vietnam have in recent years been sending observers to the Council's sessions.

In its initial stage, CEMA resembled the Warsaw Pact: primarily restrictive in purpose, it was designed to keep the European Communist states out of the Marshall Plan. . . . During this early period [1949-53], the organization concentrated primarily on redirecting the trade of its members towards each other. . . .

The steady growth of CEMA's bureaucratic machinery [since Stalin's death] has been a concomitant of its increasingly active integrative role. . . . At the present time, CEMA is doubtless the single most important organ for actively shaping policies designed to promote the Camp's unity. . . . [Since 1956] it has been the source of numerous policies designed to mold a "world socialist market" as the basis for the Camp's political and ideological unity. . . .

Two additional multilateral organizations of considerably less political importance are the Danube Commission (U.S.S.R., Bulgaria, Czechoslovakia, Hungary, Rumania, and Yugoslavia), and the Institute for Nuclear Research (all the Communist states except Yugoslavia). Brzezinski continues:

This multilateral framework is buttressed by a web of bilateral agreements. Of these, the most important are the friendship and mutual aid agreements. They are usually directed against a specific outside threat—either Germany or Japan, and their possible allies— and they contain pledges of mutual support. . . .

Only one of these mutual-aid treaties represents a meaningful alliance. That is the one between the U.S.S.R. and China. As for the rest, they are

essentially a cloak for a relationship of political subservience [to the Soviet Union], with the juridical fiction of equality serving both to mask this relationship and to perpetuate it. . . .

Bilateral trade treaties also serve to unify the Camp and are meant to create a common and enduring interest in its preservation. . . . Given overall state control of the economy, such treaties govern the totality of trade among its members, and since most of the foreign trade of the Communist states takes place within the Camp . . . these agreements have an important bearing on the future livelihood and development of the signators. . . .

Diplomatic and consular relations have been formalized and regularized by "a whole series of consular conventions" entered into during 1957-1958 between the Soviet Union and the other Communist states. In these, however, the Soviet government still exhibited its traditional reticence concerning the opening of foreign consulates on Soviet soil. . . .

The final link in the formal web of ties . . . is provided by the cultural agreements concluded between the Communist states. Since art, culture, and science are subject to state control under the Communist system, all cultural contacts between the various members of the Camp must be regulated through official and formal channels.

These agreements provided for expanded contacts in education, art, music, literature, the theater, films, press, radio, television, sports, and even tourism. In effect, they were meant to establish a broad social basis for contacts with the "first country of socialism." . . .

[All this formal apparatus] is given content by the continuous interaction of [the Camp's] members, resolving conflicts, shaping policies, developing close trade contacts, engaging in exchanges and, of course, responding to the demands of the Camp's most powerful state. . . .

[Of great importance from this perspective are the frequent meetings] between the top leaders of the various ruling parties. This practice is a relatively recent development and involves an important change in the political style of the bloc. . . . [Since Stalin's death] and particularly since [the Russian-suppressed Hungarian revolt of] October-November 1956 (which can be considered as a sort of watershed in the bloc's history), relatively frequent bilateral and multilateral consultations between the party leaders have taken place. Even more important, Soviet leaders journey frequently to the other Communist states and necessarily have become much more conscious of the problems that the other ruling parties face. While not all of these meetings are of actual policy-making importance, they do help to keep the various party leaders better informed about current difficulties and they invariably involve a measure of discussion. Since at such meetings the Soviet leadership can muster the overwhelming support of the other regimes, the multilateral meeting is a useful forum for articulating common principles and for forcing recalcitrant parties (until about 1958, the Polish; more recently the Chinese) into declarations of unity. . . .

Secondly, according to a decision reached at the November 1957 conference, an inter-party political-ideological magazine was established. . . . Since publication of its first issue in September 1958, the magazine has appeared once a month. Although it does not seem to have lived up to expectations as the vital organ for the crystallization of ideological and political unity in the bloc, it is the only inter-party publication on ideological-political matters, and in some ways a successor to the [former] Cominform journal. . . .

Little can be said without access to classified data concerning the dynamic side of military relations within the bloc. However, certain facts do stand out. Since 1956, the Soviet Union has striven to remove the most overbearing aspects of its military domination of Eastern Europe, a domination to which the Soviet leaders had to admit during the critical days of October 1956. However, these [subsequent] adjustments do not amount to close co-operation and/or military integration. In fact, it would appear that on the military level, the Soviets, possibly anxious to protect their military secrets and hypersensitive to security matters, prefer to avoid tight military integration. Apart from providing some of the satellites with technical information necessary for the production of Soviet-type weapons (thereby alleviating delivery pressures on the USSR), and general standardization of weapons within the Camp, military co-operation tends to operate primarily at the top political-military levels, through exchange of visits and a general definition of broad strategic tasks, but without real military integration or frequent and regular joint maneuvers of the various Communist forces.

The Soviets' determination to protect their military preponderance within the bloc is particularly evident with respect to nuclear weapons. Unwillingness to share them has been expressed through such maneuvers as the scheme for an atom-free Asia (coolly received by the Chinese) and by continuing equivocation in response to requests for greater nuclear assistance from the other "socialist" states, particularly China. . . .

These various high-level forms of relations testify to a steadily intensified contact between the ruling regimes. The number of visits of various ministers, . . . technical and scientific delegations, youth activists, etc., runs virtually into the hundreds. These, too, compare notes and sometimes engage in subtle communications. Recent years have also seen a marked increase in personal contacts among the several Communist states, something not possible during Stalin's era. The gradual development of tourism means that each year tens of thousands of private citizens of one Communist country visit other Communist countries. . . .

One should also note an increasing student exchange, . . . special conferences of bloc scholars, collaboration agreements between the several national academies of science . . . and circulation of bloc literature and newspapers (particularly Soviet) among the various states. . . .

The extensive efforts to promote unity, so lacking during the Stalinist phase of the Camp's development, has two further aspects which deserve mention. The first is the matter of trade, the second that of the literature of unity. The importance of close trade ties as a factor of interdependence was recognized much earlier than the need for coordinated planning and for the activization of the dormant institutions of CEMA. However, with specialization, trade has assumed an even more important role in shaping a "socialist world market," distinct from the capitalist world and fully self-sufficient. . . .

In general, in the eyes of the Communist leaderships, the emerging economic interdependence is said to have not only economic but great political and ideological significance. It is quite evident that in the thinking of the Soviet leaders, the consolidation and growth of a "socialist world market," and eventually its preponderance over the "capitalist" market, is one of the determining factors shaping the present epoch. . . .

The final aspect . . . involves the literature of unity that is mushrooming within the bloc and particularly in the USSR. By this is not meant the trite, propagandistic, and largely sterile treatments of the often illusory advantages for the various Communist-ruled countries of friendship with the Soviet Union. Such publications have been available for a long time. In the last two or three years, however [written in 1960], there have been signs that more serious thought is being given . . . to what might be called the problematics of the Communist Camp. . . . While often simplistically dogmatic in its approach . . . [the new] literature [circulating among the Communist countries] is a modest step forward in the direction of at least recognizing some of the problems involved in building "socialism" on the basis of a common ideology but within the context of several societies, ranging from the technologically most advanced to the most primitive.

All these devices are regarded as efforts to regularize and intensify transnational relationships within the Communist Camp.

While foreign affairs, military affairs, and ideology still remain primarily in the Soviet domain (excepting the special case of China), a limited measure of autonomy in regard to the tempo and specific character of domestic social and economic policies is gradually developing insofar as the other Communist states are concerned.

[Events have also] revealed a striking differentiation in the formal structure of the Camp insofar as the Asian group of Communist states is involved. They are not in the formal alliance system nor in CEMA, and their contacts with the other parties appear to be less intense. Furthermore, since much of the Soviet hope for the future political and ideological unity of the Camp is based on the present drive for closer economic interdependence, an autarkic Chinese development means that in the years to come Chinese unity with the rest of the Camp will rest almost entirely on the ideological-political plane. While this is not tantamount to disunity, it does reflect a somewhat less homogeneous reality than the Communist leaders would have the world believe.

This leads to two further points. . . . In the first place, the Camp no longer seems as monolithic and as invulnerable to change as during Stalin's lifetime. Because of that, the alternative to it seems less likely to be violent upheavals. Today, in some ways the Camp is better equipped to absorb the strains which occur in any multinational organization, and particularly in one dominated by a single national group. By suppressing such tensions through terror, accompanied also by economic exploitations, Stalin created the preconditions for a revolutionary situation. This no longer appears to be the case. On the other hand, because of the greater elasticity which now absorbs the strains and prevents an explosion erupting from stored-up frustration, the danger of a gradual erosion of the Camp's ideological unity seems greater than ever before. . . . Furthermore, to the extent that the Soviet leadership finds it necessary to mobilize the support of other Communist regimes in opposition to some Chinese stands, the relationship of political power between Moscow and the other capitals becomes increasingly less asymmetrical.

Secondly, it seems fair to note that the Camp in its first [Stalinist] phase was in effect a national empire, centrally directed and run largely to the advantage of the dominant Soviet party. . . . The present development within the Camp is increasingly transforming it into an international Communist empire, dominated by various Communist elites, bound together, to be sure, by Soviet power but also by common interests and aspirations. While united in their efforts and in their vested interest in keeping their ideologically oriented empires together and their populations suppressed, they increasingly find it necessary to express their unity through various organizational devices.

The need for such organizational devices is felt to be particularly great because in the current Communist thinking "socialist" and subsequently even Communist countries will continue to exist as separate entities until a world-wide Communist society emerges. During this transitional, but probably lengthy period, unity between the ruling parties is to be cemented through continuing effort to develop ever closer political and economic ties among the countries ruled by them. To the extent that such ties do establish normative principles (if only in theory), particularly the principle of equality and independence, they will gradually consolidate the transition from a national to an international empire. By preserving the state forms but emptying them gradually of their content, the ultimate hope is to surmount the traditional forces of nationalism and to create in effect an interlocking supra-society. While many obstacles still remain and others may arise, particularly with the further development of China, the West would do well not to underestimate the importance of the organizational development of the Communist Camp.

George Modelski (a political scientist, at the Australian National University, cited earlier in this chapter) comes to somewhat similar conclusions. But he seems to differ from Brzezinski in significant if subtle ways. Instead of an "international Communist empire," Modelski speaks of a "Communist international system." He envisages not so much an eventual Communist "supra-society" in which *national* political institutions are "emptied gradually of their content," but rather the possibility of a progressively expanding Communist system that might eventually displace (though perhaps not quite completely) the present international system which he characterizes as "pragmatic," that is, nonideological. In short, Modelski conceives of the Communist Camp as a currently less-than-global political system which possesses attributes for becoming universal without losing its essentially *international* character. These attributes Modelski identifies as follows:

(1) The expansive propensity discernible in all international political systems, but especially in the contemporary Communist system
(2) The segmentation pattern of the Communist system
(3) The insulating and boundary-maintaining properties of the Communist system
(4) The system's capacity for self-maintenance
(5) The system's conflict-containing capacity

The universal aspirations of Communism [Modelski says] . . . are well known. . . ." In this respect, he contends, the Communist system is not unlike other international systems in history which have exhibited a "tendency to expand to the limits of their 'world'."

> Such a generalization does not assert that all members of the system are expansionist, or that they always pool their resources for such purposes, or that they all work toward the goal of system expansion; it ignores questions of individual motivation and merely observes that international systems expand . . .

What gives special significance to this expansive tendency, in the case of Communism,

> is the existence of the several scores of mutually supportive Communist parties in all parts of the world . . . [This fact] makes Communism's aspirations to universality a matter of practical politics and a subject of general concern.

> The *segmentation pattern* (that is, the number of units in the system, and their relative size and political potential) have an important bearing on the system's future development. The Communist system

>> now contains, in addition to the ten small states, two Great Powers of nearly equal rank—one more powerful and prestigious; the other for the time being weaker, but potentially the stronger of the two. Until 1949 the Soviet Union was the sole Great Power of Communism and its command over the world Communist movement was unchallenged and unchallengeable. For several more years, Stalin's personal ascendancy as well as China's reconstruction problems and her direct involvement in the Korean War obscured the radical transformations that were taking place within the Communist system. . . .
>> If 1953 [the year of Stalin's death] marks the beginning of the growth of an international element in the system, the years 1956-1957, when China finally demonstrated its freedom from the Soviet Union and made her influence felt in Eastern Europe on behalf of the growth of

system-wide independence, saw the emergence of a nucleus of a potential[ly universal] international system. . . .

Since 1956 the influence, but even more the mere recognition, of
China's new status as the second Great Power has served to loosen
relations in the Communist system.

Citing the development of the formal institutional structures and adjustments in Soviet strategy since 1956, described by Brzezinski (earlier in
this chapter), Modelski concludes that the present

segmentation pattern of the system and, above all, the position of China
indicate that, provided the system itself survives, this loosening-up is
unlikely to be merely a passing phenomenon.

In other words, the segmentation pattern has become favorable to the
development of a truly *international* Communist system, and no longer
towards a Moscow-governed world empire.

The third striking feature of the Communist system is its *relative
isolation* and its *boundary-maintaining* properties. . . .

The boundaries of international systems can be plotted with the help
of the same procedures by which the boundaries of other entities,
social or otherwise, are established. . . . : States sharing a "common
fate," states "similar" in social or political make-up, and states "proxi-
mate" to each other are separable by a line from others that are not.
These boundaries, in turn, can be diagnosed in terms of such indices
as the impediments to outside influences (trade, travelers, culture)
seeking to penetrate the system, and the difficulty which such influences experience in penetrating beyond it. Within the boundaries of
the system, cultural characteristics, communications, and trade diffuse
more rapidly than outside it and in their turn help to preserve the
distinctiveness of the system and hence its boundaries.

Communist leaders have exhibited great concern to insulate their system against outside influences. This concern is reflected in restrictions of
various kinds on movements of persons, goods, and ideas across the system's boundaries.

For all members of the Communist system, exchanges with other
Communist states constitute the mainstay of their foreign trade. Some
of them—Mongolia, Albania, North Korea, or North Vietnam—have
no trade, or virtually none, with the outside world; most of the others
conduct roughly three-quarters of their trade within the system. . . .

Trade figures are a good general index of isolation because they indicate not only the movement of goods but also to a large degree the
circulation of persons: of trade representatives, delegates, and negotiators, factory servicing agents, installation men and other technicians.
. . . The movement of goods also determines the large international
transport and communication networks, such as air and shipping lines,

railway, canal, and pipeline development, and cable, radio, telephone, and news systems. It could be shown that for each of these networks a discontinuity arises when system boundaries are crossed. . . .

But let us consider for the present merely the movement of persons —for instance, in the general field of travel. . . . Although detailed figures are not available, it would seem that the greatest intensity of interchanges is, once more, within the system. It may be surmised that the larger part of the 536,732 foreigners who visited the Soviet Union in 1957 came from the other countries of the Communist system, and that most of the 716,000 Soviet citizens who traveled abroad in the same year visited those countries. . . .

Consider cultural relations. Of the 15,000 foreign students in the USSR in 1958, some 14,000 came from other Communist states. . . .

Similar considerations apply to book translations. Before the war most of the books translated into East European languages were French, English, or German; today a large part are Russian, some of them translations of political tracts but others, and in growing numbers, renderings of technical and professional literature. . . .

The same trends are observable in scientific, technical, and professional activities. Although the Academy of Science of the USSR, for instance, prides itself on contacts with all countries, its most intimate relations are in fact maintained with other Communist academies. . . . The growing numbers of Soviet-trained specialists "naturally" incline toward following the Soviet technical example. Russian is becoming the lingua franca of the system—above all, in political and in technical matters; together with Chinese it is the official language of all system-wide Communist organizations, and its adoption is another factor contributing to the relative isolation of the system.

The key to all these boundaries is the political insulation of the system, which is in essence the result of the long-standing and purpose-fully self-imposed isolation of the Communist Party, and the reverse side of the political intimacy within it. In the higher echelons of the Communist system, the political figures and the specialists are in frequent and personal contact: they meet several times a year on such occasions as the Congresses of the several "fraternal" parties, at meetings of international organizations of the system, or of the United Nations, during bilateral conferences in Moscow or the other capitals, and in the course of negotiating such routine instruments as the annual trade agreements, cultural exchange treaties, and scientific and technical co-operation pacts. The density of the network of diplomatic representation is nearly maximal, too; with the exception of Mongolia, each Communist state is represented at the ambassadorial level in the eleven other capitals of the system, a thoroughness of coverage which has no counterpart in the outside world. . . .

The decisive contacts of the Communist system occur between top party leaders and through party channels. . . . The decisiveness of party contacts and party channels is the reverse of the isolation of Communist-system processes, because "outsiders" or "non-members" have, of course, no access to such channels: they cannot cross this boundary, in contrast to the situation in the Western international system, any recognized member of which, be it a Communist or a non-Communist state, is part of the regular "diplomatic circuit," the system's primary channel of contact and communication.

Relative isolation can also be diagnosed in the field of international organization. Seven of the twelve states belong to the United Nations and the others are trying to gain admittance, but with regard to the twelve specialized agencies [of the U.N.], the Soviet Union belongs to seven, Poland to nine, most other Communist U.N. members to six, and East Germany and China to none. The U.N.'s key financial and economic agencies, the International Monetary Fund and the World Bank have no Communist members.

Modelski describes in detail the intergovernmental organizations within the Communist system, ground which has already been covered in the selection by Brzezinski. Modelski comments on these institutions as follows:

A review of international organizational activity suggests that the Communist system sets up its own functionally specific agencies whenever concrete needs make themselves felt, without however displaying undue inventiveness of its own. The number and vitality of these organizations, as well as Communist participation in the U.N. and its specialized agencies, have increased since 1953-1956. But there is no evidence that intergovernmental organizations are being created for the special purpose of serving as nuclei of possibly world-wide agencies or as shadow organizations of the U.N. . . . The strategy is one of staying in the U.N., of exploiting it for Communist purposes and eventually "capturing" it, much as Communist parties have participated in national Parliaments, using them for their own purposes without ever becoming parliamentary parties, being "in them," but never "of them."

In contrast to Communist intergovernmental organizations, each one of which has a concrete job to accomplish for member states, there are the numerous world-wide non-governmental organizations of the Communist system. Among the more important of these are the World Federation of Trade Unions (another "captured" organization) and its twelve specialized "Internationals" (such as the Miners' International, etc.), the World Peace Council, and the World Federation of Democratic Youth (responsible for the World Youth Festivals). All of these bodies are "political" in inspiration, designed not for the accomplishment of intra-system tasks, as the governmental agencies are, but to supplement the activities of the Communist movement in non-Communist countries in a variety of specialized fields with the overriding purpose of bringing the widest public possible within the range of Communist Party influence. . . .

Let us remark, last of all, upon the "cultural separateness" of the Communist system. Every international system has its own distinct culture and value systems; the cultural self-consciousness of the Greeks made them regard all non-Greeks (non-members of the classical Greek international system) as barbarians—an attitude parallel to that adopted by members of the Western international system toward "heathens" and then toward the "primitive and uncivilized" races. The Communist system, too, has its culture and its own value system, a phenomenon which is usually described under the heading of ideology. . . . Communist culture is that ensemble of norms, standards, and values which is current in the Communist system, common to Communist Party members and separating them from non-members: "reactionaries," "capitalists," "imperialists," and the like. This culture is embodied in its own prolific literature, has its own distinct language and other symbols, its own history with its own heroes, villains, and martyrs, and its own special ritual behavior. Cultural separateness has so far been most evident in political and social matters and less so in the scientific and technical fields, in which universalist and achievement norms common to all industrial systems seem strong. . . .

The Communist system is akin to the semi-isolated international systems coexisting on earth in earlier ages [for example, the classical Roman and Chinese systems]. The early isolation of those systems was the result of their inability to expand beyond a certain physical range owing to the scarcity of resources and the pointlessness of doing so. In this sense, boundaries of international systems reflect limitations on expansive power. The Communist system too has boundaries, is acutely conscious of them, and notoriously anxious to solidify them by a variety of methods. Hence, it is a relatively isolated system, its "expansion" in all cases resulting in the absorption of new members into "isolation" or, depending on the point of view, into the "family fold of the states of socialism." And as in earlier times, its boundaries mark the limits of its "expansive," or "absorptive" capacity. . . .

This isolation is no more than relative. It does not mean that the Communist system has no effect on the non-Communist world or vice versa. Contacts across the boundaries go on all the time. Many of the well-known devices of Communist "isolationism"—the "Iron Curtain," the blockage of communications, especially in the late Stalin era—have been no more than a defensive posture, a mode of consolidation of the system, procedures for excluding unwanted interference. . . .

In the past two or three years [written in 1960] the mood has changed. The spirit of the Communist system is now self-confident, expansionist. Many of the restrictive features of the Stalinist mentality, the virtual banning of private outside contacts, the morbid suspicion of visitors, the inability to treat with Asian and African nationalists, have abated. Communism is in an outgoing, expansive mood, ready to embrace new recruits. Its isolation has declined, but its boundary-maintaining properties are unchanged.

[With respect to the fourth attribute—capacity for *self-maintenance* —Modelski observes that] international systems persist over time and must therefore exhibit internal structures which insure their survival and efficient operation over a prolonged period. Every such system needs structures (1) for performing the functions of leadership and for a derived system of stratification, (2) for creating and strengthening solidarity, (3) for maintaining culture, value, and communication systems, and (4) for allocating differentiated roles and maintaining a division of labor. . . .

With respect to leadership, the Communist system has yet to develop any "permanent, system-wide, intergovernmental, and functionally-diffuse" institutions. There is no Communist counterpart of the United Nations. Thus far, integrative leadership for the system as a whole has been performed "by means of informal and transient contacts within Communist Party channels."

There is, however, no doubt as to where ultimate leadership resides.

For the time being the Communist system resembles a pyramid structure, with one Great Power wielding all legitimate authority. This is an arrangement whose stability may be questioned and the conditions under which such authority may in the future come to be shared are among the key problems of the system. Be it noted that the basis of the Soviet claim to authority is fundamentally achievement-oriented. The claim is said to rest upon priority in founding a socialist state, upon power and attainments in the military, industrial, and technological fields, and upon a front-rank position in advancing toward communism. . . .

Only the first of these claims serves as a permanent title to authority. . . .

The Chinese regime has already challenged the Soviet claim to be the front-runner towards communism. And China may in the not too distant future also challenge Soviet military, industrial, and technical primacy. This may result in a "sharing of authority by two or more Communist states (a "concert"), or the transfer of authority to China if and when it becomes the "mightiest socialist power."

The rights and duties of Communist-system leadership have not been explicitly defined. The expectation seems to be, however, that the Soviet Union provides a number of services essential to the functioning of the system: military protection against "imperialist enemies," economic and other aid for the less-developed members and for non-governing parties, path-breaking and experimentation in political and economic development, and the spearheading of the external expansion of the system. In exchange she receives deference from the other members and authority to initiate certain policies and to make ideological pronouncements. Her status is not that of an alliance leader, organizing followers in a concrete task against a concrete enemy; it resembles more that of a head of a family or of a tribe, interested in and responsible, in a sense, for all family or tribal affairs but not necessarily concretely involved in any of them.

The eminence of the leaders reduces the operating freedom of the small powers. Although the price for the services of leadership is deference and "obedience," no country, big or small, willingly accepts a price that is outrageous, for it is of the essence of an international system that its hierarchical elements should be compensated by some attention to the notions and practices of equality.

All international systems display both hierarchical and equalitarian features, but the mix varies from one system to another. Within the Communist system there is a definite hierarchy; it is exemplified, for instance, in the order in which representatives of national parties address the CPSU Congress, or the order in which "fraternal delegates" are welcomed by the key speaker on such occasions. The ranking order is not merely ceremonial but . . . provides a precise indication of the influence—or impotence—of members of the system.

Modelski concludes the discussion of this point by noting that the formerly notorious inequality within the system is still in evidence but has "decreased recently nevertheless."

With respect to devices for *maintaining solidarity*, Modelski gives first place to the "Communist Party and its international ramifications."

Another device is the "appeal of unity against a common enemy (the 'capitalist imperialists,' or sometimes *all non-Communists*) and the positive appeal of unity for the 'construction of communism.' It needs little perception to observe that the closer the system comes to its goals of universality, the lesser will be its solidarity; the larger the system, the less imposing the common enemy, the nearer 'the stage of communism,' and the greater the strains within. . . ."

Modelski warns, however, against optimistic expectations of Soviet-Chinese tensions disrupting the system.

Communist leaders are still acutely conscious that for decades they have struggled in isolation against seemingly overwhelming odds. The Soviet Union's own progress and, even more, the accession to the Communist system of China, with its huge population and rapid strides in economic growth, have now brought within striking distance the dream of a Communist world, a world in which at first the preponderance and then the monopoly of power would be held by Communists. When Khrushchev says that in a few years' time one-half of the world's industrial output will be produced in the Communist system, it is this future world which he sees as coming within his grasp through a shift in the world balance of power. Yet it is just as plain that without China—or, even less, in the face of opposition from China—such a state of affairs would be completely unattainable, no matter how powerful the Soviet union herself might become. What more compelling image could there be for Communist leaders, what more powerful incentive to unity and solidarity, than this revolutionary prospect of a Communist world, now at last within reach? . . .

Modelski also rejects the frequently expressed view that time will soon erode seriously the expansionist dynamic of the Communist system.

Today many and conflicting pressures operate within an immensely more powerful system. In the past few years, China has come to represent the radical wing of the movement and the pressure group for tension. But there are other dissatisfied regimes within the system, the East German, the North Korean, the North Vietnamese, even the Albanian, each insecure and pressing for strong action. Within the Soviet Union, too, those in charge of ideological purity are capable of generating great pressure. Nor can we ignore as influences for radicalism the scores of non-governing parties in the world, some of them carrying increasing weight in intra-system assignments. A coalition of these forces will not necessarily be dominant all the time, but its importance in lending to the system an inherent dynamism of its own, beyond the control of one man, must not be overlooked. Historical examples of ideological erosion are, moreover, merely indications of a long-term trend. It took Islam, for instance, over a century to lose its primary impulse for expansion. . . . For outsiders, it is little short of suicidal to underrate the power of the bonds of solidarity which as of this day maintain the world Communist system.

That communism disposes of its own culture and value system has already been indicated; that it disposes of structures maintaining it in a manner not incompatible with the functioning of an international system may also be argued. Once again the party is the principal structure performing this function. It serves as the chief international communications channel, the formulator, critic, and bearer of Communist values . . . and the creator of distinctive culture patterns. . . . The strength of this structure resides in the rapidity and efficiency with which messages from the centers diffuse within the system. . . .

In conclusion [with respect to the self-maintenance property of the system], let us note the growth of mechanisms stimulating division of labor . . . [Economic] specialization is . . . helping to establish within the Communist system the essentials of a "world market," the "parallel socialist world market" first discovered by Stalin in 1952. Side by side with the Western world market and its banking, insurance, commodity trade, and transport arrangements centered in London and New York, it is evolving its own independent trade mechanisms. . . .

Modelski regards the fifth attribute of international systems—capacity for *containing conflict*—as second only to the segmentation pattern in importance.

The most crucial single fact about international systems to date has been their propensity to war; they have been composed of members each having control over the means of violence, conflict between whom has always involved the possibility or the actuality of the use of force. . . . Like members of all other international systems, the states belonging to the Communist system retain individual control over the means of international violence . . .

The systemic implications of this fact are not to be discovered by analyzing the relations between the Soviet Union and the East-European satellites.

Equally absurd would be an attempt to gauge the nature of Western international relations from the conditions prevailing between the United States and Liberia. . . . The character of the Communist system . . . will . . . be shaped . . . first and foremost by Sino-Soviet relations. . . . [These are the] key to the whole system and determine the nature of all other relationships within it.

[It seems] likely, moreover, that in the near future China will begin to manufacture her own nuclear weapons, and there is also good reason to believe that she is attaching great importance to missiles, radar, and other essential components of modern weapons systems. . . . If and when China demonstrates a nuclear weapons capability, a situation of nuclear deterrence will prevail between China and the Soviet Union. Although presumably Chinese missiles will not at first be aimed at Soviet targets, the mere possibility of their being so will play a role in Communist-system relations. . . .

With respect to the military relations between the two major units, U.S.S.R. and China, and the lesser members of the system, Modelski concludes:

Direct Soviet influence over the armed forces varies from country to country; it may be dominant in Mongolia or East Germany, strong in Czechoslovakia, moderate in Poland, and non-existent in North Vietnam. Chinese control, on the other hand, may at times have been dominant in North Korea, may be strong in North Vietnam, and nonexistent in Albania. In principle, however, control of the means of violence remains in national hands, and might in some circumstances be used against the Soviet Union or the other Communist states. . . .

Modelski examines a large number of conflict situations that have occurred or may occur within the Communist system, or between members of the system and outside states. On the whole, the evidence to date convinces him that the Communist system is at least as capable of preventing such conflicts from getting out of control or endangering the system's survival as is the contemporary, universal, nonideological system. Since his discussion of this issue is long and detailed, we summarize his conclusions as follows:

Certain potential conflicts within the system relate to historic *national* claims and tensions: for example, the boundary between Poland and East Germany, the status of the Sudeten Germans in Czechoslovakia, the traditional Polish-Russian antagonism, the rights of Hungarian minorities in Rumania and Czechoslovakia, the Soviet, Chinese, and Mongolian boundaries, and others. Another type of intrasystem conflict relates to the right of interference, especially by one of the major states, in the domestic affairs and policies of other Communist countries. Both types of conflicts occur in all international political systems; but the second type is of special importance in the Communist system because of the high value placed on doctrinal conformity and the large role which government plays in all sectors of national life.

Given the abundance of potential and actual causes of dispute, it is only reasonable to expect that conflicts should at various periods coalesce into distinct and general alignment patterns; and that, as in all international systems, these alignment patterns should be shifting ones, depending on the "relationship of major tension" of the moment. The "state of the system" can, at each such stage, be represented by a simple diagram; [Figure 20.A] presents in this form four simplified, but representative alignment patterns of the Communist system.

Diagrams of the same kind can be drawn to depict the "state" of any other international system and the alignment patterns within it. For larger systems they would be more complicated but no different in principle.

Modelski cites two reasons for failure to perceive these ordinary "diplomatic alignments" within the Communist system:

The first has been the prevailing picture of the Communist system as a bloc (hence one which cannot tolerate any kind of "split") and, by implication, the treatment of each intrasystem dispute as an "exceptional," "marginal," or "special" case, bringing the system to the verge of fatal crisis—since a "split" *bloc* falls apart into two.

The second [reason] concerns Communist secretiveness and the difficulty of interpreting Communist messages. This, however, no longer presents insuperable problems. Today the outline of an alignment pattern in the Communist system can be perceived with reasonable clarity at the time it is taking place. The system, being no longer a monolith (as it probably was under Stalin), is no longer a sphinx either; since its "internationalization," it now holds a number of parties each one of which may on occasion wish to improve its position by a judicious "leak." Other, more "objective" information may be secured from a perusal of Communist information output by "content analysis" . . . or by following the activities of the top leadership, the visits they make or the receptions they attend. Nor must the more important non-governing parties be ignored in these analyses, for in the past few years they have begun to play a part in the "diplomatic" processes of the Communist system. . . .

[Modelski emphasizes the success of the Communist system to date in] insulat[ing] its intra-system conflicts from the outside world. . . . Com-

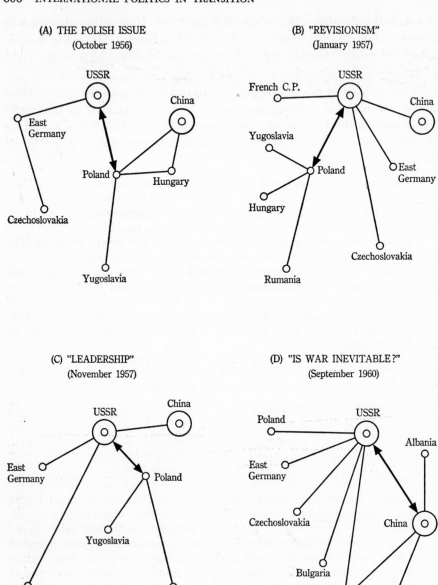

FIG. 20.A.   COMMUNIST SYSTEM ALIGNMENT PATTERNS

munist contestants do not invite support extraneous to the system and do not receive it; "external" intervention is strongly discouraged. This is the most important sense in which conflicts are "contained" within the system—important because failure to "contain" conflict rather than failure to "abolish" conflict could become the most profound cause of change and, ultimately, transformation of the system. . . .

The operation of "conflict-containment" mechanisms in the Communist system may be seen most clearly in relation to the U.N. Among the scores of disputes which the organization has had to deal with in the past fifteen years, not once has an intra-system conflict been brought before it. Whenever Communist-system matters are introduced on outside initiative—for instance, Tibet—discussion of them is always violently resisted on grounds of "interference into domestic affairs." The one exception to the rule is singularly enlightening: Imre Nagy's request for U.N. intervention in the Hungarian crisis of 1956. His execution twenty-one months later tends to suggest that the invocation of outside help may be an extremely risky step for a Communist leader to take. From the moment of Kadar's installation, the Communist Powers have violently denounced attempts to keep the Hungarian question in the world forum.

The U.N.'s record of disengagement from intra-Communist system disputes is in no way exceptional. I know of no instance of a Communist state inviting the support of a non-Communist state against another Communist state or party. When Yugoslavia was condemned by the Cominform in 1948 and then expelled from it (hence no longer bound by rules of Communist solidarity), Tito hesitated a long time before accepting American aid—and incurring the even more vicious, Moscow-led attacks against him. . . . The only partial and successful exception to this rule appears to be acceptance of American economic aid by Gomulka-led Poland immediately after the changeover in October 1956 . . . [That incident] remains important as a possible precedent for an unpunished breach in Communist solidarity. . . .

Coming finally to the crucial issue of Sino-Soviet tensions and possible conflicts, Modelski asks:

Can we not envisage a state of affairs in which the conflict between China and the Soviet Union had become so critical that one of the sides (presumably the weaker of the two), threatened perhaps by imminent invasion or in some other vital manner, would call for outside aid?

This is the model of the "split" which observers have in mind when discussing the likelihood of a break in Sino-Soviet relations. Without ruling it out altogether or in the long run, [Modelski's] own inclination would be not to assign too great a probability to it, primarily because it represents a situation whose vital components are all under the control of the leaders of the two great Communist Powers. As pointed out, there are substantial reasons for believing that the immediate incentives for unity are so great that they would tend to discourage headlong Sino-Soviet disputes, and if those are avoided, the dangers of conflicts among the smaller Communist Powers are minimal. . . .

Modelski finally considers a type of conflict-situation

in which all of the vital components no longer are under the control of the Communist leaders: the situation in which one of the Communist Powers is engaged in a sharp conflict with the outside world. As previously observed, Communist expansion cannot be viewed as a "bloc policy," the monolithic action of one bloc actor, but as a system property, carried out first by one Communist Power and then by another. Hence, whenever the Communist system is pressing upon the outside world, as likely as not one of the two Great Powers is more directly involved than the other. It would follow from the rules of Communist solidarity that the Power less directly involved must at least abstain from supporting the enemy of the other Communist Power, and is also expected to render positive aid and support. That is why the conditions under which one Communist Great Power might be induced to give aid to the opponent of a "fraternal country" become of such interest. . . .

Consider the frontier dispute between India and Communist China in 1959-1960. Right from the start, and despite considerable political and emotional commitment on the part of China, the USSR has adopted an attitude of conspicuous neutrality, violating the expectation that sympathy, if not direct aid, would be accorded to the Communist side in the dispute. . . .

The conditions which made it possible for the Soviet Union thus to ignore the demands of solidarity stem from ambiguities in the definition of membership in the Communist system. As currently conceived, that system has not only "full" and "associate" members but also what I have called "assistant" members, as listed in the 1957 Moscow Declaration. In effect these are the Asian, African, and Latin American [underdeveloped] countries. . . . The Declaration moreover enjoins "socialist states" to aid such countries "in their struggle for peace and against aggression," and in their advance along the path of national progress. In this tenuous sense, Soviet aid to India can be regarded as "intra-system" aid, rendered by a "socialist state" to a country now on the "road to socialism." But whether it is so in fact will depend just as much upon the skill of the Indian, Indonesian, and other governments as it does upon Soviet intentions.

The position has its clear dangers: an underdeveloped country soliciting Soviet aid implicitly acknowledges the Soviet claim to a share in world leadership and raises Soviet status. For certain purposes, such a country becomes part of the system, and, as usual, the price of protection is deference and there is at least the possibility that deference may lead to ultimate full membership. Collaboration with the Soviet Union strengthens the national Communist parties, increases their claim to co-rule, and hence hastens conditions for full membership in the Communist system.

But the situation also presents great opportunities: the country hard-pressed by one Communist Great Power may find that the real leverage against it is available in the capital of the other Power. Moreover, much of this contest amounts to a battle of wits: the nationalists, if they are careful, are just as likely to outsmart their local and the foreign Communists as to be outsmarted by them. Finally, it confuses members of the Communist system, including non-governing Communist parties, erodes the solidarity of the system, and breaks down the rules about "conflict-containment."

If the Communist system ever displaces the present nonideological international system,

it will do so after a series of encounters in which the line of division between the Communist system and the non-members has become blurred to the point where significant differences no longer are recognizable. . . .

In developing his thesis, Modelski contends only that the "contemporary Communist system contains, in a primitive form, all the necessary features" which might enable it progressively to displace and eventually to transform the present universal system. He does *not* assert that this is bound to occur or even that it is very likely to occur. Nor does he deny that the Communist states are simultaneously members of the existing nonideological international system. What he has done is to marshal evidence to show that inside the existing universal system there exists the "core" that could expand under certain conditions to become itself a new universal system. In short, this is one of the possibilities latent in the fluid, transitory phase through which the Society of Nations is passing in the 1960's.

Any evaluation of Modelski's thesis and supporting evidence and arguments must take account of two categories of conditions and events: those inside the Communist system, and those outside.

One of the imponderables—one that might decisively affect the future —is manifestly the outcome of a general war, should one occur. As noted in Chapter 8, it is difficult to refute the hypothesis that such a war, if it did not exterminate the human race altogether, would wreck the more highly industrialized countries, including both Russia and the United States. Assuming this to be so, one possible result of such a war might be to turn the future management of human affairs over to the less modernized peoples, with the Chinese Communists the most likely candidates to reorganize the shattered remnants of human society.

Another event that might decisively affect the future pattern of international politics would be a long leap ahead by *one* side or an accumulating advantage by one side in military or even in industrial technology. This too is an imponderable. Both the Communist Camp and the Western World, it is clear, contain the basic physical resources necessary for accelerating technological development. The scientific and engineering talent and skills available to the Communist Camp appear to be at least the equal of the West's over the long pull.

If one rules out both of the above imponderables, the issue shifts to other social levels. One of these is likewise very difficult to predict. That is whether the Communist leadership of China will be able to bring Chinese population increase under control sufficiently and in time so as not to frustrate the continued rapid modernization of China's huge population. Let us assume that this is achieved.

We come next to what Modelski calls

the "contradictions" between the monolithic organization of each Communist party, with its totalitarian control over all centers of political life, and the requirements of an international system for independence, diversity, and flexible organization.

Domestically, it seems, a monolithic party that does not tolerate any autonomous power center inside itself may, under certain conditions, work. Its operation strains the political system, but the Soviet experience demonstrates that such a party not only can keep itself in power but can propel the country through various stages of development.

Internationally, monolithic methods of politics are out of place. The functional requirements of an international system call for the toleration of a number of autonomous political systems which may be more or less similar but which inevitably maintain separateness. . . . The leadership of an international system is neither all-powerful nor total; it secures co-ordination and other forms of common action by methods and techniques profoundly alien to the domestic experience of Communist regimes.

Will the new Communist leaders succeed in the international context or will they attempt total control and regimentation, and, in the attempt, destroy the system? We have had occasion to note that in the past they have found it difficult to operate by the methods and in the style of traditional international relations in contexts where a number of autonomous political systems had to be treated on an equal footing. The creativity and flexibility of their domestic party tactics contrast sharply with the conservatism and lack of inventiveness of Communist international behavior and with its disregard for the governmental, institutionalized, and legal aspects of interstate relations. The difficulty which one has in imagining a U.N. functioning in a Communist world illustrates precisely this point, yet something like a U.N. may be indispensable to the operation of every industrial international system. . . .

As stated above, what the Communists can themselves do is only half of the picture. The other half is what happens outside the Communist Realm: both within the Anti-Communist Coalition and in the Realm of the Uncommitted Nations. To these issues we now turn.

CHAPTER TWENTY-ONE

The Anti-Communist Coalition

ARRAYED AGAINST THE Communist Camp is a coalition of forty-odd national communities, associated for the avowed purpose of common defense. Upon a map (see Figure 21.A), this Anti-Communist Coalition appears as several widely separated groupings of countries: in North and South America, in Europe, in the Middle East, in Southeast Asia, and in the Western Pacific.

The linkages between the regional groupings, both in an economic and in a military-logistical sense, are the principal sea and air ways of the globe. Hence the Anti-Communist Coalition has been called, in a geopolitical sense, the Oceanic Realm. Another common designation is the Western World, a label that is geographically inaccurate, but expresses the leadership of the North Atlantic nations in general, and of the United States in particular. Still another popular designation is the Free World, a label which, in this context (as stated previously) does NOT mean nations governed by liberal democratic principles and institutions, but simply free from Communist rule or domination. Since this concept also embraces most of the uncommitted nations (to be dealt with in the next chapter), Free World is not really synonymous with the Anti-Communist Realm. For these reasons, we prefer to speak of the nations associated for common defense against the Communist Camp as the Anti-Communist Coalition, since that is precisely what it is, and to conceive of the Anti-Communist Coalition as another less-than-universal international system. It is organized very differently from the Communist Camp, but it is none the less a subsystem of the global international political system, as these terms were defined in Chapter 2.

The countries at present included in the Anti-Communist Coalition cover about 30 percent of the earth's surface, an area slightly larger than the Communist Realm. They contain about 34 percent of the earth's popula-

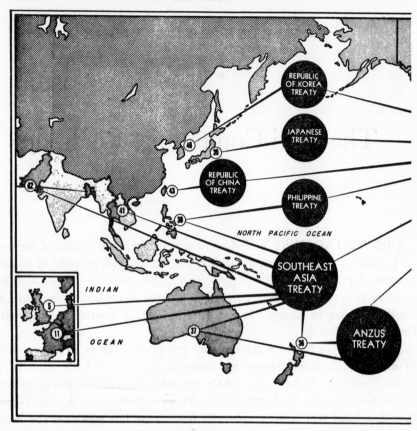

NORTH ATLANTIC TREATY (15 NATIONS)

A treaty signed April 4, 1949, by which "the parties agree that an armed attack against one or more of them in Europe or North America shall be considered an attack against them all; and . . . each of them . . . will assist the . . . attacked by taking forthwith, individually and in concert with the other Parties, such action as it deems necessary including the use of armed force . . ."

1 UNITED STATES	9 LUXEMBOURG
2 CANADA	10 PORTUGAL
3 ICELAND	11 FRANCE
4 NORWAY	12 ITALY
5 UNITED KINGDOM	13 GREECE
6 NETHERLANDS	14 TURKEY
7 DENMARK	15 FEDERAL REPUBLIC
8 BELGIUM	OF GERMANY

RIO TREATY (21 NATIONS)

A treaty signed September 2, 1947, which provides that an armed attack against any American State "shall be considered as an attack against all the American States and . . . each one . . . undertakes to assist in meeting the attack . . ."

1 UNITED STATES	22 EL SALVADOR	29 PERU
16 MEXICO	23 NICARAGUA	30 BRAZIL
17 CUBA	24 COSTA RICA	31 BOLIVIA
18 HAITI	25 PANAMA	32 PARAGUAY
19 DOMINICAN	26 COLOMBIA	33 CHILE
REPUBLIC	27 VENEZUELA	34 ARGENTINA
20 HONDURAS	28 ECUADOR	35 URUGUAY
21 GUATEMALA		

ANZUS (Australia–New Zealand–United States) TREATY (3 NATIONS)

A treaty signed September 1, 1951, whereby each of the parties "recognizes that an armed attack in the Pacific Area on any of the Parties would be dangerous to its own peace and safety and declares that it would act to meet the common danger in accordance with its constitutional processes."

1 UNITED STATES
36 NEW ZEALAND
37 AUSTRALIA

tion, as against an estimated 36 percent in the Communist Realm. The Anti-Communist Coalition includes most of the highly industrialized countries as well as some that are in the early stages of economic modernization. The Anti-Communist Realm presents extremes of affluence and poverty to a far greater degree than does the Communist Realm.

The United States is the core or nucleus of the Anti-Communist Coalition. The system has been predominately inspired, supported, directed, and

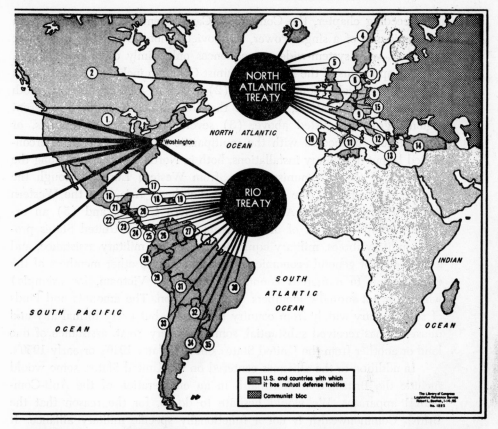

NORTH
ATLANTIC
TREATY

NORTH ATLANTIC
OCEAN

Washington

RIO
TREATY

SOUTH PACIFIC
OCEAN

SOUTH
ATLANTIC
OCEAN

INDIAN

OCEAN

■ U.S. and countries with which
   it has mutual defense treaties

▨ Communist bloc

PHILIPPINE TREATY (BILATERAL)

A treaty signed August 30, 1951, by which the parties recognize "that an armed attack in the Pacific Area on either of the Parties would be dangerous to its own peace and safety" and each party agrees that it will act "to meet the common dangers in accordance with its constitutional processes."

1 UNITED STATES
38 PHILIPPINES

JAPANESE TREATY (BILATERAL)

A treaty signed September 8, 1951, whereby Japan on a provisional basis requests, and the United States agrees, to "maintain certain of its armed forces in and about Japan . . . so as to deter armed attack upon Japan."

1 UNITED STATES
39 JAPAN

REPUBLIC OF KOREA (South Korea) TREATY (BILATERAL)

A treaty signed October 1, 1953, whereby each party "recognizes that an armed attack in the Pacific area on either of the Parties . . . would be dangerous to its own peace and safety" and that each Party "would act to meet the common danger in accordance with its constitutional processes."

1 UNITED STATES.
40 REPUBLIC OF KOREA

SOUTHEAST ASIA TREATY (8 NATIONS)

A treaty signed September 8, 1954, whereby each Party "recognizes that aggression by means of armed attack in the treaty area against any of the Parties . . . would endanger its own peace and safety" and each will "in that event act to meet the common danger in accordance with its constitutional processes."

1 UNITED STATES
5 UNITED KINGDOM
11 FRANCE
36 NEW ZEALAND
37 AUSTRALIA
38 PHILIPPINES
41 THAILAND
42 PAKISTAN

REPUBLIC OF CHINA (Formosa) TREATY (BILATERAL)

A treaty signed December 2, 1954, whereby each of the parties "recognizes that an armed attack in the West Pacific Area directed against the territories of either · of the Parties would be dangerous to its own peace and safety," and that each "would act to meet the common danger in accordance with its constitutional processes." The territory of the Republic of China is defined as "Taiwan (Formosa) and the Pescadores."

1 UNITED STATES
43 REPUBLIC OF CHINA
(FORMOSA)

Fig. 21.A.   UNITED STATES COLLECTIVE DEFENSE ARRANGEMENTS

dominated by the United States. If United States capabilities should falter, or if United States strategy should show signs of reverting to its historic isolationist pattern, the Anti-Communist Coalition would collapse like a house of cards.

This extreme dependence upon the United States contrasts with the apparent trend of events within the Communist Realm. As emphasized in the preceding chapter, the Communist Camp seems to be evolving from the dominance of a single Power, the Soviet Union, towards a Sino-Soviet bipolarity, with system-wide consequences only dimly discernible as yet.

The apparatus of the Anti-Communist Coalition includes (1) numerous United States declarations of policy, (2) a web of military alliances, both multipartite and bilateral, between the United States and the different regional groupings listed above, (3) several permanent secretariats, or headquarters, connected with the multipartite alliances, (4) an interconnected layout of military installations, both in North America and along the perimeter of the Communist Realm, from Western Europe through the Mediterranean region, the Middle East, Southeast Asia, and the Western Pacific to Japan, Korea, Alaska, and Northern Canada, and (5) an extremely complicated set of arrangements whereby the United States provides military forces, military equipment, technical military assistance, and a good deal of general economic support not only to other members of the coalition but to numerous countries (Spain and Vietnam, for example) which are not formally members of the coalition. The amounts and kinds of support vary widely from country to country, but every formal ally and quasi-ally has received substantial, sometimes very great, assistance of one kind or another from the United States since the later 1940's or early 1950's.

In addition to the alliances centered on the United States, some would include the British Commonwealth in an enumeration of the Anti-Communist apparatus. We would hesitate to do so, for the reason that the British Commonwealth is not a functionally specific military alliance. It does not exist for the purpose of defense against any specific set of postulated enemies. Moreover, it includes numerous states—India, Ghana, Nigeria, and others, with additional ones in prospect—which have explicitly rejected alignment with either side in the Cold War. The Commonwealth association may be a valuable channel of communication to some of the most influential regimes within the Uncommitted Realm, but it seems scarcely likely that the Commonwealth, as now constituted, will play any significant role in the East-West struggle.

Since the end of World War II, the United States government has periodically issued statements reiterating an intention to resist both military attacks and paramilitary or nonmilitary operations designed to bring additional countries under Communist rule or under Soviet or (more recently) Chinese domination. The first of these general policy statements was the Truman Doctrine. In 1947, with reference to Russian-supported activities which were believed to be designed to convert Greece into a Soviet satellite, President Truman informed Congress that

> totalitarian regimes imposed on free peoples, by direct or indirect
> aggression, undermine the foundations of international peace and

hence the security of the United States. . . . The United Nations and its related organizations are not in a position to extend help of the kind required. . . . I believe that it must be the policy of the United States to support free peoples who are resisting attempted subjugation by armed minorities or by outside pressures.

Since then, American Presidents and their Secretaries of State have followed up with numerous other declarations of policy. Most of these have referred to specific acts of aggression or situations in which aggression was believed to be imminent. All together these declarations can be summed up in the following propositions: (1) that the Soviet Union and its allies are engaged in a concerted effort to extend the area of Communist rule; (2) that Communist governments should be deterred from launching military attacks on non-Communist countries; (3) that, if such attacks occur, they should be resisted; (4) that indirect aggression (by which is meant Communist infiltration and take-over by conspiracy, subversion, or guerrilla warfare inside a non-Communist country) or any other actions that extend the area of Communist rule or domination constitute a threat to the security of all non-Communist peoples and should be resisted; and (5) that, in view of the inability of the United Nations to perform these functions, the United States intends to commit its own resources and to enter into such regional alliances as may be needed to achieve the above objectives.

The United States government began to implement this platform in the late 1940's. Within ten years the pattern of alliances was virtually complete. Figure 21.A. (pp. 612-3) gives some essential facts about these alliances: the signatories, dates of signing, basic terms, and the geographical pattern of the system as a whole.

The alliances have been buttressed by a huge American military deployment at home and overseas, by substantial but much smaller forces contributed by the other allied governments, and by large-scale military, economic, and technical assistance provided by the United States, and in a few instances and to a much smaller extent by the principal European members of the Coalition.

The kinds and quantities of this defense assistance exceed anything previously attempted. The United States has provided huge quantities of military equipment and funds with which to buy more. American military missions, sometimes comprising hundreds of persons, have been sent to many allied countries. Thousands of foreign officers have received advanced training in American military institutions. In addition, as noted above, the United States has supplied large funds for general economic development and to meet special emergencies in allied countries. The cash value runs to many billion dollars per year. Table 21.1 indicates the magnitude of this aid. But no set of statistics can possibly do justice to the multitude of ways in which, directly and indirectly, the United States government has labored to strengthen the Anti-Communist Coalition.

These commitments and outlays are all contrary to the historic American tradition of avoiding permanent alliances. That tradition, moreover, is far from dead. It has shown its head year after year in Congress, in attempts to pare down the annual "mutual security" appropriations. Only a widely shared and deeply felt sense of peril on the part of high executive

TABLE 21.1　UNITED STATES AID TO MEMBERS OF
ANTI-COMMUNIST COALITION
July 1, 1945–June 30, 1960 [a]
(thousands of dollars or equivalent)

NORTH ATLANTIC TREATY NATIONS		RIO TREATY NATIONS	
Canada	163,285	Mexico	410,181
Iceland	26,026	Cuba (pre-'60)	48,157
Norway	140,608	Haiti	26,017
United Kingdom	5,034,554	Dominican Rep.	
Netherlands	439,034	Honduras	6,737
Denmark	56,726	Guatemala	3,296
Belgium	242,182	El Salvador	642
Luxemburg	3,000	Nicaragua	3,267
Portugal	57,046	Costa Rica	14,945
France	2,502,855	Panama	8,059
Italy	547,916	Colombia	220,321
Greece	190,127	Venezuela	23,806
Turkey	209,256	Ecuador	43,090
Fed. Rep. of Germany	1,355,711	Peru	201,668
		Brazil	1,019,532
	10,968,326	Bolivia	44,918
ANZUS TREATY NATIONS		Paraguay	17,675
New Zealand	17,510	Chile	250,173
Australia	14,188	Argentina	288,631
PHILIPPINE TREATY		Uruguay	15,711
Philippines	196,162		
JAPANESE TREATY			2,646,826
Japan	967,415	SOUTHEAST ASIA TREATY NATIONS	
REPUBLIC OF KOREA TREATY		(United Kingdom,	
Rep. of Korea	27,562	France,	
REPUBLIC OF CHINA (FORMOSA)		Australia,	
TREATY		New Zealand,	
Rep. of China	305,173	Philippines,	
		see above)	
		Thailand	37,665
		Pakistan	209,773
	Total to members of the Anti-Communist Coalition		15,390,600
	Grand total of foreign aid		18,653,651

[a] Statistics from *Foreign Grants and Credits by the United States Government*, prepared by the Balance of Payments Division, U. S. Department of Commerce. June 1960 Quarter, No. 63. Table 6.

officials and a fluctuating Congressional majority, sharpened repeatedly by fresh Communist threats and thrusts, has kept the American military budget in the 30-50 billion-dollar bracket and maintained the continuing outflow of aid on a massive scale to our allies overseas. In short, as already emphasized, the Anti-Communist Coalition would not exist without leadership and support from the United States, and these would not have been forthcoming but for the stimulus of recurrent Communist threats, pressures, and aggressions.

The security motif runs through all American discussion of alliances, military and economic aid to allies, and other coalition business. The coalition exists because enough Americans have become convinced that the United States could not continue to survive in an international system dominated by Communist power and principles; that security for the United States depends on keeping the Free World free—free, that is, from Communist rule or dictation. If, by some miracle, the Communist Camp should disband and the Communist threats subside, the whole United States-centered system of alliances would dissolve in short order.

At the outset, the American concept of the coalition was not only defensive; it was also predominantly military. The task as originally envisaged in Washington was to build a position of such imposing strength as would deter future limited thrusts like the Berlin Blockade (1948-1949) and the Korean War (1950-1953) and also reduce the danger of any full-scale assault in Europe or elsewhere. From such a position of superior strength, it was reasoned, the United States and its principal allies should be able to negotiate in due course a durable "settlement" with the Soviet Union.

Events have not worked out as anticipated. The position of superior military strength has not been achieved. On the contrary, in strictly military terms, the anti-Communist position has certainly not improved; it may have seriously deteriorated as a result, at least in part, of economy-minded budgeting in Washington and in various allied capitals since the Korean truce of 1953. Buttressed by an improving economic and military position, the Communist Camp has stepped up the tempo of the Cold War. In the name of "peaceful co-existence," the Communist leaders have waged verbal warfare in the press and over the air waves. They have continued to harass the border countries of Asia. They have annually raised their economic bidding for the favor of the underdeveloped countries. These and other events have gradually forced a searching re-examination of the priorities given to military and nonmilitary operations in the strategy of the United States and its allies.

Partly, possibly mainly, because of the defensive state of mind widely prevailing within the United States, the Anti-Communist Coalition has lacked the dynamism which characterizes the Communist Camp. One explanation of that dynamism is the fanatic zeal which Communist ideology seems to inspire in so many of its converts and leaders. Communist statesmen are against what they call "capitalist warmongering"; and they show great concern for the defense of their countries. But they are also _for_ as well as _against_ something. They preach incessantly a vision of a new utopia, and confidently predict the triumph of "socialism" and the demise of bourgeois capitalist society.

Communism has often been characterized as a political religion. Marx and Lenin may be false gods by Western standards. But their disciples often display a dedication not unlike that which inspired the early Christian martyrs, and in more recent times the thousands of American and European missionaries who braved all sorts of physical hardships, illnesses, and even premature death to carry the Christian gospel to the heathen.

Americans appear rather generally to find it difficult to appreciate the psychological advantage which the Communist Camp derives from this religiouslike dynamism radiated by the disciplined and indoctrinated members of the Communist parties. For many Americans, perhaps for most, hostility to the Communist creed provides all the motivation needed. Indeed, the depth of this American anti-Communist feeling often baffles foreigners.

> It is always difficult in England [a British journalist writes] to imagine the depth and intensity of anti-Communist feeling in the United States. . . . Except in a lunatic fringe this anti-Communism cannot be called hysteria; it is a dogma deeply held and sincerely believed. Co-existence with such an absolute evil is hardly imaginable. To most Americans the British nuclear disarmers' slogan, "Better Red than Dead" is not [merely] a rather silly over-simplification but blasphemy.*

Another British observer, an economist on the staff of Cambridge University, commented after a visit to the United States:

> I was much struck by the extreme negativism of orthodox opinion in America. Orthodox Americans, of course, are against imperialism, against poverty, and against oppression. But they seem also to be against all means to deal with them that involve anything that can be called communism. They never say what it is that they are in favor of.†

This negativism—if one could so describe the overwhelming American hostility to Communism—coincided in the early 1960's with another, pos-

---

* J. D. Pringle, "Behind the Cuban Fiasco," in *The Observer*, May 21, 1961. Copyright 1961 by The Observer, Ltd., London; reproduced by permission.

† In "From the United States to Cuba," by Joan Robinson, in *The Listener*, Aug. 24, 1961. Copyright 1961 by the British Broadcasting Corporation, London; reproduced by permission of the publisher and author.

sibly more destructive kind of American negativism. This was a state of acute and apparently mounting frustration evoked by the course of world events, more specifically by the seeming shrinkage of American ability to manipulate world events. This frustration was manifest in various ways. It was reflected in the dangerously growing frequency of pessimistic assertions that nuclear war was inevitable and probably just around the corner. It was manifest in a still more defeatist demand that the United States government quit trying to provide leadership for the Free World and concentrate on building a Fortress America, all complete with protective tariffs and new-style cyclone cellars. This neo-isolationist mood was characterized by Chester Bowles (prominent American businessman and politician) as follows:

> Instead of strengthening our alliances, [these new isolationists] propose that we abandon our commitment to any nation which is reluctant to accept in full our interpretation of world affairs.
>
> Instead of strengthening the United Nations, they propose that we withdraw, unless its members agree to become a subservient arm of American foreign policy.
>
> Instead of seeking adjustments within our own economy which will help expand international trade, they would have us raise our tariffs to shut out those foreign goods which compete with American products; no matter how costly and inefficient our domestic production may be.
>
> Instead of working positively through the Federal Government to strengthen our national defense, to improve our schools and our highways, to help create greater opportunities for all of our people, they would have us slash our Federal budget to the bone.
>
> Instead of seeking through a sensitive balance of necessary firmness and patient negotiation to reduce the "cold war" tensions and to find some honorable basis of avoiding war, they would have us break relations with every nation that opposes us.
>
> Instead of applying our surplus food and a tiny fraction of our great wealth to help the underdeveloped non-Communist nations secure the same freedom of choice which allowed us to build our own great country, they would have us cut off foreign assistance.
>
> Such actions, Mr. Bowles said, run contrary to the lessons of American history and would constitute "total abdication of our responsibility as a world power." *

The dichotomy between a narrow isolationism and a broad concept of the United States leading the way towards a better world order based upon human freedom, dignity, and law, runs through much of the public discussion of American foreign policy in recent years.

The narrow view frequently reflects not merely a yearning to unload onerous foreign burdens and go it alone but also a more or less con-

* From *The New York Times*, November 6, 1961. Copyright 1961 by the New York Times Company.

temptuous attitude towards international law and moral principles and towards the opinions of foreign peoples. Into this pattern, for example, fell much of the American frustration evoked by the abortive United States-supported attempt early in 1961 to liquidate Castro's regime in Cuba by illegal military intervention. Provisions of inter-American treaties and the hypersensitive attitude of nearly all articulate Latin Americans towards United States intervention in any American republic were brushed aside as irrelevant. A similar apparent disregard for international law and foreign opinion was discernible in much of the American reaction to the U-2 spy plane incident in 1960. Exposure of American espionage over Soviet territory was deplored, but legal issues and foreign criticism (even criticism coming from countries most friendly to the United States) were dismissed as of no consequence. In both instances, and in others that could be cited, the narrow, incipiently isolationist view of American national interest put immediate military or political advantage ahead of conformity to international law and ahead too of a "decent respect to the opinions of mankind."

Neo-isolationists, who support this posture, often assert that "world opinion" is a figment of the imagination. They contend that what counts in the life-and-death struggle with international Communism is brute force and boldness in using it. The United States, according to this view of the national interest, would be more successful if we copied more closely the brutal and callous methods of Khrushchev and Chou En-lai. In short, they argue, it takes fire to fight fire—and forget about the opinions of mankind.

Like most convictions held by informed men, the above posture clearly has some force. It can be persuasively argued that in the present configuration of world politics strict observance of legal obligations and faithful deference to foreign criticism might lead to disaster in many imaginable contingencies. But it is one thing to deviate reluctantly from legal and moral norms from a sense of extreme urgency; it is quite a different thing to elevate defiance of norms and of world opinion (including the opinions of our most faithful allies) into a standard principle of international statecraft.

To some observers it seems dubious whether such a standard pays even expediential dividends in the long run. It is not self-evident, they argue, that Khrushchev's callous disregard for the welfare and attitudes of peoples the world over, by polluting the atmosphere with unprecedented nuclear explosions in 1961, paid off as handsomely as the admirers of "realism" and "boldness" would have us believe. Similarly, they point to the scars left in the Communist Camp by the brutal Russian suppression of renascent liberty in Hungary in 1956.

Whatever the long-run consequences of these and other exhibits of Communist disregard for international law and world opinion, there may be an even stronger reason for not emulating our Communist adversaries. The West stands for law and order and for human freedom and dignity, not for disorder, violence, and brute politics. The moment that the United States or any other Western nation abandons this posture, it forsakes its strongest claim to leadership in our divided world. Some would even go so far as to contend that it is an ineluctable principle of politics that the defenders of law and public order can never compete on equal terms with the instigators of revolution and disorder by emulating the latter's illegal methods and their callous disregard for the opinions of frightened and anxious peoples.

If, as many observers believe to be the case, mere hostility to Communism does not provide, in most of the national communities allied to the United States, the powerful impetus to action which it gives here in America, and if the United States is not to abandon its support of the Free World and retreat into a narrow isolationism, then there is manifest need for additional dynamic ideas to buttress the Anti-Communist Coalition.

There have been numerous efforts to identify the Coalition with the positive values of Western-style democracy (an ideology discussed in Chapter 17). Such efforts have run into at least two sets of obstacles. The Anti-Communist Coalition includes many kinds of political communities, including some with notoriously antidemocratic ideologies and practices. Also, there is widespread doubt as to whether Western-style democracy will work at all in some of the political communities now fighting their way up the difficult ladder of modernization (an issue dealt with in Chapter 15 and elsewhere in this book).

A more promising approach is the attempt to combine the ideas of self-determination and human dignity. Some such concept was clearly implicit in President Truman's original Point Four statement back in 1949, when he said: "I believe that we must assist free peoples to work out their destinies in their own way."

The importance of combining the requirements of national security with these broader transnational values is the point of departure in a perceptive commentary on the Anti-Communist Coalition, prepared in 1959 by Paul H. Nitze (a high official in the Truman and Kennedy Administrations and a member of the Washington Center of Foreign Policy Research):

> It is possible to look at [the question of American national security and other foreign-policy interests] from one of two viewpoints. One viewpoint is to emphasize U. S. interests, U. S. security and the direct threat to that security posed by the hostile power and intentions of the Soviet-Chinese Communist bloc. From this point of view, allies are

important to us only because of the contribution they can make to our interests and our security, and the object of our foreign policy is basically defensive. It is to keep the Russians and those whom they control from expanding into areas which would threaten our direct interests and our sincerity as a nation.

The alternative is to regard U. S. interests and U. S. security as directly dependent upon the creation of some form of world order compatible with our continued development as the kind of nation we are and believe ourselves capable of becoming. The creation and maintenance of such a system calls for a protracted and creative effort on the part of the United States—an effort going far beyond mere holding operations against Communist encroachment. From this viewpoint, the object of policy is focussed more directly on what it is we are trying to construct, and to defend while we are constructing it, rather than merely upon reaction to Communist encroachments. . . .

From the second point of view, the fundamental issue in the international arena is not merely that of U. S. security; within whatever world system of order or disorder may happen to exist, it is the question of who it is that will construct a new international order, appropriate to today's world, to take the place of the one that was shattered in the two World Wars. From this point of view, what we have been doing since 1946, whether we have been fully conscious of it or not, has been exactly that, contesting with the Soviet Union and its allies, whether it would be they, or we and our allies, who would succeed in constructing such a new system. . . .

This new structure had to have its political, its economic, and its military parts. It had to provide for certain worldwide functions. It had to foster closer regional institutions within the worldwide system. An unique role in this system had continuously to be borne by the United States because we alone had the resources and the will to tackle the job. And it had to be constantly defended against the hostile and destructive efforts of the Soviet-Chinese Communist bloc who were dedicated to the construction of quite another system.

An important part of the structure was its economic part. This had its worldwide aspects geared into the United Nations structure. The International Monetary Fund provided an institution looking toward greater stability of the world's currencies necessary for the financing of the world's commerce. The International Bank for Reconstruction and Development was to provide a pool of capital to flow to those areas needing capital and able to make sound use of it. The arrangements under GATT, the General Agreement on Trade and Tariffs, were to move toward the reduction of administrative barriers to international trade. These international institutions were reinforced by regional and bilateral actions such as the Marshall Plan, the Organization for European Economic Cooperation, the European Payments Union, the Technical Assistance Program, and the Colombo Plan. And we have tried to support these international regional and bilateral approaches through U. S. economic policies generally consistent with our new role as the world's leading creditor nation and principal reservoir of capital and of technology.

In the military sphere a similar structure compounded of international, regional and individual arrangements was gotten under way. The heart of these military arrangements had to be strength at the center, strength in the United States itself. Supplementing U. S. strength at the center, an immense effort has gone into building at the periphery, through the Organization of American States, NATO, SEATO, through the military defense assistance program and through our bilateral arrangements with the Republic of Korea, the Chinese Nationalists, and Japan. Much of the non-Communist world was tied together through a system of alliances. Even those parts of the free world outside the alliance system were given a substantial measure of protection through the strengthening of world acceptance of the principle of restraint against the use of aggressive military force—and our active support of that principle.

These economic and military measures have found their place within a political structure, the broadest aspect of which was the United Nations Organization, but the heart and driving spirit of which has been United States responsibility. A pattern of political relationships emerged, characterized by exceptionally close collaboration between the United States, England, and Canada, spreading out through close, but not so close, relationships with Germany, France, Italy, and Japan, and shading off to cooperation on certain basic matters with the uncommitted but free countries such as India and Burma.

The object has been to create a structure sufficiently flexible in its arrangements and sufficiently dynamic to house the diverse interests and requirements of the entire non-Communist world. Even with respect to the Communist world it was hoped that the structure would have something to offer and would, by its attractive power, either give room for maneuver and draw off portions of the Communist world, as it did in the case of Jugoslavia, or result in a weakening of the bonds within the Communist world, as it did in the case of Poland but failed to do in the case of Communist China.

The point of view here outlined . . . if it were to be followed consistently as a basis for U. S. policy . . . would call for a protracted and expensive effort. It [would] challenge Soviet policy not merely at a series of geographic points but overall and in its essence. It is quite understandable why many Americans have thought that [it] . . . would be more prudent if we restricted ourselves to U. S. interests, to U. S. security . . . [and avoided] getting ourselves too much mixed up in other people's business. [Such a] policy would constitute a less direct challenge to Russia. . . .

As this more restrictive conception of our interests has made itself felt from time to time, U. S. policy has fluctuated between the "modest" view of U. S. interests and security and the more ambitious target of participating in the construction of a "novus ordo seclorum," the motto that appears upon the Great Seal of the United States. Some official pronouncements have appeared to support the first point of view. Other statements, however, have implied that the object of U. S. policy should be "peace with justice." This concept of justice is hardly understandable apart from a system of order within which the principle of justice is to operate. . . .

If we fail in this objective we will still have to look to the defense of United States direct interests and security, either within a chaotic world situation or within a system basically designed and created by the U.S.S.R. and its associates. . . .*

NATO

The keystone of the system of U.S. alliances has been NATO, the North Atlantic Treaty Organization. This alliance, formed in 1949, was one of the American responses to a sequence of events which seemed to pose a severe threat to the war-damaged countries of Western Europe. These countries together constitute one of the world's most advanced and diversified industrial regions. Had this region come under Russian domination, the Communist Realm would have achieved industrial primacy at a stroke, and the United States would have been permanently isolated and outproduced in a hostile international environment.

Many events contributed to the sense of urgency. Among the more dramatic episodes, three stand out in relief: (1) the revival (in 1947) of an international association of Communist parties (Cominform) designed to subvert non-Communist political communities; (2) the coup d'état (1948) which transformed Czechoslovakia overnight into a Communist satellite of the Soviet Union; (3) the Berlin Blockade (1948-1949).

The American response was to form a military alliance with the European states and to hasten their economic recovery with massive infusions of American capital. Though Communist threats were simultaneously developing in other parts of the world, Europe was given priority because "it was an area where (a) the free world had most to lose if successful aggression took place, and (b) effective countermeasures could be most constructively and quickly taken."

The above sentence is from a report prepared for the Senate by William T. R. Fox (professor of international relations at Columbia University) and William W. Marvel (of the Carnegie Corporation). To quote further from their report:

* From pp. 1-4 of "The Purposes of United States Military and Economic Assistance," Annex A, Supplement to the Composite Report of the President's Committee to Study the United States Military Assistance Program. August 1959. Government Printing Office, Washington.

. . . until the fear of Soviet aggression that pervaded Western Europe could be dispelled, economic revival could not be expected to go forward at anything like the pace necessary to create within the foreseeable future, the foundations of long-run economic, political, and military power. To the extent that economic recovery was nevertheless achieved, this would increase the "prize for aggression" (by making these countries more valuable possessions for the Soviet Union) and at the same time gradually reduce the likelihood that communism would prevail through the tactics of subversion and infiltration. But Western Europe, unable to defend itself, was fully exposed to military aggression and the danger was believed to be that the Soviets would be tempted to try it.*

The task as envisaged in Washington was to make any attack on Western Europe, whether initially on a large or a small scale, so costly as to deter the men in the Kremlin from taking the risk. The components of this deterrent strategy were (1) to build up coalition military forces in Western Europe (with the United States initially providing the largest contribution) continuously ready for, and capable of, making a strong stand against any attack, and (2) to buttress this local military power with the superior nuclear-weapons capability of the United States.

In a geopolitical sense, NATO represented the fulfillment of a prophecy made by Sir Halford Mackinder as far back as 1924, repeated in 1930 and again in 1943. Mackinder's concept of the Atlantic Community was described in Chapter 10; and the reader may refer to the relevant passages on pages 330-31.

The history of NATO since 1949 has not been plain sailing. On the contrary, vital as it is deemed to be by most experts, European as well as American, for the defense of the West, the record is overwritten with doubts, anxieties, disagreements, and recriminations. It was inevitable, at the outset, that the United States should carry the major burden. But European military contributions to the common defense have not kept pace, in the main, with European economic recovery. Most of the French army has been continuously engaged in fruitless colonial wars, first in Indochina and then in Algeria. For a variety of reasons, the British Government has felt increasingly compelled to reduce its military commitments. West Germany's booming economic revival has not been reflected in proportionately larger military contributions. Most of the smaller nations in the

* This and other quotations from the same source are from "Military Assistance and the Security of the United States, 1947-1956," prepared under the auspices of the Institute of War and Peace Studies of Columbia University, for the Senate Committee on Foreign Relations, pursuant to S. Res. 285, 84th Cong., and S. Res. 35 and 141, 85th Cong. Government Printing Office, 1957.

Alliance have contributed scarcely more than token forces. From the American viewpoint, all this has seemed frustrating and unfair. American critics frequently point to the cold statistics which show that the United States government is allocating a higher percentage of the nation's economic product to military defense than is any other member of NATO. These disparities have already been noted in Chapter 14, Table   .

NATO has been aptly called the "strained alliance." In the following selection, Klaus Knorr (director of the Center of International Studies at Princeton) tells why this is so.*

Down the record of history, alliances have come and gone, some short-lived, some lasting over long stretches of time. We cannot predict whether NATO . . . will prove relatively durable or not. . . . From its inception, NATO has been subject to centrifugal pulls—such as French dissatisfaction over lack of NATO support in Algeria, the Franco-British invasion of Egypt in 1956, the three-cornered conflict of Britain, Greece, and Turkey over Cyprus, the fisheries dispute between Iceland and Britain—without losing fundamental cohesion. These many but minor pulls only reflect the fact that the allied nations have different interests regarding many foreign policy issues and view the external world in more or less different ways; they do not prove disruptive so long as the advantages of alliance are felt to outweigh the disadvantages.

It is also true that, by historical standards, NATO is no ordinary alliance. Strictly speaking, it is not a defense community, as it is sometimes called, for a community has common central institutions, and NATO is a compact among sovereign states. The members have only bound themselves to exercise their sovereign powers in prescribed ways, when any other member is under attack. The compact is revocable at the will of each member; decisions are made on the unanimity principle and are carried out at the will of each government.

And yet, as an alliance, NATO can claim to be in some ways unique. Outwardly, this uniqueness is expressed by a profusion of common military institutions and elaborate machinery for consultation. Before the Korean War, NATO was, as a wag put it, like the Venus of Milo —all SHAPE and no arms. Thereafter, however, arms were provided and NATO developed a network of common commands and coordinated forces, and a degree of consultation, which—though not satisfying all its proponents—go far beyond what any other alliance of free nations has achieved in peacetime, and which could not be pushed radically further without transforming the alliance into a community with supranational organs.

To some extent, no doubt, this proliferation of joint military institutions and forces reflects the recognition that, owing to the technological revolution in weapons, defense and deterrence of attack demand forces

* From pp. 3–8 of NATO and American Security, by Klaus Knorr et al. Copyright 1959 by Princeton University Press; reproduced by permission.

that are fully mobilized in time of peace. But this recognition alone would have failed to bring forth the noted results without more fundamental conditions: a similarity and compatibility of basic political orientations and the firm expectation that, among these countries, internal conflict would not be resolved by resort to military power.

Indeed, though nobody can call it a federation or confederation of states, NATO is sometimes claimed to be more than a military alliance. But if it is, it is so only to the most inchoate extent. Surely the alliance as a whole, and especially the United States and the United Kingdom, are unprepared to adopt the integrative measures with which the Community of Six is experimenting in the European Economic Community, the Atomic Energy Community, and the Coal and Steel Community; and, despite repeated attempts, it has even proved impossible to breathe life into Article II of the North Atlantic Treaty, which exhorts the members to promote close economic collaboration. In no other field of interest are the allies as united as in their interest in withstanding Soviet military moves against themselves. In its present form, NATO is primarily a defense alliance against possible Soviet aggression in Europe. And it is as such a defense alliance that, over the near future at least, it will wane or prosper.

Despite impressive military collaboration, NATO as a defense alliance has from its beginning suffered not only from minor pulls of divergent interests, but also from basic defects which now, during the current crisis of confidence [1959] are coming more sharply to the fore. First, although the military power of Soviet Russia has been menacingly great and growing rapidly, the military effort of the NATO allies as a whole has tended to be parsimonious. Though Russia has been and remains decidedly inferior to the NATO allies in population and economic resources, it has diverted to the military sector a larger proportion of its national product than they of theirs; and this, in addition to efficient use of these resources, has permitted Russia over the past ten years to gain greatly and ominously, relative to the NATO combine, in over-all military strength. This defect of not devoting to defense enough manpower and other resources varies from ally to ally. But even the United States and Britain, the two allies which during these years allocated the largest proportion of their national product to defense, have shown a disposition to place "economy before defense," as many critics put it.*

Second, short of a supranational solution requiring a merging of national sovereign powers, it is inevitably difficult for a large group of countries to develop a common and efficient strategy and balanced military forces. The main difficulty is, of course, that the military interests of the coalition partners are not sufficiently convergent and that, in the absence of federation, mutual trust in the dependability of allies is necessarily incomplete and naturally subject to doubt and corrosion. It is a weakness of the alliance that this difficulty has not been mitigated

* [In the United States this trend was at least temporarily reversed, following the installation of the Kennedy Administraion in 1961.]

by closer cooperation. And the first defect, it should be noted, aggravates the second, for the smaller the total defense effort of the alliance, the greater is the need for agreement on the most effective strategy and for the economies of complementary and interdependent forces.

In part, but only in part, the United States is perhaps especially responsible for the second defect. American predominance in decision-making in NATO and at SHAPE and the retention of SAC—overwhelmingly the mainstay of Western deterrence—as a national, rather than as part of a joint, military instrument are easy to understand and easy to justify. The United States is by far the most powerful of the allies; it has important military interests and obligations outside Western Europe; and the inherent difficulties of joint decisions over the use of SAC, or part of it, would have made it a far less efficient instrument. Nevertheless, the limits which the United States set to its sharing of military strategy and capability have tended to reinforce the independent reluctance of its partners to share the defense effort to a greater extent than they have done.

These two defects of NATO have contributed, and are contributing to the current crisis which threatens to undermine the solidarity of the NATO allies. This crisis, however, is the direct result of Russia's swift gain in strategic nuclear capability and, more recently, of her lead in the development of ballistic missiles. With Western Europe no longer protected by the umbrella of SAC's superior thermonuclear power, it is now commonly assumed in Europe that both the USSR and the United States are capable of inflicting unacceptable damage on the other and that, in fact, the American striking force is vulnerable to a Russian surprise attack, while the advantage of a surprise attack on Russia is denied to the United States because of political and moral constraints. If the Russians should add to their lead in missile development by substantially outproducing the United States in ICBM's—a contingency which is being widely anticipated by American critics of their country's defense posture—the opening "missile gap" would lend increasing substance to Moscow's claim of having achieved a decisive thermonuclear superiority over the United States.

Under these circumstances, it is not surprising that the existence of at least a strategic nuclear stand-off between the two big antagonists has cast doubt on America's readiness to protect its allies by the threat of massive retaliation, which is now viewed as a threat to commit national suicide. It is this diminished credibility of America's capability for massive deterrence which is the crux of the present crisis. Whether *in fact* the United States will be less ready in the future than it was in the past to use SAC for the protection of its allies is only one aspect of the problem and probably not the most important. How Russia and the Western Europeans assess the American potential of response may be decisive. The premise underlying the new doubt is that nations are unlikely to accept the risk of nuclear warfare except in direct self-defense.

What chiefly causes anxiety in Western Europe is not a Russian thermonuclear threat to the entire alliance, which would mean a *direct* threat to the United States itself. From this the Russians are still felt at present to be deterred by SAC—although the "missile gap," if it develops in significant dimension or is believed to have so developed, should in time prompt the additional fear of the possibility of American defeat and consequent Soviet military mastery over the entire West. The main anxiety at present is over a Soviet strategic threat or a limited ground attack on one or more of the European members of the alliance —anxiety over a Russian move, in other words, which the threat of American strategic reprisal may no longer deter. In the light of these fears, a European ally, without thermonuclear weapons of its own, would seem to be helpless in the face of a strategic bomb threat from the Soviet Union. And the possibility of a surface attack by Russian forces has raised sharp fears because of the numerical superiority of Soviet forces over NATO's shield; the destruction which Europe might suffer, especially if tactical nuclear arms were employed; and the assumption, in some allied countries at least, that what would be limited war for the United States and perhaps the United Kingdom would be total war for themselves.

Whether objectively justified or not, the diminished credibility of American massive reprisal is thus bringing out and hardening the divergent patterns of risk and interest within the alliance. Several possible consequences are foreshadowed. Certainly France will, and other allies may, follow the British example of wanting strategic nuclear deterrent power *of their own.* The bid for such independent strategic capabilities will not only confront the United States with a host of problems, including demands for American weapons; it is also possible, if not probable, that the alliance will crumble once independent strategic nuclear forces are diffused among the NATO countries. For, in that event, with too many fingers on too many independent triggers, the increased risks of alliance might well outweigh its diminished benefits. The benefits might appear to have declined because independent deterrents were available, and the risks to have been enlarged because an incautious ally could involve its partners in crises and war.

At the same time, a sharpened sense of insecurity in Western Europe, no doubt spurred by Soviet propaganda, may arise and engender, in some European countries at least, strong public pressures toward an escape from the horrible threat of destruction by seeking disarmament, arms control, and political accommodation with the Communist world. Such pressures would not only put Western governments in a feeble bargaining position vis-à-vis the USSR, possibly resulting in arrangements extremely risky to the West; they might also generate dissent and conflict among as well as within the NATO countries. Alternatively, acute feelings of insecurity may produce apathy and despair on a scale so large that the national will to stand up against aggression is broken, and Soviet inroads become feasible by means of forceful threats and diplomatic guile.

To recognize the current crisis in NATO, to worry about it, and to concede that this crisis is loosing forces which may disrupt the coalition is not the same as predicting that NATO as a going concern is about to fall apart. There is a great deal of momentum and vitality in the NATO compact, and disruptive forces will provoke remedial reactions. But successful adaptation to new circumstances depends on these circumstances being honestly faced and appraised, on constructive criticism and innovation.

Defense in Asia

Structures of the Anti-Communist Coalition in Asia and the Western Pacific have developed under quite different conditions than in Europe. In Europe the problem was to strengthen and organize a group of nations which (with certain minor exceptions) are geographically contiguous, and (again with certain exceptions) possessed large and diversified (if more or less seriously war-damaged or run-down) industrial economies. In Europe, the highest priority was given to strengthening the defensive capabilities (both military and economic) against the threat of large-scale military attack from the East. Strategy in Asia had to envisage the greater threat of disorder and subversion *inside* the political communities to be defended. These countries were widely separated geographically. Some were located upon the mainland; others occupied offshore islands. Those located upon the mainland were, without exception, traditionalistic societies, poverty-ridden, largely illiterate, with little modern industry and low military capabilities. Moreover, they were societies which, because of Japanese occupation during World War II or recent liberation from European colonialism or for other reasons, showed evidence of more or less serious internal instability. Most of them, in short, appeared to be ripe for subversion and Communist take-over, as well as highly vulnerable to military invasion of the conventional type.

American concern with this area heightened rapidly beginning about 1950. In 1949 the Chinese Nationalist government abandoned the mainland to the victorious Communists and sought refuge under American protection upon the offshore island of Taiwan. In 1950 the Communist regime of North Korea launched a military attack on the non-Communist southern part of the peninsula, an attack covertly supported by the Soviet government and joined within a few months by Chinese Communist forces. In French Indochina, internal disorder (fanned by Chinese agents and supported by Chinese equipment) flared into full-scale civil war which ended in the total destruction of French rule in Southeast Asia. Simultaneously, disorder was erupting in the Philippines, in Malaya, in Burma, in Iran, and elsewhere along the Asian periphery of the Communist Realm.

The responses of the United States developed along somewhat analogous but different lines than in Europe. American forces fought the Communists to a standstill in Korea. The United States government entered into bilateral alliances to defend Japan, South Korea, Nationalist China (Taiwan), and the Philippines. A three-party alliance was concluded with Australia and New Zealand (1951), followed in 1954 (after the French debacle in Indochina) by a multipartite alliance, remotely analogous to NATO, called the Southeast Asia Treaty (subsequently known as SEATO) which included Britain and France as well as New Zealand, Australia, the Philippines, Thailand, and Pakistan.

In the Middle East, Turkey was brought into NATO (1952). The United States government encouraged a defensive alliance between Great Britain and the northern tier of states bordering the Soviet Union: Turkey, Iraq (withdrew in 1959), Iran and Pakistan. Though remaining outside the Central Treaty Organization, CENTO (popularly known as the Bagdad Pact), because of other American interests and commitments in the Middle East, Washington actively sponsored the project designed to close the geographical gap between NATO and SEATO. The United States government has participated informally in CENTO, and has provided its Middle Eastern members with moderately large quantities of military and economic assistance.

As indicated above, American defensive thinking and arrangements have envisaged internal disorder and Communist take-over from within as the most serious threat to be met in the peripheral countries of Asia. Quoting again from the Fox-Marvel report:

> It may be of little importance whether local rebel groups are Communist led or even avowed Communists. Unfulfilled nationalist aspirations and demands made in the name of social justice can, whether or not exploited by Communists, create turmoil, disorganize national life, and undermine the stability of governments, thereby serving Soviet, whether Russian or Chinese, purposes. For this reason, military assistance policies in many Asian countries have emphasized the creation of internal-security forces. Even where the armed strength developed is no match for the Chinese or Soviet-Russian military power that could be pitted against it, these forces are helping to meet a local threat which is real and imminent.
>
> A calculation that must affect the decision to grant military aid is that of the risk that such equipment and training will finally be used against someone other than the principal target of security arrangements, as viewed by the United States, and the alternative risk that this new military power, though used against the intended target, will be used more aggressively than the United States intended, thus leaving to an ally the possibility of starting a war which the United States did not want at a time it did not want it. . . .
>
> [Noting that this danger also existed to a degree in Europe, the report continues:] Again the contrast is dramatic when the spotlight is shifted to nations on the Asiatic periphery of the Soviet world. There the chances are much greater that American supplies and equipment

may in the end be used in ways and against adversaries other than those intended by the United States. No real counterpart of NATO has existed in Asia, for there is not the same widely shared intra-regional consensus to receive expression in a mutual defense agreement. SEATO is technically a treaty of this kind; but it is self evident that, though it may have a superficial resemblance to NATO, its substance and significance are different. It does not express any real consensus on the common values being secured by military assistance and defense arrangements. No comparable degree of mutuality is a condition of aid. Furthermore, SEATO is formed of countries located at considerable distances from each other and lacking any prior experience in defense collaboration. From all reports, any advance, joint planning for greater effective military strength that may go on is but a pale reflection of this function as carried on in NATO. The Bagdad Pact may have forged closer bonds than SEATO, but its coalition military planning activities cannot be compared with those of NATO.

Finally, in Asia and the Near East there are several situations that go beyond a mere absence of consensus among neighbors. The dispute between India and Pakistan (over Kashmir) and the hostile relation-ships between the Arab states and Israel are without real parallels in Western Europe. . . . The net gain achieved from the Pakistan [assistance] program has to be calculated so as to take account of the loss suffered in our relations with India where our action has produced resentment and suspicion.

Military aid based on prior regional consensus is virtually impossible in the Israel-Arab States context since each side views the other, rather than Soviet Russia, as its mortal enemy. Assisting in an approximately equal military buildup on the two sides would support the most unprofitable kinds of arms race, while granting military aid to one side also only entails undesirable consequences: the upset of a prior balance, however tenuous, which may have prevented either side from taking the initiative, or provocation of the side that was being disadvantaged to turn to the Soviet Union or its satellites for countervailing aid. This situation is at the other end of the spectrum from the consensus among neighbors found in NATO Europe.

There is general agreement that the defensive efforts in Asia have been much less successful than in Europe. Fox and Marvel indicate some of the reasons why. But the difficulties and frustrations with CENTO and SEATO are not identical as the following commentaries indicate. John C. Campbell (director of political studies at the Council on Foreign Relations, New York, and a recognized authority on the Middle East) concludes with regard to CENTO:

A common regional defense, to be immediately effective in case of war, requires a working alliance and preferably an agreement on a joint command and joint strategy as in NATO. These were the goals of the negotiations of 1951 for a Middle East Command, which the Western Powers signally failed to achieve. The Central Treaty Organization makes possible a certain amount of common planning in the northern tier. The members are anxious to build up their armies, and the United States is acting wisely in helping them. But CENTO does not in fact offer the means of defending the Middle East against a major Soviet attack, by reason of the weakness of its members, particularly Iran, and because of the absence of cooperation on the part of Iraq, the lost partner, and the other Arab states. Unless the Western Powers were lining up the U.A.R. [Egypt] and the rest of the Arab world along with the CENTO nations, they would lack the necessary ports, railway lines, and other necessary facilities for access to the area and for the conduct of defense in depth. The political climate in the Arab world, already unfavorable to military planning with the West, would only be made more unfavorable by Western efforts to press Arab governments for bases, facilities, transit rights and joint planning.

The conclusion to be drawn . . . is that there is little point in trying to plan and prepare for an organized defense of the Middle East in a general war against the Soviet Union. It is quite apparent that the United States and its Western allies do not have ground forces for this purpose and are not likely to have them at such time as a general war broke out; that they cannot count on effective, organized "indigenous" forces now or for a long time in the future; and finally, that adequate planning on a regional basis is ruled out because of political conditions. . . .*

A Middle Eastern historian, Firuz Kazemzadeh (of Yale University), speaks even more bluntly:

The Bagdad Pact [CENTO] was built on the shaky foundation of a solidly pro-Western Turkey and a badly divided Iraq. Unlike Turkey and Iran, Iraq had never experienced Russian aggression, pressure, or occupation. Her officers, bureaucrats, and intellectuals had only the vaguest notions of what kind of society the Soviet Union really was. However, together with the other Arabs, they had experienced Turkish and British rule. An alliance with these nations, as well as with Iran, was unnatural to them. Actually, the pact was no more than an alliance among Britain, Turkey, Pakistan, and a small group of Bagdad politicians who felt that their personal fortunes depended upon British support. Yet this pact was proclaimed as the cornerstone of Anglo-American defense of the Middle East. The consequences of the West's shortsightedness are only now beginning to make themselves felt.†

* From chap. 13 of *Defense ofhe Middle East*, by J. C. Campbell. Copyright 1958, 1960 by Council on Foreign Relations; published by Harper & Brothers, New York; reproduced by permission.

† From "The West and the Middle East," by Firuz Kazemzadeh, in *World Politics*, April 1959, p. 470. Copyright 1959 by Princeton University Press; reproduced by permission.

Senator Hubert H. Humphrey (of the Committee on Foreign Relations) has spoken out even more bluntly. On returning from the Middle East in 1957, he reported:

> The foreign policy of the United States has failed to keep pace with our obligations and responsibilities in the Middle East. In an area of the utmost importance to ourselves and our allies, we have for long pursued a policy of drift and improvisation. We have confused our friends, and we have not retarded our enemies.

Noting that the United States had inherited the "responsibilities" previously carried by Britain and France in the Middle East, the Senator continued:

> Because we have shown no real initiative in dealing with the region's problems, we have also inherited the enmity and suspicion once directed toward the colonial Powers.
>
> To put it bluntly, our policy has concerned itself too much with kings and oil, too little with people and water. This is not to say that we can or should ignore or underestimate the importance of close working relationships with existing leaders in friendly Arab states. . . . However, we must not lose sight of long-range objectives. We have conceived of the security of our interests in the Middle East in terms of military pacts, arms agreements, and advance bases, when it depends in fact on our ability to win the respect and friendship of the region's 40 million people.*

The record and prospects of SEATO are no brighter. This alliance, with a permanent headquarters in Thailand, was the American response to the French debacle in Indochina in 1954. It was conceived as the Asian counterpart of NATO, though, as already emphasized, the resemblance is superficial. In the words of A. Doak Barnett (authority on the Far East, and professor at Columbia University):

> Serious internal divisions and frictions among the non-Communist nations of Asia, and even among those which have signed military pacts with the United States, have presented major obstacles to developing an effective collective security system in the region. They have made the formation of any NATO-like regional organization impossible, at least for the present. . . . Japan is only slowly overcoming the antagonisms left behind its occupation of Southeast Asia during World War II; anti-Japanese feelings have been particularly strong in the Philippines. Problems relating to the Overseas Chinese have created troublesome frictions in the relations of the Philippines, South Vietnam, and Thailand with Nationalist China. Because the non-

---

* From "The Middle East and Southern Europe," a report by Senator H. H. Humphrey to the Committee on Foreign Relations, July 1, 1957. 85th Cong., 1st Session. Government Printing Office, Washington.

aligned countries and Pakistan have recognized Communist China, Nationalist China has been bitter toward them. Burma and Indonesia are particularly hostile toward Nationalist China; both have charged Chiang Kai-shek's government with intervening in their domestic affairs. Cambodia's relations with both South Vietnam and Thailand have been tense in recent years; border disputes have been both a symbol and a cause of deep distrust. There has long been a traditional hostility between Burma and Thailand, and it has been overcome only in part by recent friendly exchanges.

SEATO represents the only attempt at a regional pact among Asian states, and it suffers from serious weaknesses. Peking's propaganda attacks, denouncing it as a symbol of American "militarism" and "interventionism" in Asia, have had a considerable effect over the past five years [written in 1960], especially since the nonaligned countries have had their own reasons for opposing SEATO. The only two Southeast Asian members of SEATO—the Philippines and Thailand—are in many respects not typical of most Asian feelings, and their membership in SEATO may have separated them more sharply from other South and Southeast Asian states. Pakistan's membership has contributed little of value to the defense of Southeast Asia and has been one major reason for India's intense hostility to the pact.

Because of the French record in Indo China, the inclusion of France has tended, in the eyes of some Asians, to identify SEATO with past European colonialism in Asia. SEATO's roster of five non-Asian members [Britain, France, U.S.A., Australia, and New Zealand] and only three Asian members [Philippines, Thailand, and Pakistan] has inevitably invited Asian criticism. It has been argued by some, in fact, that because of its divisive effects in South and Southeast Asia —in particular because of the fact that it has aroused highly critical reactions in India and Indonesia, the largest nations in that area— SEATO has brought more political losses than military gains.

The alliance has, however, produced some military advantages. It has, for example, made possible joint planning and training, exchange of intelligence, improvement of military base facilities, and standardization of weapons and military doctrine among its members. It has also made possible increased cooperation in strengthening antisubversion programs, although no general military pact was necessary for this. But in purely military terms SEATO has not resulted in a significant increase of strength in the area. The United States has not stationed new forces there, nor has any regional defense force been formed.

SEATO's main achievement has been the psychological reassurance which it has provided in mainland Southeast Asia . . . based on the United States' commitment to give support against either "armed attack" or "subversive activities directed from without." It can be argued, however, that this could have been accomplished through bilateral pacts or other arrangements which might well have had a less divisive political effect. It can also be argued that despite the SEATO pledges Southeast Asian nations may have doubts about exactly how the United States can and will honor its pledges as long as American strategy relies primarily upon mobile naval and air forces, designed to threaten nuclear retaliation against the centers of Communist power, rather than upon forces which can be brought to bear effectively within Southeast Asia in case Communist China increases its threats to that region.*

In 1958 an Australian observer, M. Macmahon Ball (professor of political science at the University of Melbourne), attempted an overall assessment of SEATO and came to some decidedly negative conclusions. For one thing, he complained:

> SEATO's policy, under American leadership, impedes the relaxation of tensions between the communist and non-communist countries of East Asia, tends to exacerbate east-west hostility, and to divide Australia and New Zealand from the Asian members of the Commonwealth.

Ball also warned:

> It is important to remember that while for us in the West the most important division in the world today is between democracy and communism, to East Asians the most important division is between the few nations that are rich and the many that are poor. If the non-communist countries of Asia are therefore resolved to give first place to reducing their economic inequality with the West, they may need to move further in the direction of authoritarianism. . . .
>
> This does not mean that the nations of Southeast Asia must accept a communist or military dictatorship. Still less does it mean that they must be integrated in an international communist bloc. The form of the authoritarianism may vary in type and degree from country to country. And the hope that there may be authority without terror, and authority based on national ambitions rather than on an international ideology hostile to the West, will surely heavily depend on economic achievement. If non-communist countries can equal or surpass the rate of economic growth in underdeveloped territories under communist control, it is unlikely that they will want to surrender their independence to Moscow or Peking. Their economic progress must depend mainly on their own efforts, but at critical points it may depend on the technical and economic aid and the political understanding and sympathy of the West. It seems more likely that the future of Southeast Asia will be decided in the fields of economics and politics than in the fields of war. But SEATO is not well designed to deal with these problems. It is designed in the West, controlled by the West, and inspired by the Western, not the Asian, view of basic values. It is not a suitable vehicle for economic or technical aid.

* From pp. 135-7 of *Communist China and Asia*, by A. D. Barnett. Copyright 1960 by Council on Foreign Relations; published by Vintage Books, New York; reproduced by permission.

If these assumptions are correct, SEATO's usefulness is strictly limited. It may provide useful opportunities for joint defense planning for countries on the periphery of Asia, and this planning would perhaps be more effective if it were carried on with the minimum of publicity and ostentation.[*]

The inter-American alliance

The oldest link in the United States system of alliances is the Treaty of Rio de Janeiro, signed in 1947. If one may judge from relative allocations of aid, the aid-dispensers in Washington have given relatively low priority to the feeding and care of the inter-American alliance. In comparison with the nearly 11 billion dollars granted to the fourteen NATO states between 1945 and 1960, and nearly 2 billions to nine Pacific and Asian allies in a rather shorter period, the twenty American republics have received slightly more than 2.6 billions, of which over half went to two countries, Brazil and Mexico.

Moreover, events (to be reviewed in a moment) indicate that United States concern in Latin America has not been with military attack from overseas, but rather with Communist-directed subversion and possible take-over inside Latin American countries.

Experts on Latin America seem to be nearly unanimous that the threat of subversion in those countries varies in proportion to social instability, and that the latter is a result, in the main, of long-standing social inequalities and discriminations. Yet until very recently the military and other aid extended to Latin American governments has had the side effect in numerous instances, if not in most, of actually obstructing long-overdue social reforms. United States aid may have tended in certain critical instances to increase rather than to reduce the recipient community's vulnerability to Communist infiltration. To make matters worse, some of the steps taken by the United States government to alert Latin Americans to the threat of indirect aggression have had the further undesirable side effect of reviving Latin American memories of "Yankee imperialism."

In order to appreciate the obstacles to building Latin America into the Anti-Communist Coalition, one needs to put the Rio Treaty into historical and social perspective. In the first place, unlike the other anti-Communist alliances negotiated by the United States since World War II, the inter-American alliance exists within the framework of the Organization of American States (OAS), which is a multipurpose regional organization. The

---

[*] From "A Political Re-Examination of SEATO," by W. M. Ball, in *International Organization*, Winter 1958, pp. 24-25. Copyright 1958 by the World Peace Foundation, Boston; reproduced by permission.

OAS itself is a product of developments reaching back well over a hundred years.

Following the early-nineteenth-century revolutions which liberated the Latin American colonies of Spain, there were rumors that the European Great Powers were preparing to send military forces to restore the colonial authority of Spain. These rumors evoked from President Monroe the famous declaration which bears his name. The essence of this declaration was that any attempt to resubjugate the liberated colonies or otherwise to extend the European "system" to the Americas would be regarded as a threat to the security of the United States.

On the basis of this declaration, revolutionary regimes in several Latin American countries sought formal alliances with the United States. But the latter would undertake no joint commitment. The Monroe Doctrine remained for over a century nothing more than a unilateral statement of policy which the United States government might or might not enforce at its own option.

North American interest in closer ties with the Latin American republics did not develop significantly until the 1880's. Then the main theme was not security but commerce. A Pan American Conference was held in Washington in 1890. This meeting featured a grand tour of the United States, lavish entertainment of the visiting Latin American delegations, and plenty of incidental advertising of American products. The commercial value of the Conference was negligible, but it did achieve two enduring results. It set a precedent for a long series of later inter-American conferences; and it led to the establishment of a permanent office which evolved into the Pan American Union. This in turn has become the permanent secretariat of the present-day Organization of American States.

For many decades United States interest in inter-American organization continued to be mainly nonpolitical. By 1890 the United States was rapidly becoming a Great Power whose leaders felt confidence in their ability to cope single-handed with any political or military threat from overseas. The United States held a great and increasing preponderance of military force within the Western Hemisphere, to which no combination of Latin American nations could present any significant political challenge. Thus, within the United States, there was no felt need for any hemispheric security organization.

For the Latin American republics the situation was just the reverse. They had profitable and deeply rooted economic ties with Europe, and the United States provided an unsolicited market for coffee, copper, and various other products. They watched with anxiety the rise of North American military potential, accompanied by increasingly frequent interference in the

Caribbean and Central American republics. Under these conditions, Latin American leaders came to fear the United States more than they did Europe. Their problem was to build legal and other barriers to neutralize the superior military and economic capabilities of the colossus of the north; and they assiduously tried to utilize the periodic inter-American conferences for this purpose.

These conflicts of interest gradually softened. Beginning in the late 1920's, the United States terminated the military occupations, financial receiverships, diplomatic protectorates, and other operations in Central America and the Caribbean which had aroused Latin American fear and hostility and evoked charges of Yankee imperialism. The Roosevelt Administration, inaugurated in 1933, preached and in the main practiced the gospel of the Good Neighbor. Latin American journalists and politicians could still win sure-fire applause by denouncing the United States. But antagonism towards the United States seemed nearly everywhere to be subsiding.

Numerous purposes inspired the Good Neighbor policy. Not the least were the ominous signs of serious trouble in Europe and in the Far East during the 1930's. Several Latin American countries contained large German and Italian minorities. German influence permeated the military establishments of certain states. German enterprise had considerable hold on commercial airlines connecting South American countries with each other and with Europe. There were disquieting reports of subversive activities by Nazi and Fascist agents throughout the Americas. There was growing anxiety in the United States lest Germany, and possibly Japan too, should acquire footholds for sabotage within reach of the Panama Canal.

World War II crystallized the need which men in Washington felt for a more united hemisphere. No treaty or other verbal instrument could abolish the enormous disparity of power which imposed upon the United States the major burden of any defense effort. But the range and scale of modern war emphasized the essential contributions of the other American republics. Vital air routes to Africa crossed several Latin American countries. The United States could use these only with the consent of the governments of those countries. Latin American raw materials were urgently needed, especially after Japanese conquest in 1942 cut off access to Southeast Asia. It was imperative that no American republic should become a center of enemy espionage, subversion, or sabotage. For these and other pressing wartime reasons, Latin American cooperation was deemed essential. To obtain that cooperation the United States for the first time accepted in principle the joint responsibility of all American states for the security of the Western Hemisphere.

This principle of joint responsibility for the common defense might easily have disappeared after the victories of 1945 but for one development: the onset of the Cold War.

Communist parties existed and were active within numerous American countries. These parties were believed to be engaged in conspiratorial activities designed to prepare the way for eventual Communist take-over. While the danger of overt military attack from overseas might be remote, the danger of Soviet-supported "internal" war was close and real. Or at least it seemed so from the perspective of Washington.

Latin American perspectives were generally somewhat different. They reflected more concern regarding possible attacks by one American state on another. In particular, there was latent fear, fed by memories of earlier United States interventions in the Caribbean and Central American countries, that Communist activities would become the pretext for future United States interference in the internal affairs of Latin American countries.

Against this background of divergent images and purposes, the Rio Treaty was negotiated in 1947. Without going into details, the essence of the Treaty is that an armed attack against any American republic "shall be considered as an attack against all the American states and . . . each one . . . undertakes . . . to assist in meeting the attack in the exercise of the inherent right of individual or collective self-defense." On the issue of indirect aggression, or subversion from within, the treaty is less specific. It merely provides that in such a contingency, the "Organ of Consultation [of the inter-American system] shall meet immediately in order to agree on measures which must be taken . . . to assist the victim of the aggression or, in any case, the measures which should be taken for the common defense and for the maintenance of the peace and security of the Continent."

As the lines of the Cold War hardened, the United States government grew more concerned over the possible consequences of Communist infiltration in Latin America. At the Tenth Inter-American Conference (held at Caracas in March 1954), the United States delegation pressed for and secured adoption of a resolution which stipulates, among other things, that the Conference

condemns the activities of the international communist movement as constituting intervention in American affairs; expresses the determination of the American States to take the necessary measures to protect their political independence against the intervention of international communism, acting in the interests of an alien despotism; reiterates the faith of the peoples of America in the effective exercise of representative democracy as the best means to promote their social and political progress; and declares the domination or control of the political institutions of any American State by the international communist movement, extending to this hemisphere the political system of an extra-continental power, would constitute a threat to the sovereignty and political independence of the American States, endangering the peace of America, and would call for a meeting of consultation to consider the adoption of appropriate action in accordance with existing treaties. [The Declaration further] reiterates recognition of the inalienable right of each American state to choose freely its own institutions in the effective exercise of representative democracy . . . without intervention on the part of any state or group of states, either directly or indirectly, in its domestic or external affairs . . .

The Declaration of Caracas was adopted against a background of Communist penetration in Guatemala, going back to the election of President Arbenz in 1950. Shortly after the Caracas Conference, the pro-Communist Arbenz administration was overthrown by a *coup d'état*, apparently with at least approval from the United States. This episode, though full of ambiguity, revived hostile memories of earlier United States interference, and revealed how fragile the spirit of Pan American solidarity still is. This fragility was further confirmed by the generally hostile reactions throughout Latin America to the heavy-footed, badly bungled Central Intelligence Agency's project of early 1961, in which the new Kennedy Administration became entangled in an abortive effort to land paramilitary forces in Cuba to destroy the Castro regime, which seemed to be drifting steadily towards the Communist Camp.

As a result of these and lesser incidents, a great many Latin American leaders appear to be quite ambivalent as to whether their fear of Communist infiltration and possible take-over is greater than their fear of United States policies and operations directed against precisely that eventuality. And their distrust seems to be scarcely less acute if such Anglo-American operations are proposed in accordance with previously agreed inter-American procedures for collective action. This viewpoint is forcefully expressed in an article by Jorge Casteñeda (a Mexican Foreign Office official). Though written several years ago (in 1956), this article indicates the dilemma which continues to plague United States efforts to build a solid anti-Communist front in the Americas. Casteñeda writes: *

> If a demonstration were desired of the political and economic dualism
> of the continent and the scanty integration of the Pan American system,
> the continental formulation of the principle of non-intervention [by one
> state or group of states in the internal affairs of another] would be a
> good proof, notwithstanding that it is considered one of the mainstays
> of Pan Americanism. It actually is, but precisely to the extent that it

* From "Pan-Americanism and Regionalism: A Mexican View," by Jorge Casteñeda, in *International Organization*, August 1956, pp. 382-6. Copyright 1956 by World Peace Foundation, Boston; reproduced by permission.

expresses the dual reality of the continent, and to the extent that its strict provisions reflect the necessities of coexistence between the United States and Latin America.

Recently a dangerous trend has come to the fore as regards the principle of non-intervention in America. It is the idea that the principle of non-intervention is to be opposed to the action of other states [acting individually], but not to the collective action which a regional agency may adopt. Thus, according to this position, the measures decreed by the OAS would not be considered intervention. . . . Under Article 2, paragraph 7, of the U. N. Charter, those "matters which are essentially within the domestic jurisdiction of any state" cannot be subject to intervention by the international organizations. Thus, there is a jurisdiction which embraces the domestic life of the state and which is "reserved," which is exempt from all foreign action, even of the international organizations, since no country would wish to be a member of the latter if their participation implied the renunciation of their domestic autonomy. This principle should be considered an essential, characteristic element that is at the very foundation of any international organization made up of sovereign states, independently of the fact that it may be expressly stated in the basic charter, as in the case of the UN, or may not be specified, as in the case of the OAS. . . .

Nonetheless, some recent developments of Pan Americanism are obviously contrary to that structural principle of the OAS. The Tenth Inter-American Conference held in Caracas adopted a resolution entitled "Declaration of solidarity for the preservation of the political integrity of the American States against the intervention of international communism," which authorized collective action against the member states in the event of certain possibilities which undoubtedly refer to and belong to the domestic jurisdiction of the states, such as the domination or control of their institutions by communism. Mexico vainly presented many amendments aimed at specifying, at the very least, that the premise for collective action should be subversive action by foreign agents. That is, it sought at least to ascribe a clear international character to those factors which form the basis for the collective action of the inter-American organization, at the same time taking them out of the sphere of domestic jurisdiction. However, all the amendments offered by Mexico were rejected. Moreover, when drafting the resolution entitled "Declaration of Caracas," Mexico tried to include as one of the guiding principles of the system the following:

"The political system and economic and social organization of the peoples belong essentially to the domestic jurisdiction of the State and, therefore, cannot be subject to any intervention, direct or indirect, individual or collective, by one or more countries or by the Organization of American States."

In spite of the fact that the Mexican draft only applied a principle already established by the UN Charter, it was rejected by the Conference, having gained four votes in favor (Bolivia, Mexico, Argentina and Guatemala), two against (United States and Brazil) and fourteen abstentions. (According to the voting system of the OAS, a resolution requires for its approval in plenary session the absolute majority of the states present in the conference, in this case eleven votes.)

The rejection of this principle signifies a frank retrogression of Pan Americanism. States are insufficiently protected in that aspect of intervention which has become most dangerous and important in our time. The American republics are coming to be less concerned about unilateral and arbitrary intervention by individual states, at least intervention of a military character. They are coming to be more concerned about intervention through collective action on the basis of votes in international meetings.

The acceptance and practice of representative democracy is one of the postulates of Pan Americanism. In the famous resolution XXXII adopted at the Bogotá Conference [1948], the peoples of the New World reaffirmed the faith that they "have placed in the ideal and in the reality of democracy," and the Charter itself of the OAS (Article 5, Paragraph *d*) declares that "the solidarity of the American States and the high aims which are sought through it require the political organization of those States on the basis of the effective exercise of representative democracy."

This is one of the Pan American principles which is most distant from reality. At present, more than half the member states do not fulfill the minimum requirements of a democratic system of government. What is worse, if the present situation is compared with that of some years ago, the democratic ideal of America seems to be increasingly distant.

Nonetheless, one cannot criticize the fact itself that the American republics pursue an ideal which they are not at present in a situation to put into practice. But it is interesting to observe, if one seeks a conclusion concerning the factors of solidarity which operate in the American continent, that the dual political composition of the continent has not historically favored nor does it favor at present the practice of representative democracy in America. The existence of dictatorships in the continent is due to a complex of causes and factors peculiar to the countries which are afflicted by them. But it cannot be denied—and that is a truth which is repeated as an axiom in Latin America—that one of the most important reasons for the perpetuation of dictatorial regimes in America is the decided moral and material support which they have been given historically by the United States. . . . What is most deplorable is that the postwar conditions have made the situation worse. The political and ideological struggle of the United States against communism has had the indirect consequence in America of strengthening dictatorships. The continental reality is not union in democracy, but disunion, the division between dictatorships and democratic countries. The postulate of representative democracy has limited value as a factor of solidarity and cohesion in America. . . .

The principle of collective defense represents a more advanced level of cohesion among the members of a regional system so far as it reveals a common desire to set up a united front against outside forces. This principle might become one of the factors of solidarity which would best contribute to building up an integrated regional community. Nonetheless, the Rio Treaty, where this principle took shape, is beginning to lose sight of its purposes in two important aspects.

The first aspect is the tendency to use the enforcement measures provided for in the Treaty, not for their fundamental purpose which is to repel armed aggression or to serve as an instrument of collective security of the UN under the authority of the Security Council, but as a means of pressure to judge, condemn and eventually to overthrow the internal regime of the states, to the extent that they do not meet with the approval of the majority of the American republics. . . . The Rio Treaty was conceived of and drawn up as an instrument which should protect the continent in the international aspects of common defense. Certainly, the extremely vague wording of Article 6 ("any other fact or situation that might endanger the peace of America") allows the Organ of Consultation a wide field of action. But the best proof that the authors of the Rio Treaty did not provide for or desire collective intervention in such domestic matters as are contemplated in the Caracas resolution is that when the Rio Treaty was drawn up [1947], two proposals to that effect were presented and they were both rejected. Uruguay proposed that the Treaty be applied to "the violation of the essential rights of man or the departure from the democratic system," and Guatemala to "any act or situation which might endanger the democratic structure of the Continent." The specific rejection of these proposals substantially supports the interpretation that the governmental regime of the American states is outside the scope of the collective action provided for in the Treaty.

Unfortunately, that is not the only respect in which the purposes of the Rio Treaty may become worthless. The new role played by the United States in world politics is changing the arrangement into a military alliance which fundamentally serves to carry out the extracontinental objectives of the United States. That is, it is being transformed from a *regional* instrument of defense to an instrument of *world* policy. The triple participation of the United States in the Rio de Janeiro Treaty, in the North Atlantic Treaty and in the defense agreements of the Pacific creates political and military risks for the Latin American states which are very different from those which are normally understood as involved in continental defense. The only *extracontinental* responsibilities which should be undertaken by our countries are those which arise directly out of the UN Charter, with precisely all the guarantees which it carries. The meaning which the Rio Treaty has for us is to prevent aggression from approaching our shores. To the extent that one of its members, which we must aid in defending, has direct interests of its own in other areas of conflict—to that extent, the war draws nearer to our continent. A defensive regional arrangement only has meaning for Latin American countries if it compels joint defense only of those countries which have no political and military interests beyond America which might bring about a war. In the past, perhaps until a few years before the last war, as long as the United States followed an isolationist policy, the advantages for the Latin American countries of a joint defense treaty with the United States would have outweighed the disadvantages. Today its benefits are not evident. . . .

Under arrangements worked out during World War II and extended under the postwar "mutual security" program, the United States has contributed heavily to raising the level and efficiency of many Latin American military establishments. The avowed purpose of this military aid has been to enable the Latin American nations to contribute more significantly to the joint defense of the Western Hemisphere, as envisaged in the Rio Treaty. However, military aid has produced side effects in Latin America, which the aid-dispensers in Washington have shown considerable reluctance to face up to.

Writing a few months after the Rio Treaty was signed, Edgar S. Furniss, Jr. (professor of politics at Princeton) observed that military equipment given to Latin American government

has been used for many purposes other than to fight the Axis [during the late war]. It has maintained dictators in power; it has overthrown governments. In an area in which military forces normally play an important political role that role has been greatly enhanced by the powerful weapons which can now be employed. The level of armaments in the Western Hemisphere has been raised [from a previous condition of virtual disarmament], with all the attendant suspicion between individual countries. . . . It is peculiar reasoning . . . which argues that peace within the hemisphere can be more effectively maintained if the American republics receive still more military equipment from the United States.*

This is precisely what has happened during the intervening years. But only quite recently have the social and political by-products of military assistance to Latin American countries begun to receive serious official attention. These effects were repeatedly brought up in the 1959 hearings on the annual Mutual Security Bill. In these hearings Senator Wayne Morse (of Oregon) was outspokenly critical of past policy. In one of several exchanges with the Secretary of Defense, Senator Morse said:

. . . this committee last year had a very interesting luncheon with a couple of parliamentarians from Chile, one an ex-senator and another a present member of their house. He put us back . . . a bit with a direct question:

* From "Recent Changes in the Inter-American System," by E. S. Furniss, Jr., in *International Organization,* September 1948, pp. 465-6. Copyright 1948 by World Peace Foundation, Boston; reproduced by permission.

"What do you send this military aid for? What good do you think it does in Latin America? Let me tell you what it does. It stirs up trouble within our countries and between our countries. Why don't you enter into an agreement with the Latin American States that you will protect our territorial integrity, you will protect us from aggression from without, and spend that money by way of loans for economic projects that will do something to help the standard of living of our people?"

We had a little difficulty on this committee . . . to punch any holes in this parliamentarian's advice to us. . . . What is so undesirable about that approach, rather than continuing to send money to Latin American dictators who give us as much trouble as they have in recent years? . . .

One of our difficulties in Latin America is that this so-called military aid money or defense money is going into too many regimes in which it in fact is used to strengthen that regime, only to have that regime later embarrass us. . . . Then the charge is made [that] the United States is in effect maintaining this regime by its arms.

It seems to me that bears upon a comment . . . that you made to this effect: If we don't maintain stable governments, then there is no justification for economic assistance.

I am troubled with that argument because I ask myself what kind of a government are we maintaining as a stable government. That is what the world is asking us in many places, and that is what the people in the parts of the world that we have got to win over to the cause of freedom are asking us.

What about maintaining some of these governments? I ask whether or not this committee should go into the consideration of whether we can justify giving military assistance to maintain a government that does not provide the people with democratic processes. I think it is a very questionable national policy. . . .

And that leads into another comment that you made [Mr. Secretary] —that one of the reasons that we supply arms is that if we don't somebody else will.

I don't buy that argument. I think we are yielding to a form of international blackmail. Let's find out if they will. Let's find out if we are dealing with that kind of a country. Let's find out if we are dealing in Latin America with a country to which we say, "We are willing to join in a pact to protect your territorial integrity. We are willing to join in a program that will give you the loans necessary to build projects that your people need. But we do not feel we can tax the American taxpayers for that kind of a program and then (as the records of my subcommittee will show) your own military expenditures run somewhere between 20 and 30 percent of your national budget, way beyond what you can afford to pay and maintain a decent standard of living for your people."

If we are supporting nations that would run to the Communist side of the world as a sort of device to blackmail us into supporting their regimes, I am for finding that out, rather than yielding to that kind of pressure. I would like to have your observation on that.

Secretary McElroy. This can be done . . . however, it seems to me that you are asking me to get into areas which are primarily the responsibility not of the Department of Defense but the Department of State. . . .

Senator Morse. I recognize that, Mr. Secretary, but I also recognize the terrific position of psychological power you men from the Pentagon Building have in this country. You come forward, as you come forward this morning, and then in effect say in these statements, this is what we have got to have to be secure. . . .

I am convinced as chairman of the Latin American Subcommittee we are going to have a lot of trouble if we don't change our course of action militarywise in regard to Latin America. . . .*

The year 1959 may appear, in retrospect, to have been the turning point in United States official thinking about the Latin American alliance and problems related to it. There was evidence of growing awareness of the unwisdom of continuing to buttress dictatorial or oligarchic regimes, however stable they might appear superficially to be, if they were opposed to overdue basic reforms or fearful of their consequences. With the dreadful example of Cuba before them, responsible policy-makers seemed increasingly to envisage the Cold War problem in Latin America as essentially social rather than purely military—a problem of helping moderate reformers to do what needed to be done before the Communists should beat them to it.

"Containment" is not enough

An overview of the East-West struggle reveals one vital difference between the Anti-Communist Coalition and the Communist Camp. Communism is unquestionably a harsh and repressive system. It bears especially hard on the individual. To most educated persons brought up in the relative freedom of Western societies, denial of individual liberty and degradation of human dignity are rejected out of hand, as foundations upon which to build a social order. But the Communist elites enjoy one very important advantage over their adversaries. They are guided by a philosophy of history, a sense of direction, a belief that they are riding the wave of the future. We have emphasized the essentially negative conception which prevails so widely in the United States. We have noted the growing conviction that it is not enough to be *against* Communism, the conviction that anti-Communism alone cannot provide the dynamism required to seize and

* From Hearings before the Committee on Foreign Relations, U. S. Senate, on the Mutual Security Act of 1959. 86th Cong., 1st Sess., pp. 206, 208-9.

hold the initiative against powerful nations whose leaders *do have* a positive philosophy of history, however repugnant that philosophy may seem to us. Because we believe this issue is the root of so many of the difficulties and frustrations recounted in this chapter, we close this discussion of the Anti-Communist Coalition with a few well-chosen words by Robert C. Tucker (formerly an official in the American embassy in Moscow, and now professor of politics at Princeton University).*

There is a feeling abroad today that Western civilization is on trial before history. One of the clearest signs of it is the increasing frequency with which we hear the word *challenge* in connection with the policies and progress of Soviet Russia and the Communist world at large. The challenge of the sputniks, of Soviet science and education, of Soviet economic development—these phrases, and variations on them, have recently grown all too familiar in America and Europe. . . .

The topic of this article is the Soviet challenge to the West in the field of theory. The term *theory* is used here in a quite specific sense. It refers not to theoretical ideas in general, and not to science, but concretely to comprehensive conceptions of the *historical process* of our time, conceptions of the direction or directions in which events are tending on a world scale. The thesis to be defended is that Soviet Russia does present a most serious challenge to the West in this particular sphere, albeit a challenge of which people in the West are not generally aware. One of the reasons why it is so serious is that "theory" in the particular meaning just specified is intimately related to policy-making, and the latter, in turn, influences or may influence the actual world trend of development.

Notoriously, we in the West tend to minimize the need for theory (and theorists) in the policy-making function, whereas the Soviet policy-makers attach considerable importance to it. In this respect they continue a tradition which goes very far back into the past, and most notably to [Lenin's thesis] that "Without a revolutionary theory there can be no revolutionary movement." . . . The Russian Communist mind has changed considerably since Lenin's time, but theory in the above mentioned sense of the word still shapes its thinking to an important degree. It is a measure of the persistence of this theoretical bias that Nikita Khrushchev, who is exceedingly theory-oriented compared with leading statesmen in most Western countries, has been criticized by certain elements within the Soviet Communist Party for being insufficiently so. . . .

The contrast between this outlook in policy-making and the characteristic Western one scarcely requires documenting. A pragmatic or instrumentalist approach to world problems typifies the Western policy-maker. Not theoretical conceptions enabling him to relate policy to the

---

* From "Russia, The West, and World Order," by R. C. Tucker, in *World Politics*, October 1959, pp. 1-4, 20. Copyright 1959 by Princeton University Press; reproduced by permission.

general trend of events, but know-*how* in the face of concrete problem-situations is what he typically emphasizes. He wants to "solve" the immediate, given problem that is causing "trouble," and be done with it. Accordingly, diplomatic *experience*—always of great importance, of course—is exalted as the supreme qualification for leadership in foreign policy. For experience is the royal road to know-how. It teaches statesmen how to negotiate with the Russians, how to co-ordinate policy with the Allies, how to respond to emergencies, and so on.

In facing foreign-policy problems it is not the Western habit to attempt first of all to form a valid general picture of the world-setting of events in which the problems have arisen. The tendency is rather to isolate the given problem-situation from the larger movement of history and ask: "What can and should we *do* about it?" . . .

So strong is the instrumentalist bias in our foreign-policy thinking that we cannot easily perceive the existence of a Soviet challenge to the West in the area of theory. We can readily see that the Russians challenge us in science, education, military power, economic growth, missiles—everything, in fact, about which we can straightway *do* something without becoming involved in the work of theorizing. . . .

However, our image of a pragmatic, technique-minded West versus a theory-conscious Soviet Russia requires some modification. For the foreign policy of the Western coalition has a certain grand design which is not devoid of doctrinal foundation. Curiously, though, this underlying philosophy of the western position derives from a single source—a rather brief essay by George Kennan, entitled "Sources of Soviet Conduct" and published in *Foreign Affairs* in 1947. Here Kennan explored the motivation of the Soviet expansionism which, as he correctly foresaw, would confront the West for years or decades ahead with a profoundly serious challenge. And he formulated the concept of "containment" of Soviet expansionism which still serves as the theoretical base of the entire structure of Western policy in the present world situation. Ironically, it was Kennanism in this form which rose to do battle with Kennan when, in his . . . lectures [in Britain in 1957], he embarked upon the search for a new perspective.

The philosophy of containment played a great and positive role during the years immediately following World War II. But, beginning in 1953, the year of Stalin's death and the Soviet explosion of a thermonuclear device, the development of events has revealed signs of its inadequacy. And looking back now upon the essay in which this philosophy was stated, I think that its essential deficiency can be stated as follows: the reasoning relates only to Russia. This is not said in criticism of Kennan, who had every right to confine himself to his announced subject—the sources of Soviet conduct. It is a criticism of the essay only in its acquired historical role as the theoretical underpinning of Western policy in the contemporary world.

The essay examined the powerful expansionist drive which was manifest in the actions of the Stalin regime in the war's aftermath, but it did so in abstraction from the over-all world setting. It did not con-

struct a broad frame of reference, did not visualize the Russian developments in relation to the general pattern of events of our time in the
world at large. The global situation and tendencies in the twentieth
century lay outside its scope. In short, the horizon of thinking was a
Russian horizon and not a world horizon. And this basic limitation
entered into the structure of Western policy as it took firm shape in the
late 1940's.

Here, I suggest, we touch upon a fundamental flaw in the Western
position and a source of the troubles which the West is increasingly
experiencing. Here too is one of the explanations for the uneasiness
which many thoughtful people in the West feel nowadays about the
established ways of thinking and acting in foreign affairs. Our response
to the global situation is an inadequate one. Lacking a world horizon
in its thinking, the Western coalition lacks an affirmative policy for the
world. To state it otherwise: the West, instead of dealing with Russia
in terms of a world policy, persists in the attempt to deal with the
world in terms of a Russian policy, this being in essence the policy of
containing Russia all over the world. The underlying orientation is
faulty.

Here is the context in which the Soviet challenge to the West in the
field of theory takes shape. For Soviet thinking and policy do not suffer
from the deficiency just pointed out. Of Soviet Russia, it cannot be said
that, instead of dealing with America in terms of a world policy, it deals
with the world in terms of an American policy. Whatever its own peculiar deficiencies may be . . . the Soviet philosophy of foreign policy
has a world horizon. That is, Soviet foreign policy and, more generally,
the policy of the Communist bloc are predicated upon a certain theory
of contemporary history, a broad conception of what is transpiring in
the twentieth century. . . .

Western thinking does increasingly reflect an uneasy awareness that
the rise and spread of Russian communism are not the whole story of
what is happening in the world in the present century, and that a
policy predicated on the one idea of "containment" of communism
scarcely suffices as the Western response to the world situation. The
efforts to fix upon these larger contours of the problem have not, however, been very successful. Present Western thinking is typified by such
phrases as "revolution of rising expectations" or "rising tide of nationalism in the world" or even "anticolonial revolution." Phrases of this kind
do have the merit of suggesting that something very consequential is
happening abroad which is not exactly Soviet-inspired even though
Moscow tries to encourage it and to capitalize upon it, and that Western
policy consequently errs insofar as it focuses *exclusive* concern on the
containment of the Soviet Union and communism. But they fail to go
to the root of the matter—to the fact that an erstwhile world scheme
of things is today in a very advanced stage of decomposition. And
while they suggest that the West badly requires a *world* policy as
distinguished from a policy of containing Soviet Russia all over the
world, they do not yield ideas as to what an effective or at least relevant Western response to the present situation might be. . . .

We shall return to this theme (in Chapter 23). But before doing so it is desirable to examine the perspectives, purposes and strategies of that large and diverse congeries of national political communities, most of them new to political independence, which thus far reject alignment with either side in the Cold War between the Communist Camp and the Anti-Communist Coalition.

★ ★ ★

CHAPTER TWENTY-TWO

The Uncommitted Realm

THE THIRD MAJOR grouping of states includes all those which reject formal alignment with either the Communist Camp or the Anti-Communist Coalition. These states are variously designated as neutral, neutralist, non-aligned, and uncommitted. Hans J. Morgenthau (professor of international relations at the University of Chicago) has classified these states into four categories:

> Neutralism may mean escapism pure and simple; it may mean political noncommitment; it may mean moral indifference. And it may mean surreptitious alignment with the Soviet bloc.*

This is blunt talk. It may or may not do justice to the motives of those who seek to resist the pressures that would formally align them with Moscow or Washington and, even more than at present, turn their countries into major battlefields of the Cold War. Leaving that question for the moment, it will suffice to recognize that the chosen international roles of these nations vary considerably. Some try simply to keep from being trampled by the giants. Others attempt to play an active but independent role upon the international stage. Some are trying to operate European-style democratic institutions. Others are experimenting with various forms of socialism. One or two have gone over to Soviet-style Communist dictatorship. Some exhibit a pro-Western orientation; others, a pro-Soviet bias. Still others say, in effect, a plague on both of you. The ideological basis of these variant attitudes has been dealt with in the section on Neutralism in Chapter 17. The only common element in the policies of all these nations is avoidance of formal identification with either the Communist

---

* From "Critical Look at the New Neutralism," by H. J. Morgenthau, in *New York Times Magazine,* August 27, 1961. Copyright 1961 by New York Times Co., New York; reproduced by permission.

Camp or the Anti-Communist Coalition. For this reason we shall designate them simply as the Uncommitted Nations, with the understanding that "uncommitted" refers only to their posture vis-à-vis the two sides in the Cold War.

The Uncommitted Realm, the geographical area occupied by these nations, covers between 50 and 60 percent of the earth's surface. Its population is about 30 percent of the world total. Most of the Realm is located within and to the south of the belt of mountains, deserts, and arid plains which extends across Africa and Asia (as described in Chapters 10 and 19). That is to say, the Uncommitted Realm includes a large part of the area which, until World War II, was comprised in the colonial empires of Britain, France, Italy, Belgium, and the Netherlands.

Like Communism, which has many disciples outside the geographical limits of the Communist Camp, neutralism too has attractions for many people outside the Uncommitted Realm. Various shades of neutralist sentiment are discernible in Western Europe and in the Latin American and Asian countries formally associated in the Anti-Communist Coalition, and also, to an extent quite impossible to ascertain, in many countries within the Communist Camp. To the degree that governments in these various regions are operated by leaders with neutralist tendencies, or are responsive to neutralist attitudes in their constituencies, such behaviors tend to weaken identification with one side or the other in the Cold War.

Neutralist sentiment in Europe has not yet forced the hand of any government associated with the Atlantic Alliance. But Drew Middleton (London correspondent of the *New York Times* and a veteran observer of the British political scene) predicted, near the end of 1960, that the neutralist movement in Britain had not yet reached its "apogee." He was confident that a general election at that time would

> result in a rout of the neutralists, but there [was] . . . no certainty that five years hence they might not win a general election fought in a worsening international atmosphere that would focus popular attention on the extreme vulnerability of this island.*

From various sources one gains the impression that the mood of passive neutralism may gain adherents, gather momentum, and become sooner or later a political force to be reckoned with, not only in Britain but also in France, the Low Countries, and elsewhere in Europe. Much depends, as Middleton and others have stressed, on the future course of the Cold War.

* From "The Deeper Meaning of British Neutralism," by Drew Middleton, in *New York Times Magazine*, December 11, 1960. Copyright 1960 by the New York Times Co., New York; reproduced by permission.

Desire to frighten more Europeans into passive neutralism, and thereby to weaken the resolve of their governments to stand firm on Berlin, may well have been one of the prime considerations which moved Khrushchev to step up the strategy of terror in the summer of 1961.

For purposes of comparison and analysis, it is useful to separate the nonaligned states of Europe from those of Asia and Africa. The overtly uncommitted nations of Europe number only five: Yugoslavia, Austria, Finland, Eire, Switzerland, and Sweden. Yugoslavia is a Communist-ruled nation, whose present government is identified with the Afro-Asian neutralists, but whose future orientation is as unpredictable as is the continued identification of Iran, for example, with the Anti-Communist Coalition. Passive nonalignment has been imposed on Austria by international agreement. Finland, a country located on the border of the Soviet Union, in which there are plenty of Communists but a democratic form of government, has maintained a precarious posture of nonalignment. For reasons largely associated with the long and unhappy history of British rule in Ireland, the government of Eire too has opted for nonalignment, though with a more pro-Western bias. Switzerland and Sweden continue to follow their historic policies of armed neutrality.

In no sense do these European states form a bloc. Nor can they be realistically lumped with the uncommitted states of Asia and Africa.

These latter present a very different picture. They are all underdeveloped countries, in various early stages of modernization. One and all, these modernizing communities are undergoing social, economic, and political changes (as described in Chapter 15). Their foreign policies are closely linked to their recent history and present condition. Most of them were parts of European empires as recently as fifteen to twenty years ago. In those with a longer history of nominal independence—Liberia and Egypt, for example—there are memories of semicolonial status under foreign "protection" and tutelage. In all of these countries such modern economic enterprises as developed before World War II were largely owned or controlled in Europe or in the United States and operated primarily for the profit of absentee stockholders.

With a few exceptions, these Afro-Asian countries are short of easily exploitable natural resources, especially cheap and easily accessible sources of energy. Coal, in particular, is generally in short supply throughout the Uncommitted Realm in Africa and southern Asia. To a rather greater extent than in the northern countries, these peoples have to cope with extremes of climate. In nearly every instance, for reasons described in Chapter 13, they are caught in the situation in which one of the by-products of socio-economic modernization is to reduce high death rates, with the resulting increase of population everywhere threatening to frustrate programs of modernization.

Most of the top political leaders of these Afro-Asian peoples harbor bitter memories of inequalities and discriminations imposed on them and their peoples by the Europeans who ruled them. Many of these leaders spent months or years in prison, sent there by colonial administrators as agitators and disturbers of public order.

Though each of these emerging nations presents its own set of problems, their respective environments and histories exhibit parallels and similarities, and their leaders—the revolutionary agitators of yesterday, the rulers of today—have reacted in more or less similar fashion to more or less similar needs, resources, obstacles, and memories.

The perspectives, attitudes, and strategies of these underdeveloped political communities, whose leaders have steadfastly refused to join the Anti-Communist Coalition, are neither well understood nor sympathetically regarded, on the whole, in the United States and in Western Europe. The late John Foster Dulles, Secretary of State during most of the Eisenhower Administration, labored to align these emerging nations with the West and repeatedly expressed exasperated frustration over their stubborn resistance to pleas, inducements, and pressures. Many Americans have reacted with scepticism, if not with cynicism, to the reiterations of their leaders that nonalignment is not a stage on the road to the Communist Camp.

We propose to let spokesmen for the Uncommitted Nations speak for themselves. For this purpose, we have passed over the top leaders who have been so much in the public view. We include no lengthy statements from Nehru, Nasser, Nkruma, Tito, Touré, Sukarno, or other heads of government, whose public behavior inevitably exhibits the characteristics of top-level politicians everywhere. Instead, we have gone both to lesser officials and to recognized scholars for statements of the purposes and strategies of the Uncommitted Nations.

The first selection is from a lecture delivered to an academic audience by Marko Nikezić, the Yugoslav ambassador to the United States. Nikezić represents the one avowedly Communist-ruled state outside the Communist Camp. His government, it will be recalled, was host to the Conference of Uncommitted Nations held in Belgrade in the late summer of 1961. His statement represents an attempt to explain to an American audience the meaning of—

Active nonalignment *

. . . Most of the uncommitted [countries] became independent after World War II with the disintegration of European colonial empires. The main feature of their foreign policy is their refusal to join the existing military alliances, although their economic weakness, their military weakness, and their former allegiances would have indicated the opposite course.

The members of the two great political and military alliances consider them neutral because they do not want to participate in pacts. Few if any of the uncommitted approve of that view, not because they think their refusal to take sides in this great controversy not moral, but because they wish actively to take part in the shaping of their own future and accordingly to influence world affairs in general.

Neutrality, as it is historically known—Swiss, Swedish, and early United States neutrality—consisted in not taking part in the political struggle and military conflicts of European powers. The uncommitted likewise refuse to fight for any one of the conflicting sides, though they have no illusions that they could avoid the consequences of a nuclear war. They refuse to take sides because they think that the present partition of the world does not settle their national problems and does not settle the problem of preserving peace. What is more important, they take an active part in the political struggles of our time, and they are vitally interested in the liberation of oppressed peoples and the prevention of a new general conflagration.

Those who regard the new nations as neutral, in the sense of being inactive in the solution of the main world problems, are those for whom the antagonism between East and West is the only major development today. That antagonism tends to polarize all the forces of the present world and, finally, to array for battle all the states into two camps, and so, being fraught with greatest danger, it naturally centers the attention of all. But we believe another development is the main and unavoidable and positive trend of our time, and that is the breakdown of imperialism. In that development, however, the uncommitted countries are far from being neutral; on the contrary, they are in the midst of events, since they are first a product and then an active agent of the decay of imperialism. . . .

In the past, declining empires were replaced by new ones, whereas today they disintegrate from inside and are destroyed by a general wave of change which dates back fifty years to the Chinese and Russian revolutions and which is now, with Africa, nearing its full completion.

In all those countries, immediately after independence—won through revolution or otherwise—there arises a question of the way they will

* From "Why Uncommitted Countries Hold That They Are Not Neutral," by Marko Nikezic, in *The Annals*, July 1961, pp. 75 ff. Copyright 1961 by the American Academy of Political and Social Science, Philadelphia; reproduced by permission.

choose in their development. This development for them, as for any other country, requires the development of industry and a sufficient rate of capital formation. Trying to achieve it as quickly as possible, they show more and more the tendency of introducing government planning and state participation into the key branches and the key projects of their economy, creating an economic and administrative pattern which we regard as a pattern of state capitalism or of socialism. It tends also to be supported by a socialist philosophy. . . .

This seems [to us] to be . . . the only way in which [the new nations] . . . can secure for themselves their fast development, and there is a proof of it, because, today, nationalists of all shades are discovering that road. With state capitalist and socialist elements playing the key role in their economic life, their thinking and political structures will tend more and more to reflect that development. And forces that lead this industrial transformation of an agricultural society, in our view, are likely to be the leading forces of the next period. . . .

It is probable that the present developments in the former colonial world have been a shock to the Western countries, who had planned a smooth transition from the colonial status into that of allies, keeping the former colonies well in the established frame of the Western world. They will probably remain tied to the West to a certain extent, in relation to the world market, but we do not expect it to be feasible in the political field. We think that these internal changes going on everywhere in the world are essential and, as in the past, no armed force could prevent the old from being replaced by the new in human societies, so we do not expect the armaments accumulated today and the existing powerful alliances to be able to prevent the decay of obsolete structures. The balance of power between the United States and the Soviet Union cannot insure the *status quo* inside countries which are ripe for change. That is why we believe that having a few more allies is far from a panacea. Building friendly relations and cooperation with really independent countries that have found their own way of development, that have a strong internal drive, that are properly using their resources, and whose governments have a real support from the population, is probably the only way to achieve peace and stability.

However, I should like to point out that we do not regard these revolutionary changes as a victory of the Soviet [Union] or of any established formula. We are aware that the Russian revolution, as the first great blow that modern imperialism has suffered, and the end of colonial rule in the great lands of Asia have had a strong influence on other countries. But we do not think that the course the events took in Russia or China or India, to mention only these greatest and most important countries, has created the only possible patterns. Every new nation is choosing its own way, being an active subject in that struggle and not a follower only. Nations stand up to fight for their liberation for reasons of their own, because of pressure accumulated on their soil and from the conditions of their own life. So, they are creating new patterns and not only illustrating the existing ones. We do not expect the result of these revolutions to be a uniform state of human society as lovers of prototypes do. Neither do we think that the antagonism between the United States and the Soviet Union as protagonists of the two sides in this divided world is the essence of the struggle between the new and the old in the world. We think that the struggle between new and old is in a state of restless activity within every society, but these unavoidable changes do not necessarily serve the national interests of existing socialist states. New nations have themselves shown, in the short period since they became independent, that they intend to serve no foreign interests. Their development could be a source of disappointment to the enthusiasts of the Cold War on both sides by the radical revolutionary essence of these movements and by their genuinely autonomous nature.

The most conspicuous feature of the foreign policy of the uncommitted countries is their refusal to join military blocs; they are against blocs, as they are aware that no bloc would genuinely defend their interests. Being economically and militarily weak they would have little influence in the councils of an alliance. On the contrary, alliances, in our view, often serve to preserve the privileges and to promote the national interests of developed states, who, besides controlling and guiding the foreign policy of alliance members, have the possibility of controlling and influencing the internal development of weaker nations.

Ten years ago that tendency to stay out of the East-West conflict could be attributed to the ideas of a few leaders. It was regarded as a kind of wishful thinking of governments that had found themselves in an awkward position, as something that could not be implemented in practical foreign policy. Today, however, bearing in mind that a number of new nations have chosen that path, we believe this to be a normal way of defending and promoting their national interests, though there are people who still call it "walking on a rope." Not only have the new nations seldom shown tendencies to join the alliances, but some of those already committed have shown a trend toward abandoning the military blocs or, at least, toward diminishing the degree of their commitment. We do not expect the uncommitted to abandon their present course. Still, it may happen that, under strong pressure, some of those countries could be forced to join the opposite side, but we consider that kind of pressure unreasonable and rather improbable today. Underdeveloped countries will depart from their course of uncommittedness, in my opinion, only in the case in which the ruling group has a special interest of its own in joining an alliance. True national interest and the public opinion expressing it seem to lead more and more of those countries towards uncommittedness.

Trying to woo and line up other nations, it is natural for the Great Powers to present their cause as just, fair, and moderate, but

I think that the underdeveloped countries see their policy from another angle—not through statements but through their own long experience. As I see it, the West can expect the uncommitted countries, the former colonial world, to cooperate with it economically, but not to follow the West in the political and military commitments. Those countries were born in a revolution against the West, and, besides that, their leaders and population are aware that the Western countries still have a strong interest in preserving their dominating position under new circumstances.

The Soviet Union, by its genesis, is probably nearer to the uncommitted, since it was, in fact, the first underdeveloped country to rise against imperialism. But the fact that the Soviet Union is today a Great Power itself, whose nature in competition with other Great Powers is mostly felt in her foreign policy, keeps the new countries on their own ground.

The Great Powers, the United States and the Soviet Union, say that they recognize the rights of nations to remain uncommitted. That is an improvement compared to the attitudes of several years ago, when our position was termed immoral. But we think that both sides in the Cold War are still far from really accepting uncommittedness. They believe that this is a temporary position which is possible only because of the present state of relations between the Great Powers and which will have to change, that is, that the uncommitted will have to join one or the other side in the competition of the powers. True uncommittedness is desirable only when it concerns that country which could rather easily join the opposite side.

Speaking of the ways and means of winning influence, I think that the Soviet Union is convinced more that the uncommitted are a political reserve of hers, than the West is convinced of the opposite. The West, on the other hand, relies more on the needs of the underdeveloped countries for capital, technical knowledge, and markets, hoping that those elements will prevail upon political reminiscences [sic].

As for the relations between the uncommitted and the Great Powers, I should like to say something, since my country is sometimes included among the former, about the accusation that the uncommitted are blackmailing the great powers. They still have little weight and little experience to do so. On the contrary, as long as they are economically weak, they are bound to be subjected to pressures. Their position is growing stronger, and, in this relation, new limitations appear every day. Their role in international affairs is bound to increase, although it cannot be expected in our lifetime to be proportionate to the part of mankind they represent. So the danger of the underdeveloped countries submerging the rest of the world, in the United Nations or elsewhere, I think, is imaginary. The increase of their role will stem to a lesser extent from their economic development, which will be rather slow, and to a greater extent from a better and more coordinated use of their political possibilities, both through the

United Nations and outside it. Among themselves, the uncommitted countries have achieved a degree of cooperation, but they are not and will not be a bloc of Powers, for trying to build up a real military force would ruin their economies and would finally force them to join one or the other side, thus intensifying the Cold War. Instead, they have found a path that serves their national interest and that, they believe, serves peace as well—which is their abstention from the alliances and their efforts to do everything they can to settle crises wherever they appear. Besides the awareness of the governments and the populations of the Great Powers that they would be the first victims of a nuclear war, which is the main brake to such an adventure, the position of the uncommitted countries is developing a restrictive influence upon the Great Powers, who can less and less afford to alienate those numerous nations. . . .

Next, a lucid, eloquent statement from an African perspective. The speaker is A. M. Ngileruma, Nigerian delegate to the United Nations. In an address to an American college audience in the summer of 1961, he put as follows the interest and role of—

Africa in the cold war *

Africa's role in world affairs has been a changing one, from that of insignificance to one of critical importance. Owing to the lack of harbors, the lack of good waterways, tropical fevers, and land rendered impenetrable by forests and desert, Africa went practically unnoticed during the age of geographical discoveries, five centuries ago. The wealth of the Far East was the center of attraction for the European adventurers. In their quest for a western sea route, the adventurers discovered America with its wealth and excellent but rigorous climate. However, the indigenous inhabitants of America were few and their mode of life was not consistent with the requirements of a vast virgin land in need of rapid development. Cheap labor was needed. Africa had such labor and it became the supplier of slaves. Thus from the very beginning Africa was destined to play an important role in the history of the United States of America. But unfortunately it was a role shorn of honor and dignity.

After the industrial revolution, the role of Africa in the world changed significantly, but it was still a role subordinated to the interests of foreigners. The industrial revolution had raised the standard of living in Europe; but to sustain that standard, it was necessary to have access to raw materials and food available in foreign lands, and a big market to absorb the manufactured goods. While I will admit that European colonial policies were not dictated exclusively by economic factors, yet they were greatly influenced by them.

While it may not be generous to deny that Africans received some

* The full text of Ngileruma's address is printed in *Vital Speeches*.

benefit from European colonialism, yet, on the balance, the scale was very much in favor of the Europeans. Africans became involuntary servants of European economies, contributing significantly not only to the profit of European capitalists, but also to the prosperity of the masses of Europe. Thus, at this stage of world history, Africa's role was still subordinated to European interests.

The contribution of Africa to peace in Europe in the last quarter of the 19th century is very often overlooked. . . . Although there were crises [among the European Powers over African issues], they did not lead to major wars. European Powers were able to reach agreement during crises by bartering African territories. The Africans themselves were not consulted before the barterings were effected. They were innocent victims on the altar of international friendship— victims of European national and imperial rivalries. . . .

After describing the breakup of European empires during and since World War II, Ngileruma continues:

There is nothing anyone can do to stem the trend of events in Africa. In fact, all independent African states, irrespective of their so-called ideological leaning, are committed to working for the total elimination of colonialism in Africa. . . . The security of Europe can no longer be based on the insecurity of Africa. The elimination of colonialism from Africa should not necessarily deprive the West of her legitimate and reasonable needs in Africa, provided the West accepts a new relation with Africa—a relationship based on equality and cooperation. . . .

The emergence of so many African states has altered, among other things, the composition of the United Nations and perhaps indirectly the urgency of the problems facing that organization. For the first time in world history, Africans are in a position to protect their own interests and to play a role in world affairs not subordinated to the interests of others.

The African members of the United Nations certainly form an interest group. The group includes most of the poorer and less developed countries, all of which share bitter recollections of colonialism, common abhorrence of imperialism. They also share a common hope and desire for economic development and social progress. . . . The question of economic development in Africa is one of war against illiteracy, poverty, and disease, and, consequently, the question assumes an emergency of the same order as the emergency of war in developed countries. It is, therefore, not surprising that with the African states, the problem of economic development overshadows ideological conflicts and the cold war. . . .

To the Africans, a strong and effective United Nations is necessary for the attainment of their aspirations. In the first place, the United Nations presents a platform from which small countries (and all African countries are small in this respect), irrespective of the level of their economic development, can make their voices heard and influence world affairs. Insofar as the United Nations performs this function, it safeguards the interests of the small countries and tends to prevent the big Powers from making their usual deals at the expense of the smaller countries, without consulting them.

In the second place, the United Nations, if even it is no more than a talking shop, promotes peace insofar as it presents a forum where the big Powers can meet to talk and even discuss. It is in this respect that the neutral group in the United Nations performs a very useful role in keeping the United Nations open as a forum of discussion. . . .

Economic development can only take place in an atmosphere of peace and security. Since the African states are very much concerned with economic development, one can understand their preoccupation with the maintenance of world peace. Reduction in world tensions, and better still, disarmament will surely release, to the benefit of all underveloped countries the much needed capital which is now tied up in armaments. Africans, therefore, seeing the hope for peace in the United Nations give their unstinted support to that organization. True enough, we think that the organization of the U.N. Secretariat, the distribution of seats in the various organs of the United Nations, etc., are anachronistic and we would like to see healthy reforms take place; but all Africans are agreed that, subject to these desirable reforms, nothing should be done to impair the efficiency and effectiveness of the organization. . . .

The discussion of every question in the United Nations in the context of the cold war tends to reduce discussions to mere formalities and stultify the efforts of the organization to promote peace. In their role as neutrals, the Africans try to bring objectivity and sanity back into discussions. Since they are not committed to either bloc, each bloc, in the effort to win a majority, has to direct its appeal to the neutrals; each bloc has to argue convincingly instead of relying on slogans. Thus, unhampered by routine commitment to either bloc, the neutrals try to judge each question with objectivity and thereby keep the United Nations open as a forum of discussion. Furthermore, the presence of the neutrals in the United Nations presents to the power blocs a venue of "letting off steam" which, otherwise, might explode into physical warfare under the pressure of the cold war

Surely, neutralism in the context that I have described is very moral and, in fact, indispensable if the United Nations is to survive. I must emphasize that neutralism does not necessarily imply indecision about choosing between different ideologies. My country, Nigeria, is a democratic country, committed to the principles of human dignity, equality, and freedom. And yet she is neutral. Similarly, a nondemocratic country can be neutral. The essential attributes of neutralism in this context are the refusal to associate itself as a matter of routine with any power blocs and the readiness to treat every question with the objectivity it deserves.

Partly because Africa has had to play a role subordinated to the interest of non-Africans and partly because Africans have confidence in their own ability to look after their interest, the new African states

are very jealous of their independence. They loathe outside interference in African affairs, as evidenced by their irritation at the prospect of the Great Powers—East and West—getting involved in the
Congo.

In every discussion of Africa by the Great Powers one often hears
terms like containment, satellite, extermination of imperialism, etc.
To the Africans these terms are mere slogans invented to camouflage
the old diplomatic concept of marking out "spheres of interest" of the
Great Powers. It will be sheer delusion to think that Africa today
will gladly accept any Great Power's influence. The truth is that
Africans do not want to be anybody's pawns. As *The Economist* . . .
[has] aptly pointed out: "It is political death for any African leader
to become labeled as a pawn of the West. Equally, Moscow has
repeatedly found its favored protégés disappointing, basically for the
same reason." . . .

The desire to be independent of the Great Powers does not necessarily mean anti-West or anti-East feeling. It is usual these days to
divide Africa into two groups: the radicals, or anti-Western group,
and the moderates, or pro-Western group. It is true that there is a
division among the new African states, but the division is surely not
[on] cold war lines. . . . If there is any anti-Western feeling in Africa
it is not due to Communist infiltration. Rather, it is generated more
by Western attitudes to such burning African and colonial questions
as Apartheid, Angola, etc. Even the so-called moderate African States
that met in Monrovia [earlier in 1961] . . . clearly showed how
sensitive they are to the seeming insincerity of the West on colonial
questions. The truth is that the future relations between Africa and
the West depend more upon what the West does than upon Communist propaganda. The tendency, on the part of the West, to regard
their military alliances as being so important as to prevent them
from supporting [the] African struggle will only antagonize
Africans. . . .

Ngileruma has spoken with candor. His words may shock a good many
Americans. But, we repeat, he speaks as an African moderate, from a moderate African national community, a community whose leaders appear to
be genuinely committed to democratic principles, a community with possibly stronger ties with the West than any other in Africa.

The gulf that separates the predominant Western image of the international scene from the viewpoints of the uncommitted nations of Africa
and Asia becomes even more apparent when one begins to explore—

Indian perspectives on the cold war

Prime Minister Nehru has steadfastly refused to enter into alliances
with either side in the Cold War. But he does not conceive this posture

to be in any sense a merely passive neutrality. Speaking on the radio in the United States in 1956, he said:

> The preservation of peace forms the central aim of India's policy. It is in the pursuit of this policy that we have chosen the path of nonalignment in any military or like pact or alliance. Nonalignment does not mean passivity of mind or action, lack of faith or conviction. It does not mean submission to what we consider evil. It is a positive and dynamic approach to such problems as confront us.

Nehru's sister, Mrs. Vijaya Lakshmi Pandit (who has served India in many top-ranking capacities—as High Commissioner to Britain, as ambassador to the Soviet Union and to the United States, and as President of the U.N. Assembly) has emphasized that

> this particular approach to peace is not new in India. It is her traditional outlook, both philosophical and historical. Philosophically it took shape . . . when Gautama Buddha condemned violence in all its forms and sought through the example of his own renunciation a solution to human suffering. . . . But an approach, however revered, must find its flowering in visible examples if it is to have a practical value for the people who subscribe to it. Mahatma Ghandi has been for us that practical example. . . . He proved that the peaceful approach still had a dynamic significance for our own era, that bloodshed was not the only way, even in an age of violence, for a nation to conduct its struggle for independence. . . . He laid the foundations for the cooperation that continues today between free India and Great Britain. . . . We are convinced not merely that [the nonviolent approach] can prove an asset on the wider international plane but that it is the only method that will guarantee a lasting peace. . . .
>
> India is an active member of the United Nations and willingly offers her service when it is needed to ease tension and promote good will. . . . Her chosen role demands that she exert herself in whatever capacity offers itself in the interests of peace. Her neutrality itself implies involvement in its cause. . . .
>
> This is the policy to which we adhere for two reasons. Firstly, because our need for peace is imperative. It is not merely desirable or preferable, it is a vital necessity and a daily prayer. We have problems to face in India that would tax the energies and resources of a nation far better equipped and developed than ours. We need peace not in order to become more powerful or more prosperous, but in order to exist. We need it in order to eat, to be clothed, and housed and made literate. We need it for these basic unadorned reasons and we will not jeopardize their realization by even a remote word or action that might add to the unhappy tensions that already exist.
>
> Secondly, we choose this way because we reject completely the psychology of threat and its byproduct, fear. We do not subscribe to the widely-held belief that the affairs of nations can be successfully

conducted on a military level. In the world's recent history there is abundant evidence to prove that neither threats of superior force nor displays of armed might have been able to create the climate in which peace can take root. The great malady which affects humanity today is fear, born of tensions following the armaments race. Fear is a bad counsellor and reduces those who fall within its grasp to a state in which no positive action is possible. To keep fear at its lowest ebb even if it cannot wholly be eliminated is India's ceaseless endeavor.

In the world of conflicting ideologies there is, to our way of thinking, no civilized method of living in harmony with those who disagree with us but that of peaceful coexistence. . . .*

Mrs. Pandit's article and certain other expositions of Indian foreign policy evoked an exchange of views between the British political scientist, Alan de Rusett (of the University of Leeds) and A. Appadorai (director of the Indian School of International Studies). The following selections give the essence of their respective arguments.

The Indian approach to the cold war: a Western view †

DE RUSETT: Prevalent Indian and Western views on the maintenance of peace appear at first sight to differ only in emphasis. Western spokesmen give primary attention to the establishment and preservation of a balance of power in international society, which demands that careful and persistent attention be given to armaments and alliances, so extensively has the power of a large and potentially expansionist part of the world disturbed past equilibrium. When and where there is a reasonably secure balance, and on innumerable matters that do not closely affect relative power, they are prepared to negotiate, compromise, and conciliate, and have done so repeatedly. In such situations they accept help and advice from all nations of goodwill, but they are fearful of doing anything that may upset the equilibrium of power—for which they have such an absolute responsibility—and this does, indeed, circumscribe the area in which they feel that compromise and acts of good faith can be safely exercised.

Indian spokesmen acknowledge the needs of national defense. . . . They also acknowledge India's moral obligation to go to the defense of others: "When a man's liberty or peace is in danger, we cannot and shall not be neutral; neutrality, then, would be a betrayal of what we have fought for and stand for" is one of Mr. Nehru's many affirmations of this position. However, all this is kept in a minor key: "Why shout it out?" asks Mr. Nehru. Instead, the whole of

---

* From "India's Foreign Policy," by V. L. Pandit, in *Foreign Affairs*, April 1956. Copyright 1956 by Council on Foreign Relations, New York; reproduced by permission.

† The selections by De Rusett and Appadorai are from *International Relations*, issues of April 1959 and October 1960. They are reproduced by permission of the David Davies Memorial Institute of International Studies, London.

Indian emphasis is placed upon the need for peaceful talk, behavior, postures, and procedures; as Professor Appadorai so well summarizes it: "To keep the peace, try peaceful means—negotiation, inquiry, mediation, conciliation and arbitration; listen to the viewpoints of both parties to a dispute expressed by their duly constituted representatives; hesitate to condemn either party as an aggressor, until facts proved by international inquiry indisputably testify to aggression; believe the *bona fides* of both until proof to the contrary; and explore fully the possibilities of negotiation and at least localize war—this is India's view."

There is no direct conflict between these two aspects of peacemaking, so long as the correct relationship between them is clearly recognized. They are supplementary; and they could lend themselves to a fruitful division of labor between the Western Powers and India. For it is basic to all Western analysis—and here scholars and statesmen are agreed—that to organize peace in a society of sovereign states power must be so distributed that its members are not tempted to seek their ends by violence; otherwise, fear stalks through the world, and its fate is in the hands of its most lawless members; and this is so in all known political communities, tribal, national, and international. This is not deemed to be a Western idea, but a universal law of political science. The best way to organize power for peace, as the history of India and all other nations has shown, is to place it under centralized community control, in the hands of a legitimate and representative government, which can guarantee the security of all members, and so free them from the fears that stifle the growth of community spirit. This spirit, so essential to peace, develops best under the protection of the sword, but never enough, so experience and observation shows, to eliminate the need for the sword.

Ideally, the society of sovereign states should secure peace, therefore, through democratic world government . . . But in the absence of world government, the balance of power system is the only other way known of distributing power so that it restrains resort to violence. It is a poor second best—a deplorable answer to a deplorable vacuum at the top. But without it, the foundations of all other peace-making are destroyed; the will to negotiate vanishes when all can freely choose between it and the violent achievement of their ends; the courage to trust disappears, when the price of miscalculation is total conquest. Therefore, to the Western mind, the code of conduct outlined by Dr. Appadorai, while it is essential to the preservation and enrichment of peaceful international relations (as peace can never rest on the sword alone), is only possible when founded on a stable power equilibrium. India, therefore, can exploit in the cause of peace a condition created by others, so long as her participation is not necessary to its successful creation. She can supplement the fundamental and indispensable spadework of the power-balancers. And that throughout history has been the role of the Mediator.

There is much evidence that this is no theoretical analysis. . . .

[India] is protected by the over-all power balance, without having to guarantee this protection by an alliance. Her size is her strength, whereas smaller nations need alliances because they can be so quickly over-run that their collective defense must be organized in advance. This is nearly the whole way to being in the position of a natural Mediator. The rest of the way is achieved by the fact, now at last acknowledged by the West, that the world balance of power can be established without India being tainted by active participation in it. The West has been helped to see this, partly through the experience of doing without India's active aid in the Korean War, and partly through realizing the strength of India's defensive will and capacity. Hence, to put it colloquially, others can do the dirty work; for maintaining power balances is a rather soul destroying task, though none the less necessary for that; and history shows how happily nations will, if they can, opt out of their duties in this respect; the United States did so for too long, not so long ago. But, unlike the United States, India can do so without disastrous results. She can keep her mediatory hands clean for the benefit of the world, and aid the West in its ultimate objectives. . . . India can now be the world's largest Mediator without false starts, while others prepare the ground, and bless her exploitation of it.

But, in fact, we should indeed delude ourselves, if we imagine that this is the way Indian statesmen or intellectuals present the situation to themselves or to their nation. . . . On the contrary, they present the role of Western Powers and of India in such a way that it is almost impossible to make this reconciliation of their policies. They present these policies as opposites; they create an antithesis between India's community-building behavior, and the West's pursuit of power balancing. They justify the former by reference to first principles of ideal conduct, and this inevitably leads them to condemn the latter, for it does not fit in with such first principles . . . Yet Indian writers do not demolish the Western analysis, and replace it with another conceptual framework, based on new insights into the way peace is organized in political societies. They ignore it, and pass on. Thus there is no meeting place, where the Western mind can find something to grapple with. Instead, we find a kind of intellectual "brinkmanship" in Indian thought on these matters: they observe and objectively record facts up to a point—and just as it would appear inevitable that they must draw conclusions that accept the fundamental basis of Western analysis, and come to terms with the balance of power, its necessity and its inevitably unpleasant corollaries and consequences, they stop dead in their tracks. No analysis follows. And so we are forced to read between the lines, to discover what framework of political principles is guiding them, and what we read, or possibly misread, is not particularly reassuring.

To illustrate: First, there is the record of Indian mediation and conciliation, which is presented as a battle against the "cold war mentality." . . . But all the examples given of India's successful work

in this field, her chairmanship of the Neutral Nations Repatriation
Commission in Korea and her chairmanship of the Supervisory Commission for Indo-China, for example, show that Indian statesmen were
exploiting in the cause of peace an equilibrium created by others, and
that she could not have done so had not the equilibrium been established. North Koreans were in no mood to listen to India, when they
poured south in June 1950. Nor would Ho Chi-Minh have refrained
from exploiting his victories in 1954, had not the threat of American
intervention helped to restore the balance in Indo-China; nor were
the French interested in conciliation earlier, when they thought their
power greater than that of Viet Minh. Similarly, all India's gallant
failures to instil reason, compromise, and good faith into the minds
of contestants in international power struggles have occurred in conditions of grave disequilibrium, or when one party has believed that
the balance was moving in its favor. But this is not stressed or even
mentioned by Indian writers; the point is not made, and therefore its
implications are not even analyzed. India's peace-loving methods are
contrasted with the West's desire for a "military" solution; their
success is attributed to others seeing reason at last; their failures to
other nations—more often the West than the East—having an obstinate
preference for "power politics."

The same analytical error—or vacuum—produces the same false
antithesis, when it comes to describing the role of the United Nations.
Here again is the contrast between the need for conciliation, mediation, and so on, and the need for organizing power to discourage
aggression. In the Western view, the West was faced with an alarming
concentration of Communist power, and sought to counterbalance it,
in the 1947-to-1952 period especially, by organizing the defensive
power of the whole "free world" through using the machinery of the
United Nations. This was certainly a risky way of doing it, because
the Charter was not designed to enable this to be done, and it could
only be achieved through the clumsy and inappropriate machinery of
the General Assembly. Moreover, it is very difficult to use the same
international organ both for enforcing peace, and for the delicate tasks
of peaceful settlement. This has always been recognized as one of
the dilemmas in the classical scheme of organizing collective security
through a kind of world parliament. But it was a mistake of idealism
or over-enthusiasm, mainly on the part of the American government
and people, that led the West to try and use the United Nations this
way; it was partly an attempt to avoid having to create an alliance
system; and all the peaceful procedures of the United Nations were
used, though when active war broke out [in Korea] they were certainly
strained by the tensions that accompany the organization of defensive
power. In the event, the Western Powers rectified their mistake, and
established a balance of power through a system of alliances, which
operated independently of the United Nations, and so gradually freed
the General Assembly to concentrate on mediation and conciliation
without danger. By 1955, the idea of international forces at the disposal

of the General Assembly had been dropped, the enforcement provisions of the 1950 "Uniting for Peace Resolution" were a dead letter, the membership deadlock was broken and the way was open to universal membership, and so on. In other words, just as India's way to becoming a great Mediator with the blessing of the West was opened by the maintenance of a power equilibrium without her, so the way of the United Nations to a similar role was opened—and by the same means. The power of each to exploit the situation for peace, however, could not have been exercised effectively until such conditions had been created.

The prevalent Indian version of this development is cast in the mould of antithesis. India is described as viewing the United Nations as "a great organization for peace"; the Western leaders as seeing it "as an organization through which war can be waged." Again, "India has emphasized the desirability of improving the machinery of the United Nations for the tasks of peace rather than those of war." And this contrast is simply achieved by equating preparation for defense with preparation for war, and heavily inferring that nations so engaged are bent on war, or prefer it to negotiation. . . . The creation of "power blocs" is without qualification described as not in the "interests of the world organization," and it is inferred that they are designed to "supplant the United Nations," as contrasted with India's desire to "supplement" it by friendly collaboration all around. Nor is the initial reason for the United States wishing to use the United Nations to counterbalance Communist power—namely, that [the American] people had strong, rather Indian, prejudices against the division of the world into military alliances after . . . [World War II]—given credit; [American] . . . policies are simply seen as attempts to "convert the United Nations into an executive agent of an anti-Communist alliance." Thus every avenue towards recognizing the need for an equilibrum of power, and acknowledging the peace-maintaining object of establishing it, is blocked. Even defense becomes "preparation for war"— and, somehow, throughout the report of the Indian Council of World Affairs [a report entitled "India and the United Nations"], it is always the West that is most anxious to make such preparation, and its antagonist, which history shows first caused it to take up these positions, gets off very lightly. . . .

Here, then, is the crux of misunderstanding. Peace rests on some unspecified social foundation; the need for equilibrum is not recognized; so even the desire for it is misconstrued. Actions taken in its pursuit are condemned whenever they conflict with a code of good conduct that is justified in the language of ideal moral values, unrelated to any particular form of society. India's chosen role, therefore, is not explained in terms of her favorable power position, but is held up as a model for all to follow, regardless of their size, position, or past experience of present neighbors. Indian freedom from fear is given a moral virtue. Thus not only is the West misunderstood, but the actions of many of India's Asian friends and neighbors misconstrued, and Western relations with them, too. Whether stated directly or indirectly, the Indian message to these [Asian] states is clear: as in the observation—"The general Indian view is that the establishment of organizations for collective self-defense, even within the framework of the Charter, only leads to the consolidation of power blocs. India is not a party to any military pact and has shown no enthusiasm to organize or join one. On the contrary the Indian government and the people have expressed their disapproval of the action taken by other powers to organize a Middle East defense organization [CENTO] and recently they have vigorously criticized the United States decision to give military aid to Pakistan. It can be safely stated that India is opposed to the conclusion of any military pact by neighboring countries which would automatically involve them in the 'cold war.' However, India recognizes the right of other Powers to establish organizations for collective self-defense of their own choosing."

In this way [DeRusett continues], weak Asian states are first warned against the idea of organizing their defense in collaboration with others. They have, however, a "right" to act less wisely or nobly, but they must not turn for help to the only source of power that can create an equilibrium in present circumstances—the Western Powers—because by some inherent law this involves them in preparation for war. Nor, of course, can they turn to India, because she has wisely shown "no enthusiasm to organize" any military pact. . . .

Yet, if one looks at the quotation just given, and at others in the same vein, one notices an emphasis which—taken in conjunction with some undertones in observations in other contexts—gives reason to believe that we may one day be presented with a new, and specially Asian theory of the causes of conflict and conditions of peace in modern international society. The implication is there that Asians do not establsh military liaisons with Western nations "of their own choosing." The will to do so is fostered or forced by the West. In other words, Asia is contaminated by European attitudes and behavior, based on a peculiarly European view of the world. This thought is reinforced by the special sense in which the term 'power politics' is used. India's faith in the United Nations, we are informed by the Indian Council of World Affairs Study Group, has been shaken by decisions of the Security Council on Kashmir, which were deemed to be "influenced by power politics"; and some members opposed strengthening the United Nations "because of the predominance of power politics in the Organization."

By Western definition, all international politics are power politics; and a relationship can only be taken outside them by its unqualified submission to the rule of law. . . . But India's international political relations are not regulated this way, and the aforementioned Group endorses this conduct. Yet, somehow, India does not, in the Group's view, indulge in "power politics"; at least, not naturally. And one is forced to conclude that consciously or subconsciously they feel that "power politics" are European or Europeanized politics, introduced into Asia, perforce copied by Asians in moments of temptation, but essentially alien to them—that is, they are superimposed on an altogether different Asian norm of behavior. . . .

An Indian response to De Rusett

APPADORAI IN REBUTTAL: India is still groping in the dark to find stable foundations for peace in an atomic age; if she had the talisman for achieving that aim we should already have secured a "peaceful" peace instead of continuing to live in the "fearful" peace in which we find ourselves now. Having admitted this, India's own view of the foundations of peace may be stated thus: (1) the balance of power, whether it was useful or not to preserve peace in the pre-atomic age, cannot preserve it in the atomic age; and (2) the approach to peace in the atomic age, while not ignoring the realities of power, is to be looked for in successfully exploring, more fully than was necessary in an earlier age, the potentialities of negotiation and other means of peaceful settlement of conflicts and in promoting active peaceful co-operation between states. . . .

The Indian approach proceeds on the assumption that peace cannot be promoted by creating positions of strength; on the contrary, the creation of positions of strength might become a threat to peace—for every party will naturally try to increase its strength vis-à-vis its competitors for power, and such an attempt is suicidal in the atomic age. Entering into military alliances and the establishment of military bases in foreign territory accentuates discord and the possibility of war. The peaceful approach—which also does not guarantee peace—has to be tried if only because there is no other. Its essential is the determination to avoid force, for the use of violence creates more problems than the one it solves if, indeed, its use does not lead to world destruction; hence discussion, negotiation and accommodation are the only way left for the settlement of differences. . . .

India's emphasis upon negotiation, it should be added, derives its *raison d'être* not only from the conditions of modern warfare but also from a belief that invariably in genuine international disputes, both the parties to a dispute are likely to have a just cause, the difference being only in degree. . . .

What does all this boil down to in terms of the question raised by de Rusett: Does such an approach guarantee peace? No, but neither did the traditional approach guarantee peace. Is it another way, a way different from the one adopted by the West, to secure peace? No, de Rusett is right in arguing that this approach is supplementary to the one based on power—but supplementary with a difference. Those who approach problems in this way do not close their door to, but emphasize, negotiation, and are careful more than others to watch for opportunities for negotiation and try to make a success of it as much as is possible in the circumstances; the truces secured in Korea and in Indo-China are cases in point. It is true that the unwillingness of the parties to the conflicts to use their destructive weapons supported, in the instances cited, the temper of peace, or perhaps vice-versa; but that exactly is the utility of the approach in present conditions in the world. The temper of peace is no panacea for the evils of international power politics but is supplementary to power. De Rusett is right, if its supplementary value is recognized to the proper degree.

The vital issue for international politics . . . then is: Are the techniques of negotiation and other peaceful methods of settlement potentially capable of yielding more successful results than they have yielded so far? War has often been resorted to in the past when peaceful means of adjustment failed; under modern conditions of warfare, war, it is recognized, cannot be a useful alternative to peaceful means of adjustment. Can we then fall back on the only other alternative available in order that adjustment of difference is possible and some satisfaction can be obtained by the parties concerned? . . .

The anatomy of negotiation suggests that when two or more parties disagree on a question, two factors play a part in resolving their differences, one, the fear on the part of any party to the dispute that superior force might be used to settle the difference, and the other, the sense of accommodation which suggests that while its own vital interests must be safeguarded, consideration must also be given to the interests of the other party or parties. It is not easy to isolate these two factors and say which has played the greater part in the final settlement of the differences at issue: there are too many variables to be taken into account in assessing the sources of fear on the one hand, and the sense of accommodation on the other. Thus force is a function of several factors: geographical position, economic resources, the strength of government and the leaders in power, diplomatic finesse, armaments, alliances, and the morale of the people of the country in question; the sense of accommodation is a compound of the innate sense of justice, the desire to placate public opinion at home and abroad, and the desire to have some stability in the settlement to be arrived at. These apart, another factor in the situation, invariably, is conflicting interpretation of the facts in question; this acts as a sort of brake on the willingness to use force, and as an ally to the sense of accommodation.

If this analysis is correct, it follows that where negotiations have been successful, the sense of accommodation has played a greater part than power, and that where negotiations have not been successful, the reverse has been the case; the sense of accommodation is itself affected by the extent of the interest that the protagonists attach to the issue in dispute.

In sum, the essence of an approach to successful negotiation, through history, has been to see that when differences of opinion have arisen between two or more parties on a matter which concerns them, an attempt must be made to settle the differences in such a manner that none of the parties suffers a significant loss; for only then would the result be stable. It would be wrong to consider this as a distinctly *Indian* approach; it is integral to true negotiation as such. . . .

The willingness to submit a dispute to a third-party judgment, as may be seen in the numerous cases referred to arbitration, can be explained only by the existence in the disputants of that spirit of accommodation and of willingness to see the other man's point of view which is so essential in order to avoid a breakdown. The Indian emphasis on negotiation as a way to peace only highlights a well-known technique and its utility in the atomic age. Indeed, the debate . . . should continue . . . not on the issue whether negotiations should be an alternative to the use of force (as there is no disagreement here) but on how to improve the techniques of negotiation and other peaceful methods of settlement so that they may yield the desired results. . . .

Some further reflections on active nonalignment

Comparison of the Yugoslav, African, and Indian views quoted above, confirms what was said earlier in the chapter, that the foreign policies of the Uncommitted Nations exhibit little in common except a determination to avoid identification with either side in the Cold War. If space permitted an examination of the attitudes and policies of spokesmen of the Arab states, Indonesia, Burma, and still others, further differences and variations would become apparent. But we have sufficient data for certain further reflections on the patterns of interactions which are taking shape within the Uncommitted Realm, and between the Uncommitted Nations and principal antagonists in the Cold War.

De Rusett argues, not that India's self-chosen role as uncommitted mediator is unworthy or undesirable, but that Indian politicians and scholars should not delude themselves into believing that their chosen role would be operable at all outside a reasonably stable military equilibrium provided thus far by others; and hence, that they should be less harshly critical of the West whose military forces and alliances have created the conditions which enable the mediator to function with some prospect of success.

On the Indian side, the drift of the argument seems to be, not a denial that a military equilibrium may create conditions more conducive to successful negotiations, but rather that those who rely heavily on military forces and alliances are apt to exhibit a self-defeating lack of faith in compromise by negotiation. The underlying premises here seem to be: (1) that compromise is always possible; (2) that compromise is always preferable to suicide; (3) that neither side to a controversy has a monopoly on justice; and (4) that adjustment by compromise, in which each side gives up something, each gains something, and neither is publicly humiliated, is more apt to produce durable and stable future conditions than victories by which one side imposes its demands on the other.

These premises, or at least some of them, contrast starkly with the theses urged by prominent theologians, professors of philosophy and politics, politicians, and others in the Western world, in the United States in particular, who contend (1) that Communism is an absolute evil, (2) that it is morally wrong to compromise with evil, (3) that any attempt to negotiate compromises with the major Communist dictators is fruitless since their appetites are insatiable, and hence (4) that compromise with the Communist Camp is tantamount in the long run to appeasement and surrender.

Here is a moral impasse which no amount of debate can resolve. The issue goes to ultimate values and beliefs which divide individuals and cultures. However, one thing is quite clear: the extreme American view is unlikely to convince many leaders of the Uncommitted Nations.

The interchange between De Rusett and Appadorai suggests a further hypothesis, that the nuclear military stalemate which hardened in the later 1950's, and seemed likely to last indefinitely, not only provides an opportunity for uncommitted mediators but also indicates a positive need for a group of uncommitted nations willing to play this role, if any mitigation of East-West tension is to be achieved through the processes of negotiation. From this perspective, the West should not deplore the stand taken by the Uncommitted Nations, but rather welcome their intermediary role while striving to maintain the military equilibrium which will make that role more fruitful.

There is evidence that some such view is gaining ground in the capitals of Europe and America. It would doubtless gain more ground and be more convincing but for two conditions: One is the new nations' continuing identification of the Western Powers with colonialism, coupled with their seeming inability to appreciate that the Soviet government is repressing certain ethnic minorities within its own borders and domineering over the populations of a number of neighboring countries with a ruthlessness comparable to earlier European colonialism at its worst. The second condition that disturbs Western observers is the Communist infiltration that goes on inside the uncommitted nations (as elsewhere) and anxiety regarding the ability of these emerging political communities to cope with subversion despite their expressed intention to do so.

On the first issue, one has to recognize that, in Asian and African eyes, great significance attaches to the fact that all the disintegrating empires of our time are on the non-Communist side of the East-West alignment.

The colonial rule with which these peoples have had any experience has been *European* colonialism. Hence all the major Western states, and several lesser ones too, are identified in the minds of Africans and Asians (and to some extent Latin Americans too) as colonial Powers. The Soviet Union and China, on the contrary, are viewed as pioneers in the assault on colonialism, however unrealistic and illogical this attitude may seem to us in the West.

In European and American perspectives, this attitude seems both unrealistic and dangerous. Western spokesmen point to the Soviet government's ruthless repression of nationality in Estonia, Latvia, and Lithuania, to its persecution of the Jews, and to its savage reprisals in Hungary and elsewhere. Westerners emphasize the aggressive expansion of China into Tibet and its imperialistic probing for weak spots in Southeast Asia. But all to little apparent avail. Rational arguments make little headway in overcoming the nearly universal disposition within the emerging nations to distrust the West, and to accept at face value the propaganda of the self-appointed Communist champions of anticolonialism.

The consequence of this state of affairs is that American and European governments open any negotiation with the emerging nations under a psychological handicap that bears little relation to their own purposes and strategies or to those of the Communist Camp. This is simply one of the international "facts of life," one of the inescapable conditions of the contemporary international environment. This state of affairs will change only slowly at best; it may persist for a long time. How long may depend a good deal, it would appear, on how quickly and how smoothly the remaining vestiges of European colonialism are eradicated in Africa, and on the course of the savage racial struggle in the Union of South Africa.

On the second issue raised above, the issue of Communist influence in the emerging nations, the "major prophets" of Communism appear to believe that these communities are all destined to arrive eventually inside the Communist Camp. The prevailing anxiety in the West is twofold: (1) that the uncommitted nations will be tempted (for reasons explained in Chapter 15) to pattern their institutions after the Soviet model and thereby deliver themselves into the Communist Camp; and (2) that acceptance of Soviet (and increasingly, Chinese) capital aid and technical assistance will push them willy-nilly in the same direction.

One of the arguments frequently cited for giving American and West European aid and assistance to these nations is that this is one means of tying them politically as well as economically to the West and thereby preventing or checking their drift toward the Communist orbit.

On these issues, the positions of African and Asian leaders are generally quite specific. They insist on freedom to choose for themselves what forms of government and economy they will adopt. They also insist on freedom to accept desperately needed capital and technical assistance wherever they can get it. Rubles are nearly as useful to them as dollars— and rubles become more useful every year. Russian technical experts are received in numerous countries more cordially than those from America and Western Europe—a further manifestation of the bitter memories of former colonial rule. In certain countries, it is claimed that American effectiveness has been impaired because of the mediocrity of many of the experts sent out from the United States and because of their insistence on living apart in a style approaching as close as possible to what they have been accustomed at home.

There is no use blinking the facts and risks involved. Russian (and increasingly, Chinese) embassies and technical assistance missions everywhere are components of the apparatus of Communist expansion. In the words of W. A. Lewis (principal of University College in Jamaica, West Indies),

> in inviting Russia into their countries even though they fear it, [African] politicians are walking a tightrope, and they know it. A Soviet embassy is not just a center of cultural relations. The Russians bring in as many of their people as they are allowed to do, flood the country with propaganda, give aid and instructions to local Communists, and try to prepare the country for membership in the Communist bloc.
> African governments hope to evade trouble in two ways. First, by restricting the activities of the embassies. . . . The second safeguard is to ban native Communist parties. . . .

Lewis, like other competent Western observers, entertains no illusions regarding the risks which the emerging nations incur in their flirtations with Communist diplomats and technical experts. But he is likewise convinced that

> there is no point in trying to oppose the entry of Russia into Africa. This is impossible, and by alienating Africa from the West it will have the opposite effect to that which is intended. African nations will have Communist embassies. They will also have Soviet economic aid, and will regard as enemies any persons who try to prevent them having such aid. To attack African neutralism or to try to stand in the way of African relations with Communist states is to play right into the hands of Russia.
> The correct policy for the West is not to try directly to weaken African ties with Russia, but rather to strengthen ties with the West. Russia has nothing to offer that the West cannot offer in greater abundance. Indeed, the West has great advantages over Russia in

competing for African support. It starts with a great fund of good will, and a thousand ties of language, education, institutions, and culture; whereas the Africans fear Russia, and look to it for aid only as a last resort. If the Soviets win out in Africa it will be only because of Western arrogance combined with Western meanness. . . .*

Many in the United States and Europe, who accept at face value the avowed African desire and intention to become satellites of no foreign Power or bloc, nevertheless have doubts as to whether these weak communities in process of radical transformations can in fact sustain their chosen uncommitted position. The argument is that these emerging nations cannot have it both ways. To accept capital and technical assistance from a powerful nation puts the recipient in some degree under the political influence of the granting Power. Historical experience is cited in support of this conclusion. In numerous instances, economic involvement has lead to serious impairment of the political independence of the weaker nation.

The channels of such influence are many. The Great Power may provide preferential markets for the exports of the recipient country. It may provide machinery or other capital goods, thereby rendering the recipient dependent on the giver for spare parts and service. The Great Power may provide bank credit and long-term loans and other investments. As Dr. Lewis emphasizes above, it may flood the country with technical experts who double as propagandists and subversionists.

Under conditions widely prevailing before World War II, such entanglements nearly always compromised more or less seriously the weaker party to the relationship. It is at least arguable that this result is less certain under conditions prevailing these days. One new factor is the enormous increase in the number of modernizing nations who share a common interest in obtaining aid without giving political hostages, so to speak, in return. A second factor is the existence of the United Nations, through which the new nations (as well as the older ones belatedly caught up in the modernizing process) are able to exert, through sheer numbers, some restraint on the purveyors of capital and technical assistance. Third, the United Nations and its associated organizations have themselves become administrators of capital and technical assistance, a channel which (if it continues to develop) provides a further check on the use of aid as a means of pressuring the emerging nations into either the Communist Camp or the Anti-Communist Coalition. Finally, perhaps the crucial factor is the Soviet-American military stalemate. In spite of superficial indications to the con-

* From "Neutralism in Africa," by W. A. Lewis, in *The Reporter*, November 10, 1960. Copyright 1960 by The Reporter Magazine Co., New York; reproduced by permission of publisher and author.

trary, this stalemate (while it continues) sets limits to the risks which Russian and American statesmen are likely to take in pressing their demands on the uncommitted nations. Such prudence and caution tend to enhance the capacity of the weak to resist demands, blandishments, and threats which, in prenuclear days, were repeatedly backed up by force or ominous display of force.

A neutralist bloc?

The Yugoslav ambassador at the close of his lecture (see page 656 above) was asked whether the Uncommitted Nations constituted a third international bloc, alongside the Communist Camp and the Anti-Communist Coalition. His reply follows:

> The uncommitted countries are not a bloc of powers. First of all, they have no power. Not only do they not want to, but they cannot build up a third bloc. If they wanted to take part in alliances, they would have to join one or the other side. That much for blocs in the sense of the military and political alliances in world competition. But, in attempting to influence the course of world affairs, the uncommitted do represent a group; their representatives get together from time to time, and there is a permanent cooperation between them. I would say, therefore, that it is not an organization, not even a group with permanent membership. On certain issues in the United Nations, there is quite a number of these countries who agree to take a joint position, because they believe this to be in their interest, as well as in the interest of the areas they represent. On some other issues, five or ten of them cooperate even more closely, not only in the United Nations but also outside it, keeping common attitudes on problems or crises, be that in Asia, Africa, or the Middle East. However, these countries have no illusions that they could build up a real bloc. . . .*

Whether the ambassador's response is satisfactory depends somewhat on how one defines a bloc. Manifestly the Uncommitted Nations do not constitute a bloc in any military sense. Furthermore, they are not linked together by a common ideology that goes beyond the vague tenets of nationalism, a determination to modernize their societies, and refusal to join either side in the East-West struggle. Nor is there any comprehensive pattern of alliances or other treaties defining their relations to each other as a group or their posture to other groupings in the Society of Nations.

But that is not the whole story. As the Yugoslav ambassador noted, representatives of the Uncommitted Nations are developing habits of consultation and concerted action on a range of issues. There have been several carefully staged meetings, with public addresses, quiet backstage

* From *The Annals,* July 1961; reproduced by permission.

diplomacy, and formal resolutions. There is increasing intercapital visiting and conferring by heads of government. There is caucusing before voting in the Assembly of the United Nations. There is a regular Asian-African Caucusing Group; and also smaller caucusing groups of Arab states and African states.

All these patterns are still fluid. But certain features begin to emerge. The Belgrade Conference (1961) demonstrated that a shared sense of weakness could bring together such left-wing regimes as Tito's in Yugoslavia and Castro's in Cuba with such right-wing governments as those of Cyprus, Cambodia, Ethiopia, Nepal, and Morocco. The Belgrade Conference also revealed close to unanimity on desire to mitigate the rigors of the Cold War.

Critics, especially those who believe that military force sets the patterns of international politics, may ask: So what? To this question, there can be no firm answer as yet. But it can be said, as we have said repeatedly in this book, that the East-West military stalemate provides an unprecedented oportunity for these weak voices to be heard; and that the more successful the United States and its allies are in their efforts to maintain a military equilibrium, however precarious and dangerous it may be, the larger will become the freedom of maneuver and the potential international influence of the Uncommitted Nations, If the military stalemate continues, and if the Uncommitted Nations produce statesmen of sufficient caliber, it would appear by no means improbable that they will play a progressively more influential role in the United Nations and at other points of leverage in the international political system.

CHAPTER TWENTY-THREE

Blueprints for the Future

ANYONE WHO HAS read this book should entertain no lingering doubt that we are living through a period of serious troubles. We are caught up in a multifaceted revolution which has no counterpart in human history. Mid-twentieth-century Americans are wont to identify Communism as the source of our troubles. For most Americans, abhorrence of Communism is so deep and so consuming as to crowd from our minds other revolutionary changes which have transformed and continue to transform our world.

Earlier chapters have dealt with some of these changes in the context of current international politics. We have emphasized the transcendent importance of rapidly enlarging scientific knowledge and its innumerable engineering applications. We have described some of the impacts of a runaway technology on geographic space and configuration, on the supply of natural resources, and on man's ability to surmount climatic and other natural obstacles. We have recounted the effect of rising living standards (which derive largely from technological advance) on the growth and distribution of populations, resulting in our day in a rate of human increase that may yet confirm the gloomy predictions of old Malthus. We have probed into the processes of social, economic, and political change which have disrupted traditional societies, raised human demands and expectations, and profoundly altered human relationships throughout the world. We have given attention to the political ideologies, the moral and legal norms, and the institutions through which many of the processes of social change are channeled. We have described the successive transformations of the international political system, tracing its evolution from a system of European monarchies to a Europe-centered system of nation-states to a Washington- and Moscow-centered bipolar system to the present fluid phase in which a new polycentrism is being superimposed upon the military bipolarity of Washington and Moscow. We have given special attention to the weapons systems which have added a wholly new dimension to the interactions of nations. Had the Communist revolutions never occurred, it seems likely that our generation would still have had to cope with most of the disruptive changes that confront us on every hand.

It is mankind's melancholy predicament that disruptive social revolutions on many fronts should have been accompanied by such lethal by-products as thermonuclear explosives, ballistic rockets, chemical and biological weapons—with climatic control (which might prove to be the most decisive weapon of all) already on the technological horizon. It would have been difficult enough to cope with social revolution in its numerous forms, without the added perils arising from this almost unimaginable increase in destructive capability.

It may be a cliché but it is none the less true to say that the scientists and engineers have created a Frankenstein monster which threatens to destroy everything, its creators included. Thus far, as is all too obvious, no one has found a way to control this monster. For the time being, our fate appears to depend mainly upon the rationality and prudence of the politicians and generals who control the superweapons on both sides of the Iron Curtain. There is widespread and probably well-grounded fear that a mistaken calculation, a human failure, or sheer accident will yet touch off the big bang, from which no one can reasonably hope to escape, and which conceivably might transmute modern man and all his works into radioactive dust drifting above a deserted and uninhabitable planet.

Thus far in the text and readings, a continuous effort has been made to keep the perspective contemplative and analytical. The book has presented a frame of concepts designed to help in identifying the processes and basic forces of international politics in our time. With this background one should perhaps be better equipped to choose among the many different proposals offered these days for coping with the successive and multi-faceted international crises. It is manifestly impossible in these final pages to deal comprehensively with these recommendations to policy makers. What follows, therefore, are simply a few samples selected either because they represent somewhat contradictory approaches to, or fresh challenging perspectives on, the international issues confronting the United States today.

The first sample is from a report prepared in 1956 for the United States Senate. This report was prepared in the Center for International Studies at the Massachusetts Institute of Technology. It has become known as the Millikan-Rostow Proposal (from the names of its principal authors, Max Millikan and W. W. Rostow, professors in the Massachusetts Institute of Technology). The report deals with conditions as these appeared several years ago. We do not know to what extent the authors of the report would modify their proposal in the light of the rapidly changing world situation. But they outlined a position in 1956 that has many supporters today, a position based upon the premise that—

Military deterrence is not enough *

We take the most fundamental American national interest to be the physical and political survival of the United States and the continued evolution of America as a society committed in its institutions, in its relations among its citizens, and in its external performance to the ideals of the Declaration of Independence, the Constitution, and the Bill of Rights. It follows that the task of American foreign policy is to foster a world environment congenial not merely to our survival but to the continuing development of America as a free society.

Specifically, American foreign policy must meet a twofold test:

First, it must prevent any diminution of relative United States military strength which might encourage a potentially hostile Power to conclude either that it might "win" a big war or that it could threaten or force us into degenerative step-by-step appeasement and isolation. Further, the United States must minimize the likelihood of war by "miscalculation"; and it must give us the capability to win a war, should one be forced on us, on politically advantageous terms.

Second, our strategy must not require us, in order to preserve a stable balance of power, to sustain a posture corrosive of our central values, procedures, and institutions. We must avoid the dilemma of being forced, for the sake of survival, to stunt our vitality as a free society. . . .

In the current context of the cold war, the meaning and implications of the first requirement, a balance of military power, are evident.

First, we must maintain sufficient offensive and defensive power to enable us to respond to a Soviet attack on the United States or on NATO by certain and devastating bombardment of the Soviet Union. We must never allow the Soviet Union a reasonable prospect of destroying our retaliatory capability by surprise attack or of neutralizing it by means of a superior Soviet air defense.

Second, we must, on military grounds alone, deny the Communist bloc any extension of its control in Eurasia. Any expansion of Soviet hegemony in East or West Eurasia could well lead to an imbalance in military power which would threaten us with ultimate military defeat. At least for the near future, even our nuclear retaliatory

* From "The Objectives of United States Economic Assistance Programs," in *Foreign Aid Program*, prepared for the Special Committee to Study the Foreign Aid Program, U. S. Senate, pursuant to S. Res. 185, 84th Cong., and S. Res. 35 and 141, 85th Congress. Government Printing Office, Washington, D. C., July 1957.

capacity hinges on overseas airbases which would be neutralized by any serious erosion of free world power in Eurasia. In the longer run, it is difficult to conceive of the United States maintaining a tenable military balance in the face of the overwhelming resource and manpower superiority of a more or less unified and hostile Eurasia. . . .

The above tasks constitute what has come to be called the policy of deterrence. Deterrence requires that we muster all means at our disposal to convince the Soviet bloc that neither overt nor "fuzzy" aggression will pay. In particular, it requires that we develop a capability to respond to local and limited pressure, if we so choose, by local and limited means. . . .

But deterrence alone will not do. It suggests a future of virtually endless cold war, of perpetual siege, with survival dependent on a costly and nightmarish weapons race. This kind of a future—with ballistic missiles which can reach targets halfway around the earth in minutes and are powerful enough to obliterate the largest of cities and poison areas the size of New Jersey; with small and immature states controlling weapons which could annihilate the greatest— is a future that fails to meet our essential interests. It implies an American political and military posture which, if sustained over two or three decades, is bound to damage the defining qualities of our society.

Moreover, there is a second, and deeper reason why a policy relying on deterrence alone is inadequate. Its exclusive focus on countering Soviet-initiated action ignores the real possibility that the two-thirds of the world's population outside the Iron Curtain just emerging into political and economic awareness may become an independent source of turbulence and change, that interaction among the "uncommitted" countries could overnight threaten the precarious stability of the East-West balance. It also neglects the longest run evolution of those countries which within two or three decades could render military deterrence either superfluous or futile. It fails, by default, to use what margin of influence the United States can muster to effect that evolution in our interest. It leaves the nonmilitary play largely to the Communists. . . . To avoid losing the cold war we must look beyond deterrence. . . .

Three themes of unequal import run through the rather discordant harmony of American thought, talk, and action of the last ten years germane to "resolution of the cold war." One rather thin proposition, which disappeared early, simply begged the issue: "Let's build situations of strength from which to negotiate" was a call to desperately needed action, and in 1949 it was surely putting first things first; but it avoided the problems of what we were to negotiate about, of what kinds of carrots and sticks we were to use to strike what kinds of bargains.

The second rather shrill theme has appeared only now and then. "Preventive war" and "liberation" are two of the labels by which it may be identified. Its essential characteristic is an implicit commitment to invoke force, or at least to threaten use of force, not just to contain or deter but to change the geographical status quo. In its more extreme form it never received serious consideration. Even during the period of U.S. monopoly in nuclear weapons the notion of trying for a decisive settlement by threatening to initiate atomic war was clearly not to be seriously contemplated. Quite apart from whether we in fact had the capability to base an ultimatum on a threat to launch a nuclear offensive—given our dependence on foreign bases this is at least doubtful—such an act, no matter how favorable its power consequences, would have been an inconceivable corruption of the American interest. An overwhelming majority of Americans understand this and sense that "preventive war" is a nonsense alternative. As of 1956 [and even more, the 1960's] this understanding is reenforced by the Soviet atomic delivery capacity. . . .

The third and much more important theme of resolution emerged as the major premise of the original containment doctrine as articulated by Mr. George Kennan in his celebrated "X" article. It was essentially a strategy of "contain and wait." If we are successful in effectively containing the Soviets, so it was argued, autonomous historical forces will inevitably bring about internal changes in the Soviet empire which will cause Soviet Russia to withdraw from her forward positions in the center of Europe, turn back on herself, and cease to be a threat to our security.

The trouble with this view is not that it is wrong, but that it is only half right. Kennan was superbly far-sighted in emphasizing the possibility of change in Soviet policy once opportunities for expansion by military means were blocked. But our attention has been focused so intensively on the bilateral relations of the Communist bloc and the Western alliance that we have failed to reckon with the tremendous potentialities of self-generated change and evolution outside the bloc and the alliance.

The point of containment is to convince the Kremlin that the game for Eurasian power hegemony is hopeless. This requires not merely a sustained demonstration that the Western allies can and will prevent Soviet takeover of the border areas. It requires, above all, that the Kremlin become convinced that the newly emerging societies of Eurasia [to which Africa would now have to be added], in search of accelerated solutions to their own problems, will not of their own account opt for one or another variant of the "Communist way." Where containment falls short is in not recognizing that the urgent search of the "uncommitted" nations offers opportunities for American action far beyond containment. . . .

This view rests on two crucial facts about the world of 1956 [and even more, of the 1960's] and on a proposition.

The first fact is that one-third of the world's peoples have come to share a determination to overcome, and quickly, centuries of social and political inertia and economic stagnation in order to achieve a larger national dignity and, in particular, to create expanding economies and rising standards of life. Embarked upon revolutionary changes in their modes of life, these peoples—including some who are our military allies—are as yet "uncommitted." Most are uncommitted in terms of the day-to-day alignments of the cold war; more important, almost all are uncommitted in terms of the kinds of societies they want to create.

The second fact is that the United States is a country of immense and fast increasing wealth, and hence in a position to deploy abroad substantial resources while continuing steadily to raise our own standards of living. Further, we have developed more successfully than most nations social, political, and economic techniques for realizing widespread popular desires for change without either compulsion or social disorganization. Although these techniques must be adapted, country by country, to fit particular local conditions, they represent a considerable potential for steering the world's newly aroused human energies in constructive directions.

The proposition is that a comprehensive and sustained program of American economic assistance aimed at helping the free underdeveloped countries can, in the short run, materially reduce the danger of conflict triggered by aggressive minor powers, and can, in say two or three decades, result in an overwhelming preponderance of societies with a successful record of solving their problems without resort to coercion or violence. The establishment of such a preponderance of stable, effective, and democratic societies gives the best promise of a favorable settlement of the cold war and of a peaceful, progressive world environment. . . .

The Millikan-Rostow Proposal has evoked various kinds of responses during the years since it first appeared. One of the more negative rejoinders has come from Arnold Wolfers (director of the Washington Center of Foreign Policy Research). In a statement prepared for the President's special committee to study the foreign aid program in 1959 (the Draper Committee), Wolfers takes issue with several theses which in one way or another appear to him to undercut an order of priorities in which—

Military defense comes first *

Many people, both inside and outside the United States, are disturbed that so much expenditure goes into building up defenses against the Soviet or Communist threat when millions of men and women are living in a state of dire poverty. In terms of American values, or human values generally, they would naturally prefer to see their country engage in economic rather than in military aid—as

* From "Questions of Priority in Mutual Security Allocation," published as Annex-B to the *Composite Report* of the President's Committee to Study the United States Military Assistance Program. Government Printing Office, Washington, D. C., August 1959.

they would prefer a national budget devoted to social welfare instead of military preparedness. . . .

However, whether the United States can afford to engage in costly humanitarian tasks abroad, given the limited funds likely to be available for foreign aid even under the best circumstances, depends obviously on the requirements for pressing nonhumanitarian tasks, and on the priorities to be allotted to the various tasks falling under foreign aid.

A second motivation behind the demand for a shift to economic aid is less clearly or not exclusively humanitarian. The Millikan-Rostow school of thought argues forcefully in favor of an aid program designed to assist all countries "in achieving a steady, self-sustained rate of growth" irrespective of the "short-run political interests of this country."

The assumption here is that "self-sustaining growth," once attained will not merely relieve human poverty, but "resolve the cold war," "render military deterrence superfluous," "convince the Kremlin that the game for Eurasia power hegemony is hopeless" and thus, in the long run, accomplish more effectively the defense task that is presently assigned to military aid and short-run economic aid.

It is necessary to determine whether the assumptions on which the MIT study rests are valid if a decision is to be reached on the relative emphasis to be placed on short-range military and economic aid, on the one hand, or long-range economic development aid on the other.

Pressure comes from a third source . . . [a group of Senators who have contended that] the primary task of the aid program . . . consisted in "strengthening the resistance of the other nations to totalitarianism." They see the danger now faced by the United States and the free world as a Sino-Soviet threat to individual freedom and civil liberties, rather than as a threat to the independence of nations from Sino-Soviet control. As a consequence their fear that military assistance may increase what they regard as the chief danger, by contributing to the maintenance in power of "regimes which have lacked broad support within their own countries we have assisted," by creating "a militaristic image of the United States" and by "creating in them perpetuating military hierarchies . . . which . . . may endanger the very value of individual freedom which we seek to safeguard."

Here the question must be answered whether, in the light of the threat of further Sino-Soviet expansion, the United States can afford to give priority to the promotion of American democratic ideals and to the defense of individual freedom against autocratic government, Communist or other, even where such defense would tend to increase the Sino-Soviet military menace. . . . The problem here is not whether the development of democracy in other countries is desirable when the necessary preconditions exist—which nobody would deny—but whether in the face of the Sino-Soviet threat the United States can afford to combat non-Communist autocratic government in situations where the short-run result would be to weaken the military defenses against the Sino-Soviet threat. . . .

The dangers of the cold war are present dangers. To meet them, efforts of the most exacting kind are needed that can be expected to produce results immediately, or within a brief period of time. Only if and after they have been met can there be room for efforts that will bear fruit at best two or more decades hence.

Concerning the short-run effects, controversy has arisen as to whether changes in the circumstances characterizing the East-West struggle have not made military assistance less valuable than it was some years ago, and economic assistance more urgent than before. . . . The United States must, it is said, be prepared . . . to meet competition in this new field rather than to emphasize the race for adequate military defenses.

Undoubtedly, East-West competition in economic aid has become a fact, but it may be asked whether it constitutes a substitute for the earlier military competition or has merely added a new dimension to the struggle. . . . The Soviet and Chinese governments can return to the method of military expansion at any time since they have not reduced but continue to increase their military striking power.

According to another argument, American strategic doctrine places chief reliance on long-range strategic nuclear striking power rather than on local forces of countries receiving military assistance. Moreover, since allied local military power is alleged to have lost much of its former value, therefore, it becomes more important to supply friends and allies with economic staying power that will help them resist indirect conquest by infiltration and subversion than to assist in building up local forces.

If we leave aside for the moment the question of whether economic aid is regularly a better means of warding off the dangers of indirect conquest, it should be noted that the strategy of deterrence and defense through strategic nuclear power is meeting mounting criticism, with many experts arguing that, in the light of the high degree of nuclear stalemate, the possibility of limited military engagements that require on-the-spot local forces should in the future be given more attention.

The argument of the eight Senators is also relevant to this point. . . . They assume that the issue today is a struggle between totalitarianism or autocracy on the one hand, and individual freedom or democracy, as we understand it, on the other, rather than a struggle between two antagonistic blocs, one of which is seeking to upset the present world balance of power in its favor. If this assumption were correct, only such aid would be justified as promised to promote democracy and freedom, and it is more than likely that economic rather than military aid would serve this purpose, although neither may be able to stem the tide of autocracy in underdeveloped countries.

Against this argument it should be said that if the struggle in fact were essentially concerned with autocracy in all of its forms, and not with Sino-Soviet expansion and control, the United States and its Western allies would have lost the battle for the time being. The West today is a democratic island in a sea of autocracy, though autocracy varying widely in degree and character, Communist here, Fascist or military elsewhere.

The struggle has not been lost for good, however, as long as the Sino-Soviet bloc remains contained within its present borders. In time many of the autocracies may become liberalized. Meanwhile, although foreign aid should be administered in a way that will promote rather than hinder a process of liberalization, democratic values would not be served if the means of containment were neglected and these countries were allowed to fall into the arms of Soviet totalitarianism, thereby becoming enemies of the West, and losing most of their chance of future liberalization.

In the defense field it makes sense to distinglish between aid intended to help countries protect themselves against *external* Sino-Soviet military attack and aid intended to help them withstand *internal* events and pressures that would withdraw them into the Soviet orbit even in the absence of any external attack. The first, which covers both military deterrence and defense, might be called aid in the context of "hot war strategy," the latter, aid in the context of "cold war strategy."

In terms of hot war strategy, there can be no substitute for military aid (including defense support) if the aim is to improve the abilities of indigenous forces of the recipient country to stand up against an external military attack. . . . Military assistance to the countries that are exposed to Sino-Soviet military attack must be looked at with a critical eye. . . . The area of the recipient country may not be worth the cost of its defense; or no amount of aid within reason could build up local forces to a level at which they would be both able and willing to take up arms against a Sino-Soviet attacker; or better military results, dollar for dollar, may come from expenditure on the American Defense Establishment; or the effort required to build up indigenous forces adequate for external defense may wreck the re- cipient country by destroying its internal political, social, or economic balance. However, where the conditions are favorable, military as- sistance adds to the defensive power of the anti-Soviet coalition and thus to the security of the United States. . . .

On occasion it makes sense to give external military defense assistance to countries that are in no danger from the Sino-Soviet bloc at all but whose survival is necessary to the stability of a regional power balance. Military assistance to Israel or Jordan falls under this heading since it serves the purpose of balancing the military power of non-Communist countries and, by making them capable of mutual deterrence, of pacifying the non-Communist world.

In respect to cold war strategy where the issue is internal rather than external defense, the relative merits of military aid, and economic aid, and the character to give to either, raise difficult and controversial questions. Unless they are answered, no decision can be reached for or against a shift to more economic aid, or from short-range economic aid to more long-range economic development assistance.

There would seem to be three distinct ways in which countries might fall under Soviet control by events short of war, or at least refuse to be aligned with the West: (*a*) The government in power may decide to shift the allegiance of its country to the side of the Soviet bloc, or to choose a course of "positive neutrality" favorable to the Soviets, or, finally to give up ties with the West based on collective defense agreements in favor of genuine neutrality. (*b*) Opposition parties may come into power and replace a pro-Western or neutral government by a pro-Soviet government. (*c*) Communist forces within the country may arise to power, presumably on the basis of considerable revolutionary public support, and turn the country into a Soviet or Red Chinese satellite. . . .

Not all of these dangers are present in each of the countries that are present or potential recipients of U.S. aid. The governments of [South Korea or Taiwan] will not and, in fact, cannot swing to the Soviet side or turn neutral. In Europe, the only conceivable danger would be a shift of a NATO country from alliance to genuine neutrality which would raise the question of the price it would be worth paying to prevent such a shift.

Almost everywhere, there are opposition forces with more or less anti-Western sentiments but whose ascendancy to power would not everywhere be sufficiently detrimental to free world defenses for the United States to let itself be blackmailed into giving unlimited support to the "friendly" in-group.

The danger of a rise of indigenous communism, supported by the Sino-Soviet bloc, differs greatly from country to country. It, too, is frequently exaggerated by a government in power as a means of obtaining whatever aid it wants. It is also doubtful in many instances whether such aid will stem the Communist tide. Some aid, in fact, tends to increase Communist strength in the recipient country, because it bolsters an unpopular regime.

It is often argued that the economic poverty of the mass of the population is the source of the major internal threat to Western interests. . . . However, of the three types of internal threats to the West listed above, none can be definitely and universally traced to the misery or aspirations of the mass of the people though a dissatisfied and rebellious populace may be a factor behind any one of the three threats. As a rule, the most effective type of aid will be aid that promises to give the greatest internal stability to the country and the greatest satisfaction to those elite groups who are eager to keep the country out of Communist or Soviet control.

In many instances military assistance may be the best means of bringing about such stability and satisfaction. A strong military establishment can be an element of order; it gives the government authority and prestige; it offers to many a chance of social and technical advancement. However, not all demands for military assistance or for "internal order and immunity against communism through military strength" are justified in terms of American interest. Military autocracies are not always stable; they may provoke rebellion led by the Communists. They are not always reliable; there have been cases where the leaders of the armed forces or influential junior officers have gone over to the Soviet camp (Syria? Iraq?). Excessive militarization may break the economies of weak countries, or may arouse fears in neighboring non-Communist countries, or split the international non-Communist camp (Pakistan-India). . . .

Short-run economic aid, or what can be called either economic emergency aid or economic defense aid, has a vital part to play in the defense against the internal dangers mentioned earlier. Here Soviet competition in economic aid becomes a major factor, though it is not the only justification for such aid.

Soviet economic competition or no competition, there is reason to fear that governments in grave financial monetary or commercial difficulties may be overthrown, or may look elsewhere for support, and that economic crises may lead to the kinds of dangerous unrest on which the Communists can capitalize. Therefore, economic emergency aid . . . to help countries overcome monetary, fiscal, or balance of payment troubles, is an important defense tool. Its significance has increased since the Soviet Union entered the economic field and now stands ready to offer emergency aid if help from the West is not forthcoming, or is not adequate. . . .

The idea of long-run economic development aid to underdeveloped countries is not only extremely appealing, because it suggests help to the underprivileged and represents a constructive effort, but also because it conforms with long-run American interests. It promises advantages to the "haves," the countries of high living standards, similar to those that slum clearance offers to the privileged parts of an urban community. However, the benefits that flow from the actual completion and successful operation of economic development schemes, for which the Aswan Dam [in Egypt] can serve as a symbol, are likely to translate themselves into benefits for the mass of the impoverished sections of a people only after decades, as the MIT report emphasizes. Therefore, even if all the assumptions of the MIT report were accepted—that the recipient country will, in fact, devote the development aid to development and not to current uses, that it has and employs the necessary skills to bring the projects to fruition, that it will survive the long interim period as a free country—the material benefits of industrialization which lie in a more or less remote future cannot in themselves remove or lessen the present dangers of the cold war. . . .

Here one runs into a serious dilemma. From the point of view of cold war strategy, a relatively phony "economic development" project, such as the paving of the streets of Kabul [capital of Afganistan] by the Soviets, may be more successful than a very costly but in the long run sound irrigation project. . . . Probably, it will be found that the competitive value of the phony is short-lived and that sound projects, if properly publicized and attractive to the elites of a country, will pay higher dividends even in the cold war.

What needs to be stressed, however, is the fallacy of thinking that the time has come to shift from "unconstructive" defense aid (military aid and short-term economic development aid) to "constructive" sound long-term economic development aid. The latter can at best have a psychological side-effect that will be valuable to the present and exacting defense effort imposed by the cold war. It is also likely to have unfavorable effects, like creating social dislocation, increasing a restless industrial proletariat, or undermining an established cultural and religious order. . . .

It may seem out of place to raise doubts about the value of underwriting the economic development of friendly but underdeveloped countries or to suggest limiting such aid, as a rule, to the amounts either needed to meet Soviet competition in development aid or likely to produce short-range psychological capital for the donor. Particularly with respect to India, it is argued that unless India, through our assistance, can match Red China's economic development, the cause of the free world and its way of life will be damaged beyond repair throughout the underdeveloped parts of the world. To this, it can be answered, that unfortunately no amount of economic aid will be able to supply India with the equivalent capital and working hours that the Communist regime can extort from its people. It can also be suggested that if external economic aid by the United States helps India over its short-run emergencies, gives her technical and educational assistance and meets Soviet psychological competition by some striking demonstrations of Western skill, the United States may be doing as much as it can to meet the dangers flowing from a Red Chinese victory in the productivity. Similar considerations would apply to other countries in which the government like that of India is genuinely concerned with economic development. Where it is not—and cannot be induced to be so concerned—favorable psychological side effects are the only worthwhile results to be anticipated from economic development aid anyway; here even the resort to "phonies" may be expedient.

If one may take Wolfers' argument at face value, he would appear to favor giving highest priority to the geographical containment of the Communist Realm by military means, and supporting anti-Communist regimes, however autocratic they may be, provided they give promise of internal stability and continued loyalty to the anti-Communist cause. These and other issues appear in somewhat different perspective in an article by Marshall D. Shulman (of the Russian Research Center at Harvard University). In this article, published in the summer of 1961, Shulman examines—

The real nature of the Soviet challenge *

Until now, if our mental image of the Soviet problem could have been projected onto a screen, it would have resembled an old-fashioned newsreel, jerky and strident. From one week to the next, our attention has been nervously shifting—from the missile gap to "prestige"; from gross national products to "the hearts and minds of men"; from space to paramilitary forces, always with the feeling that *this* was the key to the whole thing. From week to week, we have demanded to know "Who's ahead?" as though there were somewhere a giant scoreboard, now giving points to the Russians for the first man in space; later, it may be, giving points to us for the first man on the moon. . . . Discussions of our foreign policy reflect some widely prevalent and profoundly serious misconceptions about the essential nature of the conflict, which urgently need to be clarified if we are to move on to a more effective stage in our response to the Soviet challenge.

One of the most serious of these current misapprehensions stems from the effort of a number of prominent and respected people, foremost among them Walter Lippmann in this country, and some of our British friends, to find some basis for a territorial stabilization of our relations with the Soviet Union.

Their argument is that our world power position has diminished, relatively speaking, and that our political positions should be brought into line with the new power relationships. They reason that our present commitments around the world were established on the basis of the doctrine that came to be known as "massive retaliation," which in turn rested upon our unchallenged strategic superiority. Since our strategic superiority has now been neutralized by growing Soviet strategic power, according to this view, we should reduce our commitments to defend various areas, and encourage them to settle into neutralized status, whereupon the international situation could be stabilized in the familiar nineteenth-century balance-of-power style. Both Soviet and United States power and commitments would be limited to areas close to and vital to our respective homelands, and the system would be in balance, cushioned by neutral territories where we would contend with each other according to self-limited rules of conflict.

The difficulty with this approach, and with any other effort to establish a territorial settlement with the Soviet Union, is that it is based upon an archaic conception of power in spatial terms. It does not sufficiently appreciate the dynamic political element of Soviet policy.

The challenge of the Soviet Union is not the same as that once

* From "The Real Nature of the Soviet Challenge," in *New York Times Magazine*, July 16, 1961. Copyright 1961 by the New York Times Co., New York; reproduced by permission of publisher and author.

presented by the rising young nation-states of Germany and Italy to the British balance-of-power system on the continent of Europe. Soviet dynamism includes, but is more than, the bursting energy of a nation-state entering upon a virile stage of its development.

The essential characteristic of Soviet dynamism is that it transcends the plane of nation-state relations, and is closely bound to anticipated changes within the social systems it is dealing with. The central conception of Soviet policy, and the distinctive source of its dynamism, is that the world is in a process of transition; that our social order is no longer effective in the changing environment, and is therefore in a process of disintegration and replacement.

This dynamic commitment gives a non-spatial dimension to calculations of Soviet power. It requires of us an exercise of political imagination, which can be illustrated by the way one looks at maps.

Behind the familiar multi-colored representation of two-dimensional territorial divisions on a conventional map, it is now necessary to visualize a third dimension, projecting—in depth—images of the seething interplay of political and social forces particular to the areas involved. To this must be added a fourth dimension, representing the changes, with the passage of time, within these states and societies, and in their relations with each other.

Most of us will find doing this for a year or even a month ahead hard enough to do, but, in analyzing Soviet policy, it is necessary to try to think in terms of decades.

This is not to say that Soviet policy moves according to a precise timetable, or that it is always predetermined and foresighted. But only if we fully appreciate that Soviet policy is deeply rooted in a commitment to what Moscow regards as an inevitable process of social change, can we understand that relations with Russia resist stabilization in territorial terms. A stabilization obtained by agreement on territorial interests—as, for example, in Berlin—can be expected to be effective only for limited periods while the Soviet Union is consolidating recent gains. Khrushchev has explicitly described for us his conception of a status quo agreement. He sees it, in effect, as a movable partition which would be successively adjusted to accommodate the inevitable process of change.

The reason we are now facing a series of erupting situations in various parts of the world is not because our doctrine of massive retaliation has been weakened by Soviet missiles. Massive retaliation was never a sensible sanction to protect these areas from Communist infiltration, and would not protect them now, even if there were no question about our strategic superiority. The eruptions arise from the juncture of the rising ferment in these areas, and from the effective Soviet use of this ferment.

While it is certainly correct to say that we should be clearer than we have been about where a military defense is required and where the urgent vulnerabilities are political and social, it is wrong to think that this is required by a "change in the balance of power," or that this can be expected to produce a geopolitical stabilization. The primary reason why a clarification of our policies along these lines is required is that the Soviet leaders for the past five or six years have been increasing their efforts to channel the forces of social change in the world in a direction which they call "socialism," but which in fact involves the unlimited spread of the Soviet hegemony, and this we have no real choice but to resist.

Here is the nub of the conflict. We are resisting the Soviet version of change—let us be clear—not in the name of "no change," and not to spread American capitalism or control around the world, but because the independence of other nations from Soviet domination is vitally important to us.

So long as this dynamic commitment remains at the heart of Soviet policy, we cannot avoid a fundamental conflict of interest. In time, this dynamism may be moderated. Until then, we must try if we can to wage the conflict on less dangerous planes than war, but we cannot expect the situation to be stabilized by a contraction of our periphery.

Another area of misconception concerns the military component of the Soviet challenge. Some Americans think of the Soviet challenge only in terms of military conquest. Others seem blind to the role that military power plays in Soviet policy. We need a framework of thought which can deal with the military and nonmilitary elements of the Soviet challenge not as a matter of either/or but of both/and.

What does *effective* national power mean in the present state of the world?

Quantitative comparisons of missiles, aircraft, men under arms or gross national products do not give us a direct index of relative national power in the world today. These factors are all vitally important, but they are not automatically decisive in determining the relative capability of the Soviet Union and ourselves to influence significant events.

The Soviet approach to national power is a deeply political one. That is to say, it depends for its effectiveness not upon the automatic effect of any of the conventional components of power, but upon the skill and the insight with which these are used to relate underlying forces and attitudes in the world to Soviet interests.

The bitter lesson of Laos has been partly—but only partly—the effectiveness of Communist guerrilla tactics, with weapons and training supplied from the outside. But why was it that the Laotians whom the Communists were supporting had the will to fight, while those to whom we gave our support did not? Was it not because the Soviet Union had succeeded in identifying itself with what many Laotians ardently desired—a better life, "independence," freedom from corruption and exploitation, association with the "wave of the future"?

What is involved is a kind of international jujitsu. The Soviet Union uses local sources of energy as multipliers of its own efforts. This is true not only in the underdeveloped parts of the world but in Europe and Japan as well.

What are these underlying forces? Foremost among them is nationalism, not only in Asia and Africa but also in the advanced industrial areas. Many people in this country are inclined to underestimate the present potency of this force, because they would like to see the world progress to a stage of broader allegiance. "The banner of national independence," as Stalin reminded his followers in 1952, still quickens more pulses the world over than any other cause, and, ironically, the banner has been securely grasped by the Communists.

The technological revolution is another such force. The instant world-wide communication of ideas, the simultaneous organization of demonstrations the world over, the rapid transportatation of goods and people, the symbolic threat of new weapons—these are all illustrative of the ways the Soviets have used the new technology in international politics.

The powerful appeal of economic development, and with it the awakening of a restless impulse for rapid social change in the underdeveloped countries, is another such force. There are still others, including the population explosion and the disintegration of old colonial relationships. In addition, there are powerful political attitudes, such as the strong peace sentiment around the world, neutralism, feelings of hostility toward the United Statees and the emotional revulsion against imperialism, as fact and as symbol. All these are sources of energy which Soviet policy seeks to channel.

What is most striking, in considering the application of Soviet policy to any particular area, such as Cuba or Laos, is the orchestrated use of a variety of ways of manipulating local energies. In each area, the Soviets seek to make use of influential individuals or groups whose interests can—at least for the time being—be associated with Russia's.

With them—whether they be the Pathet Lao in Laos, the Left Socialists in Japan, the *Fidelistas* in Cuba, or some of the nationalist figures in Indonesia, Iraq or Egypt—the Soviet Union seeks political alliances built on powerful local issues. Soviet support varies according to circumstances—in some cases, weapons, military training and organized cadres (as in the U.A.R., Iraq, Afghanistan, Indonesia, Cuba and Morocco); in others, economic aid, technical specialists and cultural indoctrination, especially of the next generation of leaders (as in India, Africa and Latin America). In addition, Soviet policy offers local leaders prestige, recognition and the backing on the world stage of Soviet diplomacy and power.

It should be pointed out that the Soviet approach to the direct involvement of its own force in another country has been cautious. Khrushchev has many times spoken of the possibility of a rain of rockets on the West, but when the Cubans seemed to be taking him literally, he was quick to insist that the threat be interpreted as "symbolic." Military power is one vital ingredient in Soviet policy, but at the present time it is not by itself a decisive factor in Soviet gains. The significant feature of Soviet power is the way it uses military and nonmilitary means interrelatedly to play upon the forces at work in particular local situations.

A third common misconception concerns the distinctive character of Soviet short-term policies. Soviet expansionism does not necessarily involve immediate efforts to communize or take over the countries it is dealing with. The first stage of Soviet expansionism in many areas mainly seeks the manipulation of existing groups rather than a direct path to revolution. This approach reflects a balance between two considerations: the Soviet judgment of the ripeness of the local situation for take-over, and the significance of the area in the world power balance.

In order to make this point clear, it is useful to deal separately, as do the Soviets themselves, with the advanced industrial areas of the world and the underdeveloped areas.

In the short term, Soviet policy seems to be less interested in communizing advanced industrial areas—Western Europe, Japan or North America—than in influencing the orientation of their "bourgeois" governments. The reason for this emphasis in Soviet policy is that in the short term—within a decade, more or less—the world power balance can be most decisively affected by changes in the orientation of the advanced industrial countries—by their relations with each other, by the direction of flow of their industrial output, by the level of their military capabilities, by the condition of their economies.

Whether France now continues to pursue an "independent" path to "national grandeur" instead of operating within the NATO framework; whether West Germany is politically, economically and militarily oriented on Western Europe or is to be a drifting prize between the power blocs; whether Japan is effectively associated with the United States or seeks a private accommodation with the Communist world—these are among the questions whose answers could have an immediate effect upon the power of the Soviet Union relative to that of the non-Communist world.

At best, the Soviet Union seeks to help bring to power within the advanced industrial nations coalitions more favorably oriented toward Moscow. At the least, the Soviet Union hopes to encourage pressures and political forces that would circumscribe the freedom of action of the Western governments, and oblige them to incline toward policies regarded as favorable from the Soviet point of view. Neither objective requires the prior overthrow of the "bourgeois" governments of the West.

The present Soviet concern is not with the "proletariat"—which shows no sign of producing a social revolution in the near future—but with the *bourgeoisie*, which they identify as the people who really exercise power for the present and who need to be influenced.

To them, the Soviet Union addresses appeals based upon three major themes: nationalism, trade and peace.

To France, to Britain, to Japan and other advanced nations, the Soviet Union stresses the theme of "national independence"—that is, independence from the United States and opposition to such supranational institutions as the European Economic Community. The purpose of this theme is to encourage fragmentation.

The appeal of trade is used not only to fill temporary needs in the Soviet economy but to create interest groups within the *bourgeoisie* which will have a stake in improving relations with the Soviet Union.

"Peace" is used in two ways: to encourage popular pressure for unilateral disarmament (as in Khrushchev's messages to pacifist groups in the West), and to encourage an atmosphere of *detente* or relaxation of tension.

In the current strategy of "peaceful coexistence," Soviet policy is to improve its position around the world while keeping international tension at a minimum. It therefore seeks, from time to time, "atmospheric" measures to reduce tension—symbolic actions which will reduce the Western stimulus to cohesiveness and mobilization, without changing the actual situation.

In the Soviet view, the question of the transition of the advanced industrialized countries to "socialism" is by no means foreclosed, but it awaits a later stage of developments. It is not, as the Soviets would say, "on the immediate agenda."

In the case of the underdeveloped nations, it is also necessary to differentiate between immediate and long-term Soviet purposes.

Soviet short-term purposes in such places as the Congo, Cuba or Laos are more complex and dangerous from our point of view than a policy of simple expansionism. Presumably the Soviet Union would not turn away gifts that fell in its lap, but its primary intent in the short term appears to be denial to the West. What it desires is to be able to subtract the raw materials, geographical positions and political support of these areas from the Western system.

By weakening the ties between these areas and the Western powers, the Soviet Union seeks to achieve a decisive leverage effect upon the advanced industrial nations, in the expectation that the "inevitable" crisis of capitalism will be hastened as markets and sources of raw materials are cut off. It does not need to gain control over the new nations in order to achieve immediate advantages in the world power balance.

Therefore, in the current Soviet view, this is a period of collaboration with "bourgeois-nationalist" leaders, as Moscow calls such men as Kassim, Sukarno, Nkrumah and Touré. How long this temporary collaboration lasts will depend upon how useful Moscow believes they are in weakening the West, and in preparing the ground for the next stage of Communist advance in their countries.

The Chinese Communists regard this short-term policy of collaboration as short-sighted, and would proceed directly to a more revolutionary stage of action. But the Soviet Union has its eye upon what it regards as the decisive factor of the present period.

In the Soviet view, it would be less useful to bring one or another of the underdeveloped countries wholly into the "Socialist camp," with all the stimulus this would give to the mobilization of the West, than to sever the ties, one by one, between the advanced industrial nations of the West and the countries of Asia, Africa and Latin America. When this has been done, the Soviet leaders argue, the power of the United States and its allies will shrivel, and the expansion of the "Socialist camp" can proceed at minimum risk.

Whether the Soviet Union will be able to hold to its view in the face of the apparent Chinese pressure toward more militant policies is one of the major uncertainties of the present period.

Clearly, it is not enough to be anti-Soviet, not enough to be strong, not enough to want peace, not enough to seek traditional diplomatic solutions, not enough to go on improvising fix-it policies to deal with one crisis after another.

What the Soviet Union is challenging is not alone our foreign policy in the traditional sense, but the vitality and the effectiveness with which our society can grasp and respond to the fundamental conditions of a rapidly changing world.

Are we capable of understanding the forces that are at work in the world today? Can we relate our interests to them more effectively than does the Soviet Union? Are we capable of thinking ahead ten or twenty years, and of projecting a sense of the future toward which we would like to see the world move? And if we did, could we learn to bring our resources to bear upon these purposes, rationally and effectively?

It is, of course, easier to ask these questions in this general form than to translate them into specific programs and policies. Even more difficult will be the process of winning political support for such measures—for, in practice, they will involve radical departures from our present habits, and collide with private interests and private preferences. The necessary first step is to increase our understanding of what is needed.

Between futile strength and surrender

Many if not most discussions of United States foreign policy and defense strategy these days rest explicitly or implicitly upon the premise that national armaments (both conventional military forces and nuclear and biochemical weapons systems) are symptoms, not causes, of the Cold War which threatens recurrently to erupt into devastating total war. Persons who accept this premise tend also to believe that, in the present state of the international environment, the "balance of terror" provides the best possible safeguard against paralyzing attack; and that, in any case, no trust can safely be put in any weapons control agreement negotiated with the present rulers in the Kremlin.

Against these views, voices are occasionally raised to contend that present superweapons systems are themselves the most dangerous feature of the present international environment; and that the present possessors of these weapons are caught up, whether we like it or not, in a fateful race against time to prevent, at the very least, an ever wider dissemination of these engines of destruction throughout the Society of Nations. Some indeed are convinced that the most urgent task of all is to contrive means for halting the continuously expanding national stockpiles of superweapons capable of destroying modern man and all his works. To persons of this persuasion, it is difficult to imagine how any sane and rational politician, civil servant, or military officer, either in Moscow or in Washington, could envisage without extreme anxiety the prospect of the Red revolutionaries in Peking getting their hands on H-bombs and ICBM's. Yet this is precisely part of what is in store unless ways and means are devised to limit the spread of these weapons.

This problem was examined by David Frisch (physicist at the Massachusetts Institute of Technology) in an article published in the summer of 1961.* In that article, he suggests some constructive alternatives—

> Since Stalin's death, as many ideas about arms reduction seem to have come out of the East as out of the West. But as we get deeper into disarmament problems, it is likely that the situation will change and we will have to think things through not only for ourselves but for the nations of the Communist bloc as well. While their goals and ours will increasingly have in common a dominating desire to escape the destruction of large-scale international warfare, the Communists will continue to be sharply inhibited, both by their suppression of public discussion and by their dogma, from examining the problem of disarmament as freely and imaginatively as we can.
>
> When the dense verbiage is cleared away, several clear points of view on disarmament emerge.
>
> One attitude is that we should have none of it. Instead, we should stay so far ahead of all other nations in all military and economic affairs that no one will ever dare threaten us. This peace-through-invulnerable-strength approach will possibly be that folly which marks the apex of man's journey up from the primeval sludge and rapidly down again. Almost every candidate for high public office in an alarming number of countries pays at least lip service to it.
>
> Unfortunately, "invulnerable strength" is based on a dream, or rather a technical nightmare. A 50 per cent efficient defense would have been impressive against a World War II bomber attack with high explosive bombs aimed at our cities. In sharp contrast, even a 90 per cent efficient defense against a World War III missile attack with H-bombs would leave us almost inconceivably devastated. By concentrating research on some particular technical aspect of missile offense, or perhaps on a comparatively new field, such as biological warfare, a future ag-

---

* From "Between Futile Strength and Surrender," in *New York Times Magazine,* July 30, 1961. Copyright 1961 by the New York Times Co., New York; reproduced by permission of the publisher and author.

gressor would have an easy time opening a lethal 10 per cent gap in any total defense system.

Proposed reliance on "invulnerable strength" often reflects a hypnotic preoccupation with Soviet aggressiveness, to the neglect of the problem of the instability of an all-out arms race among an ever-increasing number of nations.

If, for example, Asians and South Americans get into a full scale nuclear war fifty years hence, U. S. superiority in, say, hypothetical Multiorbit Anti-Counter-Anti-Bacteriofusion Research (Project MAC-ABRE) may not be able to keep the radioactive and biological fallout from devastating North America. Furthermore, United States "superiority" very probably won't keep the political fallout from such explosive world events from changing our way of life into just what we are so firmly resisting.

A second theory of how to achieve peace is that we should disarm unilaterally and completely and win the minds and hearts of any and all aggressors by nonviolent resistance. Instead of keeping significantly ahead of everybody else in everything technical forever, we would rely on superior moral strength.

It is tempting to patronize this pacifist position as being politically impossible, but a reasonable view as to the single most probable course of events is that after two or three cycles of nuclear and biological world wars and slow recoveries, an almost fatally crippled humanity will find that nonviolent resistance is a major component of all viable political organization.

There is no denying, however, that most of us are too frail in moral strength to be confident of practicing non-violent resistance successfully. Because there has been no demonstration of its efficacy in preserving our present civilization against such tough customers as the Chinese Communists, nonviolent resistance has a negligible chance of commanding a working political majority in any democracy today, including even Gandhi's own India.

A third and less extreme approach toward disarmament is that, while keeping our present military stance, we should use whatever powers of persuasion and international moral pressure can be brought to bear to get the Communists to join us in recognizing a common conception of world order and law. For example, one serious student of disarmament problems writes: "If there can be no agreement to make the United Nations a responsible instrument of political accommodation and peaceful change, and an effective guardian of international order, I submit that we will make *no* progress in discussing the mere technique of inspection."

Every thoughtful person recognizes the dominant importance of the political environment in which technical treaties are made. But we cannot afford to postpone serious attempts at limitation of armaments until that happy day when the Soviets and the Red Chinese become deeply committed to the idea of an external authority to which a strong nation must submit against its immediate interests. Indeed, it is not clear how deeply we ourselves have accepted the inevitable loss of national sovereignty in the world of the future.

What can we do if there seems to be no clear approach which holds promise of real progress before it is too late? In order to limit the development and spread of weapons of mass destruction, do we really have to have formulated points of view which are clearly understood and agreed on by all parties to agreements? Do we have to seek master formulas which will unlock the puzzles of contemporary history and of future human behavior?

I submit that in such a difficult situation we had better *experiment* than theorize. Bold experiments in every field of human activity have ways of putting old ideas into much better perspective, of bringing out new ideas which have never been thought of or which have not seemed practical, and above all, by the very act of doing something new, of modifying the background circumstances which seemed previously to prevent any major changes.

What appears today to be immutable Soviet opposition to international control of nuclear stockpiles may soften after a few years spent helping to enforce even a fragmentary nuclear-test ban on unwilling Communist, Western and neutralist nations alike. What appears today to be Western inability to rely on other than nuclear deterrence may vanish after experience with demilitarized zones and with inspected reduction of the number of opposing long-range nuclear missiles.

Certainly we should not give up trying to solve the intellectual questions of the ultimate disposition of power in this extremely complicated world. But we are inescapably pressed by the rapid development of armaments to act on disarmament now. We must try many new arrangements, constantly re-examining them to be sure that we are not being booby-trapped. Yet at each stage of entering new agreements, we must also weigh our loss of security, if any, against the irretrievable loss that we are constantly sustaining by maintaining our present course.

What useful initial steps could we take? We should keep pressing for an inspected nuclear-bomb test-ban treaty with the British and the Soviet Union and, if necessary, a limited test ban even without the Soviets. Before giving up hope of bringing them in, however, we should be willing to give up all on-site inspections and rely entirely on the fixed detection stations and on conventional espionage to give verification of Soviet compliance in the megaton-bomb test region. The unreality of such a treaty with respect to inhibiting small bomb tests would be worth the price to us of starting some activity on Soviet soil so that they can see the workings of international law and order in controlling weapons.

This only partly inspected cessation of bomb testing may be worth the loss of privacy to the Soviets—great by their standards—if they get us to make the beginnings of a commitment to abandon nuclear weapons. It may mean to us, on the other hand, the beginning of a commitment by the Soviets to allow serious inspection of all kinds of disarmament arrangements. Neither side will really feel that it has made such a commitment, but neither side will be profoundly weakened by such a test-ban treaty. Both sides will learn a great deal from what will probably be the long, trying experience of setting up an international detection system.

Another partial step we might attempt soon, whether or not the Soviets accept any test ban, is to set up inspected troop limitations. All the countries represented in the Geneva ten-power negotiations have subscribed to the principle of limiting the total numbers of national military forces. It will take some thought and much negotiation to agree on a reasonable inspection system and to define military troops as opposed to civil police forces.

It might be wise to make an inspected troop-limitation treaty for all nations which wish to join, as the Soviet Union and Red China may refuse to come in at first, saying that they don't want to participate in piecemeal disarmament. Watching such an inspected troop-limitation system operate might be an important experience for Communist countries.

As a third example, consider that the Soviets have proposed destruction of *all* long-range missiles, aircraft and naval vessels. Whether this is to be accomplished in stages or all at once, there will remain a difficult problem of monitoring the movements and cargoes of civil aircraft and ships to ensure that they cannot be converted easily into long-range nuclear-weapons carriers.

No matter what the probability of all nations reaching such a stable inspected disarmed state, we can try now to formulate the outlines of a suitable international long-range civil-carrier agreement. When the Soviets hear details of such an agreement—even if only as listeners at conferences they refuse to take part in—they will have to take disarmament technology much more seriously than they have in the past.

As a fourth and last example, consider a much more difficult kind of step, area withdrawals. Probably Soviet and United States political expectations from inspected troop and weapons withdrawals differ widely, yet in my view we ought to try, for example, the Rapacki-Eden plan for demilitarization of the Soviet satellite countries and Western Germany. By pursuing the illusive alternative called "keeping the status quo" in Central Europe, we are in reality losing a race against time, since several of these countries can have their own nuclear and biological warfare capabilities a few years hence.

The question that arises immediately when we discuss the possibility of even partial disarmament arrangements with the Soviet Union is: Are Communists sufficiently responsive to the pressures of external or internal opinion to be at all reliable in any working agreement? This is a hard question, and one for which there is apparently no agreement on a simple answer.

But there is at least some evidence that the Soviets are sensitive to charges of legal correctness before the bar of world opinion, even more among their fellow Communist nations, and remarkably enough (as pointed out by Ithiel Pool in Donald Brennan's important collection of articles, "Arms Control, Disarmament and National Security") within the Soviet Union. But even if there were no present evidence of Soviet sensitivity to fixed legal standards, we would still have no alternative but to try to inculcate understanding and response in them by going ahead with working experiments in this field. Our ace in the hole is that they have at least as much fundamental motivation as we to change the present dangerous course.

A closely related question is whether partial measures can give substantial progress toward the goal of large-scale disarmament. Are the steps we have discussed so small as to be unable to prevent the spread of nuclear weapons? If it is true, for example, that a nuclear-test-ban treaty between the present nuclear powers will not help slow the development of nuclear weapons in other nations, then we are lost in any case. We have no choice but to try little steps when the big ones would involve changing our way of life so completely that we would rather continue to risk destruction than give up.

This brief review of a few disarmament possibilities suggests that there are many small initial steps to be taken, steps which might not necessarily require concordant approaches between East and West, but which might lead to new views on both sides. Whether or not the Soviet Government really wants total disarmament—and my impression at the International Conference of Scientists in Moscow last December was that their Government undoubtedly wants to get rid of nuclear bombs and to avoid major wars—it will be an eye-opener both to them and to us if we take their disarmament proposals seriously and make serious proposals of our own.

There is much to be done, using all our energy and intelligence, for we face a common danger.

Some years ago George Kennan (veteran Russian expert of the American Foreign Service and author of authoritative histories of Soviet foreign policy, and in 1961 appointed ambassador to Yugoslavia) proposed a series of military and other steps to achieve what he called a "disengagement" of Soviet and American relations in Central Europe, as a means of mitigating the Cold War. Kennan's proposal was received with more favor in Europe than in America. Since then the opponents of disengagement of any kind have contended that such projects are simply appeasement by another name, or, at any rate, reflect a mistaken view of the "real nature of the Soviet challenge" (see the article by Shulman beginning on page 692 above). However, the underlying idea of disengagement continues to provide a basis for thinking about how to relieve the tensions of the East-West struggle. One who has explored this approach from a rather fresh perspective and with a different kit of tools is Charles E. Osgood (psychologist, and director of the Institute of Communications Research at the University of Illinois). He presents his conclusions in an essay entitled—

The human side of policy in a nuclear age *

In this paper I will try to analyze some of the dynamics of human thinking, which, paradoxically, are driving us in a direction we do not wish to go. The analysis leads to certain suggestions for policy. These are made in the broadest possible terms. I do not believe the academician is equipped with the information or experience needed to make detailed policy proposals in concrete situations. What he can do best is raise questions about the assumptions underlying policy, ask that they be re-examined rather than simply taken for granted, and offer what may be novel ways of viewing policy problems in the hope of contributing to the discovery of alternatives not previously believed to exist.

What criteria should we use in evaluating alternative policies? If the long-term goals of a nation are not made explicit, decisions are likely to be made opportunistically in defense of the status quo. What has merely become habitual is easily seen as somehow natural and essential. What are our goals? What are we "fighting for"? To answer this question we must distinguish between two quite different wars and opponents.

One is *the "hot war" with Russia* as a nation—a war in which we are in danger of becoming involved. Our long-term goal here is, quite simply, *survival*. This may be a rather ignoble value, but it is a necessary *pre*condition for securing any other goals. Unfortunately—from the point of view of achieving rational solutions as against preserving one's peace of mind—the most common reaction to an overwhelming threat is to avoid thinking about it. This is a luxury that those concerned with a nation's welfare can ill afford. The availability of nuclear weapons with awesome capacities for destruction, to say nothing about biological weapons, may not alter the nature of international conflict, but it certainly must change radically the weights we use in evaluating alternative strategies.

The other conflict is *the "cold war" with Communism* and other totalitarian systems. This war goes on steadily in the minds of men, and it is fought as much within as across the borders of nations. Our long-term goal here is *to preserve and extend our way of life*. Stripped to its essential ideal, our way of life is one in which the state is subservient to the individuals who compose it. The development of such a political philosophy, based on the essential dignity of individual human beings, was a most remarkable step along the path to becoming civilized; it was hard come by and is all too easily lost. Again, in the interest of short-term goals and in defense of the status quo, we have often

---

* Reproduced by permission of Dr. Charles E. Osgood.

lost sight of the fact that this way of life was itself a major socio-political revolution, and it is still under way.

There are, of course, many case-hardened statesmen and well-disciplined political theorists who will say that the underlying source of international tensions is still what it has always been—the struggle for power—and weapons, whether they be clubs or atomic warheads, are simply instruments for effecting a change in the balance of power. Although the manifest behaviors of nations may often conform to this Neanderthal conception of international relations, I suspect that the Neanderthalic bluster nearly always has masked a deeper anxiety. Today, perhaps more than ever before in history, *mutual insecurity* rather than the struggle for power has become the underlying source of international tensions.

Keeping in mind these two criteria—eliminating the threat to our biological survival and maintaining our way of life—and adding a third criterion of *sheer feasibility*, let us now consider briefly the major policy alternatives currently being discussed.

The decision to wage *preventive war* implies a sufficient lead in the armament race to minimize the possibility of punishing reprisal—or a sufficient frenzy to take the gamble. Furthermore, since such a war must begin (and probably end) with a surprise attack, this decision must be reached by other than democratic procedures. On both counts this strategy is more available to Russia than to ourselves, particularly during the next critical decade. However, the great danger in the present unstable period is that the leadership of either side is liable to take the gamble, justifying its decision on the ground that the other side was obviously planning the same thing. The . . . American espionage plane incident [in 1960] clearly illustrates this kind of thinking. Even were we to gain a sufficient lead, and an elite were to make the decision for us, this solution would not serve to maintain or extend our way of life—we would have to exhaust ourselves policing a hostile globe.

The backbone of our present policy is *mutual deterrence through fear of retaliation*. The underlying notion is that, with each side capable of destroying the other with massive retaliation, neither side will make the initial move, and a prolonged if uneasy "peace" can be maintained. This does not reduce nuclear threat—indeed, it is the threat which is supposed to guarantee the peace. Quite to the contrary, this threat serves to generate a nuclear arms race, since the habitual response to external threat is to demand more and better weapons. Would the Free World be able to maintain a favorable position in such a race? I have come to the somber conclusion that to compete successfully we would have to give up our way of life as rapidly as possible. A democratic system cannot so easily channel the energies of its people into military preparations at the expense of civilian comforts; it cannot order its young people into engineering and the physical sciences; it cannot make quick decisions and changes in strategy without regard to popular opinion and vote. But should we not sacrifice our freedoms temporarily so that in the long run we might preserve them? Prolonged subjugation to a totalitarian way of life, particularly if self-imposed, would certainly result in a thorough distortion of our own social philosophy, and the policy of mutual deterrence contains no provisions for its own resolution. Its proponents have not asked themselves—*when and how does it end?*

There are also two imponderables in the situation. One is the *nth Country problem.* We can expect other nations to beg, borrow and steal the capacity to produce nuclear weapons. Just as the Colt 45 brought big men and little men to common stature in the days of the Old West, so will the atomic bomb be "the great equalizer" in the nuclear age. International tension and instability will increase geometrically with the number of nations capable of mounting a nuclear attack. Second, there is *the unpredictability of human behavior under stress.* The policy of mutual deterrence is predicated on the assumption of rationality on all sides. But as technology reduces retaliation time, decision-making must be dispersed over more and more individuals whose fingers are nearer the critical buttons, and we know that there are potentially unstable people, potentially suicidal people, who have no compunctions about taking the lives of others when they themselves are thwarted.

The complete unwieldiness of massive deterrence as an instrument of everyday foreign policy has been leading us toward the compromise policy of *limited war.* . . . The underlying notion here is that the threat of full-scale nuclear war will prevent nations from unleashing it, thereby allowing "war as usual" to be used as an instrument of foreign policy. However appealing the idea of "gentlemanly war" may be to military men, it is inconceivable under present world conditions. Modern conflicts are not viewed with the impassion of peasants watching a tourney of champions; rather, they are waged by whole populations, whose will to fight, will to produce, and involvement with even remote objectives must be whipped up and maintained by the mass media. As to the idea that the very horror of nuclear war will prevent its occurrence, one must wonder why this horror in times of relative peace hasn't led us promptly into agreements on nuclear disarmament. The proponents of limited war would ask us to literally flirt with the danger of all-out nuclear war with no more protection than fear itself.

The only problem with *mutual disarmament*—an ideal solution in all other respects—is the *feasibility* of carrying out successful negotiations when international tensions are running high. Under such conditions *logic,* which requires both sides to accept a course in which neither gains nor loses, tends to be replaced by *psycho-logic,* which operates under the guidance of "one-ups-manship" and pays more attention to the folks back home than to the folks across the table. We have behind us a long and dismal history of unsuccessful negotiations with the Russians. It is easy to blame this on the intractability of the Communists, but the same mechanisms operate on both sides.

One of these is what I call *the biased perception of what is equable.* Literally hundreds of experiments, both in the laboratory and outside of it, testify to the biasing effect of prior attitudes and motives upon how events are perceived and interpreted. Men who have experienced failure become sensitized to words signifying their state; men who are hungry are prone to perceive food objects where there are none. During Khrushchev's [1959] visit to this country, many instances of the misinterpretation of ambiguous words to fit one's purposes and expectations occurred—some quite funny and some not quite so funny. In other words, what may be seen as balanced, as just and fair, by the representatives of one nation, given its life history and present world view, is likely to be seen as unbalanced, as unjust and unfair, by the representatives of the other, given its quite different life history and world view. In fact, one could argue that an objectively equable solution would necessarily be one seen as somewhat biased toward the other's favor by *both* sides—but this is a difficult criterion of successful negotiation to put across!

The other mechanism is what has been called *the self-fulfilling prophecy*. Given existing suspicions and tensions—and the fear of losing face—each side predicts that the other will prove obdurate and unreasonable, will try to use the negotiations for advantage in the "cold war"; each side then behaves in terms of these expectations, and nothing is accomplished—in part because the predictions were made—and both sides say "I told you so!" Mutual disarmament requires commitment prior to action, and in the present atmosphere of fear and distrust it is difficult to see how commitments of any significance can be achieved.

Before turning to what I hope will be more constructive aspects of this paper, I would like to make a psychological digression—into what might be termed *some dynamics of controversy*. The essential irrationality and danger in our present course is apparent, yet we feel impelled along it. . . . What forces operate in times of controversy between human groups to push ordinary disagreement toward mutual destruction?

Assessment of human values. Nations differ in their calculus of human values. We have already seen one essential difference between Communism and our way of life—the relative value placed upon the rights of the individual as compared with the rights of the state. . . . Differences in the assessment of values produce controversy within as well as between nations. The main source of divergent opinions about strategy in the war with Communism lies here. In a recent debate in *The New Leader*, Bertrand Russell maintained that a Communist victory would not be so great a disaster as the extinction of human life, whereas Sidney Hook maintained just the reverse. . . . The difficulty does not lie in the fact that men have values and defend them, but in two quite different directions: First, values are often held so *insecurely* that we feel threatened when others disagree with us—often to the extent that we would deny them the right to express their views. Second, emotional involvement with our own values often makes it very difficult for us to accept short-term frustration for long-term achievement.

Perspective. In general, as we trace the course of evolution and particularly the development of the cortex, we find higher species capable of maintaining longer delays, employing more extended foresight, and striving for more remote goals. Within each species the more intelligent members display these capacities to a greater degree than the less intelligent. But emotion has the effect of primitivizing this capacity. The motivational conditions of controversy, e.g., our present tensions/arms-race dilemma, are precisely those designed to restrict our perspective. It sometimes proves helpful to back off from a problem and view it within a larger chunk of both time and space. . . . Taking the long view through time, one can envisage the interlacing, ever-expanding tree of human life, bearing its generations of ephemeral blooms, yet but little affected by the changing national climates in its course. The organizations among men we call "nations" come and go— a name may persist and the human content change, or the reverse— and this is as true for what we now call "Russia" and "The United States" as it was for Rome and Babylon. This is not said to minimize the seriousness of our present problems, but rather to emphasize different goals. A wide perspective makes it possible to substitute more remote goals for immediate ones. . . .

The relativity of social judgments. At least three stages can be traced in the development of clear social thinking—in "becoming civilized," if you will. At the simplest, most primitive stage *we unconsciously project our own frame of reference onto others.* Since Ego assumes Alter to share his reference frame, it follows that when Alter calls "straight" what to Ego is obviously "crooked," when he judges "tasty" what to Ego is obviously "distasteful," Alter must be evil, lying, or at least abnormal in some way. The second stage is where *we recognize the relativistic nature of Alter's frame of reference, but not our own.* This produces a more human approach toward social problems, a "forgive *them* for *they* know not what they do" attitude. We account for the disapproved behavior of others as due to the conditions under which they happened to develop. The third stage is one arrived at with difficulty and maintained with even greater difficulty. It is where *we realize the equally relativistic nature of our own frame of reference.* This is the sensitive—not "ugly"—American who realizes that his own neutral points on the clean-dirty, tasty-distasteful, or even moral-immoral scales are no more "natural" than those of the Mexican or Hindu. Social relativity does *not* mean that there are no external criteria for distinguishing good from bad; quite the reverse, it means that we must search for external criteria just because social judgments are so liable to bias.

Emotion and the restriction of alternatives. Rational behavior requires understanding one's own ultimate goals, weighing the consequences of alternatives means to these goals, and then selecting among the alternatives in terms of their success probabilities. Many laboratory and field experiments have demonstrated that animals and humans operating under intense emotion display a reduced awareness of alternatives . . . nations today are lumbering down the one *habitual* path to "security"—bigger and better weapons—gathering as they go tensions which make it less and less possible to see other alternatives. Being habitual, this course is assumed to be "realistic." Anthropologists are familiar with cultures that, through blind adherence to practices that once were realistic, have gradually committed suicide. I think we are in exactly the same spot. We are continuing to practice rites and rituals of international relations that were developed in and appropriate to the past—firmly believing them to be realistic—in a present age that renders them suicidal.

Self-delusion. We expect the normal human being to defend himself against attack—including mental attack. We expect him to try to refute any suggestion that there is anything wrong or evil about himself. But we also expect him to be accessible to facts, pleasant or unpleasant. If he is not, if he refuses to accept reality, then we place him in an institution. Unfortunately, there are no institutions for nations. If a whole group of people, including their leaders, refuse to accept reality, if their communications media consistently paint a self-righteous picture in the face of contrary facts, then there is no court to dispel the dangerous process of self-delusion. Both Russia and the United States—as well as most nations on our globe—have been steadily manufacturing their own versions of reality. The . . . spy-plane incident [in 1960] is a remarkably clear instance of this mechanism. Even before the dust of the abortive Summit Meeting had settled, Russians were being told that they were absolutely white and Americans were absolutely black, while Americans were being told that *they* were absolutely white and Russians absolutely black—each country put full blame on the other. As those of us who deal with individual humans under stress realize so well, there are seldom if ever absolute blacks and whites. But in the behavior of nations, we are continually asked to think like worms. Both sides need *intense and thoughtful self-criticism from within,* but the dynamics of mass self-justification make this very difficult to apply—and support once it has been applied.

Psycho-logic. Human thinking abhors inconsistency. As the process of self-delusion I just described clearly indicates, we continually strive toward attitudinal balance, consonance, and congruity. In the language of our lay philosophy, this is known as "the consistency of little minds" —but unfortunately the same dynamics affect big minds, too, particularly when they are operating under intense emotion. If we like Ike, and he happens to praise some congressman from Timbuktu, it is congruent for us to feel more favorably disposed toward this man, even though we know absolutely nothing else about him. But if Khrushchev were to comment on this congressman's sound ideas—popularly known as the "kiss of death"—then psycho-logically, but not logically, we would probably find ourselves more than a little dubious about this fellow. Similarly, it is psycho-logic, not logic, that leads us to conclude that Nehru must be pro-Communist because he insists on India's neutrality. It is sometimes true, of course, that psycho-logic may lead us to a valid conclusion, but this does not validate the process.

Psycho-logic runs rampant when we try to come to grips with the problems of international conflict. This can be illustrated by applying the Socratic method of questioning to a hypothetical American citizen picked at random. Suppose, says Socrates, that Russian Man were to suddenly junk all of his atomic weapons—would you, American Man, leap to destroy him in a nuclear holocaust? Absolutely not, says American Man—we are only concerned with protecting ourselves, not with destroying others. All right, then, says Socrates, do you think that Russian Man would leap to destroy *you* with atomic bombs if you were to lay down your weapons? Here there is a long pause. Finally, American Man answers that he doubts if the Russians would do this, but he certainly isn't sure enough about it to take the chance. Furthermore, he adds, Russian Man obviously would take advantage of our helplessness by over-running the world and making it a tight Communist despotism. But then, asks Socrates, am I to conclude that American Man in the same circumstances would over-run a helpless world and make a Capitalistic despotism of it? For goodness sake, American Man replies with a grin, *we* have no imperialist ambitions—and in any case, a world unified under a Capitalist system couldn't be despotic. Shaking his head in puzzlement, Socrates says—all I can conclude is that Russian Man must be somehow intrinsically different from American Man. Of course, the great philosopher would have arrived at the same conclusion had he directed his questions at a hypothetical Russian man-on-the-street.

Abrupt and complete unilateral disarmament by either side is entirely unfeasible. It asks both American Man and Russian Man to think and act in uniquely civilized ways, and human culture is not yet ready for such a big step. Nevertheless, this hypothetical case does serve to draw out what I think is the deepest objection to any non-aggressive solution.

This is *the Bogey-man conception of the enemy.* Human groups in conflict have always created their Bogey-men. What are the dynamics of Bogey-building? It comes down to psycho-logic. Given the belief by each side that WE are *good, kind, fair,* and so on—a necessary and generally valid belief as far as everyday human relations are concerned —and given also the logical opposition between WE and THEY, between FRIEND and ENEMY, psycho-logic dictates that THEY, THE ENEMY, must be *bad, cruel, unfair,* and so on through the opposites of all traits we attribute to ourselves. The failure of the Russians to see eye-to-eye with the United States on many issues, their purges, their atheism and so forth support and strengthen this Bogey-image, while it in turn provides us with a ready explanation of their un-American and anti-American behaviors.

But then we have real, live Russians visiting our homes and farms; we find them *friendly, sociable,* and in many ways just like us. Our own tourists return with reports about how *helpful, cultured,* and *sincere* the Russians they knew were. This puts the attitude system out of balance again. The typical resolution is to break the concept RUSSIAN into two parts: it is the RUSSIAN PEOPLE who are *friendly, sincere,* and *just like us;* the RUSSIAN LEADERS (in the Kremlin) are the *bad, cruel, dangerous* fellows. Psycho-logic thus fosters the hope that soon the *good* RUSSIAN PEOPLE must overthrow their *bad* RUSSIAN LEADERS. No doubt the Russian man in the street wonders why the *good* AMERICAN PEOPLE *just like him* haven't yet begun the revolution against their *bad* CAPITALIST LEADERS!

Many recent travelers to Russia, including statesmen and scholars, have been impressed by the "mirror image" of our own attitudes they find among the people and the leaders there. "Why do you Americans want war?" our informal ambassadors are asked. And when they answer that we most certainly do not want war, the Russians ask, "Then why do your leaders prepare for it? Why do they ring us about with missile bases?" When our travelers ask them why they maintain a great army and are building up nuclear weapons for long-range attack, they reply, of course, that we leave them no choice. I believe that we must accept these protestations of good faith as genuine. They blame their aggressive behavior on us just as we blame ours on them.

What, then, can we conclude about the Russian Bogey Man? I am sure it would be unrealistic to completely discount the real differences between the Russians and ourselves—particularly those concerning the value of the individual and his rights which stem from our ideological conflict. But, on the other hand, I am equally sure that this Bogey has been overdrawn in the workings of our own mental dynamics—particularly by those who fail to distinguish between Russian Communism and German Nazism. The Russian Bogey surely can be cut down to a more realistic size and shape. Russian perceptions of the present situation, and their reactions to it, may be much like our own; they probably would welcome a way out as much as we would. . . .

. . . In the remainder of this paper I will propose a policy alternative —which I call *graduated unilateral disengagement*—that derives essentially from social science considerations.

In the search for any long-term solution, we must first ask ourselves: what are the conditions that support the Communist (or any totalitarian) way of life? Here I can only list some of these conditions: *Economic scarcity.* When people exist near a bare subsistence level, little energy is left over for the development of those uniquenesses which make people important as individual human beings. *Social inequality.* Totalitarian systems display gross inequalities in civil, political, and social rights, based on the distribution of power if nothing else. *Educational deficiency.* Limited or biased education prevents people from acquiring the tools needed to better their condition. *Information restriction.* The free flow of communication, both within and across national boundaries and both among individuals and via the mass media, provides the diversity of opinion in which lies the vitality of the democratic system and the freedom of choice people need to govern themselves. Such freedom is the anathema of totalitarianism. *External threat.* Threat from outside the group impels people to accept subservience to the state and to forego individual freedoms in the interest of what they perceive as the common goal—namely survival. This is admittedly an incomplete list, but it will serve to set the problem.

Secondly, we must ask ourselves: how can these conditions be changed within the existing set-up of competing sovereign states? When scientists, working on their own much smaller-scale problems, want to change something, they operate on the conditions which produce the phenomenon. In our present, infinitely larger-scale problem we would like to so modify the background conditions in Communist and other states as to foster and support a more democratic way of life. But the world situation today is one of extremely high mutual threat perception between two coalitions of essentially sovereign states. It is a bi-polar power situation aggravated by a fundamental ideological conflict. This situation has led to intense security measures, and both sides have erected "iron curtains" through which only carefully metered dribblets of information can pass.

Therefore, it seems to me that rational policy requires two phases: *Phase I—reversal of the tensions/arms-race spiral.* Before any other policies can be employed effectively, mutual threat perception must be reduced to a level where the arms race can be halted and put in reverse. Not only is this necessary to escape from the very real danger of mutual annihilation, but it is also the only sure way to dissolve the "iron curtains" that hamper the use of other strategies. *Phase II— maintaining the peace.* It is my contention that our way of life flourishes in peacetime and the totalitarian way in wartime. If I am right, then anything that continues the peace works in our favor.

It is obvious that many of the conditions that support the Communist way of life—economic scarcity, social inequality, educational deficiency and information restriction—cannot be directly manipulated through the "iron curtains" that separate East and West. (But the Russians have been doing a very good job of modifying these conditions, and in so doing have been modifying themselves—whether they know it or not.) On the other hand, *we can manipulate the condition of external threat.* This is at least partly under our control, because we ourselves, in our words and actions, contribute to the level of threat which the Russians perceive. We can behave so as to raise this threat or so as to lower it; we can change it abruptly or in gradual stages. The solution of the critical, but very sensitive and difficult, Phase I—reversal of the tensions/arms race spiral—hinges on our intelligent manipulation of the condition of external threat.

What are the assumptions underlying graduated unilateral disengagement? I use the term *disengagement* (rather than disarmament) to emphasize the fact that we are considering a much wider range of acts than the term "disarmament" implies. This policy is based on the assumption that the Russian people and leaders are sufficiently like us to accept an unambiguous opportunity to reduce the probability of mutual nuclear destruction. It also assumes that the Russian leaders are susceptible to moral pressures, both from without and from within— since such pressures are an index of the success or failure of their system. It assumes that—unlike mutual negotiations that can easily be twisted into cold war propaganda—unilateral *acts* of a tension-reducing nature are relatively unambiguous. It assumes that each unilateral act which is reciprocated makes the next such sequence easier to accomplish. Finally, it assumes that the Communists are as convinced that their way of life will win out in non-military competition for men's minds as we are (or should be) that ours will.

What is the nature of this policy? To be maximally effective in inducing an enemy to reciprocate, a unilateral act: (1) should, in terms of capacity for military *aggression,* be clearly disadvantageous to the side making it; (2) should be such as to be clearly perceived by the other side as reducing *his* external threat; (3) should not increase an enemy's threat to our heartland; (4) should be such that reciprocal action by the other side is clearly available and clearly indicated; (5) should be announced in advance and widely publicized to ally, neutral, and enemy countries—as regards the nature of the act, its purpose as part of a consistent policy, and the expected reciprocation; (6) but should not demand prior commitment to reciprocation by the other side as a condition for its commission.

I am not going to try to specify the precise nature of such a series of graduated unilateral acts. Their selection, ordering, and timing demands a great deal of information which only people in government, not ordinary citizens, have available. However, I can give some general characterizations. The initial series of acts in unilateral disengagement would be small in magnitude of risk, should they not be reciprocated, but would increase in risk potential as reciprocations were obtained. Alternative acts would be available at each stage—one to be announced and then made if the Russians had reciprocated (a larger step) and another to be announced and then made if they had not (a smaller step). The initial series of unilateral acts would be designed to be cumulative in their tension-reducing effect upon the enemy, but noncumulative in their effect upon our capacity for massive retaliation should this policy fail—that is, the acts would not be such as to weaken us progressively in the same area, or in the "survival" area at all. I am sure that if we put even a small part of the total energy we are now pouring into armaments production into an intensive study of the possibilities for graduated unilateral actions, effective programs could be devised.

The essential differences between this proposal and Kissinger's "limited war" proposal need to be emphasized: Although both policies rely upon the capacity for massive retaliation as a psychological buffer, "limited war" would use this nuclear deterrence as the support for tension-*increasing* acts ("war as usual") whereas "graduated unilateral disengagement" would use nuclear deterrence as the support for tension-*reducing* acts. Whereas the former encourages conditions in which nuclear weapons would be more likely to be used, the latter encourages conditions in which nuclear weapons would be less likely to be used. Finally, where the policy I am proposing holds out some hope for eventual elimination of the massive nuclear deterrents themselves, the Kissinger Plan offers no such hope.

There are many deep-seated *objections to any non-aggressive policy* of this sort, and it will be wise to anticipate them. Some are largely emotional, but none the less serious for that. One of these is *the Bogey-man conception of the enemy* discussed earlier. If the Russians are in truth inherently evil and not like us, then any attempt to reduce tensions on our part will be interpreted by them as a sign of weakness and will simply encourage further aggression on their part. But if this *is* their inherent nature, then we should be sure of it before the present balance of power has shifted to any significant degree. On the other hand, it would be cause for cosmic irony if two of the most civilized nations on earth were to drive each other to mutual destruction because of their mutually threatening perceptions of each other—without ever testing the validity of these perceptions.

Some people, of course, will see any such proposal as *a Communist-inspired Trojan horse*—that it is actually proposed as a strategy to get us out of a dilemma and, in the long run, to win the real war with Communism would be incomprehensible to them. More will see this as *a coward's way*, a kind of "moral disarmament"—but men who rely on their wits rather than their brawn, especially when their brawn is peculiarly susceptible to radiation, are hardly cowards. Many people, however, will see such a policy as *an idealist's fantasy*, certainly not one that faces up to the hard realities of the world we live in. I have already said that what we call "realistic" is usually what is familiar, what is habitual. New issues force new definitions of what is "realistic," and we certainly are facing new issues today.

There are more rational objections. One is that even graduated unilateral action *involves too much risk*. But our present policy of mutual deterrence involves equal or even greater risk. I think we simply must accept the fact that there is no alternative we can choose that entails no risk; we have to weigh the risk against the ultimate security to be achieved by each alternative. Another objection is that *any unilateral act which is militarily disadvantageous must be considered a threat to our heartland*. I do not believe this follows. There is no perfect correlation between the military significance of events and their psychological impact;and further, a minimum *capacity* for deterrence may have a near-maximum deterrent *effect* on an enemy—to be able to annihilate him ten times over doesn't deter him much more than to be able to annihilate him once!

Yet another criticism is that this policy seems to amount to *a betrayal of our obligations to defend the Free World*. Just what constitutes "defending" other nations needs to be carefully studied. One could argue that the best defense would be to resolve the present bi-polar conflict and allow so-called "underdeveloped" countries to fend for themselves. Furthermore, just as our own liability to attack is coming to be independent of geographic distance, so would we now not risk all-out nuclear war for some remote, foreign objective. And it is certainly true that in the sparring of the nuclear giants in "brush-fire wars" about the perimeter of the Free World, it is the little countries on whose soil the skirmishes take place that suffer the most severe wounds.

Finally, there are some psychological objections. First, *would the Russians accept our unilateral acts, and we their reciprocations, as bona fide?* Here the distinction between unilateral *acts*, which have the status of *fait accompli* (like the satellites circling our globe), and mutual *negotiations*, which are easily twisted into cold-war propaganda, becomes important. And it should be stressed that ambiguity over the motivation of the first unilateral act tends to be resolved by commission of the next. Furthermore, there is a principle of interpersonal behavior that operates here—if American Man has made an intentional conciliatory move toward Russian Man, he is much more likely to perceive the Russian's reciprocation as bona fide than if it came unsolicited. Second, *what if one side tried to take advantage of the other's unilateral action?* Wouldn't this have the "boomerang" effect of intensifying mutual Bogey-man conceptions? This, of course, is the risk we would take. However, with *graduated* unilateral acts the initial risks are small. Actually, I believe that the pressure of world opinion, to say nothing of the growing threat of China, would soon force the Russians into at least token reciprocations. And here another principle of interpersonal behavior takes over: when people are made to keep on behaving in ways that are inconsistent with their actual attitudes (here, behaving as if they really trusted each other), their attitudes tend to shift into line with their behaviors.

In conclusion, then, what I am proposing is a psychological "primer" to initiate a reversal in the present tensions/arms-race dilemma. American Man and Russian Man have been moving out *against* each other along a narrow and teetering see-saw, each trying to match every unilateral aggressive step by the other with an outward step of his own—so as to maintain the unstable balance. It is also possible for them to move gradually and unilaterally *toward* each other, step by reciprocated step, until they meet at the stable midpoint and the danger is past.

Chapter 21 closed with a passage by Robert S. Tucker (of Princeton University) contrasting the generally negative, defensive Western approach to world policy with the positive, dynamic approach which the Communist interpretation of history instills into his apostles. Later in the same article, Tucker suggests some of the ideas which might be built into—

A more positive alternative to Communism *

If we take the disintegration of international order as the fundamental fact and trend of the twentieth century—a trend not yet really

---

* From "Russia, The West, and World Order," by R. C. Tucker, in *World Politics*, October 1959, pp. 1-23. Copyright 1959 by Princeton University Press; reproduced by permission.

checked or altered by the two great experiments in world organization undertaken during this century—the challenge to Western thinking becomes a challenge to frame a new world policy in the light of what has happened. If, further, we take international order as something supremely desirable, especially in the nuclear age and dawning space age, then it may appear that the rebuilding of order into the affairs of nations should become the master concept in the world policy of the Western coalition.

Of course, the concept of reconstitution of international order as the goal and guiding principle for Western policy requires further definition. According to one possible interpretation, it might mean the restoration of the world of 1914. But this is scarcely a tenable interpretation. On any realistic view, it has to be recognized that the nineteenth century is beyond resurrection, that the era of Western world hegemony is over. The processes which have produced this result run too deep and have gone too far to be subject to reversal now. The contemporary West can hope that certain values of its civilization, centering in its liberal political ideas, will take route and flourish in former dependencies that have now become or are on their way to becoming independent nations. It can work by certain methods to achieve this, not least by the force of example, by a conscious effort to show how successful the open society can be in solving its serious problems and how exciting and satisfying to live in. It can strive to cultivate close and productive relations with these nations in commerce and culture and many other fields. But it is out of the question to resubordinate them to Western political influence or control.

Practically speaking, then, the issue is whether or not the Western mind and spirit are capable of one more supreme historic impulse of political initiative, whether the West can proceed, first in its thinking and then in the action that flows from thought, beyond the nationalist principle to a concept of international order not predicated upon the hegemony of any one great Power or group of Powers, or upon the universalization of any one form of internal social-economic system. To make international order in this historically new sense the conscious goal of national policy would evidently mean placing greater and greater emphasis upon the existing machinery of the world community, particularly the United Nations and its associated agencies, such as the World Court. But the positive content of such a new internationalism would by no means be confined to that. International order and international organization are related but distinguishable concepts. Given the existence of several dozen national sovereignties in the present world, international order essentially means the establishment of certain operative norms of orderly behavior of national states in their relations both with each other and with their own peoples. It is open to the Western countries, and above all to the United States, to take the initiative in many ways toward the growth of international order so conceived. The force of American and Western example is potentially a very great force indeed.

To take one concrete example, there appears to be a growing consensus among well-informed Americans that a far greater effort is needed in the area of aid for economic development than America is presently putting forth. The difficulty with the proposals that have been offered so far for a greatly increased effort is that they are not coupled with a large political idea capable of generating the requisite will to sacrifice on the part of the American public and its elected representatives. The Marshall Plan experience stands as a reminder of what it means to associate economic assistance with a positive and unselfish political idea. How might the United States make an expanded economic assistance program the instrument of a policy dedicated to the growth of international political order? One way of doing this might be to predicate the program upon the new principle that aid for economic development of underdeveloped lands should *not* be used as a means of competing for political influence over the recipients, and in this connection to internationalize the administration of the aid program. This in turn would strengthen the insistence of the donors upon the willingness of the recipient nations to use the assistance in the manner best calculated to attain positive results, to submit to the requisite supervision, etc. Beyond this, the "depoliticized" economic assistance might well be offered on condition that the recipients live up to certain norms of behavior in their relations with other states, as dictated by the requirements of international order in their part of the world.

In short, under this approach the West would not be working to line up the uncommitted countries on *its* side, but rather to line up *itself* as well as them on the side of a higher goal and principle—the growth of international order in the relations among states. Recognizing that the freedom of the uncommitted nations includes the freedom to remain uncommitted as between East and West if they so desire, it would ask them to commit themselves only to those norms of behavior in international relations to which it is committing itself in deeds as well as words. The practical adoption of such a philosophy of Western foreign policy would, moreover, put the present policies of Soviet Russia to the test in a politically most potent manner. Refusal of the Soviet Union to co-operate in measures to promote the growth of international order would expose the discrepancy between the "selfless" aims of Soviet foreign policy and its actual motivation. It would clarify for those who may need such clarification, and continually remind the whole world, that the grand design of Soviet foreign policy is not, as its exponents claim, a world-wide commonwealth of nations on a new, higher plane of order, but rather the transformation of the twentieth century into a greater replica of the nineteenth—with Russia as the new hegemonic center of the international system.

In times of rapid and confusing change, when passions run high and fear blurs clear vision, a few voices are sometimes raised, voices of men distinguished for their wisdom and their humanity. Such has been the

voice of Raymond B. Fosdick (former president of the Rockefeller Foundation). He has now passed from the world of affairs, but the words that
he uttered, back in 1947, have lost nothing in relevance and significance.
It is fitting, therefore, to close this book on the foundations of international
politics with Fosdick's—

Perspective for a revolutionary age *

All centuries are dangerous, said Professor Whitehead; and he added:
"It is the business of the future to be dangerous." This was written in
1925, and certainly there can be no question of the accuracy of the
prognosis as it applies to our generation. The challenge of today's crisis
is the most commanding which Western society has ever faced. We
have always known that knowledge was a perilous possession, because
it could equally well work in the wrong direction; but the knowledge
that has been placed in the hands of this age is so supremely capable
of misuse—and misuse could so easily reduce the hopes and monuments
of men to drifting dust—that the impact of the challenge finds us confused, uncertain and fearful.

Like all frightened people everywhere and in all ages, our first reaction is physical force, and our instinctive faith is given to military power.
Let us grant at once that in this unprecedented crisis a measure of
physical force is essential. We do not live in a utopia, and it would be
suicidal to act as if we did. Equally suicidal, however, is the assumption that the crisis can be met solely on the level of force, or that
mechanisms, power, and dollars constitute the essential elements of
the solution.

The present is one of the supreme moments of challenge, in which, as
Toynbee says, the character of our response determines the chances of
survival. The past is littered with the wreckage of nations and empires
which tried to meet the crises of their times by physical means alone.
Our response today cannot be confined to this lower level. Unless we
can rise to greatness and lift our answers to an intellectual and ethical
plane, our fate will be the fate, not only of the nations that preceded us
in history, but of all species, whether birds or brontosaurs, which
specialized in methods of violence or defensive armor.

One of the difficulties in putting our response on a higher level of
human searching is our emphasis here in America on the task of raising
the material standards of living. In this ambition we have been incomparably successful; our productive and consuming capacity is
greater than that of any other country in the world. But the result is
that our principal standards are standards of quantity: we have more
of everything than anybody else—automobiles, refrigerators, radios,
railroads. Consequently our vision is not so much of a world peopled by

* From the *Annual Report of the Rockefeller Foundation, 1947,* by R. B. Fosdick,
president.

wise and honorable men as it is of a world in which "every family has its automobile and every pot its chicken." We have too easily made the assumption that other values would automatically follow our material well-being, that out of our assembly lines and gadgets the good life would spontaneously be born.

One of our leaders recently said that Europe could prosper in the long run only as she adopted what he called the American philosophy of consumption. This uncritical identification of consumption with social value is, of course, not characteristic of this country alone or of this age alone; but the extent of the confusion in America today is disquieting. Although our religion and ethics have long tried to enlighten us, many of us are still only dimly aware that purchasing power is not the measure of a great society, and that wisdom and cultural values are not the inevitable consequences of an increased capacity to consume.

It is, of course, obvious that a solid material foundation is an essential basis for a high civilization; but it is a basis, not a superstructure. Our tendency is to confuse one with the other, to mistake the foundations for the towers and turrets of the new city. There is a spiritual hunger in the world today that is not being satisfied by American exports. "God knows we need food and coal to survive," said a European delegate to Lake Success, "but unless America can take the lead in providing a vital faith, in giving us a song that mankind can sing, all her exports will merely postpone the day of reckoning, and the world will die anyway."

Another aspect of the difficulty which we face in placing on a higher level our response to the challenge of our time, is our superstitious reverence for the physical sciences. They have become sacrosanct—the dispensers of the gifts of life. The doctrine that "civilization can be bred to greatness and splendor by science" is widely accepted. Even our universities have succumbed to this twentieth-century worship of methods which give mastery in the physical world. In contrast with the money available for the humanities and the social studies, far greater sums are today being allocated to the physical sciences by our educational institutions than ever before. From government and business, as well as from college budgets, money in increasing amounts is being poured into the teaching of chemistry and physics. "This is the Century of Science," one characteristic college announcement proclaims, "and we must orient our students to the prevailing interest of their time." A prominent eastern university reports its enlarging plans with these words: "In the face of the increasing impact of science on our society it is widely agreed that an essential aim of general education is to impart to the university undergraduate an appreciation of the methods of the sciences." Of course, a decent obeisance is always made in the direction of the humanities and the social studies. The fact remains, however, that in terms of endowment, research facilities and teaching staffs, these studies are far outdistanced by the physical sciences, and the gap is growing wider.

But the gap should be closed rather than widened. We cannot escape the obligation, in this scientific age, to comprehend science; but in the supreme question which faces our generation, physics and chemistry and engineering have no answers for us. They are ethically neutral. They are preoccupied with physical matter. They can give us more horsepower; only the naive, however, will claim that horsepower can develop within itself the means by which our runaway technologies can be brought under control. They can help more men to better health and longer life; but they have little relationship to the problem of discovering a new set of human purposes, or to the art of human relations, or to the winning of social and moral wisdom, upon which peace and successful government depend.

It is scarcely necessary to acknowledge our vast indebtedness to science in giving us the methods and patterns of research in human relationships. Every contribution of science to the problems of society is to be welcomed. But the enlightenment of science is bringing with it a tendency to reject the limitations of science. To expect that exact measurement and exhaustive definition will relieve us of the necessity of ethical inquiry, or that the meaning and values of human life will somehow or other crystallize as physics crystallized around the concepts of mass and energy, is a form of superstition as deadly as any we have known.

The issues of our time and of human destiny will be determined, not at the physical, but at the ethical and social level. Material power and dollars and military ascendancy may preserve us temporarily; but the dynamic tensions of our society can be relieved only by moral and social wisdom, and that kind of wisdom cannot be precipitated in a test tube nor can it be won by the brilliant processes of nuclear physics.

In the same essay which was quoted at the beginning of this section, Professor Whitehead went on to say: "It must be admitted that there is a degree of instability which is inconsistent with civilization. But on the whole, the great ages have been the unstable ages." This is the ray of hope that lightens the darkness of the present hour. It is not in times of security that men build a Chartres Cathedral or write a *Hamlet* or push their boats across an unknown ocean to discover a new continent. Oddly enough these achievements occur in years of instability.

Danger and hazard mark our age today. But in Professor Whitehead's phrase, it can be a great age, like other ages that have been born out of fear and challenge. Its greatness, however, if achieved, will consist in its search for an enlightened humanism and for rational and ethical values that will rise above our time as the spires of Chartres rose above the twelfth century. . . .

The conflict of ideologies—what Gibbon called "the exquisite rancor of theological hatred"—divides the world today in bitter partisanship, just as Europe was divided by its religious wars of the sixteenth century. As a matter of fact, ideologies have always divided mankind; the rifts are centuries old; there has never been one world. What we are attempting today is something that has never in recorded history been accomplished. We have barely begun on what is unquestionably the noblest as well as the most discouraging task which statesmen and nations have ever undertaken.

If the aim were to iron out all the differences which exist among men—to achieve a utopia of unruffled unanimities—it would be fatuous even to begin it. The world of the future—if any world survives—will be a world of diversity, held together by a conception of common interests. It will be a world in which many political faiths and economic creeds are tolerated and widely differing points of view fertilize each other for the common good.

Our challenge in this generation is to discover the common interests, the terrain of possible collaboration, the overlapping areas of curiosity and sympathy, of aspiration and mutual advantage, that bind the human race together regardless of ideologies or boundary lines. The search for these rallying points of unity, the development of new techniques and areas of cooperative action where ideas and experience can be pooled and combined—this is the immediate task; this comes first; this is the foundation of the ultimate structure of a united society.

The activities of the World Health Organization of the United Nations furnish a pertinent illustration; for health is something that all men desire and there is no limited supply for which nations must compete. Public health work carries no threat to anybody, anywhere. Cancer and scarlet fever have no political ideology. There is no Marxian method of eliminating gambiae mosquitoes as distinguished from a Western democratic method. The principles of sanitary engineering do not bear a Russian or an American label. No difference exists between tuberculosis in the Soviet Union and tuberculosis in the United States. Infantile paralysis is the same thing in Moscow and in Washington, and human sorrow is no less poignant in one city than in the other. The world of disease and misery is not divided; it is a common world. In terms of human suffering the world is truly and tragically one world.

What is true of medicine and public health is true also in the fields of science and humanism. There are no French or English enzymes, no German or American electrons. The second law of thermodynamics is not the property of any group or nation. Tolstoy and Shakespeare and Beethoven and Tschaikowsky belong to the world, just as the spiritual ideals of Gandhi have now become the heritage of mankind. These are some of the common interests whose waves are breaking over the old flag-marked boundaries and are bringing to the world a conception of civilization and of the intellectual life of man as a cooperative achievement.

In spite of all evidence to the contrary the things that divide the world are trivial as compared with the things that unite it. The mutualities of human beings everywhere far exceed their divergencies. In all the countries which representatives of the [Rockefeller] Foundation have visited over these recent years, one outstanding fact has emerged: the people are dominated by a passionate hope for peace, security, and a better life. They seek a world in which men may growth in strength and dignity. They want no world in which war periodically tears to pieces the bright promise of the future. That is the pattern of thinking and planning everywhere. Men differ as to the means by which these ends are to be secured, but as to the goal itself there is little diversity of opinion.

This substantial unanimity of aim, sharpened and oriented in our time to a new point, is at least a gleam of hope in a dark age. Mankind is conscious as never before of common roots and common potentialities, of common basic desires and appetites and the common skills required for their satisfaction. A recognition of kinship exists which wars and clashing ideologies can blur but cannot eliminate. Slowly but perceptibly there is developing a conception of the intermeshed interests of men, of the universality of human need, of the single destiny that awaits life on this planet, whether it be good or evil. This is the principle that lies behind the United Nations, the incentive that gives moral and intellectual greatness to the work of this generation in clearing the ground for the new advance.

It is idle, of course, to minimize the towering difficulties that confront us or the heart-breaking frustrations through which we shall live in the years immediately ahead. But we must push toward the ultimate goal of world unity with iron determination and fanatical patience. We must believe in it against all discouragements, against all failures, against all betrayals. There is indeed nothing else we can do. For the long pull there is no alternative. Or rather, the only alternative involves a price in terms of cosmic disaster which, unless the world is overwhelmed by a Gargantuan madness, it will not consent to pay.

Benjamin Franklin, writing in 1789, said: "God grant that not only the Love of Liberty, but a thorough Knowledge of the Rights of Man may pervade all the Nations of the Earth, so that a Philosopher may set his Foot anywhere on its Surface, and say, 'This is my Country.'"

That was the dream of 160 years years ago; that was the faith that inspired our forefathers as they hammered out the larger loyalty of the federal union; and today as we face the necessity of building that loyalty on even wider foundations, we must not let the song die on our lips. It is not the mistakes of our idealists, but the cynicism of our realists that will defeat us. . . .

Index